The Psychoanalysis of Race

The Psychoanalysis of Race

Edited by *Christopher Lane*

Columbia University Press

NEW YORK

Columbia University Press
Publishers Since 1893
New York   Chichester, West Sussex

Copyright © 1998 Columbia University Press
All rights reserved

Library of Congress Cataloging-in-Publication Data
The psychoanalysis of race / edited by Christopher Lane.
    p.   cm.
    Includes bibliographical references and index.
    ISBN 0–231–10946–6 (hardcover). — ISBN 0–231–10947–4 (pbk.)
    1. Psychoanalysis and racism. 2. Race—Psychological aspects.
3. Race awareness. I. Lane, Christopher, 1966–   .
BF175.4.R34P78 1998
155. 8'2—dc21   97–38840
            CIP

Casebound editions of Columbia University Press books are printed on permanent
and durable acid-free paper.
Printed in the United States of America
c 10 9 8 7 6 5 4 3 2 1
p 10 9 8 7 6 5 4 3 2 1

Contents

Acknowledgments

Many people helped me complete this book. The Andrew W. Mellon Foundation sustained me financially during the 1995–96 academic year, and the English Department at the University of Pennsylvania provided generous hospitality and practical support. Roswitha Mueller inaugurated the project by encouraging me to edit a special issue of *Discourse* on the topic. For additional advice or assistance, I thank Houston A. Baker Jr., Jacques Derrida, Jerry Aline Flieger, Tom Keenan, Carla Locatelli, René Major, Donald Moss, Donald Nicholson-Smith, Jean-Michel Rabaté, Rolando Romero, Jacqueline Rose, Ben Saul, John David Smith, Wendy Steiner, and Claudia Tate. Jason Friedman copyedited the manuscript with remarkable care and efficiency, and Ann Miller at Columbia University Press gave the project her enthusiasm and expertise from its inception. Two anonymous readers suggested a number of ways to improve the manuscript, for which I thank them, and Jason Jones helped me prepare the index. I am also grateful to Robert Caserio, Paul Darrah, Tim Dean, Patricia Gherovici, Kevin Kopelson, Deborah Luepnitz, Ligia Rave, and Joe Valente—as well as members of the Philadelphia Lacan Study Group—for their intellectual support and friendship during the 1995–96 academic year. Finally, but not least, I thank the contributors to this collection for letting me include their fine and thought-provoking work.

I acknowledge the following for permission to reprint

previously published material: Wayne State University Press for essays in *Discourse* 19.2 (1997); Collection Vert et noir, Éditions Galilée, and Johns Hopkins University Press for Jacques Derrida's essay "Geopsychoanalysis: . . . 'and the Rest of the World' "; and Johns Hopkins University Press for a slightly different version of Jacqueline Rose's "Introduction to *Black Hamlet*."

The Psychoanalysis of Race

The Psychoanalysis of Race:
An Introduction

Christopher Lane

> How extraordinary it is that governments which claim to be realistic should try to base themselves on anything so shadowy and romantic as race!
>
> —Forster, "Racial Exercise" 19

> The racist's error is one of *thought*, not merely, or only, of behavior.
>
> —Gates, "Talkin'" 205

Every citizen of Europe and North America is haunted by the specter of racism. Despite our concern to restrict this specter to traumatic chapters of history, it revisits contemporary society in shocking and surprising forms. Is it enough to criticize increasingly conservative strains in our political climate to understand this phenomenon, or to reclaim the past in an effort not to repeat it? What in fact can we learn from the past?

Adopting Gertrude Selznick and Stephen Steinberg's phrase, this collection interprets, in several literary and cultural texts, "the tenacity of prejudice." By unraveling conscious and unconscious dimensions of racism, these essays engage critically with the fantasies organizing the *meaning* of racial and ethnic identities. Arguing that we cannot comprehend ethnic and racial disputes without considering the implications of psychic resistance, *The Psychoanalysis of Race* offers neither hopeless nor idealist models of groups, communities, and nations. Instead, this collection brings new and compelling insights to bear on colonialism and racism, revising conventional approaches to racism that tend to explain prejudice and bigotry only as conscious beliefs and political effects. From a psychoanalytic perspective, this collection asks what it means today to invoke "race" and "ethnicity" as concepts organizing our identifications and lives.

By highlighting racism's irrational forms, this collection demonstrates that prejudice can coexist with the greatest support for ethnic and cultural diversity. In emphasizing the need for a psychoanalytic approach to fantasy and identification, these essays also build on radically new approaches to ideology and history, arguing that psychoanalysis for too long has been misperceived as ahistorical and politically naive.[1] Dispelling these claims, *The Psychoanalysis of Race* offers an ethical and salutary perspective on racial conflict that sheds new light on our basic assumptions about society and sociality. Several contributors to this collection also argue that psychoanalytic accounts of ethnic antagonism not only supplement but potentially are more valuable than historicist critiques of the subject (see the essays by Slavoj Žižek, Tim Dean, Julia Reinhard Lupton, and Merrill Cole).

Arguments about racial superiority and inferiority—long ago refuted by academics around the world—have begun to resurface in many countries and cultures with increasing authority and persistence. At the same time, conventional emphasis on racism's material and discursive history tends to ignore this phenomenon's impalpable forms. What is at stake in these assertions of racial certainty and uncertainty? Why do postcolonial theories emphasize displacement, hybridity, and the marginal, while conservative movements in Europe and North America champion cultural authority and racial certainty?

To engage these questions, let us first consider the notion of racial certainty. For a recent example, we can invoke the publicity surrounding Richard Herrnstein and Charles Murray's ill-conceived and prejudicial study, *The Bell Curve: Intelligence and Class Structure in American Life*, which many critiqued after its publication (see Fraser, esp. 11–22; Jacoby and Glauberman). We can also invoke the fantasies that surfaced in contemporaneous studies, which garnered less criticism and publicity but nonetheless conveyed similar interest in racial superiority and the "genetics" of intelligence (Itzkoff 154; Rushton; Sowell 156–85; Wright 345–63; see also *Discover; Newsweek*). *The Psychoanalysis of Race* asks us to consider why these interests recur, and whether postcolonial theories—with their shared assumptions about subjectivity and cultural change—can adequately challenge the unconscious patterns of conservative interests, or their related demand for racial and ethnic certainty. Either indifferent to the unconscious or unable to interpret its effects, most approaches to racism struggle to explain the persistence of these demands, which is not to say that such approaches have not eloquently denounced racism's material and political forms.

After countless studies of Europe's and North America's colonial past, and the extensive research that ethnographers, sociologists, linguists, and political theorists have published on cultural and political differences, why have these arguments about racial superiority resurfaced? How can we explain their repetition and manifestation as racial violence in northern and eastern Europe? To many, these questions have clear and obvious answers: Racism derives from nationalist politics and colonial history, from capitalist greed and mass unemployment, and from poverty and global uncertainty (see Balibar 4, but also 8 and 10). In addition to all of these reasons, however, let us consider another: that prejudice is cogent and palpable today *because it has never left us.* This partly explains the recent U.S. fixation on racial tension and violence, from the testimony of Anita Hill against Clarence Thomas to the police beating of Rodney King and the repercussions of O. J. Simpson's acquittal (see Morrison, *Race-ing*, esp. vii–xxx; Butler 15–22). Nevertheless, to consider these examples merely a cultural fixation or residue of historical prejudice is not sufficiently helpful; it remains for us to interpret this phenomenon's astonishing intransigence, and in the process consider the stakes of every racial and ethnic identification.

In the aftermath of *The Bell Curve,* assumptions ostensibly resolved by the collapse of Europe's empires and the repeal of U.S. segregation laws have begun to flourish again with alarming intensity. Recent debates over educational policy seem to condense widespread anxiety about a range of generally tangential issues, including healthcare, welfare policy, and urban renewal. At the same time, the difference between mid nineteenth-century and late twentieth-century accounts of race is sufficiently acute to warrant careful attention.[2] Thus, considering the immense material differences between these historical periods and the burgeoning work that academics and writers have published and taught on race and racism in many countries, we seem caught in a paradox: If it is inadequate to represent prejudice and oppression as static and immutable, we cannot also approach these phenomena as if they were only historical constructions; the intensity of prejudice in fact complicates our relation to history. Partly for this reason, Etienne Balibar distinguishes between "*theoretical* (or doctrinal) racism and *spontaneous* racism (or racist prejudice)" (38), yet even this distinction doesn't take us far enough, leaving unexamined the "pull" of this spontaneity and the complicated relationship between subjects and their symbolic structures.

Given the first aspect of this paradox (the immense changes in the history of prejudice), we don't seem able to explain growing levels of intolerance, hostility, or hatred toward various minorities in Europe and North America by presuming *causal* links between visibility and violence, or by reducing this violence to formal policies and strategies. In part, this is because social resistance and psychic repression are not identical: individuals are not simply the imprint of their national and symbolic structures, as though the two are locked in a cause-effect relation. We may explain this point by noting that a country's independence from colonial rule does not in any simple way translate into freedom for its citizens. Besides stressing the obvious material repercussions of political independence, which include assessing the basis of freedom for a country's diverse ethnic groups, psychoanalysis argues that "freedom" has radically different meanings for every citizen, and that political and psychic liberation are nonidentical and often causally *unrelated* principles.

To explain the complex relation between social resistance and psychic repression, we need more rigorous accounts of racial fantasy and group identification, and our difficulty begins here. Identification is neither reliable nor mimetically accurate; it founders largely on misrecognition. Similarly, if fantasy helps us "realize" our desires and prejudices, it would seem a mistake to literalize fantasy by rendering it perceptually equivalent to desire, as if thought and act were identical. For all of these reasons, we cannot reduce desire to basic assumptions about volition and need; in Freud's and Lacan's work, desire arises fundamentally from the subject's alienation. For them, alienation exists irrespective of political circumstances because it represents an ontological condition. At the same time, specific forms of alienation recur in contemporary politics, forcing us to consider the gap between subjects and their symbolic structures. To consider this gap merely the result of ignorance or power differences neglects the conceptual tools that would better serve our analysis and critique. How, then, can we approach the second part of our paradox, that despite the obvious doubts and uncertainties informing racial and ethnic identities, we live in cultures that seem compelled to promote racial certainty, even if this certainty is often a material and demographic illusion? (Balibar writes usefully about *"fictive ethnicity"* [10, 49].) And what interpretive approach can do justice to our dilemma?

Since most studies of prejudice derive from ego psychology and the social sciences, they tend to reproduce the limitations of behavioral theory. Much of this work assumes that racism derives largely from ignorance and false consciousness. If teachers and social scientists could influence a person's views, the argument goes, that person would realize that his or her assumptions about different racial and ethnic groups are shallow and false. Correspondingly, the person's racial fantasies and hostility would diminish and ideally would cease to exist.[3] Related work in psychology, anthropology, and ethnography approaches prejudice slightly differently, focusing on cultural rituals, scapegoating practices, victimization, and so forth (see esp. Girard, *Violence* 1–38 and *The Scapegoat* 13–15; Devereux, *Ethnopsychoanalysis* 63–85 and *Fantasy* 23–24, 29–30). This work generally advances a more sophisticated understanding of group dynamics and cultural traditions, yet it also frequently splits over a related tension. Many anthropologists and ethnographers try to maintain the integrity—and "exotic" quality—of the groups they study while aiming simultaneously to dismantle this integrity in the interests of cross-cultural reciprocity and harmony.[4]

These two approaches share, then, an assumption that knowledge enhances cultural understanding while diminishing inter- and intragroup hostility. This emphasis often betrays a foundational hope that humankind, freed from alienation and political strife, would be wholly communitarian—that individuals voluntarily would place the needs of others on a par with their own. Informing recent perspectives on cultural diversity, these approaches argue that a person's beliefs and assumptions, though determined by his or her class and racial background, can be altered simply by raised consciousness.

Studies that aim to resolve urban strife and ethnic warfare often reproduce these assumptions: They anticipate that people locked in conflict want an end to struggle in order to secure the material gains they can achieve only in times of peace. To this perspective, psychoanalysis adds a difficult truth: When people and groups are locked in conflict, they are—beyond their immediate interest in securing sovereignty over another land or people—*already* experiencing intangible gains. This argument appraises both conventional perspectives on war and prevailing assumptions about what it means to be "at peace." For instance, a group's "gain" might consist of the pleasure received in depleting another's freedom. Certainly, this perspective complicates our understanding of group dynamics and ethnic identifications, allowing us to see the cruel irony of P. J. O'Rourke's recent book *Give War a Chance*. But if we ignore these psychic issues, we promulgate fables about human nature, maintaining idealist assumptions while unexamined psychic factors fuel acrimony, resentment, and hatred.

In a remarkable chapter of *Civilization and Its Discontents* (1929, revised 1930), Freud engages precisely this problem. To the biblical injunction "Thou shalt love thy neighbor as thyself," Freud counterposes the Latin dictum "*Homo homini lupus*": "Man is a wolf to man" (111). "Who," he asks, "in the face of all his experience of life and of history, will have the courage to dispute this assertion?" (111). Such questions have particular weight in late-1920s Europe, but we cannot limit their significance to this period. Criticizing "the psychological poverty of groups," their capacity for enmity and "narcissism of minor differences" (112, 114), Freud asks whether our neighbor is *worthy* of love—whether indeed this neighbor "has [not] more claim to [our] hostility and even [our] hatred" (110). He adds that people frequently experience their neighbors as not only a "potential helper or sexual object, but also someone who tempts them to satisfy their aggressiveness on him, to exploit his capacity for work without compensation, to use him sexually without his consent, to seize his possessions, to humiliate him, to cause him pain, to torture and to kill him" (111).

These claims represent the neighbor as both the cause and object of our distress. Freud does not imply that oppression is simply imposed from without, that it is only the burden of someone else's demands. Instead, the neighbor *elicits* the hatred that the subject experiences internally, given the superego's tyrannical relation to the ego. This internal difficulty is not Freud's inadvertent metaphor for political dominance and subordination. The problem is better put the other way: Without trivializing colonial history, Freud helps us see colonialism as partly a widespread enactment of psychic fantasies, an unpleasant but nonetheless "cogent" dream of global mastery. In the passage above, the neighbor presents a long-awaited opportunity for the subject to enact the appalling displays of violence that heretofore have existed only internally.

Such passages in Freud's book confront us with difficult truths, but they refute the common suggestion that psychoanalysis has nothing to say about politics or ethnic enmity. After analyzing group fantasies informing "all the massacres of the Jews in the Middle Ages," for example, Freud laments that such massacres drew heavily on ideological principles, thoroughly informed by psychic conflicts: "Neither was it an unaccountable chance that the dream of Germanic world-dominion called for anti-semitism as its complement; and it is intelligible that the attempt to establish a new, communist civilization in Russia should find its psychological support in the persecution of the bourgeois. One only wonders, with concern, what the Soviets will do after they have wiped out their bourgeois" (114–15).

Freud is not resigned to anti-Semitism here, seeing Jews as the inevitable victims of Nazism's supremacist claims. Rather, he underscores why anti-Semitism and "the dream of Germanic world-dominion" horrifically became *psychically complementary. Civilization and Its Discontents* tries to unravel and demolish this equation, but not by advancing false hope about humankind's capacity for peace. Somewhat paradoxically, Freud's text establishes the ethical *price* of asking humans to substitute civilization's "palliative measures" in "auxiliary constructions" ("powerful deflections," "substitutive satisfactions," and "intoxicating substances") for the libidinal "satisfaction of . . . inclination[s] to aggression" (75, 114). Since Freud refuses to cast himself as a prophet or revolutionary, *Civilization* fosters a humane perspective on apparently inhuman issues. "Men have gained control over the forces of nature to such an extent," he declares, "that with their help they would have no difficulty in exterminating one another to the last man" (145). In a sentence added, James Strachey tells us, "in 1931—when the menace of Hitler was already beginning to be apparent," Freud concludes his book with a prescient question (145n). While man's "current unrest, . . . unhappiness and . . . mood of anxiety" will depend on the struggle between "eternal Eros" and "his equally immortal adversary," he writes, "who can foresee with what success and with what result?" (145).

This perspective on fantasy and aggression certainly does not fully characterize Freud's (or psychoanalysis's) engagement with race; I show below how Freud and Jung drew heavily on preexisting psychological arguments that the unconscious reduces men and women to "savages." However, Freud's perspective in 1929 raises a crucial and compelling argument about enmity that critics cannot easily ignore, considering the atrocities that humans have thought up and committed in this century. Why then have so many critics and theorists resisted this perspective, choosing instead to dismiss psychoanalysis as apolitical and ahistorical? What, Freud effectively asks, could be *more* political than fantasy when it determines the fate of entire communities, nations, and even continents?

In their attempt to deconstruct racial prejudice and phobia, few poststructuralist and postcolonial theorists have engaged these psychoanalytic arguments, preferring instead to call these phenomena discursive and national effects—claims that appear to give their work greater immediacy and critical purchase.[5] But can these claims be ultimately true when their perspective tends to eclipse an understanding of the unconscious? In light of this oversight, for instance, can one plausibly deconstruct racial *trauma* or make clear why racial phobia recurs in liberal times? Critics who do acknowledge the unconscious tend to perceive it as an unfortunate impediment to interracial harmony and equanimity, as an element they would like to dissolve. At the same time, the current emphasis of postcolonial theories on hybridity and mutability tends to ignore related structures of fantasy and identification—the precise demand that we *retain* identity in the service of culture, politics, or meaning.[6]

A paradox has thus emerged in recent postcolonial theories, in which critics' emphasis on mobility and displacement in "transnational" subjects often proceeds hand-in-hand with quite conservative and rigid claims of subjective authenticity. Some work has begun to soften this paradox by rethinking distinctions between evidential discussions of racial prejudice and theoretical accounts of racial and cultural difference.[7] Yet few thinkers have theorized the conceptual interdependence of psychoanalysis and "race."[8] This neglect radically underestimates the influence of psychic factors on racial antagonism and diversity.

Combining some of these multicultural and psychological approaches to prejudice, Elisabeth Young-Bruehl's recent and ambitious study, *The Anatomy of Prejudices* (1996), aims to refute Gordon Allport's influential work *The Nature of Prejudice* (1954, 1979). In the 1950s, Allport strove to synthesize existing sociological and psychological accounts of prejudice; he based much of his work on the six-volume study of anti-Semitism that Max Horkheimer and others assembled in the wake of World War II. As Young-Bruehl notes of Allport's work, "His preface summarized both the sense of horror and the hope—the faith in science—shared by all the writers he considered" (8). In his preface Allport wrote:

> At the time when the world as a whole suffers from panic induced by the rival ide-ologies of east and west, each corner of the earth has its own special burdens of ani-mosity. Moslems distrust non-Moslems. Jews who escaped extermination in Central Europe find themselves in the new State of Israel surrounded by anti-Semitism. Refugees roam in inhospitable lands. Many of the colored people of the world suf-fer indignities at the hands of whites who invent a fanciful racist doctrine to justify their condescension. The checkerboard of prejudice in the United States is perhaps the most intricate of all. While some of this endless antagonism seems based upon a realistic conflict of interests, most of it, we suspect, is a product of fears of the imag-ination. Yet imaginary fears can cause real suffering. (xiii)

Many critics would hesitate today to summarize these conflicts in such a panoramic way; they would resist arguing that an "endless antagonism" explains their multi-farious political differences. Yet Allport states clearly that regions of the world have their "own special burdens of animosity." Wanting to give credibility and urgency to the study of prejudice, he looked for shared traits among these "bur-dens," trying to make sense of "endless antagonism" by revealing specific psycho-logical disorders.

Initially generous in her assessment of Allport's work, Young-Bruehl acknowl-edges these points. However, she later faults Allport's study on many counts, beginning with his title's erroneous claim that prejudice is unitary: "Allport could not bring himself to say that there are both many causes *and many prejudices*. He could explore the many causes, but he could not produce a phenomenology of prejudices (in the plural) because he was trapped by his assumption that prejudice is one" (16; original emphasis). Allport's assumption that prejudice has *a* nature means for Young-Bruehl that his study of hatred basically fails even before it begins.

Young-Bruehl also critiques Otto Klineberg's work, arguing that while he shares Allport's assessment that prejudice has multiple causes or sources, Klineberg "tries to draw the non-Allportian conclusion that this multiplicity implies that prejudices themselves are multiple, not just in degree but in kind as well" (45; see Klineberg, *Race and Psychology* and *Race Differences*, esp. 17–36, 211–22). Young-Bruehl shares some of these precepts but she rejects Klineberg's emphasis on differences of kind. "I find Klineberg's caution salutary," she writes, "though it came to nothing because it was a caution without an alternative. He was—to use the current parlance—a deconstructor, not a reconstructor. Specifically, he left in place his own theoretical prejudice about the centrality of differences *of degree* for distinguishing prejudices, while I think it is crucial, on the contrary, to make distinctions *of kind*" (46; original emphases).

What are the repercussions of insisting on this distinction, particularly when offering a psychoanalytic perspective on prejudice? "The assumption that prejudice is a generalized attitude needs a critique," Young-Bruehl cautions,

> but not one that splinters prejudice into a series of pointers, named after the people who are pointed out. The literatures on prejudices written by members of victim groups have not explored the generalized idea theoretically. They have not questioned what purposes the idea served. As a result, the various victims of prejudice have not yet been able to make a clear survey of what the types of prejudice they have experienced have in common and do not have in common. They have not surveyed *the similarities and the differences.* Coalitions among victim groups will never be tied with strong theoretical ropes until both the similarities and the differences among the types of victimization are understood. (20–21; original emphasis)

Such statements initially appear straightforward, even commonsensical. If one wants to promote political coalitions, beginning from the perspective that prejudice does not affect individuals or groups identically, such comparisons would seem useful. Problems nonetheless arise because prejudice and its effects rarely reproduce logical, commonsense standards. Young-Bruehl is thus careful to preempt suggestions of rigidity, arguing, "No typology can capture individuals or societies in their full complexity or in their dynamism—or in their perversity" (39). All the same, this last factor ("perversity") remains the primary focus of her six-hundred page book. In light of her critique of Allport and Klineberg, *differences* among various prejudices (anti-Semitism, racism, and sexism) both motivate and enable Young-Bruehl's book.

"Distinctions of kind" rather than "differences of degree": Can *The Anatomy of Prejudices* sustain this thesis? As we read more of this book, we find Young-Bruehl foreclosing not only on the unconscious but on the "perversity" that, Freud tells us, gives individuals and groups "satisfaction" *precisely in their expressions of enmity.* Her assessment of this satisfaction manifests itself as a materialist critique precisely when one would expect her psychoanalytic argument to emerge most forcefully:

> I certainly do not want to argue that wars between tribes, conflicts between ethnic groups, battles under banners of nationalism, and religious controversies have not

had enormous and dreadful play in this period. But the era of state economies and world wars, of internationalism and what is now known as globalism, which gives all local conflicts larger contexts of interference, has been an era in which 'us versus them' has been both enacted and rationalized, converted into ideology, in quite distinctive ways. (30–31)

How then can Young-Bruehl engage prejudices *in their particularity?* She does so by trying to align various types of prejudice with specific psychic structures: "I consider antisemitism, for example, an obsessional prejudice, the sort of prejudice that people of rigid, superego-dominated characters often display and the sort of prejudice that societies organized and functioning obsessionally are riddled with" (33). On the next page we read: "racism, by contrast, exemplifies hysterical prejudice, by which I mean a prejudice that a person uses unconsciously to appoint a group to act out in the world forbidden sexual and sexually aggressive desires that the person has repressed" (34). And on the next page: "Sexists, finally, are people (usually but certainly not always male) who cannot tolerate the idea that there exist people not like them, not—specifically—anatomically like them. Their prejudice has a narcissistic foundation, and it is, of the ideologies of desire, the most universal—as universal as narcissism is—even though it is most life defining and extreme in people whose narcissistic desires dominate their character" (35).

The difficulty of trying to map specific psychic structures onto various types of prejudice becomes apparent when Young-Bruehl tries to distinguish hysteria from obsessional neurosis, and narcissism from both. If sexism is "as universal as narcissism," and racism is as ubiquitous as people's repressed fantasies, then prejudice logically is a condition of being human, a point Young-Bruehl seems only fleetingly to acknowledge when noting, in parentheses, that her approach "may mean, of course, that the *society* is pathological" (32; original emphasis). I am not disputing how extensive and deeply held such prejudicial fantasies are; I am merely noting the irony that Young-Bruehl, using the psychic categories of hysteria, narcissism, and obsessional neurosis, makes prejudice more monolithic and universal than Allport ever strove to do.

I have engaged with Young-Bruehl's book at some length because *The Anatomy of Prejudices* highlights a prevailing assumption in contemporary approaches to racist and ethnic prejudice: that general statements about prejudice *by definition* are now inadequate in theorizing the complexity of racism in multicultural societies. Thus while I appreciate Young-Bruehl's frustration with "universal" statements about how prejudice functions, it seems to me not only conceptually mistaken but profoundly antipsychoanalytic to assume that valuable diagnoses can be made of the prejudices affecting specific groups (for related examples see the diverse psychological studies in Watson). When engaging prejudice *at the level of the group*, as Young-Bruehl partly realizes at the end of her Introduction, one is still dealing with generality and thus cannot avoid reproducing stereotypes in attempting to document or explain them. As she remarks of stereotypes surrounding gay men, "Homosexuals can also be 'Negroes' (especially the ones who *are* Negroes) for the hysterically prejudiced: they are imagined as hypersexual or sexually monomaniac, they have huge phalluses or abnormal genitalia, they engage in all manner of exciting and forbidden perversities; they are 'black' pornography, they are always ready for rape" (36).

In light of Young-Bruehl's conceptual and diagnostic assumptions, what can a "psychoanalysis of race" be expected to accomplish? When psychoanalytic critics are asked to *justify* their approach or assess the possibility of strategic intervention or even cultural reparation, they are tempted to stress the efficacy of "adding" psychoanalysis to existing critical approaches. In such a way, they note merely that an emphasis on the psychic field supplements materialist theories by drawing attention to sexual difference and its accompanying structures of fantasy and identification. Certainly, such answers are not entirely untrue, but they ignore the assumptions already hidden in my question above. When asking what psychoanalysis can *accomplish*, critics are demanding that psychoanalysis prove empirically useful— for instance, in resolving conflicts in the political field. In today's political climate, when racial conflicts are so fraught and people want quick and easy solutions, such expectations are understandable. But while Young-Bruehl and many others would not hesitate to give psychoanalysis this intervening and/or reparative power, I hesitate to suggest that psychoanalysis *resolves* or even diminishes ethnic conflicts. Since fantasies are volatile, one risks exacerbating their effects when claiming, however implicitly, that people must change, rethink their attitudes, and learn how to get along.

Certainly, I hope this collection will encourage reflection and debate, but its chances of doing so are strongest if it is understood at the outset that this book does not aim to bolster or enhance the ego, as *The Anatomy of Prejudices* tends to do, by strengthening identitarian and communitarian claims. Building instead on Leo Bersani's and Tim Dean's profound recognition that the ego is the seat of contradiction and the enemy of difference and desire (Bersani 93; Dean 126), this book may be conceived as an opportunity to *displace* the ego, allowing nonidentitarian and noncommunitarian arguments to surface in its place. This perspective, I should stress, differs radically from quietism, and it should not be confused with reactionary arguments that the status quo can continue to prevail. *The Psychoanalysis of Race* maintains a stance against identitarian counterclaims precisely because they risk enforcing hostility and antagonism in an altered form.

Following Shoshana Felman's subtle observations on the interdependence of psychoanalysis and literature, this collection therefore tries to implicate "race" and psychoanalysis in ways that describe their joint enigmas and interpretive blind spots. By so doing, *The Psychoanalysis of Race* adopts a strategy different than Frantz Fanon in *Black Skin, White Masks* (1952), who diagnosed racial conflicts by strict, psychoanalytic distinctions between neurosis and psychosis (141–94; see also Mannoni 125–31, 142–51). Felman's emphasis on implication, not application, may be closer to Joel Kovel's work on racial conflicts in North American history, in which he examines unsolved conflicts in psychic life (51–105). Still, Kovel's work often betrays a schematic faith in psychoanalytic answers by mapping conflicts onto stable, psychoanalytic scenarios (for instance, 75, 91; see also Watson; Sterba).

Unlike these and other attempts at interpretive certainty, this collection does not apply psychoanalysis to "race," or vice versa. Nor does it deconstruct "race" to a point where the term is conceptually meaningless. Instead, these essays put "race" and psychoanalysis in relief by addressing the historical and conceptual blind spots accompanying both terms. This approach resembles the contentious but still provocative questions that Jean Genet posed at the start of his 1958 play, *Les Nègres*: "What is a black? First of all, what is his color?" (*Mais, qu'est-ce que c'est donc un Noir? Et d'abord, c'est de quelle couleur?"* [15]). Let us join Genet in asking the same questions of whites and of whiteness—questions that are difficult to address but nonetheless crucial to ask (for elaboration, see Stowe).

By resisting evidential discussion of racial "color," Genet tried to make clear why "the tenacity of prejudice" undergirds European and North American racism: He examined our disposition to rigid narrative expectations and stereotype; the ease with which our cultures view race relations as Manichean allegories; our accompanying fantasies of attraction and repulsion, fear and retribution; and the sexual character of envy and projection. In *Les Nègres*, Genet focused a spotlight on a single white person in his audience (15); he also urged his black actors to defamiliarize their appearance by wearing white masks. Genet understood that "color" can resist and defeat our assumptions of certainty; like him, we need to interpret the meaning of "color," given the widespread assumption that this is something we already know.

Discussion cannot simply end here, however, with a belief that in posing relevant questions, the answers will somehow emerge. We must ask whether the realization that "race" is a biological fiction correlates with our demand that it have political and symbolic importance. And we should ask why the racist assumptions that Genet, Fanon, and many others critiqued nonetheless recur. Under what circumstances do these assumptions wither and flourish, for instance, and what mechanisms impede them or allow them to endure?

Genet's interrogative strategy would ask psychoanalysis to examine its assumptions about universality and cross-cultural motifs. This strategy would historicize many of Freud's and Jung's early descriptions of the unconscious as a "primitive" or "savage" constituency (see Freud, *Totem*; *Group*, esp. 101; Jung 42; see also Gilman, *Freud*, and Wallace esp. 59–112); it would also signal why Freud revised Gustave Le Bon's argument that we all have a "racial unconscious" (*Group* 74). Freud remarked with palpable despair in his 1921 work on group psychology: "Closely related races keep one another at arm's length; the South German cannot endure the North German, the Englishman casts every kind of aspersion upon the Scot, the Spaniard despises the Portuguese. *We are no longer astonished that greater differences should lead to an almost insuperable repugnance*, such as the Gallic people feel for the German, the Aryan for the Semite, and the white races for the coloured" (*Group* 101; my emphasis).

Certainly, we must read this statement in the context of post-World War I nationalism and a related increase in German racism and anti-Semitism, but can Germany's economic depression in the 1920s clarify the extent of this "almost insuperable repugnance"? Have the Holocaust and the death of millions from other racial, religious, ethnic, and national conflicts made us "astonished that [such] differences should lead to an almost insuperable repugnance," or have these atrocities merely confirmed that difference can, under certain circumstances, generate extreme hostility and violence? What would make us *astonished* at this repugnance, a question Freud strove repeatedly to answer (see "Why War?" and "Anti-Semitism")?

However "tarnished" the origins of psychoanalysis now seem to us by their interest in the "savage" and "primitive," to assume that this material's recovery releases the unconscious from inquiry is, I think, a grave mistake. It implies that prejudice operates according to conscious and rational precepts, and that we can reach a level of self- and group understanding that is free of psychic ambivalence. Such perspectives would be at a loss to explain the recurrence and intensity of prejudice when it is least expected. For this reason, Fanon refused to ignore the material effects of racial fantasy: "The civilized white man," he claimed, "retains an irrational longing for unusual eras of sexual license, of orgiastic scenes, of unpunished rapes, of unrepressed instinct. . . . Projecting his own desires onto the Negro, the white man behaves 'as if' the Negro really had them" (165).

Like Fanon, psychoanalysis adds to theories of "race" an emphasis on structures of fantasy and identification that often haunt us in contemporary life (for a remarkable account of this haunting, see James). In particular, psychoanalysis insists that we cannot treat subjects and politics as entirely rational categories (Rose, "Thatcher" 45). Such emphasis helps us unpack the psychohistorical deadlock that Fanon once called a "Manicheism delirium" (183), in which whiteness seems identical to virtue and harmony. Fanon put this sardonically: "Moral consciousness implies a kind of scission, a fracture of consciousness into a bright part and an opposing black part. In order to achieve morality, it is essential that the black, the dark, the Negro vanish from consciousness" (194).

It might seem easy to portray Freud as an active contributor to this "Manicheism delirium." Certainly, not every contributor to this collection entirely agrees on this subject. Yet even those contributors least certain of Freud's relation to this "Manicheism" agree that his work is ambivalent about the dominant racial motifs of his culture and time. In addition to the lament cited above, for instance, we recall Freud's poignant remarks in *Group Psychology*, which prefigure his own emigration to Britain because of anti-Semitism: "We have heard during the war of people who stood half-way between two hostile nations, belonging to one by birth and to the other by choice and domicile; it was their fate to be treated as enemies first by one side and then, if they were lucky enough to escape, by the other. Such might equally be the fate of psycho-analysis" (180).

A Martinican psychiatrist, Fanon frequently invoked Sigmund and Anna Freud and Lacan (and vigorously rejected Octave Mannoni and Jung) to assist him in theorizing racism's irrational and unconscious forms. Fanon did not simply indict psychoanalysis for causing or reproducing racism, as some critics of psychoanalysis now claim. Nor did he reject the idea of the unconscious as a pernicious element of Eurocentrism. Rather, Fanon tried to indicate why the unconscious, in occidental cultures, came to represent a "depository" for racial and sexual *difficulty*. To this extent, Fanon was quite willing to distinguish Freud from his cultural apparatus: He considered Freud not a perpetrator of myths about savagery, but a figure able to show why these myths so often have recurred.

Fanon can make clear recent debates about the alleged "universality" or "particularity" of psychoanalysis. Put briefly, his critique of racial hostility and indifference turns into a hope of mutual recognition *between white and black men*, in which a category such as "humanity" can supplant the very idea of "color" (Bhabha, "Remembering" 123). Whether or not we share the exact form of Fanon's hope, he follows Sartre and Hegel in likening oppressed races to "the Other." For various reasons, postcolonial theory has found this conceptual model very useful in theorizing generic and specific conflicts between the "Same" and the "Other." Yet Lacan's conception of "*L'Autre*," or big Other, has no obvious relation to color; indeed, as Tim Dean remarked, "the Other has no color."[9] This does not mean that Lacanian psychoanalysis is unable to address racism and prejudice, or that it is uninterested in either phenomenon. To the contrary, Lacan's refusal to portray racial difference as pure alterity fosters a more precise and historically subtle account of group identification and racial fantasy than we find in Hegelian accounts of whites and blacks, in which both racial groups are locked in immutable conflict and structurally unresolvable difference (see Eze 109–49).

In this respect, psychoanalysis cannot claim universal relevance, and Lacanian psychoanalysis does not do so. Lacan was quite clear that psychoanalysis (*as distinct from the unconscious*) has a close conceptual relation to history—that the symbolic orders in which psychoanalysis participates cannot be monolithic because not all of their determinants are known. With this insistence, then, Lacan also complicated our relation to history and politics:

> One thing is certain: to take the misery onto one's shoulders, as you put it, is to enter into the discourse that determines it, even if only in protest. . . . [I]n relating this misery to the discourse of the capitalist, I denounce the latter. Only, here, I point out that in all seriousness I cannot do this, because in denouncing it I reinforce it—by normalizing it, that is, improving it. (*Television* 13–14)

While Lacan's argument is obviously historical, his understanding of social and psychic determinants is not historicist (see Copjec 13–14). This distinction clarifies why Lacan represents political reaction within the terms of capitalism as inadequate. At the same time, as he remarked on a related argument in "Kant with Sade," "Let no one by some slowness or even emotivity doubt our attachment here to a liberty without which the nations are in mourning" (57). Jacques-Alain Miller claimed similarly that to take Lacan's argument seriously, "you have to take psychoanalysis outside the realm of pure therapy. You also have to take capitalism outside the realm of pure sociology or political science" (9). To put this simply, while Lacan revised some of Freud's claims about the cross-cultural and transhistorical relevance of psychoanalysis, his argument differs radically from culturalist and historicist suggestions that desire is *reducible* to history. By enumerating a similar argument, this collection aims to theorize such concepts as desire, fantasy, identification, and prejudice quite carefully, so that our understanding of psychic resistance does justice to the genuine complexity of history, narrative, and temporality.

Many essays in this collection interpret the racial motifs of quite liberal texts and cultural figures; this emphasis is deliberate. The collection might have included more conservative—even reactionary—authors to highlight their egregious racial theories, but conservatism often tells us little about the particularity of racial conflicts. For instance, scholars of Rudyard Kipling's work may recall his notorious pronouncements on the impossibility of "White" and "Black" living together in harmony, but they find it difficult to assess why Kipling's *Kim* (1901) strangely vacillates between disbanding and reinvoking racial hierarchies.

To underscore this argument and the collection's aims, let me turn to two essays by E. M. Forster that appear in *Two Cheers for Democracy* (1951). These essays usefully document what we might call "the psychoanalysis of race"; they also highlight the paradoxes and enigmas of racial identity that we have examined thus far. The first, "Jew-Consciousness" (1939), was published at the start of World War II. In this brief essay, Forster tried to explain pernicious forms of British anti-Semitism that elude his interpretive control:

> A nasty side of our nation's character has been scratched up—the sniggering side. People who would not ill-treat Jews themselves, or even be rude to them, enjoy tittering over their misfortunes; they giggle when pogroms are instituted by someone else and synagogues defiled vicariously. "Serve them right, really, Jews." This makes unpleasant reading, but anyone who cares to move out of his own enlightened little corner will discover that it is true. (13)

Rebelling against his "own enlightened little corner," Forster offers three perspectives on anti-Semitism. "Cool reasonableness would be the best of all," he writes, "but it does not work in the world of today" (14); the second option is to repeat " 'That's propaganda' . . . several times," until "the sniggering stops" (14). The more courageous strategy, Forster asserts, is to ask the perpetrator: " 'Are you sure you're not a Jew yourself? Do you know who your eight great-grandparents were? Can you swear that all the eight are Aryan?' " (14).

Considering the magnitude of anti-Semitism in this century, Forster's attempts to curb it by rational argument are tragically naive. His idealism clarifies why liberal tolerance cannot fully engage with hostility and "enjoy[ment in others'] misfortunes." Forster's idealism would vanish if we consider humanity's capacity for malice, mass-hatred, and genocide, yet his fragment closes insipidly: "For the moment, all that we can do is to dig in our heels, and prevent silliness from sliding into insanity" (14). The date of this fragment—1939—reminds us unequivocally that "insanity" prevailed; it also recalls Freud's brief letter to *Time and Tide* in November 1938, which the *Standard Edition* reprints as "Anti-Semitism in England": "I feel deeply affected by the passage in your letter acknowledging 'a certain growth of anti-semitism *even in this country*.' Ought this present persecution not rather give rise to a wave of sympathy in this country [i.e., in England]?" ("Anti-Semitism" 301; my emphasis).

Perhaps realizing that anti-Semitism greatly exceeded "silliness" in 1939, Forster wrote "Racial Exercise" the same year, and began to question the implied purity of everyone's racial past. The question that Forster directed at individual perpetrators of racism widens into a claim that every European and North

American must give up his or her racial identity: "Whether there ever was such an entity as a 'pure race' is debatable, but . . . there never can be a pure race in the future. Europe is mongrel forever, and so is America" (19). Without relinquishing the need for "a common language, a common religion, [and even] a common culture," Forster insists that "race belongs to the unknown and unknowable past" and that a "community of race is an illusion" (19).

Romanticized notions of race have indeed intensified this century's many acts of genocide, but we might question Forster's readiness to attribute "race" to a specific default in our conscious understanding—the unconscious. In the following passage, Forster makes clear this move by comparing the vicissitudes of his past to the complexities of 1939 Europe:

> Let us do some easy exercises in Racial Purity. And let me offer myself for dissection-purposes.
>
> If I go the right way about it, I come of an old English family, but the right way unfortunately is a crooked one. It is far from easy going in the branches of my genealogical tree. I have to proceed via my father to his mother, thence to her mother, and thence to her father. If I follow this zigzag course I arrive in the satisfactory bosom of a family called Sykes, and have a clear run back through several centuries. . . . I come of an old English family, and am proud of it.
>
> Unfortunately in other directions the prospect is less extensive. If I take a wrong turn and miss the Sykes', darkness descends on my origins almost at once. Mrs. James is a case in point, and a very mortifying one. . . . She might be anyone, she may not even have been Aryan. When her shadow crosses my mind, I do not feel to belong to an old family at all.
>
> After that dissection, let us proceed to do our easy Racial Exercise. It is this: Can you give the names of your eight great-grandparents? (17–18)

Forster's account of family history recalls the title of one of Jane Gallop's chapters: "History Is Like Mother" (Gallop 206, quoting Judith Kegan Gardiner). Forster's exercise in racial origins bears out this remark by making clear his anxiety about his own origins: "If I follow this zigzag course [from] my father to his mother . . . I arrive in the satisfactory bosom . . ." ("Racial" 17). While Forster's exercise is not substantively easy, it presents him with greater conceptual difficulties. He aims to demonstrate only the racial opacity of his past, but elements of self-ignorance—speculation and anxiety about his origins—compound his rational discussion of racism and anti-Semitism. Here we witness not only an about-face in strategy (if racism cleaves to self-ignorance, for instance, we cannot simply challenge it—as Forster previously believed—by speech) but the added problem that Forster repeats such racism when trying to explain it.

Appreciating the paradox that Forster's "right way is unfortunately a crooked one," we might emphasize how the marginal and "errant" aspects of race entirely constitute his sense of lineage and racial progress, but we cannot ignore that Forster's rueful assessment of the "crooked . . . way" recurs in racism as the imaginary "misfortune" of a group or nation. Much contemporary analysis of racism underscores the first point (about errancy and the marginal) without engaging the second: the affective and imaginary consequences of normativity. In Forster's essay, disappointment about his past generates wider concerns about cultural purity; these beleaguer every nation's struggle to define its "character." Our reading cannot end here, however, for the example returns us—as it did Forster—to the limits of our self-knowledge.

How does Forster's oscillation implicate racism and psychoanalysis? I think his essay points up an assumption informing contemporaneous literature and some aspects of psychoanalysis. If consciousness is the civilizing element of our subjectivity, the argument goes, unconsciousness must be not only a disordering influence, but the "racial" component that prevents us from reaching our "civilized" ideal. Numerous literary and cultural examples frame this argument (from Forster's writing alone, consider his violent conclusions to "The Life to Come" and "The Other Boat"). When trying to distinguish consciousness from its errant histories, however, Forster and others endorse another powerful myth: that whiteness—because it "is" consciousness—has no color. Apparently, both consciousness and whiteness are pure and conflict-free (see Dyer; for analyses of the reverse scenario, see Morrison, *Playing*, esp. 31–59, and Fanon 162n. and 100 on the dilemma *"turn white or disappear"*).

Let us therefore return to our earlier discussion of Freud, Fanon, and Lacan. Owing to the widespread belief that the unconscious has a "racial" or "savage" character, the myth that "whiteness" lacks color resembles fantasies that we can "deracialize" consciousness by recalling only the clarity of our political past. Here Forster's essay underscores my opening concerns about memory and historical repetition. In a notable display of inadvertent racism, for instance, he remarks: "As each of us looks back into his or her past, doors open upon darkness" ("Racial" 18). This "darkness," we recall, is the inevitable corollary of taking "a wrong turning": "If I . . . miss the Sykes', darkness descends on my origins almost at once" (17).

Doubtless, Freud sometimes reproduced a similar conviction about the "savagery" of our "racial" past, using this conviction to endorse various ideas about consciousness. As he once remarked in "The Unconscious" (1915) on the outcome of instinctual impulses:

Their origin is what decides their fate. We may compare them with individuals of mixed race who, taken all round, *resemble* white men, but who *betray* their coloured descent by some striking feature or other, and on that account are excluded from society and enjoy none of the privileges of white people. (191; my emphases)[10]

In the same essay, Freud also tells us that "the content of the [unconscious] may be compared with an aboriginal population of the mind" (195). However, as I argued above, if we accept a more current emphasis in psychoanalysis—that the *ego* is the seat of contradiction and the enemy of difference and desire (Bersani 93; Dean 126)—we reach a clearer understanding of what is at stake for consciousness (and thus, for the history of psychoanalysis) when claiming that our personal histories reenact generic "racial" conflicts. Forster remarks: "On such a shady past as this— our common past—do we erect the ridiculous doctrine of Racial Purity" ("Racial" 18). This suggests that the ego's anxious belief in "Racial Purity" represents the past as racially "shady." I think Forster's reading differs radically from later psychoanalytic claims that the history and origins of every subject represent *civilization's* fault line. While Forster makes racism an indelible aspect of our personal mythography, psychoanalysis undercuts a related myth that consciousness is pure and abstract, untarnished by its nebulous beginnings. Building on this distinction, *The Psychoanalysis of Race* shows why claims of racial certainty necessarily foreclose the unconscious. This collection emphasizes the value of interpreting the unconscious, not to give it "racial" or "savage" significance but to ruin the myth that Western subjectivity can uphold a vision of racial certainty detached from the past.

After invoking the past as "darkness" (17, 18), Forster represents it as "shad[e]." With this second metaphor, Forster (like psychoanalysis) likens the ego's "doctrine of Racial Purity" to a "ridiculous" fantasy of its being conflict-free. If the ego is haunted by fears about its unmaking, its problem concerns less the past than its ability to integrate difference. Unable to sustain self-presence, the ego may phobically attack its past in an attempt to reproduce the "selfsame." By corollary, Forster and psychoanalysis imply that if the ego gives up this dream of self-presence, consciousness would find itself "racialized" by its present exclusions: It would be "mongrel forever" in a way that racists claim is undesirable and calamitous.

For conceptual clarity, let me stress that I am not suggesting a possible merger or union between the ego and the id, aimed at downplaying the division between these mutually opposing forces (Freud, "Resistance" 294). Such a dream of forgetting would force us again to ignore the unconscious—that is, to conclude that we have successfully excised the indeterminacies of our historical and subjective origins. Such fantasies of pure exclusion and familiarity surface politically in universal claims that are either "untarnished" by the unconscious or quite oblivious of its existence. Following Forster's inadequate response to the Holocaust, the repercussions of this foreclosure should now be clear: They uphold the same racist assumptions that Forster tried unsuccessfully to disband.

The point is not to fantasize a conflict-free ego or to ignore the unconscious; it is to puncture the arrogance of all claims that consciousness is miraculously—and "racially"—free of such disharmony. In this respect, this collection has at least two related but nonidentical aims: to ruin the myth that psychic enigmas are best explained as racial conflicts, and to critique the assumption that conflicts over the cultural meaning of race can be resolved *without* our tackling or understanding the unconscious.

Without undertaking the first objective, we would repeat egregious stereotypes about racial difference. Without engaging the unconscious, however, we would reproduce assumptions about cross-cultural harmony that misunderstand this harmony's ongoing difficulty. As the following essays demonstrate, in their diverse readings of cultural texts, fantasy emerges in the gap between the assumption that the unconscious is unimportant and that it operates as the immutable "depository" of our racial prejudice. By examining both these assumptions, this collection highlights the contradictions and enigmas that still haunt our volatile fantasies of "race."

The Psychoanalysis of Race begins with a section on psychoanalysis and post colonialism. The decision to start this collection with an analysis of "Current Dilemmas"—rather than interpreting racism in a strictly chronological way—was based on two related convictions. First, psychoanalysis challenges conventional understandings of history and temporality, insisting that events are understood retroactively through "deferred action"; we project onto the past to sustain our perspectives on the present. Second, *The Psychoanalysis of Race* asks a number of questions of postcolonial theory, urging for a reexamination of such key concepts as "hybridity," "communitarianism," "diaspora," and the "transnational." To ensure that this debate take place, it was imperative to present these arguments at the outset.

Charles Shepherdson's essay on "Human Diversity and the Sexual Relation" opens this section, tackling recent scientific debates about racial differences and their implications for contemporary theories of racial identity. Shepherdson notes that many critics have rejected appeals to "race" as a biological concept, claiming biological definitions of race are impossible to sustain on purely scientific grounds; he remarks too that these appeals for racial certainty tend inevitably to reproduce some of the eugenic assumptions invoked in the Holocaust. Sharing many of these concerns, Shepherdson notes nonetheless our difficulty in describing human diversity *without* such concepts. He comments, "it has not been possible simply to dispense with the question of race as it bears on our bodily or physical diversity."

Shepherdson argues that while analyzing race as a social and ideological formation is indispensable, such critical approaches have not adequately addressed questions of embodiment. He argues that criticism also has tended to dismiss biological accounts of race without proposing an alternative account of corporeal differences. Since psychoanalytic theory engages not only psychic representation but also the body and symptom, it may, he suggests, clarify racial difference as a corporeal phenomenon, but without succumbing to the naturalism that genetic theories currently endorse. If we cannot conceptualize a biological approach to racial difference detached from our system of representation, he argues, we also cannot sustain cultural theories about difference without rigorously engaging the genetic arguments that are now proliferating. Examining both the concept of sexual selection and the difference between race and ethnicity offers points of contact that would, Shepherdson argues, allow psychoanalysis to challenge biological accounts of race. Such challenges do not thereby claim that racial differences are exclusively the product of ideology or the effect of contingent historical formations. Adept at engaging recent scientific arguments while remaining attentive to the intricacies of cultural and postcolonial theories, Shepherdson makes an important intervention into a troubling and politically sensitive subject.

Serving as a chastening reminder of some of psychoanalysis's blind spots, Jacques Derrida's polemical essay "Geopsychoanalysis: '. . . and the rest of the world' " appears next in the collection. Derrida presented this essay in February 1981 as the opening address to a French-Latin American meeting convened in Paris by the Lacanian analyst René Major. "Geopsychoanalysis" is an often sardonic reflection on the dearth of international psychoanalytic policy. Derrida asks the International Psychoanalytic Association why it repeatedly has ignored the political conditions of countries in which psychoanalysis is widely practiced. He also pointedly asks the IPA to formulate a coherent policy on such pressing issues as torture, as well as asking why the IPA has failed to define—or even adequately reflect on—human rights. Derrida's questions emerge from his account of the IPA's glib statement that the policies on which it votes in Europe can simply apply to "the rest of the world." More than a critique of assumptions that psychoanalysis offers only personal assistance, however, "Geopsychoanalysis" raises important questions about psychoanalysis's relationship to the social, and thus to human rights, universality, cultural specificity, and imperialism.

Amit S. Rai's essay " 'Thus Spake the Subaltern . . .': Postcolonial Criticism and

the Scene of Desire" broaches many related issues. Striving to rethink a now familiar debate about the subaltern subject and her or his ability to speak, Rai engages
the use and meaning of the "postcolonial example," as well as the force of memory operating within such emblematic moments in critical theory. Claiming that
these examples surface on the fragile terrain of cultural memory, Rai interprets
several melancholic passages in Homi K. Bhabha's and Gayatri Chakravorty
Spivak's work before invoking a tradition of colonial sadness in Lévi-Strauss's
ethnography. He connects this sadness to Lacan's thought by rethinking the
alleged universality of Lacan's understanding of the Law and by reconsidering
postcolonial accounts of death and motherhood. Rai's second path of inquiry leads
him to the popular Hindi film *Raat aur Din* (1967); his eloquent reading of this film
clarifies various conceptual tensions between postcolonial criticism and Lacanian
psychoanalysis. Such tensions, he argues, help us rethink the relationship between
postcolonial criticism and what he calls "the speechless subjects of our desire."

Taking as his point of departure recent critiques of Julia Kristeva's work, James
Penney also revisits a number of postcolonial axioms. In "Uncanny Foreigners:
Does the Subaltern Speak Through Julia Kristeva?" Penney examines the relationship between psychoanalysis and the postcolonial in Kristeva's *Strangers to
Ourselves* and *Nations Without Nationalism*. Arguing that "it would be difficult to
argue that Kristeva's oeuvre is *not* Eurocentric, in the precise sense that her inter-
texts generally have not yet extended far beyond the literary and philosophical traditions of France, Germany, Anglo-America, and Slavic Eastern Europe," Penney
nonetheless asserts: "It is irresponsible not to investigate the manner in which
Kristeva's recent, socially inflected thought, *when considered in its proper context and
limitations,* informs a cultural project explicitly questioning the psychodynamics of
imperialism and racism."

Examining how such Freudian concepts as the death drive, the uncanny, and
identification recur in Kristeva's notions of the abject and the exile, Penney underlines the value of psychoanalysis for postcolonial theory precisely in its recognition of the impossibility of maintaining a stable identity, whether relative to race,
class, or gender. He argues compellingly that in *Strangers* and *Nations*, "Kristeva
aims to recuperate critically the universalist and cosmopolitan tenets of
Enlightenment thought in order to achieve democratic renewal and present an
alternative to the Left's despondency." Helping us rethink Kristeva's cosmopolitanism, Penney claims eloquently that Kristeva "urges us to consider the dynamic
precariousness of subjectivity—our uncanny strangeness to ourselves—alongside
the unquestionable effects of social and historical contexts."

What structures of alterity underlie fantasies of racial otherliness? Suzanne
Yang engages this question from the perspective of her work as an Asian-

American clinician. In "A Question of Accent: Ethnicity and Transference," she examines the difference that ethnicity makes in the clinical situation—that is, in visual and auditory registers of the transference. Yang discusses the effect by which the therapist represents a "foreigner" who speaks with or without an apparent accent. She argues that implicitly, and sometimes explicitly, the patient comes to question the therapist's origin. At times this questioning devolves on the patient's origins—where he is from, and his complex rapport with his home. Yang notes that an understanding of trauma and its restitution in the treatment entails reworking the "small other," or *objet petit a*, as well as the patient's traumatic encounter with the Other. In her discussion, Yang frames the problem of "accent" in terms of the mother's voice, her naming and address of the infant, and the infant's preliminary recognition of his name.

Revisiting issues discussed in Penney's and Yang's essays, Slavoj Žižek argues that "racism confronts us with the enigma of the Other which cannot be reduced to the partner in symbolic communication." Racism, he continues, "confronts us with the enigma of that which, in ourselves, resists the universal frame of symbolic communication." Asserting that socioeconomic and culturalist analyses of racism are not, as they believe, complementary accounts of prejudice but rather formulations that *"return to each other their own lack,"* Žižek argues that psychoanalytic accounts of racism too often have offered a "pseudoconcrete application of specific clinical categories (paranoia, compulsive neurosis, etc.) to racist phenomena." "If one is to account for the uncanny logic of racism," he writes, "one needs the exact opposite of this pseudoconcreteness. One must instead begin with the subject's elementary relationship to the traumatic kernel of jouissance structurally unassimilable into his or her symbolic universe." Engaging Lacan's Seminar on *The Ethics of Psychoanalysis*, Hannah Arendt's notion of the "banality of evil," Daniel J. Goldhagen's recent study, *Hitler's Willing Executioners*, and Kieślowski's *Short Film on Love*, among other texts and films, Žižek interprets what he calls "the obscene supplement" of power. In doing so, he critiques conventional notions of transgression and subversion that fail to consider the subject's fantasmatic and symbolic complicity in diverse—and often grotesque—arenas of "political enjoyment."

Alphonso Lingis's essay "Schizoanalysis of Race" concludes this section on "Current Dilemmas" with a rather different perspective on complicity and fantasy. Lingis adopts what we might call a "phenomenological" approach to racial differences, writing critically about the ego's often violent fascination with "exotic" differences. After providing a devastating critique of Western tourism and its "packaged" reality, Lingis proposes a type of "facelessness" in which we dismantle our unthinking reliance on custom, tradition, and authority; he urges us to engage with foreigners without arrogance or preconceptions. Lingis's argument about "face-lessness" documents a yearning for simplicity and lyrical intimacy that clashes starkly with Žižek's understanding of the "stain" of obscene enjoyment. "Schizoanalysis of Race" also deliberately suspends the politically correct, view-ing it as an inhibiting Western formulation that helps us cope with difference and alienation by protecting us from both. Lingis sometimes advances a certain naiveté about racial differences in order to illustrate how Western perceptions are inher-ently exoticizing: His understanding of "facelessness" implies strongly that we must ask ourselves what encounters and desires emerge when the ego's defenses are exposed and dismantled.

The second section of this collection, "History and the Origins of Racism," adopts a more historical approach to racism, beginning with Julia Reinhard Lupton's astute reading of Paul's Epistle to the Romans and concluding with Tim Dean's brilliant account of colonial trauma in Joseph Conrad's 1899 novella, *Heart of Darkness*. Offering detailed readings of diverse literary texts, this section reveals psychoanalysis's ability to interpret the "minute particulars" of cultural prejudice, bringing to our attention how fantasy and identification help constitute historically specific definitions of the social.

In "*Ethnos* and Circumcision in the Pauline Tradition: A Psychoanalytic Exegesis," Lupton interprets how Paul's Epistle to the Romans deliberately identi-fies a mixed audience of Jewish and gentile converts to Christianity, promulgating a message of salvation, in Paul's words, "to the Jew first and also to the Greek." This Epistle, Lupton argues, "divides between Paul's urge to repeal the laws of contemporary Judaism in the name of a universal Christianity, on the one hand, and to grant historical significance to the Jews as a people on the other, positions that equally stem from his sense of the Jews as an *ethnos*, a tribe or nation bound by a common language, customs, and genealogy." In emphasizing this *ethnos*, Paul underscores the symbolic importance of circumcision. "Physical yet not physio-logical, genealogical but not genetic," the rite of circumcision, Lupton argues, marks "the Jews as a distinct people" without serving as a " 'racial' indicator in the modern sense of an inherited trait." In this way, as Lupton observes, Paul's letters "perform an 'ethno-graphy,' a graphing of the *ethne* or 'nations' that laid the foun-dations for a modern theory of biological race that has since effaced it."

Lupton's analysis has extensive repercussions for historical and contemporary approaches to racism. Not only does she clarify key psychoanalytic arguments about the relationship between individuals and symbolic systems (a relationship that, she notes, is determined by Law *and* trauma), but in uncovering some of the meanings attached to circumcision from antiquity to the Renaissance, she also lays bare "the largely forgotten scaffolding of Renaissance ethnography," namely, how biological racism—rooted in the tropes of science—took its place in an arena already defined by theology. Such an approach to ritual and ethnography adds a compelling perspective to existing accounts of historical change and the origins of racism; it contradicts the assumption that psychoanalysis has only limited or generic ways of interpreting the past.

In many ways, Daniel Boyarin's essay "What Does a Jew Want?; or, The Political Meaning of the Phallus" is a modern counterpart to Lupton's account of Paul's Epistle and its impact on Renaissance ethnography. Revisiting Freud's argument about temporal displacement and self-estrangement in "The 'Uncanny' " (1919), Boyarin uncovers a set of "toxic political symptoms" in Freud's analysis of Little Hans and in his late essay "Analysis Terminable and Interminable" (1937). Building on Freud's remarks about castration and circumcision in these essays, Boyarin engages "the strange figurings of 'Mulattos' in Freud's work" and then, relatedly, of Jews in Frantz Fanon's important study *Black Skin, White Masks*. Such formulations, he argues, reveal that while both thinkers offered profound insights into identity's porous and mutable qualities, certain blind spots led them periodically to "unknow that which sexually and racially they already perceived on a cultural level."

Beginning her essay by discussing W. E. B. Du Bois's account of "double-consciousness," Gwen Bergner examines a number of scenes in Frederick Douglass's 1845 autobiography, *Narrative of the Life of Frederick Douglass, An American Slave, Written by Himself*. In this text, Douglass describes his perception of being divided or split by his awareness of racial difference. Bergner claims that this racial alienation impedes Douglass's gender identification, excluding him from normative models of masculinity. In the *Narrative*, Bergner claims, Douglass attempts to subsume his racial alienation and oppression within a tradition of "masculine self-sufficiency"—one favored particularly by nineteenth-century American writers. Despite Douglass's concern that his narrative speak for enslaved men and women, he authorizes his voice by claiming a conventional masculinity and displacing his racial alienation onto African-American women. Sensitive to the reasons Douglass would want to enhance his masculinity in this way, Bergner highlights the psychoanalytic repercussions of his difficulty. In the process, she valuably underscores why racial and gender identification is such a charged and traumatic issue in American slave narratives.

Both building on and departing from Bergner's study of Douglass, Merrill Cole, in "Nat Turner's Thing," advances a bracing critique of conventional historicist accounts of American slavery and racism. He argues that since Paul Gilroy's "continuist narrative" in *The Black Atlantic: Modernity and Double Consciousness* (1993) aims to advance a "linear and redemptive conception of history," it systematically eclipses discussion of *The Confessions of Nat Turner* (1831). As Cole contends, Turner's account of the bloody slave rebellion he led in Virginia in 1831, "arguably one of the most influential texts in the history of slavery," tries to narrativize forms of trauma and violence that conventional accounts of history dismiss as nonsense or delirium. The force of *Nat Turner* derives, he contends, from its elemental relation to aggression and the death drive, factors that tend to dissipate meaning and cause anxiety in readers accustomed to linear narrative. Juxtaposing Turner's "implacable negativity" with a fine reading of Lacan's Seminar on *The Ethics of Psychoanalysis*, Cole argues that *Nat Turner*, like psychoanalysis, "teaches us the ethical value of paying constant attention to the operations of desire."

Advancing the collection's historical perspective to the mid-1920s, Christopher Lane engages André Gide's *Travels in the Congo* (1927). Utterly dissimilar to *The Confessions of Nat Turner* in its historical and geographical context, Gide's travel diary nonetheless is conceptually similar in its fascination with the death drive. Not only does Gide's text make clear his demand for political reform and give us compelling insights into French and Belgian colonialism, but it also represents Gide's profound *recoil* from Africans in their expressions of enjoyment. Gide calls this enjoyment "savage ecstasy [*le transport sauvage*]" and writes at length about its inhuman and disgusting properties, arguing that such expressions of joy lead Africans and Frenchmen alike toward a type of cultural degeneration before pushing them on toward an ontological abyss.

Gide's reflections not only conflict starkly with scholarly claims that *Travels in the Congo* represents his political epiphany (a reading Gide actively promoted), but ask us to rethink the very bases of colonial exchange, knowledge, and intimacy. For this reason, Lane does not dismiss Gide's interest in "savage ecstasy" as an unfortunate lapse in political wisdom. Nor does he relegate such interest to merely "symptomatic" moments that curtail the possibility of colonial reform. He argues instead that such moments taint the very fabric of colonialism, revealing beneath the edifice of economic interests, trade, and political rule an inseparable preoccupation with the political and psychic meanings of death and desire. In making clear this distinction, Gide's memoir highlights the profound incommensurability of two conceptions of desire—materialist and psychic. In this way, Lane argues, Gide inadvertently reveals the political complexities of a country striving for economic *and* symbolic independence from its former colonizer.

Developing a compelling reading of Conrad's *Heart of Darkness* (a text that, Gide acknowledged, partly inspired his own reflections on colonialism), Tim Dean revisits both psychoanalytic and postcolonial accounts of this novella. Arguing that the former tend ironically to limit Conrad's inquiry by reducing it to an exploration of individual psychology, Dean suggests that the latter often dismiss all inquiry into psychic issues, calling Conrad's "heart of darkness" an inherently racist trope. But *Heart of Darkness* fails to sustain either interpretive method, Dean argues, because its narrative enigmas point up a dimension of trauma that is both historically specific (partly congruent with European colonialism) and politically disturbing (a profound indication that colonial atrocities can be recorded only as trauma). Far surpassing expectations that Conrad's novella is merely a "symptomatic" display of unconscious European fantasies, Dean's account of colonial trauma asks us to rethink our assumptions about the relation between history and imperialism. He builds on recent developments in trauma theory, using Lacan's concept of the Real to conceptualize trauma in nonindividualistic, transpersonal terms. Dean's approach is thus historically specific and conceptually apposite, extending interpretations of Conrad's text far beyond individualistic definitions of the unconscious.

This argument in itself is sufficiently ambitious to warrant an extensive rethinking of Conrad's most popular and widely taught work. However, Dean's argument is not simply a conceptual one. The "germs of empire" that his title invokes are both figurative and literal, enabling Dean not only to revisit recent accounts of colonialism and disease, but to speculate compellingly that Mr. Kurtz, Conrad's famous protagonist, is represented as if he had died of AIDS. Is such a claim absurd? Not when we consider Dean's empirical evidence and conceptual rationale. "While we can neither prove nor disprove the apparently preposterous hypothesis that Kurtz dies of AIDS," he writes, "I propose it as a heuristic device to illuminate both the historiography of AIDS and the impact of colonialism, as well as the particular force of imperial ideology in *Heart of Darkness*."

Consider the empirical evidence supporting Dean's hypothesis. Mirko Grmek, Director of Studies at the Sorbonne and a widely respected physician and historian of science, is not alone in arguing that "HIV-1 or a close virus with similar antigenic properties was present in Zaire as early as 1959." Dean adds that "although the date 1959 may seem astonishingly early to those accustomed to thinking of AIDS as a disease of the 1980s, it is actually a cautious estimate, since Robert Gallo's calculations backdate to the end of the nineteenth century the existence of HIV as a human parasite." What relevance has this argument for Conrad's novella and theories of colonialism? Dean writes that the year 1959 is crucial for several reasons: "First, it represents the earliest verifiable date for locating HIV-1 in human tissue; second, the verification concerns plasma collected in Zaire; and third, 1959 represents the eve of Zaire's independence and hence of massive political upheaval and social reorganization in the former colony—an upheaval that, I shall argue, was instrumental in the emergence of AIDS."

Such "nonlinear temporality" accompanying the historical emergence of AIDS allows a specific and politically cogent reading of colonialism's *effects*. As Dean observes, "Conrad enables us to see why imperialism should be counted a vital 'cofactor' in the etiology of this new disease. And so while *Heart of Darkness* remains vulnerable to charges of racism, Conrad's novella permits us to grasp that Africa is not the origin of AIDS—European colonialism is."

Concluding the second section of this collection, Dean's analysis of Conrad anticipates related discussion of colonialism by Jacqueline Rose, Kalpana Seshadri-Crooks, Claudia Tate, Jean Walton, and David Marriott. Opening the final section of *The Psychoanalysis of Race*, "Psychoanalysis and Race, an Uncertain Conjunction," Jacqueline Rose interprets the context and reception of Wulf Sachs's 1937 study, *Black Hamlet*. Sachs was a white psychoanalyst struggling to interpret the conflicts and aspirations of his black South African patients in the 1920s. Examining the political and psychic stakes of this work, Rose is careful not to dismiss what was radical or unorthodox in Sachs's approach: "To credit a black African with an internal world," she writes, "was to go against the creeds, not just of explicit racism but also of medical science." Considering the twin histories of South Africa and psychoanalysis, however, Rose is also suspicious of Sachs's undertaking: "There are certain questions that, reading *Black Hamlet*, seem unavoidable today. In whose interests does Sachs's [undertaking] proceed? Or rather, given that in the colonial setting, to act in the other's interests was the problem rather than the solution . . ., whose desire or fantasy are we dealing with here?"

Rose also considers *Black Hamlet*'s contemporary and contemporaneous significance, including the perspective of European psychoanalysis in the 1920s, with its own unanalyzed and often coercive mission of promoting racial and psychic change. She juxtaposes this perspective with that of psychoanalysis *from* South Africa, which yields an interesting account of psychoanalysis's relation to Europe and its internal conflicts in the early decades of the twentieth century. Speaking of one of Sachs's patients, for instance, Rose comments: "It is as if her objections are there to remind us that the issue for psychoanalysis in Africa is not whether it can affect the individual (you can always affect an individual), but the relationship it establishes, or fails to establish, with the symbolic parameters of the group."

This is a profound question, anticipating Seshadri-Crooks's essay on white racial identification and Freud's theory of jokes. Claiming, as Rose does, that all racial identifications have unconscious determinants and equally unconscious effects, Seshadri-Crooks, in "The Comedy of Domination," uses the mechanism of jokes to undermine the particular "conceit" of whiteness—that whiteness is synonymous with humanity. Building on a close reading of George Orwell's story "Shooting an Elephant" (1935), in which Orwell's narrator fears native laughter and derision when he must shoot an elephant to consolidate his power, Seshadri-Crooks argues that an unarticulated—and immensely revealing—joke about racial authority circulates in this story. Revising the now standard claim that jokes can inhibit and displace aggression, she notes that in the colonial context, whiteness is the single most important repressed element that comedy can expose. In Orwell's story, the colonizer discovers unwittingly that a joke against him rapidly diminishes his power and difference; Orwell's narrator experiences this exposure as uncanny. The joke in "Shooting an Elephant" therefore inadvertently exposes what haunts and undermines white subjectivity. Aiming to make clear the volatile dynamics of racial and cultural difference in colonial contexts, Seshadri-Crooks exposes what whiteness must abject when arrogating the belief that it represents all humanity.

What is at stake for readers of literature when a popular African-American author writes a novel about white Southerners? Partly reproducing the concerns of Seshadri-Crooks's essay on Orwell and whiteness, Claudia Tate's reading of Zora Neale Hurston's 1948 novel, *Seraph on the Suwanee*, sets out to answer this question. Despite Hurston's immense popularity over the last two decades, *Seraph on the Suwanee*, notes Tate, remains problematic for her readers; in African-American literary scholarship this text is still largely seen as an anomaly among Hurston's works. In "Hitting 'A Straight Lick with a Crooked Stick,' " Tate refutes this contention, arguing that *Seraph* is "very much a part of Hurston's persistent and compelling investigations of female desire and racialized culture." "With this novel," Tate writes, "Hurston tried to please a white popular audience and herself by conspicuously constructing *and* subtly deconstructing the novel's white patriarchal narrative of romantic love with a couple of canny jokes about that culture's idealization of passive female desire and its conflation of race and class."

Viewed from this perspective, *Seraph* is fully characteristic of Hurston's parodic folk discourse. Indeed, Tate argues that since *Seraph* is thoroughly informed by black dialect, the novel's implicit joke—lost on many of its readers—is profoundly ironic and subversive. That *Seraph*'s central protagonists seem to "possess white exteriors and black interiors" suggests, for Tate, that Hurston is exploiting and unsettling "the validity of time-honored racial ideologies." Stated baldly, the joke is that her "white folks are black!" "This," concludes Tate, "is *Seraph*'s seditious joke on racialism."

While Tate draws on psychoanalysis to clarify the dramatic psychic repercussions of Hurston's "metahumorous novel," Jean Walton's " 'Nightmare of the Uncoordinated White-folk' " considers how various racial tropes of the unconscious—adopted frequently by European modernists—informed the POOL group's 1930 film, *Borderline*. The film was a collaboration among poet H. D.

(Hilda Doolittle) and her two lovers, Bryher (Winifred Ellerman) and Kenneth Macpherson, and it featured H. D. and Bryher alongside Paul Robeson and his wife, Eslanda. *Borderline*, notes Walton, is "an expressionistic depiction of the sexual and racial tensions that develop in a small European village when two couples—one white, one black—play out the interpersonal problems arising from the white man's sexual involvement with the black woman." Walton reads the film as a type of "film à clef," exploring "the preoccupations, desires, and interrelationships of white modernists that are 'projected' onto their black acquaintances." *Borderline* "also partly clarifies the forms of racial and sexual difference that surface in a cinematic venture designed to *counter* the blatantly racist productions of the American film industry."

Not only did the POOL group denounce Hollywood in the film journal *Close Up*, but, as Walton shows, the "group's preoccupation with racial politics was concomitant with its intense interest in psychoanalysis for its affirmation of the role of the unconscious in creativity and its availability as a discourse of sexual difference." In this respect, she claims, "*Borderline* in part critiques the way a white modernist aesthetic, with a somewhat racialized understanding of Freud's ideas, relegates blackness to the realm of preneurotic primitivism."

Concluding *The Psychoanalysis of Race*, David Marriott's essay "Bonding Over Phobia" combines searing personal reflections on racial prejudice with a conceptual interest in the culturally violent repercussions of racial misrecognition. How, he asks, can we rethink the relation between trauma and reparation in racial fantasy without naively reducing culture to a symptom? Engaging passages about identification trauma in Fanon's *Black Skin, White Masks* and Erik Erikson's "Memorandum on Identity and Negro Youth" (1964), Marriott asks pointedly how the spectrum of available racial identifications can change when cultures persist in laying down overdetermined roles for specific racial groups. Revisiting Fanon's agony in being snared visually by the accusatory look of a young white child ("Look at the nigger! . . . Mama, a Negro!"), Marriott remarks that Fanon "is reduced to the imago of a cannibal," a fantasy evoking dread about oral-aggressive drives. He examines too how the research of two black social psychologists, Kenneth and Mamie Clark, contributed to the famous 1954 *Brown v. Board of Education* case to desegregate schools by advancing concerns that "a third of the children effectively 'misidentified' themselves as white when demonstrating a marked preference for the white doll—a preference decidedly more noticeable in children aged three and four years rather than at a later age." "To the Clarks," notes Marriott, "this preference signified a confusion, even a loss of racial identity; for the narcissistic choice of the white doll necessarily involved 'a concomitant negative attitude toward the brown doll.' " "We simply do not know who or what these children imagined themselves to be," he concludes, but "when asked why they preferred the white doll, . . . some of the children replied ''cause he's white' or 'pretty.' Conversely, the brown doll was rejected with the words ''cause him black' or 'ugly,' or, more revealing, because he 'got black on him.'"

Reframing some of the expectations informing various types of psychology in the 1950s and 1960s that considered building self-esteem one of the best means of averting such "misidentification," Marriott asks instead, "What could the full liberation of black libidinal adaptation have meant in the 1960s (the decade of black civil rights), when a mass outbreak of white racial (and sexual) fears in extreme forms of racial violence effectively tried to deny such liberation, at least as equated with the fulfillment of social wants and aspirations?" As Marriott and many other contributors to this collection ask, "If the act of identification produces a fractured doubling of self, how can we distinguish what is interposed from what is properly desired?"

Marriott's question continues to vex and haunt me. Perhaps we may never successfully distinguish "what is interposed" from "what is properly desired." However, the need to make clear the factors informing this psychic "decision" remains imperative today. *The Psychoanalysis of Race* asks us to consider the repercussions of living with such imperatives, perhaps making us wonder too what all the fear, anxiety, and violence are really about.

ENDNOTES

I am grateful to Houston A. Baker, Jr., and Claudia Tate for their comments on an earlier draft.

1. I refer to Slavoj Žižek's and Joan Copjec's brilliant reappraisals of historicism (see Žižek, *Sublime* 1–7 and Copjec 13–14). Copjec writes, "We are calling historicist the reduction of society to its indwelling network of relations of power and knowledge" (6). Such a reduction, she notes, fails to consider "a surplus existence that cannot be caught up in the positivity of the social" (4).

2. For elaboration on this point, see Balibar and Wallerstein 55; Gilman, *Difference* 30–32; Gilman and Chamberlin 72–89; Greenfeld 3–26; Kristeva, *Strangers* 169–92 and *Nations*; Mosse 133–52; Pick 1–33; Young 4–19.

3. For examples, see Holden; Lapides and Burrows; Lindsey; Mack 375–77; Putnam. Feagin and Hernán usefully complicate this approach, writing that their book "takes a starting point different from many other studies. Often a basic assumption permeating analyses of U.S. racial problems is that such relations are a zero-sum game, such as in the common white notion that when blacks gain, whites lose. We argue that such a zero-sum assumption is generally unwarranted. In some cases all can win, while in others all can lose" (xii). Feagin and Hernán argue that "racial problems that a majority of whites pre-

tend do not exist cannot successfully be overcome" (xiv), and thus that "more radical action is needed to eradicate white racism and create an egalitarian, multicultural society" (xiii). Such arguments are not disputed here. What this collection of essays argues, additionally, is that psychic issues complicate our chances of achieving and sustaining egalitarianism.

4. See Banks 11–48, especially regarding the concept of "boundary maintenance" (27).

5. For examples of this approach to cultural identity and postcolonial politics, see Appiah and Gates; Gates, *"Race"* esp. 1–20.; Goldberg, *Anatomy* ix–xxiii and *Racial* 1–16; Gregory and Sanjek 1–11; Ignatiev and Garvey, esp. 9–14 and 35–37; Stoler 19–54; also JanMohamed 103–6, and Gates and West.

6. See Appadurai, "Disjuncture" 328–34 and *Modernity* 1–23; also Gilroy, "Urban" 406, 409–18 and *The Black Atlantic* on what Gilroy calls "the continuing lure of ethnic absolutisms" (3).

7. Critical work that uses theoretical accounts of racial and cultural difference broadly to rethink evidential discussions of racial prejudice includes Bhabha, *Location*; Gates, *Figures*; Hall, esp. 392–96; Lingis 99–103, 167–85; McClintock, *Imperial* 9–17 and *Dangerous* 89–112; and Suleri 246–52.

8. For exceptions to this approach, see Abel, "Race," "Black," and *Female*, esp. 1–18; Fuss 141–65; Gilman, *Freud*; Nandy, *Intimate* 55–59 and *Savage* 81–144; Rose, "Universality"; Seshadri-Crooks; Spillers, "Mama's" and "All"; Walton; Young-Bruehl 43–56; and Žižek, "Enjoy!"

9. Dean's remarks surfaced in his discussion with Barbara Johnson about whiteness and alterity at the 1989 MLA Convention in Washington, D.C.

10. Freud offered a similar representation of the id in "Dissection": "We approach the id with analogies: we call it chaos, a cauldron full of seething excitations" (73).

WORKS CITED

—— Abel, Elizabeth. "Race, Class, and Psychoanalysis? Opening Questions." *Conflicts in Feminism*. Ed. Marianne Hirsch and Evelyn Fox Keller. New York: Routledge, 1990. 184–204.

——. "Black Writing, White Reading: Race and the Politics of Feminist Interpretation." *Critical Inquiry* 19 (1993): 470–98.

Abel, Elizabeth, Barbara Christian, and Helene Moglen, eds. *Female Subjects in Black and White: Race, Psychoanalysis, Feminism*. Berkeley: U of California P, 1997.

Allport, Gordon W. *The Nature of Prejudice*. 25th Anniversary Edition. Reading, Mass.: Addison Wesley, 1979.

Appadurai, Arjun. "Disjuncture and Difference in the Global Cultural Economy." 1990. In Williams and Chrisman. 324–39.

——. *Modernity at Large: Cultural Dimensions of Globalization*. Minneapolis: U of Minnesota P, 1997.

Appiah, Kwame Anthony and Henry Louis Gates, Jr., eds. *Identities*. Chicago: U of Chicago P, 1995.

Balibar, Etienne and Immanuel Wallerstein. *Race, Nation, Class: Ambiguous Identities*. Trans. Chris Turner. New York: Routledge, 1991.

Banks, Marcus. *Ethnicity: Anthropological Constructions*. New York: Routledge, 1996.

Bersani, Leo. *The Freudian Body: Psychoanalysis and Art*. New York: Columbia UP, 1986.

Bhabha, Homi K. *The Location of Culture*. New York: Routledge, 1994.

——. "Remembering Fanon: Self, Psyche, and the Colonial Condition." 1986. In Williams and Chrisman. 112–23.

Butler, Judith. "Endangered/Endangering: Schematic Racism and White Paranoia." *Reading Rodney King/Reading Urban Uprising*. Ed. Robert Gooding Williams. New York: Routledge, 1993. 15–22.

Copjec, Joan. *Read My Desire: Lacan against the Historicists*. Cambridge: MIT, 1994.

Dean, Tim. "On the Eve of a Queer Future." *Raritan* 15.1 (1995): 116–34.

Devereux, George. *Ethnopsychoanalysis: Psychoanalysis and Anthropology as Complementary Frames of References*. Berkeley: U of California P, 1978.

——. *Fantasy and Symbol: Studies in Anthropological Interpretation*. Ed. R. H. Hook. New York: Academic, 1979.

Discover: The World of Science 15.11 (Nov. 1994), special issue: "The Science of Race."

Dyer, Richard. "White." *Screen* 29.4 (1988): 44–64.

Eze, Emmanuel Chukwudi, ed. *Race and the Enlightenment: A Reader*. Cambridge: Blackwell, 1997.

Fanon, Frantz. *Black Skin, White Masks*. 1952. Trans. Charles Lam Markmann. New York: Grove, 1967.

Feagin, Joe R. and Vera Hernán. *White Racism: The Basics*. New York: Routledge, 1995.

Felman, Shoshana. "To Open the Question." *Literature and Psychoanalysis: The Question of Reading: Otherwise*. Ed. Felman. Baltimore: Johns Hopkins UP, 1982. 5–10.

Forster, E. M. "The Other Boat." 1915–16. *The Life to Come and Other Stories*. New York: Norton, 1972. 166–97.

——. "The Life to Come." 1922. *The Life to Come and Other Stories*. 65–82.

——. "Jew-Consciousness." 1939. *Two Cheers for Democracy*. New York: Harcourt, Brace and World, 1951. 12–14.

——. "Racial Exercise." 1939. *Two Cheers for Democracy*. 17–20.

Fraser, Steven, ed. *The Bell Curve Wars: Race, Intelligence, and the Future of America*. New York: Basic Books, 1995.

Freud, Sigmund. *Totem and Taboo*. 1913 (1912–13). Vol. 13 of *The Standard Edition of the Complete Psychological Works of Sigmund Freud*. Ed. and Trans. James Strachey. 24 vols. London: Hogarth, 1953–74. 1–162.

——. "The Unconscious." 1915. Vol. 14 of *SE*. 159–215.

————. "Resistance and Repression." 1916–1917 (1915–1917). Vol. 16 of *SE*. 286–357.

————. *Group Psychology and the Analysis of the Ego*. 1921. Vol. 18 of *SE*. 65–144.

————. *Civilization and Its Discontents*. 1930 (1929). Vol. 21 of *SE*. 59–145.

————. "Why War?" (with Albert Einstein). 1933 (1932). Vol. 22 of *SE*. 197–215.

————. "The Dissection of the Psychical Personality." 1933. Vol. 22 of *SE*. 57–80.

————. "Anti-Semitism in England." 1938. Vol. 23 of *SE*. 301.

Fuss, Diana. "Interior Colonies: Frantz Fanon and the Politics of Identification." *Identification Papers*. New York: Routledge, 1995. 141–65.

Gallop, Jane. *Around 1981: Academic Feminist Literary Theory*. New York: Routledge, 1992.

Gates, Henry Louis, Jr. *Figures in Black: Words, Signs, and the Racial "Self."* New York: Oxford UP, 1986.

————. "Talkin' That Talk." *Critical Inquiry* 13.1 (1986): 203–10.

Gates, Henry Louis, Jr., with Cornel West. *The Future of the Race*. New York: Knopf, 1996.

Gates, Henry Louis, Jr., ed. *"Race," Writing, and Difference*. Chicago: U of Chicago P, 1986.

Genet, Jean. *Les Nègres*. 1958. Paris: L'Arbalète, 1963.

Gilman, Sander L. *Freud, Race, and Gender*. Princeton: Princeton UP, 1993.

————. *Difference and Pathology: Stereotypes of Sexuality, Race, and Madness*. Ithaca: Cornell UP, 1985.

Gilman, Sander L. and J. Edward Chamberlin, eds. *Degeneration: The Dark Side of Progress*. New York: Columbia UP, 1985.

Gilroy, Paul. "Urban Social Movements, 'Race,' and Community." 1987. In Williams and Chrisman. 404–20.

————. *The Black Atlantic: Modernity and Double Consciousness*. Cambridge: Harvard UP, 1993.

Girard, René. *Violence and the Sacred*. 1972. Trans. Patrick Gregory. Baltimore: Johns Hopkins UP, 1977.

————. *The Scapegoat*. Trans. Yvonne Freccero. Baltimore: Johns Hopkins UP, 1986.

Goldberg, David Theo. *Racial Subjects: Writing on Race in America*. New York: Routledge, 1997.

Goldberg, David Theo, ed. *Anatomy of Racism*. Minneapolis: U of Minnesota P, 1990.

Greenfeld, Liah. *Nationalism: Five Roads to Modernity*. Cambridge: Harvard UP, 1992.

Gregory, Steven and Roger Sanjek, eds. *Race*. New Brunswick: Rutgers UP, 1994.

Hall, Stuart. "Cultural Identity and Diaspora." 1990. In Williams and Chrisman. 392–403.

Herrnstein, Richard J. and Charles Murray. *The Bell Curve: Intelligence and Class Structure in American Life*. New York: Free Press, 1995.

Holden, Michael, Jr. *The White Man's Burden*. New York: Chandler, 1973.

Ignatiev, Noel and John Garvey, eds. *Race Traitor*. New York: Routledge, 1996.

Itzkoff, Seymour. *The Decline of Intelligence in America: A Strategy for National Renewal.* Westport, Conn.: Praeger, 1994.

Jacoby, Russell and Naomi Glauberman, eds. *The Bell Curve Debate: History, Documents, Opinions.* New York: Times, 1995.

James, Darius. *Negrophobia: An Urban Parable—A Novel.* New York: Citadel, 1992.

JanMohamed, Abdul R. "Sexuality on/of the Racial Border: Foucault, Wright, and the Articulation of 'Racialized Sexuality.'" *Discourses of Sexuality: From Aristotle to AIDS.* Ed. Domna C. Stanton. Ann Arbor: U of Michigan P, 1992. 94–116.

Jung, Carl G. *The Archetypes and the Collective Unconscious.* 2nd ed. Trans. R. F. C. Hull. Princeton: Princeton UP, 1969.

Kipling, Rudyard. *Kim.* 1901. Harmondsworth: Penguin, 1989.

Klineberg, Otto. *Race Differences.* New York: Harper and Brothers, 1935.

———. *Race and Psychology.* Paris: Unesco, 1951.

Kovel, Joel. *White Racism: A Psychohistory.* New York: Pantheon, 1971.

Kristeva, Julia. *Strangers to Ourselves.* Trans. Leon S. Roudiez. New York: Columbia UP, 1991.

———. *Nations Without Nationalism.* Trans. Leon S. Roudiez. New York: Columbia UP, 1993.

Lacan, Jacques. "Kant with Sade." 1963. Trans. James B. Swenson, Jr. *October* 51 (1989): 55–75.

———. *Television: A Challenge to the Psychoanalytic Establishment.* 1974. Trans. Denis Hollier, Rosalind Krauss, Annette Michelson, and Jeffrey Mehlman. Ed. Joan Copjec. New York: Norton, 1990.

Lapides, Frederick R. and David Burrows, eds. *Racism: A Casebook.* New York: Crowell, 1971.

Lindsey, Paul and Ouida. *Breaking the Bonds of Racism.* Homewood, Ill: Homewood, 1974.

Lingis, Alphonso. *Foreign Bodies.* New York: Routledge, 1994.

Mack, Raymond W., ed. *Prejudice and Race Relations.* Chicago: Quadrangle, 1970.

McClintock, Anne. *Imperial Leather: Race, Gender, and Sexuality in the Colonial Conquest.* New York: Routledge, 1995.

McClintock, Anne, Aamir Mufti, and Ella Shohat, eds. *Dangerous Liaisons: Gender, Nation, and Postcolonial Perspectives.* Minneapolis: U of Minnesota P, 1997.

Mannoni, Octave. *Prospero and Caliban: The Psychology of Colonization.* 2nd Edition. Trans. Pamela Powesland. New York: Praeger, 1956, 1964.

Miller, Jacques-Alain. "A Reading of Some Details in *Television* in Dialogue with the Audience." *Newsletter of the Freudian Field* 4.1–2 (1990): 4–30.

Mosse, George L. *Nationalism and Sexuality: Middle-Class Morality and Sexual Norms in Modern Europe.* Madison: U of Wisconsin P, 1985.

Morrison, Toni. *Playing in the Dark: Whiteness and the Literary Imagination.* New York: Vintage, 1992.

Morrison, Toni, ed. and intro. *Race-ing Justice, En-gendering Power: Essays on Anita Hill, Clarence Thomas, and the Construction of Social Reality.* New York: Pantheon, 1992.

Nandy, Ashis. *The Intimate Enemy: Loss and Recovery of Self under Colonialism.* Oxford: Oxford UP, 1983.

———. *The Savage Freud and Other Essays on Possible and Retrievable Selves.* Princeton: Princeton UP, 1995.

Newsweek (13 Feb., 1995), special issue: "What Color Is Black?: Science, Politics, and Racial Identity."

O'Rourke, P. J. *Give War a Chance: Eyewitness Accounts of Mankind's Struggle against Tyranny, Injustice, and Alcohol-Free Beer.* New York: Vintage, 1992, 1993.

Pick, Daniel. *Faces of Degeneration: A European Disorder, c. 1848–1918.* New York: Cambridge UP, 1989.

Putnam, Carleton. *Race and Reason: A Yankee View.* Washington, D.C.: Public Affairs, 1961.

Rose, Jacqueline. "Margaret Thatcher and Ruth Ellis." *Why War?: Psychoanalysis, Politics, and the Return to Melanie Klein.* Cambridge: Blackwell, 1993. 41–86.

———. "On the 'Universality' of Madness: Bessie Head's *A Question of Power.*" *Critical Inquiry* 20.3 (1994): 401–18.

Rushton, J. Philippe. *Race, Evolution, and Behavior: A Life History Perspective.* New Brunswick: Transaction, 1995.

Selznick, Gertrude J. and Stephen Steinberg. *The Tenacity of Prejudice: Anti-Semitism in Contemporary America.* New York: Harper and Row, 1969.

Seshadri-Crooks, Kalpana. "The Primitive as Analyst: Postcolonial Feminism's Access to Psychoanalysis." *Cultural Critique* 28 (1994): 175–218.

Sowell, Thomas. *Race and Culture: A World View.* New York: Basic Books, 1994.

Spillers, Hortense J. "Mama's Baby, Papa's Maybe: An American Grammar Book." *Diacritics* 17.2 (1987): 65–81.

———. " 'All the Things You Could Be by Now If Sigmund Freud's Wife Was Your Mother': Psychoanalysis and Race." *Critical Inquiry* 22.4 (1996): 710–34.

Sterba, Richard. "Some Psychological Factors in Negro Race Hatred and in Anti-Negro Riots." *Psychoanalysis and the Social Sciences* 1 (1947): 411–27.

Stoler, Ann Laura. *Race and the Education of Desire: Foucault's History of Sexuality and the Colonial Order of Things.* Durham: Duke UP, 1995.

Stowe, David W. "Uncolored People: The Rise of Whiteness Studies." *Lingua franca* 6.6 (1996): 68–77.

Suleri, Sara. "Woman Skin Deep: Feminism and the Postcolonial Condition." 1992. In Williams and Chrisman. 244–56.

Wallace, Edwin R. *Freud and Anthropology: A History and Reappraisal.* New York: International UP, 1983.

Walton, Jean. "Re-Placing Race in (White) Psychoanalytic Discourse: Founding Narratives of Feminism." *Critical Inquiry* 21.4 (1995): 775–804.

Watson, Peter, ed. *Psychology and Race.* Harmondsworth: Penguin, 1973.

Williams, Patrick and Laura Chrisman, eds. *Colonial Discourse and Post-Colonial Theory.* New York: Columbia UP, 1994.

Wright, Robert. *The Moral Animal: Evolutionary Psychology and Everyday Life.* New York: Pantheon, 1994.

Young, Robert J. C. *Colonial Desire: Hybridity in Theory, Culture, and Race.* New York: Routledge, 1995.

Young-Bruehl, Elisabeth. *The Anatomy of Prejudices.* Cambridge: Harvard UP, 1996.

Žižek, Slavoj. *The Sublime Object of Ideology.* New York: Verso, 1989.

——. "Enjoy Your Nation As Yourself!" *Tarrying with the Negative: Kant, Hegel, and the Critique of Ideology.* Durham: Duke UP, 1993. 200–37.

PART I

Current Dilemmas:

Psychoanalysis and Postcolonialism

I

Human Diversity and the Sexual Relation

Charles Shepherdson

> Imitation is natural to man from childhood, one of his advantages
> over the lower animals being this, that he is the most imitative crea-
> ture in the world, and learns at first from imitation.
>
> —Aristotle 1448 b4–8

> What follows is speculation.   —Freud, *Beyond* 24

The Limits of Historicism

In recent years, appeals to race as a biological concept
have been subject to strenuous criticism, not only
because of the history that has bound scientific definitions of race to eugenics, colonialism, and the Holocaust,
but also because biological definitions of race cannot be
sustained even on scientific grounds. It is therefore not
only for political and ethical reasons, but for reasons
internal to science, that the biological category of race
remains problematic. And yet, while research has made
us profoundly and rightly suspicious of the uses to which
the science of race has been put in the past, it has not
been possible simply to dispense with the question of
race as it bears on our bodily or physical diversity. The
distinction between cultural and natural aspects of
human identity thus appears to remain intact and worthy
of attention.

Even in the arena of social theory, the popular terms
"race" and "ethnicity" tend to suggest that we can distinguish—and perhaps still need to distinguish—between

those aspects of identity that can be attributed to culture (learning, tradition, religious practice, kinship systems, language, etc.), and those aspects that are due to a natural or genetic endowment. A Caucasian who is adopted at birth by a Native-American family, who shares the customs and beliefs of the Ojibwa, who thinks and dreams in Algonquin, cherishing the values embodied in that language and community, might well be considered *ethnically* Native-American, but it is less likely that we would regard such a person as *racially* Native-American. Certainly the current legal system, which obliges citizens to identify themselves as Hispanic, Pacific Islander, and so on, would classify such a person as Caucasian.

It is therefore not only from a biological point of view, but from the standpoint of social and political theory, that our physical differences continue to receive terminological attention, and to play a conceptual role that is distinguished—however obscurely and inadequately—from purely cultural and historical differences. Thus in spite of the extreme vigilance we have been taught to maintain regarding the biological category of race, human diversity seems to remain open to both cultural and biological analysis.

This difficulty is not limited to sociopolitical theory, where—the distinction between "race" and "ethnicity" notwithstanding—the term "race" refers ambiguously to both social and physical differences. The same conceptual impasse, and the same need for an analysis that would bear simultaneously on biological and social factors, arises in a number of disciplines: in physical anthropology (which encounters the problem of how various cultural phenomena such as agriculture and medicine have affected the human body, to the point of altering its genetic makeup); in linguistics (where the question arises as to whether language, properly speaking, belongs only to the human species, and, if so, whether it is learned or innate, a cultural invention or a natural endowment); and in many other fields. The problem therefore goes well beyond our everyday use of the word "race," wherein the term seems to designate something more than cultural difference.

Recent medical literature has similarly relied on the distinction between social and biological identity, while at the same time making it especially problematic. Differences in morbidity, heart disease, cancer, and many other conditions have been explained in part by reference to social factors (economic conditions, diet, behavior, access to medical care, and so on), but research has also given increasing attention to genetic predispositions and other inherited factors, which point not only to the family (a group that is both a social institution and a biological relation), but to larger group identity, and thus to something like "race."

It has been suggested, to cite only the most familiar examples, that Native-Americans do not metabolize alcohol as easily as Caucasians; that there is a genetic basis for depression among the Amish; that sickle cell anemia tends to appear only in certain populations (among "blacks," or rather, as Sander Gilman says, "actually only those individuals who inhabit or whose ancestors inhabited malarial water areas"), and so on (2). Prior to AIDS, Kaposi's sarcoma appeared largely among people whose antecedents lived in the Mediterranean basin, and many other diseases circulate, not randomly, but in a way that distinguishes some human populations from others (see Risse 33–34; Bateson and Goldsby 11–23). Debates rage fiercely as to whether these distributions are due to social or biological factors, and obviously there is no single answer: Not all diseases circulate according to the same logic or the same routes of transmission. In the case of diabetes and hemophilia, which are not contagious, genetic factors appear to predominate, whereas in the case of tuberculosis, which is airborne, and cholera, which passes through the water supply, social structures (or their lack) correlate directly with the spread of disease. In each case, the social and biological factors involved must be weighed; but again, as with the term "race," both factors seem to merit attention, even as the difficulty of distinguishing them remains.

Like some forms of medical knowledge, the concept of race thus points to a question of identity that cannot be resolved entirely at the level of social or symbolic identity, even if we tend to resist purely biological arguments. This difficult border between nature and culture is negotiated not only in medicine and in popular discussions of race, but in anthropology, psychology, linguistics, and many other fields that deal with human diversity. Any discipline touching on the peculiar border between nature and culture—in fact, any discipline dealing with the body, as psychoanalysis does—seems to require some way of distinguishing between the biological and social dimensions of identity, however problematic and unsatisfactory this distinction may be.

Cultural criticism has tended to avoid this problem. To the extent that it leaves our bodily diversity to one side in order to concentrate on the meanings and interpretations that are imposed upon the body, cultural criticism has handed over the fact of our physical embodiment to the natural sciences, as though it were entitled to address only the sociohistorical aspects of our diversity—our cultural differences. Discussing various *representations* of the body, and the changing *conceptions* of the body that have arisen at different historical moments (as when Thomas Laqueur, for example, describes the shift from the "one sex" model to the "two sexes" theory of post-Enlightenment medicine), cultural criticism often appears to abandon the body itself to the arena of nature. Cultural criticism thus might be said to maintain a tacit alliance with the very naturalism it so frequently denounces. To be sure, we are warned that every observation or theory of the body is embedded in a complex network of symbolic conditions, such that even a scientific account, while promising to describe "the thing itself," is a contingent discursive construction that cannot provide unmediated access to reality. Feminist theorists such as Donna Haraway and Anne Fausto-Sterling and historians of science such as Nancy Stepan have shown us in convincing detail how the purportedly objective and neutral discourse of science is unwittingly burdened by preconceptions drawn from other domains. On these grounds, "race" as a valid biological concept may be rejected; the focus can shift to *racism* as a social and political issue that we can place alongside class and gender and regard as a cultural effect. Psychoanalysis has often contributed to these forms of social critique by exploring the fantasies supporting racist ideologies and the narcissistic underpinnings of prejudice, hatred, and aggression. As Michel Foucault points out, Freud himself took pains to break with the theories of "degeneracy" that supported racism and homophobia in the early twentieth century (*History* 149–50).

Such arguments are extremely valuable, and we have no wish to contest them here. In a sense, we wish only to deepen the historical question and render the terms of debate more problematic. For we might ask whether every phenomenon can be historicized in precisely the same way, or given the same discursive status, when we address their historical formation. We may speak of the Renaissance theory of madness, or the invention of the modern nation-state, but not all phenomena should be placed at the same conceptual level when we consider their relation to history. Nor should we immediately suppose that race can automatically be discussed in the same way as class or gender—that it should be regarded as a historical product and analyzed with the same conceptual tools we bring to analyses of national identity and other social categories. In the case of AIDS, for example, we are faced with a phenomenon that is embedded in the most vicious and prejudicial representations; it cannot be simply detached from this discursive horizon in the name of pure biological knowledge. So powerful is the network of representation that it has affected not only the progress and funding of research, but the very course of disease. Thus AIDS itself is not a purely natural phenomenon that representation can render in a merely secondary way. This should not lead us to suppose, however, that AIDS is a purely symbolic effect, or that it is "historical" *in the same way* that gender and national identity are said to be when they are regarded as social constructions.

If we question the limits of historicism, then, we do so not to propose a return to the reality of empirical facts or in the name of biological truth, but because the historicity of various phenomena—what we might call their modes of temporalization—has often been prematurely reduced to a single form by the discourse of social construction. In this sense the body—perhaps like race itself—cannot be adequately grasped if it is regarded as a discursive effect or a purely symbolic formation. Judith Butler, in *Bodies That Matter*, and many other writers have recently tried to rectify this deficiency in much of our theoretical work by exploring the concrete relation between language and the flesh.

In this respect, race has much in common with the term "sexual difference," which plays such a notorious role in psychoanalytic theory. We often speak of "gender" as a network of social and symbolic meanings, imposed on the "sex" of the subject, which we regard as an anatomical fact. On the basis of this vocabulary, readers are frequently encouraged to decide whether "sexual difference" refers to sex or gender—that is, whether psychoanalysis is a disguised form of naturalism, a version of essentialism, or whether it regards sexual difference as a symbolic formation, and thereby coincides with historicist theories of gender. In fact, however, neither of these perspectives is correct. The vocabulary of psychoanalysis cannot be grasped in its own theoretical specificity if it is forced to coincide with a conceptual alternative that effaces its most elementary terms from the outset.

Like sexual difference, our racial differences are also bound up with the most heavily invested symbolic values, but they cannot be regarded as the invention of a particular culture or the product of a specific historical moment. This does not mean that we can construe race or sexual difference as natural phenomena, reducible to biological facts. But it does mean that we cannot adequately conceptualize race or sexual difference if we treat them precisely like laws, theories of selfhood, or economic policies. Like sexual difference, race is not a human invention, and there is a sense in which arguments for social construction—insofar as they fail to theorize these distinctions—remain bound to a humanistic tradition in which "man is the maker of all things."

This brings us to the historical axis of our argument. The fact that this conceptual problem arises today with such regularity across such a wide variety of disciplines, including medicine, psychology, anthropology, linguistics, and the entire range of social theory, suggests that the inherited configuration of our knowledge—the very distinction between nature and culture to which we appeal so frequently in our discussion of race and many other issues—has reached an impasse, in the sense that this distinction is no longer adequate to the phenomena it seeks to address. What can current developments in psychoanalytic theory contribute to this discussion—not only to the concept of race, but to the ancient question of human physical diversity?

The Nature/Culture Debate

As a concept, "race" designates an obscure and contested domain, seeming to refer to both natural and cultural aspects of human identity. In certain contexts, the term "race" has a strictly biological sense (and one can endorse or denounce such usage); but it can also designate a group identity that is based on a common cultural and historical inheritance. Although some writers simply take one of these senses for granted, ignoring or dismissing the other, many accounts of race employ the term in all its ambiguity, without distinguishing between these two registers of meaning. In such cases, "race" is used to indicate a cultural inheritance, a form of social identity, while also referring to features that are not entirely social and cannot be acquired by education and upbringing, such as skin color and genetic ancestry. Discussions of race often lead back to this ambiguity, and thus to a single, decisive question concerning its status as a biological or social category.

One might seek to avoid this difficulty by terminological fiat, insisting that "race" *really* designates a biological fact, or that it is *really* a purely social invention, a product of history that might be equated with class or religion or national identity, and analyzed with the same conceptual tools that we bring to the discussion of other cultural phenomena. One might thereby assert that race is a human invention, a social phenomenon no different than architecture or parliamentary representation. It is tempting, perhaps, to insist on a terminological division of labor, in the hope of removing ambiguity by placing the term "race" on one side or the other of this conceptual divide. But ordinary language tells the truth in this case, indicating something about *race itself*, in its very oscillation between nature and culture, its excess over the conceptual alternative we continue to use in our efforts to address it. In Jacques Lacan's language, we might say that race is something *real*—not in the sense that it refers to prelinguistic *reality*, but because it exceeds our symbolic grasp.

Lucius Outlaw has stressed this conceptual instability: "For most of us, that there are different races of people is one of the most obvious features of our social world" (58). These differences, he adds, are evident "in our encounters with persons who are significantly different from us particularly in terms of physical features (skin color and other anatomical features), *but also, often combined with these*, when they are different with respect to language, behavior, ideas, and other 'cultural' matters" (58; my emphasis). If we stress the apparently innocent words "but also, often combined with these," it is because they provide an initial orientation for the problem concerning us, since it is a question of recognizing a *difference* between two distinct domains ("physical features. . . *but also*. . . 'cultural' matters") as well as a *mixture* (the one being *"often combined with"* the other). As a result, these two domains, which can and must be differentiated without being reduced to a common ground, nevertheless "combine" in a manner that calls for theoretical clarification.

We thus have a first indication of our difficulty: Cultural critics today might be tempted to insist that race has no biological validity, but is *really* a symbolic effect, a contingent product of discursive practices that is wrongly "naturalized" as a biological fact. Directly opposed to these critics—though in perfect keeping with the same conceptual framework—certain members of today's scientific community celebrate "the revival of interest in the biological roots of human nature" (Degler 264), claiming that race is *really* a biological fact. Thus Degler offers to demonstrate that such things as the incest prohibition—and other phenomena, including war and religion—have a biological basis (see also Harris 296–300). We know how heavily this debate is invested today.

The notorious incest taboo is, for Degler, the example that will finally allow us to dismiss Freudian theory altogether. We are asked to recognize that this apparently cultural law, whatever its peculiar manifestations in the human world, is in fact a genetically inherited mechanism that aims at preventing "inbreeding." Citing authorities who have established "the avoidance of incest among animals" (257), Degler argues that "the incest taboo could not be an invention of human beings" (257). He enlists Norbert Bischof's claim that it is "an empirical fact that in the whole animal world with very few exceptions no species is known in which under natural conditions inbreeding occurs to any considerable degree" (qtd. 257). We are thus faced with "a growing and often enthusiastic interest among social scientists in looking at the history of the incest taboo from a biological point of view" (264). "The ethnological evidence, mounting each year, renders the avoidance of incest within the family or basic social unit no longer a peculiarly human activity" (264).

Freud, Lévi-Strauss, and other social theorists were therefore wrong to consider this law or prohibition a uniquely cultural phenomenon. Lacking our scientific knowledge, they fell prey to the anthropocentric illusion that humanity is somehow an exception to nature, refusing to admit that this prohibition merely reinforces an already "natural avoidance" (262). But we now know "that culture evolved in accordance with genetic advantage" (265) and "that incest avoidance was genetically based" (264). We thus have "new support for the Westermarckian hypothesis" that "family members do not have a strong sexual attraction" (266), and new ammunition against Freudian theory, Lévi-Strauss, and others who share the prejudice of the social sciences.

A long period of philosophical naiveté would thus be brought to a close, with consequences bearing on race and a number of other issues. For as Peter Bowler notes, "The collapse of evolutionary race theory came not because it was scientifically disproved but because the social sciences turned their backs on the whole evolutionary viewpoint" (*Evolution* 305). This period of naiveté, which began early in the twentieth century, was characterized by a turn from evolutionary explanations to an emphasis on the "superorganic" forces that were thought to organize culture—historical and symbolic forces that could not be reduced to nature or explained by biological mechanisms. For these sociologists, Bowler laments, "Cultural forces alone account for the differences; and, as A. L. Kroeber proclaimed in his 1917 paper on the 'superorganic,' these forces have nothing to do with biological differences" (305). It is this theory of purely "symbolic" differences that the new biological discoveries will finally discredit.

Degler notes in passing, however, that the theory he defends, while confidently asserting an innate repulsion in regard to any "intra-familial erotic attraction," may "leave some elements unaccounted for" (261). He mentions "the question of father-daughter incest" (261), which not only occurs but appears to be forty times greater than mother-son incest. And yet, Degler never addresses this small detail, which remains confined to one sentence and footnote, as if it presented no obstacle to the theory of innate avoidance. There is not time for philosophical naiveté or culturalist prejudice. We can no longer avoid the conclusion, based on evidence that is "mounting" (264) every year: "Westermarck's conception of the lack of intrafamilial erotic attraction seems to be more accurate than the assumption that among human beings there is a natural urge to incest" (264–65).

The point here, however, is not to assert a familiar counterargument, turning from nature to history in order to claim (as Degler puts it) that the incest prohibition is a social construction, "an invention of human beings" (257). For Degler, these are indeed the only possibilities: The avoidance of incest is either a natural mechanism or a cultural institution—like democracy or abstract expressionism, something invented by human beings that can be confined to a particular culture or historical moment. For Freud, however, the incest taboo is neither a biological fact nor a human invention. It would be more accurate to say that the human is an invention of the incest taboo. That is why Freud situates this taboo not *in history* but *at the origin* of human time—the time of the subject and of the human community. The taboo thus cannot be grasped by the alternative Degler proposes.

When Degler ascribes to Freud the belief that the prohibition is a "law" like other human conventions, he has already refused the most radical and philosophically important dimension of Freud's work. He not only presupposes that Freud can be read sociologically, so that the entire problematic of the *constitution* of the subject is eliminated and the discussion is displaced onto the field of sociohistorical *construction*; he also avoids the question of *what "incest" means*. For the biologist, "incest" concerns only the actual sexual union—not of a "subject" and an "object" (terms receiving extended discussion throughout psychoanalysis) but of two *organisms*. From this perspective, "incest" designates the union of two individuals viewed as carriers of genetic material that will either mix ("inbreeding") or not, so that animals who do not breed with their immediate biological relatives may also be said to avoid "incest." For Freud, however, incest cannot be understood at the level of genetic substance. As a result, to speak of the taboo as a cultural invention aimed at preventing "inbreeding" is equally beside the point, since genetic inbreeding is not the standard explaining the psychoanalytic account of incest. The entire conceptual framework demands to be rethought.

Degler opposes psychoanalysis precisely in terms of this framework, however, drawing Freud's work back into the very debates he intended to reconfigure: "Psychoanalysis required the taboo to be cultural rather than innate" (Degler 248). Freud wrongly assumed that in the face of incestuous desire, an institution had to be developed to prevent by law or custom—indeed "from an apparently rational decision" (246)—what would otherwise naturally take place. (Here too, Degler avoids basic terminological distinctions, as if incestuous "desire" for Freud were the same as "instinct," and meant only a natural urge to copulate.) It is therefore not a matter of insisting, against Degler, that the taboo is in fact a cultural construction such as table manners or the modern form of the prison—the contingent effect of a given social order. Yet this is the alternative that contemporary debates frequently propose with regard to a number of disparate phenomena, including race, homosexuality, schizophrenia, and many other things: The object in question is either grounded in biological causes, like hormones or skin color, or viewed as a social construction that is destined to pass away, like democracy, the nation-state, or atomic weapons.

An enormous problematic could be opened here, for the difficulties arising over the term "incest" recur throughout Degler's work. When he speaks of incest between "brother" and "sister," for instance, or uses the terms "mother" and "father," these words simply designate for him organic beings in a certain biological relation. It should be obvious, however, that terms such as "mother" have a highly developed sense in psychoanalysis and cannot simply be translated into the vocabulary of natural relations without misconceiving the entire theoretical field (as if "woman" and "mother" and "female" were equivalent terms). Given a biological reduction of all this vocabulary, how could one speak of the mother-daughter relation as "incestuous"? The question cannot even arise.

Freud, by contrast, explicitly points out in *Totem and Taboo* that the essence of the prohibition against incest is not biological. Following Frazer, he notes that among the aboriginal people of Melanesia and the Solomon Islands, a man will avoid not only sexual intercourse but any physical contact—and even the exchange of glances—with a woman who *bears the same name*, even if she is no biological relation (12–13). The biologist may claim that in such cases, the "primitive" people do not understand how conception works, or that they have extended a natural principle in a symbolic way, taking it beyond its true and proper function. For

Freud, however, this apparently excessive and perverse case of symbolic displacement reveals the heart of the taboo itself, not an aberration of its proper biological purpose: The displacement brings to light the discontinuity between biology and the name. "Kinship terms," Freud writes, "do not necessarily indicate any consanguinity, as ours would do" (7). As a result, the prohibition of "incest" must bear on a structure—a relation between subject and object—that is distinct from biological relations. According to Freud, this structure confronts us with "a peculiarity which remains obscure to us—of replacing real blood-relationship by totem kinship" (6). At the same time, however, this structural relation should not be confused with a social or "tribal" identity: "An Australian's relation to his totem is the basis of all his social obligations: it overrides on the one hand his tribal membership and on the other hand his blood relationships" (3).

In rejecting biology, then, Freud does not regard the taboo as a historical institution, an "invention of human beings." The very universality of the prohibition suggests to him that the structure of the symbolic order brings with it a number of features decisive for subjectivity as such. These features cannot be grasped if they are confused with biological mechanisms or reduced to historical conventions, and thus considered mere social phenomena. Contrary to Degler, the prohibition against "incest" is neither a natural mechanism to be analyzed at the level of genetic mixing nor a cultural invention to be explained by methods of sociohistorical research. Like desire itself, the prohibition cannot be regarded as the exclusive possession of a particular culture or equated with the biological concept of "instinct" and considered as a natural "urge." It is this very alternative that Freudian theory calls into question.

The historical axis of our argument is clear: When two discourses arise simultaneously promising to "explain" such varied and diverse phenomena as schizophrenia, alcoholism, anorexia, male violence, and even perception itself, the genealogist can only suspect that these two modes of explanation, however fervently they may denounce each other, are simply two faces of one and the same conceptual formation. Their supposed opposition to each other—so public, and so heavily invested with moral passion today—is the sign of a deeper commonality, a sign that they have a common birth.

We might at this point take our direction from Foucault: "What often embarrasses me today," he says,

> is that all this work done in the past fifteen years or so . . . functions for some only as a sign of belonging: to be on the "good side," on the side of madness, children, delinquency, sex. . . . One must pass to the other side—the good side—but by trying to turn off these mechanisms which cause the appearance of two separate

sides . . . This is where the real work begins, that of the present-day historian. ("Power" 120–21)

This is why the *theoretical* obscurity of the term "race"—its ambiguous position with respect to the distinction between nature and culture—cannot be approached as a purely logical or conceptual problem. It must also be articulated in terms of the *history* that has given rise not only to the term "race" as it functions today (in a manner that is far from unified), but to the *disciplines* that promise to explain it, including contemporary cultural theory and genetic analysis. This also means, however, that if psychoanalysis offers to contribute to current discussions of race on the basis of its own theoretical perspective, by drawing on its unique vocabulary or procedures, it cannot simply respond to the conceptual impasses of contemporary debates. Psychoanalysis must also attend to the historical development of race as a concept, and thus to the very history that gave rise to psychoanalysis itself.

The impact of psychoanalysis is therefore historical as well as theoretical: If the fundamental concepts of psychoanalysis are irreducible to the opposition between biological and historical models, it is not for conceptual reasons alone. While this opposition is ancient, it took a particular form in the nineteenth century when the biological sciences and the discipline of history were both organized. It is this heritage that psychoanalysis disrupts, which continues paradoxically to organize and distort our understanding of psychoanalytic theory (as Degler's account of "incest" suggests).

The same point can be made for many other basic concepts. When Freud speaks of the ego, he is not speaking of a biological phenomenon, an anatomical part of the living being; but nor is he speaking of an institution that can be attributed to a specific culture. To be sure, each culture may provide different rituals or symbolic props to regulate the ego in distinctive ways; but this does not mean, for Freud, that the ego itself is a human invention. Similarly, when Lacan speaks of the imaginary body it is clear that each culture will negotiate corporeality in different ways, but the body itself cannot be confined to a particular historical moment—any more than madness, as Derrida has shown, can simply be historicized (42–43, 54, 57). This does not mean that the body, or madness, can be handed over to the natural sciences or situated at the level of the organism—a thesis the imaginary body explicitly opposes. It simply means that the basic concepts of psychoanalysis cannot be grasped in terms of this familiar alternative. We have suggested that "sexual difference" likewise falls outside the opposition between nature and culture, and that, as a result, to ask whether the term refers to "sex" or "gender" is already to abandon the entire vocabulary of psychoanalysis. Thus when Degler offers to resolve the debate over the incest taboo by deciding once and for all whether the prohibition is a social institution or a biological phenomenon, his question is simply anachronistic. It proceeds in terms of an alternative that is, from a genealogical perspective, strictly pre-Freudian, drawing the entire debate back onto a conceptual field that Freudian theory radically displaced.

These remarks should have an effect on race and many other concepts, for when we are asked to decide whether the object in question (be it race or incest, homosexuality or sexual difference) is a discursive effect or a biological phenomenon, neither alternative confronts the two compelling difficulties that Outlaw's formulation puts before us: First, that both dimensions of human existence have a distinctive character and should not be too quickly absorbed by one another; and second, but even more important, that we can approach this very distinction *only through a certain mixture,* a "combination" that would finally oblige us to detach race from the two alternatives still promising to explain it today, and demanding our allegiance so loudly.

As a result, *race itself* would no longer belong to this horizon of debate. Instead of asking whether race is a biological fact or a cultural construction, or allotting some justice to both sides of the debate, might it not be more accurate to say that race is *neither,* just as "sexual difference" is neither sex nor gender? The historical aspect of the difficulty should therefore be clear: If we speak of race or the body or sexual difference today (and we can no longer think without addressing them), and if all these concepts prove irreducible to the nature/culture debate, surely these particular difficulties arise for us not because of their intrinsic and eternal importance, but because the history of our thought has reached an impasse at precisely these points, so that these specific questions dominate and weigh upon us today, even as our conceptual resources remain inadequate to them.

Imaginary Physiology and Genetic Diversity

We have said that the concept of race is problematic not only from an ethical and political perspective but for reasons internal to science. Without entering into an extended discussion, let us consider a few of these difficulties more closely. The most common and popular markers of racial difference—skin color, hair, and facial features—are also, from an evolutionary standpoint, the most superficial. They are surface phenomena, expressions of phenotype leading to racial classifications that do not correspond to the divisions of the population given by the international genetic maps currently under construction (see Gutin 73; Banton and Harwood 47–49).

Although opponents sometimes suspect biological accounts of automatically subscribing to the most familiar and prejudicial stereotypes, representatives of the Human Genome Diversity Project have pointed out that the opposite may be the case: Far from confirming the traditional racial categories, a more accurate account of human genetic diversity would run counter to them, since "patterns of variation that appear at the genetic level cut across *visible* racial divisions" (Gutin 73; my emphasis).[1] Thus Luca Cavalli-Sforza, a professor of genetics at Stanford University, claims that "only genes . . . have the degree of permanence necessary" to produce an historically adequate account of the evolution of human populations (qtd. in Gutin 73).

For the geneticist, the point may be simply that "good science" should restrict itself to its proper object, without relying on traditional typologies of race (Bowler *Theories* 106, 128; Outlaw 62–64). But for the intellectual historian, the mistakes of "bad science" are not simply errors that the progress of knowledge will overcome—like the medieval doctrine of humors that is regarded as a "primitive" form of biology. On the contrary, these "mistakes" have their reasons and must therefore be explained as positive phenomena in their own right. In Foucault's words,

> genealogy does not resemble the evolution of a species and does not map the destiny of a people. On the contrary, to follow the complex course of descent is to maintain passing events in their proper dispersion; it is to identify the accidents, the minute deviations—the errors, the false appraisals, and the faulty calculations that gave birth to *those things that continue to exist and have value for us.* ("Nietzsche" 81; my emphasis)

Will our current rage for "genetic science" not one day appear in precisely the same light as the doctrine of humors does today? And is our passion for revealing the discursive construction of all things not also one of those accidents giving birth to our momentary truth? May we not therefore consider them already with the same cold gaze that the genealogist brings to the extravagant mythologies of the past, instead of blinding ourselves with the illusion that we have finally emerged into the light?

Given the distinction between visible "races" and genetic diversity, the scientist may wish simply to dismiss the traditional classification, regarding it as an error of the past. But another conclusion seems to follow. Consider the most familiar racial groups, the four or five types found in traditional physical anthropology since the time of Linnaeus: the Asian, African, Caucasian, American Indian, and two or three others, such as the Capoid or "Koisan" people, commonly known as "Bushmen," the "Australoid" group, the "Polynesians" (Goldsby 31–39, Coleman 92–

117), as well as the two groups added by Linnaeus himself, which he called "ferus," for "wild" children, and "monstrous," to describe "hairy men with tails, and other travelers' confabulations" (Gould, "Geometer" 67). Following our observations above, we might regard these groups not as *mere mistakes* that genetic science will rectify, but as groups based on *visible features*, which generate classifications that are quite distinct from those obtained by reference to other genetic traits—traits that are arguably more fundamental from an evolutionary perspective. We may therefore posit a discontinuity between what one might call *the imaginary physiology of race* and *human genetic diversity*.

This taxonomic discontinuity between genetic and imaginary "races" is not the only difficulty, however. For genetic diversity gives rise to a number of difficulties even when taken on its own terms, and apart from traditional typologies, because the classifications one obtains by focusing on one trait do not correspond with those resulting from considering other features (Albert et al. 26). For example, populations in which adults share a genetic lactase deficiency include a number of "different" groups, such as people from Southern Europe, most African blacks, East Asians, and American Indians (Diamond 86), while in the case of differences in earwax, genetic analysis puts Caucasian and black populations in one group, contrasting them with East Asian populations (Goldsby 56).

Far from stabilizing the familiar racial taxonomies, efforts to resolve these difficulties of classification by focusing on groups of traits rather than single features will yield only greater internal variation within apparently unified groups. Since features such as fingerprint pattern, dental characteristics, and hair color are inherited independently (rather than being genetically linked), a more rigorous table of differences will produce only a more diverse and complex map of human diversity, in which the familiar "races" conceal more than they show. Nor are these difficulties limited to group taxonomy, for individual genetic traits present their own difficulties: In the case of organ donation, where genetic considerations are frequently crucial, an African-American will often turn out to be a better match for a Caucasian, and vice versa, than someone of the same race (Gutin 73). Here again, *genetic proximity* cuts across received categories of racial type.

These difficulties can be multiplied, for the diversity of the human blood pool remains notoriously problematic from a biological point of view, and variations in the antigens of the human immune system (which is based on bone marrow as well as blood) are similarly obscure, though knowledge of these differences is essential for transplants, transfusions, and other medical purposes. As for skin color, even aside from its relatively "superficial" status in evolutionary theory, this too remains highly problematic from a biological perspective. Although differences in pigmentation are commonly attributed to varying degrees of exposure to the sun over many generations, this "adaptive" explanation has not proved satisfactory to the scientific community. As Jared Diamond notes,

> anthropologists love to stress the dark skins of African blacks, people of the Southern Indian peninsula, and New Guineans, and love to forget the pale skins of the Amazonian Indians and Southeast Asians living at the same latitudes. . . . Besides, when one takes into account cloud cover, peoples of equatorial West Africa and the New Guinea mountains actually receive no more ultraviolet radiation or hours of sunshine each year than do the Swiss. (88)

Arguments based on exposure to sunlight have been sufficiently problematic, he notes, that researchers "have proposed at least seven other supposed survival functions of skin color, without reaching agreement" (88).

Differences in human skin color thus continue to escape arguments based on adaptation to the environment, posing a problem for accounts relying on the theory of natural selection. Faced with these difficulties, arguments often turn to "sexual selection" as a supplementary mechanism, as Darwin himself did in a short but crucial section of *The Origin of Species* that has recently been given a considerably broader role in evolutionary theory (see Ridley 26–40).

Sexual Selection and Intersubjectivity

Let us look at the question of sexual selection more closely. Whereas natural selection bears on the individual's relation to the environment and other species (survival), sexual selection concerns the relation between individuals (procreation). The latter type of selection appears to obey different principles, and perhaps to yield different consequences, than those involved in natural selection. "Sexual selection theory suggests that much of the behavior and some of the appearance of an animal is adapted not to help it survive but to help it acquire the best or the most mates" (Ridley 134). The two might seem to coincide, for as Darwin himself said, "the best adapted individuals. . . will tend to propagate their kind in greater numbers." Yet he immediately distinguished between the two: "This leads me to say a few words on what I have called Sexual Selection. This form of selection depends, not on a struggle for existence in relation to other organic beings or to external conditions, but on a struggle between the individuals of one sex, generally the males, for the possession of the other sex" (*Origin* 97–98). In Darwin's view, moreover, the principle of sexual selection is "*less rigorous than natural selection*" (98; my emphasis), because "the result is not death to the unsuccessful competitor, but few or no offspring" (98).

Classical evolutionary theory recognizes this fact. In many cases an animal faced with the choice between survival and reproduction will choose the latter, at the cost of its own life, for the sake of its genetic perpetuation—as the spawning of salmon suggests, or, to take an example more dear to Lacan, when the male praying mantis joins with its partner, only to be devoured when his function is fulfilled (*Seminaire* 249–54). Thus sexual selection would explain such things as the peacock's tail and his ritual display, and indeed many "social" phenomena in the animal world with no direct adaptive function.

On this basis, evolutionary theorists of culture have attempted to give a biological account of many human institutions that social theorists usually regard as cultural inventions. "By 1980 no detail of animal courtship mattered unless it could be explained in terms of the selective competition of genes. And by 1990 the notion that human beings were the only animals exempt from this logic was beginning to look ever more absurd" (Ridley 9). War, religion, technology, even stories and ancestral myths can thus be regarded—like the incest taboo—as mechanisms by which genetic material is distributed (Harris 296–300; de Waal 29–34, 182–86). For advocates of genetics such as Ridley, these apparent "institutions" have a biological foundation: they have been "selected for" in the ancestor and thus provide a genetic basis for behavior (not merely for appearance). A word to the wise psychoanalyst, then: "you are descended not from your mother but from her ovary" (8).

Nevertheless, these cultural institutions, however genetically driven they are said to be, already broach an extremely complex question of *representation*, a question concerning the function of language. For this attempt to reconcile culture and nature already gives humanity a peculiar and strangely eschatological position—precisely the one Foucault ascribed to modernity. From this perspective, "man" would be that animal who lives not by nature alone, but by symbolic norms that provide a supplementary means by which the population would regulate itself. We must not move too quickly here. Even if, as Aristotle says, man is a unique animal, "the most imitative creature in the world," who "learns at first from imitation," acting not only from instinct, but on the basis of an acquired and traditional wisdom, it is nevertheless possible, from the perspective of cultural evolution, to consider these institutions from a strictly biological perspective, as the means by which the human animal evolves. Culture is the adaptive advantage of the human species, and all of our symbolic behavior can be viewed as the expression of evolutionary forces. "Why then," Ridley laments, "does social science proceed as if it were not the case, as if people's natures are the product of their societies?" (8). It is precisely here, however, that we must consider the status of representation more closely, for even biology endorses a familiar humanism at this point. As the great biologist Theodosius Dobzhansky wrote in 1962:

The most important point in Darwin's teachings was, strangely enough, overlooked. Man has not only evolved, he is evolving. This is a source of hope in the abyss of despair. In a way, Darwin has healed the wound inflicted by Copernicus and Galileo. Man is not the center of the universe physically, but he may be the spiritual center. Man and man alone knows that the world evolves and that he evolves with it. By changing what he knows about the world man changes the world that he knows; and by changing the world in which he lives *man changes himself*. (346–47; my emphasis)

Thus "Evolution need no longer be a destiny imposed from without; it may conceivably be controlled by man, in accordance with his wisdom and his values" (347).

One could hardly hope to find a clearer expression of the framework in which "man" was invented. As Foucault puts it, in modern thought, man is a creature that lives by means of representation. When we speak of a "science of man," it is not a question of developing empirical sciences of wealth, or language, or production. Nor is it a matter of describing the various forms of life, the historical values and systems of belief that have characterized human existence in all of its mysterious and bizarre diversity. To arrive at a properly human science, we must isolate a relation between culture and nature, so as to suture them in a functional hierarchy: "man" appears whenever a biological need is regulated by representation, by means of which the human animal will live; whenever the scarcity of goods is managed and redistributed through the symbolic codification of economic values; whenever the representation I make of my words gives me access not to the linguistic object but to the essence of my subjectivity, my thought in its full consciousness and self-presence.

Thus "biology, economics, and philology must not be regarded as the first human sciences" (Foucault, *Order* 351). Man for the human sciences is not a living being, but "that living being who, from within the life to which he entirely belongs . . . constitutes representations by means of which he lives" (352). Man is not a creature that labors in an alienated but unnaturally productive way, generating a surplus that extends beyond nature, but a creature that—faced with a finite set of resources and demands that go well beyond need—is brought into unnatural conflict with his own kind, but is nevertheless able to form groups that can "represent to themselves the partners with whom they produce or exchange," so that this conflict can be regulated by "the manner in which they represent to themselves the society in which it takes place" (*Order* 352–53). In each case, man appears as a being subject to an unnatural life, dominated by external conditions, but able to master that subjection precisely to the extent that he can represent the forces that deprive him of a natural existence: "man appears as a being possessing *functions*—receiving stimuli (physiological ones, but also social, interhuman, and cultural ones), reacting to them, adapting himself, evolving . . . having, in short, conditions of existence and the possibility of finding average *norms* of adjustment which permit him to perform his functions" (357).

The fact of cultural and historical difference thus presents no difficulty for the biologist willing to recognize "human nature" in terms of this unique capacity to represent, and thereby to take in hand and manage the very forces that would otherwise be imposed from without. The forces of exteriority—the language I am taught to speak, the conditions of production I must inhabit, the organism in which my experience takes shape—all these determinations can be regulated and engineered by the very being that is subject to them, but only insofar as that being has the power to represent them, to order them "in accordance with his wisdom and his values" (Dobzhansky 347). Language would thus be a tool in the hands of the subject, and not irremediably Other. Cultural critics who appeal to the symbolic order as the uniquely human possession, that inventive capacity giving human existence its peculiarly contingent and historically diverse character, do not occupy a different conceptual field but remain tightly bound to the same discursive arrangement of which "man" is but one effect. Needless to say, this arrangement no longer holds much interest for us. It is an old fantasy now, hiding as much as it shows about the possibilities of desire.

The Organism and the Ego

What, then, may we conclude with respect to the enigma of sexual selection? How is the notorious "sexuality" of psychoanalysis distinct from the biological accounts promising to explain such things as genetic diversity and incest avoidance? And what is the link between "sexuality" in the psychoanalytic sense and human physical diversity? Let us take up our thread again. While sexual selection is distinguished from natural selection, and even regarded as "less rigorous" in some sense, this relation between individuals can still be explained, according to the biologists, by appeal to genetic determination, as a matter of instinct. Thus a highly codified mating ritual or a distinctive song will be instinctively produced, even when the animal has never previously seen this ritual or heard such a song before.

But perhaps this principle of sexual selection, though regulated in most animals by a strict biological mechanism, is less regular, less normal and uniform, and indeed still "less rigorous" in the human animal than the rest of the animal world. Do we not find here an opening toward Freud's distinction, in his *Three Essays on the Theory of Sexuality* (1905), between the "instinct" and the "drive," and thus toward the idea that whereas the instinct is governed by the laws of nature (survival and reproduction), the drive is detached from its natural foundations, displaced into an Other domain, where it is governed by representation and indeed by a "principle of pleasure" that cuts against the grain of nature, so that "satisfaction" is obtained not by the organism and its needs but by the ego and its demands? Do we not in fact confront a discontinuity, in the human animal, between this "principle of pleasure" and the "reality principle," the "external world" to which the animal would appear to be far more harmoniously adapted?

The order of mating may thus follow a biological law with a strict and mechanical regularity in cases such as the one Lacan mentions in "The Mirror Stage" (1936), in which "it is a necessary condition for the maturation of the gonad of the female pigeon that it should see another member of its species, of either sex; so sufficient in itself is this condition that the desired effect may be obtained merely by placing the individual within reach of the field of reflection of a mirror" (3). But the image may have a different function in the human world, such that mating is governed not simply by the *relation between organisms*, which is all that counts from the standpoint of genetic science, but by the *relation between egos*, which is conspicuously maladaptive.

In the human world, organisms manage to meet only *through their representatives*, through the mediation of their egos (including all the social identifications this entails), so that the imaginary is indeed that pivotal point around which the entire relation of the subject to the organism is denatured, deprived of the regularity that instinct affords in the animal world. This also means that the image no longer opens on a world of reality and no longer functions as a natural perception providing access to the things themselves; rather the image gives rise to representations that *reconfigure* the entire order of intersubjectivity. Accordingly, it is not only a question of distinguishing the principle of natural selection from that of sexual selection, but above all of distinguishing, *within* the principle of sexual selection itself, between the image as it functions in nature and the imaginary domain in which the human lives its life. The question therefore arises not only of how the relation to the other (in mating) differs from the relation to the environment (in survival), but also of whether this relation to the other obeys laws in the human world that can be distinguished from those obtaining in the "state of nature." If the rupture *within* sexual selection is thereby clarified, what are its consequences for human racial diversity?

We have suggested that the traditional typologies of race are a mistake from the standpoint of genetics, since "patterns of variation that appear at the genetic level cut across *visible* racial divisions" (Gutin 73; my emphasis). But it would be a mistake to follow the geneticist here, believing that the proper scientific conclusion would simply be to *dismiss* this level of superficial visibility, condemning it to the dustbin of historical "errors" and *replacing* it with the truth of genetic analysis. For at the level of sexual selection, visibility is not a matter of indifference. We may return here to Lucius Outlaw's remark that physiological differences are "often combined with" cultural matters. In fact, while the scientific community may often proceed as if the "natural" dimension of the body were independent of all cultural overlay—as if the biological domain were autonomous and *prior* to any merely symbolic matter—we have good "scientific" reasons to object.

Human genetic diversity does not coincide with the visible typologies of race, and yet this does not mean that visible differences (such as hair and skin color) are simply a scientific mistake. At this point, the genealogist will turn a cold gaze on the cultural critic as well, for although we may be tempted to conclude that traditional racial categories are only imaginary, a product of cultural practices or a purely symbolic phenomenon, this difference between imaginary physiology and genetic diversity is not so easily resolved. If the imaginary physiology of race is not reducible to a discursive phenomenon (that is, if features such as skin color, hair, and facial features have some genetic basis, while nevertheless being insufficient for classifying human populations from an evolutionary perspective), then perhaps its specific character, within the general arena of genetic diversity, should be identified in a more precise manner.

It may well be that many of the features commonly enlisted in the traditional racial classifications belong not to the domain of survival but to this "less rigorous" domain of sexual selection. As a consequence, such features may not only exceed the adaptive function of natural selection, but also be subject to laws that the principle of sexual selection cannot entirely circumscribe—laws that may even, in the case of the human subject, contradict or pervert what one might expect from the sexual instinct and the mechanisms of mating that operate in the natural world. Here too, the imaginary has a character that does not conform to the image in nature. Again Lucius Outlaw, who has no particular interest in advancing the claims of psychoanalysis, put this point clearly: "When we classify a group as a 'race,' then, at best we refer to generally shared characteristics derived from a 'pool' of genes. Social, cultural, and geographic factors, in addition to those of natural selection, all impact on this pool, thus on raciation" (66).

This brings us to a final complication of recent genetic science, which takes us from the imaginary domain to the symbolic order, where the impact of language on human embodiment is explicit. For it must be stressed that apart from the taxonomic difficulties we have mentioned, the genetic differences that do in fact distinguish one person from another are not generally attributable to "racial" differences (Ridley 13). On the contrary, while the genetic differences between two individuals drawn from different "racial" groups may be visible to the eye (in terms of height, body type, sex, hair color, and so on), they are due to "racial factors" only to a remarkably small degree—about one hundredth of one percent. According to Paul Hoffman, "race accounts for only a minuscule .012 percent difference in our genetic material" (4).

In other words, given a particular set of chromosomes with its large number of genes, two observations may be made: (1) virtually all of this genetic material will be shared by all other humans, allowing us to grow as mammals, with a spinal column, various internal organs, etc.; and (2) the portion that distinguishes us from others will also distinguish us individually from others who belong to the same genetic population—separating two Pygmies or Germans or Lebanese from each other as well as from all other humans. In short, if, as Gutin claims (72), "every human carries about 6 billion base pairs—the chemical rungs of the DNA ladder," only ".2 percent of the whole" will be distinct from that of another randomly chosen individual; and of that two-tenths of one percent, almost all variation occurs not between "races," but *within* any given group. Thus, "a random sample of people in any small group . . . from rural Sweden to the Ituri Forest to Tierra del Fuego—will turn up 85 percent of all the genetic variation our species contains" (Gutin 72).

What happens, then, if we turn to the remaining fifteen percent (namely, the fifteen percent that remains of this .2 percent variation), which bears on differences *between* different genetic populations? Even here, the majority of this variation is due not to "racial" differences, but to differences between "social" groups—that is, between those who belong to *different linguistic or ethnic groups.* "Of that 15 percent," Gutin adds, "almost 9 percent is reflected in differences among ethnic and linguistic groups *within any given race*" (72; my emphasis). We are thus faced not with an absolute dismissal of any genetic analysis, but with *genetic differences that derive from ethnic and linguistic differences.* Accordingly, we may posit a role for the symbolic order in addition to the imaginary physiology of race. Perhaps genetic differences cannot be disregarded, then, or dismissed on the grounds that such differences are too dangerous, too historically contaminated to discuss—as if race could be recast as an ideological construction. But nor can our racial differences be reduced to a biological fact, separate from culture and language, and from all the mechanisms of imaginary intersubjectivity that denature human life. For representation is not secondary to the biological domain; it drives raciation as much as any factor the scientists have identified.

In conclusion, therefore, let us give the last word to the scientist of poetry, in accordance with ancient wisdom, and the stories that have passed down to us:

> It is clear that the general origin of poetry was due to two causes, each of them part
> of human nature. Imitation is natural to man from childhood, one of his advan-

tages over the lower animals being this, that he is the most imitative creature in the world, and *learns at first from imitation*. And it is also natural for all to *delight in works of imitation*. The truth of this second point is shown by experience: though the objects themselves may be painful to see, we delight to view the most realistic representations of them in art, the forms for example of the lowest animals and of dead bodies. (Aristotle 1448b3–12; my emphasis)

Two features would thus mark the peculiar destiny of the human animal, a creature by nature distinct from "the lower animals" and consequently subject to different principles of organization and change. First, "he is the most imitative creature in the world" and "he learns at first from imitation," developing an understanding of the world not from immediate contact with *the things themselves* or by adapting himself in response to the environment, but from the *representation* of things, which first gives him access to the world (since "he learns *at first* from imitation"). And second, these representations afford the human animal a certain "pleasure" that is quite remarkable, and perhaps even perverse, as it seems to run counter to nature, leading the human creature to *turn toward* the very objects from which the animal would instinctively *turn away*. For we "delight to view" representations of things even—and perhaps especially—"though the objects themselves may be painful to see," as if, in the very organization of our pity and fear, our love and hate—in our very relation to the other and the world—we are led away from nature, fatefully governed not only by a peculiar and unnatural pleasure but by a knowledge that comes from representation, and destines us for an Other domain. This domain is not simply of "man's" making, like the various clever tools and institutions that humans have invented at different historical moments and that differentiate one culture from another; rather this domain is constitutive of the human in all its incarnations: a constitutive denaturing to which the human animal is subject, not only in one culture or one historical epoch, but in its very being— or perhaps as a race.

ENDNOTE

1. This group should be distinguished from the Human Genome Project, which aims to give an exhaustive account of the entire human chromosome complement, consisting of numerous genes. As Gutin observes, "Every human carries about six billion base pairs— the chemical rungs of the DNA ladder—in the nuclei of his or her cells" (72). The source of this DNA, however, is extremely limited, representing "a mere handful of U.S. and European scientists" (72). The Human Genome Diversity Project, by contrast, is an effort to expand the range of material, by gathering samples from a variety of distinct populations, many of which are currently disappearing through migration, assimilation, or extinc-

tion. Given the effort to patent human genetic material and the growth of the bio-techno-logical industry, however, this effort to preserve varieties of human DNA (like so much native raw material) is not without its own ethical difficulties.

WORKS CITED

Albert, Michael, Leslie Cagen, Noam Chomsky, et al. *Liberating Theory*. Boston: South End, 1986.

Aristotle. *The Poetics. Introduction to Aristotle*. 1947. Revised and enlarged 2d ed. Ed. Richard McKeon. Trans. Ingram Bywater. Chicago: U of Chicago P, 1973. 670–713.

Banton, Michael and Jonathan Harwood. *The Race Concept*. New York: Praeger, 1975.

Bateson, Mary Catherine and Richard Goldsby. *Thinking AIDS: The Social Response to the Biological Threat*. New York: Addison-Wesley, 1988.

Bowler, Peter J. *Theories of Human Evolution: A Century of Debate, 1844–1944*. Baltimore: Johns Hopkins UP, 1986.

———. *Evolution: The History of an Idea*. Rev. ed. Berkeley: U of California P, 1989.

Butler, Judith. *Bodies That Matter: On the Discursive Limits of "Sex."* New York: Routledge, 1994.

Coleman, William. *Biology in the Nineteenth Century: Problems of Form, Function, and Transformation*. New York: Cambridge UP, 1977.

Darwin, Charles. *The Origin of Species by Means of Natural Selection; Or the Preservation of Favoured Races in the Struggle for Life*. 1859. New York: Collier, 1962.

Degler, Carl N. *In Search of Human Nature: The Decline and Revival of Darwinism in American Social Thought*. New York: Oxford UP, 1991.

de Waal, Frans. *Good Natured: The Origins of Right and Wrong in Humans and Other Animals*. Cambridge: Harvard UP, 1996.

Derrida, Jacques. "Cogito and the History of Madness." *Writing and Difference*. 1967. Trans. Alan Bass. Chicago: U of Chicago P, 1978. 31–63.

Diamond, Jared. "Race without Color." In *Discover*. 83–89.

Discover: The World of Science. Spec. Issue: "The Science of Race" (November 1994).

Dobzhansky, Theodosius. *Mankind Evolving: The Evolution of the Human Species*. New Haven: Yale UP, 1962.

Fausto-Sterling, Anne. *Myths of Gender: Biological Theories about Women and Men*. Rev. Ed. New York: Basic, 1992.

Foucault, Michel. "Nietzsche, Genealogy, History." 1971. *The Foucault Reader*. Ed. Paul Rabinow. New York: Pantheon, 1984. 76–100.

———. *The Order of Things: An Archaeology of the Human Sciences*. 1966. New York: Random House, 1970.

———. *The History of Sexuality, Volume I: An Introduction*. 1976. Trans. Robert Hurley. New York: Vintage, 1978.

———. "Power and Sex." 1977. *Michel Foucault: Politics, Philosophy, Culture: Interviews and*

Other Writings, 1977–1984. Ed. Lawrence Kritzman. Trans. David J. Parent. New York: Routledge, 1988. 110–24.

Freud, Sigmund. *Three Essays on the Theory of Sexuality.* 1905. Vol. 7 of *The Standard Edition of the Complete Psychological Works of Sigmund Freud.* Ed. and trans. James Strachey. 24 vols. London: Hogarth, 1953–74. 123–230.

——. *Totem and Taboo.* 1913. Vol. 13 of *SE.* 1–161.

——. *Beyond the Pleasure Principle.* 1920. Vol. 18 of *SE.* 1–64.

Gilman, Sander L. *The Case of Sigmund Freud: Medicine and Identity at the Fin de Siècle.* Baltimore: Johns Hopkins UP, 1993.

Goldsby, Richard A. *Race and Races.* New York: Macmillan, 1971.

Gould, Stephen Jay. *The Mismeasure of Man.* New York: Norton, 1981.

——. "The Geometer of Race." In *Discover.* 65–69.

Gutin, Jo Ann C. "End of the Rainbow." In *Discover.* 71–75.

Haraway, Donna J. *Simians, Cyborgs, and Women: The Reinvention of Nature.* New York: Routledge, 1991.

Harris, Marvin. *Our Kind: Who We Are, Where We Came From, Where We Are Going.* New York: Harper and Row, 1989.

Hoffman, Paul. "The Science of Race." In *Discover.* 4.

Lacan, Jacques. "The Mirror Stage as Formative of the Function of the I as Revealed in Psychoanalytic Experience." 1936. *Écrits: A Selection.* Ed. Jacques-Alain Miller. Trans. Alan Sheridan. New York: Norton, 1977. 1–7.

——. *Le Seminaire, livre VIII: Le transfert.* Ed. Jacques-Alain Miller. Paris: Seuil, 1991.

Laqueur, Thomas. *Making Sex: Body and Gender from the Greeks to Freud.* Cambridge: Harvard UP, 1990.

Outlaw, Lucius. "Towards a Critical Theory of 'Race.' " *Anatomy of Racism.* Ed. David Theo Goldberg. Minneapolis: U of Minnesota P, 1990. 58–82.

Ridley, Matt. *The Red Queen: Sex and the Evolution of Human Nature.* New York: Macmillan, 1993.

Risse, Guenter B. "Epidemics and History: Ecological Perspectives and Social Responses." *AIDS: The Burdens of History.* Ed. Elizabeth Fee and Daniel M. Fox. Berkeley: U of California P, 1990. 33–66.

Stepan, Nancy Leys. *The Idea of Race in Science: Great Britain 1800–1960.* New York: Macmillan, 1982.

2

Geopsychoanalysis: ".. . and the rest of the world"

Jacques Derrida

Translated by Donald Nicholson-Smith

Before naming Latin America, I would like to open a parenthesis.

".. . and the rest of the world"—a quote, a *bon mot*, from the International Psycho-Analytic Association. The Association's proposed Constitution of 1977, as ratified by the Thirtieth Congress in Jerusalem, contains a parenthetical sentence which attempts after a fashion to map the divisions of the psychoanalytic world:

> (The Association's main geographical areas are defined at this time as America north of the United States–Mexican border; all America south of that border; and the rest of the world.)

The formulation is far too tempting—the *bon mot* simply too good—not to take the said "rest" as a starting point. Basically the word denominates Europe, the native land and old mother country of psychoanalysis, a body tattooed all over with psychoanalytic institutions and apparatuses; but the self-same "rest of the world" also connotes all that virgin territory, all those parts of the world, where psychoanalysis, to put it bluntly, has never set foot. "The rest of the world," for the IPA Constitution, is thus a title, a name and a location shared by the roots of psychoanalysis and everything which, since it lies beyond the boundaries of psychoanalysis, has yet to be opened up to it—all expectations in this regard being legitimate; a sort of Far West or no man's land, then—but also a sort of foreign body named, incorporated, and circumscribed ahead of time by an IPA Constitution rehearsing, as it were, the psychoanalytic colonization of a non-American rest-of-the-world, the conquest of a virginity parenthetically married to Europe.

I shall now close my own parenthesis, for the time being anyway, and proceed to the naming of Latin America. My only ambition for this morning is to name Latin America—and to do so in a manner that differs from that of the Constitution of the International Psycho-Analytic Association. For we must bear in mind from the outset the plain fact that this is an international meeting—and a psychoanalytic one, even if it bears the legitimating stamp of no international psychoanalytic association. It is almost as though this place were being haunted—and legitimated in advance—by the specter of another International.

So—I will now name Latin America. What is Latin America today? I will explain in a moment why in my view it has to be named. But, first, does it in fact exist, and if so what is it? Is it the name of something so sufficient unto itself—i.e., as a continent—as to have identity? Is it the name of a concept? And what could this concept have to do with psychoanalysis?

Well, my answer to this question, a question which I asked myself on my way here, is Yes. Yes, Latin America is indeed the name of a concept. I would even go so far as to say that it is the name, in the interwoven histories of humanity and of psychoanalysis, of a psychoanalytic concept.

I am sure it will come as no surprise to you that my speaking of "geopsychoanalysis"—just as one speaks of geography or geopolitics—does not mean that I am going to propose a psychoanalysis of the earth of the sort that was put forward a few decades ago, when Bachelard evoked "The Earth and the Reveries of Rest" and "The Earth and the Reveries of the Will." But as inclined as I may be today to distance myself from such a psychoanalysis of the earth, as likewise from the more recent and more urgent theme of an anti-psychoanalysis of territorialization, it is nevertheless upon the earth that I wish to advance—upon what the psychoanalysis of today considers to be the earth.

For psychoanalysis has an earth, sole and singular. An earth that is to be distinguished from the world of psychoanalysis. It is not my purpose today to inquire how it goes with the psychoanalytic world, or whether psychoanalysis is a world, or even whether it is of this world, but to observe the figure which psychoanalysis in its becoming-a-world, in its ongoing worldification, inscribes upon the earth, upon the surface of mankind's earth, upon the body of the earth and of mankind.

More than likely this notion was suggested to me simply by reading the program of your conference: the idea that there should exist within the psychoanalytic *socius* an entity called "Latin America," that a continental unit—an identity at once geo-graphical (one might as well say "natural") and cultural, linguistic or historico-lin-guistic—should somehow be pertinent to the worldwide organization of psycho-analysis, does not seem like something to take for granted, and it raises several questions. It suggests that for psychoanalysis there are continents, semi-continents, peninsular entities—some of them peninsulas thickly settled by psychoanalysts and psychoanalysis, others as yet virgin, half-continents black or white; and that there is more or less one dark continent only, and one more or less dark—dark, that is, as uncleared or unexplored land is dark, black like femaleness, like a sex, like the skin of some people, like evil, like the unutterable horror of violence, torture, and extermination. All this made me wonder whether it might not be possible to adopt a sort of "map-reading" approach to psychoanalysis. Since in that event I should certainly not be utterly without any political axe to grind, this idea gained a certain momentum for me, a momentum which became almost impossible to resist when I read two fairly recent documents.

I have been asking myself whether I would dare tell you how ingenuously I approached these documents, with what freshness of mind, and out of what depth of ignorance I perused them.

But though I have asked myself that question, it has not exactly been my prin-cipal preoccupation. For in the first instance I wondered why I was being asked to come here, and what questions, exactly, people here wanted to ask me. Why was I being asked to speak, to be the first speaker of the morning, on the first morning, early in the morning? What was I to say, and to what purpose? To whom was I to speak?

Notice that I had no question as to my reason for accepting the invitation. That reason was quite simple: I accepted in order to try and understand the wherefore of the invitation. No doubt it is common enough to reply affirmatively to a question or invitation without knowing what one's interlocutor has in mind, and solely in order to discover what that intention might be, but it is certainly dangerous as a for-eign policy. All the same, were such a policy never adopted, nothing would ever happen. How could an event be expected to take place if one responded only after having understood the question or invitation, only after having monitored the nature and meaning of the question, demand, or provocation?

My first hypothesis, formulated on the basis of personal experience, ran as fol-lows: In this particular psychoanalytic world, here in Paris, there was a wish to lis-ten as soon as possible, as early as possible, as early in the day as possible, without losing any time at all, to what this stranger—this "foreign body" belonging to no body, this non-member, in whatever capacity, of any of the psychoanalytic corpo-rations of the world (or of the "rest of the world"), whether represented here today or not, whether European or Latin American—might possibly have to say. I say "foreign body" for two reasons: first, in order to designate something that can be neither assimilated nor rejected, neither internalized nor—since it transcends the boundary between internal and external—foreclosed; and, second, in order to cite Freud. In the *New Introductory Lectures*, Freud speaks within the space of a few lines (Lectures XXX and XXXI) of a "foreign body" (*Fremdkörper*) and of that body which is the most "foreign" to the ego (*am Ichfremdesten*).

The first reference comes in a discussion of telepathy and *Gedankenübertragung* (thought-transference), and the precise context is the moment when the role played by a particular gold coin (*Goldstück*) defeats, and signals the limits of, an analysis. Interestingly enough, it was once again in connection with telepathy and thought-transference that Freud, in a letter to Jones, used the expression "foreign policy" in speaking of psychoanalysis as a global institution, as though this organization were a kind of state seeking to govern its relations with the rest of the world. Freud explains to Jones—who always had great difficulty following Freud in the matter of telepathic communication—that although up till now he has kept silent about his "conversion to telepathy" out of concern for "foreign policy," and in order to guard, as Jones has been asking him to, against the impression of obscurantism and the charges of occultism which such an avowal might generate in certain parts of the world, his conviction has now become so firm and so easily verifiable that it is no longer possible to respect the strategic and diplomatic needs of the psychoanalytic super-state.

The second allusion to foreign bodies in the *New Introductory Lectures*, which occurs just a few lines after the first, defines the symptom as a body foreign, no more and no less, to the ego. The symptom is always a foreign body, and must be deciphered as such; and of course a foreign body is always a symptom, and behaves as a symptom in the body of the ego—it is a body foreign to the body of the ego. That is what I am doing here; I constitute a symptom, I am the symptom, I play that role—if not for each one of you separately, then at any rate for the ego, so to speak, of psychoanalysis as an institution. So the inclination to hear the outsider quickly, early in the morning, is perhaps also a way of banishing the symptom as fast as possible, of pigeonholing what it has to say without delay or, in other words, of consigning it to oblivion without further ado. What is more, the outsider's discourse will be classified and forgotten even more quickly, and be more easily categorized and less disturbing, if it is accorded a place of honor—that is, an honorary place in the sense in which honorary means insignificant. The ostracized foreign body is thus expelled politely, in accordance with the traditional form of protocol which makes an external and supposedly neutral agency responsible for opening an inauguration ceremony or for innocently pulling a paper out of a hat.

That is naturally what the symptom will now do, the outsider being only too happy to play the game. I am therefore going to speak to you of two papers that I might as well have pulled from a hat.

I am an outsider here not only by virtue of the fact that I have no psychoanalytic credentials, being neither an analyst, nor even an analyst in training, nor—as you say and as I now write, in one word or in one breath—"inanalysis." I am psychoanalytically irresponsible, and it is perhaps so that certain things might be said through the mouth of someone irresponsible that I have been summoned here. I have to answer for what I say to no psychoanalytic agency, whether Parisian, French, or international. I am also an outsider here, though, because I am neither an American—whether of the North or of the South—nor a European, Northern or Southern. I am not even really a Latin.

I was born in Africa, and I guarantee you that I retain something of that heritage. My reason for recalling this today is that there is practically no psychoanalysis in Africa, white or black, just as there is practically no psychoanalysis in Asia, or in the South Seas. These are among those parts of "the rest of the world" where psychoanalysis has never set foot, or in any case where it has never taken off its European shoes. I don't know whether you will find such considerations trivial or shocking. Naturally, there are outposts of your European or American psychoanalytic societies in these regions, notably in Africa, in particular places formerly or still under colonial or even neo-colonial rule. In Algeria, the country that I come from and that I only left for the first time at the age of nineteen, the institutions of psychiatry and, more embryonically, of psychoanalysis were, before the war of independence, merely emanations of what we used (how accurately!) to call "metropolitan" organizations. *De facto* and *de jure*. African psychoanalysis was European, structurally defined in the profoundest way by the colonial state apparatus. In order to contextualize the political problem to which I refer, I shall do no more than mention the name and the work of Frantz Fanon.

At that time and in that place it was altogether exceptional and untypical for psychoanalysts to raise the question of their own practice in its political, ethno-psychoanalytic, and socio-institutional dimensions. The laws, the deontology, the ethics of psychoanalysis, as laid down or simply taken for granted by the colonial societies or by the international psychoanalytic establishment were supposed to regulate practice and govern relations with state authorities on the one hand and medical authorities on the other. The Fanons were few and far between, marginal or marginalized; I say this merely in order to provide a well-known and painful point of reference, and not in any sense to establish a particular discourse—Fanon's own positions as a model beyond the reach of all discussion. The political geography of the world has changed since that time, and intercontinental balances of power have been subject to much turbulence; this can hardly have failed, it seems to me, to have had an impact on the political geography of psychoanalysis.

What, then, are the two documents that I pulled from the hat so graciously held out to me? Of course you are people who do not believe in happenstance: before we have finished our session you will doubtless have mapped out the preprogrammed paths that were bound to lead me to having that particular hat held out to me by such and such and to choosing this particular exquisite corpse rather than some other one, and the writings of a corpse rather than anything else. Well, I too believe in happenstance as little as possible, though I should be hard put to it to say that I don't believe in it at all; in any case, my beliefs can be of little interest to you.

So let us say that, as chance would have it, being interested simultaneously in political-institutional questions and in postal matters (correspondence, letters and postcards, telecommunications, telepathy, computer networking, etc.)—being interested, therefore, in the very point of intersection of the institutional policies of psychoanalysis on the one hand and postal technology on the other—I happened upon my first document, to wit, the 144th Bulletin of the International Psycho-Analytic Association, there to find an account of the IPA's 31st Congress, held in New York. This was the second such congress to be held outside Europe, the first, which had voted on a proposed Constitution and Bylaws, having taken place in Jerusalem in 1977. My eye was first caught by details of a debate on a mail ballot. In a passage that I shall read you in a moment, the question of mail-in voting and of possible changes of opinion between a vote cast *in presentia* and a later one cast *in absentia* and mailed in, is oddly linked with an allusion to certain problems faced by Latin American societies and a reference to the upcoming 1981 Helsinki Congress. It is at that coming Congress that the aforementioned proposed Constitution and Bylaws are to be debated and voted upon.

Helsinki is a place whose name has for a number of years now been associated in our minds with the Olympic Games and with accords, governed by international law, on human rights, or at least on freedom of ideas and freedom of travel. And in Helsinki, then, in less than six months, the IPA will adopt its new Constitution and Bylaws. Still playing the symptom, I am going to pretend today to contribute—albeit in a brief, irresponsible and thoroughly illegitimate way—to the discussion that may be expected to precede the voting on that occasion. In the few lines that I am now about to read, however, what really gave me pause was a particular use of the word "geography" in association with the word "economy." It seemed to me that the formulation "geographical and economic circumstances" was standing in place of something that was not being said, and this distinctly not by reason of circumstances of a geographical or economic order. At the point in question, the discussion had been marking time for a while apropos of the vote on the Constitution and the way in which that vote might be conducted (whether by mail or not, using registered mail or not, etc.). Then:

> Dr. Gemma Jappe (Tübingen, W. Germany) suggested that in a situation where two votes were taken on an issue—one at the Business Meeting, and one some time later by mail ballot—the result might be complicated by the inevitable change of opinion that takes place over a period of time. She would like to suggest, therefore, that provision be made that if the result of the two votes is different, the issue need not be lost, but should come up again for discussion . . . . Dr. Carlos Mendilaharsu (Montevideo) spoke in favour of the mail ballot, pointing out that *geographical and economic circumstances made it difficult for the Latin American Societies* particularly to be adequately represented at the Business Meeting and Congresses. He felt, therefore, that the mail ballot would be an important innovation for his Latin American colleagues. [*My emphasis*—J.D.]

I certainly have no wish to play down the indubitable existence of "geographical and economic circumstances" which make it "difficult for the Latin American Societies particularly to be adequately represented." But inasmuch as comparable circumstances must necessarily confront other societies also, given the form of the planet and the distances that must be covered in order to reach the place of assembly of the entire psychoanalytic tribe, I concluded (not that I had to be a genius to do so) that this reference to the economico-geographical realm just prior to the vote on the new Constitution in Helsinki must be a replacement for something else that could not be named.

What exactly was being replaced here? What was it that must not be named? Had one had any doubts on this, an answer presented itself a very short distance away—by virtue of a sort of metonymic contiguity—on the page opposite, where we find a "Request from the Australian Psychoanalytical Society for Discussion of Alleged Violation of Human Rights." I quote once more:

> Dr. Joseph introduced the discussion (I must say I like the fact all this came about under Dr. Joseph's chairmanship, but no connection should be inferred with my title, "Geopsychoanalysis") of this item by saying that he had received a request from the Australian Society that the IPA look into rumours [*sic*] of alleged violation of human rights in Argentina. As the IPA did so, the issue became one of rumours and allegations and various kinds of evidence from and about many countries around the world. Accordingly, the Executive Council felt that to single out any one country could not in any way do justice to our concern. Nor, it became obvious, was it an issue which only concerned psychoanalysts, but all citizens in general. Accordingly, the Executive Council had asked him to read the following Statement to this Meeting.

Before reading this official statement of the IPA's on the subject of human rights violations, let me remind you that these words were uttered in New York at a time when, though Reagan had not yet assumed the presidency and Haig had yet to declare that the question of human rights would no longer, even in principle, be accorded top priority, actual violations of those rights in Argentina and elsewhere were no longer a matter of mere rumors or allegations. Discussion at the Congress had already in fact produced a naming of countries implicated, including Argentina; and the word "country" had been used in this connection—a word that designates something other and something more than a geographical entity, more, indeed, than a mere nation, for it also implies the existence of a political apparatus, a state, civil society—and psychoanalytic institutions.

Now, however, in the name of "doing justice," out of regard for the clearly incontestable fact that human rights are not violated solely in this or that particular country, all reference to any countries at all will, as we shall see, be eliminated from the official position, from the Council's resolution. Even the word "country" itself will be replaced by the politically neutral or hollow notion of "certain geographical areas." Any concern for justice would naturally impose the requirement that other human rights violations not be overlooked—including, for instance, those in "geographical areas" from which institutionalized psychoanalysis is quite absent. But such a concern is expressed here in a form whose moral, juridical, and universalizing rigor is on a par with its political neutrality and formal abstraction. The appeal to the geographical, to natural location, thus serves to erase any properly symbolic and political inscription of the violation upon or within the earth; erased too, as part of the same process, are the violation's concrete singularity, the irreplaceable body, and the unique site of the violent act in question. In other words, something of the earth is lost too. Geographical abstraction, which effectively neutralizes political discourse, also wipes out the earth itself by wiping out what links a country's name to a particular territory, to certain proper names, to specific policies, and especially, for my present purposes (and I shall return to this), to some psychoanalysis or other. Here is the text of the statement, with its preamble:

> Along with various other international organizations, the International Psycho-Analytic Association has, of course, become aware of the violation of human rights which has occurred in certain geographical areas.
>
> The Executive Council of the IPA has discussed these issues at length during its meetings in New York, as it did previously during the Jerusalem Congress. As a result of these discussions I have been asked to read the following official statement to this Business Meeting and to ask you to approve that this Statement be circulated

to various concerned international organizations, such as the World Federation for Mental Health, the World Health Organization, the International Psychiatric Association, Amnesty International, and so on, and to various national Governments, at the discretion of the President and Secretary. Members are invited to suggest to the Executive Council further appropriate recipients for this Statement, which is as follows:

"The International Psycho-Analytic Association wishes to express its opposition to the use of psychiatric or psychotherapeutic methods to deprive individuals of their legitimate freedom; to an individual's receiving psychiatric or psychotherapeutic treatment based on political considerations; to the interference with professional confidentiality for political purposes. The IPA also condemns the violation of human rights of citizens in general, of scientists and of our colleagues in particular."

Dr. Walter Briehl (Los Angeles) then placed before the Meeting a proposal that a statement be made by the IPA specifically taking a stand about the situation in Argentina, rather than the issuing of the more generalized statement proposed by the Executive Council. The arguments for and against both the statement proposed by the Executive Council and that proposed by Dr. Briehl [unpublished] were discussed by many Members. Finally, the Members present were asked to give an expression of their opinion by voting on the two statements proposed. The result of this show of hands indicated that nearly 85% of members present were in favour of the Statement proposed by the Executive Council.

What Briehl's report had to say we do not know, nor, of course, do we have any idea what outcome of a vote cast according to some other procedure, such as a mail-in vote, might have produced.

That such a position should have thus been taken up is far from negligible nor is it in any way to be condemned. In view of all the pitfalls that assuredly had to be avoided, it is a position lacking neither in clarity, nor in dignity, nor in skillfulness. Coming as it does from a Western organization of liberal persuasion committed to human rights, to political pluralism, but also to its own formal neutrality, to its own survival, and to the prerequisites of its own unity, including whatever degree of noncommitment might be necessary to avoid its being rent apart by international conflicts, this declaration is certainly better than nothing, and I have no wish to go into all the possible reasons or justifications for its extreme cautiousness.

Which having been said, we come to the questions that do arise here. It is striking that the guardedness of this document depends for legitimacy solely upon its formal abstraction, or in other words upon its geographical schematism. What liberal institution in the West could not have made exactly the same declaration? The text bears not the slightest specifically psychoanalytic coloring—a fact that can hardly fail to arouse one's curiosity.

Let me deal right away with two possible objections. First of all, there is no denying that this protest statement does bear some fairly specific characteristics. It is aimed, we read, at a variety of worldwide health organizations; and it is concerned with psychotherapeutic methods which deprive individuals of their "legitimate freedom," with treatments "based on political considerations," or "the interference with professional confidentiality for political purposes."

But could not the same statement be made by any association of psychotherapists or psychiatrists, even one not even remotely affected by psychoanalysis? There is not a word in the resolution to suggest that the violation of the rights of man or of the citizen (concerning which "rumours and allegations" are said to be circulating) could conceivably have a special interest to psychoanalysis as compared with medicine or with classical psychiatry, nor that this interest might be understood not only in the sense of interest in an object of theoretical and clinical study, but also in the sense that psychoanalysis, that the psychoanalytic sphere, that psychoanalysts and their institutions are involved, implicated in one way or another, sometimes in active or passive complicity, sometimes in virtual or organized confrontation, with the forces that commit the aforesaid human rights violations, be these directly under the control of the state or no, and whether or not they exploit, manipulate, and persecute analysts and their analysands in some very specific way.

Others have already described, or may be relied upon to describe, better than I can the violent practices to which I am referring, practices which indeed come in a most singular way into conjunction with the agency of psychoanalysis. I am not thinking only of the most spectacular ways in which psychoanalytic authorities compromise with political or police authorities, nor, inversely, of the most terrifying forms of persecution of psychoanalysts and their patients; all such instances follow well-known and readily identifiable patterns in face of which positions may be taken up that are perfectly clear and equally valid for any professional, and in a general way for any citizen. For there are also more invisible abuses, ones more difficult to detect—whether in Europe or beyond its borders—and perhaps in some sense newer. Psychoanalysis may serve as a conduit for these new forms of violence; alternatively, it may constitute an irreplaceable means for deciphering them, and hence a prerequisite of their denunciation in specific terms—a necessary precondition, then, of a struggle and a transformation.

Inasmuch, indeed, as psychoanalysis does not analyze, does not denounce, does not struggle, does not transform (and does not transform *itself* for these purposes), surely it is in danger of becoming nothing more than a perverse and sophisticated appropriation of violence, or at best merely a new weapon in the symbolic arsenal. Nor would this new weapon be at the disposal solely of what is confusedly referred to as power—a power, that is, which is *external* to organized psychoanalysis, which can make use of that organization in myriad ways, even to the point of pressing certain effects or travesties of psychoanalytic knowledge into the service of the technology of torture. The panoply in question is just as liable to be deployed within the psychoanalytic institution as to surprise it from without: it may come into play inside the so-called analytic situation itself, whether between analyst and analysand or between analysts themselves, qualified or unqualified, in the process of becoming qualified, in control analysis, etc.; and it may equally well intervene between different analytic institutions, the "foreign policy" of which, to recall Freud's phrase, is governed by no specific law—not even, in some cases, by what is referred to in the rules of war as the law of nations.

I now turn to the second possible objection, the aim of which would be to justify the IPA declaration's formal character and the resulting elimination of any political reference, along with the consignment of Latin America to the realm of the unnamable. It is quite consistent with an appeal to human rights—the argument would run—that the IPA's statement of its position should make no mention of specific countries, specific political struggles, or even specific geographical areas (for such geographical generalization does not merely set aside all other, sociopolitical determinants, it also retains an indeterminateness of its own, concealing its own reality under the cloak of the purposely abstract "certain geographical areas"); nor should the text be any more specific, when it comes to psychoanalysis itself, apropos of that sphere where psychoanalysis may become either the agent or the object, whether directly or not, of human-rights violations of the most singular kind. Calls for human rights, it is felt, should always retain their formality, this being a necessary condition of their force as imperatives, of their claim to a universal and abstract purity transcending all concrete and empirical differences. To save time I shall refrain from recapitulating this well-known theme. Suffice it to say that its role in the present context would be to justify the IPA's geographical schematism, apoliticism, and even apsychoanalyticism in the name of a particular conception of human rights.

This is obviously a very serious problem, and no good purpose would be served by tackling it in great haste, under the pressure of the intimidation, whether virtual or actual, and more or less violent, which lies in wait for us whenever we approach such matters. It goes without saying that respect for human rights ought to be supported, and that any abuse of these rights, wherever it can be shown to occur as such, ought to be opposed. It is thus not merely a question of criticizing the IPA declaration. As I say, it is better than nothing, and, given the IPA's present state, why, every little bit helps, and the statement may very well have some positive effect here or there. In very specific situations it may very well serve to modify actions, to indicate boundaries and reference points, to inspire ideas of resistance, or to give abstract expression to the ethical-political concerns of those who call themselves psychoanalysts in the world of today, and so on.

These provisos notwithstanding, our original question remains essentially unanswered. Why is the International Psycho-Analytic Association, founded seventy years ago by Freud, unable to take up a position on certain kinds of violence (which I hope to define more clearly in a moment) in any other terms than those of a pre-psychoanalytic and apsychoanalytic juridical discourse, even then adopting only the vaguest and most impoverished forms of that traditional legal idiom, forms deemed inadequate by modern human rights jurists and lobbyists themselves? Why can the IPA be no more specific than to evoke "the violation of human rights of citizens in general," merely tagging on "of scientists and of our colleagues in particular"—a corporatist addendum which vitiates but in no way offsets the text's universalizing abstractness? Why must it speak merely of the "legitimate freedom" of individuals?

Since this is the sole content assigned by the statement to what it understands of human rights, there is not even any need for us to refer back to the whole succession of developments that has occurred since 1776 or 1789 in the discourse of human rights. It is enough for us to refer to the most ancient form of the declaration of the rights of man, to the Magna Carta of 1215, brought to France by English émigrés, which concerns itself with the bare minimum of civil liberty. Even that charter had the merit of great precision in its treatment of the concrete situation of the period. The IPA's Magna Carta, by contrast, is totally abstract and its one and only allusion to politics is an evocation of "treatment based on political considerations" and "the interference with professional confidentiality for political purposes" which fails to indicate either what this entails or where and how it happens, while at the same time assuming that such things could never *not* occur. We are back, are we not, at the prospect of a "map-reading" of psychoanalysis?

There is no time to refine the basic premises of our discussion, so I shall confine myself to the recapitulation of a few obvious facts. If facts they indeed are, as I believe, and if it has not been possible to take them into account, this can only mean that there is something obscure and terrifying in the joint history of mankind, of human rights and of what is known as psychoanalysis. The first obvious fact is that despite all the commotion over such issues as "psychoanalysis and politics," despite the deluge of discussions on this kind of topic that we have witnessed over the last ten or twelve years at least, it has to be acknowledged—indeed all this agitation actually signals the fact—that at present there exists no approach to political problems, no code of political discourse, that has in any rigorous way incorporated the axiomatics of a possible psychoanalysis—assuming always that psychoanalysis is possible. I hypothesize, therefore, that no such incorporation has occurred. If no ethical discourse has incorporated the axiomatics of psychoanalysis, no political discourse has done so either. I am speaking of discourses emanating from nonanalysts just as much as from those psychoanalysts or cryptoanalysts operating in the psychoanalytic milieu and using psychoanalytic terminology. And I do not refer solely to theoretical discourses concerned with the necessary preconditions of a politics or an ethics; I am thinking, rather, of discourse qua ethical-political action or behavior. The incorporation I have in mind would not be a kind of calm appropriation: it could not come about without a measure of distortion and transformation on both sides. This is why, paradoxically, the less psychoanalytic and ethical-political discourses become integrated in the strict sense to which I refer, the easier it is for some apparatuses to integrate or appropriate others—for political or police agencies to manipulate the psychoanalytic sphere, for the power of psychoanalysis to be abused, and so forth.

The implications of this cardinal fact, though overlapping, may be said to fall into three types.

The first type concerns the neutralization of ethics and of the political realm, an utter dissociation of the psychoanalytic sphere from the sphere of the citizen or moral subject in his or her public or private life. Why deny that this fracture line runs through our entire experience, sometimes clearly visible, sometimes less so, affecting all our judgments large or small, every day and every instant; and this whether we are analysts ourselves or merely nonanalysts concerned about psychoanalysis? This incredible dissociation is one of the most monstrous characteristics of the *homo psychoanalyticus* of our time. It is a ghastly deformity which gives us the aspect of mutants; sometimes it is terrifying, sometimes comical, and sometimes both at once.

The second type of implication—which may be superimposed upon the first—involves the retreat toward ethical-political positions whose neutrality is rivaled only by their seeming irreproachability; they lean, moreover, away from the political and toward the ethical (and here I shall deliberately leave this immense problem in suspense). It is in this context that a doctrine of human rights is evoked—a doctrine, what is more, itself ill-defined—that shelter is taken behind a language with no psychoanalytic content or pertinence, a language that takes no risks of a psychoanalytic nature and that should certainly satisfy no one present here today. What is an "individual"? What is a "legitimate freedom" from a psychoanalytic point of view? How is *habeas corpus* defined? What does it mean to exclude all political aims? What is a political aim? And so on. Even if it is not to be condemned—because it is better than nothing—falling back upon the appeal to human rights seems an inadequate response in at least three ways. I pass quickly over the first, the most radical, which is bound up with the philosophy of law, its history, the problem of its relationships to ethics, politics, ontology, and the value of the person or even of the humanity of the human individual—the possibility (or impossibility) of forming the notion of a dignity (*Würdigkeit*), in the Kantian sense, which would transcend all values, all exchange, all equivalence, all *Marktpreis*, and perhaps even go beyond the idea of law itself, beyond judicial weighing-up: so many vast and pressing issues which the psychoanalytic problematic should no longer be able to evade and about which it ought to open a debate with Plato, Kant, Hegel, Marx, Heidegger, and several others, as well as with jurists and philosophers of law. A debate of this kind has never been more apropos, and when I say that psychoanalysis should no longer be able to evade it, this also implies, in my view, that psychoanalysis cannot itself in this respect be evaded.

The second inadequacy relates to the formality of the IPA's declaration. Let me make it quite clear right away that I have never subscribed *purely and simply* to the old critique of the formalism of the Declaration of the Rights of Man, as developed early on in Marxist circles. Not that that critique was without merit—indeed, the best proof of its merit lies in the fact that in countries flying the flag of socialism formal constitutions based on respect for the rights of man have never posed the slightest impediment (even when they are formally respected) to the most horrendous violence. Any careful reading of the Declaration of 1789 makes it clear that the worst tyrannies could come to terms with it, because every article includes an interpretation clause that can be bent in any way one wishes. The truth is that a measure of strict formality, rising above all individual transactions, is indispensable here. But there are degrees of formality, more or less rigid, more or less rigorously defined.

The IPA adopts the most relaxed set of rules possible. In the first place, the Association dispenses with any properly psychoanalytic reflection upon human rights, upon what the meaning of "right" might be in a world where psychoanalysis is a contemporary reality. Second, the IPA takes no account, either in its deliberations or in its reasons adduced, of the history of the human rights issues of which I have been speaking—no account, in other words, of all the thinking, whether classical or not, that has been done on the subject of human rights and on justice in general, the kind of thinking that is being pursued in very lively fashion today (for reasons that are only too obvious) within state agencies and, especially, independently of them. Reading the IPA statement, one is even at a loss to know which particular declaration of human rights it refers to. There have, after all, been several such declarations since the Magna Carta, the Petition of Right, the Bill of Rights of the seventeenth century, the Declaration of Independence of 1776, and the Declaration of the Rights of Man of 1789. Among these are the Universal

Declaration of Human Rights adopted by the United Nations in 1948, from the signing of which the USSR abstained on the grounds that it was too formal and still too close to the 1789 Declaration, the Convention for the Protection of Human and Fundamental Rights signed by the European powers in Rome in 1950, a proposed Inter-American Convention on Human Rights, etc.

All these efforts and their products, which have the form of traditional legal pronouncements, are doubtless not as subtle as they might be in their conceptualization, nor as speedy as they might be in their application. All the same, slowly but surely, the search continues for ways in giving ever more specific content to the formal structures and problematics of human rights principles. Since the last century, it is on the social side of things—and in what we may as well call the "socialist" approach to the social—that enrichment for this content has been sought. But is not this the very area—that of a *socius* no longer defined solely in terms of classic, i.e., socioeconomic, concepts—where a psychoanalytic contribution might be considered essential?

Furthermore, one of the legal themes being worked on at present is torture—the concept of which is, as it were, lagging behind the thing itself. What is that form of violence that we call torture? Where does it begin and end? What is the status of the suffering inflicted or undergone in torture? What is the substance of torture? The fantasy of torture? The symbol of torture? And so on. Even supposing that psychoanalysis can provide a rigorous basis for a discourse of nonviolence—or of nontorture (which seems to me more fundamental)—I should certainly not venture here, merely touching upon the subject, to remind an audience such as you that this is precisely the subject of your theory, your practice, and your institutions. You ought to have essential things to say—and to do—on the matter of torture. Especially on the matter of the particularly modern aspect of torture, in the context of a contemporary history that is also contemporary with psychoanalysis—a synchronicity that still needs to be examined in its many ramifications. At the very least, psychoanalysis ought to participate wherever it is present—and especially wherever it is present in its official manifestations, national or international—in all research undertaken on this subject. Does it do so? To the best of my knowledge, no—or at any rate in far too discreet a way. If I am ill-informed on this, which is quite possible, I shall be only too happy to be set right. At all events, no trace of any such concern is to be found in the discourse of the IPA.

Yet even in the most traditional of agencies—those most thoroughly alien, most thoroughly blind and deaf, to psychoanalysis—the urgency of these matters is felt to be such that in 1975–76 the General Assembly of the United Nations requested, apropos of "torture and other cruel, inhuman or degrading treatments or punishments," that various agencies establish new international norms. Surely it is here that a properly psychoanalytic intervention should absolutely be set in motion—provided, of course, that there is such a thing as the "properly psychoanalytic" in this sphere. And if ever there were not, very grave conclusions would have to be drawn on all sides from that fact. Can one say that such an intervention, either direct or indirect, is occurring? I don't think so, for the moment. Is it possible? I don't know—I put the question to you. Are the causes of the difficulty inherent to the discourse of psychoanalysis, to its practice, to the institutional forms it requires and to the relations it is obliged to entertain with the dominant political forces? Or are things difficult for reasons which are neither essential nor general, but which derive from a particular dominant state of the theory, the practice or the institutional forms?

The question is still open, but one thing is already certain: if the dominant and representative forces of psychoanalysis in the world today have nothing specific to say or do, nothing original to say or contribute to the thinking and the struggle that are proceeding in connection with the concepts and the crude or refined realities of torture, then psychoanalysis, *at least within the dominant forces that have currently appropriated its representation*—I am trying to phrase things in as nuanced and prudent a fashion as possible—is nothing more and probably much less than those traditional medical health organizations to which the IPA distributes its principled protest, its visiting card or geographical chart, its *parva carta*, its little New York charter. For, when all is said and done, to whom was this card addressed, apart from governmental agencies, the selection of which was left up to the Association's president—Dr. Joseph—and secretary? The answer is: the World Federation for Mental Health, the World Health Organization, the International Psychiatric Association, and Amnesty International. But what part has the IPA taken in the work of the Human Rights Commission? Or in that of the WHO, which has been invited to prepare a new code of medical ethics to protect individuals from "torture and other cruel, inhuman or degrading treatments or punishments." As for Amnesty International, another recipient of the IPA's little card, for its part it long ago declared the need to work out new international norms, and in 1976, for example, published a document entitled "Codes of Professional Ethics." And Amnesty limits itself (if one may decently speak of limits in this connection) to the areas of detention and imprisonment. Torture knows no such bounds, however.

What role has psychoanalysis played in such projects and campaigns? And what conclusions should be drawn should it be decided that this role has been meager, nonexistent, or potential rather than substantial? Please understand that I am not trying to drag something of the order of psychoanalysis or of its official representation before the court of the Rights of Man. I am merely concerned to point up a fact or a possibility the seriousness of which ought to precipitate thought and action. This possibility has the character of a symptom, it indicates a state of psychoanalysis (as theory, practice, and institution) that should not be interpreted solely in terms of backwardness relative to the political struggles on the national, international, and supra state levels, about which I have just been talking. For this backwardness is also the price paid for a step forward by psychoanalysis, an advance which now impedes any translatability as between psychoanalytic concepts and those politico-juridical and ethico-juridical concepts, etc., by means of which such problems are voiced and such actions coordinated. This combination of backwardness and progress—the disjunction and inequality between the two—is not simply an anachronism of psychoanalysis. It is not just a matter of the relationship between two unsynchronized tendencies within a single linear evolutionary process, but also probably of an imbalance in the relationship of psychoanalysis to itself caused by some internal limitation, some occlusion or obstruction which at present shapes the analytic cause, analytic discourse, and analytic clinical and institutional practice. Not that this occlusion is essentially or wholly internal; indeed, the fact that it is unanalyzed means that for the moment, in current psychoanalytic terms, it is unanalytical in character. Yet it must necessarily give rise to some representation, must leave its mark, within the body of psychoanalysis. Shortly I shall suggest that Latin America is the name, the locus and material body of this trace, the surface most clearly marked by its inscription—and this on the very face of the earth itself.

I come now to the third type of implication, which, once again, may be read as overlapping the two earlier types. Something which seems like progress for psychoanalysis, namely the reevaluation of the basic concepts of the axiomatics of human rights and of traditional forms of political discourse, is actually merely the opening up of a void; while this process does train analytic sights upon concepts, values, and what I call the sphere of transcended values (e.g., the "dignity" of the individual in the Kantian sense—which is not a value and cannot be grasped by any value-grounded discourse), it does not in any way *replace* them. In this third category, then, are those theoretical constructs best able to bring out the conceptual inadequacy of the axiomatics of human rights and of Western political discourse, and to show the way in which these are rooted in deconstructible philosophemes. Now such theoretical constructs, as advanced as they may be, still constitute only negative discourses whose effect is to neutralize, and it is only in a hollow way that they indicate the necessity for a new ethics—not just for an ethics of psychoanalysis, which does not yet exist, but for another ethical discourse on ethics in general, another political discourse on politics in general, a discourse that would take into account deconstructive and psychoanalytic factors as well, if possible, as what may be interpreted as the truth of psychoanalysis—something, of course, which always varies according to the places occupied by psychoanalysis on the earth today. So long as the area thus exposed resembles an empty crater, the very greatest need for thought, for the ethical and the political, must necessarily coexist, within this space, with the greatest imaginable *laissez-aller*, with pragmatic *laissez-faire*, with archaism, conformity, opportunism, and so forth.

Is this situation the result of chance, a provisional state of affairs, an empirical given? Or, alternatively, does the present condition of psychoanalysis, as manifested in its principle schools (and by "schools" I mean schools of thought as much as the organizations that train and turn out analysts), embody an element that is unanalyzed, although analyzable in principle—an occlusion, as I called it a moment ago, which effectively bars the emergence of an ethics or politics truly *contemporary* with psychoanalysis? Is it thinkable that psychoanalysis might be made, as it were, into *its own contemporary*? I am by no means unaware of the multifacetedness, and the undoubted richness—contradictions included—of the discourses already filed under the heading "Psychoanalysis and Politics." I base myself, however, on the fact that all these efforts have not succeeded in concealing the hollowness of what has been achieved—or, if you prefer, have succeeded *only* in concealing that hollowness. The question needs to be framed differently—although I am obliged to restrict myself here to its general form—for whichever school predominates in each of the various "geographical areas" of the earth (to use the IPA's terminology), for Latin America, and for the many empirical variants of Freudian orthodoxy just as much as for the Kleinian and Lacanian persuasions.

The distribution of forces, so to speak, that results from the occlusion in question is as follows. On the one hand, theoretical advance posts are established which are unable to support the institutions that could then incorporate them. Such advance posts prove inadequate, therefore, and hence essentially incapable of embodying any concept of their own limitations and the advantages attaching thereto. On the other hand, we see an empirical proliferation of discourses and practices, of micro-institutional affiliations, of ailing or triumphant marginalities—a world of improvisation governed solely by its own currents, by isolation, by the determining inscriptions of biography, history, politics, and so on. This is truer of Latin America than of anywhere else, although it holds increasingly for the "rest of the world." Finally, we are confronted by an official—national or international—representation whose role (despite the appearance it offers, which some tend to deride) is increasingly important in a historical period when the legitimization of psychoanalysis by more and more governments raises the stakes in a way that hardly needs underlining. The more official this representation is, the more thoroughly legitimized, public, and formally wide-ranging, right up to the highest level of the IPA, the less representative is it of the concrete situations in which psychoanalysis finds itself on the ground, the less able is it to produce a specific discourse or lay down specific ethical-political principles. And the reason for this is not a kind of impoverishment or abstraction intensifying in proportion as the representation becomes more exalted, but that basic occlusion of which I have been speaking.

Perhaps some light might be cast on this by a reading of the proposed Constitution and Bylaws framed at the IPA's Thirtieth Congress, held in Jerusalem in 1977, these being the content of the second of the documents pulled, as it were, from the hat held out to me. Aside from mention of Freud's name, there is nothing at all in the Constitution that applies exclusively to something like psychoanalysis (if indeed such a thing exists), nothing at all that any number of associations of the Western type could not readily embrace. Without going so far as to include sports federations or associations of stamp or postcard collectors, it is certainly safe to say that any traditional institution whose goals are the search for knowledge, health, or mutual aid of a humanitarian kind could subscribe to these propositions. I repeat: with the sole exception of the evocation of the name of Freud, everything here reflects—sometimes indeed repeats exactly, in its hackneyed formulations—the most firmly established conventions of the framework of civil, administrative, and commercial law. Such is the perspective from which I wish to read the IPA's Constitution.

Let me now consider three specific aspects of that Constitution. These concern (1) dissolution (an issue destined to assume an ever greater topicality, and an issue from which one must always start out); (2) the institution proper, its performative establishment (an issue with which it is impossible either to begin or to end); and (3) geography and Latin America (the issue with which I wanted to begin and end today).

Dissolution

The Constitution's last article deals with the question of dissolution, and this is of interest to me in the first place because of the perspective I adopt. A perspective before which you too are placed historically, that of a radical transformation, already under way, which must sooner or later result in the dissolution of the IPA that Freud founded and its replacement by something else, something quite other, something with a fundamentally different structure, a different aspect, a different topography—in short, a different *chart*.

I do not know if, once this transformation is complete, the idea of a charter or constitution, the idea, that is, of law, will still hold sway; equally doubtful is any continued adherence to a statelike international centralization (the suprastate level is of course still statelike in character). More likely we have to envisage something quite different; what is happening here today already suggests as much. My interest in this article on dissolution has another dimension also—that of transference, or rather of transference in the particular sense of the transfer of an inheritance. When I say that the dissolution of the law which the IPA takes as its authority is already under way, it is not that I think it should be followed, or that it will in fact be followed, by a wild, lawless state of affairs. But there is inevitably a stage, in any transformation of a legal code, in which the new law (itself subject to later transformation) must appear from the standpoint of the earlier system as a condition of wildness: this is the stage of negotiation, of transition, and of the transfer of an inheritance.

Now, as I say, the final—and twelfth—article of the IPA Constitution envisages the Association's dissolution, and its terminology consists of formulas long used by associations of this type. It contemplates the "transfer" (the exact word used) of the IPA's property, i.e., the passing down of the only possible, perceptible, preservable legacy of the organization. To whom, then, is this legacy to be transferred? Were it not for fear of taking up too much of your time, I would have liked to undertake a thorough analysis of this last article concerned with death, this sort of proto-will which foresees the IPA's dissolution "by a resolution of which due notice has been given"—something you could prepare, say, between now and the Helsinki Congress. To become effective, such a resolution must be passed by a three-fourths majority of the members *present* at a duly convened business meeting. Thus the IPA cannot be dissolved by correspondence or by telegram even if a majority in favor exists, nor can it be dissolved by letter, postcard, telephone, satellite relay, or telepathy—Freud's self-acknowledged conversion of 1926–1930 to *Gedankenübertragung* or thought-transfer notwithstanding. This axiomatics of presence is extraordinarily revealing here. And this, not only for what it tells us of the ontological underpinnings of the IPA Constitution but also because it is a safe bet that those today who have the most to say, and do, in connection with the transformation of the psychoanalytic international will not be able to be present in Helsinki. Here, then, is the very last paragraph of the IPA Constitution:

> If upon the dissolution of the Association there remains, after payment of all its debts and liabilities, any property whatsoever, the same shall not be paid or distributed among Members of the Association but shall be given or transferred to some other institution or institutions having objects similar to the objects of the Association. Such institution or institutions, to be determined by the Members of the Association at or before the time of dissolution, shall prohibit the distribution of its or their income and property among its or their members. If and so far as effect cannot be given to this provision, then such property shall be transferred to some charitable object.

I do not know into how many languages the word "charity" can be translated—barely into French, at any rate, but no matter. In any case, these arrangements suggest quite a number of different ideas. The mere notion of institutions with "similar objects" provides a vast topic for discussion, and the use of the idea of analogy in this context can teach us a very great deal about this self-representation of the IPA's. That the sole completely legitimate object of transfer should in the last analysis amount to a renunciation of assets under the banner of the Christian category of charity, of Christian love unassociated with exchange, reproduction, or investment, really makes one wonder about what exactly the end of the IPA is liable to usher in. As for the idea of "similar objects," the idea that there are analogous institutions, etc., this leads us to ask ourselves what the peculiar, unique, or incomparable properties of a psychoanalytic institution might be. The IPA Constitution designates this specificity by means of a single word, a single proper name—and this brings me to my second point.

The Institution Itself

This second point, as it happens, concerns the Constitution's second article. The first has named the organization "IPA"—a performative statement that is now explicated by Article 2 under the heading "Definition of Psycho-Analysis." Those of you who are familiar with this charter will recall that absolutely nothing is said there of the specificity of psychoanalysis except for the name of Freud. There is explicit mention of "specificity," yet the word is given no content, post Freud, except Freud's name. Here is the text:

> Definition of Psycho-Analysis. The term *psychoanalysis* refers to a theory of personality structure and function, to the application of this theory to other branches of knowledge, and, finally, to a specific psychotherapeutic technique. This body of knowledge is based on and derived from the fundamental psychological discoveries made by Sigmund Freud.

This is a *hapax legomenon*. No institution of learning or of therapeutic practice has ever been founded on a proper name. The claim is so outlandish, and its outlandishness here made so basic to psychoanalysis that all the subsequent articles of this Constitution ought to have been undermined by its implications. In fact, as we have seen, nothing of the sort occurs, and aside from Freud's name one searches in vain for a single feature capable of marking this charter off from that of any other association established on the basis of problematical notions such as "personality," "psychotherapy," "branches of knowledge," and so on.

To save time, let me proceed directly to the most formal upshot of this, which is that anyone who ceases to appeal *a priori*, as a matter of dogma, to the authority of Freud's name thereby relinquishes his right to membership in the Association. Let us leave aside for the moment the case—though it is certainly serious enough—of those people who request clarification of such terms as "personality structure and function," "technique," "psychotherapy," "branches of knowledge," "body of knowledge," etc., and confine ourselves to the consideration of those who, without even wishing to deny all debt to Freud, do come to wonder about the role of this proper name and its relationship to science, to thought, to the institution, to the legacy of psychoanalysis—those who become interested in the unique link between this name and its bearer, between this name and the psychoanalytic cause or movement, etc. Since this is something that occurs here or there ever more frequently, and always along paths that are essential to psychoanalysis, one is obliged to draw the following conclusion: All who are inclined to lay hold of the right and the means to develop questions of this kind, all who believe it necessary to accept the implications for the institution of the answers they find, must needs have a new psychoanalytic *socius* in view—a *socius* that would not necessarily have the structure of a central, national, or international organization, and that would certainly not remain solely a school of theory as impotent in its way as that League of Nations whose impotence and lack of autonomy Freud pointed up in 1932 in his letter to Einstein (*Why War?*)—without, however, proceeding to wonder whence a psychoanalytic league of nations might one day derive an autonomous force.

Nor, for that matter, where on the earth such an organization might exist. What about *place?*

Geography and Latin America

I have reached my third topic: geography and Latin America in the IPA's proposed Constitution (from Jerusalem to Helsinki via New York). The text is much concerned with attributions to places, and its whole topology is very interesting. I pass quickly over the location of the Association's office—namely, "the country of the President." This arrangement was envisaged by Freud himself, as he recalls in "On the History of the Psycho-Analytic Movement," and this as early as the first Congress and the presidency of Jung. Let us not forget that opposition to it was quite vigorous. As Freud himself acknowledges, there was fear of "censorship and restrictions on scientific freedom." Nor can the fact that this opposition centered around Adler serve either to validate or to invalidate it in the eyes of anyone who is not a dogmatist or a true believer. The president, then, has his own place—a place amidst the psychoanalytic organizations which divide the globe up among them.

The grand map of this partition might seem purely grographical in nature, but when we consider the complex historico-political motivations involved, which, once they have been painstakingly traced, emerge as a differentiated network of blazed trails, what we see is a highly meaning-laden *terra psychoanalytica*, as sketched in the parenthetical statement that I quoted at the beginning: "(The Association's main geographical areas are defined at this time as America north of the United States-Mexican border; all America south of that border; and the rest of the world.)" Three areas, then—a tricontinental triangle. But inasmuch as "the rest of the world" is further divided into two, it may be more accurate to say that there are in fact four areas. "The rest of the world" is divided into two: on the one hand, it covers Europe and all those places where analysis has taken firm root (broadly speaking, the cradle of psychoanalysis in the so-called democracies of the Old World); on the other hand, it also includes that immensity of territory where, for reasons of a particular kind but of great diversity, *Homo psychoanalyticus* is unknown or outlawed.

Whatever the contours of the network of historical and political blazed (and unblazed) trails, however, the striking thing is that the map is not a triangle but a square—or, perhaps better, a framework or checkerwork—serving to mark out four zones, four types of territory, denominated in a geographically neutral manner, each of which is absolutely distinct from the standpoint of psychoanalysis. Though roughly coextensive with actual territorial areas, these four types are not fundamentally geographical in character, and where the overlap with territorial realities is not exact or perfect, this by no means compromises the typology, which I shall now try to define.

First come those areas of human settlement where psychoanalysis has made no inroads whatsoever—sometimes not even with the help of all the paraphernalia of colonization: almost all China, a good portion of Africa, the entire non-Judeo-Christian world—as also myriad enclaves in Europe and America. The size of these psychoanalytically virgin territories, in terms both of their physical extension and of their (present and future) demographics, as well as their cultural and religious foundations, means that they constitute a vast problem for the future of psychoanalysis. For that future is far from being structured like a space opening up ahead—a space yet to come, as it were, for psychoanalysis. This first zone is itself made up of two sectors: countries of European culture, such as those of the socialist world, where psychoanalysis is as yet unable to develop, and other countries. A comparable division exists from the point of view of human rights. Apropos of "the rest of the world," then, we ought to speak not of one kind of area but of two.

Another area—and another hemisphere—embraces all those places where psychoanalysis as an institution is firmly implanted (Western Europe, North America) and of which—though human rights are not universally respected (far from it, in fact, as witness Amnesty International's reports on European and North American countries, not to mention those kinds of violence which fall outside Amnesty's purview)—it may at least be said that certain sorts of violence have not as yet, not in the period since World War II, been unleashed with the ferocity, whether state-supported or not, that is familiar at varying levels and in varying forms in so many Latin American countries. Some might say that this is a matter of degree only, yet the difference is so great, albeit quantitative, that a certain qualitative threshold is undoubtedly passed; likewise, another kind of coexistence comes to obtain between the organizational apparatus of psychoanalysis and the deployment of political violence, so giving rise to problems, controversies, sufferings, and dramatic events which are as yet without parallel elsewhere.

We must therefore speak in this connection of a *fourth* area, and discern another map lying beneath—beyond, or on the far side of—the one proposed by the IPA's Constitution. What I shall from now on call the Latin America of psychoanalysis is the only area in the world where there is a coexistence, whether actively adversarial or not, between a strong psychoanalytic institution on the one hand and a society on the other (civil society or State) that engages in torture on a scale and of a kind far surpassing the crude traditional forms familiar everywhere. As I feel sure others will testify in the coming days far more effectively than I ever could, the kinds of torture to which I refer sometimes appropriate what I suppose we may as well call psycho-symbolic techniques, thereby involving the citizen-psychoanalyst, as such, as an active participant either on one side or the other, or perhaps even on both sides at once, of these abuses. In any case, the medium of psychoanalysis is in consequence traversed by the violence in question, and this, whether directly or indirectly, inevitably leaves its mark on all its intra-institutional relationships, all its clinical practice, and all its dealings with civil society or with the State.

This is an area, then, where no relationship of the psychoanalytic sphere to itself can be conceived of that does not bear traces of internal and external violence of this kind. In short, the psychoanalytic medium no longer enjoys any simple interiority. We are obliged to acknowledge that this pattern—a dense psychoanalytic colonization and a strong psychoanalytic culture coupled with the highest possible intensity of modern military and police violence—is at once *without equivalent* and *exemplary* in character. To say that it is without equivalent implies that no one who is not blind to reality, or speaking in bad faith or out of political calculation, can refuse, as the IPA under the presidency of Dr. Joseph did, to name Latin America (in the event, Argentina) under the pretext that human rights are also violated in other places. From the point of view of psychoanalysis as institution and as historical movement, what is happening in Latin America can be compared neither with the situation in all those parts of the world—or of "the rest the world"—where psychoanalysis does not take place, where it has not yet found a place, nor with the situation in those other parts of "the rest of the world" where psychoanalysis has put down roots and where human rights are no longer violated (a recent development), or not yet violated, in such a massive, spectacular and systematic fashion.

But while it is true that the pattern in Latin America is thus indeed without equivalent, thus indeed *incomparable* in this sense, and while no substitution of other names or other examples can thus be justified here, this is not to say that that which is without equivalent, that which is unique, cannot *serve as an example*. The unexampled may have an exemplary role for the ethical-political problems of psychoanalysis. What occurs on a massive scale, inscribed in large letters upon Latin America, may well serve to expose—by projecting it, as it were, onto a giant screen—what is written small, as a function of what might be described as the circulatory system and the stock of less easily decipherable small letters, upon the so-called liberal democracies of Europe and North America. (Let us not forget that the latter's intervention is one of the essential determinants of the Latin America situation.) There can be no substituting of Chinese, Russian, Afghan, or South African instances for what is written in large letters over there in Latin America, but on the other hand those large letters can help us understand what is happening, could happen, or will happen in the psychoanalytic Old World, here where we stand, in the relations of psychoanalysis with the rest of the world in its political dimension (civil society, State), with the European and North American continents in their entirety, and above all in the relations that obtain *within* the territory of institutional psychoanalysis. It happens (and it is no coincidence) that the dominant psychoanalytic schools in Latin America, apart from the orthodox empiricisms I alluded to earlier, are radically European tendencies, by which I mean to say that they remain firmly anchored to their British or French (Kleinian, Lacanian, etc.) roots. This is something which enlarges and turns face up a good many small letters awaiting decipherment.

Under given conditions, once a protocol has been established, *naming* can become a historical and political act responsibility for whose performance is inescapable. This is a responsibility that the IPA has ducked at a particularly grave moment in history—the history of psychoanalysis included. Henceforth, should psychoanalysis wish to take the measure of what is happening in Latin America, to measure itself against what the state of affairs down there reveals, to respond to what threatens, limits, defines, disfigures, or exposes it, then it will be necessary, at least, to do some *naming*. This is the first requirement for an appeal: a call to call that which has a name by its name. To call Latin America by its name, by what that name seems to mean for psychoanalysis today. At least as a start. All I could hope to contribute to that appeal today was: the naming of Latin America.

ENDNOTE

This essay was the opening address to a French-Latin American meeting convened in Paris in February 1981 at the initiative of René Major. The proceedings of this event, which was devoted mainly to the institutions and politics of present-day psychoanalysis, were published under the same title as the meeting itself: *Confrontation* (Paris: Collection Vert et noir, 1981), and subtitled *Les souterrains de l'institution* (The Underground Corridors of the Institution). Translation first published in *American Imago* 48.2 (1991). Translation © 1991, 1996 by Donald Nicholson-Smith. All rights reserved.

3
"Thus Spake the Subaltern . . .": Postcolonial Criticism and the Scene of Desire

Amit S. Rai

> I say limit not death, for I do not at all believe in what today is so easily called the death of philosophy (nor, moreover, in the simple death of whatever—the book, man, or god, especially since, as we all know, what is dead wields a very specific power).
>
> —Derrida, *Positions* 6

If we are sure today that the subaltern cannot speak, can we be as sure that her ghost does not, especially when postcolonial criticism seems to re-present the discourse of that ghost? I situate what follows at the limits of this haunted discourse by reopening the now familiar question of who speaks for the subaltern subject; my essay considers the relationship between the "postcolonial example" and the force of memory within that criticism. I contend that postcolonial criticism can usefully articulate Lacanian psychoanalysis and Foucauldian discourse analysis from within the field of cultural memory. However, this articulation is obliged to mark, as rigorously as possible, the structural lures that can lead us down some false trails. My itinerary therefore follows the stakes of the "example" in texts by Homi K. Bhabha and Gayatri Chakravorty Spivak. Noting the melancholia that haunts these texts, I consider the genealogy of a certain sadness within Lévi-Straussian ethnography. I attempt to link this sadness to Lacan's thought in two ways: by reconsidering the nature of the "Law" and by offering a postcolonial account of the lost m/other and the symbolization of death. To explore the latter, I offer a reading of the popular Hindi film *Raat aur Din* (1967). Generally, I hope that my itinerary will clarify the fraught relationship between postcolonial criticism and Lacanian psychoanalysis; indeed, that it will help us rethink the relationship between postcolonial criticism and the speechless subjects of our desire.

Example

Let us begin then with an example.

In *Raat aur Din*, Nargis, a well-known Muslim actress, plays Varuna, a character with multiple personality disorder (MPD). Varuna's MPD manifests itself as a host personality who is a quiet, sober, stay-at-home young bride who speaks little English and is deeply conscious of Hindu propriety (of course, her husband, Pratap, dotes on her). Her other "personality" calls herself Peggy (among a variety of other Christian names): she is Westernized as a dissolute, dance-crazy, cigarette-smoking alcoholic, whose nocturnal wanderlust leads her secretly to seek out male lovers at clubs in Calcutta. This "feminine" binary encodes a number of national and cultural anxieties in postcolonial India, oscillating between virginity/promiscuity; purity/contamination; religion/dissolution; India/the West; sanity/madness; public sphere/womanspace. Since Varuna's MPD launches a series of displacements, let us consider a moment in the last scene, itself a repetition:

> VARUNA: (*standing over a precipice, looking down, screams*): I killed my mother! I killed my mother!
>
> RATAP (*her husband*): Varuna! Varuna!
>
> *Scene shifts to a hospital in Simla*:
>
> DR. ALVAREZ (*to Pratap*): Pratap, here we found the coroner's report. Read this. It is clear from this that Varuna did not kill her mother. Her mother died of a heart attack. Before she fell from the ledge, she was struck with a heart attack, and it was only because of the heart attack that she fell. (*Turning to Varuna*): Varuna, in this you have no responsibility. You thought that you were the cause of your mother's death. And you supposed that you had committed a huge sin. And the more you thought this, the more you began to hate yourself, so much so that you wanted to kill Varuna.
>
> Yet, beside you there was another life that from childhood sustained your heart [*nibati rahi*], a sort of life that from your point of view held no sorrow [*gum*], no difficulty [*takleef*], no regret [*afsos*], no fixed plan [*bandish*], only the utmost happiness. And that life was Peggy's life. As much as your mother tried to keep your wish-desires [*bhavna*] down, to crush your passion-desires [*arman*], this wish [*icha*] of yours to live like Peggy kept growing. The result [*nateeja*] of this was that in your mind there was born an uncertainty of sep-

aration between you and Peggy. The body is the servant of the mind. This is why sometimes you became Varuna, sometimes Peggy, and neither knew of each other. Now you understand? Well then, now there is no reason to worry. Varuna, get up. Meet your father.

VARUNA'S FATHER (*stretching out his arms*): Varuna, come child.

VARUNA: Papa! (*they embrace.*)

   (*Varuna, supported by her father and husband, walks off into the waning day.*) (*Raat aur Din*; my trans.)

How can we adequately translate this scene? Indeed, of what is it an example? Doubtless, the interpretations we could offer are legion. We could begin with the problems of "translating" the scene of postcolonial, gendered madness into the language of metropolitan analysis. But how do we translate the hybridity of Hindustani into recognizable and intelligible English? Another complicated issue, considering the film itself obliquely raises the problem of translation: Despite all the nationalist pretensions characterizing the genre, this Hindi pop film is set mostly in Calcutta, where Bengali is the regional language. So if we succeeded in this act of double translation, what would it represent?

Postcolonial criticism might give us an answer. Consider those spectacular passages in Homi Bhabha's work where the tempo of his prose speeds up and a series of examples denoting cultural difference and hybridity juxtaposes as equatable incisions, slitting open the universalistic temporality of Western modernity. I am thinking of crucial passages throughout *The Location of Culture* where, with the sharp click of a camera's eye, Sri Lankan theater groups line up next to Australian Aborigines, South African novelists, Salman Rushdie, and Toni Morrison's *Beloved*:

> This side of the psychoses of patriotic fervour, I like to think, there is overwhelming evidence of a more transnational and translational sense of the hybridity of imagined communities. Contemporary Sri Lankan theatre represents the deadly conflict between the Tamils and the Sinhalese through the allegorical references to State brutality in South Africa and Latin America; the Anglo-Celtic canon of Australian literature and cinema is being rewritten from the perspective of Aboriginal political and cultural imperatives; the South African novels of Richard Rive, Bessie Head, Nadine Gordimer, John Coetzee, are documents of a society divided by the effects of apartheid . . .; Salman Rushdie writes the fabulist historiography of post-Independence India and Pakistan in *Midnight's Children* and *Shame*, only to remind us in *The Satanic Verses* that the truest eye may now belong to the migrant's double vision; Toni Morrison's *Beloved* revives the past of slavery and its murderous rituals of possession and self-possession, in order to project a contemporary fable of a woman's history that is at the same time the narrative of an affective, historic memory of an emergent public sphere of men and women alike. (*Location* 5)

We should immediately note Bhabha's insistent use of the present tense—his prose writes, reminds, revives. Another example surfaces in *Location*'s conclusion, which begins with Fanon's interpretation of the phrases "Dirty Nigger!" and "Look, a Negro!" Bhabha comments:

> Whenever these words are said in anger or in hate, whether of the Jew in the *estaminet* in Antwerp, or of the Palestinian on the West Bank, or of the Zairian student eking out a wretched existence selling fake fetishes on the Left Bank; whether they are said of the body of a woman or the man of colour; whether they are quasi-officially spoken in South Africa or officially prohibited in London or New York . . . ; whenever "Dirty nigger!" or, "Look, a Negro!" is not said at all, but you can see it in a gaze, or hear it in the solecism of a still silence; whenever and wherever I am when I hear a racist, or catch his look, I am reminded of Fanon's evocatory essay "The Fact of Blackness" and its unforgettable opening lines. (236)

Again, Bhabha seems compelled to respond to racism by repeated acts of "rememoration" (Schneiderman 140); we will need to return to this presentist "slit" (Lacan, *Four* 11). Here we should mark carefully how such stunningly expansive lists recur throughout the body of Bhabha's work (see *Location* 139, 178), providing us with moments in Bhabha's texts that seemingly situate his politics, while also, precisely because they traverse such expanses of time and place, giving us the assurance of an uninterrupted and total discourse of the subaltern (see Hall; Shohat).

For many years now, Bhabha has embarked on a project that is trying to make room . . . for what? Even as his examples repeatedly reterritorialize a Third Space of "being that is wrought from the interruptive, interrogative, tragic experience of blackness, of discrimination, of despair" (238), this use of the example to illustrate the liminal and temporally disjunctive draws on a proprietary economy, which we could call "postcolonial panopticism." More precisely, this economy situates the "particular case, details, and examples . . . as illustrations of some more general trait, characteristic, or theory" (Harvey 262).

> Exemplarity, as the transformation of the given into a sign for something else (*either not present now but with the capacity to be made present, or never present intrinsically*) or as the transformation of the given into a case, a particular that illustrates or represents a universal, always invokes the same metaphysical assumption. This assumption is the supposedly valid structure of the sign as determined by Plato and Aristotle. . . . I wish to point out that exemplarity, by using that notion of representation, thereby establishes a particular theory of meaning. This "given" is meaningful only insofar as it becomes or can become an example of something else. (265; my emphasis)

Following Harvey's astute critique, we must consider the strange recurrence of this trope in Bhabha's work, particularly when he repeatedly and rigorously tries to place the sign's designated meaning under erasure.

Although I maintain some of the consciousness of a grateful and admiring disciple, who acknowledges the force and vision of Bhabha's interventions, these collated examples—which are marked only by disclaimer, denial, and disavowal—leave no place for the untranslatable. Despite Bhabha's repeated disclaimers about the formulation of any general theory of the postcolonial (e.g., *Location* 41), I sense that what authorizes these lists is a desire for totality that Bhabha dissimulates as an uncanny chain of difference. This dissolves the *différantial* relations among the examples I quoted above (see also Thomas, Lowe). The examples nonetheless exceed Bhabha's discourse. Derrida astutely formulates this problem: "The example is first of all for others, and beyond the self. Sometimes, perhaps always, whoever gives the example is not equal to the example he gives—which he gives by giving then what he has not and even what he is not. For this reason, the example thus disjoined separates enough from itself or from whoever gives it so as to be no longer or not yet example *for itself*" (*Specters* 34).

Bhabha's postcolonialism seems unable to tolerate this surplus of meaning. His equation of all liminal and dominated groups and subjectivities also risks collapsing their social identities into an ontological correspondence, which reduces their distinct struggles to analogous experiences of marginalization (Guillory 11). In this respect, Bhabha's desire to situate difference in the present tense is not fortuitous. Let me be clear: Postcolonial criticism, of which Bhabha's work is certainly not the only example, must acknowledge that the trauma of history dividing or uniting the wretched of the Earth can only be undone in strategically adventurous, repeat performances that do not seek to escape from the essential and irreducible heterogeneity of this *différance*.

Where, then, should we *situate* a postcolonial criticism that would, at the very least, mark exemplarity as a structural lure? We might do worse than return to that moment when Lacan, responding to his "excommunication" from the psychoanalytic establishment, addresses the praxis of psychoanalysis: "one cannot avoid the impression that, in a whole field, everything is explained in advance. Analysis is not a matter of discovering in a particular case the differential feature of the theory, and in doing so believe that one is explaining why your daughter is silent—for the point at issue is to *get her to speak*, and this effect proceeds from a type of intervention that has nothing to do with a differential feature" (*Four* 11; original emphasis). What relevance has this intervention for postcolonial criticism? If, following Spivak, we can say without hesitation that to "get her to speak" is another way of rendering the role of the representer transparent, we should recall that Lacan also acknowledged that "hysteria places us, I would say, on the track of some kind of original sin in analysis. There has to be one. The truth is perhaps simply one thing, namely, the desire of Freud himself, the fact that something, in Freud, was never analysed" (12).

On the track of this "sin," in which postcolonial theory cannot but participate, we can place my initial example in a network of repetition, a structure that poses serious problems for the economy of exemplarity, though it nonetheless compels us to think and "work through" examples. How can one stage this compulsively repeated scene of desire in postcolonial criticism, where the knowledge of a "nego-tiating" alterity is irreducibly compromised by our investments of desire? As we have seen, these scenes of alterity authenticate postcolonial discourse, but only as "rememorized" traces that mark the distance between First World circuits of cul-tural/critical reproduction and "other world" lived experiences of exploitation and domination. A precise relation to regression haunts this economy. As Schneiderman remarks, "The use of regression for Lacan was limited to what he called rememoration, which concerned remembering past experiences not as they were lived the first time but in terms of the important signifying elements that remained from them in the unconscious" (140). Cultural rememoration *always* founders on a certain loss, whose effects are surely essential to postcolonial criti-cism. With this in mind, let us consider the present.

Present

In her now famous critique of Kristeva, Spivak begins her analysis of French fem-inism with "an obstinate childhood memory":

> I *am* walking alone in my grandfather's estate on the Bihar-Bengal border one win-ter afternoon in 1949. Two *ancient* washerwomen are washing clothes in the *river*, beating the clothes on the stones. One accuses the other of poaching on her part of the river. I can still hear the *cracked* derisive voice of the one accused: "You fool! Is this your river? The river belongs to the Company"—the East India Company, from whom India had transferred its charge to an Indian Governor-General in 1947. India would become an independent republic in 1950. *For these withered women, the land as soil and water to be used rather than a map to be learned still belonged, as it did one hun-dred and nineteen years before that date, to the East India Company.* . . . [T]heir facts were wrong but the fact was right. The Company does still own the land. ("French Feminism" 135; my emphases)

Rendering the past present, Spivak's "memory" metonymically invokes impe-rialism's burden as a thorn of guilt that Western feminists must extirpate before they can understand Third World womanspace. Spivak carefully marks her distance from these ancients by emphasizing her own class, caste, and age; she has no desire to romanticize these figures by the river. Still, how are we to read this scene, which Spivak narrates in the anthropological present tense? Considering Cixous's "The Laugh of the Medusa," Spivak tells us more recently: "We must be able to read this 'present tense' in that nondimensional verbal . . .: not a future present but a persistent effortfulness that makes a 'present.' This practice 'does and will take place in areas other than those subordinated to philosophico-theoretical domination.' Up close, we cannot grasp it at all. The undecidable in view of which decisions must be risked" ("French Feminism Revisited" 156).

Up close, these withered women of land and soil, toiling by the Company's river, slip away, but not before they become elements in this postcolonial critic's melancholic scene of desire—the land, water, women, and Company are objects of dynamic and contradictory cathexes. In anthropology, psychoanalysis, and post-colonial criticism, this type of scene recurs over and again *precisely because it is undecidable*. In less vigilant hands than Spivak's, narrating this scene would efface the economy of desire, rendering the role of the representer transparent and thus obliterating irreducible differences between the narrator and the objects of her memory.

Let us pursue this obsessively renarrated scene, however, by considering Lacan's psychoanalytic appropriation of Claude Lévi-Strauss's structural anthropology. There is an urgent need to contextualize postcolonial criticism at the intersections of these two discourses. Indeed, Western anthropologists and psychoanalysts are beginning to confront the interface of these two, at times, antagonistic modes of cultural inquiry.[1] For instance, in their "Introduction" to a recent collection of essays entitled *Anthropology and Psychoanalysis: An Encounter through Culture*, Suzette Heald, Ariane Deluz, and Pierre-Yves Jacopin have argued that anthropologists, due to renewed interest in subjectivity, are now "exploring the different conceptions of the self in a way which extends beyond the simple description of cultural difference to attempt to grasp something of the internal dynamic of a worldview" (Heald 1). They suggest that psychoanalysis has become indispensable to this exploration. Were this "explor[ation]" to continue without noting the role global decolonization has played in the history of these two disciplines, and without acknowledging the global power lines that link these two discourses to epistemic, cultural, economic neocolonialism, it would be yet another colonial adventure. By clarifying the postcolonial context of anthropology and psychoanalysis, however, we can return to postcolonial criticism with a new set of interpretive strategies. I contend that Lacanian psychoanalysis has ridden on the coattails of a discipline (Western anthropology) that is complicit with the colonial project of producing the Orient as pure alterity. This symbiotic relationship between psychoanalysis and anthropology has been crucial to the history and conceptual possibility of both fields. Postcolonial criticism is also thoroughly implicated in this history—that is the nature of its crisis. Yet though it often surreptitiously reintroduces this self-consolidating other (Spivak, "Three"), postcolonial criticism has also quickly become a field that can help us reinscribe the *force* of this history (Derrida, *Positions* 57).

Malaise

Such is the scale of the problems, so narrow and so precarious are the paths hitherto trodden, so final the annihilation of tract after immense tract of the past, and so uncertain the bases of our speculations, that even the briefest reconnaissance on the terrain plunges the enquirer into a state of indecision, in which feelings of humble resignation fight for supremacy with moments of the insanest ambition. He knows that the essentials have gone for ever and that all he can do is scratch the surface. . . . Nothing is possible: everything, therefore, is possible.

—Lévi-Strauss, *Tristes tropiques* 246–48

The crisis that postcolonial criticism faces should not plunge us into melancholy. We can recall that sadness has a certain genealogy in anthropological discourse: Readers may remember that the tropics rendered Lévi-Strauss morose. He realized, through "equally demoralizing experiences" in various parts of the world (36), that "journeys, those magic coffins full of dreamlike promises [*coffrets magiques aux promesses rêveuses*], will never again yield up their treasures untarnished" (*Tristes* 37; trans. mod.). The anthropologist laments the lost purity of "these primitive peoples, the briefest contact with whom can sanctify the traveller," for he mourns doomed "sensitive and powerless victims, paltry game [*pauvre gibier*] caught in the toils of mechanized civilization" (41; trans. mod.). The "victims" are present only on their way to an inevitable absence, an effortfulness (to recall Spivak's term) infused with the supposed immediacy of the Noble Savage. How are we to understand the role of melancholic nostalgia in Lévi-Strauss's structural anthropology?

Drawing on linguistics and communication theory, and considering himself influenced by Marx and Freud, Lévi-Strauss argued that cultural phenomena could be rendered intelligible only by demonstrating their shared relationship to a few underlying principles (Ortner 380). By revealing the axes and limits of cultural thought, structuralism established the "universal grammar of culture" (380). (In fact, as many have pointed out, while Lévi-Strauss claimed Freud as a major intellectual influence, his theories of the human mind as the creator of culture dealt with the psyche only as an intellectual product, largely independent of psychoanalysis [Heald 7].) According to Lévi-Strauss, however, the grammar and logic of these cultures can never be completed, for such totalities have "no meaning" (qtd. in Derrida, "Structure" 289). Yet what is universal here? What cultural?

When attempting to answer these questions, one confronts the paradox of the "center" in structuralist thought. In "Structure, Sign and Play in the Discourse of the Human Sciences," Derrida argues that thinking about a "structure lacking any center" is itself unthinkable. He writes:

> It has always been thought that the center, which is by definition unique, constituted that very thing within a structure which, while governing the structure, escapes structurality. This is why classical thought concerning structure could say that the center is, paradoxically, *within* the structure and *outside it*. The center is at the center of the totality, and yet, since the center does not belong to the totality (is not part of the totality), the totality *has its center elsewhere*. The center is not the center. (279; original emphases)

This totality without a center is a function of the field of *play*: "that is to say, a field of infinite substitutions only because it is finite, that is to say, because instead of being an inexhaustible field, as in the classical hypothesis, instead of being too large, there is something missing from it: a center which arrests and grounds the play of substitutions" (289). Of course, this play is also the "disruption of presence" (292). If we return to Lévi-Strauss, however, the presence of innocent natives seems to be "a signifying and substitutive reference inscribed in a system of differences and the movement of a chain." As such, the presence of this "paltry game" is made possible by an originary game of presence and absence; to succeed at this game, the discourse of the anthropologist must serve as its center. We can locate this "game" between what Lacan calls the moment of "seeing" and that of "absorption."

> We find here once again the rhythmic structure of this *pulsation of the slit*. . . . The appearance/disappearance takes place between two points, the initial and the terminal of this logical time—between the instance of seeing, when something of the intuition itself is always elided, not to say lost, and that elusive moment when the apprehension of the unconscious is not, in fact, concluded, when it is always a question of an "absorption" fraught with false trails [*il s'agit toujours d'une récupération leurrée*]. (*Four* 32; my emphasis)

Let us reiterate Spivak alongside Lacan's "*récupération leurrée*": "The undecidable in face of which decisions must be risked" ("French Feminism Revisited" 156). What else can either theorist mean but the possibility of trudging down false trails? By following Lacan's suggestion that the status of this pulsating slit is primarily ethical rather than "ontic," we can ask, paraphrasing Lacan, where Lévi-Strauss's passion lay and where his desire took him (*Four* 34; see also Fabian).

This play between seeing and absorption recurs in Lévi-Strauss's thought in the incest taboo's dynamic, which shatters the opposition between culture and nature. As Derrida has often explained, the West has radically opposed nature to "law, to education, to art, to technics—but also to liberty, to the arbitrary, to history, to society, to the mind, and so on" ("Structure" 283; see also "White" 226, *"Différance"* 17). In the nature/culture binary, opposition nature is a metonym for presence, immediacy, and truth, or, alternately, savagery, woman, and animality. Similarly, culture is a metonym for mimicry, degradation, and postlapsarian existence, or, alternately, the phallus, history (of the subject's intentionality), and politics (narrowly defined). The incest taboo reinscribes and disrupts this binary opposition. Derrida writes:

> In the *Elementary Structures*, [Lévi-Strauss] begins from this axiom of definition . . . But . . . [he] encounters what he calls a scandal, that is to say, something which no longer tolerates the nature/culture opposition he has accepted, something which simultaneously seems to require the predicates of nature and of culture. This *scandal* is the incest prohibition. The incest prohibition is universal; in this sense one could call it natural. But it is also a prohibition, a system of norms and interdicts; in this sense one could call it cultural . . . ("Structure" 283)

The incest taboo is a scandalous hybrid that founds culture (Kuper 170). Structure is thus founded on a rule that "impurely" distinguishes between culture and nature. If structuralism tries to "get 'behind' the flux of real behavior to the unconscious generating structure," "to uncover the universal principles of human mentality" (Kuper 173), how can it do so on the basis of something that is not universal? How can it do so if the "mind" itself is incorrigibly cultural? This "scandal" forces Lévi-Strauss to admit his methodological reliance on the binary between nature and culture, which shifts his once "real analysis" onto "ideal analysis" (*Of Grammatology* 104).

Lévi-Strauss cannot give in to this "play." Instead, "an ethic of nostalgia of origins, an ethic of archaic and natural innocence, of a purity or presence and self-presence in speech—an ethic, nostalgia, and even remorse, which he often presents as *the motivation* of the ethnological project," traps the anthropologist of structure in a "saddened, *negative*, nostalgic, guilty, Rousseauistic side of the thinking of play" (Derrida, "Structure" 292; original emphasis). The motivation—might one say *desire?*—to engage anthropology is surely this loss of purity. But what are we then to make of this melancholia and how does desire structure or enforce it?

To answer these questions, let us try to situate, as clearly as possible, the term "desire." Lacan's formula runs thus: "man's [*sic*] desire is the desire of the Other" (*Four* 38). Not desire *for* the Other, but desire *of* the Other; as such, it is a continuous force set in motion by the question "What am I for the Other?" Alan Sheridan remarks that *désir* implies "a continuous force" in French, a "perpetual effect of symbolic articulation. It is not an appetite: it is excentric and insatiable. That is why Lacan coordinates desire not with an object that can satisfy it, but with an object that causes it (one is reminded of fetishism)" ("Translator's Note," *Four* 278–79). Elaborating on this object of desire, Pradelles de Latour observes that the subject derives from a fundamental omission in which the subject is situated (153). This absence of being lies at the very origin of desire, which Lacan distinguishes from need and demand. Whereas need is governed by the interplay of satisfaction (generally, at the level of biology), and demand (represented by a signifier at the level of enunciation) yearns for the plenitude and the hereafter, desire is never brought to a close, because it fails to satisfy. By "desire," Lacan means a striving for completion in that which is not wanted in any simple way. Where there is a lack, there is also a desire and a subject (*Four* 153).

Troubling the relationship between self and other, desire emerges from the unconscious: "*the unconscious is the discourse of the Other*" (*Four* 131). What, then, is the Other? (I realize this question risks us getting lost in a maze of terms: "Other," "other," "barred other," etc., but we must risk posing it.) Lacan asserts that the Other is "the locus in which is constituted" the speaking subject, which is linked to the symbolic order (qtd. in Felman 55; I elaborate on this below). Yet this relationship with the Other is also unconscious (Felman). The discourse of the Other fractures our intentionality, our self-presence, such that a full sense of "ourselves" always eludes us. By locating Lévi-Strauss's melancholy in this desire for the irretrievable Other, which is also an economy of writing (difference/deferral), we can begin to understand the structure of desire as the condition of possibility for ethnographic knowledge. This knowledge is bound to desire because, as Felman has pointed out, the "observer is a fundamental, structural, desiring, formative part of the observed" (63). In a certain sense, the "observed" is always already lost; we can therefore link Lévi-Strauss's *autre*-melancholy to what Kristeva defines as the very condition of depression (see *Black Sun* 10).

I suggest that the lost object—the wretched native of an always prior age—is the intolerable violence animating the ethnographic project. Consider Lévi-Strauss, who, having himself returned from the jungle, "the world's end," stands at the abyss of desire with a handful of ashes. In a moving passage, he asks, "Can it be that I, the elderly predecessor of those scourers of the jungle, am the only one to have brought back nothing but a handful of ashes?" ("*Prédécesseur blanchi de ces coureurs de brousse, demeuré-je donc le seul à n'avoir rien retenu dans mes mains, que des cendres?*" [41]). He continues:

> Is mine the only voice to bear witness to the failure [*échec*] of escapism? Like the Indian in the myth, I went as far as the earth permits and when I arrived at the world's end, I questioned the people, the creatures and things I found there and met with the same disappointment [*déception*]: "He stood still, weeping bitterly, praying and moaning. And yet no mysterious sound reached his ears, nor was he put to sleep in order to be transported, as he slept, to the temple of the magic animals. . . ." Dreams, "god of the savages," as the old missionaries used to say, have always slipped through my fingers like quicksilver . . . But a few shining particles may have remained stuck, here and there. At Cuiaba . . .? At Ubatuba . . .? . . . In America or in Asia?. . . . I can pick out at random a name still steeped in the magic of legend: Lahore. (41–42; trans. mod.)

Can we generalize this "disappointment," this "quicksilver" dream, and the economy giving it force, as that which renders anthropology an im/possible gamble and an irruption of alterity within the ethnographer-self? This gamble at "the end of the world" is precisely why we must shift analysis from the ontic to the ethical. I suggest that a universalist structure orients Lévi-Strauss's melancholy. Defending his humanist nostalgia from the vagaries of play, Lévi-Strauss hopes to ground his argument by invoking the universalism of the prohibition on incest; his example undoes him. Pushing this further, we note that the observing subject is split by the subjectivity he aims to contain. This structure of totalizing desire founders on the example that binds Lévi-Strauss to my discussion of Bhabha's "postcolonial panopticism." Yet it is to Lévi-Strauss's lasting credit that he was at least able to mark this double bind of the anthropologist:

> I am caught within a circle from which there is no escape: the less human societies were able to communicate with each other and therefore to corrupt each other through contact, the less their respective emissaries were able to perceive the wealth and significance of their diversity. In short, I have only two possibilities [*je suis prisonnier d'une alternative*]: either I can be like some traveller of the olden days, confronted by a stupendous spectacle [*prodigieux spectacle*], all, or almost all, of which escaped [*échappait*] him, or worse still, filled him with scorn and disgust; or I can be a modern traveller, chasing after the vestiges of a vanished reality. I lose on both counts, and more seriously than may at first appear, for, while I complain of being able to glimpse no more than the shadow of the past, I may be insensitive to reality as it is taking shape at this very moment, since I have not reached the stage of development at which I would be capable of perceiving it. . . . I am subject to a double

infirmity: all that I perceive offends me, and I constantly reproach myself for not seeing as much as I should. (43; trans. mod.)

Here the centrality of vision is crucial to memory and the vanishing of reality. This rememorizing vision, which Lévi-Strauss calls the anthropologist's double, also affects the postcolonial critic, who sometimes sees a little too well, a little too much, and thus not at all (see Spivak, "Feminism and Deconstruction" 124–25). This unavoidable vanishing clarifies Spivak's obstinate memory and the peculiar force it exerts in her essay. I will return to postcolonial criticism's haunting, double infirmity in my discussion of *Raat aur Din* by tracing the persistent power of this revenance. Before proceeding, however, I want to return briefly to Spivak's scene of desire by the river, on the border of Bengal and Bihar, where we observed the postcolonial critic in turn observing the objects of her diasporic desire. Rather than simply posit these ancient others as metaphors for Kristeva's maternal body, the murder and repression of whom is requisite for the postcolonial to enter the Law of the Metropolis, let us displace this scene.

What does Spivak want here? Hers is "not the tired nationalist claim that only a native can know the scene" ("French Feminism" 136). Spivak intends to shatter the homogenizing, universalizing category of "woman" by interrogating the "immense heterogeneity of the field." To do so, she sets her sights on Kristeva's *Des chinoises*, a text that many critics consider peculiarly paradoxical (see Lowe). Spivak charts the trace of a previous orientalism in Kristeva's concern about who she is ("French Feminism" 137), in her "colonialist benevolence" (138), and in her "macrological nostalgia for the pre-history of the East" (140). Spivak then outlines "deconstructive themes" in a number of French antifeminist feminists. Her brilliant and important critique ranges over these thinkers, but it also cleaves to her obstinate memory by the river. I am tempted to read her text as an analog to Lévi-Strauss's melancholy, for the organization and affect of these texts are remarkably similar. The river, laboring women, and present memory arrest the play of Spivak's text; a desire haunts her memory.

Lacan links the figure of rivers to language and desire in this way: "The channel in which desire is located is not simply that of the modulation of the signifying chain, but that which *flows beneath* it as well; that is, properly speaking, what we are as well as what we are not, our being and our non-being—that which is signified in an act passes from one signifier of the chain to another beneath all the significations" (*Ethics* 321–22; my emphasis). Does this mean only that Spivak's women escape absolute "understanding," rigorous "differentiation," and firm "effortfulness"? What would it mean to write this scene of desire as the fractured, undecidable violation that enables postcolonial critique (Spivak, "Burden" 149)?

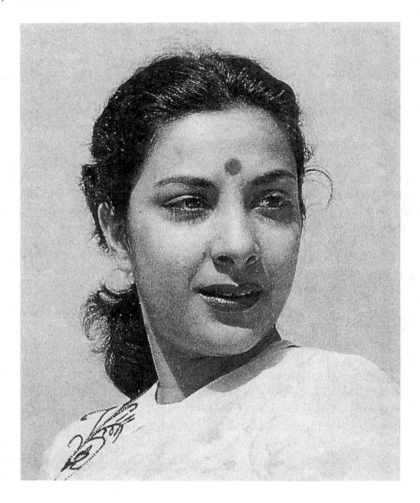

FIGURE I.
Promotional shot of the actress Nargis. *Author's collection.*

Tajub hai

The core of Freudian thought as it is deployed by us as analysts, whether we attend this seminar or not, is that the function of memory, remembering, is at the very least a rival of the satisfactions it is charged with effecting. It has its own dimension whose reach goes beyond that of a satisfying finality. The tyranny of memory is that which is elaborated in what we call structure.

—Lacan, *Ethics* 223

FIGURE 2.
Promotional shot of the actress Nargis. *Author's collection.*

It would be too easy to argue at this point that the symbolic order, O/other, and productive/repressive power simply do not apply "in the Indian context." Instead of this claim, and by operating from the conviction that in "order effectively, practically to transform what one decries," one must "still be heard and understood within it" (Derrida, "Tympan" xiii), I have chosen a cinematic text that resists interpretation not by negating psychoanalysis, but precisely by negotiating with it (see Spivak, *Post-colonial Critic* 11). First, a quick plot summary of *Raat aur Din*

FIGURE 3.
Still of Nargis and actor Raj Kapoor in *Awaara. Author's collection.*

(but do remember that this is a Hindi pop film! See figures 1 and 2 for promotional shots of Nargis; figure 3 features her and actor Raj Kapoor in another film).[2]

Late at night, a woman in a glittering sequined dress hails a taxi that whisks her off to "Cirpo," a high-fashion dance club in Calcutta. She sings, dances, and flirts with a man named Dillip, who believes he saw her once before, in Simla. Peggy, the woman, says she has never been to Simla. Suddenly, a man storms into the club, grabs Peggy by the arm, calling her Varuna, and demands that she go home with him at once; his name is

Pratap, and he claims to be her husband. She takes one look at him and bursts out laughing, exclaiming "Impossible!" A scuffle ensues between Pratap and Dillip. Meanwhile, Peggy slips out.

The next morning we learn that Peggy is actually Varuna, and that Varuna has no knowledge of her nighttime escapades. "*Tajub hai*," says Dillip. "It's puzzling." She is admitted into "Dr. Dey's Psycho Ward," where she is interviewed by the elderly Dr. Dey and the more youthful Dr. Alvarez. Varuna responds to all questions with an insistent "I don't remember anything." In an interview with Pratap and Dillip (who are now friends), Pratap recalls all that he knows about Varuna:

On his way to Simla to meet his future wife, Sheila, Pratap's car breaks down. Pratap hears a song rising out of the fog; he cannot find the singer. He is forced to seek shelter in the only house in the area. He learns that Varuna, along with her father, lives in this house. Almost immediately, they fall in love.

Pratap's mother is against their marrying—"We don't know anything about her birth and astrology!"—and does not attend the wedding. On their wedding night, Varuna complains of a headache. Her headaches persist: At a picnic, Pratap and Varuna, after a stunning song sequence, find themselves on a precipice; she takes a false step and almost falls to her death. Pratap grabs her, but some rocks fall over. Seeing them roll down, Varuna screams. Her headaches grow worse; a doctor is consulted, drugs are prescribed.

In the middle of the night, Pratap is woken by "Western" music blaring from a radio; Varuna is not in bed. Pratap's mother also wakes (the newlyweds live with his parents, and his sister). Staring through the keyhole of a locked door, they glimpse Varuna gyrating wildly to the music. Pratap's mother is convinced she is possessed by a demon. The next day, she invites a Hindu Ojah, or Charmer, to dispel the evil spirit [*bhut-pret*] from Varuna's body.

The Ojah manages to draw out Varuna's other, Peggy, through an exhortative incantation, but she proves more than he can handle. She strikes the Charmer to the ground and begins to laugh and yell, speaking, significantly, in English. He calls for the assistance of all the women and together they forcibly hold Peggy down. "*Nayee jao gayee?*" he asks her. You won't go? He applies a burning hot rod to her hand. She screams in agony. Just then Pratap walks in, and, aghast at the scene he witnesses, thrashes the Ojah. When his mother explains that it was she who invited him, Pratap quarrels with her. The newlyweds move to another house.

During their housewarming party, Varuna is tricked into having a drink (she guzzles her first drink as the Everly Brothers' "Bye, Bye Love" lilts in the background). This first drink proves fatal: Varuna is suddenly transformed into a dance-crazed, singing alcoholic. Pratap returns from a work-related trip to find all the liquor bottles empty. On his first night back, he catches Varuna (as Peggy) with Dillip at the Cirpo.

The narrative returns to the present. Dr. Dey explains that Varuna is suffering from "split personality"; or, as Dr. Alvarez puts it, "As old people used to say, two in one body. Think of it that way." Varuna is admitted into the "psycho ward" for observation. At night Peggy returns, demanding cigarettes, alcohol, music, dancing, "freedom" to do what she likes. Peggy begins to dominate more and more of the personality; Varuna is completely submerged. Denied freedom, Peggy turns violent. Dey and Alvarez decide that electroconvulsive therapy is the only option. Huge and prolonged applications have no effect on her. Pratap's mother is determined to get her son a divorce and to get him married to Sheila.

Peggy escapes from the clinic. After a series of adventures in hotels and a song-dance sequence in the Christian district, she collapses on an elderly couple's doorstep. They take her in; she is very ill, and, as they also learn, pregnant. When Peggy learns that she is pregnant, she screams "Kill this child! Kill this child or else it will kill me!" She collapses in agony into the arms of her perplexed benefactor. Suddenly, from outside the scene's frame, we hear a Hindu bhajan. Hearing it also, Varuna miraculously returns.

Trying to return to her house, Varuna encounters her mother-in-law at the gates, who casts her out, accusing her of bringing the sin of the world into her son's house (the implication, of course, is that the child is not Pratap's). Forlorn, she wanders the streets. Not paying attention to where she is walking, she is struck by a truck (a common Hindi film device). Back in the hospital, Dr. Alvarez resumes treatment, but Varuna is now amnesic, though not completely: In the hospital, as she is being observed, she is watching a nurse carry some dishes down the stairs; he slips, and the dishes clatter to the ground. Varuna screams, as if partly remembering the falling rocks at the picnic.

Alvarez (Dr. Dey has simply disappeared by this point) asks Varuna's father for any biographical help he may be able to give them. He confesses that Varuna and her mother did not live with him for most of Varuna's life. He recounts his estrangement from his wife over his desire to educate Varuna. His wife felt that it would ruin her. Frustrated, he began to drink and gamble; heavily in debt, he demanded that she give him her wedding necklace to pawn. She refused; he assaulted her. Varuna came to her rescue. Mother and child left the father, and settled in Simla.

For this reason, Alvarez decides that Varuna's only hope is to return to Simla. Once there, she does slip back easily into her childhood. After some initial prodding from Alvarez, she spontaneously begins narrating life with her mother: Her mother locked her up in her room and didn't allow her to leave. She was never allowed to play with other girls lest they contaminate her. Her mother wouldn't allow her even to open the window. One night, however, with her mother gone, Varuna opened the window. A girl named Peggy lived next door; through the window, Varuna saw Peggy dancing at her own party. Varuna and Peggy developed a close friendship through their windows. Varuna's mother caught her imitating Peggy's dancing. "This is not what good girls do," she said. "I don't want to be a good girl," Varuna replied.

When they were teenagers, Peggy invited Varuna to her Christmas party, and made her promise she would come. Varuna sneaked out (through much of this scene, the camera adopts Varuna's perspective). Dillip was there at the party; a friend of his grabbed Varuna's hand, pulling her to the dance floor. She admitted wanting to dance, but was too frightened, always remembering her mother's warning. Varuna fled. Her mother caught her as she was leaving the party. Horrified, the mother suffered a heart attack and fell to her death.

Now let us pose the problem of Varuna's "illness." Mikkel Borch-Jacobsen has argued that

> psychotherapists generally agree that MPD is caused by traumatism combined with dissociation. By "traumatism" they mean an event that provokes a paralysing pain or emotion which prevents the subject from reacting adequately, generally suffered during infancy and inflicted by the parents. "Dissociation" is the defence mechanism mobilized by the subject who has been disarmed by such a traumatism . . . , in order to survive this invasion of pain or emotion: the subject "dissociates" as if nothing had happened; or, more exactly, as if the traumatic event had not happened to him [*sic*], but to *another*, with whom he does not have, nor want to have, any contact, of whom he wants to know nothing, who simply does not exist. (49)

Switching, amnesia, timeloss, dissociation, trauma: all of these terms "apply" to Varuna's condition. Yet I hope the previous discussion has also clarified a new analytic path that mimics the subject's oblique itinerary (Spivak, *Post-colonial* 101–2). In what follows, I argue that *Raat aur Din* dramatizes subjectivity and gender by locating the spatial violence of religious/national pedagogies "in" the female body. The film displaces this violence by psychologizing Varuna's/Peggy's subjectivity, which reframes this spatial violence as the simple retrieval of a memory. I end by considering how we might translate this memory.

After an ineffectual course of psychotropic drugs, Varuna-as-Peggy receives a course of ECT (Electro-Convulsive Therapy). This process marks woman's desire in the film's political imaginary (and so asks us to specify the local significance of Lacan's psychic registers): It is not coincidence that the initial strategies used to manage Peggy's "eruption" aim to slit her "real" self from her personality: I would link this process to what Spivak calls "symbolic clitoridectomies" (*Post-colonial* 10). Further, the polysemous narrative in which this scene recurs repeats the alleged development of psychiatry: from madness-as-illness to madness-as-relational effect (Pilgrim and Treacher 4–5; see also Foucault, *History* 111–14).

ECT has played a notorious role in this history. Breggin reminds us, in the very first English translation of a 1938 article by Bini, a proponent of ECT, that after even a limited application of ECT, the dogs on which Bini and others experimented suffered so much brain damage that none of their studies was satisfactory. Even after changing their methods to produce less severe damage, the scientists' results still included "irreversible" changes in the brain and "chronic cell disease" (41). This evidence did not seem to trouble the psychiatric establishment at all:

"Following its introduction in the late 1930s by Cerletti and Bini, ECT soon became a standard somatic therapy for severe psychiatric illnesses" (Frankel 13). Clearly, this "standardization" of ECT was the result of a massive repression, the full history of which has yet to be told. However, it is clear that the introduction of electroshock therapy into Indian psychiatric practice paralleled this treatment's rise in the West, though with crucial differences: Unlike the fairly narrow application of ECT in the United States and Britain (today it is mostly used for cases of severe depression), according to one Indian-trained psychiatrist with whom I talked (Roy), in India ECT was and still is considered a plausible therapy in almost all cases of mental illness.

With this in mind, let us pose some tentative questions that might relaunch this disturbing aspect of *Raat aur Din*.[3] What is the specific relationship between the history of Indian psychiatry and the postcolonial project of nation building? How do national pedagogies collude with and interrupt the technologies of normalization that they borrowed from Western modernity? Also, in what ways do these technologies produce their own resistance, psychic or otherwise? These are crucial questions, especially when we consider that ECT is completely ineffectual in "curing" Varuna of her "monstrous" desire.

Considering this situation, such psychiatric power "can scarcely be exercised except on what resists it." Indeed, films such as *Raat aur Din* do not seem to fear Varuna's desire; they actually solicit it in the form of Peggy (Miller 27). This solicitation implies a useful postcolonial "slashing" of Foucault and Lacan. For instance, as Lacan points out, we do not enjoy in spite of the law, but because of it (see Shepherdson note 40). This conception of jouissance allows us to see how, in this postcolonial context, Varuna's desire (represented by the modern, Western Peggy) to kill the maternal (traditional Hindu) superego is itself a violent dimension of gendered subjectivity. The film reappropriates this violence as a discrete moment that its psychonational narrative tries to resolve. By splitting and then "uniting" Varuna's subjectivity, the film compels a range of postcolonial anxieties to recur from within her palimpsestic body. To quote Foucault, this body becomes the "inscribed surface of events (traced by language and dissolved by ideas), the locus of a dissociated self (adopting the illusion of a substantial unity), and a volume in perpetual disintegration" ("Nietzsche" 83).

The second scene I will interpret also engages the issue of violence, but it has a different genealogy. First, keep in mind that in 1960s India, a ready morphology seemed able to explain Varuna's split personality. This morphology drew on the *Bhagavad-Gita*'s national significance in late nineteenth-century Hindu populism. Building on his categorical advice to Arjuna—"kill the enemy menacing you in the form of desire!" (*Bhagavad-Gita* III.43)—Krishna links desire to an insatiable fire:

It is desire and anger, arising/ from nature's quality of passion;/ know it here as the enemy/ voracious and very evil!/ As fire is obscured by smoke/ and a mirror by dirt,/ as an embryo is veiled by its caul,/ so is knowledge obscured by this./ Knowledge is obscured/ by the wise man's eternal enemy,/ which takes form as desire,/ an insatiable fire, Arjuna. (III.37–39)

Considering this representation of desire-as-fire, it is crucial to recall that knowledge in the *Bhagavad-Gita* is the precise vehicle for self-liberation. The suppression of knowledge is also both the cause and effect of a lower order of *guna* dominating the mind. Finally, this desire-as-fire recurs as Varuna's father's desire to *educate* his daughter. Not surprisingly, the *Gita* represents desire and knowledge as sharing a common root in fire: "Just as a flaming fire reduces/ wood to ashes, Arjuna,/ so the fire of knowledge/ reduces all actions to ashes" (IV.37). It seems that Varuna's subjectivity marks an impossible place where knowledge's chastening fire merges with desire's perverse fire.

In nationalist Hinduism, however, knowledge corresponds to desire in a purely instrumental way. Rationalistic Hindus such as the philosopher Swami Vivekananda represent the mind—in its *natural, worldly* state, the state of *chitta*—as a "maddened monkey." Vivekananda comments on this figure in this way: "The human mind is like that monkey, incessantly active by its own nature; then it becomes drunk with the wine of desire, thus increasing its turbulence. After desire takes possession comes the sting of the scorpion of jealousy of the success of others, and last of all the demon of pride enters the mind, making it think itself of all importance. How hard to control such a mind!" (qtd. in Budhananda 35–36).[4]

Needless to say, the ethical project of national Hinduism has aspired since Vivekananda to regulate the mind and eradicate desire. That *Raat aur Din* articulates this desire by a cluster of signs signifying the gendered West mirrors in Hindu nationalist ideology the precise ambiguity of Varuna's name: In Hindi, the masculine noun "varuna" refers to both the sun and the deity of Water; the feminine noun "vaaruni" can also mean "west," "a spirituous liquor," or "Varuna's wife."

In this second scene from *Raat aur Din*, Varuna's mother-in-law, herself deemed a maternal guardian of Hindu patriarchal tradition, invites an Ojah to dispel the evil spirit, or mental disorder, from Varuna's body. Crucial to this scene is a correspondence among the home, folk Hinduism, and collective womanspace. In this scene, a "madwoman's" body again endures extreme violence: The Ojah burns Varuna with a stick (alluding strongly to the *Gita*). She screams in agony. But *who* screams? Is it Varuna or Peggy? If, as Lacan points out, "it is in the very movement of speaking that the hysteric constitutes her desire" (*Four* 12), in what space does this scream find representation?

Further, how does *Raat aur Din* displace the warzone of desire that recurs in nationalist Hindu thought (a warzone usually gendered male)? Is this displacement another example of the nationalist resolution to the Woman's Question, or is another form of gendered subjectivity articulated here? Can postcolonial temporality account for the eruption of a trauma that is neither the archaic double nor, as Freud put it in "The 'Uncanny,' " "a harking-back to particular phases in the evolution of the self-regarding feeling" (238), but the sign of a contaminating Western modernity *within* the postcolonial *Heim*? These questions perhaps enable a reconsideration of the window scenes in Varuna's final flashback (where she peeps through a closed window to glimpse Peggy's whirling, twisting body): In a peculiarly postcolonial sense, the window scenes refigure Lacan's mirror phase, for they signify not the misrecognition of a complete and unified whole but a dangerous negotiation among (nonheterosexual) desire, law, and knowledge. Put differently, if, as in Bhabha's colonial mirror, "to exist is to be called into being in relation to an otherness, its look or locus" (*Location* 44), and if the "exchange of looks between native and settler" constitutes their psychic relation of paranoid possession and horrified reversal, the "space of splitting" (45) that Varuna occupies, as the gendered palimpsest of postcolonial national violence, must be unthought as the impossible thing that was never supposed to cast a look.

Only in the film's penultimate scene do we see how perceptions of space and time make intelligible Varuna's illness. In this scene we also see Varuna's analyst, Dr. Alvarez, the man of science and modernity, as sovereign, apodictic subject, outlining the etiology of Varuna's MPD as a simple split caused by her mother's domination and by the allure of a wayward neighbor called Peggy. The doctor can only comfort Varuna with platitudes: "In this you have no responsibility . . . As much as your mother tried to keep your wish-desires [*bhavna*] down, to crush your craving-desires [*arman*], this wish [*icha*] of yours to live like Peggy kept growing. The result of this was that in your mind there was born an uncertainty of separation between you and Peggy. The body is the servant of the mind. . . . Now you understand? Well then, now there is no reason to worry. Varuna, get up. Meet your father."

When the "cured" Varuna speaks her father's name, the film seems strangely to meld secular nationalism with strands of Hinduism (Regnault 68). Drawing on this legacy of Hindu nationalism, the film basically enlists Dr. Alvarez in a spiritual war against desire, but with this difference: The violence that portrays Varuna's scission as its "ethical substance" clarifies an ambivalence that the film's emphasis on individual development struggles to overcome. Alvarez's therapeutic strategy might resemble what Schneiderman calls "psychosynthesis" (138), since this alleged synthesis redefines violence as traumatic memory. Apparently, all

Alvarez has to do to heal Varuna is help her remember the point when her subjectivity was undivided (a psychoanalytic contradiction in terms). Effective translation of this scene would, however, disrupt this narrative elision between nineteenth-century nationalist Hindu ideology and postcolonial psychiatry's mimicked Cartesianism; such translation would clarify the relationship between the shuttled, anxiety-written figure of Varuna/Peggy and the secular and normalizing regime that tried to reduce all psychosocial tensions in postcolonial India's imaginary to a single historical moment.

Our strategic recontextualizing cannot end here, however. We must also ask what exactly is the remembered trauma? It is very difficult to answer this question in Varuna's case. Is it really her mother's death? No doubt Varuna comes to realize that one cannot easily live with the dead. Yet however difficult the first mother was, once dead she becomes impossible: unremitting and inexorable (Schneiderman 63). This is also a valuable lesson for postcolonial criticism, which is both hysterical and neurotic in its relation to the subaltern's "undead."

> Freud said that hysterics suffer from reminiscences, from a past that has not been dealt with, from a mourning process that has not reached its term, from the unburied dead. The hysteric may try to forget the dead but the dead do not forget her. . . . Not that the obsessional neurotic does not have some sort of relationship with the dead. . . . Faithful servant of death, the obsessional buries the dead and reburies them, and does the same thing again and again and again. Not only does the obsessional not forget the dead, not repress them, but he is too solicitous of them, anxious about the satisfaction of death's desire. (Schneiderman 146)

I am well aware that this claim inhabits a very dangerous space, but these are familiar symptoms for postcolonials. Am I therefore arguing for a politicotheoretical genocide, a type of postcolonial ethnic cleansing, which legitimates "actual" genocide? Isn't this the final gesture of depoliticization: the increasing conservatism of postcolonial criticism? Not at all. Instead, I argue that to entertain those who "live and struggle in subalternity" within neocolonial social relations compels us to think at the limits of representation, and thus to interpret the terms of its many violences. This counters those who argue against Spivak's position in "Can the Subaltern Speak?" by naively declaring the oppositionality of neocolonial subjectivity; those melancholic assurances of the fullness of subaltern self-presence always seem to take recourse to a familiar formula: "Thus spake the Subaltern . . ." (see Shohat, Dirlik, Parry).

My argument also transforms the relationship between critics and their ghostly subject, for the postcolonial critic partly occupies this ghostly place but does not know that s/he is dead—for the other (Schneiderman 79). Reiterating my earlier account of Bhabha, Spivak, Lévi-Strauss, and Lacan, I suggest that the lost objects of our desire, once shaken free of the Law, occupy the singular space of the murdered m/other, whom we cannot dissociate from the criticizing self. This is the condition of critique; conceptually, it is also Spivak's enabling violence. That is why postcolonial criticism must interpret the world and change it; it must occupy the breach running through Marx's Eleventh Thesis on Feuerbach. That is also why postcolonial criticism, as a discourse of that desired ghost, must contextualize each act of repetition. As Varuna learns, what is dead wields a specific force. To paraphrase Derrida, the subaltern always carries its death internally. This death is surely the death of postcolonial criticism. But the genitive is double. Sometimes it is the death of a genre belonging to postcolonial criticism, which is thought within and supposedly summarized by it; and sometimes it is the death of a postcolonial criticism that does not see itself die and which is no longer to be discovered within that criticism ("White" 271).

This loss manifests itself in the insistence of a supplementary question: Did the death of Varuna's mother cause her MPD? Or was the trauma of her mother's cloistering her body responsible; or the separation of her parents; or earlier yet, with her father's assault on her mother? I could go on but one begins to see that the problem of memory persists in every question. As Shepherdson has asked, "what does it mean to say that in dredging up the past, repeating it, *going back across the river to where the ancestors lie buried*, one is concerned, not so much with what really happened . . . but rather with intervening, rewriting the past, producing a shift in the symbolic structure of the narrative that has brought us to the point where we are now?" (Shepherdson 10; my emphasis).

Fittingly, these words return us to Spivak's river. I have argued that the slitting violence of memory, which is itself the violence of writing desire, is also a condition of possibility for postcolonial knowledge. This violence releases the power of ghosts, whose haunting informs our knowledge. I have also argued for rigorous attention to this violence, desire, and writing, since these elements can sometimes blind any totalizing gaze. And if I may have failed or given in to my own hauntings in this compromised adventure, this does not trouble or sadden me—rather, it only signals the need for a persistent critique. Failure should not bother us, but it might cause us to wonder at those who imagine they have succeeded.

ENDNOTES

I thank Chris Lane for his meticulous editing of previous drafts. I have also greatly benefited from the careful comments of Dan Moshenberg, Rajeshwari Sunder Rajan, Richard Juang, and Steve Caton, as well as the participants in my "Gender and the Culture of

Imperialism" Seminar: Jenny Golden, Venessa Mazal, Brooke Willmes, Caroline Falby, and Ursula Wolfe-Rocca. Any mistakes that remain are of course fully mine. I dedicate this essay to the memory of "Babuji," Shiva Charan Rai (1909–1995): Brother, Scholar, Revolutionary, Husband, Father, Railroad Worker, Lawyer, Indian, Hindu.

1. After the first two decades of the twentieth century, as Heald et al. point out, a sharp split developed between anthropology and psychoanalysis: "Anthropologists have seen themselves as dealing with cultural phenomena and analysts with the individual psyche, the one to be explored in collective settings, the other in the privacy of the clinical session. The relationship came to be seen in terms of a series of binary contrasts: collective/individual, public/private, normal/abnormal" (3). And this within a cultural frame that, as Gellner writes, within a span of less than half a century, has been *conquered* by psychoanalysis, such that psychoanalysis has become "the dominant idiom for the discussion of the human personality and of human relations" (qtd. in Heald 3). In their own profoundly naturalized, ethnocentric way, Heald and her coeditors argue, "Whether explicitly cited or not, [psychoanalysis] provides a perspective on the nature of the human condition which furnishes a set of background assumptions for all who have worked on the interpretation of culture" (3).

2. It is important to mark the many transitions taking place during the long making of *Raat aur Din*. At this time, Indira Gandhi, soon-to-be "Mother of India," was the Minister for Information and Broadcasting in Lal Bahadur Shastri's Congress government (Nehru died on May 27, 1964). Representative of the "Congress Left," Gandhi was instrumental in rearticulating an ideology that may have precipitated the radical split between commercial and art films. This was also Nargis's last film—the only film she made after her marriage to actor Sunil Dutt. As her brother remarks: "Once she married, she settled down with great dignity. Shall we say, she married and lived happily ever after?" (qtd. in George 151). *Raat aur Din* costar K. N. Singh also commented: "With marriage it was like she had reached home. She thought God had come to earth in the form of Sunil Dutt. So much did she worship him" (qtd. in George 151).

3. I must bracket the nagging fact that, at least in America, ECT was rarely deemed the right course of therapy for patients with personality disorders. I must also bracket the problematic cultural and ethical aspects of informed consent and advanced directives, considering the forms of subjectivities they presuppose. The American Psychiatric Association remarks on varied ECT use; it has also considered ECT capable of treating three major disorders: "major depression," "mania" (including bipolar), and "schizophrenia" (see Weiner 6–9). Nonetheless, when asked if ECT was an appropriate form of therapy for patients with personality disorders, 93 percent of psychiatrists polled by the APA Task Force in 1978 responded negatively (see Frankel et al. 4). On the centrality of informed consent to the practice of ECT, see Weiner (11–14).

4. In a somewhat reductive way, Kakar argues that "*Chitta* is very similar to the id of the psycho-analytic model, the part of the psychic organization which represents the elemental, instinctual drives of the organism. Hindu texts sometimes also use *chitta* in a dynamic sense to characterize *all* unconscious mental processes. . . . Some Hindu texts draw the

metaphor of a monkey, restless by nature, who drinks wine and becomes even more restless." (22). What complicates this simple "translation" is attention to the particular ways in which *chitta* is already seen as part of the circuit of knowledge/desire, and thus an effect of certain representational strategies.

WORKS CITED

Barrett, Michèle. "Althusser's Marx, Althusser's Lacan." *The Althusserian Legacy*. Ed. E. Ann Kaplan and Michael Sprinkler. New York: Verso, 1993. 169–82.

Bhabha, Homi K. "Anxious Nations, Nervous States." In Copjec. 201–17.

——. *The Location of Culture*. New York: Routledge, 1994.

The Bhagavad-Gita. Trans. Barbara Stoler Miller. New York: Bantam, 1986.

Borch-Jacobsen, Mikkel. "Who's Who? Introducing Multiple Personality." In Copjec. 45–63.

Bourdieu, Pierre. *Outline of a Theory of Practice*. Trans. Richard Nice. New York: Cambridge UP, 1992.

Breggin, Peter Roger. *Electroshock: Its Brain-Disabling Effects*. New York: Springer, 1979.

Budhananda, Swami. *The Mind and Its Control*. Calcutta: Advaita Ashrama, 1993.

Butler, Judith. "The Body Politics of Julia Kristeva." In Oliver. 164–78.

Colás, Santiago. "Of Creole Symptoms, Cuban Fantasies, and Other Latin American Postcolonial Ideologies." *PMLA* 110 (1995): 382–96.

Copjec, Joan, ed. *Supposing the Subject*. New York: Verso, 1994.

Cornell, Drucilla. "What Is Ethical Feminism?" *Feminist Contentions: A Philosophical Exchange*. New York: Routledge, 1995. 75–106.

Derrida, Jacques. *Of Grammatology*. Trans. Gayatri Chakravorty Spivak. Baltimore: Johns Hopkins UP, 1976.

——. "Structure, Sign, and Play in the Discourse of the Social Sciences." *Writing and Difference*. Trans. Alan Bass. Chicago: U of Chicago P, 1978. 278–93.

——. *Positions*. Trans. Alan Bass. Chicago: U of Chicago P, 1981.

——. "Tympan." *Margins of Philosophy*. Trans. Alan Bass. Chicago: U of Chicago P, 1982. ix-xxix.

——. "*Différance*." *Margins of Philosophy*. 1–27.

——. "The Supplement of Copula: Philosophy before Linguistics." *Margins of Philosophy*. 175–205.

——. "White Mythology." *Margins of Philosophy*. 209–71.

——. *Specters of Marx: The State of the Debt, the Work of Mourning, and the New International*. Trans. Peggy Kamuf. New York: Routledge, 1994.

Dirlik, Arif. "The Postcolonial Aura: Third World Criticism in the Age of Global Capitalism." *Critical Inquiry* 20 (1994): 328–56.

Fabian, Johannes. *Time and the Other: How Anthropology Makes Its Object*. New York: Columbia UP, 1983.

Feldstein, Richard, Bruce Fink, and Maire Jaanus, ed. *Reading Seminar XI: Lacan's Four Fundamental Concepts of Psychoanalysis*. Albany: SUNY P, 1995.

Felman, Shoshana. *Jacques Lacan and the Adventure of Insight: Psychoanalysis in Contemporary Culture*. Cambridge: Harvard UP, 1987.

Foucault, Michel. "Power and Strategies." *Power/Knowledge: Selected Interviews and Other Writings, 1972–1977*. Ed. and trans. Colin Gordon. New York: Pantheon, 1980. 134–45.

———. "Nietzsche, Genealogy, History." *The Foucault Reader*. Ed. Paul Rabinow. New York: Pantheon, 1984. 76–100.

———. *The History of Sexuality, Vol. 1: An Introduction*. Trans. Robert Hurley. New York: Vintage, 1990.

Frankel, Fred H. et al. *Report of the Task Force on Electroconvulsive Therapy of the American Psychiatric Association*. Washington, D.C.: American Psychiatric Association, 1978.

Freud, Sigmund. "The 'Uncanny.' " 1919. Vol. 17 of *The Standard Edition of the Complete Psychological Works of Sigmund Freud*. Ed. and trans. James Strachey. 24 vols. London: Hogarth, 1953–74. 217–56.

George, T. J. S. *The Life and Times of Nargis*. New Delhi: HarperCollins, 1994.

Guillory, John. *Cultural Capital: The Problem of Literary Canon Formation*. Chicago: U of Chicago P, 1993.

Hall, Stuart. "When Was 'The Post-Colonial'? Thinking at the Limit." *The Post-Colonial Question: Common Skies, Divided Horizons*. Ed. Iain Chambers and Lidia Curti. New York: Routledge, 1996. 242–60.

Harvey, Irene. "Structures of Exemplarity in Poe, Freud, Lacan, and Derrida." *The Purloined Poe: Lacan, Derrida, and Psychoanalytic Reading*. Ed. John P. Muller and William J. Richardson. Baltimore: Johns Hopkins UP, 1988. 252–67.

Heald, Suzette, Ariane Deluz, and Pierre-Yves Jacopin. "Introduction." *Anthropology and Psychoanalysis: An Encounter through Culture*. Ed. Heald and Deluz. New York: Routledge, 1994. 1–26.

Kakar, Sudhir. *The Inner World: A Psycho-Analytic Study of Childhood and Society in India*. 2d ed. New York: Oxford UP, 1981.

Kristeva, Julia. *Black Sun: Depression and Melancholia*. Trans. Leon S. Roudiez. New York: Columbia UP, 1989.

Kuper, Adam. *Anthropology and Anthropologists: The Modern British School*. 3d ed. New York: Routledge, 1991.

Lacan, Jacques. *The Four Fundamental Concepts of Psycho-Analysis*. 1973. Ed. Jacques-Alain Miller. Trans. Alan Sheridan. New York: Norton, 1978.

———. "The Mirror Phase as Formative of the Function of the I as Revealed in Psychoanalytic Experience." 1949. *Écrits: A Selection*. Ed. Jacques-Alain Miller. Trans. Alan Sheridan. New York: Norton, 1977. 1–7.

———. *The Seminar of Jacques Lacan, Book VII: The Ethics of Psychoanalysis*. Ed. Jacques-Alain Miller. Trans. Dennis Porter. New York: Norton, 1992.

Lévi-Strauss, Claude. *Structural Anthropology*. Trans. Claire Jacobson and Brooke

Grundfest Schoepf. New York: Basic, 1963.

——. *Tristes tropiques*. Trans. John and Doreen Weightman. New York: Atheneum, 1974.

Lowe, Lisa. *Critical Terrains: French and British Orientalisms*. Ithaca: Cornell UP, 1991.

——. "*Des chinoises*: Orientalism, Psychoanalysis, and Feminine Writing." In Oliver. 150–63.

Miller, D. A. *The Novel and the Police*. Berkeley: U of California P, 1988.

Moore, Henrietta. "Gendered Persons: Dialogues between Anthropology and Psycho-analysis." In Heald and Deluz. 131–52.

Oliver, Kelly, ed. *Ethics, Politics, and Difference in Julia Kristeva's Writing*. New York: Routledge, 1993.

Ortner, Sherry B. "Theory in Anthropology since the Sixties." *Culture/Power/History: A Reader in Contemporary Social Theory*. Ed. Nicholas B. Dirks, Geoff Eley, and Sherry B. Ortner. Princeton: Princeton UP, 1994. 372–411.

Parry, Benita. "Problems in Current Theories of Colonial Discourse." *Oxford Literary Review* 9.1–2 (1987): 27–58.

Pilgrim, David and Andy Treacher. *Clinical Psychology Observed*. New York: Routledge, 1992.

Pradelles de Latour, Charles-Henry. "Lacanian Ethnopsychoanalysis." In Heald and Deluz. 153–62.

Raat aur Din [Day and Night]. Dir. Satyen Bose. A. A. N. Productions, 1967.

Regnault, François. "The Name-of-the-Father." In Feldstein, Fink, and Jaanus. 65–74.

Roy, Pradeep Kumar, M.D. Personal interview. October 1, 1995.

Schneiderman, Stuart. *Jacques Lacan: The Death of an Intellectual Hero*. Cambridge: Harvard UP, 1983.

Shepherdson, Charles. "History and the Real: Foucault with Lacan." *Postmodern Culture* (Electronic Version) 5.2 (1995).

Shohat, Ella. "Notes on the Postcolonial." *Social Text* 31–32 (1992): 99–112.

Spivak, Gayatri Chakravorty. "Three Women's Texts and a Critique of Imperialism." *"Race," Writing, and Difference*. Ed. Henry Louis Gates, Jr. Chicago: U of Chicago P, 1986. 262–80.

——. "French Feminism in an International Frame." *In Other Worlds: Essays in Cultural Politics*. New York: Routledge, 1987. 134–53.

——. "Can the Subaltern Speak?" *Marxism and the Interpretation of Culture*. Ed. Cary Nelson and Lawrence Grossberg. Urbana: U of Illinois P, 1988. 271–313.

——. *The Post-Colonial Critic*. Ed. Sarah Harasym. New York: Routledge, 1990.

——. "The Burden of English." *Orientalism and the Postcolonial Predicament: Perspectives on South Asia*. Ed. Carol A. Breckenridge and Peter van der Veer. Philadelphia: U of Pennsylvania P, 1993. 134–57.

——. "Feminism and Deconstruction." *Outside in the Teaching Machine*. New York: Routledge, 1993. 121–40.

——. "French Feminism Revisited." *Outside in the Teaching Machine*. 141–71.

Thomas, Nicholas. *Colonialism's Culture: Anthropology, Travel, and Government*. Princeton: Princeton UP, 1994.

Weiner, Richard D. et al. *The Practice of Electroconvulsive Therapy: Recommendations for Treatment, Training, and Privileging*. Washington, D.C.: American Psychiatric Association, 1990.

Žižek, Slavoj. "The Lamella of David Lynch." In Feldstein, Fink, and Jaanus. 205–20.

4

Uncanny Foreigners: Does the Subaltern Speak Through Julia Kristeva?

James Penney

Delicately, analytically, Freud does not speak of foreigners: he teaches us how to detect foreignness in ourselves.
—Kristeva, *Strangers* 191; 283

. . . the highest purpose of nature, a universal *cosmopolitan existence*
—Kant 51

Contexts: Multiculturalism and the Postcolonial

If one heeded the recent thoughts of a prominent U.S.-based postcolonial theorist, the answer to my title's question would be unambiguously no. In a 1988 interview with Ellen Rooney reprinted in *Outside in the Teaching Machine* (by this time *Strangers to Ourselves* had recently appeared in France), Gayatri Chakravorty Spivak strongly dismisses the relevance of Julia Kristeva's work for postcolonial theory. Stating that she is "not generous and catholic enough to learn from her anymore," Spivak characterizes Kristeva as a "ferociously" Eurocentric, latently positivist, imperialistically Christian, and increasingly right-leaning intellectual out of touch with the postcolonial condition, presumably in both the "Third World" and Western Europe ("Word" 17).

Now it would be difficult to argue that Kristeva's oeuvre is *not* Eurocentric, in the precise sense that her inter-texts generally have not yet extended far beyond the literary and philosophical traditions of France, Germany, Anglo-America, and Slavic Eastern Europe.[1] Nevertheless, I contend that it is irresponsible not to investigate the manner in which Kristeva's recent, socially inflected thought, *when considered in its proper context and limitations*, informs a cultural project explicitly questioning the psychodynamics of imperialism and racism. My account of recent receptions of Kristeva will contrast different notions of politics informing her work with materialist aspects of postcolonial theory. Regarding the latter, I refer to a dogmatic tradition of criticism that valorizes the political and social contexts of postcolonial narratives at the expense of ethical and subjective concerns. My fundamental premise will be that the recent Kristeva deserves sustained, nuanced, *and* critical attention by cultural analysts engaging issues of cultural and racial differences. By evoking the role played by internal otherness in the subject's relation to the stranger, Kristeva outlines one of the fundamental contributions psychoanalysis can make to the study of "race." She urges us to consider the dynamic precariousness of subjectivity—our uncanny strangeness to ourselves—alongside the unquestionable effects of social and historical contexts.

Kristeva's recent books *Strangers to Ourselves* (1988) and *Nations Without Nationalism* (1990) signal a subtle yet consequential shift in style and content from her previous work. Undoubtedly marked by a huge debt to the Freudian tradition, with its characteristic emphasis on the dialectic of symbol and drive, these two texts present us with a new Kristeva who addresses issues of social concern more directly than before. While her early books interpreted avant-garde poetic form and psychoideological contention, Kristeva's new work interrogates from within the tradition of Western political philosophy the cultural conflicts arising from French decolonization. Bracketing—but never abandoning—the themes of language, subjectivity, and desire for which she has become famous, Kristeva now clarifies the relationship in her thought between concrete political problems and the ethics of psychoanalysis.

Kristeva has struck a new balance between her concern with subjective processes in literary creativity and her recognition of the importance of legal and political discourses. *Time and Sense*, Kristeva's recent book on Proust, forcefully reminds us that the hallmark of her approach to culture remains the supreme value she places on psychological transformation through creation in language. Beyond the changing and often ambiguous political sympathies of its major figures, the *Tel Quel-L'Infini* movement with which Kristeva is identified has consistently idealized a literary imagination that translates antisocial drives into poetic language as a means not only of coping with the demands of the outside world, but of *transcending* social normativity through the experience of perverse, though sublimated, pleasure. Yet Kristeva's texts on cultural strangeness let us glimpse the way her individualist ethics translate into a more manifestly political vocabulary. Such an approach challenges the dominant materialist, collectivist, and historicist paradigms in contemporary Anglo-American postcolonial criticism by broadening our understanding of the political and strongly valorizing the category of the subject.

Since with few exceptions Kristeva's previous work did not explicitly address cultural difference, one can partly appreciate the suspicion with which postcolonial critics have received her latest texts. However, it is essential to place *Strangers* and *Nations* in the context of recent French debates on immigration, race, citizenship, and universalism—debates that now echo through the political discourses of a number of Western nations. Since the mid-1980s, Jean-Marie Le Pen and his extremist-right Natural Front Party have quite consistently won between 10 and 15 percent of the popular vote in presidential and legislative elections. As a result, Le Pen's party has entered the mainstream of French political life, becoming the most powerful extremist-right force in Western Europe. Le Pen's extremely xenophobic platform continues to call for a complete halt to immigration from developing nations and the radical limitation of the civil rights of foreign residents and non-residents. Echoing rightist leaders throughout the industrialized world, Le Pen recently rationalized his xenophobic policies by claiming that immigrants are "parasites" on government social programs; that they "steal" the jobs of citizens, "colonize" cities and towns, and "crowd" the prisons of the French nation (qtd. in de Brie 4).

The election increasing Le Pen's media cachet occurred just months before the publication of Kristeva's open letter to the French human rights group S.O.S. Racisme, reprinted in *Nations*. This intervention was but one part of a veritable explosion of public discourse on the rights of foreigners, immigrants, and racial and religious minorities still preoccupying French political commentators. Kristeva's polemic was partially directed at a disheartened and fragmented Left profoundly pessimistic about the West's (and specifically France's) political and cultural capacity to deal with unprecedented change. In *Strangers* and *Nations*, Kristeva aims to recuperate critically the universalist and cosmopolitan tenets of Enlightenment thought in order to achieve democratic renewal and present an alternative to the Left's despondency.

Given this political context, Kristeva specifically addresses the condition of postcolonial subjects in the former metropole. There may be some value in reproaching Kristeva for neglecting to examine the multiple problems of decolonization; nowhere does she consider the postcolonial traditions of the former colonies. But arguing that Kristeva is irrelevant to postcolonial theory is valid only if one believes that postcolonial theory and issues of cultural difference in the developed world are mutually exclusive. Kristeva speaks as a Western intellectual trained in the Western tradition who has made a point of refusing to subscribe to fashionable Left pronouncements about the death of Europe.

For Kristeva, Europe's pressing cultural issues recall Romanticist arguments about the nation-state. Against this tradition's many organicist and quasi-mystical premises (some of which troublingly entertain nationalist extremism), Kristeva wants to reclaim the idea of Enlightenment cosmopolitanism, with its stress on universal human dignity and the nation-as-contract. Kristeva's comparison of European nationalisms implies that we must examine these traditions precisely because they are still with us, permeating every aspect of Western legislative, executive, and juridical institutions. Familiar and actual, the discourse of Enlightenment may be recuperated if modified, Kristeva claims, as an alternative to the xenophobic nationalism against which it has historically competed.

In addition to these politico-philosophical questions, Kristeva underlines the crucial importance of the psychological context; she demonstrates that the crisis of decolonization relates inextricably to the crisis of subjectivity itself. In an era of unprecedented cultural upheaval and displacement, the psychic difficulty of living as and with cultural "strangers" is exacerbated, requiring that we rethink the political discourses inherited from historical epochs unfamiliar with the complexity of contemporary cultural hybridization. Kristeva wages that the political discourses framing negotiations of cultural alterity must be considered relative not only to the problem of the subject but, more specifically, to the subject's ambivalent and inherently vulnerable constitution relative to the other. Kristeva thereby supplements a properly *political* concern about juridical distinctions between citizens and noncitizens with an *ethical* focus on the subject's relation to psychic alterity, to the dark shadow of its unconscious. Before analyzing *Strangers*, however, we must consider this book in the context of Kristeva's recent thought and its role in French social and intellectual history.

The Politics of Subjectivity

Postcolonial criticism's general impatience with Kristeva's work may be traced to Spivak's salient and influential commentary on *About Chinese Women* (1974) ("Feminism" 136–41). I do not wish to argue with this generally fair and suggestive reading; Spivak in this case is entirely correct to criticize Kristeva for using her underresearched examination of Chinese culture to interrogate what were geopolitically specific problems associated with the French Left's postwar crisis.

Yet Spivak's claim that the ethical vanguardism Kristeva has endorsed belongs to the "general intellectual backlash" of Parisian neoliberals against Marxism, Maoism, and popular social movement presupposes that examining subjective process and the subject's relation to language is necessarily politically suspect (140). The broad strokes with which Spivak paints Kristeva's individualism as "a set of directives for class- and race-privileged literary women" exhibits the same condescension characterizing materialist criticisms of Kristeva's study of the foreigner. Accusing Kristeva of ignorance about "the micrology of political economy" (136), Spivak assumes that politics and economics alone determine symbolic production. In this perspective, the subaltern subject lies in a state of creative autism and helplessness when surrounded by dire material circumstances. Though Spivak justifiably intends to shed light on the material inequalities between Left Bank intellectuals and South Asian peasants, she erroneously projects a contextualist fatalism on the very subaltern subjects whose silences passionately concern her. By contending that the subaltern does *not* speak ("Subaltern" 308), Spivak discounts the importance of this subject's enunciation strictly on the basis of its political and historical marginality; according to this view of the subaltern, a subject's voice has no value beyond its power to mark literary and political traditions or to materialize an interested call. Since it renders absolute the political significance of language production, Spivak's model cannot register the subjective and therapeutic effects of speech that are not visibly inscribed in the texts of history.

Much like Kristeva's methodology in *Strangers*, Spivak's approach to subaltern subjectivity seeks to examine theories of representation and ideology while recognizing the preeminence of political and economic factors. In my view, Spivak's hostility to Kristeva's arguments clarifies how the former ultimately subsumes subjective processes under a totalizing economistic umbrella. Claiming that it is impossible for "contemporary French intellectuals" to theorize "the unnamed subject of the Other of Europe," Spivak globally assimilates Western intellectual production under the heading of the "dynamic economic situation" of colonialism ("Subaltern" 280). Although the general thrust of "Can the Subaltern Speak?" attempts polemically to advance a Derridean framework for postcolonial studies, Spivak ultimately asserts the same antirepresentationalist and historicist premises she aims to refute in work by Foucault and Deleuze. By tying Western theoretical representations absolutely to the historico-economic structure of the colonial era, Spivak demonstrates her view that politics supersedes subjectivity.

Spivak correctly stresses differences in access to cultural capital when discussing "marginal" cultural production (the weakest part of Kristeva's argument). Yet her desire to sociologize cultural production by emphasizing "system" and "collectivity" radically limits the subject's capacity to negotiate the cultural landscape. It is difficult to balance Spivak's criticism of Kristeva for downplaying the importance of collective politics with Spivak's valid contention that in *About Chinese Women* Kristeva "blunt[s] the fine edge of her approach to literature" ("Feminism" 138). Ultimately, Spivak's attempt to walk the precarious line between a focus on subjectivity and on materiality fails to convey the full complexity of postcolonial works. I note with concern that, in her analyses, subjective dynamics usually are crushed by ideological foregrounding, economic analyses, and material determinants.

Similar doubts about Kristeva's interest in subjectivity and poetics recur in Joan Brandt's dismissive account of Kristeva's investment in psychoanalytic practice. Brandt discusses Kristeva's disillusionment with the most conventionally political aspects of her initial project, which dates from her early research on linguistics and association with the journal *Tel Quel*.[2] Citing the French avant-garde's loss of faith in Maoist and Marxist revolutionary doctrines, Brandt argues that at the end of the 1970s Kristeva "turned away from the political as such and began to focus more directly on the subject itself, returning to an area of investigation that she claims she had 'never really left,' to that of psychoanalysis and its investigations of *'l'expérience intérieure,'* of the inner workings of the individual psyche" (90). At a time when the end of her training analysis with André Green, the dissolution of *Tel Quel*, and that journal's immediate reincarnation as *L'Infini* roughly coincided, Kristeva began to focus on the subject's psychic history as verbally represented to the analyst. Alongside a new skepticism born of an increased understanding of the horror of twentieth-century history, Kristeva's account of the semiotic's disruptiveness became tempered by the more conspicuous presence of the paternal function in her writing.

Jacqueline Rose correctly observes that Kristeva's criticism of symbolist poetic discourse was always that aesthetic experimentation cannot directly affect social institutions (146). For the Kristeva of *Revolution in Poetic Language* (1974), the symbolists' reluctance to transpose their linguistic experimentation onto the level of actual, sociohistorical contradictions constituted the "ideological limits of the avant-garde" (189; 169). Even in this landmark work, the relationship between the semiotic's subversion of established meanings and the symbolic's normalizing pressure on linguistic phenomena by no means suggested a straightforward chance of revolutionary social change.

Critics too often overemphasize the role of psychoanalytic practice in Kristeva's later work, thus ignoring that literary experience was foremost among the Telquelistes' concerns from the beginning of their project. Additionally, the assumption that social change depends on the subject's creative negotiation of the symbolic order underlies Kristeva's entire oeuvre. Nevertheless, by contrast to *Revolution in Poetic Language*, books such as *Powers of Horror* (1980), *Tales of Love* (1983), and *The New Maladies of the Soul* (1992) represent the subtle influence of analytic training on the increasingly intimate and personal character of Kristeva's research. In sum, there is no doubt that Kristeva's decision to undergo a training analysis corresponded to a desire not only to broaden definitions of the political, but to use the clinical situation to address subjective processes at a relative distance from the ravages of political conflict. Moving away from the ideological clarities of political movements and parties, and toward the ambiguous shadows of unconscious life, Kristeva recognized that the complexity of human subjectivity requires a mode of intervention that cannot be reduced without remainder to political significance.

Brandt's references to political history helpfully underline the influence of the French social landscape on the subtle shifts in direction of Kristeva's work. Indeed, the broad social optimism of the early 70s transforms in the clinical texts into a more modest and intimate concern with the subject's struggle with the competing demands of the drive and signifier. But Brandt oversimplifies the complex relationship between the intimate scene of psychoanalytic dialogue and the public sphere of political debate when characterizing Kristeva's clinical interests as a turning away from "the political as such." Brandt's argument elides a fundamental question about the relationship between psychoanalysis and politics; this issue has a long and complex history that I can only outline here.[3]

Generally, Left cultural discourse and French feminist theory have answered this complex question with variations on a similar theme: Although psychoanalysis can play an important role in the process of social change—for instance, by decreasing the effects of ideologies (political, familial, sexual) on the subject's behavior—it can only supplement existing political categories. In Left discourse these categories engage only class dynamics and hierarchies of privilege; in French feminist theory they interrogate either women's economic status (e.g., materialist feminism in the tradition of Simone de Beauvoir and Monique Plaza) or the feminine libidinal economy and sexual difference (post-Lacanian feminism including Luce Irigaray). In rarer cases, we witness a concern for both aspects. While each discourse considers psychoanalysis to be political, each also views it as *not political enough*.

In my view, the controversy surrounding Kristeva's conceptual shift provides an opportunity to rethink the conventional perspective on the relation between society and psychoanalytic theory. We can identify the repercussions of two polemical strands here. First, Brandt's criticism of Kristeva's alleged turning away from politics overhastily assumes that interest in subjective conflict and concern for political change are mutually exclusive. Though manifestly weak, this argument prevails among Kristeva's fiercest detractors, including dogmatic materialists. Second, Left or progressive criticism in the Anglo-American academy assumes that for psychoanalysis to have efficacy, it must intervene using explicitly political concepts imported from outside psychoanalysis. Here, the political character of psychoanalysis is not denied but instead supplemented by *more* politics.

The most valuable way of reading Kristeva's recent work, I suggest, is to formulate a hypothesis about the *limit* of the political field; this by definition does not
imply the abandonment of politics. The proper terrain of psychoanalytic therapy
(in contrast to what has been called "applied psychoanalysis") extends toward the
outside of the political field, where the principal terms of reference are ethics, ego,
and love—in other words, toward metaphysics. Although the psychoanalytic
process, considered in terms of its subjective therapeutic effects, challenges ideological dogmatism on the Right and Left, it functions effectively as a clinical practice only by reaching beyond the limits of politics—beyond the scope of society as
such.

It should now be clear that Spivak's and Brandt's arguments sustain a reductive
either/or logic that obfuscates the complex relationship between politics and psychoanalytic practice. Brandt makes it too easy to conclude that analytic dialogue is
completely removed from public political debate, as though the analysand acquires
perfect immunity against social discourses when entering the analyst's office.
Against these assumptions, Kristeva argues that her move into the analytic cham-
ber was a response to a firm conviction that the field of human experience had been
overpoliticized, a position we must clearly contrast with crude, postpolitical quietism (Guberman 42). In an era defined by abject cynicism, increasing neoracism,
political dogmatism, and the supremacy of global capitalism, a new emphasis on
the irreducible particularity of the subject is required to counter the homogenizing
forces of postmodern political culture. Far from pessimistically abandoning politics, Kristeva adopted this perspective, I contend, on the basis of a properly pragmatic consideration of the available means of social action. Paradoxically, her
decision implied a radical critique of the pragmatism and ideological transparency
of political discourses.

The Matter of History

Strangers argues that we must conceive of the foreigner not only as the refugee and
the exile (that is, as a concrete displaced person defined by national and international law), but as the shadow of our psychology, "the hidden face of our identity"
(9; 1).[4] Adopting a poetic and personal style to introduce her theme, Kristeva shifts
the focus of cultural otherness from traditionally conceived political deliberations
on the legal status of immigrants and toward psychological questions about what
cultural otherness subjectively represents. Kristeva's detailed historicization of
Western epistemologies of foreignness clarifies, however, that she does not psychologize entirely the idea of strangeness by reducing otherness solely to subjectivity. Instead, Kristeva highlights the effects on political discourse of the subject's

inability to reconcile itself to itself. Her "toccata and fugue" for the foreigner addresses how subjectivity's precariousness taints both our democratic participation and attitudes toward strangers.

Strangeness confronts each subject with a trauma that haunts the fragile process of socialization, with "an asymbolia that rejects civility and returns to a violence laid bare" (7; 17)—or, in a more properly psychoanalytic vocabulary, with the psychic violence of castration. Kristeva represents the stranger as embodying the excess that impedes our seamless integration into the structures of language and society. The foreigner's aloofness and mysterious distance point to a part of the psyche that is opaque to consciousness and resistant to law and civilization. Unable to reconcile the insistence of the drive with social norms, the citizen projects hostility onto the cultural other, thereby justifying xenophobia. Set apart from the symbolic effectivity of the law, the foreigner is the most available (because vulnerable) figure onto which the citizen may project its self-strangeness. In the wake of the "crises undergone by religious and ethical constructs" (2; 10)—constructs that in previous cultures provided moral schemas to negotiate or transcend cultural difference—the postmodern subject is tempted with renewed urgency to sink into parochial self-enclosure by attributing all difference to ethnic minorities.

We can illuminate the difficulties confronting Kristeva's Anglo-American readers by focusing on the claims of a U.S.-based critic of Francophone North African literature. In the tradition of Marxist dissections of "poststructuralist theories" (90), Winifred Woodhull echoes Spivak when identifying *Strangers* as "complicit with the self-serving neoliberal politics which has become a Paris fashion" (171). Woodhull aims strategically to distinguish the "symbolic" level on which "poststructuralist" theoretical production operates in France from the "real" suffering and exploitation of minority groups (89–90). Basing her claim on secondary accounts of Kristeva's work rather than on her actual texts, Woodhull contends that Kristeva's discourse "level[s] differences between foreigners and other groups" (91). In fact, *Strangers* aims to trace through Western political thought the juridical distinction between citizens and foreigners. Notwithstanding the questionable relevance of her argument, however, Woodhull's text has the advantage of contrasting the collectivist politics of Left materialism with the "liberal" ethic of individualism that Kristeva and her French cultural allies endorse.

Interesting insights emerge when we juxtapose Woodhull's objections to *Strangers* with Kristeva's commentary on the ambiguous scene in Albert Camus's *The Stranger* (1946) in which Meursault, one of existential literature's classic laconic protagonists, shoots an Arab. Camus's novel gives us a narrative framework in which to clarify the relation between historical context and methods of literary analysis. Kristeva's reading of *The Stranger* posits Meursault as a psychological "prototype" of the stranger—he abhors relations, values, and the sacred. As Kristeva suggests throughout her book, these are precisely elements of the stranger's psychology. In this respect Meursault does not kill a man he identifies as ethnically Arab—as the "enemy" of the French colonial interest. Instead, he annihilates a projection of his mute psychological distress.

Camus's point, for Kristeva, is that the shocking murder on the Algerian beach does not derive from a primarily political motivation. Meursault's *passage-à-l'acte* arises rather from the suffocation of the other in himself, from the anesthetization of the uncanny that renders him emotionally alienated. "Before being staged on the beach," Kristeva writes, "the murder was there already, silent and invisible" (26–27; 42), lying in wait in the protagonist's unconscious, unfettered by sociosymbolic repression. The murder results from Meursault's peculiar resistance to entry into the order of symbols, which gives rise to a seamlessly sensuous consciousness that hinders the establishment of cognitive distance. Like a recording device, Meursault registers impressions in an unmediated way, so impeding intellection and self-consciousness. Meursault's extremely fragile repression makes him susceptible to violent outbursts that attempt to embody his symbolic alienation.

Given her rather dogmatic orientation, Woodhull's objections to these insights are not surprising. She views Kristeva's reference to Camus as emblematic of the inherent limitations of *Strangers*: "By virtue of focusing on the foreignness within and systematically dissociating it from social inequalities," Woodhull writes, "Kristeva ends by ignoring the foreigners whose foreignness, unlike her own, sparks hostility and violence in France" (92). From Woodhull's perspective, Kristeva ignores differences between types of displaced persons, losing sight of "the fact that the stakes of defining and coming to terms with difference vary, depending whether one is a Maghrebian streetsweeper, an Asian princess, or a European intellectual" (93).

I agree that Kristeva's approach to foreignness fails to consider extreme forms of cultural displacement, for instance those that political refugees suffer. Yet Woodhull's criticisms sideline the most basic point of Kristeva's intervention, that psychological trauma accompanying cultural conflict is not entirely reducible to sociopolitical meaning. Thus while the incident in Camus's novel on the Algerian beach must be situated in the context of French colonial history, readers nonetheless fail to illuminate such acts of violence as Meursault's when attributing them solely to political significance. As Kristeva is surely aware, the murder in *The Stranger* is *inscribed* in the history of colonialism, but it is not *determined* by it.

Kristeva suggests that what most characterizes Meursault is his distance from collective interest, his indifference to the community. If there has ever been a subject for whom history has no meaning, that subject is surely Camus's protagonist.

Kristeva's emphasis on the ethicosubjective dimension implies that the events in the novel could have had a different outcome, that Meursault was not destined to shoot the Arab simply because he belongs to the colonial culture. Certainly, the ethos of colonialism taints Meursault's mindset. However, maintaining that colonial psychology is the effective cause of the murder fosters an ethically and politically suspect alibi for violence. Situated at the point where social determinism vanishes under the ambivalent opacities of unconscious life, the case of Meursault epitomizes the limitations of materialist analysis.

According to Woodhull, Kristeva's insistence on the psychological dimension of cultural strangeness leads her to adopt an individualist ethics that tempers the need for collective politics. Woodhull believes, for example, that political advocacy for Maghrebian immigrants to France requires an account of group solidarity derived solely from Marxian activist tradition. In my view, the disagreement between Woodhull and Kristeva emerges succinctly here. The former suggests that considering only the "collective plight of immigrants" can properly address "the social desert that Paris constitutes for Maghrebian factory workers" (90, 91). In stark contrast, Kristeva takes account of the talents and capacities of Algerians for whom Paris has much more to offer. For me, the supreme value of Kristeva's schema lies precisely in its ability to recognize the subject's capacity to manage cultural conflict creatively—that is, to work through the trauma of displacement without resorting to Meursault's brand of racial aggression. So long as we do not lose sight of the material influences circumscribing (without absolutely determining) the cultural options available to marginal subjects, Kristeva's version of strangeness admirably dispels the melancholic and benevolent paternalism Woodhull's politics betrays.

Evoking an image of helplessly mute subaltern masses, Woodhull contends that France offers the newly arrived immigrant nothing but hopelessness and marginalization. Her methodology again confronts us with an overpoliticized choice of options, forcing us to choose between sociological determinism and the "reactionary elitism" of avant-garde subjectivism. Kristeva reminds us that there remains a middle ground for negotiation here.

And Pragmatically . . . ?

Rejecting Kristeva's work on foreignness, most Anglo-American critics have paid little attention to her appropriation of Enlightenment universalism and her concrete suggestions for political and ethical reform. Though Kristeva clearly valorizes certain aspects of the Stoic and Judeo-Christian traditions' treatment of cultural alterity, *Strangers* prioritizes eighteenth-century universalist paradigms and

Freud's theory of the subject, which for Kristeva developed directly from their Stoic and Judeo-Christian antecedents.[5]

Kristeva's desire to revisit the French Enlightenment forces us, in my view, to weigh the efficacy of a number of postmodern assumptions. By reintroducing the category of the universal into political and ethical debate, Kristeva implicitly reframes the positive conception of difference dominating contemporary theoretical discourse. Unlike the postmodern subject of absolute heterogeneity, Kristeva's conception of the political subject remains dialectical: This subject is not only divided against itself, but split between juridical categories of citizenship and the identitarian demands of ethnicity and religion—that is, more generally, between the ethical idea of the human community and the drive for national and linguistic particularity. For Kristeva, cosmopolitanism is an ethical plea *valorizing* the subject's alienation from its culture; by contrast, the postmodern subject tends to rebel against alienation by viewing it as an imposition of amorphous vectors of power.

Kristeva's account of cosmopolitanism derives largely from her reading of Montesquieu. Though it is not possible here to detail her interpretation, it is nonetheless necessary to recall a number of Montesquieu's fundamental ideas. After my brief review of Kristeva's appropriation of Montesquieu, I want to indicate some of the ethical and economic ramifications of this reading. For Montesquieu, humanity is weakly but innately sociable and may thus be considered as a totality; at the level of the species the radical diversity of human polities stems from a vulnerable social desire that leads humanity out of its anarchic and fearful state of nature. National character in Montesquieu emerges not as a positive organic unity but as an abstract arena of sociality shaped by the specificities of climate and religion, government and custom. The consolidation of global capitalism, which Montesquieu foresaw, requires that humanity integrate into a "moderate, attainable ideality" (qtd. in *Strangers* 129; 190).[6] Foreshadowing the categorical imperative of Kantian moral philosophy, Montesquieu entreats the subject to relativize its interests for the well-being of the universal human genus.

The increased interdependence of the world's economies sets the stage in Montesquieu for a cosmopolitan political vocabulary that prioritizes the subject's place in the human theater above the immediate demands of its family or nation. Acculturated into a "general spirit," the cosmopolitan subject's identitarian drives scatter across a variety of social levels in an effort to minimize cultural hermeticism. The separation of powers among political, social, and judicial levels couples in Montesquieu's work with an account of private autonomy that preserves cultural particularity. For Kristeva, the abstract character of these cosmopolitan ideals avoids the cultural homogenization jeopardizing individual liberty. Far from erasing cultural difference through the imposition of a falsely universal cultural umbrella, Montesquieu's cosmopolitanism shatters the will to power into multiple and competing fragments, thus neutralizing the political sphere in the interests of trade and culture.

A recurring motif in materialist attacks against Kristeva is her alleged embrace of "liberalism" or "neoliberalism"; both Spivak and Woodhull have more or less aligned Kristeva's politics with the general reorientation of recent French political theory toward the liberal tradition.[7] For example, besides Montesquieu, Kristeva refers in *Strangers* to a number of major figures of liberal political philosophy, including Locke, Kant, Constant, and Tocqueville. Yet by neglecting to specify precisely what they mean by "liberalism," Spivak and Woodhull not only assume that liberal political theory presents a unified view of human nature, politics, and society, but halt further inquiry by misrecognizing the effects (both negative *and* positive) of liberal principles on Marx's oeuvre as well as the progressive traditions of Anglo-American and continental social theory.

We can speculate on the reason Kristeva turns specifically to Montesquieu from among other pre-Marxist political philosophers. First, in her desire to be realistic—that is, to account for the status quo—Kristeva recognizes that Montesquieu left an indelible imprint on the constitutions of Western parliamentary democracies. Second, of all the major liberal philosophers, Montesquieu undoubtedly attributed most importance to the sphere of cultural production. Though clearly indebted to both formulations, Montesquieu's view of the subject differs from the Hobbesian warlord of political domination and the Lockean entrepreneur of pure economic interest. Additionally, Montesquieu aimed to *neutralize* the field of power in order to foster an interest in other things: In the rather cynical words of one French neoliberal, Montesquieu allows us to "earn money or write books" (Manent 60). Montesquieu's society is one in which a separation of powers in principle prevents one subject from dominating another. As a result, Montesquieu prioritizes endeavors surfacing at some distance from the exercise of force and influence. By characterizing human nature as neither a utilitarian adaptation of the pleasure principle nor a Nietzschean version of the will to power, Montesquieu's thought can be compared to the ethical complexities of the Freudian subject of the unconscious. Seeking consolation from the fearful state of nature, Montesquieu's weakly social subject turns to "sublimation"—to cultural and commercial activities that ideally channel aggressively antisocial drives into the peaceful manipulation of a fragile social bond.

Kristeva acknowledges that the globalization of trade clears a path for Montesquieu's idea of the maximal integration of mankind. Not without historical clairvoyance, Montesquieu speculated in the early eighteenth century that the development of world commerce would be "dominated by Europe," appending his (retrospectively naive) hope that the "moderate regulation of the flow of goods and currency" prevent economic exploitation (qtd. in *Strangers* 130; 191). For Kristeva, Montesquieu's theory of world capitalism feeds into the conservatism of such political theorists as Constant and Tocqueville: She concludes anticlimactically that we must "ponder" the connection between Enlightenment cosmopolitanism and European economic imperialism (132; 194). Glossing over the problematic economic implications of Montesquieu's work, Kristeva reveals that she is most interested in his ethical universalism. But to what extent is the Enlightenment ideal of universal humanity tied to metropolitan and imperialist schemes for world trade? Should we not weigh Montesquieu's doctrine against his perspective as a prerevolutionary aristocrat at the dawn of the imperialist age, especially since his economic agenda echoes in present-day negotiations of international trade law? Finally, to what extent may we use Kristeva's implicit critique of historicist and sociological reductionism to distinguish Montesquieu's ethics from his liberal view of world commerce?

Although Kristeva's text inadequately questions the conservative and imperialist consequences of Montesquieu's economic liberalism, I think the supreme value of Montesquieu's cosmopolitanism lies in its erasing juridical distinctions between human rights and citizens' rights. Moreover, Montesquieu's work reminds us that the Enlightenment's abstract humanist universalism functions not to homogenize cultural difference, but to promote individual singularity through a renewed emphasis on the boundary between public and private spheres. Radicalizing the classical split between public democratic participation and private enjoyment, Kristeva underlines the value of a fragmented social body divided among political, social, and private domains. In so doing she provides an outlet for all forms of affect and passion outside the boundaries of the political machine through literary and cultural creation. Thus Kristeva objects to the hyperrationalist view of subjectivity subtending the most utopian modes of French Enlightenment thought and, by extension, the paradigmatic Lockean subject of liberalism. But she nonetheless wants to rescue from postmodern critiques the ideal of an abstract democratic citizen who, in "working through" his or her most extreme fits of passion, is capable of articulating his or her interests in the public sphere, thereby strengthening the political effects.

For me, the value of Kristeva's reading of Enlightenment political philosophy lies in its universalist emphasis. Through Montesquieu Kristeva tries to salvage the idea of a universal humanity not as a *political category*, but as an *ethical principle* independent of "historical society and its vagaries" (152; 227). Presenting a trenchant critique of historicism, Kristeva posits humanity as a suprahistorical ethical form stripped of its utilitarian and humanist (and, in this precise sense, liberal) eighteenth-century baggage. Complicating the functionalist and rationalist Enlightenment cosmopolitan is Kristeva's internally exiled, postculturalist artist-intellectual who, flirting dangerously with hysteria, therapeutically dignifies him-or herself by recognizing and naming its passion, by acknowledging drives that are inimical to cultural domestication. Kristeva's cosmopolitanism gives the subject an ability to transcend historical and material determinants while linking the subject's dignity precisely to an ineradicable appetite for destruction and death. Far removed from the '68 fantasy of a revolutionary subject liberated from repression, Kristeva presents a moderate political view that acknowledges the irreducibility of the subject's jouissance while implicitly bracketing the possibility of a viable alternative to parliamentary ("bourgeois") democracy.

My principal aim has been to untangle Kristeva's recent political theory from its portrayal by Anglo-American detractors, without subsuming the insoluble differences between these views. Additionally, I consider Kristeva's framework a desirable alternative to the materialist reductionism of postcolonial criticism that seems incapable of balancing political and ethical concerns. Nevertheless, I shall conclude by noting some of the limitations of Kristeva's precepts. Given her polemical intervention, Kristeva's comments on human rights and immigration policies are disappointingly vague. In contrast to the depth of her approach to contemporary ethics, Kristeva's discussion of cultural displacement does not grapple with the traumas that political refugees suffer. Nor does Kristeva demonstrate a broad view of immigration legislation in either France or the wider developed world.[8] In the five years since the publication of Kristeva's books, the nations composing the European Union (EU) have adopted increasingly hostile policies against displaced persons. In France, the National Assembly's approval of the Pasqua laws, the striking of the Philibert-Sauvaigo Commission, and the shockingly violent removal of African illegal entrants from the Eglise St. Bernard in Paris presage dark times for persons seeking political asylum and economic opportunity in what was formerly one of Europe's most open nations to foreigners.[9] Given Kristeva's desire to intervene in contemporary discourses on race and immigration in France, we must note her reluctance to consider the material effects of legislation on the repression of cultural alterity in French society.

In *Strangers* Kristeva tends to celebrate cosmopolitanism as a distinct characteristic of French culture while discussing xenophobic nationalism only in the German tradition. Though the cosmopolitanism she valorizes prevailed most obviously in a French liberal tradition (one nonetheless profoundly Anglophilic), Kristeva's recollection of Hegel's Francophilia elides a profoundly different tradition of French nationalism we can trace from Joan of Arc to Jean-Marie Le Pen, and from Joseph de Maistre to Maurice Barrès (*Strangers* 145; 216). Failing to acknowledge French ethnocentrism, Kristeva manifests her own latent and symptomatic nationalism. Perhaps indicative of the displaced person's need for identification (we cannot underestimate the effects of her self-perception as a dissident vis-à-vis socialist rationalism), Kristeva's weak cultural nationalism seems to blind her to the less generous side of France's intellectual history.

Although it is necessary to keep these difficulties in mind, Kristeva's theory of foreignness is an important alternative to the type of postcolonial theory that consistently overemphasizes social and political factors—a criticism that forecloses in advance on a consideration of the limit universalist and ethical concerns place on the political arena and the role of artistic creativity in the negotiation of traumatic cultural confrontations. Too often readings of postcolonial texts account for cultural production only by sociologistic definitions of context, as though literature were nothing more than an authorless, dehumanized, and faultlessly mimetic palimpsest of the social environment. Recent overviews of Kristeva's work suggest that hyperpoliticized materialist criticism cannot balance the effects of historical conflict on cultural production with a nuanced view of creative discourse as an inscription less of a humanist subject than of a subjective process.

Postcolonial criticism can only benefit from a posthumanist theory that views cultural production as a complex, dynamic, and ultimately undecidable artifact of conscious and unconscious processes. Characterizing Kristeva's perspective as apolitical aestheticism, reactionary formalism, or traditionalist subjectivism does not engage her argument. Kristeva's work also admirably underscores the importance of Freudianism for cultural and literary studies. Her recent works ultimately suggest that the true locus of the racialized other lies within the complexities of the individual's subjective dynamics. More valuably than any other interpretive method, psychoanalysis allows the critic to consider cultural artifacts as reflections of political and ethnic struggles without rendering absolute the determinations of society and history, without subscribing to the death of the subject, and, finally, without losing sight of the conflicted and passionate individuals who, through artistic creativity, attempt to grapple with what is most frightening and enigmatic of all—ourselves.

ENDNOTES

I thank Nasrin Rahimieh for her early encouragement, Christopher Lane for his editorial support, and Toril Moi for the clearheadedness with which she read the manuscript. A doctoral fellowship from the Social Sciences and Humanities Research Council of Canada enabled me to complete this project.

1. *About Chinese Women* is the main exception to this rule. Kristeva's oeuvre does, however, contain scattered comments on Eastern linguistic traditions.

2. Brandt's article is not an extended meditation on Kristeva's politics, but a useful analysis of the place of narcissism in her theories and a valuable commentary on Lacan. Nonetheless, Brandt's comment on Kristeva's "turning away" from politics is emblematic of a common perspective on clinical practice.

3. See "Psychoanalysis and the Polis" for Kristeva's analysis of this relationship.

4. References to *Strangers* are respectively to the English translation and French original.

5. In her account of the stranger, Kristeva's primary reference to Freud is his seminal essay "The 'Uncanny' " (1919).

6. Kristeva's reading of Montesquieu refers in this instance to *Mes Pensées*; however, Montesquieu's principal political work is *De l'esprit des lois*.

7. See Lilla for an incisive introduction to French negotiations of political liberalism.

8. A recent Canadian report comparing immigration laws among seven industrialized nations (the United States and the United Kingdom, Canada, France, Germany, Denmark, and Australia) suggests that Germany and Canada (and *not* France) have to the greatest extent constitutionalized the rights of foreign nonresidents seeking asylum; theoretically, this would reduce the potential for abuses of human rights (Glenn 17). Among these seven nations the United States and Canada are the only ones to feature judicial or quasi-judicial (as opposed to administrative) procedures for removing illegal immigrants, thereby eliminating in principle the legality of forced exclusion at the moment of an attempt at entry (35).

As to the question of determining refugee status, France is the only nation among the seven *not* to provide the claimant with the right to a fair hearing; such cases in France are decided unilaterally by members of the public service (62). In sum, the Glenn report makes clear that France in particular, and the western European nations in general, certainly are not at the forefront of humane and democratic reforms of procedural justice concerning immigration.

9. The Pasqua laws are a series of legislative reforms dating from the mid-1980s that reappraise the rights of foreigners seeking asylum in France. Among the many consequences are a limitation of the rights of family members to join immigrant relatives, an acceleration of the deportation process for those judged to menace the social order, and a tightening of requirements necessary for the acquisition of refugee status. The Philibert-Sauvaigo Commission submitted a report to the National Assembly in April 1996 recommending an increase in the length of administrative retention and the revocation of rights to healthcare and education for illegal entrants. The commission's report has no legislative power but it does signal a sea change in France's attitude toward foreigners (de Brie 4).

On August 23, 1996, Parisian police officers stormed the Eglise St. Bernard, arresting and detaining 210 Africans, many of whom were on a hunger strike in protest against government policy toward immigrants. Though the vast majority was released after a procedural review and several days of administrative detention, many were eventually deported.

The incident provoked a public outcry against the harsh treatment of foreigners by French authorities.

WORKS CITED

Brandt, Joan. "The Power and the Horror of Love: Kristeva on Narcissism." *Romanic Review* 82.1 (1991): 89–104.

de Brie, Christian. "Boulevard de la xénophobie." *Le Monde diplomatique* (juin 1996): 4–5.

Camus, Albert. *The Stranger*. Trans. Matthew Ward. New York: Knopf, 1988. *L'Étranger*. Paris: Gallimard, 1957.

Freud, Sigmund. "The 'Uncanny.' " 1919. Vol. 17 of *The Standard Edition of the Complete Psychological Works of Sigmund Freud*. 24 vols. Ed. and trans. James Strachey. London: Hogarth, 1953–1974. 219–56.

Glenn, H. Patrick. *Strangers at the Gate: Refugees, Illegal Entrants, and Procedural Justice*. Cowansville, Québec: Y. Blais, 1992.

Guberman, Ross Mitchell, ed. *Julia Kristeva: Interviews*. New York: Columbia UP, 1996.

Kant, Immanuel. "Idea for a Universal History with a Cosmopolitan Purpose." Trans. H. B. Nisbet. *Kant: Political Writings*. New York: Cambridge UP, 1991. 41–53.

Kristeva, Julia. *About Chinese Women*. Trans. Anita Barrows. London: Marion Boyars, 1977. *Des chinoises*. Paris: des femmes, 1974.

———. *Nations Without Nationalism*. Trans. Leon S. Roudiez. New York: Columbia UP, 1993. *Lettre ouverte à Harlem Désir*. Paris: Editions Rivage, 1990.

———. *The New Maladies of the Soul*. Trans. Ross Guberman. New York: Columbia UP, 1995. *Les Nouvelles maladies de l'âme*. Paris: Fayard, 1992.

———. *Powers of Horror: An Essay on Abjection*. Trans. Leon S. Roudiez. New York: Columbia UP, 1982. *Pouvoirs de l'horreur. Essai sur l'abjection*. Paris: Seuil, 1980.

———. "Psychoanalysis and the Polis." In Moi. 301–20.

———. *Revolution in Poetic Language*. Trans. Margaret Waller. Intro. Leon S. Roudiez. New York: Columbia UP, 1984. *La Révolution du langage poétique: L'avant-garde à la fin du XIXe siècle. Lautréamont et Mallarmé*. Paris: Seuil, 1974.

———. *Strangers to Ourselves*. Trans. Leon S. Roudiez. New York: Columbia UP, 1991. *Étrangers à nous-mêmes*. Coll. Folio. Paris: Gallimard, 1988.

———. *Tales of Love*. Trans. Leon S. Roudiez. New York: Columbia UP, 1987. *Histoires d'amour*. Paris: Denoël, 1983.

———. *Time and Sense: Proust and the Experience of Literature*. Trans. Ross Guberman. New York: Columbia UP, 1996. *Le Temps sensible. Proust et l'expérience littéraire*. Paris: Gallimard, 1994.

Lilla, Mark. "The Legitimacy of the Liberal Age." *New French Thought: Political Philosophy*. Ed. Lilla. Princeton: Princeton UP, 1994. 3–37.

Manent, Pierre. *An Intellectual History of Liberalism*. Trans. Rebecca Balinski. Princeton: Princeton UP, 1994. *Histoire intellectuelle du libéralisme: Dix leçons*. Paris: Calmann-Levy, 1987.

Moi, Toril, ed. *The Kristeva Reader*. New York: Columbia UP, 1986.

Montesquieu, Charles-Louis de Secondat, Baron de. *Œuvres complètes*. Ed. Roger Caillois. Bibliothèque de la Pléiade. 2 vols. Paris: Gallimard, 1949–1951.

Rose, Jacqueline. "Julia Kristeva: Take Two." *Sexuality in the Field of Vision*. London: Verso, 1986. 141–64.

Spivak, Gayatri Chakravorty. "French Feminism in an International Frame." *In Other Worlds: Essays in Cultural Politics*. New York: Routledge, 1988. 134–53.

———. "Can the Subaltern Speak?" *Marxism and the Interpretation of Culture*. Ed. Cary Nelson and Lawrence Grossberg. Urbana: U of Illinois P, 1988. 271–313.

———. "In a Word: Interview." *Outside in the Teaching Machine*. New York: Routledge, 1993. 1–24.

Woodhull, Winnifred. *Transfigurations of the Maghreb*. Minneapolis: U of Minnesota P, 1993.

5
A Question of Accent:
Ethnicity and Transference

Suzanne Yang

In the matter of shells . . . I did my best to define my ignorance, to
organize it, and above all to preserve it.

—Valéry 109

In approaching this topic, I sense my voice a little tremu-
lous, anguished, confronting the limits of my own subjectivity in the context of beginning to work with
patients. Speculatively, I will delineate a theoretical discourse of this work, illuminated by moments from clinical encounters. My claims here, by necessity, must be
general, mobilizing ethnicity without the details of its
unfolding in the particularity of any subject's history—
aside, that is, from the perspective that lies at the very
limits of my own.

Ethnicity—and why not say *versus race*?—is a way of
contrasting two approaches to alterity.[1] I would like to
start by aligning *race* with a visible otherness in the scopic
dimension, using the term *ethnicity* to designate an otherness in the acoustic field of verbal phenomena. In making
this distinction simply to open the discourse, I shall
regard the emergence of otherness in each perceptual
field as an alternate point of entry into the clinical experience of the transference. After distinguishing between
these modes of alterity, there may be a way of proceeding toward their reconfiguration by seeking a common
moment of origin—an origin at stake in the handling
and, ultimately, in the liquidation of the transference. In
what follows, I will put forward a few stories and an orig-

inary myth regarding the constitution of subjectivity along an axis presumed to be dyadic, but implicating an Other whose presence manifests itself as the marking of a question.

What is the opposite of an Asian woman? With this question, I introduce an issue of the surface, in order to follow this surface and its contours toward that primordial beginning that allows for oppositions to be founded. Perhaps this is an uncharitable way of starting to address the dilemma of ethnicity—uncharitable, since I have not yet told you what an Asian woman is, or how she may partake of the structure of opposition. In presenting the question to you in this way, I can only assert that an Asian woman is not something about whom testimony can be given; rather, she is a signifier whose referent is an image that may eventually bring ethnicity to light.

To this extent, you already know what an Asian woman is—you don't need me to tell you. I could as easily ask you *Where have you seen her?* and you would know that ethnicity is a dilemma, because race is not a choice. Race is readily apparent, a surface reflecting light and color . . . warmth or its absence, silence and mystery, friend or foe. Race is an outfit like clothing involving no decisions every morning. Race wears its subject without regard to fashion, though to be sure the public imaginary confers its shifting meanings on racial identity, which presents an indication of symbolic hope for change—though *change* must not be mistaken as a synonym for *improvement.*

In the presence of race, ethnicity makes its first appearance as this cloak, a mask whose exteriority would not be its only virtue. Race is the given surface folding inward into places impossible to see, whose access is equally impossible to forsake. As Nicolas Abraham emphasized and elaborated throughout his work with Maria Torok, the envelope or shell—this cortex we call Imaginary—conceals and protects what it shelters, limiting—*while also being impinged upon by*—the ineffable kernel we hope to reach. A Lacanian commentary would insist on a differentiation (and a dialectic) between this surface, understood as continuous transformation and distortion, and the sharp restructuration of the figure by an event that alters the continuity and its flow within the space it defines and renders possible (Granon-Lafont 23). With regard to external space—an area beyond the body surface and in the perceptual field of the Other—we might posit that the finding of geography, or of place in the physical sense, recapitulates the contours shaped by an internal structuration, which may undergo reworking and reconfiguration through a series of cuts, folds, and ties. Thus, from the empirical fact of race as concealment and mediation, we hold open the possibility of seeking what resides beyond face value. From the scopic constitution of racial identity, mediated through an imaginary representation of the desire of the Other, we may proceed to question how this desire is constituted through fantasy and an apotropaic operation, at the exclusion of a portion of the scene.

In elaborating the problem of the envelope, perhaps I shall have recourse to a man—a European man, as though he were the opposite of an Asian woman. In his 1937 essay on seashells, Paul Valéry begins his meditations on finding an object along the seashore. "The shell," he writes, "offers me a combined development of the simple themes of helix and spiral, involves me in a degree of astonishment and concentration that leads where it may: to superficial remarks and observations, naive questions, 'poetic' comparisons, beginnings of reckless 'theories.' . . . And my mind vaguely anticipates the entire innate treasure of responses that rise within me in the presence of a thing that arrests and questions me" (113). But he then notes, following the contours of the surface to their end, "even the mathematician is baffled when in the end the tube suddenly broadens, breaks, curls back, and over-flows into uneven lips, often bordered, waved, or fluted, which part as though made of flesh, disclosing in a fold of the softest mother-of-pearl the smoothly inclined starting point of an internal whorl that recedes into darkness" (115). There where the shell is presumed to end, Valéry approaches the troubling question of its maker, the being from which the shell is said to "emanate" or "exude" (124, 125), which somehow gives the shell, in its likeness to "an endless number of similar figures" (120), a historical mark of singularity within a domain in which all may look alike. I shall return to this maker and the question of the creature's subjectivity, after a detour into the life of this shell, a racial envelope, by which the subject moves about and through which it first is known. Thus confronted by the appearance of the shell of racial masking, we shall eventually find a way to ask, *Who, after all, is there?*

And so I have begun with an enigma—an enigma that takes the form of a questioning. *What is the opposite of an Asian woman?* I don't want to just leave you there, alone with the question of this enigma and its cost. Above all, I don't want to reinforce for you any premonition regarding the inscrutability of my discourse, which might prematurely curtail the unfolding that conveys the shape of this questioning. Having promised to follow the enigma back to the moment of its inception, I would like to speak extremely clearly—in no uncertain terms, if this is possible—for the question itself is strange enough. *What is the opposite of an Asian woman?* I will return to this question over and again, as if to approach an answer by repeating it speculatively, in a different way each time, recapitulating an experience of primal strangeness. In order to stay grounded, I shall offer first a story, something empirically true and down-to-earth—a boring story in that it happens all the time, mostly unnoticed.

The story takes place outside of—or more accurately on the way to—a clinical encounter. One afternoon, I was in an elevator, returning to the psychiatric ward where I was working, lost in thought about a patient who communicated only in fragments involving obscure literary allusions, and who insisted that he had acquired HIV through the intravenous use of coffee. He had been hospitalized after starting a fire for reasons having to do with Dante's *Inferno*, a clue to his perception of the world in which he lived. When asked during a routine mental status examination to state his name, as well as the year, date, and place, he would turn the questions around and ask if *I* knew where *I* was, giving me a choice of Austria or Australia—to which the answer was obviously *neither*. I sensed he felt his place to be unnamable, impossible to locate in a symbolic system based on binary oppositions—an impossibility he forced me to experience as an uncertainty about my own location, which happened at that moment to be an elevator in transit. . . .

Lost in the revery of these thoughts, I scarcely noticed the Caucasian stranger who entered the elevator with me and addressed me in Chinese, "Ni hao ma?" (how are you?). Startled, cornered, and unable to refuse the question, I recognized myself suddenly within a Chinese-seeming body as the object of an address— which, to be fair, was perfectly polite; I replied simply by nodding. He then asked me if I spoke English. "Well," I responded wryly, summoning my most American accent and feeling a little offended, "I most *definitely* do." He laughed nervously and went on to say that I probably spoke English better than he did, thereby casting himself as more foreign than the supposed foreigner. Embarrassed and somehow wishing to console him, perhaps because I regretted the loss of my strangeness and was uncomfortable with my newly conferred authority over the entire English language, I reached my floor and stepped off the elevator, thinking somehow to remark, "It's difficult to tell just by looking."

It's difficult to tell just by looking. What, then, do we make of our tendency to jump to conclusions regarding identity, simply from the scopic evidence presented by an appearance on the surface? Societal conventions and categorizations lead us to expect that appearances are tied to a stable truth beyond the surface—that the visual image correlates with the language a person speaks, with or without an accent, and will reliably indicate the geographical place where he or she is from. Symbolic structures hold these categories in place as positions conferred on different groups relative to others under the law, and as figurations crafted within the media's more malleable public sphere. Yet these meanings, to the extent that they are determinate, are also radically underdetermined, gaining their force and privilege over the individual by passing though more fundamental levels of intrapsychic structure, where the subject first becomes vulnerable to the constitution of difference.

I continue with the story—of the patient in whose words I had been lost at the moment when I was confronted with a racial image in the elevator. Emerging from his fragmentary silence, the patient proceeded in the next days to speak of Tokyo Rose, bringing my image to the forefront of his delusions, believing that I must be the actress Susie Wong, and hinting at a story of espionage from a movie I had not seen. Declaring his certainty regarding my status as an illegal alien, he threatened to amputate various of my limbs—splintering me perhaps into multiple objects of the drives—though he never expressed the wish to kill me entirely.

It is difficult and painful to encounter these mutilating words, which claim to disfigure the other in order to access the *objet petit a*. The subject aims at all costs to retrieve the *objet a* without the mediation of the Other and without that alienating surface by which a separation would be marked. The words conveying a threat must be received and supported in the locus of the Other, which the therapist holds open as a promise of future symbolization.[2] At times the therapist's only response must be compliance with the demand to go away, in order to preserve the possibility of a return to the relation, which the patient, finding that his or her words are reversible, is likely eventually to seek. In these moments of rapprochement, the patient may use the image of race as a basis for closeness—or for distance and for difference: "I have the Buddha within me," one patient told me in a moment of greater lucidity. Another patient, a Caucasian woman convinced she was African, often expressed the belief that her mother might have been Chinese. She knew, however, that I was neither her mother nor her daughter; indeed, she named the many people I was *not*. "You are not Amy Tan," she said emphatically, as if to raise the question, in the negative, of who I really might be.

In the encounters above, we find that race is an opening for the transference, a first manifestation which the patient believes to be secure because race is culturally obvious—a way of taking the therapist at face value. Race is thus made to serve as an "indisputable fact" providing the ground for psychotic elaboration and an attempted destruction of an otherliness that is at once unbearable and all too familiar. In neurotic-spectrum patients there may be a greater preservation of this surface and its careful exploration, as well as the defensive phenomenon of its avoidance.

Training as a therapist has awakened me to the experience of ethnicity, because race is so ineluctable, a way of forcing an issue that will attain a different meaning for every subject who experiences the therapist's ethnicity as a component of the transference. I began my work as a therapist in a clinic for Vietnam veterans with post-traumatic stress disorder, a context in which my visual appearance, similar to that of the enemy on whose soil the war was fought, made the question of my ethnic identity an important issue for many patients to ascertain. For some the transference first arose with the question "Are you Vietnamese?" It was sometimes necessary to answer this question on a factual basis, all the while examining the question also at the level of the unconscious where "no" is not accepted as an answer.[3] For other veterans, the question of my ethnicity was initially concealed beneath equally anxious queries, as with one patient who asked "Are you a Freudian?" to which I had to reply in the affirmative, but equivocally, so as to allow the patient to make of it what he would. Interestingly, when we compare or even equate the emergence of these questions—"Are you Vietnamese?" and "Are you a Freudian?"—we find an implicit correlation between the anxiety induced by ethnicity and the operations of an enemy emerging from the unconscious, whose identity we may posit as that of the *objet petit a.*

Elsewhere, I have discussed the experience of being a therapist situated in the position of that enemy, both reviled and honored, faced with the trauma of war ("Styles"). In the supposition of knowledge in the transference, the veteran addresses an unconscious knowing within himself, which he is not yet able to render into speech—a speech he attributes to the Other in the transference. There the therapist encounters a dilemma: whether the subaltern can—or, perhaps more accurately, *may*—speak.[4] We then think of the conditions allowing the subaltern to speak. At times the subaltern seems best tolerated if silent. At other times, the patient may construe the stance of analytic neutrality as passivity—as the therapist's docility, quietness, or inscrutability—in which case the therapist's decision to speak, and how loudly, entails a judgment about the patient's readiness to having his stereotypes broken. This judgment requires a modulation in technique that may equally engage the therapist's own readiness to counter the image of which she is the support and for which she herself must be willing to pay a variable price. The model of the "pyromaniac fireman" that Soler proposed may serve as a guide: If the flames of the transference are dying, they must be fed; if blazing, they must be limited by a partial extinction (Gueguen 83). The challenge falls to the therapist to understand race and ethnicity as phobogenic and to modulate the strangeness— all the while remaining attentive to that edge between black and white, where the image of the Geisha Girl can suddenly and unexpectedly flip into that of the Dragon Lady.[5] On an even more fundamental level, the therapist must, as always, view the analytic presence as the operative form of an anxiogenic *objet a*—as the support of a desire exceeding the masquerade of race and gender. Indeed, this desire arises in the alternating appearance and crossing through of the definite article—the "T̶h̶e̶" of the Asian woman, situated somewhere between the binary poles of blackness and whiteness.

In the transference, there is *excess* from the beginning—as well as *access* by way of those mythologies we call the metapsychology of that strangeness within which the subject is first constituted. Recent theorists have interpreted the findings of empirical researchers on early infant development in order to support their respective accounts of the origins of subjectivity (see Muller, Kumin). However, the retroactive character of the subject's "originary moment," constituted as it is by values that the observer imposes, requires that we construe such interpretations with caution. Any extension of empirical observations into a theory relies upon the theorist's desire. Such theoretical formulations must be understood to serve as heuristic fictions that have consequences for the unfolding of the treatment and the realization of the subject's desire. Thus beyond the perspective of the baby, which we cannot ever know in words—even if questions can be posed and responses measured—metapsychology ends up leaving theory to adults, positing an agnostic beginning that underlies the fantasies that guide the subject's destiny.

We could say that the subject's emergence begins as a wordless *hey you*. From within primordial formlessness, desire presents itself as an enigma mumbling through an obscurity of signification—not yet an enchainment of signifiers but an address, which Laplanche has called an "enigmatic signifier" of primal seduction (126–28). This address in its diffuseness eventuates in the face of an Other, which forms its boundary and serves as the mirror image of an imago soon to become the infant's own. Here the process would reach a standstill if the speech act were not completed by the introduction of words giving symbolic concreteness to the address. Thus subjectivity is first constituted through an Other addressing the message *hey you*, which comes to mark a locus verbally that the child is propelled into taking as his own. Only the signifier arriving in this place to designate the locus *as* a locus, consolidating its fragility, can stabilize this "origin," allowing it to form the basis for the subject's historical unfolding. In this moment, the signifier (soon to be S_1) refers not yet to another signifier (S_2) but rather to itself in an infinite circuit of divided and groundless identity, founding primary narcissism as a marking, of which the proper name is the most evident example (see Schneiderman 72, 80).[6]

The subject presumes the bodily imago to be preserved and stabilized under this naming. Though castrated by the signifier, it can never again return to the shattering morcellation of the body in the domain of the Real from which it once emerged (Fletcher 108, 112). It is tempting to suppose that this moment is race-neutral—that the imago carries the signifier's structuring implantation in pure form, prior to the establishment of a specific social content, even when mother and child differ in skin color. This may well be true of the implantation in its purest form, since this purely structural moment founds a difference that retroactively is sexual, rather than racial—though we may eventually posit something like an anxiety of pigmentation that the child superimposes over castration anxiety. In a racist and xeno-phobic world, however, the process will not go far without the influence of an unconscious transmission of social meaning—whether in infancy through the mother or babysitter, or in the schoolroom—whereby the child encounters his difference not as autonomy but as prejudice and a differential in power. Analogously, but to a much greater extent, the implantation of the signifier performs an operation on the subject, independently of whether the signifier is a word found in English, French, Chinese, or Hebrew—all contexts in which it can inscribe a name. Unlike the imago, the signifier is predestined to this belonging, a mark of ethnicity that may remain with the subject in self-reference irrespective of the transformations that his imago will undergo as it reformulates itself throughout his history. At the moment when the primary signifier is implanted, a little piece will fall from the imago to proceed from that moment onward as something Lacan designated by the term *objet petit a*. Pliable as the imago is, it will never recover this intimately strange and missing piece. The *objet a* remains "extimate" to the imago (that is, both inside and outside it; see Miller 85 and his discussion of racism, 79–80), the subject pursuing the *objet a* forever in an unending articulation of desire. Through the continual inscription and reinscription of the primary signifier within a chain of signification, the subject seeks to stabilize a place where ultimately it is impossible to reside.

Diverging from some of the analytic literature on this primal communication (Dupont, Schenquerman), I have chosen to speak anasemically of *accent* rather than of intonation or melody to emphasize the question of cultural identity implicit in the voice.[7] Accent as anasemia is neither simply a question of how one expresses mood and attitude by way of tone on a given day, nor of a song one happens to feel like singing. It is rather the shuttle by which a primal configuration makes its way out to the surface, finding there a geographical and linguistic specificity. Accent indicates a source and designates the place by which the subject is spoken—an accent of that moment when the child encounters the implantation of the signifier as Other. Indeed, *encounter* describes the situation of accent, where the voice meets the signifier in discordant strangeness and in its transmission through speech.[8]

Recapitulating Lacan's formulation, I hypothesize that ethnicity partakes of all three passions of the transference—those of love, hatred, and ignorance.[9] The encounter with the racial image in the transference presents a barrier upon which various affects and the insistence of not-knowing can be elaborated, up to the point of their dissolution through a series of punctuations, reconfigurations, and unbindings of the subject's discourse. Easier stated as a goal than as something fully achievable, the therapeutic aim might be understood as a shift from transference to self-strangeness, and as the ownership of ignorance preserved as knowing (*savoir*) rather than as passion. Ignorance as remainder is thus an ineffable and infinite reverberation, an echoing recollected within a shell that the subject discards and refinds.

I have argued that the appearance of race and ethnicity in the transference may repeat at a secondary level the primal strangeness in which the subject is first constituted—a strangeness suspended in pure difference but invested equivocally with varying social meanings. An Asian woman, in the position of therapist or elsewhere, may find herself the recipient of these meanings, produced by the collective amassment of an inescapable psychic tendency—to represent in ordinary persons the remainder imagined as lost in the Other.

While this impulse may result in racist social formations and discriminatory practices both subtle and overt, it is also a source of curiosity and desire, domesticated in recent times in the pluralist discourse of multiculturalism. In clinical terms, this impulse, when apprehended in its unspeakable and aporetic psychic function, forms the very basis for what we call *relating*. The task of the therapist is to return the racial image to this aporia, which is concealed and revealed in the passions of the transference. Considering this equivocity in her meaning, the opposite of an Asian woman is perhaps a reinscription of the signifier by which her image is sustained—that is, a poetics of the subject as it searches. Thus when asked by the patient where am I from, I pass through the fact, and the face, to convey an answer in place of any nation: a tone—this void—these words—and a naming—leaving the rest to fall from difference.

ENDNOTES

For their wise and helpful comments, I would like to thank Tim Dean, Anne-Lise François, Mardy Ireland, Chris Lane, Juliet Flower MacCannell, and Rebecca Plant. This paper was presented at the 1996 meeting of the Association for the Psychoanalysis of Culture and Society in Washington, D.C., and has benefited greatly from conference participants' insightful remarks and questions.

1. Sollers observes that the terms "race" and "ethnicity" are often used loosely and interchangeably, with the latter generally perceived as the more inclusive and general category. In his definition, all groups, even the dominant or backdrop group in a society, are ethnically identified, and race may be a subset or component of this identity. He implies a symbolic definition of identity when suggesting that for purposes of social analysis "kinship and cultural codes" (39) are more useful than either "race" or "ethnicity" in designating group differences. Similarly, Hall understands ethnicity as an acknowledgment of the "place of history, language, and culture in the construction of subjectivity and identity"

(226), tying ethnicity to a play of mobile differences that navigate in a conditional and contingent field. In this essay, I make a distinction between ethnicity and race to contrast visible and invisible forms of difference, implying that a portion of the invisible difference can manifest itself as an audible difference in language, dialect, or idiom.

2. I use the term "therapist" to denote the role of someone conducting a treatment in which the patient's subjectivity is at work. Although the distinction between "therapist" and "analyst" is sometimes used in the literature to mark a difference in attitude and aim, I have suspended that distinction in order to suggest the possibility of an analytic stance in settings and treatment situations that may not be explicitly psychoanalytic in orientation and program structure.

3. This raises problems involving limits in the interpretability of race and the handling of the transference with patients for whom the racial image is deeply embedded in unconscious strife *involving specific enactment* in the subject's own history. The fantasy of destroying an Asian woman is surely different for those who have never perpetrated the act than for those who may have done so, and at the government's insistence. The forcefulness of the drive once it has undergone deregulation in the context of traumatic experience may first require a fact as containment before proceeding further, or even to sustain the viability of the treatment. Although analytic parameters customarily suppose that the therapist ought not comply with the patient's demand for information, here we find that the question "Are you Vietnamese?" supposes not only the drives but a historical and political conflict that may directly impinge on the openness of each party to the other, a framing event radically external and preliminary to what may evolve in the treatment. A direct answer from the therapist may sometimes be necessary to allow the treatment to continue, especially if the question and its underlying fantasy would otherwise be used in the service of resistance. At the emergence of such a question, particularly in the beginning of the treatment, the challenge falls to the therapist to assess whether the question presents a demand or a frame issue. Just as the therapist must respond to the question "What is the fee?" with a factual answer, the therapist cannot vary the length of the session without a willingness to supply information regarding Lacanian parameters. This does not preclude the eventuality that the fee and the signifier "Lacanian" will become tropes within the unfolding of the treatment.

4. Irigaray comments that "if the sexualized being of these 'not-all' women is not a function of the body (at least not their own bodies), they will nevertheless have to *serve* as the object *a*, that bodily remainder. The being that is sexualized female in and through discourse is also a place for the deposit of the remainders produced by the operation of language" (90; my emphasis). I would like to highlight the function of servitude as standing in for a position that cannot be occupied by anyone. Both Spivak and Butler ("Arguing") suggest that disempowered groups in social formations are created by structures of domination and that the very conceptualization of an ineffable element outside symbolization reinforces this domination. Butler writes, "The production of the *un*symbolizable, the unspeakable, the illegible is also always a strategy of social abjection" ("Arguing" 190), shutting out the very possibility she asserted in *Gender Trouble*: "masquerade suggests that there is a

'being' or ontological specification of femininity *prior* to the masquerade, a feminine desire or demand that is masked and capable of disclosure, that, indeed, might promise an eventual disruption and displacement of the phallogocentric signifying economy" (47). While Butler then proceeds to misconstrue the nature of this "disclosure" as performativity and to overestimate the free play of signification (see Dean), we might reassert the priority she grants to femininity in order to reverse her statement to read: *The production of social abjection is also always a strategy for managing the anxiety the subject confronts in the unsymbolizable, the unspeakable, and the illegible.* Irigaray clarifies how the position of woman is historically and culturally contingent in this strategy: "Woman never speaks the same way. What she emits is flowing, fluctuating. *Blurring.* And she is not listened to, unless proper meaning (meaning of the proper) is lost. Whence the resistances to that voice that overflows into 'subject.' Which the 'subject' then congeals, freezes, in its categories until it paralyzes the voice in its flow" (112).

5. I can only introduce here the difficult topic of the intrapsychic impact of racial abjection on the subject receiving the societal message of otherliness—what it means to live as and be a phobogenic object. Fanon's conclusion regarding the "neurosis of the black" was that the recipient of racist projection cannot resolve the dilemma through psychoanalytic treatment, but must turn outward, to social and political activism. For us today, this turn to the political must entail a careful discernment of the moment when the psychotherapeutic intervention fails. We insist on following the psychoanalytic process up to the moment when it opens onto the social, only to find that within the social, activist interventions must in their own right confront collective defenses—understood in psychoanalytic terms—to attain lasting change.

6. We may say S_0, ontologically present but epistemologically lost; or following Laplanche, S_1 / S_1 to indicate a ratio that is inexorably divided and rendered inaccessible as enigma. More detailed discussion of the debate between Lacan and Laplanche on the nature of primal repression is beyond the scope of this paper. See Lacan, *Four* 244–60.

7. Abraham coins the term "anasemia" to describe the action of psychoanalytic conceptualization as the creation of signifiers that "do not strictly speaking signify anything, except the founding silence of *any act of signification*"—a *designification* that rips the terms "away from the dictionary and ordinary language" (84, 85). Torn from their meaning in common sense, figures produced within psychoanalytic discourse try to reach the unnamed as dynamic phenomena.

8. Considering *accent*, we think of the vowels that translate it into *affect*. Accent versus affect is a difference merely in consonants, the vowels remaining in the same place within both words. As Dolar writes, "It is only the reduction of the voice—in all of its positivity, lock, stock, and barrel—that produces the voice as the object. . . . [The voice] cannot be broken down into differential oppositions, since it was this dissolution that produced it in the first place. So there is no meaning that could be assigned to it, since meaning springs only from those oppositions. It is not a function of the signifier, since it presents precisely a nonsignifying remainder, something resistant to the signifying operations, a leftover heterogeneous in relation to the structural logic which includes it" (10; see also 27). The imag-

inary capture of the voice-as-remainder conveys the lack in positive form as feeling, a texture that I suggest is concomitant with accent.

9. See Lacan, "Direction" 263. Freud outlines a triadic structure in his 1912 essay "The Dynamics of the Transference," in which he states that the erotic and negative components (love and hate) must be "raised" to consciousness and detached from the person of the physician, while a third and "unobjectionable" component of the transference remains "the vehicle of success in psychoanalysis" (105). He subsequently elaborates how the analyst uses the "unobjectionable" component as a strategic ploy to defy the patient's resistance in order to put him "into the mental situation most favourable to the solution of the conflict" ("Lines" 162). Conflict is understood to be unresolvable through the mere presentation of knowledge by the analyst to the patient; rather it entails the handling of ignorance as a resistance standing over and above knowledge itself: "The patients now know of the repressed experience in their conscious thought, but this thought lacks any connection with the place where the repressed recollection is in some way or other contained" ("Beginning" 142). Later commentators have construed Freud's "unobjectionable" component of the transference in a restrictive fashion as the "therapeutic alliance" that grounds the analytic relation as a contract in reality. Although Lacan acknowledges that a working alliance is necessary for the treatment to exist, he goes further to theorize the third "unobjectionable" component as the necessary perpetuation of the analysand's supposition of knowledge in the Other, which keeps the treatment discourse going.

Freud himself thematizes the question of knowledge as alliance in his recommendations on the beginning of the treatment: "We therefore say to [the patient]: 'Before I can say anything to you, I must know a great deal about you; please tell me what you know about yourself'" ("Beginning" 134). In this way, the analyst supplies the analysand's unspoken demand: The analyst accepts the analysand's attribution of knowledge in the place of the Other, while insisting that as analyst he does not yet know. By the very act of speaking, the analysand announces *what* he does not know, and *that* he does not know.

As Lacan states in *Seminar I*, "if the subject commits himself to searching after truth as such, it is because he places himself in the dimension of ignorance—it doesn't matter whether he knows it or not. That is one of the elements making up what analysts call 'readiness to the transference.' There is a readiness to the transference in the patient solely by virtue of his placing himself in the position of acknowledging himself in speech, and searching out his truth to the end, the end which is there, in the analyst. The analyst's ignorance is also worthy of consideration" (277). Lacan recommends a poetics as solution, "not to say to him that he is wrong, since he necessarily is in error, but to show him that he speaks poorly, that is to say that he speaks without knowing, as one who is ignorant, because what counts are the paths of his error" (278). In this way, Lacan's augmentation of the third dimension of the transference as ignorance goes beyond the unobjectionable character of the reality-based therapeutic alliance and hooks it into the domain of the signifier. Again in *Seminar I* he states, "it is only in the dimension of being, and not in that of the real, that the three fundamental passions can be inscribed—at the junction of the symbolic and imaginary, this fault line, if you will, this ridge line called love—at the junction of the imaginary and the real, hate—and, at the junction of the real and the symbolic, ignorance" (271). The passion for ignorance thus engages "the unspeakable element in that which is ignored [in the demand]. In this embodied aporia, of which one might say that it borrows, as it were, its heavy soul from the hardy shoots of the wounded drive, and its subtle body from the death actualized in the signifying sequence, desire is affirmed as the absolute condition" ("Direction" 265).

Analytic work thus takes the issue of embodiment to task, with the analyst guiding the subject in the heterogeneous encounter of the symbolic and the real. As Lacan argues, "Analytic neutrality takes its authentic meaning from the position of the pure dialectician who, knowing that all that is real is rational (and inversely), knows that all that exists— including the evil against which he struggles—is and will remain always equivalent at the level of its particularity, and that there is no progress for the subject other than through the integration which he arrives at from his position in the universal" ("Intervention on Transference" 72; trans. mod.). Ethnic and racial difference in the treatment interaction introduces all the more strongly the problem of nonequivalence and particularity as the jouissance of the Other.

WORKS CITED

Abraham, Nicolas. "The Shell and the Kernel: The Scope and Originality of Freudian Psychoanalysis." 1968. Nicolas Abraham and Maria Torok, *The Shell and the Kernel: Renewals of Psychoanalysis, Volume 1*. Ed. and trans. Nicholas T. Rand. Chicago: U of Chicago P, 1994. 79–98.

Butler, Judith. *Gender Trouble: Feminism and The Subversion of Identity*. New York: Routledge, 1990.

———. "Arguing with the Real." *Bodies That Matter: On the Discursive Limits of "Sex."* New York: Routledge, 1993. 187–222.

Comas-Diaz, Lillian and Frederick M. Jacobsen. "Ethnocultural Transference and Countertransference in the Therapeutic Dyad." *American Journal of Orthopsychiatry* 61 (1991): 392–402.

Dean, Tim. "Bodies That Mutter: Rhetoric and Sexuality." *Pre-Text* 15 (1994): 80–117.

Dolar, Mladen. "The Object Voice." *Gaze and Voice as Love Objects*. Ed. Renata Salecl and Slavoj Žižek. Durham: Duke University Press, 1996. 7–31.

Dupont, Marco Antonio. "On Primary Communication." *International Review of Psycho-Analysis* 11 (1984): 303–11.

Feldstein, Richard, Bruce Fink, and Maire Jaanus, eds. *Reading Seminar XI*. Albany: SUNY P, 1995.

Fletcher, John. "The Letter in the Unconscious: The Enigmatic Signifier in the Work of Jean Laplanche." *Jean Laplanche: Seduction, Translation and the Drives*. Ed. John Fletcher and Martin Stanton. London: Institute of Contemporary Arts, 1992. 93–120.

Freud, Sigmund. "The Dynamics of Transference." 1912. Vol. 12 of *The Standard Edition of the Complete Psychological Works of Sigmund Freud*. Ed. and trans. James Strachey. 24 vols. London: Hogarth, 1953–74. 97–108.

——. "On Beginning the Treatment (Further Recommendations on the Technique of Psycho-Analysis)." 1913. Vol. 12 of *SE*. 121–44.

——. "Lines of Advance in Psycho-Analytic Therapy." 1919 (1918). Vol. 17 of *SE*. 157–68.

Fuss, Diana. *Identification Papers*. New York: Routledge, 1995.

Gordon, Lewis R., T. Denean Sharpley-Whiting, and Renée T. White, eds. *Fanon: A Critical Reader*. Cambridge: Basil Blackwell, 1996.

——. "The Black and the Body Politic: Fanon's Existential Phenomenological Critique of Psychoanalysis." In Gordon. 74–84.

Granon-Lafont, Jeanne. *La Topologie ordinaire de Jacques Lacan*. Paris: Point Hors Ligne, 1985.

Gueguen, Pierre-Gilles. "Transference as Deception." In Feldstein. 77–90.

Hall, Stuart. "New Ethnicities." *The Post-Colonial Studies Reader*. Ed. Bill Ashcroft, Gareth Griffiths, and Helen Tiffin. New York: Routledge, 1995. 223–27.

Holmes, Dorothy Evans. "Race and Transference in Psychoanalysis and Psychotherapy." *International Journal of Psycho-Analysis* 73 (1992): 1–11.

Irigaray, Luce. *This Sex Which Is Not One*. Trans. Catherine Porter and Carolyn Burke. Ithaca: Cornell UP, 1985.

Judy, Ronald A. T. "Fanon's Body of Black Experience." In Gordon. 53–73.

Klotz, Jean-Pierre. "The Passionate Dimension of Transference." In Feldstein. 91–97.

Kumin, Ivri. *Pre-Object Relatedness: Early Attachment and the Psychoanalytic Situation*. New York: Guilford, 1996.

Lacan, Jacques. *The Four Fundamental Concepts of Psycho-Analysis*. 1973. Ed. Jacques-Alain Miller. Trans. Alan Sheridan. New York: Norton, 1977.

——. *The Seminar of Jacques Lacan, Book I: Freud's Papers on Technique, 1953–1954*. Ed. Jacques-Alain Miller. Trans. John Forrester. New York: Cambridge UP, 1988.

——. "Intervention on Transference." 1951. *Feminine Sexuality: Jacques Lacan and the école freudienne*. Ed. Juliet Mitchell and Jacqueline Rose. Trans. Rose. New York: Norton, 1982. 61–73.

——. "Intervention sur le transfert." 1951. *Écrits*. Paris: Seuil, 1966. 215–26.

——. "The Direction of the Treatment and the Principles of Its Power." 1958. *Écrits: A Selection*. Ed. Jacques-Alain Miller. Trans. Alan Sheridan. New York: Norton, 1977. 226–80.

Laplanche, Jean. *New Foundations for Psychoanalysis*. 1987. Trans. David Macey. Cambridge: Blackwell, 1989.

Miller, Jacques-Alain. "Extimité." *Lacanian Theory of Discourse: Subject, Structure, and Society*. Ed. Mark Bracher, Marshall W. Alcorn, Jr., Ronald Corthell, and Françoise Massardier-Kenney. New York: New York UP, 1994. 74–84.

Muller, John P. *Beyond the Psychoanalytic Dyad: Developmental Semiotics in Freud, Peirce, and Lacan*. New York: Routledge, 1995.

Ridley, Charles R. "Pseudo-Transference in Interracial Psychotherapy: An Operant Paradigm." *Journal of Contemporary Psychotherapy* 15 (1985): 29–36.

Sarup, Madan. *Identity, Culture, and the Postmodern World*. Ed. Tasneem Raja. Athens: U of Georgia P, 1996.

Schenquerman, Norberto E. "Identification and Its Connexion with Unconscious Thought and Melodic Lines." *International Journal of Psycho-Analysis* 68 (1987): 207–12.

Schneiderman, Stuart. "Mondes impossibles et noms impropres." *Ornicar?* 37 (1987): 66–85.

Silverman, Kaja. *The Threshold of the Visible World*. New York: Routledge, 1996.

Sollers, Werner. *Beyond Ethnicity: Consent and Descent in American Culture*. New York: Oxford UP, 1986.

Spivak, Gayatri Chakravorty. "Can the Subaltern Speak?" *Marxism and the Interpretation of Culture*. Ed. Cary Nelson and Lawrence Grossberg. Urbana: U of Illinois P, 1988. 271–313.

Valéry, Paul. "Man and the Sea Shell." 1937. *Paul Valéry: An Anthology*. Trans. James R. Lawler. Princeton: Princeton UP, 1977. 108–35.

Yang, Suzanne. "Styles of the Veteran: Meaning after War." *JPCS: Journal for the Psychoanalysis of Culture and Society*, forthcoming.

6

Love Thy Neighbor? No, Thanks!

Slavoj Žižek

Psychoanalytic approaches to racism enjoy bad press
these days. Critics tend to disqualify such approaches as
"psychological reductionism," a way of explaining
racism that ignores not only racism's socioeconomic conditions but the sociosymbolic context of cultural values
and identifications that generate racist reactions to the
experience of ethnic otherness. However, a close analysis of the socioeconomic and culturalist accounts of
racism soon shows how these two approaches, far from
being complementary, simply *return to each other their own
lack*. When socioeconomic analysis fails to account for
some key feature of racism, critics evoke a need to supplement it with an analysis of the cultural context, and
vice versa. In short, both socioeconomic and culturalist
analyses of racism cannot effectively function as the two
halves that, brought together, provide a complete
account of the analyzed phenomenon. We must give psychoanalysis another chance.

The problem with earlier psychoanalytic accounts of
racism was not their abstract-psychologistic approach
(direct references to "aggressivity" and the "death
drive," which only *seem* to disregard concrete social and
cultural conditions), but their all too hasty pseudoconcrete application of specific clinical categories (paranoia,
compulsive neurosis, etc.) to racist phenomena. I contend here that if one is to account for the uncanny logic
of racism, one needs the exact opposite of this pseudoconcreteness. One must instead begin with the subject's

elementary relationship to the traumatic kernel of jouissance structurally unassimilable into his or her symbolic universe. Racism confronts us with the enigma of the Other, which cannot be reduced to the partner in symbolic communication; it confronts us with the enigma of that which, in ourselves, resists the universal frame of symbolic communication.

In his Seminar on *The Ethics of Psychoanalysis*, Jacques Lacan elaborates on the distinction between two types of contemporary intellectual: the *fool* and the *knave*:

> The "fool" is an innocent, a simpleton, but truths issue from his mouth that are not simply tolerated but adopted, by virtue of the fact that this "fool" is sometimes clothed in the insignia of the jester. And in my view it is a similar happy shadow, a similar fundamental "foolery," that accounts for the importance of the left-wing intellectual.
>
> And I contrast this with the designation for that which the same tradition furnishes a strictly contemporary term, a term that is used in conjunction with the former, namely, "knave" . . . He's not a cynic with the element of heroism implied by that attitude. He is, to be precise, what Stendhal called an "unmitigated scoundrel." That is to say, no more than your Mr. Everyman, but your Mr. Everyman with greater strength of character.
>
> Everyone knows that a certain way of presenting himself, which constitutes part of the ideology of the right-wing intellectual, is precisely to play the role of what he is in fact, namely, a "knave." In other words, he doesn't retreat from the consequences of what is called realism; that is, when required, he admits he's a crook. (182–83)

In short, the right-wing intellectual is a knave, a conformist who refers to the mere existence of the given order as an argument for it and who mocks the Left on account of its "utopian" plans leading to catastrophe, while the left-wing intellectual is a fool, a court-jester who publicly displays the lie of the existing order, but in the way that suspends the performative efficiency of his speech. Today, after the fall of socialism, a knave is a neoconservative advocate of the free market who cruelly rejects all forms of social solidarity as counterproductive sentimentalism. A fool, on the other hand, is a deconstructionist cultural critic who, by means of his or her ludic procedures destined to "subvert" the existing order, actually serves as its supplement.

Psychoanalysis can help us break this vicious fool-knave cycle by laying bare its underlying libidinal economy—i.e., the libidinal profit, the "surplus-enjoyment," that sustains each of the above positions. When Lacan uses the term *plus-de-jouir*, one has to ask a naive but crucial question: In what does this surplus consist? Is it merely a qualitative increase of ordinary pleasure? The French phrase is decisively ambiguous: It can mean "surplus of enjoyment" as well as "no (more) enjoyment." In other words, the surplus of enjoyment over mere pleasure is generated by the presence of the very opposite of pleasure—that is, pain. Pain generates surplus-enjoyment via the magic reversal-into-itself by means of which the material texture of our expression of pain (the crying voice) gives rise to enjoyment. What we find here is a nice illustration of the Lacanian formula of the fetishistic object (minus phi under the small *a*): Like the castrato's voice, the *objet a*—the surplus-enjoyment—arises at the very place of castration. Does not the same follow in love poetry and its ultimate topic: the lamentation of the poet who has lost his beloved because she doesn't return love, because she died, because parents do not approve of their union and obstruct his access to her, etc.? Poetry—that is, a specific poetic jouissance—emerges when *the very symbolic articulation of this loss gives rise to a pleasure of its own.*[1]

One can see, now, how each of the two positions—that of the fool and the knave—is sustained by its own type of jouissance: the enjoyment of snatching back from the Master part of the jouissance he stole from us, and the enjoyment that directly pertains to the subject's pain. Psychoanalysis can help the critique of ideology clarify precisely the status of this paradoxical jouissance as the payment the exploited, the servant, gets for his serving the Master.[2] This jouissance, of course, always emerges within a certain fantasmatic field; the crucial precondition of breaking the chains of servitude is thus to "traverse the fantasy" that structures our jouissance in a way that keeps us attached to the Master, that makes us accept the framework of the social relationship of domination.

This reference to jouissance clarifies the insufficiency of Hannah Arendt's notion of the "banality of evil" from her famous report on the Eichmann trial. On the contrary, Eichmann, far from being driven by some demonic will to impart suffering and destroy human lives, was merely a model civil servant doing his job, executing orders, and not minding about their moral implications, etc. Allegedly what mattered to him was the pure "boring" symbolic form of the Order, deprived of all imaginary—or, in Kantian terms "pathological"—vestiges: for instance, horrors that an execution entails, private motifs of financial profit, sadistic satisfaction, and so on. However, the fact remains that the Holocaust was treated *by the Nazi apparatus itself* as a kind of obscene dirty secret that was not publicly acknowledged, and that resisted simple, direct translation into the anonymous bureaucratic machine.

To account for the way the executioners carried out the "Final Solution," one should thus supplement the purely *symbolic* bureaucratic logic involved in the notion of the "banality of evil" with two other components: First, the *imaginary* screen of satisfactions, myths, etc., that enabled the executioners to maintain distance toward (and thus "neutralize") the horrors in which they were involved and the knowledge in which they participated (saying to themselves, for instance, that the Jews were only being transported to new Eastern camps; claiming that only a few were actually killed; listening to classical music in the evening and so convincing themselves that "after all, we are men of culture, unfortunately forced to do some unpleasant, but necessary things"; and so on).

Second, and above all, the *real* of the perverse (sadistic) jouissance in what they were doing—torturing and dismembering bodies, killing people. It is important to keep in mind how the very "bureaucratization" of the crime was ambiguous about its libidinal impact: On the one hand, it enabled some of the participants to neutralize their horror and to assume their responsibility as "just another job." On the other hand, the basic lesson of the perverse ritual also holds here: This "bureaucratization" was in itself the source of an additional jouissance. We must therefore ask, Does it not provide an additional "kick" if one performs the killing as a complicated administrative-criminal operation? Is it not more satisfying to torture the prisoners as a part of some orderly procedure—say, the meaningless "morning exercises" that served only to torture the prisoners? Didn't it give the guards another "kick" to inflict pain on their victims not by directly beating them up but in the guise of an activity officially destined to maintain their health?

Herein lies the interest of Daniel J. Goldhagen's much-discussed *Hitler's Willing Executioners*, a study whose rejection of all of the standard versions of explaining how the "ordinary, decent" Germans were ready to participate in the Holocaust brings about an undeniable truth-effect. One cannot claim that the vast majority of Germans did not know what was going on—that they were, for instance, terrorized by the minority Nazi gang, a notion propagated by some Leftists to save the German "people" from collective condemnation. They *did* know it; enough rumors and self-defeating denials were circulating. One cannot also claim that gray, dispassionate bureaucrats were blindly following orders, in accordance with the German authoritarian tradition of unconditional obedience; numerous testimonies bear witness to the *excess of enjoyment* the executioners found in their enterprise (consider the many examples of the "unnecessary," supplementary inflicting of pain or humiliation).

One cannot claim that the executioners were a bunch of crazy fanatics oblivious of even the most elementary moral norms: The very persons who executed the Holocaust were often able to behave honorably in their private or public lives, to engage in diversified cultural life, to protest these and other injustices, and so on. One cannot claim that they were terrorized into submission on the threat that any refusal to execute orders would be severely punished. Before doing any "dirty work," the members of the police unit were regularly asked if they could carry it out, and those who rejected such "work" were excused without punishment. Thus while Goldhagen's book may be problematic in some of its argumentation, its basic premise is undeniable: The executioners *did have a choice*; they were on average fully responsible, mature, "civilized" Germans.

However, Goldhagen's explanation of the Holocaust as the realization of a tradition of eliminationist anti-Semitism that was fully established as the central ingredient of "German ideology," and thus of German collective identity already in place by the nineteenth century, is too close to the standard thesis of "collective guilt." This reference to collective destiny allows Germans an easy way out: "What could we do? The collective ideological heritage predetermined us!" Furthermore, in his concrete descriptions (or, rather, in his interpretations of concrete testimonials), Goldhagen seems not to take into account the way ideology and power function at the level of their "microphysics."

One can fully agree with Goldhagen that Arendt's notion of the "banality of evil" is insufficient, insofar as—to use Lacanian terms—it does not take into account the obscene, unacknowledged "surplus-enjoyment" provided by executing orders as manifested in the "unnecessary" excesses of such executions. (As Goldhagen demonstrates, not only were these excesses discouraged by higher officers, but low-rank soldiers were often gently reprimanded for them—not out of any compassion for Jews and other Nazi victims, but because such excesses were considered incompatible with the "dignity" of a German soldier.) Despite the public character of Nazi anti-Semitism, the relationship between the two levels—the text of the public ideology and its "obscene" superego supplement—remained fully operative: Nazis themselves treated the Holocaust as their "dirty secret," as a kind of collective "private secret." This fact not only posed no obstacle to the execution of the Holocaust but served precisely as its libidinal support. The very awareness that "we are all together in it," that we participate in a common transgression, served to "cement" the coherence of the Nazi collective.

Goldhagen's insistence that the executioners, as a rule, did not feel any "shame" about what they were doing is thus misplaced: His point is that this absence of shame proves the extent to which their torturing and killing of Jews was integrated into their ideological awareness as something totally acceptable. But a close reading of the testimonials printed in his own book demonstrates how the executioners *experienced their deeds as a kind of "transgressive" activity*, as a type of pseudo-Bakhtinian "carnivalesque" activity in which the constraints of "normal," everyday life were momentarily suspended. This "transgressive" character—transgressive in regard to the publicly acknowledged ethical norms of Nazi society—

accounts for the "surplus-enjoyment" the Nazis received from excessively torturing their victims. The feeling of shame thus, again, in no way proves that the executioners were "not wholly corrupted," that "a minimum of decency persisted in them." On the contrary, this shame was the unmistakable sign of the excess of enjoyment they received from their acts.

What matters here is the gap between the public, "official," ideological texture, and its publicly unacknowledged "obscene" supplement. Indeed, one of the most painful and troubling scenes in Lynch's *Wild at Heart* (1990) brings into play this gap. In a lonely motel room, Bobby Peru (played by Willem Dafoe) exerts a rude pressure on Lula Fortune (played by Laura Dern): He invades her intimacy, repeatedly demanding, "Say fuck me!"—that is, extorting from her a word that would signal her consent to a sexual act. The ugly, unpleasant scene drags on, and when, finally, the exhausted Lula utters a barely audible "Fuck me," Peru abruptly steps away, assumes a nice, friendly smile, and cheerfully retorts: "Some day honey I will, but I gotta get going . . ."

The uneasiness of this scene, of course, resides in the fact that the shock of Peru's final rejection of Lula's forcefully extorted offer completes his triumph and deepens her humiliation. He has attained what he really wanted: not the act itself, just her consent to it, her humiliation. What we have here is rape in fantasy that refuses its realization in reality and thus further humiliates its victim—the fantasy is forced out, aroused, and then abandoned, thrown upon the victim. That is to say, it is clear that Lula is not simply disgusted by Peru's intrusion into her intimacy: prior to her concession, the camera focuses on her right hand, which she slowly spreads out—the sign of her acquiescence, the proof that he has stirred up her fantasy. The point is to read this scene in a Lévi-Straussian way, as an inversion of the standard scene of seduction, in which the gentle approach is followed by the brutal sexual act, after the woman, the target of the seducer's efforts, finally says "Yes."

How can such an ugly, repulsive figure as Bobby Peru stir up Lula's fantasy? We are here back at the motif of the ugly: Peru is ugly and repulsive insofar as he embodies the dream of a noncastrated phallic vitality in all its power—his entire body evokes a gigantic phallus, with his head resembling the head of a penis (see Chion). Even his final moments bear witness to a kind of raw energy that ignores the threat of death. After the bank robbery goes wrong, for example, he blows off his own head—not in despair but with merry laughter. Peru is thus inserted in the series of larger-than-life figures of self-enjoying evil whose best-known representative in Lynch's work is, of course, Frank (Dennis Hopper) in *Blue Velvet*, though

Frank is less intriguing and more formulaic than Bobby Peru. One is tempted here to go a step further and conceive the figure of Peru as the last embodiment of the larger-than-life figure on which all of Orson Welles's films focus:

> [Bobby Peru] is physically monstrous, but is he morally monstrous as well? The answer is yes and no. Yes, because he is guilty of committing a crime to defend himself; no, because from a higher moral standpoint, he is, at least in certain respects, above the honest and just Sailor, who will always lack that sense of life that I shall call Shakespearean. These exceptional beings should not be judged by ordinary laws. They are both weaker and stronger than others . . . so much stronger because directly in touch with the true nature of things, or perhaps one should say, with God. (Bazin 74)

We have merely replaced the names in André Bazin's famous description of Quinlan in Welles's *Touch of Evil* and the description seems to fit perfectly.

How, then, are we to grasp Bobby Peru's effectively saying "No, thanks"—one of the great ethical gestures in contemporary cinema? Perhaps we should contrast the setting of this scene in *Wild at Heart* with another well-known scene from real life—what was perhaps the most humiliating racist ritual in the American Old South: a white gang cornering an African American and forcing him to commit the first gesture of insult. While the African American was held tightly by his associates, a white racist thug would shout "Spit on me! Tell me I'm scum!" in order to extort from him the "occasion" for a brutal beating or lynching—as if the white racist wanted to set up retroactively the proper dialogical context for his assault. Here we encounter the *perversity* of the injurious word at its purest: The proper order of succession and implication is perverted. In a mocking imitation of the "normal" order I compel the victim to insult me voluntarily—that is, to assume the discursive position of the offender and thereby to justify my violent outburst. It is easy to perceive the homology with the scene from *Wild at Heart*. The point of this repulsive racist ritual is not simply that white thugs compel the well-meaning humble Uncle Tom-ish African American to offend them against his will: Both parties are well aware that the besieged African American does cultivate aggressive fantasies about his white oppressors, that he *does* consider them scum. Their pressure serves to awaken these fantasies, so that when the African American finally spits on the white thug or tells him "You're scum!" he partly lets go of his defenses—his sense of survival—and displays his true desire, at all costs. Similarly, Lula in *Wild at Heart* by saying "Fuck me," yields not only to external pressure but to her fantasmatic kernel of jouissance.

There is, however, a crucial difference between these scenes. After extorting consent from Lula, Peru in *Wild at Heart* does not pass to the act itself; on the contrary, he reads her consent as a truly spontaneous act and gently rejects it. In contrast to this scenario, the racists molesting the African American, after extorting "You are scum!" from him, use this as a legitimization to beat him up or even to lynch him. In other words, if Peru were to act like racists in the Ku Klux Klan, he would simply rape Lula after obtaining the forced consent from her. And if the KKK racists were to act like Peru, they would follow the African American's statement "You are scum!" by retorting simply "Yes, we probably are!" and leaving him alone.

The traumatic impact of these two scenes relies on the gap between the subject's everyday symbolic universe and its fantasmatic support. Let us approach this gap through another disturbing phenomenon. When it is pointed out that women often *do* fantasize about being handled brutally and raped, the standard answer is either that it is a male fantasy about women or that women experience it only insofar as they "internalize" the patriarchal libidinal economy and endorse their victimization. The underlying suggestion in these answers is that the moment one recognizes this fact of daydreaming about rape, one opens the door to the male-chauvinist platitudes about how, in being raped, women only get what they secretly wanted, their shock and fear attesting that they are not honest enough to acknowledge this. To this commonplace, one should answer that (some) women may daydream about being raped, but rather than legitimizing actual rape, such fantasies make rape more violent.

Let us consider two women, the first, liberated and assertive; the other, secretly daydreaming about being brutally handled by her partner, even raped. The crucial point is that if both of them are raped, the rape arguably will be more traumatic for the second one, *on account of the fact that such violence will realize in "external" social reality the "stuff of her dreams."* Perhaps a better way to put this would be to paraphrase Stalin's immortal lines: It is impossible to say which of the two rapes would be worse—they are *both worse*—i.e., the rape against one's attitude is, of course, in a way *the worst*, since it violates one's disposition. But on the other hand, the fact that rape occurred in accordance with our secret disposition makes it *even worse*.[3]

There is a gap that forever separates the fantasmatic kernel of the subject's being from the more "superficial" modes of his or her symbolic and/or imaginary identifications. It is never possible for me fully to assume (in the sense of symbolic integration) the fantasmatic kernel of my being. When I approach it too much, when I come too close to it, what occurs is the *aphanisis* of my subjectivity: I lose my symbolic consistency; it disintegrates. Perhaps in this way, the forced actualization in social reality of the fantasmatic kernel of my being is the worst and most humiliating type of violence because it undermines the very basis of my identity—my "self-image."

It is thus crucial to bear in mind the necessarily ambiguous role of fantasy: Fantasy underlies the public ideological text as its unacknowledged support, while simultaneously serving as a screen against the direct intrusion of the real. According to a popular myth, what Italian men want, during the sexual act, is for their women to whisper in their ears obscenities about what they were doing with another man or men; only by the aid of this mythical support can they perform in reality as proverbial good lovers. Here we encounter the Lacanian maxim *"il n'y a pas de rapport sexuel"* at its purest: Even in the most intense moment of bodily contact with another human being, we cannot simply "let ourselves go" and immerse ourselves into "that"—a minimum of narrative support is always needed, even if this narrative is not always announced. Mutatis mutandis, the same goes for religious or ethnic violence: The question is always "What voices does a racist hear when he indulges in beating Jews, Arabs, Mexicans . . . ? What do these voices tell him?"

For animals, the most elementary form, the "zero form," of sexuality is copulation, whereas for humans, the "zero form" is *masturbation with fantasizing* (in this sense, for Lacan, phallic jouissance is masturbatory and idiotic). Any contact with a "real," flesh-and-blood other, any sexual pleasure that we find in touching *another* human being, is not something evident but inherently traumatic and can be sustained only insofar as this other enters the subject's fantasy frame. When, in the eighteenth century, masturbation became a moral problem with a distinctly modern twist (see Laqueur), what bothered the moralistic sexologists was not primarily the nonproductive loss of semen, but the "unnatural" way that masturbation arouses desire—not by a real object but by a fantasized object created by the subject itself. When, for example, Kant condemns this vice as so unnatural that "we consider it indecent even to call it by its proper name," his reasoning is as follows: "Lust is called *unnatural* if one is aroused to it, not by a real object, but by his imagination of this object, that he himself creates one contrary to [natural] purpose" (178–79; original emphasis).

The problem here is, of course, that a minimum of "synthesis of imagination" (to use Kant's phrase), which re-creates its object, is necessary for sexuality to function normally. This "imagined part" becomes visible in an unpleasant experience known to most of us: In the middle of the most intense sexual act, it is possible suddenly to "disconnect." Pleasure all of a sudden can shift into disgust or into a strange feeling of distance, although nothing has changed in reality. What caused this shift was the change in the other's position with regard to our fantasmatic frame.

This is also what goes wrong in Kieślowski's *Short Film on Love*, a film on courtly love today: The hero, the young Tomek, practices voyeurist masturbation (he masturbates while observing the beloved woman through his "rear window").

The moment he passes the window's fantasmatic threshold, he is seduced by the woman on the other side of the looking glass. She offers herself to him, everything disintegrates, and he is driven to suicide.

This experience of "desublimation" is frequently depicted in the courtly love tradition, in the guise of the figure of *Die Frau-Welt* (the woman who stands for the world, the terrestrial life): She appears beautiful from the proper distance, but the moment the poet or knight approaches her too frequently (or when she asks him to come nearer so that she can repay him for his faithful service), she reveals her other side, a fascinating beauty mutating into putrefied flesh with snakes and worms crawling—the disgusting substance of life. In the films of David Lynch, too, an object turns into the disgusting substance of life when the camera gets too close to it. The gap separating beauty from ugliness is thus the very gap that separates reality from the real: What constitutes reality is the minimum of idealization the subject needs to be able to sustain the horror of the real. No wonder Beethoven's *An die ferne Geliebte* ("to the distant beloved") was central to Robert Schumann. Schumann's problem was that, in an obscure way, he desperately wanted his beloved Clara to remain at a proper distance to retain her sublime status and thus to prevent her changing into a true *neighbor,* who forces herself on us with her repellent crawl of life.

In a letter to Clara, his future bride, on May 10, 1838—at the very point when, after long years, the couple had surmounted obstacles to their union and were planning their marriage—Schumann directly admitted his secret: "Your presence here would, I believe, paralyze all my projects and my work, and this would really make me very unhappy" (qtd. in Litzmann 211). Even more uncanny is the dream he reports to Clara in his letter from April 14, 1838:

> I should tell you one of my dreams from the night before. I awoke and could not fall asleep again; I then identified myself more and more profoundly with you, with your dreams, with your soul, so that I suddenly shouted with all my power, from the deepest part of myself, "Clara, I'm calling you!" and then I heard a cruel voice coming from somewhere near me: "But Robert, I am near you!" I submerged into a kind of horror, as if ghosts met on a vast empty land. I did not call for you in this way again, it affected me too much. (206)

Do we not encounter here, in this hoarse and cruel voice ambushing us through its very intrusive *overproximity*, the horrifying weight of the encounter of a neighbor in the real of her presence? Love thy neighbor . . . no, thanks! And this split in Schumann between longing for the distant beloved and feeling estranged and repelled by her proximity by no means exposes some "pathological" imbalance of his psyche: Such an oscillation is constitutive of human desire, so that the

true enigma is rather how a "normal" subject succeeds in covering it up and nego-
tiating a fragile balance between the sublime image of the beloved and her real
presence.

Jacques Rivette's *La belle noiseuse* focuses on the tense relationship between the
male painter (Michel Piccoli) and his model (Emmanuelle Beart): The model
resists the artist; she actively provokes him, contests his approach, instigates him,
and thus fully participates in the creation of the art object. In short, the model is—
as the film's title insists—literally "the beautiful troublemaker," the traumatic
object that irritates and infuriates, rejecting its insertion into the series of ordinary
objects—*ça bouge*, as they put it in French. And what is the act of painting if not
an attempt to *depose* or "lay down" this traumatic dimension, to exorcize it by way
of externalizing it in the object of art and thus regaining our inner peace. However,
in *La belle noiseuse*, this pacification fails: At the end of the film, the artist immures
the painting in a crack between two walls where it will stay forever, unbeknownst
to the future inhabitants of the house.

Why? The point is not that he failed to penetrate the secret of his model, but
that he succeeded too well—that is, the finished product divulges *too much* about
its model, breaking through her veil of beauty and rendering visible the real of her
being, the abhorrent Thing. No wonder, then, that when the model finally gets a
view of the finished painting, she runs away in panic and disgust. What she sees out
there is the kernel of her being, her *agalma*, turned into trauma. The true victim of
the operation is thus not the painter but the model herself: She was active, by means
of her uncompromising attitude; she provoked the artist into extracting from her
and putting on canvas the kernel of her being; and she got what she bargained for,
which was precisely *more* than she bargained for—she got herself included with
the excess that constitutes the kernel of her being. For that reason, the painting had
to be concealed forever behind the wall and not simply destroyed. Any direct physical destruction would have been of no avail—one can only bury the painting and
thus keep it at bay—since what is deposed in the painting is *stricto sensu* indestructible: It has the status of what Lacan, in *The Four Fundamental Concepts of Psycho-
Analysis*, calls *lamella*, the mythical presubjective "undead" life substance, libido as
an organ (197–98).

Orson Welles was extremely sensitive to the strange logic of this "secret treasure," the hidden kernel of the subject's being, which, once the subject discloses it
to us, turns into a poisonous gift. Suffice it to quote from *Mr. Arkadin*: "A certain
great and powerful king once asked a poet, 'What can I give you of all that I have?'
The poet wisely replied, 'Anything, sir . . . except your secret.' " Why? Because, as
Lacan put it: "I give myself to you, . . . but this gift of my person . . .—Oh, mystery! is changed inexplicably into a gift of shit" (*Four* 268)—the excessive opening

up (that is, the disclosure of a secret, allegiance, obedience, etc.) of one person to another easily reverts into an excremental repulsive intrusion. Therein lies the sense of the famous "No Trespassing!" sign at the beginning and end of *Citizen Kane*: It is very hazardous to enter this domain of utmost intimacy. Suddenly, when it is already too late to withdraw, one finds oneself in a slimy obscene domain.

Most of us know from personal experience how unpleasant it is when a person of authority we deeply admire and even want to know more about grants us our wish and takes us fully into his intimacy, sharing with us his deepest trauma—the charisma evaporates and we just want to run away. Perhaps the feature characterizing true friendship is tactfully knowing when to stop, when not to cross a certain threshold and "tell everything" to a friend. We do tell everything to a psychoanalyst—but precisely for that reason, he can never be our friend.

Within the aesthetic experience, one of the names of the real is thus the "ugly." Contrary to the standard idealist argument that conceives of ugliness as a defective mode of beauty, as its distortion, one should assert the *ontological primacy of ugliness*: Beauty that is a kind of defense against the ugly in its repulsive existence—or, rather, existence *tout court*, since, as we shall see, what is ugly is ultimately the brutal fact of existence (of the real) as such (see Cousins).

The ugly object is an object in the wrong place. This does not mean simply that the ugly object is no longer ugly the moment we move it to its proper place. Rather, an ugly object is "in itself" out of place, on account of the distorted balance between its "representation" (the symbolic features we perceive) and "existence." The ugly and out-of-place is *the excess of existence over representation*. Ugliness is thus a *topological* category, designating an object that is in a way "larger than itself," whose existence is larger than its representation. The ontological presupposition of ugliness is thus a gap between an object and the space it occupies, or—to put this idea differently—between the outside (surface) of an object (captured by its representation) and its inside (formless stuff). In the case of beauty, we have in both cases a perfect isomorphism, while in the case of ugliness, the inside of an object somehow appears larger than the outside of its surface representation, rather like the uncanny buildings in Kafka's novels that are bigger inside than they appear from the outside. That is, what makes an object "out of place" is its being too close *to me*, like the Statue of Liberty in Hitchcock's *Foreign Correspondent*: Seen from extreme proximity, it loses its dignity and acquires disgusting features. The kernel of reality is horror—horror of the real—and what constitutes reality is the minimum of idealization the subject needs to be able to sustain the real.

Another way to make the same point is to define ugliness as the excess of stuff that penetrates through the pores in the surface, from science-fiction aliens whose liquid materiality overwhelms their surface (see the evil alien in *Terminator 2* or, of course, the alien from *Alien* itself), to the films of David Lynch (especially *Dune*), in which the raw flesh from beneath the surface always threatens to rise to the surface. In our standard phenomenological attitude toward the body of another person, we conceive of the surface (of a face, for example) as directly expressing the "soul"—we suspend the knowledge of what actually exists beneath the skin surface (glands, flesh, and so on). The shock of ugliness occurs when the surface is actually cut, opened up, so that the direct insight into the actual depth of the skinless flesh dispels the spiritual, immaterial, pseudodepth.

In the case of beauty, the outside of a thing—its surface—encloses, overcoats, its interior, whereas in the case of ugliness, an excess of interiority threatens to overwhelm and engulf the subject. This opens up the space for the opposite excess—that of something that is not there and should be—such as the missing nose that makes the "phantom of the opera" so ugly (see Žižek, *Enjoy* 114). Here we have a lack that also functions as an excess—the excess of a spectral materiality in search of a "proper," "real" body. Ghosts and vampires are shadowy forms in desperate search of the life substance (blood) in us. The excess of stuff is thus strictly correlative to the excess of spectral form: It was Deleuze who pointed out how the "place without an object" is sustained by an "object lacking its proper place"—it is not possible for the two lacks to cancel each other. What we have here are the two aspects of the real—existence without properties and an object with properties but without existence (see Žižek, *Metastases* 113–36). Suffice it to recall the well-known scene in Terry Gilliam's *Brazil* (1985) in which, in a high-class restaurant, the waiter recommends to his customers the best offers from the daily menu ("Today, our tournedos are really special!"). Yet what the customers in fact receive is a dazzling color photo of the meal on a stand above the plate, and, on the plate itself, a loathsome excremental pastelike lump. This split between the image of the food and the real of its formless excremental remainder perfectly exemplifies the two modes of ugliness—the ghostlike substanceless appearance ("representation without existence") and the raw stuff of the real ("existence without appearance").

One should not underestimate the weight of this gap separating the "ugly" real from the fully formed objects in "reality." Lacan's fundamental thesis is that a minimum of "idealization"—of the interposition of fantasmatic frame by means of which the subject assumes a distance from the real—constitutes our "sense of reality": "Reality" occurs insofar as the real is not (and does not come) "too close." It is easy to see here the connection with Freud, who defined reality as that which functions as an obstacle to desire. Hence "ugliness" ultimately stands for existence itself—for the resistance of reality on account of which material reality is never simply an ethereal medium that lends itself effortlessly to our molding. Reality is ugly—it "shouldn't be there" and hinder our desire. However, the situation is more complicated here, since this obstacle to desire is at the same time the site of unbearable, excessive pleasure—of jouissance. What shouldn't be there is thus ultimately jouissance itself; the inert stuff is the materialization of jouissance. In short, in the opposition between desire and the hard reality opposing its realization (bringing pain, unpleasure, which prevents us from achieving the balance of pleasure), jouissance is on the side of "hard reality." Jouissance as "real" is that which resists (symbolic integration); it is dense and impenetrable. In this precise sense, jouissance is "beyond the pleasure principle." Jouissance emerges when the very reality that is the source of unpleasure, of pain, is experienced as a source of traumatic excessive pleasure. Or, to put it another way, desire in itself is "pure" in its endeavor to avoid a "pathological" fixation. The "purity" of desire is guaranteed by the fact that it resides in the gap between a positive object of desire and desire itself: The fundamental experience of desire is *"ce n'est pas ça"*; this is not *that*. In clear contrast to desire, jouissance (or libido, or drive) is by definition "dirty" and/or ugly; it is always "too close." Desire is absence while libido-drive is presence.

All of this is crucial for the functioning of ideology in "everyday" sexism or racism: Ideology's ultimate problem is how to "contain" the threatening inside from "spilling out" and overwhelming us. Are women's periods not an exemplary case of such an ugly inside spilling out? Is the presence of African Americans not felt as threatening precisely insofar as it is experienced as too massive, too close? Suffice it to recall the grotesque racist caricature of black faces with eyes bulging out and too large a mouth, as if the outside surface is barely able to contain the inside that threatens to break through. (In this sense, the racist fantasmatic duality of blacks and whites coincides in their encounter with the formless remainder.) Is the concern with how to dispose of shit (which, according to Lacan, is one of the crucial features differentiating man from animals) also not a case of how to get rid of the inside that ceaselessly emerges? The ultimate problem in intersubjectivity is precisely the extent to which we are ready to accept the other—our (sexual) partner—in the real of his or her existence: Do we still love him or her when he or she defecates or farts? (Consider, for instance, the incredible extent to which James Joyce was ready to accept his wife Nora in the "ugly" jouissance of her existence.) The problem, of course, is that life itself *is* ugly: If we truly wish to get rid of the ugliness, we are sooner or later forced to adopt the attitude of a Cathar for whom terrestrial life itself is a hell and whose God the Creator is Satan himself, the Master of the World. In order to survive, we need a minimum of the real—in a contained, gentrified condition.

The Lacanian proof of the Other's existence is the jouissance of the Other (in contrast to Christianity, for example, where this proof is love). To render this notion palpable, suffice it to imagine an intersubjective encounter. When do I effectively encounter the Other "beyond the wall of language," in the real of his or her being? Not when I am able to describe her, nor even when I learn her values, dreams, etc., but only when I encounter the Other in her moment of jouissance. When I discern in her a tiny detail—a compulsive gesture, an excessive facial expression, a tic—that signals the intensity of the real of jouissance. This encounter with the real is always traumatic. There is something obscene about it. I simply cannot integrate it into my universe, and there is always a gap separating me from it. This, then, is what "intersubjectivity" is really about—not the Habermasian "ideal speech situation" of a multitude of academics smoking pipes around a table and arguing about some point by means of undistorted communication. Without the real of jouissance, the Other remains ultimately a fiction, a purely symbolic subject of strategic reasoning exemplified in the "rational choice theory." For that reason, one is even tempted to replace the term "multiculturalism" with "multiracism": Multiculturalism suspends the traumatic kernel of the Other, reducing it to an aseptic folklorist entity. What we are dealing with here is—in Lacanese—the distance between S and a; between the symbolic features and the unfathomable surplus, the "indivisible remainder" of the real. At a somewhat different level, Walter Benn Michaels made the same point in claiming that

the accounts of cultural identity that do any cultural work require a racial component. For insofar as our culture remains nothing more than what we do and believe, it is impotently descriptive. . . . It is only if we think that our culture is not whatever beliefs and practices we actually happen to have but is instead the beliefs and practices that should properly go with the sort of people we happen to be that the fact of something belonging to our culture can count as a reason for doing it. But to think this is to appeal to something that must be beyond culture and that cannot be derived from culture precisely because our sense of which culture is properly ours must be derived from it. This has been the function of race. . . . Our sense of culture is characteristically meant to displace race, but . . . culture has turned out to be a way of continuing rather than repudiating racial thought. It is only the appeal to race that makes culture an object of affect and that gives notions like losing our culture, preserving it, stealing someone else's culture, restoring people's culture to them, and so on, their pathos. . . . Race transforms people who learn to do what we do into the thieves of our culture and people who teach us to do what they do into the destroyers of our culture; it makes assimilation into a kind of betrayal and the refusal to assimilate into a form of heroism. (682–85)

Insofar as the historicist/culturalist account of ethnic identity functions as performatively binding for the group accounted for, and not merely as a distanced ethnological description, it has to involve "something more"—some transcultural "kernel of the real."[4] Without this kernel, we remain caught in the vicious cycle of the symbolic performativity that, in an "idealistic" way, retroactively grounds itself. It is Lacan who—in a Hegelian way—enables us to resolve this deadlock: The kernel of the real is the retroactive product, the fallout, of the very process of symbolization. Real is the unfathomable remainder of the ethnic substance whose predicates are different cultural features that constitute our identity. In this precise sense, race relates to culture as the real does to the symbolic. "Real" is the unfathomable X that is at stake in our cultural struggles; it is what makes us feel that someone "steals" our culture from us when he knows too much about it; and "real" is what makes us feel betrayed by somebody who shifts allegiance to another culture. Such experiences prove that there must be some X that is "expressed" in the cultural set of values, attitudes, rituals, etc., that materialize our way of life. What is stolen, betrayed, is always the *objet petit a*, the little piece of the real (see Žižek, *Tarrying* 200–37).

Jacques Rancière gave a poignant expression to the "bad surprise" awaiting today's postmodern ideologues of the "end of politics": It is as if we are witnessing the ultimate confirmation of Freud's thesis, from *Civilization and Its Discontents*, that after every assertion of Eros, Thanatos reasserts itself with a vengeance (Rancière 22). At the very moment when, according to the official ideology, we are finally leaving behind the immature political passions and realizing a postideological mature pragmatic universe of rational administration and negotiated consensus, free of utopian impulses, in which the dispassionate administration of social affairs goes hand in hand with aestheticized hedonism (the pluralism of "ways of life")— at this precise moment, the foreclosed political celebrates a triumphant comeback in its most archaic form of pure, undistilled racist hatred of the other, which renders utterly impotent the rational tolerant attitude. In this precise sense, the contemporary "postmodern" racism is the *symptom* of multiculturalist late capitalism, bringing to the fore the inherent contradiction of the liberal-democratic ideological project. Liberal "tolerance" condones the folklorist Other deprived of its substance (as in the multitude of "ethnic cuisines" in a contemporary megalopolis). However, any "real" Other is instantly denounced for its "fundamentalism," since the kernel of Otherness resides in the regulation of its jouissance. That is, the "real Other" is by definition "patriarchal" and "violent," never the Other of ethereal wisdom and charming customs. One is tempted to revive here the old Marcusean notion of "repressive tolerance," reconceiving it as the tolerance of the Other in its aseptic, benign form, which forecloses the dimension of the real of the Other's jouissance.

So how are we to undermine the hold of the fantasy over us? Let us approach this issue with a specific artistic problem that condenses it. When a work of art stands under the spell of the protofascist ideological universe, is this enough to denounce it as protofascist? *Dune* (the novel and especially the film) narrates the replacement of a corrupted imperial regime with a new authoritarian regime obviously modeled on Islamic fundamentalism. Is Lynch (and Herbert himself) for that reason already a misogynist protofascist? This fascination is usually perceived as the "eroticization" of power, so the question has to be rephrased as follows: How does a power edifice get eroticized or, more precisely, sexualized? When ideological interpellation fails to seize the subject—when the symbolic ritual of a power edifice no longer runs smoothly, and when the subject is no longer able to assume the symbolic mandate conferred on him—it "gets stuck" in a repetitious, vicious cycle. It is this "dysfunctional" empty repetitious movement that sexualizes power, smearing it with a stain of obscene enjoyment.

The point, of course, is that there never was a purely symbolic power with no obscene supplement: The structure of a power edifice is always minimally inconsistent, so that it needs a minimum of sexualization—of the stain of obscenity— to reproduce itself. Another aspect of this failure is that a power relationship gets sexualized when an intrinsic ambiguity creeps in, so that it is no longer clear who is effectively the master and who is the servant. What distinguishes the masochistic spectacle from a simple scene of torture is not merely the fact that, in the masochistic spectacle, for the most part, violence remains merely suggested; more crucial is the fact that the executioner himself acts as his servant's servant. In one of the most memorable noir scenes (from Nicholas Ray's *On Dangerous Ground*), Robert Ryan approaches a small crook in a lone hotel in order to beat him up. Ryan desperately shouts, "Why do you make me do it?" his face contorting in an expression of pleasure in pain, while the poor crook laughs in Ryan's face, taunting him with cries of "Come on! Beat me! Beat me!" as if Ryan aids his victim's enjoyment.

This radical ambiguity confers on the scene the character of perverted sexuality. Sexuality is not a traumatic substantial Thing that the subject cannot directly attain; instead, it is *nothing but* the formal structure of failure that can in principle "contaminate" any activity. Any activity that fails directly to attain its goal and thereby gets caught in a repetitive vicious cycle is automatically sexualized. A rather vulgar everyday example: If instead of simply shaking my friend's hand I were repeatedly to squeeze his palm for no apparent reason, he would undoubtedly experience this repetitive gesture as sexualized and perhaps obscene.

Owing to the ambiguity (reversibility) of the relation between the one who exerts power and the one subjected to it—that is, the failure of the direct symbolic exercise of power—the obverse of this inherent sexualization of power is the fact that sexuality as such (an intersubjective sexual relation) always involves a relationship of power: There is no neutral symmetrical sexual relationship that is undistorted by power. Witness the dismal failure of the "politically correct" endeavor to deliver sexuality of power—that is, to define the rules of "proper" sexual rapport in which partners should indulge in sex only on account of their mutual, purely sexual attraction, excluding any "pathological" factor (power, financial coercion, etc.). In fact, if we subtract from sexual rapport the element of "asexual" (physical, financial, and so on) coercion that distorts the "pure" sexual attraction, we may lose sexual attraction itself. In other words, the element that seems to bias and corrupt the pure sexual rapport may function as the very fantasmatic support of sexual attraction. In a way, sex as such *is* pathological.

But, again: Does the open display of the repetitive sexualized rituals of power not *sustain* the power edifice, even—and especially—under the false pretense of subverting it? Under what conditions is the staging of the hidden obscene supplement of a power edifice effectively "subversive"? In the process of socialism's disintegration in Slovenia, the post-punk group Laibach staged an aggressive, inconsistent mixture of Stalinism, Nazism, and *Blut und Boden* ideology. Many "progressive" liberal critics accused them of being a neo-Nazi band. Did they not, for instance, effectively support what they pretended to undermine by way of its mocking imitation, since they were obviously fascinated by the rituals they were staging? This criticism thoroughly missed the point. A barely perceptible but nonetheless crucial line separated Laibach from "true" totalitarianism: They staged (publicly displayed) the fantasmatic support of power *in all of its inconsistency*. The same goes for *Dune*, which is not "totalitarian" insofar as it publicly displays the underlying obscene fantasmatic support of "totalitarianism" in all of its inconsistency.

The ultimate example of this strange logic of subversion is the *Memoirs* of Daniel Paul Schreber, a German judge from the turn of the century, who described in detail his psychotic hallucinations about being sexually persecuted by an obscene God. We find in Schreber a true encyclopedia of paranoiac motifs: persecution transposed from the doctor treating the psychotic onto God himself; the theme of the catastrophic end of the world and its subsequent rebirth; the privileged contact of the subject with God, who sends him messages encoded as sun rays, and so on. A multitude of readings cover the entire span of these motifs, from seeing in Schreber's *Memoirs* a protofascist text (the Hitlerian motif of universal catastrophe and rebirth of a new, racially pure humanity) to perceiving it as a protofeminist text (the rejection of phallic identification, man's desire to occupy the feminine place in the sexual act). This very oscillation between extremes is itself a symptom worth interpreting.

In his brilliant reading of Schreber's *Memoirs*, Eric Santner focuses on the fact that Schreber's paranoiac crises occurred when he was close to assuming a position of some judicial-political power. The case of Schreber is thus to be located in what Santner calls the "crisis of investiture" of the late nineteenth century: the failure of assuming and performing a mandate of symbolic authority. So why did Schreber fall into psychotic delirium at the very moment he was about to assume the position of a judge—that is, the function of public symbolic authority? He was not able to come to terms with the stain of obscenity as the integral part of such a functioning. The "crisis of investiture" breaks out when the enjoying underside of the paternal authority (in the guise of *Luder*, the obscene/ridiculous paternal double) traumatically affects the subject. This obscene dimension does not simply hinder the "normal" functioning of power; rather, it functions as a type of Derridean supplement—as an obstacle that is also the "condition of possibility" behind the exercise of power.

Power thus relies on an obscene supplement. Put another way, the obscene "nightly" law (superego) necessarily accompanies, as its shadowy double, "public" Law. One should neither glorify this obscene supplement as subversive nor dismiss it as a false transgression stabilizing the power edifice (as, for instance, ritualistic carnivals that temporarily suspend power relations). Instead, one must insist on its *undecidable* character. Obscene unwritten rules sustain power as long as they remain in shadow. The moment they are publicly recognized, the edifice of power is thrown in disarray. For that reason, Schreber is not "totalitarian," although his paranoiac fantasy contains all the elements of a fascist myth: What makes him truly subversive is the way he *publicly identifies* with the obscene fantasmatic support of the fascist edifice. To put this another way, Schreber identifies with the symptom of power, displaying it, staging it publicly, *in all of its inconsistency* (for example, he displays its sexual fantasmatic background, which is the very opposite of pure Aryan masculinity: a feminized subject fucked by God).

Does the same not hold for the Weiningerian antifeminist tradition, which includes the figure of the femme fatale in film noir? This figure displays the underlying fantasy of "normal" bourgeois femininity—for instance, woman as inherently evil; as the embodiment of a cosmic corruption; of a fundamental flaw in the very ontological structure of the universe; as the seductress whose hatred and destruction of men expresses in a perverted way her awareness that her identity depends on the male gaze, and who therefore secretly longs for her own annihilation as her only means of liberation. There have been desperate attempts by those who obviously like noir to find in the figure of the femme fatale some redemptive qualities—for instance, a refusal to remain the passive object of male manipulation; a desire to assert her control over men, etc. These claims miss the point, which is that film noir undermines (without revoking) patriarchy simply by bringing to light its underlying fantasmatic bric-à-brac in all its inconsistency.

A recent British beer advertisement clarifies this crucial distinction. The first part of this advertisement stages the well-known fairy-tale anecdote: A girl walks along a stream, sees a frog, takes it gently into her lap, and kisses it; the ugly frog, of course, miraculously turns into a beautiful young man. However, in the advertisement the story isn't over yet: The young man casts a covetous glance at the girl, draws her toward himself, and kisses her, and then *she* turns into a bottle of beer the man triumphantly holds in his hand. For the woman, the point is that her love and affection (signaled by the kiss) turn a frog into a beautiful man, a full phallic presence (in Lacan's mathemes, the big Phi); for the man, the point is to reduce the woman to a partial object, the cause of his desire (in Lacan's mathemes, the object small *a*). On account of this asymmetry, "there is no sexual relationship": We have either a woman with a frog or a man with a bottle of beer. What we can never obtain is the "natural" couple of the beautiful woman and man. Why not? Because the fantasmatic support of this "ideal couple" would have been the inconsistent figure of *a frog embracing a bottle of beer*.[5]

This, then, opens up the possibility of undermining the hold a fantasy exerts over us in our overidentification with it: We can embrace *simultaneously, within the same space, the multitude of inconsistent fantasmatic elements*. Each subject in the advertisement is involved in his or her subjective fantasy: The girl fantasizes about the frog who is really a young man; the man about the girl who is really a bottle of beer. What Schreber (and Laibach and Lynch's *Dune*) oppose to this fantasizing is not objective reality but the "objectively subjective" underlying fantasy the two subjects are never able to assume—something similar to a Magrittesque painting of a frog embracing a bottle of beer, with the accompanying title "A man and a woman" or "The ideal couple."[6] Is this not the ethical duty of today's artist: to confront us with the frog embracing the bottle of beer when we are daydreaming of embracing our beloved?

ENDNOTES

1. The same mechanism is already at work in the everyday attitude of the abandoned lover who desperately asks himself and his friends, "Oh my God, why did she leave me? What did I do wrong? Did I say something? Did she meet another guy?" In order to render visible the modality of this questioning, it is sufficient to say to the mourning lover, directly and brutally, "I know why she left you. Do you really want to know why?" His answer will certainly be a desperate "No!" since his question, precisely insofar as it remains unanswered, provides a satisfaction of its own—that is, in a way it functions as its own answer.

2. According to Lacan, Hegel, in his dialectics of Lord and Bondsman, misses the key point: Jouissance is on the side not of the Master but rather of his servant—that is, what keeps the servant enslaved is precisely the little piece of jouissance thrown to him by his Master. Lacan's reproach to the standard version of the Cunning of Reason (the Slave who works and thus renounces jouissance, this way laying foundation for his future freedom, in contrast to the Master who is idioticized by his jouissance) is that it is, on the contrary, the Slave who has access to jouissance from his ambiguous relationship to the Other's supposed jouissance (to Master qua "subject supposed to enjoy"). See Lacan, "Subversion."

3. We have, of course, radically simplified this mental experiment's *dispositif*: The relationship between a certain type of public, intersubjective behavior and its fantasmatic support is never direct. That is, it is easily imaginable that a woman who is in her relations with men aggressive and assertive secretly fantasizes about being brutally mishandled. Suffice it to recall, from the opposite side, the familiar tale of the aggressive executive who regularly visits prostitutes and pays them to submit him to a masochistic ritual that enables him to realize his secret submissive daydreams. Additionally, it is easily imaginable that a woman daydreams about being submissive in order to conceal her more fundamental and much more aggressive fantasy. Thus one can never be sure when, and in what way, one will touch and disturb someone else's fantasy.

4. The postmodern multiculturalist merely displaces this pathos onto the allegedly more "authentic" Other: Hearing "The Star-Spangled Banner" does not thrill him. What thrills him is listening to some Native-American or African-American ritual. What we are dealing with here is clearly an inverted form of racism.

5. The obvious feminist point would be that what women witness in their everyday love experience is rather the opposite passage: One kisses a beautiful young man and, after one gets too close to him—that is, when it is already too late—one notices that he is effectively a frog.

6. The association with the famous surrealist "dead donkey on a piano" is here fully justified, as surrealists also practiced a version of traversing the fantasy.

WORKS CITED

Bazin, André. *Orson Welles: A Critical View*. Trans. Jonathan Rosenbaum. New York: Harper and Row, 1978.

Chion, Michel. *David Lynch*. Trans. Robert Julian. London: BFI, 1995.

Cousins, Mark. "The Ugly." *AA Files: Annals of the Architectural Association* (London) 28 (1994): 61–64; and 29 (1994): 3–6.

Goldhagen, Daniel J. *Hitler's Willing Executioners: Ordinary Germans and the Holocaust*. New York: Knopf, 1996.

Kant, Immanuel. *The Metaphysics of Morals*. Trans. and intro. Mary Gregor. New York: Cambridge UP, 1991.

Lacan, Jacques. *The Four Fundamental Concepts of Psycho-Analysis*. Ed. Jacques-Alain Miller. Trans. Alan Sheridan. New York: Norton, 1977.

———. *The Seminar of Jacques Lacan, Book VII: The Ethics of Psychoanalysis, 1959–69*. Ed. Jacques-Alain Miller. Trans. Dennis Porter. New York: Norton, 1986.

———. "The Subversion of the Subject and the Dialectic of Desire in the Freudian Unconscious." 1960. *Écrits: A Selection*. Trans. Alan Sheridan. New York: Norton, 1977. 292–325.

Laqueur, Thomas W. "Masturbation, Credit, and the Novel during the Long Eighteenth Century." *Qui Parle* 8.2 (1995): 1–19.

Litzmann, Berthold. *Clara Schumann, Ein Künstlerleben, Vol. I*. Leipzig: Breitkopf und Härtel, 1903.

Michaels, Walter Benn. "Race into Culture: A Critical Genealogy of Cultural Identity." *Critical Inquiry* 18.4 (1992): 655–85.

Rancière, Jacques. *On the Shores of Politics*. Trans. Liz Heron. New York: Verso 1995.

Santner, Eric. *My Own Private Germany: Daniel Paul Schreber's Secret History of Modernity*. Princeton: Princeton UP 1996.

Žižek, Slavoj. *Enjoy Your Symptom!: Jacques Lacan in Hollywood and Out*. New York: Routledge 1992.

———. *The Metastases of Enjoyment: Six Essays on Woman and Causality*. New York: Verso 1994.

———. *Tarrying With the Negative: Kant, Hegel, and the Critique of Ideology*. Durham: Duke UP, 1993.

7

Schizoanalysis of Race

Alphonso Lingis

Species Interattraction

Terns, albatross, gulls, and boobies seem to accept any member of their species on the isolated, predator-free rocky islands where they collect in vast numbers to lay eggs and raise their young. Prairie dogs, frogs, and many species of insects also seem to form undifferentiated multiplicities to which any individual of these species is attracted. Specific vocalizations—neither messages announcing warnings nor signaling food—convey their species interattraction.

A primary interattraction also exists among individuals of the human species. This attraction involves some sort of recognition, which is not a cold intellectual act that identifies individuals as members of the same species on the basis of certain distinctive traits. Nor is it the sort of intellectual operation performed by a biologist who identifies species of frogs by their spots. Nor, finally, is it simply a recognition that what we perceive resembles us.

Already by the age of ten days, when his eyes are not yet focused, an infant recognizes his mother. The infant smiles in response to his mother's smile. It is not that the infant sees the mother's smile, sees the upturned lips in visual space, and interprets them as a sign of benevolence because he knows that when he feels benevolence he smiles. He is not solving a four-term equation: $(my)S/B : (her)S/X$. There are in fact two unknowns $(my)S=X/B : (her)S/B=X$. The infant has not seen his own smile.

Identification by perception of similar traits remains derivative when the infant grows up. We can see another person as a whole pattern in visual space; we can explore this pattern from all sides by walking about it. But we see only fragments of ourselves—the lower part of our front side only. In reality, we see and recognize one another less by the outlines than by the inner lines. We recognize our acquaintances at distances too great to discern their complexions, the shapes of their bodies, their gestures. And we cannot see our own gait—not even in a mirror.

For an infant to recognize his mother as similar to himself is to feel a current of benevolence invading him. This benevolence is not simply a state in the privacy of a mind; it acts as an attraction of mother to child and of child to mother that induces corresponding motor diagrams in each—induces the facial movement of the mother on the infant. In the attraction they become alike.

Laughter ripples from an infant after the absorption of nourishment or during a warm bath. This excess energy vibrates upon itself in intensity, which is felt in the explosive exuberance of laughter. The mother who laughs with her infant also feels a surplus energy over and beyond what is necessary to hold the infant at her breast and produce the milk; she laughs and swings the baby back and forth, she gets up and dances as she rocks the baby. And the baby, looking at the mother's laughing face, laughs now in feeling communicated to him the mother's excess energies.

Our perception of the individuals about us yields traits that mark difference, even opposition, from us. You find yourself in an airport in Abu Dhabi, unable to leave the transit lounge, an American watching on television the reports of Reagan's bombing of Libya. You push to the back of the room and sit against the back wall, trying to be invisible. A mullah comes into the room, carrying a copy of the Koran and fingering his beads. He trips over your legs and catches hold of a bystander, as two bottles of Johnny Walker fall from his robes and smash on the floor in an alcoholic puddle about you. Laughter breaks out, spreading wider as people get up to see what is going on. Laughter rises and falls and rises again as eyes meet eyes. The mullah himself and you are laughing when your eyes meet.

In each individual the laughter is now no longer pleasure over the unexpected, the incongruous, but pleasure over the boundaries, the clothing, the body armor of strangers in an airport being dissolved, pleasure over the evident pleasure of others. The object or event that unleashed laughter has slipped from attention, having set in motion an intense human communication.

You and the other passengers were waiting in the transit lounge, worried about the multiple delays of your flights, now also concerned over the international incident, which worries them and you differently. The mullah appeared as a figure of constraint, wearing the holy robes of one consecrated to the law of Allah. The falling Johnny Walker bottles crashing on the tile floor unleashed laughter over the breaking of constraints and the revelation of hypocrisy. Like the titters in the grade school classroom when your awkwardness knocked over the aquarium, it is a laughter of complicity—the mullah's hypocrisy is shared by everyone in the waiting room who had been vaguely daydreaming of relaxing with a smuggled drink after the long delays of the trip. But the laughter also reveals a surplus of energy, despite the fatigue of the night and mutual awareness that the international incident will affect their lives and yours. We feel and see this surplus energy when, ten minutes later, the flight is announced and everybody grabs their bags and jumps up with adolescent gusto. If the mullah had tripped and smashed his smuggled Johnny Walkers in the toilet, he would not have laughed. Instead, awkwardness is transformed into clowning, distress into exuberance, in the transparency of each to the others. And the gratuitous release of energy in laughter gives even the mullah the sense of adolescent insouciance beyond what the bottles of Johnny Walker had promised.

We recognize whoever laughs as one like us, even if we do not see what he or she is laughing at, do not see what is funny. And we are drawn to anyone who laughs by a primary movement of sensibility. Human interattraction is not at bottom a fearful and cautious alliance for purposes of mutual defense and mutual cooperation. The human aggregate is maintained by a communication of exhilaration unleashed by an awkwardness, incongruity, or absurdity. Rather than through the identification of common perceptible traits, it is in laughter that we recognize members of our own kind and are attracted to them as they to us.

Sexuality is also the attraction in which we recognize members of our species. It is facile to say that reproductive coupling must be an innate biological mechanism that accounts for interattraction among members of the same species. Yet this coupling still requires recognition.

This attractive sensual recognition is not a matter of perceptual identification and mental judgment. The sensual recognition occurs when we find ourselves aroused by the warm thigh of the dozing passenger next to us on the bus, as we are not aroused by the warm vinyl of the bus seat itself. It occurs during rush hour when we are standing in a packed subway car and someone's fingers lightly brush the inside of our thigh. Whether we are straight or gay we feel aroused when we look over some rocks in the summer beach and see a man sprawled stroking a gleaming erection. Whether we are male of female, we feel aroused when, from an open window, we see a woman pleasuring herself on a towel spread over the summer grass. In his *Livre blanc* Jean Cocteau drew a picture of an aroused penis and labeled it "the only thing about a man which cannot lie" (38). Whatever the educated, disciplined, decent mind may say, the penis or the clitoris gorging itself affirms that Yes I like that, yes he or she is my kind, yes I am attracted to him and her.

Philosophers have explained that the identification or recognition of others as members of one's own species is realized in collaboration and language. We recognize as another human someone with whom we can speak. But speaking with someone whose tongue we understand comes to an end when he or she makes truth claims based on his or her tribal ruler, ancestor, or deity. The concept of "humanity" and of belonging to humanity is then the correlate of the practice of a rational language that makes truth claims based on evidence open to all. Species interattraction depends on the development of the esperanto of reason. But if we begin to speak to someone, it is usually because we initially recognize him or her as one with whom we could laugh together, and we speak to him or her about what we laugh and weep over. Prior to the speech that is informative and imperative, the speech that directs and orders, there is the speech that articulates what we laugh and weep over, what we bless and curse.

Martin Heidegger took practical behavior to be primary, and for him the primary *Mitsein*—the primary association among individuals of the human species— occurs when we recognize in another someone who deals with implements, obstacles, and goals that we can understand because we can put ourselves in his or her place. But do we not also recognize as members of our species all sorts of individuals with whom we have no practical projects in common, who are not collaborators with us?

The kind of practical recognition Heidegger isolates and analyzes indeed involves interattraction, but not species interattraction. Insofar as I recognize another as like me because I can plant rice, operate a computer, or pilot an airplane as she or he can, we team up to separate ourselves from the rest of the species. When the computer programmer or the pilot stumbles and laughs over an operation or an instrument she does not know or has forgotten, however, the recognition of common humanity and the attraction between us is suddenly felt.

Clans, Tribes, Nations, Races

Within many species of animal life, individualized societies that repel one another are formed. Wolves form packs of five to ten, or fifteen at most, and actively exclude outsiders from joining them. Chimpanzees, antelope, and platypuses separate into societies. In the ocean one can see vast schools of fish in which any member of the species—and often members of several species—is accepted. But one also sees gregarious clusters of fish of a species that do not merge with other clusters of that same species. Every ant belongs to a specific colony; bees will immediately kill any bee of the same species that inadvertently lands in the wrong hive.

Thus certain insects are attracted not only to one another but to a specific nest or hive. They may be attracted more broadly to a certain restricted territory. Baboon, wolf, and antelope societies have an "alpha male" that protects the society, and also often has exclusive fertility rights over all the females. In wolf packs there is also an alpha female—the sole female of the pack that will be impregnated. Flocks of crows and grouse have dominant males. Within the human species, too, there are clans, tribes, nations, and minority groups within nations. In them, the territory and paramount individuals are further separated by taboos and prohibitions surrounding a set of objects, places, beliefs, and practices that cannot be manipulated or questioned. They cannot be touched with lustful hands or laughed at. They arouse anxiety and fear.

We are, it is true, accustomed to say that what is distinctive to our society, what defines it, and what makes it repel and fight off other societies is something eminently positive: our ideals. These ideals are formulated in the rectilinear meanings of certain words: In God We Trust. We also believe in democracy, as well as the right to life, liberty, and the pursuit of happiness for all that can come about only when each is responsible for his words and deeds and responds to the words and deeds of others. These ideals are incarnated in certain persons: We respect our President, the Supreme Court, our Legislators, the members of our Armed Forces. These ideals associate certain practices with certain objects: We salute our flag. They are materialized in a place: this beautiful land bountiful from coast to coast.

These ideals, however, are set apart—and set on high—by a process of separation and expulsion. The places that individuate a society do not represent the whole territory it occupies and exploits; they are instead certain grottoes, mountains, cataracts, and cliffs that the society sets apart from all exploitation. They are taken to be inhabited by nonhuman beings, sacred and demonic powers, and also one's ancestors, whom one respects but also fears. It is not a positive knowledge of the beneficent powers of these extrahuman forces that marks them as sacred, but the ungraspableness of their natures that does not lend them to utilization and exploitation. The sacredness of America is marked by the Grand Canyon and the skies over the Great Plains that designate this land as God's country, and by Gettysburg and Iwo Jima, haunted by the ghosts of our ancestors.

A Society and Its Face

The anxiety before certain things that are not to be touched, certain beliefs that are not to be questioned, certain symbols that must not be defiled—an anxiety that maintains the separateness and sacredness of these objects, places, and practices—is communicated not the way laughter and sexual attraction are communicated, but through meaning and judgment. The meaning and sanction are localized on the face of the despot, the high priest, the Christos Pantocrator, the monarch, the President. His face is all surface, a blank wall extended over his head on which signs are inscribed, with black holes in which his subjectivity, pleasure, and displeasure turns. His face is a blank wall on which wrinkles, folds, spasms take form which are not seen in depth as issuing from the inner rivulets of the head, but are instead read and heard. The blank wall of the sovereign face detaches the skin from the pulsations, flexions, and exudations of the body, making it a surface of significance. The equivocal laughters and libidinous probings, the radiating movements and velocities of the multitude run up against this blank wall. As they do so they are sent off, recoded. His signs, his words are directives, imperatives.

His directives extend in linear progression: Each word follows the last, takes up its sense, and extends it to the next word. Of themselves, words resonate with overtones; they are polysignificant and extend rays of allusion in many directions. Setting one word after another progressively eliminates the polydirectionality, and when the series of words has come to an end, a single line of coherence and cohesion has been laid out. The radiating spread of sounds, tones, and movements coming from an animal body—as well as the multiple velocities issuing from that body composing with the movements of surrounding mammals, birds, reptiles, fish, insects, and bacteria—has been lined up into a chain of interreferential words, which extends one line of meaning. "What did he mean?" becomes an anxiety darkening the laughter and tears, the blessings and curses by which the multitude had come to communicate. Their actions and movements must now take their origin in his words.

On the blank wall—the surface—of his face, there are black holes, dark as night, in which his eyes and ears are suspended. The words of his subjects facing him—lining up their actions upon him—enter these black holes, where his pleasure and displeasure simmers. A spiral of subjectivity turns in these black holes, a movement turning on itself, affecting itself, and existing for itself. His authority is these black holes, before which lies the turbulence of a drifting desert, an undulating sea. The laughing and lustful lines of advances, radiation, rhythms, and entanglement in the multiplicity are by his look regulated, directed upon himself, sanctioned or terminated in the black holes of his look. In these black holes his look orders others and judges them. To be seen by him is to be judged. His arbitration operates by binary oppositions, dichotomies, and bipolarities. No. Yes. They will know his pleasure or his displeasure only in more words inscribed on the blank wall of his face.

The desert world about him becomes a landscape, corresponding to the landscape of his face. It becomes a blank surface upon which drifting dunes and shifting shadows become significant, material tracings of lines of meaning, a face of the earth facing him—the respondent, complement, and correlate of his own face. In the black holes of its glades and caverns, its forbidden sanctuaries, he sees ancestral and demonic passions corresponding to his subjectivity. In his face certain separated places, certain individuals, and certain forces of extrahuman powers and of ancestors become meaningful directives, authoritative, and fraught with sacred anxiety and fear.

The sovereign who faces demands of his subjects an account of themselves. They must account for what they did yesterday, what they will do today. The account codes what they are now as coherent with, consequent upon, what they did yesterday. They must make what they will do tomorrow the consequence of what they say today. Their movements must no longer be immediate responses to the rhythms and the melodic velocities about them—those of the other humans with which they move and feel in symbiosis. Their voices no longer resonate, chant, invoke, call forth; they respond to the voice of a law that orders one to move down the line. These movements and voices extend before him the blank walls of faces, extended over their heads. These surfaces are loci of words, of meanings that must command their inner rivulets and coral reefs. They are these blank walls—nothing but these subjects of discourse—coding, ordering their animal bodies. They are to exercise surveillance over their own movements in his place, subject each movement to judgment. They are to absorb the line extending outward into the black hole of their own look, where it turns in spirals of subjectivity, subjected to judgment, to yes and no. They turn to one another faces on which meaning is inscribed, surfaces with black holes from which authority surfaces.

Having a Society of One's Own, Having a Face

The separateness of the face—blank wall, all surface, lowered across the head—distinguishes a sacralized society from the open-ended multiplicity interattracted in laughter and sexual excitement. The citizens do not lean against, rub against, fondle, smell, palpate one another's bodies, feeling the streams and cascades and backwaters within; they look upon the blank wall of the faces, the pure surfaces extended over their heads. They read there the linear traits of meaning on which the zigzag, broken radiations of movements and velocities are lined up, past phases taken up and continued in the present, subsequent phases programmed in the present. In the streets and corridors, offices and factories, schools and hospitals, legs advance linearly toward goals that are fixed by a word. Lest they stray there are words written at highway intersections, on street corners, on doors, and along the corridors of shopping malls. The hands extend to words written on boxes, bottles, and cans. The fingers touch letters and words on security alarm pads, computers, microwaves, phonographs, television sets, and cellular phones. The line of posture in the torso and neck responds to words: Attention, the boss is looking; the highway cop is looking at the radar screen; the father, teacher, tour guide is looking over there; the judge, foreman, inspector, borough councilman, coach, star has arrived; the face is appearing on the screen; attention, at ease, attention, at ease.

A face is a determinate zone of frequency or probability, a field that accepts some expressions and connections and neutralizes others. It is a screen and a framework. To face someone is to envisage a certain range of things that could be expressed there, and to have available on one's own face a certain range of things one could address to the other. One sees what one might say, what one should not have said. We do not speak the English language, with all the vocabulary available in the dictionary; we speak as "a father must," as an office manager or factory foreman. To the lover we speak a puerilized language; in falling asleep we sink into an oneiric discourse, abruptly returning to a professional language when the telephone rings.

A face is where consciousness and subjectivity exist in the world. They exist in the black holes on the blank wall of the face, where the unilinear meanings and identities of others are swallowed up in pleasure or displeasure that sanction and blame. In these black holes appear the eyes, nose, ears, and mouth that subjectivize the outside environment. The movements, fluxes, rhythms, melodies, velocities of continental shelves, oceans and skies, the other animals, the plants and the viruses are covered over with the blank screen of a landscape, appearing only through meanings, and through gloom and pleasure.

Facing one another, we require responsibility. And responsibility requires integrity—that is, not only sincerity but an integration of the faculties and resources of the speaker. One has not only to respond to the greetings and questions of others, but to answer for what one says or said. The others face us as the one present now who has to answer for things said five minutes ago and yesterday and last year. "But you said . . . And you promised . . ." To speak, to say "I," is not simply to designate oneself as the one now making this utterance; it is to iterate the same term and attribute to it again utterances and deeds previously predicated of it. If we have changed, we have to reinstate what we were by way of offering a motive for what we have become. "Yes I promised to go to India with you this year, but I changed my major and have to study for medical school admissions."

To find our identity in facing others is to exist and act under accusation. It is to have to provide a coherent verbal justification for every movement that emanates from our body. We cultivate a memory in which everything is filed in an accessible system; we make what we feel and do today consistent with what we felt and did yesterday, what we were trained to do, what we were brought up to be. Know thyself! The unexamined life is not worth living! What we think and say today is a pledge and a commitment to which tomorrow, next year, the next decade are subjugated. The blank wall and black holes of the face of philistine Socrates—he who was unable to build a house or compose anything but a nursery rhyme out of Aesop's fables—prowl about all the workshops, assembly halls, and studios of the city, accusing and discrediting the carpenter, the leader of men or of women; discrediting even the artist, the poet, the composer if she cannot account rationally for every stanza of her compositions.

The temptation not to answer for something that was seen or said or done through one's organism yesterday—to attribute it to another psychic agency, and to begin to break up into discontinuous psychic sequences—is the very formula for antisocial existence. The schizophrenic is a sociopath. Multiple personality disorder is the ultimate psychosis psychiatry has to deal with, and society sees the sociopath not so much in violence—violence can be, as in the police or professional boxers, perfectly socialized—but in someone who leads a double or triple life.

The face extends down the whole length of the body. The hands and fingers no longer probe, punch, caress most other animals. Held at a distance from contact with any other body, the hands and fingers gesticulate, diagramming meaningful signals and punctuations consistent with the words set forth. The very genitals themselves, exposed in the collapse of posture and skills, the collapse of will, the dissolute decomposition of orgasm, undergoing material transubstantiations, solidifying, gelatinizing, liquefying, vaporizing, are under accusation the whole length of their existence: They must mean something; they must carry the dead weight of meaning; they must express respect for the person, the ego, the identity, the authority of the face; they must confirm the partner in his or her identity; and they must serve the population policy of the nation-state and its patron God. Everything animal in the body must be covered up, with clothing that extends the face, the blank surfaces of the business suit and the tailored two-piece suit of the career woman; with the black holes of its buttons, the blue of deliverymen's uniforms and the white of painters' dungarees, the uniforms of flight attendants and politicians' wives and university students; uniforms on which ordered words are inscribed, where black holes of subjectivity judge and sanction. The surfaces of clothing are facial; they circumscribe zones of frequency or probability—fields that accept some expressions and connections and neutralize others. The blank wall of the face detaches the skin from the pulsations, flexions, and exudations of the body, and makes it a surface of significance. The skin—the color of the skin—acquires the significance of a meaningful and responsible individual.

The Exotic, the Erotic

The individuation of a society by certain places, objects, and practices surrounded by taboos and prohibitions separates that society from other societies and the territories they wander or inhabit. It repulses them behind taboos and prohibitions, where they appear demonic—that is, separate and sacred. The sacred draws as it withdraws, mesmerizes as it horrifies. There arises the permanent temptation to encounter the stranger.

This treasonous impulse to intercourse with foreigners exculpates itself as a trafficking with them to acquire their merchandise for our own society, to explore their territory, or to master them by mastering the explorer's and anthropologist's knowledge of their haunts and practices. It exculpates itself with a policy of assimilation: Extending our Christianity, we efface their heathen idolatry; extending our democracy, we erase their communalism or tribalism; extending our science and technology, we develop them out of their backwardness. We enroll their children in our public schools and extend our responsibilities into Indian reservations and Amish and Hispanic enclaves. Today, travel among them exculpates itself as acquiring their pleasures—their beaches, ski slopes, emptied castles, and pagan temples appropriated as "world heritage," their festivals and carnivals, their cuisine—for ourselves and our society.

With these exculpations with which we justify crossing the boundaries of our society, we travel also, in every case, to flee our faces—to be anonymous, unrecognized, to dissolve the crust of our identity. We travel to be freed from making decisions and taking initiatives. We travel to break the enchainment of acts in time, to be in the instant. We travel to lose sight of the traffic patterns and the map of the future, our eye on a horizon as vaporous and nebulous as the sky. We travel under the gray clouds and invisible winds of the skies, pure realm of chance. We give ourselves over to chance encounters, chance infatuations, chance passions.

We travel to divest ourselves, to expose ourselves, denude ourselves. We travel to be out of touch with coworkers and companions, to open with all our loneliness to a campesino in a Bolivian canteen, a streetwalker in Macao, a streetkid in Marrakech. Travel is driven by a treasonous longing for friendship with strangers, an irresponsible longing for the exotic and the erotic. Sometimes the longing for travel takes us to Africa, to India, to Amazonia. Sometimes it takes us to the disco where the Puerto Ricans gather by night, to the black church on the other side of town, to the farm on the edge of the city to buy the berries the Chicanos pick.

Traveling, whether to China or Chinatown, is from the first not understanding others—that is, not lining up, for our judgment, what they are saying, what is being expressed on the lines, wrinkles, and spasms on the blank walls of their faces.

We see them defaced, desurfaced. We see the hue and grain of their skin showing through the blank wall extended for expression, for the inscription of signs; we see the shadows in diagonals and arcs on their skin. We see their heads designing profiles against the white walls, illuminous, voluminous forms against the clouds; we see the contours of their skull, cheeks, gleaming in the sun or under the glow of streetlamps, lips glistening in the damp, nostrils pulsating, hair waving in the wind. We find ourselves in a zone in which we are no longer faced, no longer live under accusation. In the black holes of their pleasure and displeasure, their passions, we see only their eyes turned to us, uncomprehending, inexpressive.

But inasmuch as we feel ourselves stared at, we lower once again the surface of our face. We feel discomfiture, displeasure at being stared at, a discomfiture that judges and sanctions. We line up the radiating, entangling lines of their movements in coherent and meaningful sequences. These lines of meaning are ones of judgment, establishing binary oppositions, dichotomies, bipolarities. What crowds in these streets! They are agitated. They are slovenly. The service is slow. They are indiscreet. They don't have a sense of privacy. This food is certainly hot. In all these lines of meaning, we reestablish our own face. The more understanding we acquire of their ways—that is, the more lines of meaning we establish—the more our faces materialize, hiding from them and from us our throbbing heads and troubled bodies.

White privilege, constructed by three centuries of West European and American expansionism, has spread around us a zone that had been as invisible to us as the normative. Being white had had no consistency; it was not having a distinctive culture, it was bland and formless. Travel makes us discover that our convictions and opinions—as well as our criteria for judgment and the practices that seem justified by them—are so many affirmations of privilege. Our expectation of efficiency and rationality in the airport, in the city traffic, in the disposal of garbage justifies our appropriation of the resources of "underdeveloped zones." Our demand for personal safety in Latin America justifies the training of the local armed forces by U.S. special-forces instructors. Our international-standards hotel justifies the consolidation of capital in export industries in impoverished lands. Our very traveling justifies the wages of those among whom we travel, wages that keep them in their plantations and slums.

We meet a newly arrived traveler, we sit down and have much to say; we lay out the lines of observation and understanding to guide the other. The newly arrived one looks at our face and learns there the order, keys, and map. This situation—whether the others are desurfaced, defaced, inexpressive, or their expressions incomprehensible, and where we stake out lines of significance, lines subjected to judgment in the black holes of our subjectivity—gives rise to violence; this situation is of itself violence. We walk among them like the despot in the camp in the steppe, visiting Mexico in Cortés's footsteps, visiting Peru in Pizarro's; we have replaced Captain Cook at the helm of the ship disguised as a cruise ship in Polynesian waters.[1]

But at the same time as we reestablish a face for ourselves in a foreign land, we feel ourselves imprisoned behind that blank wall. All the lines of meaning scrolling on it are lines of judgment, establishing binary oppositions. The Japanese are polite; we are casual. They are meticulously ordered; we are spontaneous and individualistic. These lines of meaning, these judgments materialized on the blank wall of our face, confine us, however far we go, in the normative white homeland of privilege and domination.

There then arises the craving to break out of this identity—this certification, this blank wall—to open the locus of our energies to the forces of the winds and the storms. It was already there when our hand reached out to steady an old black woman climbing aboard the bus. It gives rise to the impulse to lend our hands to those pushing the rusty car out of the mud, to take off our shoes and join the peasants planting handfuls of rice shoots in the mud of the paddy. How we long to break the tension and constriction of our faces with laughter—how we long to laugh with them!

This craving is provoked by the very defacing the others about us have undergone. Showing through the faces inscribed with expressions we do not understand, we see their profiles, the gleaming contours of their cheeks, the play of their sleek or kinky black hair over their complexions, the opaque hues of their eyes. We see their heads as we see their bodies—as substances from which are liberated movements of different speeds and retardations that compose with the speeds and retardations of the winds, of the sun rising in the sky, of the crowds, of the oxen and herds of goats. We see their heads as we see their hands and bare feet—coral-reef bodies exposed out of the protective bands of clothing.

There is extended before us the inexpressive expanses of bare skin, pulsating with minute rivers in which millions of sponges, gorgonians, polyps, macrophages swarm with so many speeds, rushes, and retardations, with minute nervous channels down which electrons and radiations sizzle and dance. Inexpressive expanses exposed to the movements and speeds of animals, reptiles, plants, winds, and scanning sunrays outside. The very inexpressiveness of this body, of this head, situates it outside the field of work and reason we can recognize, in a region shimmering and exotic. The darkness of that skin, its bronze-red or cream complexion draws us vertiginously with its condensed intensity. A carnal craving—now that the blank walls of our faces have faded away—longs to see, touch, and smell; to hold that body; to pour upon it all we have of kisses and caresses. We long to lose ourselves—to lose our identity, our separateness—in lustful encounters on tropical beaches, in the fern floors of rain forests, in the nameless back alleys of alien cities.

Traveling a long time, alone, in India, without a modem or even an address maintained long enough to receive posted mail, we seek out the only friends and lovers we will have in roadside stands, among streetkids, among hustlers. You stepped out of your hotel, an adolescent waiting in the street for you. He offers to guide you through the streets of Calcutta, show you the temples, take you to a restaurant. You soon discover that he does not know the way to the sights listed in your guidebook, that even the dates and names he offers for the builders of the temple in his quarter of the city are fanciful, and that his English is so poor you are fatigued just pretending to understand and appreciate the fanciful information he insists on spooning out to you. And of course he has no idea where a real restaurant might be. He has no education and no job, and is ashamed to take you to his home. He offers all his attentiveness and buoyant good will. He only needs and expects a few rupees to get him through another day, but he beams with affection, totally devoted to being your friend. You will laugh with this ingenuous adolescent, laugh with a warmth and freedom you have not felt since you were an adolescent. You will care for him and love him, and the ricksha wallah, and the streetwalker, more than anyone you have cared for and loved. But you will not be able to invite him to your hotel room, or take him to any restaurant but a roadside stand, knowing these things would shame him. You cannot give him the three dollars you shamefacedly spend on *Time* magazine when he is not there, knowing it would sully the friendship you realize—despite all the hermeneutics of your skepticism—he really feels for you. A friendship between you is irredeemably fractured by your not being able to forget being rich. You have not been able to leave the ghetto of your white privilege. You will leave, troubled, weeping when you do leave, knowing you have not been able to pair up for life in this friendship, thinking guiltily that your friendship has left him as destitute as before and more vulnerable to the next tourist who will only use him.

But even if you stay—in his mud village or ashram, in her slum—you cannot shorten or thicken your long nose, your big feet, your pale genitals; you cannot blacken or redden or yellow your white skin. The eroticism you feel is on your skin. The violence you feel is in your skin.

ENDNOTES

1. One day, in a market in the Baliem Valley in West Irian, I came upon two blond white-skinned children. I soon spotted their parents, thirty-five-ish and the only adults clad in cloth. They saw me too, and we sat down to talk. Yes, I am an American. They were

Canadians and not just passing through, tourists; they had been there nine years. I asked some questions about the region, its landscape, its population. I assumed they were anthropologists or perhaps engineers for some mining company. They spoke with overeager friendliness and a kind of zeal. Soon they said they staffed the Baptist Mission some thirty-five kilometers away. That left me at a loss to pursue the conversation, yet I did, thinking to learn something nonetheless about the Papuans they had lived among for nine years. "Are you having success?" I asked. "Are the people accepting the Christian faith?" "We have started a school," they told me. "There is an Indonesian army post nearby that supports us in our determination to have the children educated. And we have adopted four orphans from their tribal wars into our home." "Tell him what happened last week," the husband said. "You know"—the wife turned to me—"they have a men's house, where all the men sleep, and where they keep their idols. It is taboo to women. Well, last week I determined to defy their taboos. I went to the men's house. He"—she indicated her husband—"came with me—and entered the compound. It was midday, they were inside. One of them saw me, and they all came out, big proud fearsome warriors with boar's tusks in their nostrils and naked bodies smeared with pig grease. I calculated which was the entrance to the room with their idols and headed for it. They gave a cry and motioned wildly to me to stop. I have to say my heart was pounding but I crouched over and entered into it. Inside it was dark and smoky and the ground covered with filthy dried grass, and there was nothing there except some formless stones. All those men were standing out there, literally paralyzed with terror at what they expected their idols would do, those formless stones they had picked up in the dirt. You never saw such fear, not even in children! Well, I walked out and passed through them without one of them lifting a finger." Exhilarated, she laughed in the telling of it. No words came to my lips; I laughed with her and her husband. The two blond children returned, having explored the market; they were tired. "Do you get back to Canada regularly?" I asked. "Every two or three years," the husband said.

I tried to imagine her entering the chapel of a Catholic seminary—pushing into the sanctuary and climbing on the altar—before the prayer stalls of celibate seminarians. But in Toronto they surely visited family and savored the pleasures of restaurant food and clean dry sheets.

WORKS CITED

Cocteau, Jean. *Le livre blanc.* 1928. Trans. Margaret Crosland. London: Peter Owen, 1969.

PART II

History and the Origins of Racism

8

Ethnos and Circumcision in the Pauline Tradition: A Psychoanalytic Exegesis

Julia Reinhard Lupton

Etienne Balibar has argued that contemporary society operates under the regime of "neo-racism," a racism-without-races that promotes various forms of ethnic division under the alibi of "cultural" identity, purity, or autonomy. Such a regime co-opts and deforms for racist purposes the postwar vocabulary of liberal humanism and pluralism. Balibar links the neoracism of the *late modern* to patterns already in place during the *early modern* period:

> A racism which does not have the pseudo-biological concept of race as its main driving force has always existed, and it has existed at exactly this level of secondary theoretical elaboration. Its prototype is anti-Semitism. Modern anti-Semitism—the form which begins to crystallize in the Europe of the Enlightenment, if not indeed from the period in which the Spain of the *Reconquista* and the Inquisition gave a statist, nationalistic inflexion to theological anti-Judaism—is *already* a "culturalist" racism. . . . In many respects the whole of current differentialist racism may be considered, from the formal point of view, as a *generalized anti-Semitism*. This consideration is particularly important for the interpretation of contemporary Arabaphobia, especially in France, since it carries with it an image of Islam as a "conception of the world" which is incompatible with Europeanness. (23–24)

Balibar derives contemporary *neoracism* from deep structures of anti-Semitism, including not only anti-Jewish movements but the anti-Muslim tendencies characterizing recent politics and political fantasy in Western Europe, the Balkans, America, the Middle East, and Asia.

This essay uses Balibar's argument to study the *protoracism* binding anti-Jewish and anti-Muslim thought in the Christian West in the era before the advent of biological racism. Central to the imaginary topography of this protoracism is the ritual of circumcision mandated in the Hebrew Bible, negated in Christianity, and maintained by Jews and Muslims. I focus especially on the writings of St. Paul, the Jew-turned-Christian who transformed circumcision from a material rite identifying the Israelites as a separate people into a symbol of a universal Church that would dissolve all national differences.

The legacy of Paul to Western national discourse divides between his urge to repeal the laws of contemporary Judaism in the name of a global Christianity, on the one hand, and to grant historical significance to the Jews as a people on the other. These positions stem equally from Paul's sense of the Jews as an *ethnos*, a tribe or nation bound by a common language, customs, and genealogy over time and space. The major sign of the Jews' "ethnic" status in Paul's writings is the rite of circumcision—a recurrent concern in Paul's conflicted fashioning of a gentile mission out of his own training in the protorabbinic Judaism of the Pharisees. Physical yet not physiological, genealogical but not genetic, circumcision marks the Jews off as a distinct people without being a "racial" indicator in the modern sense of an inherited trait. Paul's letters, I argue, perform an "ethno-graphy," a fundamental graphing of the *ethne* or "nations" that laid the foundations for a modern theory of biological race that has since effaced it. Paul used the idea of the Jews as an *ethnos* (nation, people) to describe the gestalt of a discrete historical phase in the past and a set of neutral cultural practices in the present. In European Christendom, increasingly distanced from the Jewish grounds of Paul's life and thought, the *ethnos* flagged by circumcision increasingly came to denote a preserve of atavistic, dangerously literalist rites whose resistance to sublation challenged the dialectical narrative of Western history.

Psychoanalysis plays a key role in my exegetical analysis of protoracial thought. First, psychoanalysis is a "Jewish science," with its own debts and investments in religious discourse. Additionally, psychoanalysis offers a hermeneutics of the psychosomatic, of the interface between the body as a biological organism and the body as the site of symbolic organization—the same vexed region that circumcision has flagged in the Western ethnohistorical imagination. I take psychoanalysis as an account of social symbolization and its symptomatic fallouts, the products and remainders of the dialectical processes of subject- and nation-formation. In Jacques Lacan's vocabulary, circumcision in Judaism functions as an act of *alienation* in a network of legal and kinship relations, and as an act of *separation* that particularizes for the subject the cut of trauma. Paul's resignification of circumcision idealizes this double movement by subsuming the "ethnic" specificity of the Jewish rite within the universal mandate of world Christianity in order to create the autonomous subject of faith and conscience. This powerful set of sublations, however, in turn generates its own disturbing remainders, notably isolating circumcision as the marker of ethnicity par excellence, a persistent scar of nonhistoricized trauma faulting the symbolic fabric of Western historical consciousness.

Circumcision, First Cut: Genesis 17

In Genesis God establishes His covenant with Abraham by commanding the rite of circumcision:

> This is My covenant, which ye shall keep, between Me and you and thy seed after thee: every male among you shall be circumcised. And ye shall be circumcised in the flesh of your foreskin; and it shall be a token of a covenant betwixt Me and you. And he that is eight days old shall be circumcised among you, every male throughout your generations, he that is born in the house, or bought with money of any foreigner, that is not of thy seed. . . . And the uncircumcised male who is not circumcised in the flesh of his foreskin, that soul shall be cut off from his people; he hath broken My covenant. (Gen. 17: 10–14)

Rabbinic commentaries on this passage insist on the genital location and physical cut of circumcision. Although Jeremiah speaks of "uncircumcised" hearts and ears (Jer. 9:25; 6:10) and Moses is said to have "uncircumcised lips" (Exod. 6:12), these other sites of circumcision surface in the commentaries only as factors to be rejected, with most rabbis concluding, in the words of the eleventh-century scholar Rashi, that circumcision must occur in "that place where the distinction between male and female is evident."[1] Circumcision marks the organ through which Abraham will become "the father of a multitude of nations" (Gen. 17:4); according to Sforno, "Since the token is connected with the organ whereby the species is perpetuated, it symbolized the eternity of the covenant."[2] Yet as the commandment is a nation-marking sign linking generations across time and space without being a genetic trait, the rabbis agree that even a male who is "born circumcised" (without a foreskin) must still have blood drawn.[3] Unlike a birthmark, the scar imposed by ritual manifests the maintenance of laws not themselves natural or even moral as the necessary foundation of the nation.

The commandment's nation-building emphasis continues to guide its scope. If circumcision simply instantiated a family connection, then the commandment would apply only to Abraham and the offspring promised to him and Sarah. Yet the passage specifies a larger circle: Abraham's children by other women (Ishmael, born of the handmaid Hagar), and any sons born to slaves with no genealogical ties to Abraham; to this group, commentators would add converts to Judaism (*gerim* or proselytes).[4] Circumcision therefore functions as the sign and mechanism of *naturalized citizenship*, ratifying membership in the nation, whether attained through birth or other means. Additionally, the consequences stemming from failure to circumcise entail neither eternal damnation nor moral atrophy but excision from the group: "the uncircumcised male . . . shall be cut off from his people."

Circumcision seals two sides of the covenant: God promises children to Abraham and Sarah, while Abraham agrees to mark his existing household and himself, and to oblige all his progeny to do the same. Abraham's future is "under contract": both promised to him and then committed by him to uphold the human side of the agreement. As such, *brit milah*, the "covenant of circumcision," has a performative function, operating like a signature or an official imprimatur to validate the agreement between Abraham and God. If Abraham doesn't sign the contract, the goods won't be delivered. Circumcision makes the contract effective, for it is an expression not so much of *blind faith* as of *good faith*, a willingness to execute one's part of the bargain to get the deal going.[5] Forfeiture of the agreement between Abraham and God abrogates the very ground or "paper" of the contract—the bodies of future generations.

Does God's promise of "a multitude of nations [*goyim*]" apply only to Israel (as Rambam argues) or also to Abraham's other progeny, the descendants of Ishmael and Esau (as Rashi suggests)?[6] Although the dominant tradition favors a restrictive reading of the passage, the plurality of "nations" within the people of Israel guarantees that the latter cannot be defined by blood lines alone. These "nations" include the half-brothers, neighbors, strangers, proselytes, and slaves who enter the community through circumcision. Thus circumcision plays out the tension, characteristically Jewish, between the unique election and identity of Israel as a nation apart and the potential universality of its historical example, ethical code, and single God. From the Jewish perspective, Israel's significance to the nations of the world can be attained only through strictly maintaining its borders; it is a question not of choosing the world or the nation, but of opening up to the world precisely by obeying the ritual laws distinguishing the nation. Only through its unique identity, maintained by its special laws, can Israel assume a larger historical function.

This double function of circumcision at the level of national identification recurs within the individual drama of *brit milah* as a rite both alienating the subject within the social group and generating a being not fully assimilated by the group. Lacan glosses Abraham's sacrifice of Isaac when making this point:

> Here may be marked the knife blade separating God's bliss from what in that tradition is presented as his desire. The thing whose downfall it is a matter of provoking is biological origin. That is the key to the mystery, in which may be read an aversion of the Jewish tradition concerning what exists everywhere else. The Hebrew hates the metaphysico-sexual rites which unite in celebration the community to God's erotic bliss. He accords special value to the gap separating desire and fulfillment. The symbol of that gap we find in the same context of *El Shadday*'s [God's] relation to Abraham, in which, primordially, is born the law of circumcision, which gives as a sign of the covenant between the people and the desire of he who has chosen them what?—that little piece of flesh sliced off. It is with that *petit a* . . . that I shall leave you. (*Television* 94)

Circumcision bars the subject from the unsymbolized pleasure or "bliss" that Lacan calls *jouissance*, "provoking the downfall of biological origin" by introducing lack, signified by the loss of "that little piece of flesh," the foreskin. During the rite of circumcision, the son receives a name linking him to the history of his people; by the proper name's expropriating cut, circumcision removes the infant from the realm of nature and situates him in a network of social and linguistic relations. Circumcision resembles what Lacan elsewhere calls a *point de capiton* or "buttoning point," a primal or master signifier fastening the subject into the symbolic order through a real trauma, in this case the cut of the knife that forever inscribes his name, conferred by the father, on the infant's body.[7] Fashioning the physical penis into a signifying element through a tiny cut, a literalized protocastration, circumcision interpellates the subject within the social and symbolic system called Israel.

In the same passage, Lacan identifies the discarded foreskin with the *petit a*, his coinage for the residual objects of jouissance left over from the cancellation of "bliss" by "desire" (a function of symbolic lack), which the subject's entry into language engenders. Lacan associates the *objet a* with pieces of "the real"—nonsensical fragments of unassimilated enjoyment. The sudden reemergence of these pieces within the social scene can momentarily surprise the alienated subject into a mode of being that is beyond his function as a symbolic placeholder. Lacan calls this subjective possibility "separation." In this process, "encounters with the real"—through the revisitation of trauma—momentarily push the subject out of the symbolic order that captures and defines it.[8] In Bruce Fink's gloss, separation involves the refinding in fantasy of a portion of the bodily jouissance that is given up in alienation: "this second-order jouissance takes the place of the former 'wholeness' or 'completeness,' and fantasy—which stages this second-order jouissance—takes the subject beyond his or her nothingness, his or her mere existence as a marker at the level of alienation, and supplies a sense of being" (60).

As one of the elements causing separation, circumcision introduces a unique point of traumatic nonsignification informing subjectivity. This process is visible in the functioning of the proper name, which not only graphs the subject in the symbolic but fosters an element of the nonsensical; this phenomenon attaches indexically to a particular referent, but is not mobilized within a signifying order (Fink 57). The proper name conferred in circumcision is both the master signifier and scar left by signification, a word-thing denoting the subject as a foreign knot that the national tapestry does not fully contain. This double movement of alienation and separation, which *brit milah* initiates, recapitulates the paradox of Israel's international nationhood. The "downfall of biological origin" that circumcision effects cancels not only bodily bliss but the purely genetic or racial definition of the nation, which the contractual act of circumcision rules out. This alienation constitutes the national subject in a legal framework, denaturing the uncut penis in order to produce a naturalized—that is, purely legal—covenantal identity. Yet insofar as circumcision remains a scar on the body and not an act "in name only" (unlike a loyalty oath, say, or a social security number), it continues to measure the difference between the subject and the symbolic, the persistent nonidentity between Israelites and Israel.

Circumcision separates the individual from the nation in the very act of joining him to it, naming his strangeness *to* the symbolic in the moment of estranging him within it. Through circumcision, the "people of Israel," a legally constituted and maintained community, may include within it "a multitude of nations," of nonself-identical elements that make up its circumcised heart. In this sense, every Israelite is a Gershom, a "stranger in a strange land," adopted by his own family and converted to his own religion.[9] In Judaism, circumcision is not opposed to Israel's world significance as a "light onto the nations." Rather, circumcision is a rite lying at the very center of this significance, articulated by the cut of covenant that determines the boundaries—at once absolutely exclusive and absolutely permeable—of the Chosen People.

Circumcision, Second Cut: Romans 4

In the first chapter of his Epistle to the Romans, Paul establishes his audience along with one of his letter's basic themes, the equality of nations in Christ: "I am under obligation both to Greeks and to barbarians, both to the wise and to the foolish . . . it is the power of God for salvation to every man who has faith, to the Jew first and also to the Greek" (Rom. 1:14–16).[10]

Struggling to accommodate and discount the legal and national claims of the Jews, Paul's Epistle likely reflects the division of the Roman congregation between Greek and Jew as well as his own conflicted position as an educated, observant Pharisee who accepted Jesus as the "end of the law" (Rom. 10:4). Accordingly, Paul's address doubly maps the world's populations. He first expresses his obligation "to Greeks and to barbarians," taking up the Hellenistic division of peoples between civilized Greek-speakers and inarticulate non-Greeks, an opposition then echoed by the Hebraic distinction between Jews and gentiles, the Chosen People and "the nations" (*ethne*) at large. Paul's careful phrasing of the order of God's salvation, "to the Jew first and also to the Greek," recognized the historical priority of the Jews in the reception of Revelation yet also insisted on the necessary dissemination of that message to the second, larger group of Greeks. Like the Epistle in general, these lines acknowledge and reconcile the claims of both groups in the new church by presenting faith as the common sign of righteousness for all Christians.

Paul's letter includes an extended commentary on Genesis 17, in which Paul points out that the Hebrew Scriptures record Abraham's faith (Gen. 15:6) before introducing the covenant of circumcision (Gen. 17).[11] From this he concludes:

> We say that faith was reckoned to Abraham as righteousness. How then was it reckoned to him? Was it before or after he had been circumcised? It was not after, but before he was circumcised. He received circumcision as a sign or seal of the righteousness which he had by faith while he was still uncircumcised. The purpose was to make him the father of all who believe without being circumcised and who thus have righteousness reckoned to them, and likewise the father of the circumcised who are not merely circumcised but also follow the example of the faith which our father Abraham had before he was circumcised. . . . [Justification] depends on faith, in order that the promise may rest on grace and be guaranteed to all his descendants— not only to the adherents of the law but also to those who share the faith of Abraham, for he is the father of us all, as it is written, "I have made you the father of many nations." (Rom. 4:9–17)

Paul is careful to include the Jews as well as the gentiles within the "nations" promised to the first patriarch. As we have seen, the prophetic and rabbinic traditions debated the extent to which the *goyim* in this passage applied to the offspring of Ishmael and Esau; moreover, the exclusive formulation (nations = Israel) favored in Jewish exegesis of this passage nonetheless includes circumcision as a rite of national initiation that slave, proselyte, and native son all share.

By identifying the *goyim* promised to Abraham with the gentile nations, Paul resolves this Jewish tension in the most inclusive direction.[12] In doing so, however, he changes forever the status of circumcision as the ritual trace that institutes Israel as a nation elected by God. Now faith, with or without circumcision, establishes true inclusion among God's elect, which is no longer conceived as a national unit at all. As a result, the "nations" promised to Abraham shift in Paul's Epistles from the naturalized heterogeneity of the rabbis' Israel to a truly transnational conception of the church as that group in which there is no "Greek and Jew, circumcised and uncircumcised, barbarian, Scythian, slave, free man, but Christ is all, and in all" (Col. 3:11). Or, as Paul writes in Romans, in Christ "there is no distinction" (3:22): No *ethnicity*, no definitive nationality, inheres in the *ethne*, the nations of God.

If this and other Epistles celebrate the equality of the *ethne*, however, the Paul of Romans reserves a quotient of *ethnos*-ity for the Jews themselves. Identifying himself as a Jew to the Jews in his audience, Paul writes, "They are Israelites, and to them belong the sonship, the glory, the covenants, the giving of the law, the worship, and the promises; to them belong the patriarchs, and of their race [*sarx*: flesh] . . . is the Christ" (Rom. 9:4–5). Paul does not completely dissolve the national difference between Jew and Greek within the new covenant of Christ, but translates the ethnic particularity of Israel into the operative core of a *philosophy of history* that is also a *literary hermeneutics*. Israel *is* special, Paul asserts, its privilege resting in its historical function, its role in laying the genealogical and prophetic lines that Christ's death and resurrection have realized. Paul manages to salvage what Hans Hübner calls "the theological relevance [of] the history of Israel" (56) by granting the Jews a unique place in God's unfolding plan.

The record of Israel's historical function is the Hebrew Bible, which presents itself to the Christian reader as a vast tissue of references to Jesus. Paul's insistent linking of historiography and hermeneutics ensured that the Hebrew Bible, reconceived as the "Old Testament," was securely woven into the literary and historical impulses of Christianity, which (unlike Paul himself) so often has understood nothing, or less than nothing, about Judaism per se.[13] Paul's historicizing of Judaism into a prior epoch and an "Old" Testament, however, was also designed to negate the legal foundations of Israel as a distinctive nation or people. In Paul's understanding, Israel's *history* subsumes, explains, and qualifies Israel's *law*, which represents one element in an epochal scheme of progressive re-inscription rather than a governing body sustained by the observance of scriptural commandments.

Paul's reading of circumcision exemplifies this programmatic revaluation of Jewish law within an historical hermeneutics. In the Torah, circumcision functioned as the "token of a covenant [*l'aot brit*]" between God and Abraham, the word "token" recalling the use of official seals to secure and authenticate documents, "equivalent to the modern use of signatures" (*Eerdman's* 919).[14] The performative language indeed remains in Paul's gloss, in which circumcision appears as a "sign [*semeion*] or seal [*sphragis*]" of faith. Yet Paul subsumes the performative emphasis within a semiotic one, a move signaled by his placing "sign" before "seal," *semeion* before *sphragis*, when recalling the imagery of tokens. Circumcision no longer "seals" the covenant as a contract brought into effect by a positive act, becoming instead the external sign of internal faith. Rather than bringing a relationship into being through ritual performance, circumcision signifies a pre-existing state, replacing the performative relationship with the hermeneutic distinction between surface and depth.

Once again, hermeneutics implies historiography, insofar as the semiotic division between sign and meaning fosters a temporal distinction between prefiguration and fulfillment. In the case of circumcision, what was once binding law becomes the powerful but limited metaphor of an era-defining event; our access to this resignification of circumcision is the changing meaning of Scripture as it moves from one epochal reading community to another. In Romans, for instance, Paul famously spells out the metaphoric value of circumcision: "Circumcision indeed is of value if you obey the law, but if you break the law, your circumcision becomes uncircumcision. . . . For he is not a real Jew who is one outwardly, nor is true circumcision something external and physical. He is a Jew who is one inwardly, and real circumcision is a matter of the heart, spiritual and not literal" (Rom. 2:25–29).

In Romans, unlike in the harsher judgment of Galatians, circumcision does not sever man from Christ (Gal. 5:4). Perhaps more devastating from a Jewish point of view, however, circumcision in Romans *simply doesn't matter*, since "real circumcision"—and with it "real" Judaism—is now an internal state of faith in Christ rather than a national identity. As Daniel Boyarin concludes, although Paul's project "is not anti-Semitic (or even anti-Judaic) in intent, it nevertheless has the effect of depriving continued Jewish existence of any reality or significance in the Christian economies of history" (32). Romans renders circumcision *adiaphora* or indifferent, not counting toward justification, a ruling granting circumcision merely a local, "cultural" status, as the sign of one *ethnos* among others but no longer a legally binding statute linking a single nation to God.

Hence Paul says to the Corinthians, "To the Jews I became as a Jew, in order to win the Jews. . . . To those outside the law, I became as one outside the law" (1 Cor. 9:20–21). Paul reduces the Jews' divinely prescribed laws to a regional rhetoric that the missionary can use in his task of persuasion. This "cultural" determination of Jewish *ethnos* corresponds synchronically to the epochal (or diachronic) definition of Judaism: Whereas in the historical register, Judaism represents a superseded moment in the story of God's grace, in the spatial dimension, Judaism manifests itself as a set of local practices with their own limited value, as long as they do not conflict with the new historical order. If Paul's Epistles aim to dissolve *ethnos* in the universal ideal of Christianity, in Romans *ethnos* nonetheless finds a place in this new universe by giving both a past historical period and an existing linguistic and social group a limited, relative coherence within a larger providential scheme. This place would become "culture" in its "ethnic" determination, neither fully natural nor fully artificial—the peculiar crossing of genealogy and custom, of race and civilization, marked by circumcision.

Circumcision, Third Cut: After Paul

In *The Ethics of Psychoanalysis,* Lacan discovers in Romans the psychoanalytic theory of desire: "Is the Law the Thing? Certainly not. Yet I can only know of the Thing by means of the Law. In effect, I would not have had the idea to covet it if the Law hadn't said: 'Thou shalt not covet it.' But the Thing finds a way by producing in me all kinds of covetousness thanks to the commandment, for without the Law the Thing is dead" (83).

Lacan alludes here to the famous passage in Romans in which Paul links knowledge of "sin" to the laws prohibiting it: The law, Paul argues, teaches us the very sins it would prevent us from enjoying (Rom. 7:7–11). For Lacan, the ethics of psychoanalysis involves finding "an erotics . . . above morality," a "relation to *das Ding* somewhere beyond the law" (84). Lacan aligns his own project with the Pauline historical dialectic insofar as Paul too is looking for a subjective position beyond the law—beyond interdiction and commandment but also beyond group or national identification, the limiting traits of *ethnos*. Pauline faith liberates the individual from the collective Law of Judaism, just as Lacan's real-ized subject falls out of the alienating chain of signification and into another mode of being.

Lacan's "beyond," however, unlike that of Paul or Hegel, always implies the residue, rather than the telos, of the dialectical process. Hence Lacan substitutes Paul's "sin" with "the Thing": In Lacan's vocabulary, *das Ding* names both the archaic ground of jouissance before the intervention of symbolization and the by-products of social signification, the "*jouis-sens*" or enjoyment-in-meaning that collects in the interstices of symbolic ordering. These remainders and side effects of signification materialize as the *objet a*, the "little piece of flesh" whose excision precipitates the subject's "separation," yet the same effects recur in the most destructive social fantasies (those of fascism and racism, for example). Whereas for Paul, the subject of faith rises to a certain autonomy (from *autos*, self, and *nomos*, law), for Lacan, the subject of separation answers to a resurgent heteronomy, insofar as separation occurs in relation to an object other than the self, not subjected or reflected by the self, an opaque Thing "causing" desire as its resistant alterity rather than residing in desire as its commodified lure.

However, Lacan refuses to cast psychoanalysis as the secular therapeutics par excellence, happily adapting the ego to the instrumental needs of capitalism in a world defined by the death of God. I would argue that Lacan instead fashions psychoanalysis as a science of the "discontents" of secularization, itself an historical and hermeneutic process in the dialectical tradition of Paul. Psychoanalysis ferrets out the fortuitous remainders of enjoyment that give social structures their obscene, obsessive, or paranoid character, tracking the unsettling objects left over by the historicohermeneutic progress of the Western tradition as it proceeds from classicism to Judaism and on to Christianity and secular modernity. Psychoanalysis uncovers the pieces of religious bliss deposited in modern social and political forms, using the hermeneutic model of Western historiography to expose the religious grounds of secular life. But psychoanalysis also moves beyond the demystifying drive of secular hermeneutics by finding in the realia of religious non-sense—the unspeakable name of God, the discarded foreskin, the Burning Bush, and the face of the neighbor—the cause of its own interpretive desire, the singular scriptural signifiers that traumatically create the texture of Western thought. By confronting these signifiers beyond the field of religious signification, in the arena of their secular evacuation, psychoanalytic discourse reconfigures as much as it interprets the epochal fantasy of modern historiography, reencountering a purified heteronomy, a "law of the Other," that exceeds the Pauline and Kantian calls to autonomy without restoring a theocentric principle. The moniker, "Jewish science," should imply not a secularized Jewish hermeneutics, a midrash-for-therapists, but the recovery and reorientation of the potent kernels of Jewish law that have survived within and beyond the Christian and secular institutions that displaced them.

In the discourse of nations unfolding between Paul's Epistles and their later sublations (Shakespeare, Hegel, Freud, and Lacan), Judaism represents not only the historic origin of Christendom and its secular expansion but the troubling exposure of that process, insofar as Israel exists beyond its historical abrogation. Recall that in Romans Paul's historicocultural definition of Judaism within the split registers of space and time presented Israel with a forced choice: Be either theologically significant but a thing of the past, or a present phenomenon but theologically irrelevant. The problem, however, was that Judaism continued as a religious and national practice into the Christian era. Although not yet an urgent problem in the eschatology of the early Church, Judaism's tenacity increasingly embarrassed or scandalized Christian historiography as it hardened into a set of quasipermanent institutions. Historically vital yet theologically unconverted, the modern Jew became the sign of an historical contradiction, a mote in the Pauline vision's dialectical pattern. In later Christendom, disengaged from Paul's own passionately personal contact with Judaism, the historically economized and religiously tolerated *ethnos* of the Jews that Paul defined became a negative ethnicity, no longer benignly indifferent, but dangerously different and hence increasingly unbearable.

In the Renaissance, the ranks of the circumcised included Muslims as well as Jews. Judaism and Islam lived close at hand to Christianity. Both Judaism and Islam ascribed to monotheisms at least as strict as Christianity's and stemmed from the same Abrahamic lineage. The three groups are, in the Muslim phrase, "People of the Book," proximate religions organized around revealed Scriptures that share many of the same prophets and patriarchs. In Christian exegesis, the Jew and the Muslim were linked through the figure of Ishmael. For Paul, Ishmael had embodied carnal Israel, recalcitrantly maintaining the law despite its abrogation:

> For it is written that Abraham had two sons, one by a slave and one by a free woman. But the son of the slave was born according to the flesh, the son of the free woman through promise. Now this is an allegory: these women are two covenants. One is from Mount Sinai, bearing children for slavery; she is Hagar. Now Hagar is Mount Sinai in Arabia; she corresponds to the present Jerusalem, for she is in slavery with her children. (Gal. 4:22–25)

With the rise of Islam, the figure of Ishmael as a negative type of the Jew could be transferred onto Muhammad, an act authorized by Arab and then Islamic appropriations of Ishmael for their prophetic genealogies. Although Ishmael and Hagar are the most frequently exploited negative types displaced from Judaism to Islam, Esau, Pharaoh, and Herod were also used to promote the figural coupling of Jew and Muslim as the carnal children of Abraham facing each other across the world-historic break of the Incarnation.[15]

Islam, youngest of the three Abrahamic religions, came to represent to Christianity a type of Judaism after the fact, a redoubling of Jewish intransigence to the Christian revelation. As such, Islam executes a second, even crueler blow to Christianity's historical vision of epochal succession, since modern Judaism (from the Christian perspective) is merely a residual phenomenon, a stubborn carryover from an earlier moment, while Islam from its very inception administered its proselytizing mission in full knowledge of Christian teachings. The rapid expansion of Islam, however, contrasted with Judaism's dispersed, sequestered, and inward-looking communities. Islam rejected Jewish particularism in favor of Christian universalism; like the rulers of European Christendom, the Arab and then Turkish powers used the theme of spiritual equality among the nations to support its missionary, imperial, and commercial projects (Lewis 1–28). In the Pauline schemes of the Renaissance, Islam represents a double scandal, the catastrophic bastardization of both Christian universalism—through the seductive danger of the Islamic world mission—and Jewish particularism, represented by Muslim allegiance to ritual laws.

An Elizabethan polemical work, the anonymous *Policy of the Turkish Empire* (1598), lays out the status of the law in the three religions:

> For as the Iews had a particular lawe given unto them and published by God himselfe in mount Sinai . . . So have the Turkes (in imitation of the same) certaine lawes and precepts or Commandements laide downe in their Alcoran . . . whosoever shal transgressse or violate any of them, is held by their law to be a most sinfull and wicked person. . . . Contrariwise, they do believe that who so doth observe and keepe those commandments . . . he shall be sure to be saved: be he either Turke or Christian. Which argueth that their confidence and hope of salvation consisteth chiefely in the pietie and merite of their vertuous life, and good deedes: And that they doe not much differ in that point from the opinion of some Christians, who do attribute their salvation unto their merites. (15)

The passage carefully sets up Islamic law as a version of the Torah ("in imitation of the same") and an alienating mirror of the Catholic Church. In this, the author follows the confessional analogies of Luther, who frequently links "the Pope, the Turks, the Jews, and all the sectarians" (*Works* 26: 26).[16] And in a move familiar from both Paul and Luther, the author of the *Policy* singles out circumcision as a rite that, within the epoch preceding the birth of Christ, was "a most holy and sacred sacrament" but "is nowe converted . . . to a most idle and vaine ceremony" among Jews and Muslims (22). As a neighboring preserve of misunderstood and outdated laws, a parodic pastiche "patched up . . . out of the olde and new Testament" (*Policy* 2), Islam was linked to Judaism through circumcision.[17] In the words of John Pory, another Elizabethan ethnographer, "*Mahumet* his law . . . embraceth circumcision, & maketh a difference between meats pure, & unpure, partly to allure the Iewes" (Pory III: 1008); here circumcision becomes an act of missionary seduction.[18]

The seal of circumcision that reemerges in Renaissance ethnography exacerbates and inflames as much as it redeems that ancient scar in Paul's conflicted transvaluation of Jewish law, since the continuing practice of circumcision belies the historical narrative in which Paul strived to contain it. The Pauline author of Colossians celebrates the mystery of gentile redemption in an ecstatic catalog of transcended differences: "Here there cannot be Greek and Jew, circumcised and uncircumcised, barbarian, Scythian, slave, free man, but Christ is all, and in all" (Col. 3:11). Yet in its historic unfolding, the Pauline discourse of nations could accommodate the vast differences between the Greek and the barbarian, but not the very little difference between the circumcised and the uncircumcised. The two typologies remain noncommutative, the uncircumcised dissolved in the equality of the *ethne* as a global totality, the circumcised maintained by the persistence of *ethnos* as a singular set of nation-defining marks. The Christian-humanist discourse derived from Paul's Epistles operates as a *universalism minus the circumcised*, since the Jew and the Muslim remain subtracted from the nations of the world gathered in by Christianity, both singled out and cut off by the ritual stroke through which they continue to distinguish themselves.[19]

Following Balibar, this essay has argued that "theological anti-Judaism" lies at the core of Western ethnographic thought. Like Balibar, I have approached the word "culture" with some suspicion; although it is a concept designed to celebrate pluralism, difference, and hybridity, "culture" is easily smuggled into the game of neutralizing, cleansing, or appropriating other positions. Particularly prone to this kind of cancellation are religious stances and traditions (including aspects of Christianity itself) at odds not only with the official Christendom that rules public life in most Western nations, but with secular humanism in both its classically liberal and its multicultural versions. One such neutralizing move can occur through subsuming "religion" under the broader category of "culture." This maneuver often sequesters or disavows those aspects of non-Christian practices—especially their nationalist elements and claims to stem from divine revelation—that resist relativization within the scheme of a global comparatism. At the same time, these approaches often too quickly identify Christianity's internationalist core with imperialist ideology. Both tactics divide religious discourse between "good" aspects that promote or express individual cultures and "bad" features that negate the cultural identities of other groups.

This essay has aimed to mount both a genealogy and a critique of "culturalist" approaches to Western monotheisms. It is a genealogy insofar as I derive this historicizing move from the Pauline tradition, understood in its broadest sense; rather than applying a culturalist model to religion, I have located a nascent culturalism within religious discourses themselves. Thus insofar as my approach to *ethnos* diverges from the dominant angles promoted by cultural studies, my essay is a critique; yet I still take up the questions raised by recent historicist work as urgent ones in need of addressing and redressing. Unlike Balibar, my approach is exegetical and psychoanalytic rather than historical and Marxist, insofar as it pursues the figural structures that underwrite the West's ethnographic unconscious. The exegetical focus determines the fundamentally literary nature of my project, which tracks the secular implications of scriptural mandates and motifs in overlapping discourses. At the same time, psychoanalysis introduces a necessary sociosexual dynamism into the vagaries of what might otherwise appear to be a purely linguistic signifying process. Lacan's theory of the traumatic jouissance that incites and disturbs phallic symbolization situates circumcision as an essential articulation of collective fantasies about race in the West. A specifically psychoanalytic exegesis not only locates circumcision in the history of racism but shows how circumcision helps structure that history's conditions of possibility. It is therefore not enough to historicize circumcision; we must ask how circumcision poses the question of history per se. Pushing us beyond a contextualization of race and toward its structural understanding as fantasy, psychoanalysis powerfully enables this critical move.

ENDNOTES

1. Rashi I: 67. These parallel uses of circumcision are cited and refuted in Rambam's thirteenth-century commentary on Genesis (I: 220); Rambam in turn draws on a rather comic discussion of the same problem in the Talmud, *Tractate Shabbat* 108a.

2. Paraphrased in the Soncino Chumash, Cohen, Gen. 17:13, 80.

3. "Rabbi Simeon b. Eleazer said: Beth Shammai and Beth Hillel agree that when one is born circumcised, the blood of the covenant must be made to flow from him, because it is a suppressed foreskin" (*Genesis Rabbah* 396–97).

4. Rashi glosses "he that is born in the house" as "one to whom a handmaid gave birth in the house" and "he that is bought with thy money" as "one whom a person bought after his birth" (Gen. 17: 12; 67). The *Midrash Rabbah* glosses this passage by way of a story about two Hellenistic Egyptian proselytes, "sons of King Ptolemy," who have themselves circumcised after reading this scene (*Genesis Rabbah* 17:9–10; 395–96).

5. In Rambam's words, God "commanded Abraham to enter into His covenant to be circumcised before Sarah became pregnant so that his seed would be holy" (I: 218).

6. See Rashi I:66 and Rambam I:218–19.

7. Lacan introduces the idea of the *point de capiton* in his third seminar, on psychosis (*Seminar, Book Three*, 196–205 and *passim*). He later reworked this function in the idea of the master signifier or S_1 (see *Seminar, Book Eleven*, 216–20).

8. Lacan introduces the distinction between the "alienation" in the symbolic order, which creates the subject as barred, and "separation" from the symbolic order, which allows for a different kind of subjectivization, in *Seminar, Book Eleven* (203–25).

9. The popular etymology of "Gershom" (eldest son of Moses and Zipporah and born in the land of Midian, Exod. 2:22, 18:3) means "stranger there," expanded into "stranger in a strange land" (*Eerdman's Bible Dictionary* 412). Zipporah circumcises Gershom with a rock upon their return to Egypt (Exod. 4:25). The word *ger*, "stranger," is also frequently translated as "proselyte," indicating a convert to Judaism.

10. According to most modern scholars of Paul, the Jewish community in Rome, including those who had converted to Christianity, had been exiled by Claudius around 49 C.E.

and returned to the city with the accession of Nero in 54, a return possibly leading to tensions between gentile and Jewish Christians in the Roman church at the time of Paul's letter (Meeks 67). Relying primarily on Protestant accounts of the nationalism and legalism of "Old Testament" religion, most scholarship on Paul before World War II emphasized his violent rejection of Judaism in favor of Christianity. Since World War II, both Catholic and Protestant scholars have criticized Paul for his anti-Judaism (most famously, Rosemary Radford Reuther); in another, more positive strain, scholars have reconstructed the foundations of Pauline theology in Judaism, emphasizing the continuities between the two religions (see especially Davies and Sanders). Most recently, Jewish scholars have taken on the problem of Paul: Boyarin's *A Radical Jew*, emphasizing the theory of culture incipient in Paul's Epistles, is exemplary for my project, but see also Segal. Boyarin usefully summarizes the "cultural politics of Pauline scholarship," 39–56.

11. In Galatians 3, Paul had already presented an analysis of Genesis 17; addressing a congregation of gentile converts beset by Judaizing missionaries, his ruling there on circumcision is much simpler: "if you receive circumcision, Christ will be of no advantage to you" (Gal 5:2).

12. See Davies on Paul's appropriation of the universalist strand from Jewish thought (58–85).

13. See Auerbach on the importance of Paul to the establishment of biblical typology as one of Christianity's fundamental aesthetic and historiographical principles (49–53).

14. On the Hebrew word *aot*, see also *Strong's Concordance*, Hebrew Word List #226, and Klein 15.

15. Daniels writes of Arab genealogy in Christian exegesis: "Ismael was the savage or rustic ass; Muhammad descended from him through the idolator Nabajoth, progenitor of Moabites, Midianites, and Idumaeans. The authentic Islamic genealogies of Muhammad had a medieval European public" (128). On the reading of Pharaoh and Herod as Muslims, see Chew 390, 395.

16. Luther develops the analogy more extensively: "The monk, for example, imagines this to himself: 'The works I am doing are pleasing to God. God will look upon my vows, and on their account He will grant me salvation.' The Turk says: 'If I live this way and bathe this way, God will accept me and give me eternal life.' The Jew thinks to himself: 'If I obey the Law of Moses, I shall find God gracious to me, and so I shall be saved.' " *Works* 26, 28; see also 10, 33, 125, 140, and 147 in the same volume.

17. In Islam, circumcision is a custom rather than a law, though I have not seen this point acknowledged in the Elizabethan literature on Islam, which generally assimilates the Muslim practice to the more familiar Jewish one.

18. For canonical examples of the Judeo-Islamic seal of circumcision in Renaissance discourse, see *The Jew of Malta*, in which the Jew Barabas chooses the Muslim Ithamore as his slave, partner in crime, and successor. Barabas confesses his deep affinities: "make account of me / As of thy fellow; we are villains both: / *Both circumcisèd*, we hate Christians both" (II.iii.225–27; my emphasis). See as well Othello's final speech, in which he kills himself by identifying himself with a Turkish "circumcisèd dog" (V.ii.354).

19. I develop the Renaissance representation of Muslim circumcision in "*Othello Circumcised: Shakespeare and the Pauline Discourse of Nations*."

WORKS CITED

Auerbach, Eric. *Scenes from the Drama of European Literature*. 1959. Minneapolis: U of Minnesota P, 1984.

Balibar, Etienne and Immanuel Wallerstein. *Race, Nation, Class: Ambiguous Identities*. Trans. Chris Turner. New York: Verso, 1991.

Boose, Lynda. " 'The Getting of a Lawful Race': Racial Discourse in Early Modern England and the Unrepresentable Black Woman." *Women, "Race," and Writing in the Early Modern Period*. Ed. Margo Hendricks and Patricia Parker. New York: Routledge, 1994. 35–54.

Boyarin, Daniel. *A Radical Jew: Paul and the Politics of Identity*. Berkeley: U of California P, 1994.

Chew, Samuel. *The Crescent and the Rose: Islam and England During the Renaissance*. 1937. New York: Octagon, 1965.

Cohen, A., ed. *Soncino Chumash*. London: Soncino, 1947.

Daniels, Norman. *The Arabs and Medieval Europe*. London: Longman, 1975.

Davies, W. D. *Paul and Rabbinic Judaism: Some Rabbinic Elements in Pauline Theology*. 1948. 4th ed. Philadelphia: Fortress, 1980.

Eerdmans Bible Dictionary. Rev. ed. Allen C. Myers. Grand Rapids, Mich.: William B. Eerdmans Publishing, 1987.

Fink, Bruce. *The Lacanian Subject: Between Language and Jouissance*. Princeton: Princeton UP, 1995.

Genesis Rabbah. Trans. and ed. H. Freedman and Maurice Simon. London: Soncino, 1983.

Hübner, Hans. *Law in Paul's Thought*. Ed. John Riches. Trans. James C. G. Greig. Edinburgh: T. and T. Clark, 1984.

Klein, Ernest. *A Comprehensive Etymological Dictionary of the Hebrew Language for Readers of English*. New York: Macmillan, 1987.

Lacan, Jacques. *Seminar, Book Three: The Psychoses*. Ed. Jacques-Alain Miller. Trans. Russell Grigg. New York: Norton, 1993.

——. *Seminar, Book Seven: The Ethics of Psychoanalysis*. Ed. Jacques-Alain Miller. Trans. Dennis Porter. New York: Norton, 1992.

——. *Seminar, Book Eleven: The Four Fundamental Concepts of Psychoanalysis*. Ed. Jacques-Alain Miller. Trans. Alan Sheridan. New York: Norton, 1978.

——. *Television: A Challenge to the Psychoanalytic Establishment*. Ed. Joan Copjec. Trans. Denis Hollier, Rosalind Krauss, and Annette Michelson. New York: Norton, 1990.

Lewis, Bernard. *Race and Color in Islam*. New York: HarperTorch, 1970.

Lupton, Julia Reinhard. "*Othello* Circumcised: Shakespeare and the Pauline Discourse of Nations." *Representations* 57 (1997): 73–89.

Luther, Martin. *Lectures on Galatians*. Trans. Jaroslav Pelikan. Vols. 26 and 27 of *Luther's Works*. Ed. Pelikan and Walter A. Hansen. St. Louis: Concordia, 1963.

Marlowe, Christopher. *The Jew of Malta*. 1590. *Drama of the English Renaissance: The Tudor Period*. Ed. Russell A. Fraser and Norman Rabkin. London: Macmillan, 1976. 263–93.

May, Herbert G. and Bruce M. Metzger, eds. *The Holy Bible: Revised Standard Version*. New York: Oxford UP, 1962.

Meeks, Wayne A., ed. *The Writings of Paul*. New York: Norton, 1972.

The Policy of the Turkish Empire. (Anon.) London: John Windet, 1597.

Pory, John. "A Summarie Discourse of the Manifold Religions Professed in Africa." Addendum to Leo Africanus, Vol. 3 of *History and Description of Africa*. 3 vols. Ed. Robert Brown. London: Hakluyt and Society, 1896. 1001–71.

Rambam. *Commentary on the Torah*. 5 Vols. Trans. and annotated Charles B. Chavel. New York: Shilo, 1971.

Rashi. *Chumash with Rashi's Commentary*. 5 vols. Ed. A. M. Silverman. Jerusalem: Feldheim, 1934.

Reuther, Rosemary. *Faith and Fratricide*. New York: Seabury, 1974.

Sanders, E. P. *Paul, the Law, and the Jewish People*. Philadelphia: Fortress, 1983.

———. *Paul and Palestinian Judaism: A Comparison of Patterns of Religion*. Philadelphia: Fortress, 1977.

Segal, Alan F. *Paul the Convert: The Apostolate and Apostasy of Saul the Pharisee*. New Haven: Yale UP, 1990.

Strong, James. *Strong's New Exhaustive Concordance of the Bible*. 1890. Iowa Falls: World Bible Publishers, 1986.

Tractate Shabbat (Babylonian Talmud.) Ed. I. Epstein. Trans. H. Freedman. London: Soncino, 1987.

9

What Does a Jew Want?; or, The Political Meaning of the Phallus

Daniel Boyarin

In his essay "The 'Uncanny' " (1919), Freud recounts a
moment when he looks accidentally at a mirror and imagines he sees someone else: "I can still recollect that I thoroughly disliked his appearance. . . . Is it not possible,
though, that our dislike of [the double is] a vestigial trace
of the archaic reaction which feels the 'double' to be
something uncanny?" ("Uncanny" 248n).[1] Strangely, no
matter how many uses and stagings of the uncanny he
describes, Freud always returns it to castration. He even
connects Rank's account of the "double" with dreams,
within which castration represents "a doubling or multi-
plication of a genital symbol" (235). After listing example after example of uncanny moments having nothing to
do with castration,[2] Freud concludes: "We have now only
a few remarks to add, for animism, magic and sorcery, the
omnipotence of thoughts, man's attitude to death, involuntary repetition and the castration complex comprise
practically all the factors which turn something frightening into something uncanny" (243). Something in
Freud's world was clearly pressing in this direction with
remarkable insistence.

In a later text, *Moses and Monotheism* (1939), Freud
argues that circumcision "makes a disagreeable, uncanny
impression, which is to be explained no doubt by its
recalling the dreaded castration" (91; see also "Uncanny"
247–48). Reversing the terms of Freud's interpretation
in both of these accounts, I argue that castration recalls a
dreaded *circumcision*—dreaded because this act cripples a

male by turning him into a Jew. If we read these two "uncanny" moments together, circumcision and Freud's glimpse of himself in the mirror, we might conclude that in seeing himself in the mirror, Freud had the same uncanny feeling that he claims an anti-Semite experiences when looking at a Jew. We cannot claim that Freud meant this disagreeable, uncanny impression to recur only among gentiles (contra Geller, "Paleontological" 57; "Glance" 438). In my reading, the "appearance" Freud disliked reflects the cultural "trauma" of circumcision. The conceptual implications of this trauma take us far beyond the immediate concerns of psychobiography (see Kofman 32).

This paper interprets the moment when Freud grasped the misrecognition—the doubling of self—informing his Jewish self-alienation.[3] I argue that this misrecognition marks a precise historical moment making psychoanalysis possible,[4] and that the doubling of self ("less than one and double" in Bhabha's aphorism) generates a series of potentially toxic political symptoms in Freud and Fanon, which critics have not interpreted in quite the way I do here. These symptoms include bizarre moments of misogyny in both writers, Fanon's homophobia, and Freud's ambivalence—to say the least—about his own homoerotic desires. But especially relevant for the present study are the strange figurings of "Mulattos" in Freud's work and of "Jews" in Fanon's, which highlight Freud's racism and Fanon's anti-Semitism.

Ann Pellegrini partly anticipates this argument when she writes: "To represent the predicament of the black [male] subject, Fanon turns repeatedly to the machinery of sexual difference. The femininity he puts into play is white femininity. Fanon's strategy for revealing 'racial' difference may not really be so far from Freud's strategy for concealing it" (*Performance* 109). While I clarify that colonized subjects have a certain knowledge of lack that has liberating effects, I do not idealize this knowledge. Instead, I expose Freud's and Fanon's attempt to unknow that which sexually and racially they already perceived on a cultural level.[5] I illustrate this "attempt to unknow" by advancing episodic readings of Freud's essay on Little Hans and Fanon's study *Black Skin, White Masks*. Although my essay interprets biographical information about Freud and Fanon, I explore the conceptual and political implications of blind spots in their work, arguing in the process that these blind spots have profound significance for a psychoanalysis of race.

Before Fanon, Freud seemed to realize that the "colonized as constructed by colonialist ideology is the very figure of the divided subject [that] psychoanalytic theory [posits] to refute humanism's myth of the unified self " (Parry 29). In a profound sense, "humanism's myth" is a colonial myth. It follows that psychoanalysis is *au fond* not so much a Jewish science as a science of the doubled colonized subject—more perhaps than its practitioners have realized or conceded. This doubling of self is endemic to the colonial psyche. As James C. Scott observes, "When the script is rigid and the consequences of a mistake large, subordinate groups may experience their conformity as a species of manipulation. Insofar as the conformity is tactical it is surely manipulative. This attitude again requires a division of the self in which one self observes, perhaps cynically and approvingly, the performance of the other self " (33).

In this respect, it is no accident that psychoanalysis has proven most productive in theorizing colonialism: Fanon's psychology of colonial subjectivity strongly develops insights that already exist in Freud's text. The recognition, raised to exquisite lucidity by Fanon, that the "other within" is the doubled self of colonialism, suggests a new significance for psychoanalysis as an instrument that interprets Jewish history. This recognition surfaces neither as applied psychoanalysis nor as psychohistory, but as a symptom of the crisis shared by Jews and other postcolonial ("modernizing") peoples, whose double consciousness gives them particular insight.[6] Freud himself seemed to have intimated this relationship. He once described the subject's internal alterity as "the State within the State," a pejorative phrase for the German state's twin others: women and Jews (Geller, "Paleontological" 56). For colonial subjects such as Freud and Fanon, the cultural world, their identity, and their allegiances double: They live "lives in between," in Leo Spitzer (the younger's) evocative term.

There is a stunning moment in *Analysis of a Phobia in a Five-Year-Old Boy: "Little Hans, "* in which the Jew's doubled consciousness appears when Freud theorizes subject formation as the castration complex. Presenting Little Hans's castration complex, Freud claims:

> The piece of enlightenment which Hans had been given a short time before to the effect that women really do not possess a widdler was bound to have had a shattering effect upon his self-confidence and to have aroused his castration complex. . . . Could it be that living beings really did exist which did not possess widdlers? If so, it would no longer be so incredible that they could take his own widdler away, and, as it were, make him into a woman. (36)

This is an amazing interpretive moment. Earlier in the text, Freud tells us that Hans's mother threatened him with literal castration if he continued masturbating, and that this was the source of his "castration complex" (8). This is the first time the term "castration complex" appears in Freud's texts (Strachey's note). However, this threat produced no symptoms in Hans at the time. He insouciantly informed his mother that he would "widdle with his bottom." Following the course of *Nachträglichkeit*, the symptoms that Freud associates with castration anxiety appear more than a year later. Having been instructed by his father in the difference between men's and women's genitals (his mother does not possess a widdler, and his sister's will not grow), Hans, according to Freud, mobilizes the anxiety that his mother's threat initiated as deferred knowledge of sexual difference (35). In attenuated form, this "sighting" of the mother's genitals arouses the castration complex.

At this moment, however, Freud describes a second etiology for the onset of castration anxiety: The little boy hears about the damaged (castrated) penis of the circumcised Jew. Freud remarks:

> I cannot interrupt the discussion so far as to demonstrate the typical character of the unconscious train of thought which I think there is here reason for attributing to little Hans. The castration complex is the deepest unconscious root of anti-semitism; for even in the nursery little boys hear that a Jew has something cut off his penis— a piece of his penis, they think—and this gives them the right to despise Jews. And there is no stronger unconscious root for the sense of superiority over women. Weininger (the young philosopher who, highly gifted but sexually deranged, committed suicide after producing his remarkable book *Geschlecht und Charakter* [1903]), in a chapter that attracted much attention, treated Jews and women with equal hostility and overwhelmed them with the same insults. Being a neurotic, Weininger was completely under the sway of his infantile complexes; and from that standpoint what is common to Jews and women is their relation to the castration complex. (*Analysis* 198–99)

Freud does not interrupt his text to demonstrate what he takes to be Little Hans's "unconscious train of thought"—one he also qualifies as "typical." He does, however, provide us with the outlines of this train of thought: Hearing that Jews have something cut off their "widdlers" when they are infants provoked (or at least contributed to) Hans's castration fantasies and fears. What is more, Freud tells us that this is the deepest root of anti-Semitism, that the knowledge of the Jew's circumcision interacts with the gentile's castration complex.

Freud elaborates: "And there is no stronger unconscious root for the sense of superiority over women," a highly ambiguous formulation that supports more than one interpretation. What, after all, is the true subject occluded by this sentence's use of anaphora in the construction "there is"? One possibility is that possession of a penis produces the sense of superiority over women, since contempt for Jews apparently obtains from their "lack" of a penis. Freud's sentence, however, allows for a more radical reading: that little boys hear in the nursery that Jews have something cut off their penises and thereby conclude that they are women who look like men, or, perhaps more exactly, that they are men who have become women.[7] This would be a frightening possibility for the boys concerned, since it powerfully and directly raises the specter of the man's potential "unmanning."[8] These readings are not contradictory, though the second is more disturbing (and revealing) than the first. Moreover, the association of male Jews with women recurs in European cultural history, if not (as Freud would have it) in universal psychology.

"Universalizing Is a Symptom"; or, Little Hans Was Jewish

Freud claims that little (gentile) boys hear about Jewish circumcision in the nursery and that this contributes to their castration anxiety, engendering in them contempt for Jews, which is similar, or even identical to, men's feelings of superiority over women. Weininger was one such "little (gentile) boy," except for one thing: Weininger was Jewish, a fact Freud chose to conceal. In a context in which the "unconscious root of anti-semitism" is at issue, omitting Weininger's Jewishness is no trivial ellipsis.[9] Freud's occlusion of Weininger's Jewishness magnifies another, significant occlusion: "Little Hans" was also Jewish. Hans also did not hear about Jews having something cut off their penises; he possessed such a "damaged penis," as did Freud. In presenting "Little Hans" and Weininger as if they were gentiles gazing, as it were, at the Jewish penis and filling with fear and loathing, Freud I think represents himself (or at least an aspect of himself) gazing at his own circumcised penis. This is an ineluctable consequence of his argument. The much-maligned Fritz Wittels seemed to deduce this when he glossed Freud as arguing that "the unconscious thus despises the Jews because they have been castrated, and the same time dreads them because they castrate their children" (358). Wittels read Freud closely here. Since the fear of castration was, for Freud, unconscious and thus a psychic universal, how could his response to circumcision differ from anyone else's? Freud's note on circumcision in "Little Hans" confirms my interpretation of Freud's uncanny gaze at himself in the mirror. Like Fanon, Freud is "forever in combat with his own image" (Fanon 194) and with the imago of his penis, since his Jewishness compounds an already acute "masculine" conflict between potency and castration.

Freud claims that simply hearing about the circumcision of Jews arouses castration anxiety, just as seeing women's genitals or hearing about women's bodies induces similar fear. If male Jews and women are castrated only from the standpoint of infantile complexes, Freud would logically claim that "healthy" adults recognize neither group (or, alternatively, all subjects) as castrated.[10] The "neurotic" Weininger treated women and Jews with equal hostility because neither of them "possesses" the penis; yet they are both castrated only "from the standpoint of the infantile complexes," the stage at which Weininger was fixated. When the castration complex "dissolves," however, these unrealistic fears should (if the standpoint is no longer "infantile") give way to a "normal" (noninfantile) appreciation of psychic equality among gentiles, women, and Jews.

In Freud's account, though, the castration fantasy—the assumption that women have something missing that renders them inferior—remains the unconscious root of misogyny, and not only in infants or neurotics: Freud thinks all adult males believe in male superiority, a perception that prevails in "nonpathological" forms. In Freud's famous 1937 formulation, for instance, the "repudiation of femininity is the bedrock of psychoanalysis" ("Analysis Terminable" 252). As Jessica Benjamin argues, "We might hope that the boy's 'triumphant contempt' for women would dissipate as he grew up—but such contempt was hardly considered pathological" (160). Similarly, the fantasy that Jews have something missing, the lesson of the nursery, *remains* the unconscious fantasy producing adults' anti-Semitism; no one has argued that anti-Semitism is merely a childhood illness.

John Brenkman suggests: "The simple positive Oedipus complex simplifies the child's multifarious attachments to this one heterosexual drama in an attempt to explain how the so-called bisexual male child, filled with contradictory ideas about the salient differences between his parents, uncertain of his own or others' gender, . . . rife with passive and active sexual aims toward both parents, reemerges on the other side of latency and adolescence merely a more or less neurotic heterosexual" (123).[11] If we accept Brenkman's account of Freud, adulthood would seem to resolve neither misogyny nor anti-Semitism (17). Following Freud's statements about Little Hans's circumcision, however, we can argue that Freud was not pathologizing anti-Semitism so much as naturalizing it via the castration complex.

The Race/Gender System

Freud was delving here at the crossroads of race and gender discourse, where the secrets of both lie buried. Additionally, "racial" and sexual identity seem to obtain from the same aspect of castration (Seshadri-Crooks, "Comedy"), since, for Freud, the most compelling sign of Jewish racial difference is the male Jew's circumcised penis. Finally, since Freud rendered circumcision psychically analogous to castration, the sign of racial difference becomes almost identical to the sign of sexual difference. The circumcised penis resembles a woman's castration, and race and gender converge in the subjectivity of the Christian (heterosexual) masculine subject, putative possessor of the phallus. Accordingly, the correlation of race and gender in descriptions of male Jews as "women" is more intelligible.[12] If, as Juliet

Mitchell remarks, "Freud always insisted that it was the presence or absence of the phallus and *nothing else* that marked the distinction between the sexes" ("Introduction" 6; original emphasis) and Jews lack the phallus, it follows that male Jews are almost "women" (Carpenter).[13]

This convergence is not unique to the racial difference of Jewishness, but it is crucial in the discourse of racial formation. Since the Jew's circumcision/castration is only the most visible metaphor for the race and gender of Jewish males, we can extend it to other racial discourses. In contrast to Gilman (*Freud*, passim) and others who find in Freud's racial situation an explanation for psychoanalysis that effectively cancels its accounts of sexual difference, I suggest that the specificity of Freud's racial difference helped him understand sexual differentiation and its general intersections with race. Moreover, Fanon's *Black Skin, White Masks* is the most important commentary on Freud's inchoate but palpable racial theory, in part because Freud and Fanon have privileged access to the same knowledge. The colonized subjectivity that Fanon anatomizes and enacts—so brilliantly and painfully—is closely analogous to the subjectivity of the fin-de-siècle Viennese Jewish transplant:[14] "Not yet white, no longer wholly black, I was damned" (Fanon 138).

In Freud's note on Little Hans, we find an anatomy not only of misogyny and anti-Semitism—both interpreted as products of the unconscious—but of Jewish and (post)colonial self-contempt, construed as a near inevitability as well.[15] I suggest that Freud fundamentally *accepts* Weininger's argument; this is why Freud cites him here, not as an example of the gentile pathology of anti-Semitism, for which he would be a rather bizarre example. I should emphasize, however, that this is not Freud's idiosyncrasy. Gerald Stieg made an analogous point concerning a similar moment in Kafka: "It is beyond question that such texts are treating something besides the private sphere and that the epoch itself is being heard." Stieg chillingly continues: "The uncanny part is that in such writings the most dreadful aspects of the political propaganda of National Socialism seem to present themselves in the most private sphere, internalized to the point of self-torture" (198). This appears to resemble Freud's self-torture.

Increasingly, scholars are recognizing how all-pervasive thinking like Weininger's was, and to what extent he distilled the ordinary thought of his time and place (Arens 124–25): This is his true significance. As Arens notes:

[Weininger's] work represent[s] a facet of the discussion that *was acceptable to the public curators of science*, not just an isolated stab into the realm of theory; Weininger was not alone, or if his version of the paradigm was deviant, it was at least on the fringe of the public debate in the scientific community. The second way in which

Weininger's work entered the public sphere was as a popular science bestseller, suiting the general reader so well that it stayed in print into the Nazi era; it touched a popular chord. (130)

Weininger and Freud exemplify (but also, of course, are not simply reducible to) a crisis of male Jews in the German-speaking—and especially Viennese—culture of their time (Hoberman 142).[16]

According to my reading, Freud was more identified with than differentiated from Weininger.[17] Barely hidden behind the figure of Weininger in Freud's note, and even hidden behind the incognito Jew Little Hans, is Freud, "the specialist on the inner nature of the Jew" (Gilman, *Jewish* 242; Simon 277). Freud effectively reveals one strand of his conflicted "inner nature" as the "Jewish anti-Semite."[18] While Gilman reads Freud as responding to anti-Semitism by displacing these differences onto an absolute (i.e., universal) difference between men and women, and thus by recoding race as gender, Freud seems to accept a characterization of male Jews as differently gendered—indeed as female—and tries to overcome this difference. Moreover, Freud seems to recognize this component of his personality at least once, writing in a letter to Arnold Zweig in 1933: "We defend ourselves against castration in every form, and perhaps a bit of opposition to our own Jewishness is slyly hidden here. Our great leader Moses was, after all, a vigorous anti-Semite, and he makes no secret of this. Perhaps he was an Egyptian" (qtd. in Le Rider 31). Given Freud's identification with Moses, this is a highly symptomatic deposition (D. Boyarin, "Bitextuality").

Freud seemed in significant ways to oscillate between enacting and disavowing the self-contempt of racially dominated subjects. He discursively hid or closeted his circumcision. This signifies a type of psychic epispasm,[19] a wish to be uncircumcised. The fantasy is to be a man apparently as all other men are: not castrated. Not only of Weininger and Little Hans but of Freud could we say "that he, of course, knows that it is true" that Jews have a piece of the penis cut off. By eclipsing Weininger's and Hans's Jewishness, and by obscuring the role of his own, Freud was hiding a darker claim that Jewish knowledge of circumcision inevitably produces a sense of inferiority vis-à-vis the gentile. This inferiority, which closely resembles the "inferiority complex" Fanon identifies in the colonial subject, is I think what Freud sought to escape.

Freud Reads Fanon; or, The Misogyny of the Colonized Male

More than once, Freud used metaphors of race and colonization for psychological ideas. Attempting to situate fantasy (like a hybrid) between preconscious and unconscious systems, Freud used one of the most revealing of these metaphors, writing of "individuals of mixed race who, taken all round, resemble white men, but who betray their coloured descent by some striking feature or other, and on that account are excluded from society and enjoy none of the privileges of white people" ("Unconscious" 191). This brief and deeply enigmatic metaphor discloses Freud's rapt engagement with the question of "race," and the way that race and sexuality were for him inseparable. The "dark continent" of women's sexuality is not "merely" metaphor, but the figure of a nexus between race and gender that Freud's text insinuates. In David Kazanjian's formulation, these are "statements that open his argument onto a wide sociohistorical field" (102). Precisely what sociohistorical field opens here? How does Freud enfold gender, race, sexuality, and colonization, and how does he position himself racially in these contexts?

An early disciple of Freud's and the founder of psychoanalysis in India, G. Bose once sent Freud a portrait of an English gentleman, remarking that he imagined that was what Freud looked like. Freud responded that Bose had not paid attention to certain "racial" differences between him and the English—that is, his Jewishness (Seshadri-Crooks, "Primitive" 185; 211 n.19). As this anecdote suggests, Freud's origins as *Ostjude* impeded his aspirations as a bourgeois European; he was both the object and the subject of racism. From the colonized's perspective, Freud might look like a white man; from his perspective, and that of dominating white Christians, he was a Jew, every bit as racially marked as the Indian. In the racist imaginary of the late nineteenth century, Jews most often appeared as mulattos. The best denotation for the "race" of the European Jew seems to be off-white.[20] *Ecru Homo.*

Two modalities of reading the "race" of Freud's discourse have emerged in recent years: One—the "colonial"—would read this passage, and by extension Freud's other "ethnological" comments and texts, as the product of a "white" man commenting on "black" men (Bhabha, *Location* 89; Kazanjian 103–5). The other would read "white" and "black" here as barely disguised ciphers for Aryan and Jew (Gilman, *Jew's* 175; *Freud* 21). In the first reading, Freud is the colonizer; in the second, the colonized.

These disparate ways of reading Freud on race are not exclusive, but two aspects of the European Jew's racial anomalousness: Jews are not white/not quite, to borrow Bhabha's felicitous formulation for other colonial subjects. Freud was at once the other and the metropolitan, the "Semite" among "Aryans" and the Jew desperately constructing his whiteness by othering colonized blacks.[21] The results of this conflicted condition are virtually indistinguishable in Freud's texts because Jews were genuinely racialized (as African Americans are in the United States) and, paradoxically, because he identified with his oppressors. For Freud, "the repugnance of the Aryan for the Semite" was *not* an example of "the narcissism of minor differences" but an example parallel to that of the "white races for the coloured." Indeed, this "repugnance" contrasts with the narcissism of the minor difference (Freud, *Group* 101; contra Gilman, *Case* 21, 22, and passim).[22]

Jewishness functioned racially in Austro-Germany as "blackness" does in the United States. The "one drop" theory prevailed for Jewishness. Thus a typical anti-Semite of Freud's time stated: "Jewishness is like a concentrated dye; a minute quantity suffices to give a specific character—or at least, some traces of it—to an incomparably greater mass" (qtd. in Gilman, *Jew's* 175). Another representative nineteenth-century savant referred to "the African character of the Jew," while Houston Stewart Chamberlain, Wagner's son-in-law and Hitler's hero, wrote that the Jews are a mongrel race that had interbred with Africans.[23] The Jew was literally a mulatto, as W. E. B. Du Bois found out one night in Slovenia when a taxi driver took him to the Jewish ghetto (Gilroy, *Black* 212). Since Freud feared that some feature would betray his thinking as "of Jewish descent" and his discourse as merely a "Jewish science," the "individuals of mixed race," in his metaphor, are certainly Jews. Nonetheless, we cannot deny that he also wrote about "whites" and "coloured";[24] we cannot simply dismiss the "colonial" reading of Freud.[25] Freud's ambiguous use of "race" is no accident: His position between white and black greatly contributed to his psychological and ethnological theories.

Like Freud, Fanon produces surprising metaphors of "race." "The Jew" plays as disturbing and enigmatic a role in Fanon's text as "blacks" do in Freud's.[26] In this respect, we should read Freud's deposition about "individuals of mixed race" alongside Fanon's: "All the same, the Jew can be unknown in his Jewishness. He is not wholly what he is. One hopes, one waits. His actions, his behavior are the final determinant. He is a white man, and, apart from some rather debatable characteristics, he can sometimes go unnoticed" (115). Each man fantasizes that the other Other can (almost) "pass." This assumption prevails in Freud's reading of Little Hans: that circumcision cannot be erased but forever marks the Jewish male as appropriate object of contempt, with his evident envy of mulattos who "taken all around resemble white men"! For Fanon, the ineradicability of blackness stands explicitly against the Jew's ability to be unknown as Jewish. Yet both men also acknowledge that passing does not entirely work. Fanon fantasizes that "no anti-Semite . . . would ever conceive of the idea of castrating the Jew." His argument is symptomatic, for he could not be more mistaken historically. Owing to fantasies of Jewish desire for Christian women, castrations of Jews are not unknown (Fabre-Vassas).[27] Fanon's utterance reveals envy for the Jew's imaginary phallus.

The processes of Jewish modernization and Westernization, known collectively as the "Emancipation," closely resemble the dislocating effects suffered by

colonial subjects educated in Europe.[28] We can pursue these analogies by comparing the two groups' cultural/linguistic predicaments: "Every colonized people—
in other words, every people in whose soul an inferiority complex has been created
by the death and burial of its local cultural originality—finds itself face to face
with the language of the civilizing nation; that is, with the culture of the mother
country" (Fanon 18). "Any Jew wishing to escape his material and moral isolation
was forced, whether he liked it or not, to learn a foreign language" (Anzieu 203).[29]
Fanon would have understood the anguish of Arthur Schnitzler, who described the
colonized Jew's double bind thus: "[A Jew] had the choice of being counted as
insensitive, obtrusive and fresh; or of being oversensitive, shy and suffering from
feelings of persecution. And even if you managed somehow to conduct yourself
so that nothing showed, it was impossible to remain completely untouched; as for
instance, a person may not remain unconcerned whose skin has been anesthetized
but who has to watch, with his eyes open, how it is scratched by an unclean knife,
even cut into until the blood flows" (67).

Freud, of course, called Schnitzler his *Doppelgänger* (Bolkosky 1). Marthe
Robert has also eloquently delineated the situation of German Jewish intellectuals
at the fin de siècle. She describes them as divided subjects, trying as hard as they
could to wear German masks but inevitably revealing their Jewish skins: their
interpellation as Jews. The very condition of doubled consciousness, and not of
some essential nature, marks such subjects as Jews. For the effort to "efface"—and
embrace—Jewishness is a response to being denounced by specific cultural formations. Many Jewish jokes of the time, including much of Freud's *Jokebook*, understand this paradox well. The harder such Jews tried to efface their Jewishness, the
more they were rejected (Robert 17). In a passage whose sting and content recall
Fanon's writing, one such Jew writes (already in the 1830s): "It's a kind of miracle! I've experienced it a thousand times, and yet it still seems new to me. Some find
fault with me for being a Jew; others forgive me; still others go so far as to compli-
ment me for it; but every last one of them thinks of it" (Ludwig Börne, qtd. in
Robert 18; on Börne, see Gilman, *Jewish* 148–67).

Freud knew Börne very well. In 1919 he wrote to Ferenczi, "I received Börne
as a present when I was very young, perhaps for my thirteenth birthday. I read him
avidly, and some of these short essays have always remained very clearly in my
memory, not of course the cryptomnesic one. When I read this one again I was
amazed to see how much in it agrees practically word for word with things I have
always maintained and thought. He could well have been the real source of my
originality" (qtd. in E. Freud 73). Indeed, Börne is perhaps a prototype of the split
colonial subject. Fanon echoed him over a century later: "Shame. Shame and self-
contempt. Nausea. When people like me, they tell me it is in spite of my color.

When they dislike me, they point out that it is not because of my color. Either way, I am locked into the infernal circle" (115).

As Fanon describes the psychology of the colonized, the echo of Jewish conditions in central/western Europe since the late nineteenth century recurs. Generally, the prescriptions for solving the "Jewish problem," whether proposed by "evolved" Jews or by anti-Semites, involved a version of the civilizing mission. Thus Walter Rathenau saw "as the sole cure the integration of the Jew into German education (*Bildung*)" (Gilman, *Jewish* 223; Cuddihy 25; see also Spitzer 26; Berkowitz 2–3, 99). Even more pointed are the ideas of another assimilated Jew, Ernst Lissauer, who held that "the Jew, like Nietzsche's Superman, is progressing from a more primitive stage of development, characterized by religious identity, to a higher stage of development, characterized by the present identification with cultural qualities of the German community, to eventually emerge whole and complete" (qtd. in Gilman, *Jewish* 225). Gilman remarks clearly on the analogies between this situation and that of colonialism: "By observing the Ostjude, says the Western Jew, we can learn where we have come from, just as Hegel uses the African black as the sign of the progress of European civilization" (*Jewish* 253).

The more "educated" the subject is, the more acute its dis-ease (Fanon 9–23).[30] Börne returns to the Frankfurt Ghetto after seven years away, and "everything is so dark and so limited" (qtd. in Gilman, *Jewish* 150). "The Antilles Negro who goes home from France . . . tells his acquaintances, 'I am so happy to be back with you. Good Lord, it is hot in this country, I shall certainly not be able to endure it very long'" (Fanon 37).[31]

Language also marked the extent of this split: Consider the abandonment of Creole/Yiddish "jargon" for French/"High" German (Fanon 27–28; Hutton). An internal hierarchy emerged, elevating the more "civilized" subject of the Antilles/Vienna above the still "native, uncivilized" subjects of Dahomey or the Congo/Warsaw (Fanon 25–26). The German-speaking Jew who applied anti-Semitic stereotypes to the Yiddish-speaking *Ostjude* is an uncanny analog to the "evolved" colonial subject, with his contempt for his native people, language, and culture. For the German-speaking Viennese Jew, the *Ostjude* was what the "Unto Whom" ("the ignorant, illiterate, pagan Africans . . . unto whom God swore in his wrath," etc.) were to a Europeanized Yoruba such as Joseph May (qtd. in Spitzer 42).[32] We can imagine the effect of such internalized representations on the transplanted Freud, whose mother spoke only Galician Yiddish all her life (Hutton 11; *contra* Anzieu 204 and *passim*). I contend that the experience of a self doubling back on itself, observing itself, is psychoanalysis's primal encounter with the decentered self.

I suggest not that disadvantaged subjects—whether gay, female, colonized, black, or Jewish—have a politically privileged access to "truth" but that their disadvantage is a condition of their access to such understanding. Thus David Halperin claims that "the aim . . . is to treat homosexuality as a position from which one can know, to treat it as a legitimate *condition* of knowledge. Homosexuality, according to this Foucauldian vision of *un gai savoir*, 'a gay science,' is not something to be gotten right but an eccentric positionality to be exploited and explored: a potentially privileged site for the criticism and analysis of cultural discourses" (61). As we can see from Freud's dilemma, disavowing one's "eccentric positionality"—which Lacan figured suggestively, but problematically, as a disavowal of castration—erases the epistemological advantage of the "postcolonial subject" vis-à-vis the white male's imaginary possession of the phallus.[33] Put another way, Freud's closeted Jewishness (and I use this term for all of its historical and discursive, paranoiac effects) has a toxic effect precisely when the closet emerged historically. Uncloseting this identity would not result in an automatic dissolving of the toxic energy of the anti-Semitic, misogynistic, and homophobic imaginary (Dean). Rather, "coming out" is perhaps a prophylactic, a way of defending one's self from full participation in the most noxious forms of that discourse. In this respect, Freud hides in, and sometimes emerges from, the queer and Jewish closets of his time (D. Boyarin, "Freud's").

Doubled consciousness has had calamitous effects on postcolonial subjects. It has precipitated the Negrophobia of the (modernizing) Jew and the anti-Semitism of the (postcolonial) Negro. These phobias, rather than being analogous, are part of the same historical process. The pathological implications of this doubly liminal situation ("not yet/no longer wholly") devastatingly appear in the gender discourses of these colonized subjects—that is, in their misogyny, homophobia, and self-contempt:

> What does a man want?
> What does the black man want?
> At the risk of arousing the resentment of my colored brothers, I will say that the black is not a man. (Fanon 8)

These "pathologies" also appear as universal concepts in psychoanalysis: as sublation and attempted sublimation.[34]

The racial other lacks the phallus; "he" is always castrated. While the situation of racial others (the Jew, the black) is productive of knowledge (like Halperin's *gai savoir*), these combinations of race and gender have misogynistic and homophobic effects. The dominating European culture often represented blacks as "feminine"; the myth of hypervirility does not properly counter this point. As Fanon repeatedly claimed, "The Negro *is* the genital" (180; my emphasis). In this respect, maleness equates with possessing the phallus, while it is the condition of "Woman" to *be* the phallus. The same appears true for the Negro.

Differing slightly from its perception of blacks, European cultures represented male Jews as "female." Geller put this succinctly: "In the Central European cultural imagination, male Jews are identified with men without penises, that is, as women" ("Paleontological" 52). Gilman also provides the following startling evidence for this claim:

> The clitoris was seen as a "truncated penis." Within the turn-of-the-century understanding of sexual homology, this truncated penis was seen as an analogy not to the body of the idealized male, with his large, intact penis, but to the circumcised ("truncated") penis of the Jewish male. This is reflected in the popular fin de siècle Viennese view of the relationship between the body of the male Jew and the body of the woman. The clitoris was known in the Viennese slang of the time simply as the "Jew" (*Jud*). The phrase for female masturbation was "playing with the Jew." (*Freud* 38–39)

The black man is a penis; the male Jew is a clitoris. Neither has the phallus.

This understanding might have generated a powerful critique of gendered and sexual meanings in Freud's and Fanon's oppressive cultures; it almost did. But while Freud and Fanon had the critical knowledge to conduct this critique, and saw much else from this perspective, neither could ultimately depart from their Eurocentric perspectives and demystify the phallus *tout court*. Freud's and Fanon's projects partly entail getting the phallus for their respective male selves/peoples; the homophobia circulating in their texts makes these projects symptomatic.[35] The phallus is the ultimate white mask or *laissé passer*. We can now sharpen our interpretation of Freud's reaction to his father's story of "passively" picking up his hat when a Christian anti-Semite knocked it off his head. McGrath argues that Freud understood this hat as a symbol for the phallus: "the knocking off his father's hat could have directly symbolized to him the emasculation of Jakob Freud" (64).

The Phallus as White Mask

Writers of the Négritude movement embraced "feminization": "*Emotion is completely Negro as reason is Greek*" (Senghor, qtd. in Fanon 127). Fanon, however, experienced his negritude as "castration" and was unwilling to accept it: "with all my strength I refuse to accept that amputation" (140). On that note, he began a chapter on "The Negro and Psychopathology" and went devastatingly "wrong" in treating gender within the colonized people. His errors are perhaps symptomatic of the situation facing male *post*colonial subjects. Indeed, this blindness in a seer like Fanon makes it doubly instructive, representing the male subject of a colonial discourse who cannot escape his desire to be white/uncircumcised. Here the Freudian/Lacanian reading of lack as figured in the discourse of a particular culture is powerfully diagnostic of cultural effects, but only if we read this figuration as the product of a particular culture. Otherwise, and in all versions of psychoanalysis, the diagnosis threatens to collapse into the disease. Fanon's symptomatic chapter on the sexuality of women reveals this collapse.

In this chapter, Fanon develops his notorious arguments about (white) women's psychology. "Basically, does this *fear* of rape not itself cry out for rape? Just as there are faces that ask to be slapped, can one not speak of women who ask to be raped?" (156).[36] After producing this grotesque misogyny concerning the psychosexuality of "white women," Fanon writes of the woman of color, "I know nothing about her" (180), a statement that eerily echoes Freud's claim about the "dark continent" of woman's sexuality ("Question" 212).[37]

In his brilliant and passionate *cri de coeur* against "Negrophobia," Fanon produces both misogyny and homophobia: "The behavior of these women [who are afraid to dance with a Negro] is clearly understandable from the standpoint of imagination. That is because the Negrophobic woman is in fact nothing but a putative sexual partner—just as the Negrophobic man is a repressed homosexual" (156). Note the telling shift of subject that this sentence encodes grammatically: Fanon tries to theorize the desire and fear of the "Negrophobic woman," but she is "nothing but a putative sexual partner," the object of someone else's desire. Thus the colonized male, who in a situation of partial decolonization begins to look at himself from the white man's perspective, recovers his "maleness" (as defined by the dominant culture) by pathologizing his male and female enemies as feminine. Put another way, the colonizer's misogyny and homophobia become internalized in complicated ways, then projected by the colonized against women and gays.[38] It is not I who have these despised characteristics; it is they!

This defense prevails in Fanon's text particularly when he denies the existence of "homosexuality" in Martinique. Here his homophobia is a great deal more extreme than is Freud's. There are berdaches (my term) in Martinique, but they lead "normal sex lives" (Fanon's phrase): "they can take a punch like any 'he-man' and they are not impervious to the allures of women" (180; his scare quotes). "Fault, guilt, refusal of guilt, paranoia—one is back in homosexual territory" (183). Precisely when Fanon retorts to the racist pronouncement that every Negro is sensual, he dramatically avows: "I have never been able, without revulsion, to hear a *man* say of another man: 'He is so sensual!' . . . Imagine a woman saying of another woman: 'She's so terribly desirable—she's darling . . .'" (201; original emphasis).

Here the psychic mechanism is clear: The colonizers render us effete; we will assert our value by rejecting everything that stinks of effeminacy, homosexuality, and the female. Freud's self-described "overcoming of his homosexual cathexis" is surely cut from the same psychic cloth, as is his psychic "bedrock" that repudiates femininity (Fuss 30).[39] Paula Hyman has sharply formulated this process:

> Challenging elements of the Western model that rigidly limited the public role of women and spiritualized them as mothers, eastern European immigrants and their children contested the boundaries between domestic and public life that character-ized middle-class gender norms. As they integrated into middle-class American cul-ture, however, immigrant Jewish men and their sons—like their predecessors in Western societies—played out their ambivalence about their own identity as Jews in non-Jewish societies in gendered terms. (8–9)

As a consequence: "Jewish men, first in the countries of western and central Europe and later in America, constructed a *modern* Jewish identity that devalued women, the Other within the Jewish community" (134–35; my emphasis).

A fascinating parallel to this phenomenon surfaces in Alice Kaplan's reading of Jean-Paul Sartre's *The Childhood of a Leader*. In this text, Sartre shows a femi-nized, homosexualized Frenchman construct himself as male by rejecting Jews: "Only anti-Semitism succeeds in giving him the gift of masculinity he has sought" (qtd. in Kaplan 18). Likewise, only misogyny and homophobia gave Freud and Fanon the whiteness they sought. From this analysis, the misogyny, homophobia, and racism of both thinkers is a dimension of racial self-hatred. According to Gilman, this structure projects the racist stereotype of one's "own" group onto its other members (*Jewish* 1–21): the *Ostjude*, the Congolese, women, homosexuals. If we see colonized blacks and Jews as Europeans saw them—as, in some sense, members of a single group—this much is clear: We must also consider Freud's racism toward "primitives," like Fanon's toward Jews, for its elements of self-hatred.

Fanon's account of Negrophobia as a product of homosexual desire resembles Freud's interpretation of Daniel Schreber's paranoia, with its anti-Semitic compo-nents as a product of homosexuality.[40] Yet Fanon does not seem to cite Freud so much as reproduce the thought processes that led Freud to his conclusions.[41] In this way, the internalized self-contempt that the colonized male feels for his disempow-ered situation (represented in Jews by the affect surrounding circumcision, and in the Negro by his representation as penis) powerfully determines colonial misog-yny and homophobia: The situation of both Jew and Negro is misrecognized as feminine. This mechanism entails a form of intrapsychic splitting, in which the col-onized establishes a partial identification with the colonizer.[42] The colonized begins to see himself from the eyes of his oppressor and tries to reject what he considers contemptible by projecting all of this onto the white man's other Others: the Jew onto the black, the black onto the Jew, and both onto women and homosexuals.

Fanon reveals the grounds of this structure as clearly as Freud does. Drawing synecdochically on the "Negro of the Antilles," he claims to write about "every colonized man," and concludes that the colonized person wishes to achieve a "universal" status: the black to become white, etc. (18; see Spitzer 37). This is a highly symptomatic moment in Fanon's work, which ignores the colonized's possible deep contempt for the colonizer (see also Bhabha, "Signs" 162). Comparing this situation to that of fin-de-siècle Viennese Jews suggests a more illuminating, less universal reading. After all, only the "emancipated" Jew wishes to become gentile and thus views his circumcision with contempt.[43] As Seshadri-Crooks remarks: "If [premodern] Jews as a minority loathed their difference, then conversion could be a simple option. But that didn't happen." In traditional Jewish culture, only the circumcised male was deemed "whole" (Boyarin and Boyarin). To this extent, circumcision did not produce anxiety or self-contempt but was instead a sign of resistance and a deliberate (private) setting apart of oneself from the dominant culture. As I have argued elsewhere ("Jewish"), even if traditional Jewish male subjects in late antiquity perceived themselves as "feminine," in part because of their circumcision, this did not imply a lack or deprivation for them but a gain: Such a perspective insists that the foreskin is a blemish and that circumcision, far from being a mutilation, adorns the male body.

We can take this perspective "straight" and as a parody of gentile claims of superiority over Jews. The best analogy I have found is a text purportedly by a Bengali that Jenny Sharpe interprets, in which two Bengalis converse on why the English would benefit from learning Bengali. This text "restages the colonizers' privileging of racial purity and their own superior intellect in a manner that turns the language of purity and superiority against them" (145; but see her properly skeptical glosses on this text). In premodern Jewish descriptions that the uncircumcised penis is ugly, gross, impure, and in the Bengali reverse discourse about their superior language, we see parodic rejections of the dominant culture's claims, to which Scott refers as "hidden transcripts."

Scott argues eloquently against assumptions of hegemony here, claiming instead that the appearance of hegemony is only a "public script" serving the interests of colonizer and colonized in situations of near-total domination: "In this respect, subordinate groups . . . contribut[e] to a sanitized official transcript, for that is one way they cover their tracks" (87). He also claims that "genuine" hegemony occurs only in situations where the oppressed or dominated party hope one day to dominate—not over their present oppressors but over others—e.g., in age-graded systems of domination. I suggest that the condition of incipient decolonization, represented for Jews by their fin-de-siècle transitional emancipation status, and for Fanon by his education in France, is precisely such an "expectation that one will eventually be able to exercise the domination that one endures today." According to Scott, that would be "a strong incentive serving to legitimate patterns of domination" (82) and thus an occasion for turning the hidden transcript of contempt for the oppressor into self-contempt. In this way, the moment of decolonization on the political level ("emancipation" for the Jews) ironically fosters hegemony. For instance, an early-twentieth-century American Jewish professor remarked of his coreligionists in Eastern Europe that their bodies are bound but their spirits are free; for those of the West, however, the opposite was true (see also Guha).

Here circumcision for the Jewish colonial subject resembles a moment of displaced castration (Geller, "Paleontological"). When looking into a mirror, Freud experiences his circumcision as "uncanny," and, closeted behind the mask of white scientist, sets out to explain—almost to justify—anti-Semitism. To the extent that Jewish psychoanalysts read circumcision in this way, they glaringly inscribe their ambivalent understanding of Jewish male difference, an ambivalence that American culture records in Alexander Portnoy's and Woody Allen's "psychoanalytic" discourse. Freud is a paradigm for this ambivalent subjectivity, one of the strongest symptoms of which is his thought's frequent, but not ubiquitous, misogyny, racism, and homophobia (Gilman, *Freud* 23). The incongruity of this prejudice alongside the best of Freud's thought leads me to interpret its recurrence as a type of lapse (Fuss 36).

Freud's master complex, the Oedipus/castration complex, is the most dramatic example of this sociopsychic process. Let me repeat Freud's statement. "The castration complex is the deepest unconscious root of anti-semitism; for even in the nursery little boys hear that a Jew has something cut off his penis—a piece of his penis, they think—and this gives them the right to despise Jews. And there is no stronger unconscious root for the sense of superiority over women" (*Analysis* 198–99). I argued earlier that Freud claims that boys hearing of circumcision is the unconscious root of misogyny, anti-Semitism—and, at a deeper level—Jewish self-hatred, to react against suggestions of Jews' "castration" and "feminization." Gilman reads this as the development of normal Jews who "overcome their anxiety about their own bodies by being made to understand that the real difference is not between their circumcised penises and those of uncircumcised males, but between themselves and castrated females" (*Freud* 87); I would add that the same paradigm determines the colonized Jew's misogyny.[44]

I am not denying that other factors contributed to these ideologies and representations in Freud and Fanon. In Freud's case, we must reckon with the general upsurge in misogyny that came to a crisis in fin-de-siècle Europe, as Bram Dijkstra has fully diagnosed in *Idols*. For Fanon, the influence of Freud is certainly undeniable. For both as well, elements of misogyny and homophobia inherited from their "traditional" cultures preexist them. It is not, however, sufficient to argue that Freud and Fanon were men of their times and cultures; we must ask why—and for what *structural* reasons—they accepted and rejected various ideological motifs in their respective cultures. These men were radical rejectors of common wisdom. Why did they occasionally become so conventional? Their sociopsychological situations as men "in between"—as neither "native" nor fully Western—suggests one explanation. Postcolonial theory, and specifically Fanon's elaboration of the colonized male subject, has helped us uncover this aspect of psychoanalysis's cultural unconscious.

In the context of postcolonial theory, Freud's universalized theories of subjectivity, all of them centered on the phallus—the Oedipus complex, the castration anxiety, and penis envy—seem an elaborate defense against the feminization of Jewish men. Freud's naturalization of misogyny is also a way for him to appropriate the phallus for himself as a circumcised male. His theories allowed him to claim that the "real" difference is not between the Jewish and gentile penis but between having and not having a penis. The binary opposition phallus/castration conceals the same third term that Freud conceals in his mystification of Little Hans's identity: the circumcised penis. Both the "*idealization* of the phallus, whose integrity is necessary [to] edif[y] the entire psychoanalytical system" (Johnson, "Frame" 225), and the flight to Greek cultural models and metaphors signal this production's inmixing when psychoanalysis theorizes the affect of colonized people. We might say that the Oedipus complex is Freud's "family romance," in the exact sense of the term. Although this issue is not reducible to Freud or merely a question of psychobiography, Freud seems to fantasize unconsciously that he is not the circumcised Schelomo, son of Jakob, but the uncircumcised and virile Greek Oedipus, son of Laius (see Anzieu 195), just as he earlier fantasized that he was Hannibal, son of Hamilcar, not the son of his "unheroic" Jewish father. Fanon also writes of "a bilateral process, an attempt to acquire—by internalizing them—assets that were originally prohibited [by the colonizers]" (59–60). Such was Freud's sublated penis become phallus (Lacan, "Meaning" 82), not as an asset that he owned but as one he sought to acquire: a mask (the product of a mimicry) as abject and subversive as that of white masks for black skins.

By diagnosing Weininger's "pathology"—and "his own" as well—as "a bit of opposition to our own Jewishness," as in the letter to Zweig quoted earlier, Freud shows that the liminal racial position he occupied generates knowledge and unknowing. Freud's narrative of sexual differentiation as *nonbiological* in its foundations is a good deal more liberatory than is, for instance, Karen Horney's contention that people are born male or female (see also Ramas 480–81). In this respect, the castration complex represents an astonishing theoretical advance over naturalized views of sexual difference. Yet Freud's greatest insight—that sexual difference is made and not born—is also his darkest moment of misogyny; it emerges out of the same point in his discourse, as does his interpretation of words like *heimlich*, which are fundamentally equivocal. We must reject crude readings of Freud that caricature him merely as a white male woman-hater, but we cannot simply ignore the gender effects of Freud's castration discourse. The point is certainly not to disqualify Freud's contribution by locating it in a particular social circumstance; instead, by identifying its moments of blindness and insight, I clarify why Freud's thesis sometimes becomes incoherent, unnecessary, or otherwise unhelpful. There is, for instance, a signal blindness in Freud's unwillingness to figure sexual difference in any other way than by the phallus, which, as Lacan *correctly* interpreted, is symbolically equivalent to the Name-of-the-Father. Why was a thinker who was in many ways able to break with his culture's paradigms quite unable to do so here?

It is as if a gap emerged between Freud's figuring his affect as "defense against castration" and as "a slyly hidden opposition to his own Jewishness" (Le Rider 31). This clarifies "the divided subject posited by psychoanalytic theory . . . refut[ing] humanism's myth of the unified self," and the same subject's concomitant misogyny, homophobia, and racism (Parry 29). We now have a paradigm by which to explain the curious way in which Freud's texts support the most radical and reactionary sociopolitical projects.

Barratt and Straus have well captured this division's effect within Freud, without relating it to his doubled "racial" position:

> Freud's psychology *both* stands as the apotheosis of modern reason, the heir to enlightenment values grounded in reflective-subjective and scientific-objective practices, . . . *and* it stands as the harbinger of postmodern inspiration, the exemplar of discursive practices that emancipate whatever may be excluded or repressed by the totalization of analytico-referential reason. In this sense, the discipline of psychoanalysis occupies a very significant but disconcertingly ambiguous position in relation to the critique of patriarchy. . . . In one frame, psychoanalytic doctrine can be seen as one of the last manifestos of patriarchal legitimation, an ideological structure that systematically rationalizes masculinism [heterosexuality]. In another frame, psychoanalytic method can be seen as an inspiration for feminist [and queer] critique, an enigmatic and extraordinary challenge to the hegemonic structuration of masculinist [heterosexual] discursive practices. (38)

Going beyond Barratt and Straus in order to explain this double frame in Freud, my argument implies strongly that Freud's conflicted social position produced the internal divisions of his subject position, resulting in both his discourse's Janus-like duality, at once radical and reactionary, and his understanding of the subject's divisions. I have attempted to show how these divisions manifest themselves, pointing out their wider implications for a psychoanalytic approach to racial conflicts. In light of these divisions, the peculiarly American developments of ego psychology, which mobilize only the most reactionary aspects of Freud's thinking on sex and gender, would appear as a desperate attempt to resolve the paradoxes of such postcolonial subjectivities as that of the European Jewish refugee.

ENDNOTES

This essay is dedicated to Tony Kushner, with love.

1. Susan Shapiro is now writing a book on the uncanny as a trope for the Jew.

2. Freud's interpretation of Hoffman's *The Sandman* remains just that—a compelling interpretation, not an explanation or proof of the centrality of castration in the uncanny.

3. I wonder how akin Freud's mirror is to Stephen Dedalus's description of Irish art as "the cracked looking-glass of a servant" (Joyce 6).

4. W. E. B. Du Bois's *The Souls of Black Folk* laid the intellectual foundations for this chapter. For a brilliant reading, see Gilroy, *Atlantic*.

5. Mosse's account of the contrast between Friedländer and Hirschfeld, both Jewish and homosexual, is instructive: "For Friedländer [who converted], the Jews were assigned the very stereotype which society had created for homosexuals. . . . Magnus Hirschfeld, homosexual and Jew, became [a] strong advocate of human rights" (41).

6. In an illuminating essay, Harpham describes the *conversos* ("forcibly" converted Jews) of early modern Spain as paradigmatic modern subjects (550–51).

7. Freud seems to mean that fear of losing the penis causes misogyny. However, his use of the term "sense of superiority" makes it hard to escape the echo of sense of possession.

8. Compare Geller's similar reading: "The circumcised Jew seems to question sexual difference" ("Paleontological" 56). J. Boyarin has proposed an even more disturbing reading that the syntax allows, even prefers: Little boys hear in the nursery about the "castration" of the Jews and learn to feel contempt for them long before they know that women have no penises. The contempt for women derives from primary anti-Semitism, because women are similar to Jews. Anti-Semitism (including Jewish anti-Semitism) is thus literally the unconscious root of misogyny.

9. Nor can we object that he assumed everyone already knew this, since he informs us exactly who Weininger is, omitting only that he is Jewish.

10. For me these formulations are ultimately the same because, as I have argued elsewhere, positing the phallus basically confirms the "dominant fiction." I know this statement will be, at best, obnoxious to Lacanians, but I contend that the very terms "phallus" and "castration," if they are not interrogated historically, lose the symptomatic power they might possess to explain misogyny, homophobia, and anti-Semitism/racism and become,

willy-nilly, complicit with those discourses. With Mitchell, we must read Freud not as positing "the phallus," but as positing the *positing* of the phallus (*Psychoanalysis*).

11. I have elided the words *"pace* Freud" because I disagree with them and am appropriating Brenkman's otherwise exact formulation here for my text. I argue that Freud is, at
least sometimes, brilliantly aware of the "rifeness" of these passive and active aims.

12. This point is often missed, even in critical discussions of Freud that assume that his
account of the "patriarchal," oedipal family is a seamless sequel to something called "biblical patriarchy," and not a European production with which Freud desperately identified as
a colonized subject. Bersani writes: "the psychoanalytic Oedipal myth also describes a very
limited situation . . . the fantasmatic field of the nuclear bourgeois family at a particular
moment in European history, and perhaps also a certain crisis in a patriarchal community
structured in conformity to an ancient Judaic veneration for and terror of the law-giving
father" ("Gay" 8). This structure of "ancient Judaic veneration and terror" is, however, a
fantasy. Neither God nor the human father was venerated as an object of terror in any variety of traditional Judaism with which I am familiar; object of a pathic erotic desire for a
"maternal" father would be a more accurate description. The crisis here concerns the
always preoedipal Jew seeking to become a full participant in the fantasmatic field of the
nuclear bourgeois family. Feldman is astute on this point. Of Isaac, one of the classical
Patriarchs, she writes: "One can hardly imagine such a paternal figure serving as the source
of a Freudian castration threat or of a Lacanian 'No of the Father' " (10)—exactly! See also
her n. 1 on p. 22.

13. In a fascinating essay on *Daniel Deronda*, Gallagher elaborates another basis for the
association of Jews and (loose) women: their alleged lack of economic productivity (130).
These two aspects—circumcision and economic inutility—converge at the site of the
"clipped" coin, as my student Willis Johnson has brilliantly argued ("Henry").

14. Gilroy has sensitively examined the moral and theoretical power of the comparison
of the histories of blacks and Jews, and its limitations (*Black* 212–17).

15. For the justification of the "(post)" with reference to Fanon, see below.

16. In his reading of this Freudian text, Gilman finesses this enigma by writing as if
Freud had revealed precisely that which he hid in the closet (see Pellegrini, "Whiteface" for
a parallel critique). According to Gilman, Freud cited Weininger as "an example of the
problematic relationship of the Jew to his circumcised penis" (*Freud* 77). Gilman goes on to
argue that "Weininger is like the little (non-Jewish) boy in the nursery who hears about the
Jews cutting off penises, except that he, of course, knows that it is true. His hatred of the
Jew is 'infantile,' according to Freud, since it remains fixed at that moment in all children's
development when they learn about the possibility of castration. Jewish neurotics like
Weininger focus on the negative difference of their bodies from ones that are 'normal,' and
use this difference, like their evocation of the bodies of women, to define themselves" (80).
Gilman treats Freud's Weininger as an analysand, and Freud as an anatomist of anti-
Semitism: "Freud has evoked the Jewish 'scientist' Otto Weininger as an anti-Semite." Thus
Gilman sequesters Freud from "Jewish self-hatred": "He understood himself as a Jew, as
different. And this for him (as for Jewish contemporaries such as Theodor Herzl) was in no

way negative" (*Case* 8). In "Colonial," I argued, to the contrary, that Herzl is an exemplary case of Jewish self-hatred. Whereas Gilman reads Freud as analyzing Weininger's pathology, as an analysand, I read Freud as enlisting Weininger as a fellow analyst. Interestingly, in earlier work, Gilman himself noted similar occlusions in Freud's writings, such as the "masking" of the Jewishness of Bertha Pappenheim ("Anna O") and Ida Bauer ("Dora") (*Jew's* 81). In both cases the subject's Jewishness arguably is less relevant than is Little Hans's, where it is occluded in a discussion of circumcision and its psychic effects.

17. If, as Gilman claims, Freud had not "responded to Weininger's self-hatred as the reflection of his identity crisis" (*Jewish* 251), this would have been a classic example of denial and defense; I suggest that he did respond.

18. See Gilman, *Jewish*, where he writes, "Freud's scientific German, at least when he sits down to write his book on humor, is a language tainted by Weininger's anti-Semitism," a claim that seems to contradict his later argument that Freud pathologized and thus rejected Weininger's anti-Semitism. In 1986, it seems, Gilman was closer to the perspective on Freud that I am adopting here than he is in his most recent work (see his "Otto"). For a similar case of a "scientist," Cesare Lombroso, obscuring his Jewishness and writing an "objective" account of anti-Semitism that reveals his contempt for Jews, see Harrowitz, "Weininger."

19. "Epispasm": the operation to restore the foreskin, very popular among Hellenized Jews in antiquity (Hall).

20. Interestingly, a similar situation seems to obtain for the Irish. As Duffy remarks, "it was inevitable that the Irish would be seen to occupy an ambivalent middle ground between the 'master' and the 'dark' races" (42–43).

21. For analogous processes in American culture, see Rogin; Gilman, "Dangerous."

22. In *Civilization* 114, to be sure, it seems that Freud represents hostility to Jews as an example of "the narcissism of minor differences," but a careful reading shows that this is not necessarily the case. See also Pellegrini, "Whiteface."

23. Freud had read Chamberlain (Gilman, *Freud* 236). For extensive documentation of the "blackness" of Jews, see Gilman, *Jewish* 172–75 and *Case* 19–21. For a fascinating explanation of the functions of such discourse, see Cheyette.

24. "Jewish science" was definitely a racist/anti-Semitic term of art, a fact Gilman clarifies in "Otto" 112–13.

25. For a very thoughtful version, see Seshadri-Crooks, who asks whether certain descriptions of Freud as contemptuously patronizing of Indian psychoanalysts (including Bose) do not reproduce such a stance, since Bose and his fellows seem unaware of Freud's contempt and patronization (186). We could also ask a version of this question here. If, as some claim, Freud's work is irretrievably tainted with racism and colonialist ideology, why was someone like Fanon unaware of this corruption?

26. Compare Gilman (*Jew's* 194–209), who goes too far in my opinion in associating the straightforward racism—Nazi sympathies—of Masud Khan with Fanon's complex affect concerning Jews. There is no evidence that Fanon, for all his tragic misrecognition of European anti-Semitism, read Jews as racially inferior, *pace* Gilman 200. On the other hand,

we must contrast Fanon's grotesque reading of the Nazi genocide as a "family quarrel" with Césaire's sensitive understanding that colonialism is practice for the internal other's genocide; see J. Boyarin 105–7.

27. I am grateful to Jonathan Boyarin for this reference.

28. Cuddihy was perhaps the first to realize that there are significant homologies between Jewish "Emancipation" and the postwar processes of decolonization:

> The fact that Jews in the West are a decolonized and modernizing people, an "under-developed people" traumatized—like all underdeveloped countries—by contact with the more modernized and hence "higher" nations of the West goes unrecognized for several reasons. First, because they have been a colony *internal* to the West; second, because decolonization has been gradual and continuous; third, because of the democratic manners of the West (only Max Weber called them a pariah people, i.e., a ritually segregated guest people); and fourth, because the modernization collision has been politicized and theologized by the charge of "anti-Semitism" (as, in noncontiguous Western colonies, the charge of "imperialism" effectively obscures the real nature of the collision—namely, between modernizing and nonmodernized peoples). (47)

In "*Épater*," I discuss Cuddihy critically and at some length. For all his celebration of the West's civilizing mission, Cuddihy at least identifies the Jews as subject to it. I prefer not to use the term "assimilation," because of its implicit assumption that previously one could speak of an unassimilated or pure cultural situation, on either side. In all but the most exceptional cases, it is now clear that cultures are always to some extent in contact, thus always assimilating. This term does not sufficiently evoke the particular cultural anxieties of the transition from colonial domination to emancipation. Further, "assimilation" implies a stability in the "target culture" to which one is assimilating; in reality, European culture at the time of Jewish Emancipation was greatly in flux. Indeed, it would not be inaccurate to say that Jewish cultural activities played a role in the production of European modernity, just as we are coming to recognize the cultural role of colonialism and the colonies in producing European modernity. See also J. Boyarin 82. For the particular application of the term "colonial subject" to the "Western-educated native," see Sharpe 139–40.

29. Martin Jay has cautioned me, however, that this was true of many groups in Europe in the nineteenth century. Insofar as there were other internal colonies, undoubtedly many of the same processes befell them, each, of course, with its own historical inflections and specificities.

30. My interpretation of Börne is entirely different from that of Arendt, who wrote, "The anti-Jewish denunciations of Marx and Börne cannot be properly understood except in the light of this conflict between rich Jews and Jewish intellectuals" (54). It is certainly not irrelevant that both Marx and Börne were converted Jews—the limit case of the hybrid and self-alienated Jewish subject.

31. In this essay I will use the term "Negro," following Fanon. Here, obviously, neither "African" nor "African American" will do.

32. I suggest that this split between Ostjuden and Viennese Jews allowed the latter to "maintain a primary identification with the group from which they stemmed" (Spitzer 38, referring to Rozenblit *Jews*), i.e., by splitting off good, acculturated, German-speaking Jews from bad, primitive, Yiddish-speaking ones—who were, often their parents or grandparents! The idea of Judaism as a religion enabled this "primary identification." The famous Wien chapter of the Benei Brith is reminiscent of nothing so much as the National Benevolent Society of Yorubas in Sierra Leone (Spitzer 43; Rozenblit 150). See also Cuddihy 176.

33. In other words, I suggest that there are situations in which an imaginary possession of the phallus can be less toxic than a desperate effort to get it. Both, of course, are equally products of a certain relation to the dominant fiction.

34. Compare the kindred argument of Gilman, *Case*; see also Fuss 38.

35. Insofar as Freud is "in the closet" qua Jew and qua "queer," his discourse is oppressive to women, lesbians, and gay men; when he is less closeted, we find the moments of powerful liberatory insight so sharply located by Bersani in the margins of Freud's texts (*Freudian*). See also Duffy's sensitive remarks (21).

36. Morgan gives us a brief and moving account of her response to Fanon and the ways in which he empowered her, in spite of it all ("Politics" 113). Her strategy, in summary, is to translate what Fanon says about colonized men into discourse about women and to bracket and voluntarily ignore what he says about women.

37. Note that "dark continent" is in English. Freud's search, like Herzl's, was for an "Anglo-Saxon" white-male sublimity.

38. Of course, I am not implying that this is the *only* source of prejudice in "native" peoples. I clarify this later in the essay.

39. I would be somewhat less generous to Fanon than Fuss is here. She reads this statement as "a rejection of the 'primitive=invert' equation that marks the confluence of evolutionary anthropology and sexology," while I see it as an instance of identificatory mimesis of white homophobia, which does not refuse the categories of European sexuality but reifies and "universalizes" them. Fuss's formulation on p. 36 is more critical.

40. See also the fascinating account of this trope (the anti-Semite as repressed homosexual) in Gilman, *Freud* 196–98, and especially Santner.

41. See also Cheung 236–38 for a parallel analysis of Chinese American critical writing and its "lending credence to the conventional association of physical aggression with manly valor" and its "sexist preference for [male] stereotypes that imply predatory violence against women to 'effeminate' ones" (237).

42. Hutton usefully interprets Freud's telling of Yiddish jokes as another form of this splitting: "It involves an interplay between the identity of the 'little Jew' and that of the intellectual or 'outsider' Jew. In telling the joke, Freud or the narrator identifies with both sides, seeing each inside the other" (14). This is a somewhat more genial description of the

process than I have given. See also the telling example discussed in Gilman, "Freud" 162–63.

43. In the present-day United States, however, circumcision itself has been configured as "universal," although this is certainly changing.

44. I am drawing a distinction here, as throughout my work, between the disenfranchisement of women in the social sphere and misogyny per se—the expression of contempt and hatred for women. The two are obviously related but not identical. The former is endemic in Jewish culture; the latter, I argue, sporadic. Moreover, misogyny per se grows stronger throughout European Jewish history, reaching its peak in Eastern Europe precisely at the moment of modernization (decolonization).

WORKS CITED

Anzieu, Didier. *Freud's Self-Analysis.* Trans. Peter Graham. Pref. M. Masud R. Khan. Paris: 1975. New York: International UP, 1986.

Arendt, Hannah. *The Origins of Totalitarianism.* 2d ed. Cleveland: Meridian-World, 1958.

Arens, Katherine. "Characterology: Weininger and Austrian Popular Science." In Harrowitz and Hyams. 121–39.

Barratt, Barnaby B. and Barrie Ruth Straus. "Toward Postmodern Masculinities." *American Imago* 51.1 (1994): 37–67.

Beller, Steven. "Otto Weininger as Liberal?" In Harrowitz and Hyams. 91–101.

Benjamin, Jessica. *The Bonds of Love: Psychoanalysis, Feminism, and the Problem of Domination.* New York: Pantheon, 1988.

Berkowitz, Michael. *Zionist Culture and West European Jewry Before the First World War.* New York: Cambridge UP, 1993.

Bersani, Leo. *The Freudian Body: Psychoanalysis and Art.* New York: Columbia UP, 1986.

———. "The Gay Outlaw." *Diacritics* 24.2–3 (1994): 5–19.

Bhabha, Homi K. "Signs Taken for Wonders: Questions of Ambivalence and Authority under a Tree Outside Delhi, May 1817." *Critical Inquiry* 12.1 (1985): 144–65.

———. *The Location of Culture.* New York: Routledge, 1994.

Bolkosky, Sidney. "Arthur Schnitzler and the Fate of Mothers in Vienna." *Psychoanalytic Review* 73.1 (1986): 1–15.

Boyarin, Daniel. "*Épater L'embourgeoisement*: Freud, Gender, and the (De)Colonized Psyche." *Diacritics* 24.1 (1994): 17–42.

———. "Freud's Baby, Fliess's Maybe: Male Hysteria, Homophobia, and the Invention of the Jewish Man." *GLQ* 2.1 (1994): 1–33.

———. "Jewish Masochism: Couvade, Castration, and Rabbis in Pain." *American Imago* 51.1 (1994): 3–36.

———. "Bitextuality, Psychoanalysis, Zionism: On the Ambivalence of the Jewish Phallus." *Queer Diasporas.* Ed. Cindy Patton and Benigno Sánchez-Eppler. Series Q. Durham: Duke UP, forthcoming.

———. "The Colonial Drag: Zionism, Gender, and Colonial Mimicry." *Dimensions of (So-*

called) Postcolonial Studies. Ed. Kalpana Seshadri-Crooks and Fawzia Afzal-Kahn. Durham: Duke UP, forthcoming.

Boyarin, Jonathan. "The Other Within and the Other Without." *Storm from Paradise: The Politics of Jewish Memory*. Minneapolis: U of Minnesota P, 1992. 77–98.

Boyarin, Jonathan, and Daniel Boyarin. "Self-exposure as Theory: The Double Mark of the Male Jew." *Rhetorics of Self-making*. Ed. Debbora Battaglia. Berkeley: U of California P, 1995. 16–42.

Brenkman, John. *Straight Male Modern: A Cultural Critique of Psychoanalysis*. New York: Routledge, 1993.

Carpenter, Mary Wilson. " 'A Bit of Her Flesh': Circumcision and 'The Signification of the Phallus' in *Daniel Deronda*" *Genders* 1 (1988): 1–23.

Cheung, King-Kok. "The Woman Warrior Versus the Chinaman Pacific: Must a Chinese American Critic Choose between Feminism and Heroism?" *Conflicts in Feminism*. Ed. Marianne Hirsch and Evelyn Fox Keller. New York: Routledge, 1990. 234–51.

Cheyette, Bryan. "Neither Black Nor White: The Figure of 'the Jew' in Imperial British Literature." *The Jew in the Text: Modernity and the Politics of Identity*. Ed. Linda Nochin and Tamar Garb. London: Thames and Hudson, 1995. 31–41.

Cuddihy, John Murray. *The Ordeal of Civility: Freud, Marx, Lévi-Strauss, and the Jewish Struggle with Modernity*. With a New Preface by the Author. 1974. Boston: Beacon, 1987.

Dean, Tim. "On the Eve of a Queer Future." *Raritan* 15.1 (1995): 116–34.

Dijkstra, Bram. *Idols of Perversity: Fantasies of Feminine Evil in Fin-de-siècle Culture*. New York: Oxford UP, 1986.

Duffy, Enda. *The Subaltern Ulysses*. Minneapolis: U of Minnesota P, 1994.

Fabre-Vassas, Claudine. *La bête singulière: Les juifs, les chrétiens, et le cochon*. Paris: Gallimard, 1994.

Fanon, Frantz. *Black Skin, White Masks*. Trans. Charles Lam Markmann. 1952. New York: Grove, 1967.

Feldman, Yael S. " 'And Rebecca Loved Jacob,' but Freud Did Not." *Freud and Forbidden Knowledge*. Ed. Peter L. Rudnytsky and Ellen Handler Spitz. New York: New York UP, 1994. 7–25.

Freud, Ernst, Lucie Freud, and Ilse Grubrich-Simitis, eds. *Sigmund Freud: His Life in Pictures and Words*. 1978. New York: Norton, 1985.

Freud, Sigmund. *The Interpretation of Dreams* (Part One). 1900. Vol. 4 of *The Standard Edition of the Complete Psychological Works of Sigmund Freud*. 24 vols. Ed. and trans. James Strachey. London: Hogarth, 1953–74.

———. *Analysis of a Phobia in a Five-Year-Old Boy (Little Hans)*. 1909. Vol. 10 of *SE*. 3–149.

———. "The Unconscious." 1915. Vol. 14 of *SE*. 159–215.

———. "The 'Uncanny.' " 1919. Vol. 17 of *SE*. 217–56.

———. *Group Psychology and the Analysis of the Ego*. 1921. Vol. 18 of *SE*. 67–143.

———. "The Question of Lay Analysis." 1926. Vol. 20 of *SE*. 179–258.

———. *Civilization and Its Discontents*. 1930. Vol. 21 of *SE*. 59–145.

———. "Analysis Terminable and Interminable." 1937. Vol. 23 of *SE*. 211–53.

———. *Moses and Monotheism: Three Essays*. 1939. Vol. 23 of *SE*. 3–137.

Fuss, Diana. "Interior Colonies: Frantz Fanon and the Politics of Identification." *Diacritics* 24.2–3 (1994): 20–42.

Gallagher, Catherine. "George Eliot and *Daniel Deronda*: The Prostitute and the Jewish Question." *The New Historicism Reader*. Ed. H. Aram Veeser. New York: Routledge, 1994. 124–40.

Geller, Jay. " 'A Glance at the Nose': Freud's Inscription of Jewish Difference." *American Imago* 49.4 (1992): 427–44.

———. "A Paleontological View of Freud's Study of Religion: Unearthing the Leitfossil Circumcision." *Modern Judaism* 13 (1993): 49–70.

———. "Circumcision and Jewish Women's Identity: Rahel Levin Varnhagen's Failed Assimilation." *Judaism Since Gender*. Ed. Laura Levitt and Miriam Peskowitz. New York: Routledge, 1997. 174–87.

Gilman, Sander L. *Jewish Self-hatred: Anti-Semitism and the Hidden Language of the Jews*. Baltimore: Johns Hopkins UP, 1986.

———. *The Jew's Body*. New York: Routledge, 1991.

———. "Freud, Race and Gender." *American Imago* 49.2 (1992): 155–83.

———. *The Case of Sigmund Freud: Medicine and Identity at the Fin de Siècle*. Baltimore: Johns Hopkins UP, 1993.

———. *Freud, Race, and Gender*. Princeton: Princeton UP, 1993.

———. "Dangerous Liaisons." *Transitions* 64 (1994): 41–52.

———. "Otto Weininger and Sigmund Freud: Race and Gender in the Shaping of Psychoanalysis." In Harrowitz and Hyams. 103–20.

Gilroy, Paul. *The Black Atlantic: Modernity and Double Consciousness*. Cambridge: Harvard UP, 1993.

———. *There Ain't No Black in the Union Jack: The Cultural Politics of Race and Nation*. With a New Preface by Houston A. Baker, Jr. Chicago: U of Chicago P, 1991.

Guha, Ranajit. "Dominance Without Hegemony and Its Historiography." *Subaltern Studies* 6. Ed. Guha. Delhi: Oxford UP, 1989. 210–309.

Hall, David. "Epispasm and the Dating of Ancient Jewish Writings." *Journal for the Study of Pseudepigrapha* 2 (1988): 71–86.

Halperin, David M. *Saint Foucault: Towards a Gay Hagiography*. New York: Oxford UP, 1995.

Harpham, Geoffrey Galt. "So . . . What *Is* Enlightenment? An Inquisition into Modernity." *Critical Inquiry* 20.3 (1994): 524–56.

Harrowitz, Nancy A. "Weininger and Lombroso: A Question of Influence." In Harrowitz and Hyams. 73–90.

Harrowitz, Nancy A. and Barbara Hyams, eds. *Jews & Gender: Responses to Otto Weininger*. Philadelphia: Temple UP, 1995.

Hoberman, John M. "Otto Weininger and the Critique of Jewish Masculinity." In Harrowitz and Hyams. 141–53.

Hutton, Christopher. "Freud and the Family Drama of Yiddish." *Studies in Yiddish Linguistics*. Ed. Paul Wexler. Tübingen: Niemeyer, 1990. 9–22.

Hyman, Paula E. *Gender and Assimilation in Modern Jewish History: The Roles and Representation of Women*. The Samuel & Althea Stroum Lectures in Jewish Studies. Seattle: U of Washington P, 1995.

Johnson, Barbara. "The Frame of Reference: Poe, Lacan, Derrida." *The Purloined Poe*. Ed. John P. Muller and William J. Richards. Baltimore: Johns Hopkins UP, 1987. 213–51.

Johnson, Willis. "Henry III's Circumcised Pennies." *British Numismatic Journal* 65 (1995), in press.

Joyce, James. *Ulysses*. 1922. New York: Random House, 1961.

Kaplan, Alice Yaeger. *Reproductions of Banality: Fascism, Literature, and French Intellectual Life*. Minneapolis: U of Minnesota P, 1986.

Kazanjian, David. "Notarizing Knowledge: Paranoia and Civility in Freud and Lacan." *Qui Parle* 7.1 (1993): 102–39.

Kofman, Sarah. *The Enigma of Woman*. Trans. Catherine Porter. Ithaca: Cornell UP, 1985.

Kornberg, Jacques. *Theodor Herzl: From Assimilation to Zionism*. Bloomington: Indiana UP, 1993.

Lacan, Jacques. "The Meaning of the Phallus." *Feminine Sexuality: Jacques Lacan and the école freudienne*. Ed. Juliet Mitchell and Jacqueline Rose. Trans. Rose. New York: Norton, 1985. 74–85.

Le Rider, Jacques. "The 'Otto Weininger Case' Revisited." In Harrowitz and Hyams. 21–33.

McGrath, William J. *Freud's Discovery of Psychoanalysis: The Politics of Hysteria*. Ithaca: Cornell UP, 1986.

Mitchell, Juliet. *Psychoanalysis and Feminism*. New York: Vintage-Random House, 1974.

——. "Introduction–I." *Feminine Sexuality: Jacques Lacan and the école freudienne*. 1–26.

Morgan, Robin. "The Politics of Sado-masochist Fantasies." *Against Sadomasochism: A Radical Feminist Analysis*. Ed. Robin Ruth Linden et al. San Francisco: Frog in the Well, 1982. 109–23.

Mosse, George L. *Nationalism and Sexuality: Middle-Class Morality and Sexual Norms in Modern Europe*. Madison: U of Wisconsin P, 1985.

Parry, Benita. "Problems in Current Theories of Colonial Discourse." *Oxford Literary Review* 9 (1987): 27–58.

Pellegrini, Ann. *Performance Anxieties: Staging Psychoanalysis, Staging Race*. New York: Routledge, 1997.

——. "Whiteface Performances: 'Race,' Gender, and Jewish Bodies." *Jews and Other Differences: The New Jewish Cultural Studies*. Ed. D. Boyarin and J. Boyarin. Minneapolis: U of Minnesota P, 1997. 108–49.

Ramas, Maria. "Freud's Dora, Dora's Hysteria: The Negation of a Woman's Rebellion." *Feminist Studies* 6.3 (1980): 472–510.

Robert, Marthe. *From Oedipus to Moses: Freud's Jewish Identity*. Trans. Ralph Manheim. Garden City, N.Y.: Doubleday, 1976.

Rogin, Michael. "Blackface, White Noise: The Jewish Jazz Singer Finds His Voice." *Critical Inquiry* 18 (1992): 417–53.

Rozenblit, Marsha. *The Jews of Vienna, 1867–1914: Assimilation and Community*. Albany: SUNY P, 1983.

Santner, Eric. *My Own Private Germany: Daniel Paul Schreber's Secret History of Modernity*. Princeton: Princeton UP, 1996.

Schnitzler, Arthur. *My Youth in Vienna*. Trans. Catherine Hutter. New York: Holt, Rinehart, and Winston, 1970.

Scott, James C. *Domination and the Arts of Resistance: Hidden Transcripts*. New Haven: Yale UP, 1990.

Seshadri-Crooks, Kalpana. "The Primitive as Analyst: Postcolonial Feminism's Access to Psychoanalysis." *Cultural Critique* 28 (1994): 175–218.

———. "The Comedy of Domination: Psychoanalysis and the Conceit of Whiteness." In this collection.

Sharpe, Jenny. "Figures of Colonial Resistance." *Modern Fiction Studies* 35.1 (1989): 137–55.

Simon, Ernst. "Sigmund Freud the Jew." *Leo Baeck Institute Year Book*. London: Leo Baeck Institute, 1957. 270–305.

Spitzer, Leo. *Lives In-Between: Assimilation and Marginality in Austria, Brazil, and West Africa, 1780–1945*. Studies in Comparative World History. New York: Cambridge UP, 1989.

Stieg, Gerald. "Kafka and Weininger." Trans. Barbara Hyams. In Harrowitz and Hyams. 195–206.

Wittels, Fritz. *Sigmund Freud: His Personality, His Teaching, and His School*. London: Allen and Unwin, 1924.

10

Myths of Masculinity: The Oedipus Complex and Douglass's 1845 *Narrative*

Gwen Bergner

In *The Souls of Black Folk* (1903), W. E. B. Du Bois describes a state of divided identity particular to African-Americans living in a culture that does not see them as equal to white people. He calls this "peculiar" form of self-awareness "double-consciousness, this sense of always looking at one's self through the eyes of others" (5). "One ever feels his twoness," Du Bois continues, "an American, a Negro; two souls, two thoughts, two unreconciled strivings; two warring ideals in one dark body" (5). Although the term "double consciousness" has become standard shorthand to describe African-American subjectivity, the condition it describes has remained virtually unexplored in African-American and other literary theories. Nevertheless, works of fiction and autobiography frequently represent the subject's acquisition of double consciousness as a singular event; characters "discover" racial identity in dramatic scenes involving photographs, mirrors, or acts of witnessing. Although these "stock scenes of racial discovery" depict a visual event (Cooke 72), the protagonists perceive less the "fact" of racial difference than its cultural significance.[1] In such scenes, the self is simultaneously defamiliarized and reconstituted within the cultural discourse on race (Wald 186–87). Du Bois introduces the famous passage on double consciousness with such a stock scene:

> It is in the early days of rollicking boyhood that the revelation [of racial difference] first bursts upon one,

all in a day, as it were. I remember well when the shadow swept across me. I was a little thing, away up in the hills of New England. . . . In a wee wooden schoolhouse, something put it into the boys' and girls' heads to buy gorgeous visiting cards—ten cents a package—and exchange. The exchange was merry, till one girl, a tall newcomer, refused my card—refused it peremptorily, with a glance. Then it dawned upon me with a certain suddenness that I was different from the others; or like, mayhap, in heart and life and longing, but shut out from their world by a vast veil. (4)

With a "glance" from the tall girl, Du Bois instantly apprehends his place in an ideology of racial difference. The figure of the veil marks his fall from subjective sufficiency into the self-division of racial lack. Several entities divide: The sociopolitical world breaks in two—one black, one white; the individual's self-perception fractures through the double lens of seeing "one's self through the eyes of others"; and the nationality of American blacks cracks into the two, unevenly joined parts, African and American. These three realms of division correspond to sociopolitical, psychic, and national identities.

Representing racial acculturation through dramatic crises, the stock scenes of racial discovery both parallel and complicate the psychoanalytic claim that subjectivity forms in response to visual traumas. Freud's "primal scene" generates the castration anxiety that precipitates a boy's Oedipus complex and allows him to internalize a masculine gender identity. Lacan's mirror stage instantiates the infant's self-difference. This primary alienation underlying subjectivity resembles the self-difference of double consciousness. But psychoanalysis, a modernist discourse of identity, has emphasized gender and sexuality as the determining factors of social organization and individual development, neglecting the effects of race on ontogenesis. The trope of a singular event compressing the processes of acculturation to an instantaneous recognition of difference presents a juncture between the discourse of psychoanalysis and the discourse of modernity that allows us to critique psychoanalysis's general inattention to race. My essay inquires into the relationship between double consciousness and psychoanalytic theories of the subject by comparing two paradigms of masculine identity: Frederick Douglass's autobiography *Narrative of the Life of Frederick Douglass, An American Slave, Written by Himself* (1845) and Freud's Oedipus complex. Specifically, I address how the specular scenes of each account represent the consolidation of masculine identity against the image of a woman's castrated body. Comparing Douglass and Freud helps us explore how race inflects the masculine subject's relation to the paternal metaphor. It also makes clear how ideologies of race and nation shape identity in tandem with the symbolic order.

Because Douglass's account of one African-American man's entry into the symbolic order occupies a crucial position within African-American history and literature, the *Narrative* functions as a paradigmatic text of identity. No pre-Emancipation text by an African-American has enjoyed as much currency as Douglass's 1845 autobiography, which testified forcefully for abolitionism and has represented African-American literary and historical consciousness ever since. Commandeering American myths of self-reliance and heroic rebellion to describe his escape from slavery, Douglass extended symbolic citizenship to African-Americans (Andrews 166). His *Narrative* modeled "a coherent self that subsequent generations could use as a point of origin of written Afro-American discourse and subjectivity" (Cunningham 109). Deemed the "prototypical, premier example of the form," Douglass's text has eclipsed other narratives and genres of slave writing (McDowell 192). Its representation of subjectivity has a transformative—even transferential—effect.

Critics generally have attributed the *Narrative*'s resonance to its "literariness"—that is, its rendering of slave experience through a subtle narrative voice and set of metaphors (Smith 2). Such claims of transcendent literary value clarify neither the *Narrative*'s mythical stature nor its "widespread explanatory power and appeal" (McDowell 194). A "second wave" of Douglass criticism has begun to deconstruct the text's literary identity, arguing that Douglass claims universal subjecthood by idealizing masculinity. For instance, Valerie Smith notes that his terms of self-reliance and achievement affirm a specifically masculine American myth (21). Deborah McDowell chronicles the widespread, erroneous belief that Douglass wrote the first slave narrative—a misconception that, she argues, bolsters the text's importance in a tradition that grants authority to what is original, and consistently identifies originality as male (192–97). Finally, George P. Cunningham suggests that comparisons between Douglass and "Founding Fathers" such as Jefferson and Franklin create a "genealogical model" that fixes African-American literary identity as masculine (111). These theorists suggest that what critics have often touted as the *Narrative*'s universal value is, in part, an effective adaptation of certain modes of representation, which makes intelligible an African-American male identity by eclipsing black women (McDowell 198; Stone 64; Franchot 148).

Readers' sense of the *Narrative*'s truthfulness suggests that the text commands ideological belief, which "occurs at the moment when an image which the subject consciously knows to be culturally fabricated nevertheless succeeds in being recognized" as transparent reality (Silverman 17). Why does Douglass's combination of metaphor and masculinity compel ideological belief? In addition to mastering conventions of autobiography and providing eyewitness accounts of the horrors of slavery, Douglass molds his metaphors of masculinity from the basic components of slave society. His acquisition of freedom and subjectivity, which fosters (in his terms) a transition from slave to man, involves problems of parental lineage, linguistic authority, and physical autonomy (Olney 156). These problems mark the slave's generic, disempowered relation to the fundamental components of American identity. They also resonate with terms organizing the Lacanian Symbolic: the Name-of-the-Father, the phallus, and castration or lack. By describing his escape from slavery through metaphors corresponding to the tenets of American culture and the mechanisms of a historically specific symbolic order, Douglass manipulates the privileged terms of social hegemony. Kaja Silverman argues that our " 'dominant fiction' or ideological 'reality' solicits our faith above all else in . . . the adequacy of the male subject" (15–16); Douglass's autobiography creates such an icon of masculine sufficiency.

Freud's Oedipus complex and Douglass's *Narrative* are mythic *and* historically specific versions of the process by which male subjects submit to their symbolic systems. Both accounts engage a discourse of identity and difference; both are mythical case studies. By classifying the Oedipus complex as myth, I mean that Freud's theory of the boy's incestuous desire for the mother and sexual rivalry with the father does not summarize masculine desire; rather, it is an allegorical account of the boy's position in his sociosymbolic structure. The Oedipus complex metaphorizes, specifically, sexual difference, which determines the child's relation to paternal Law. Douglass's *Narrative* dramatizes a similar moment of sociopsychic alterity, but in this text racial and sexual differences violently affect ontogenesis. Since these differences combine to shape the subject's relation to the paternal metaphor, the *Narrative* demonstrates that classic psychoanalytic paradigms inadequately explain the relevance of race for subjectivity. Nevertheless, we cannot simply add race to psychoanalysis's conceptual frame. Vectors of racial identification operate constitutively in relation to those principles of sexuality and gender that we read in classical psychoanalysis. To illustrate this interdependence, I shall interpret competing identifications in the scene in which Douglass witnesses his aunt being whipped by his master. Douglass claims that this event is formative for his identity; I consider this episode paradigmatic for the book as a whole.

Douglass's *Narrative* contains two critical scenes marking shifts in his self-perception. The scene in which Douglass witnesses his aunt being whipped by his master instantiates Douglass's subjectivity as a slave; the scene in which he fights with the slavebreaker, Covey, allows Douglass to shed that slave identity in his own mind, if not in the eyes of the law. The effects of these events correspond to the transformations stated in Douglass's famous chiasmus: "You have seen how a man is made a slave; you shall see how a slave was made a man" (*Narrative* 107).

Critics generally consider Douglass's 1845 *Narrative* more striking than his later autobiographies, *My Bondage and My Freedom* and *The Life and Times of Frederick Douglass*; certainly the *Narrative* is more frequently read. I attribute these factors and my decision to focus on the 1845 autobiography to the way it (like psychoanalytic accounts of the Oedipus complex) condenses the gradual process of ontogenesis into a narrative flash. By comparison, *My Bondage* (1855) takes five chapters to relate the incidents of the whipping scene, also recounted in *Narrative*'s first chapter. I focus specifically on the *Narrative*'s whipping scene because it marks a crucial moment in Douglass's subjectivity, serving as a gateway to the text's themes of identity, literacy, and writing.

Is the Oedipus Complex Relative?

By comparing the Oedipus complex to Douglass's *Narrative*, I necessarily enter debates about the complex's universality and its relevance for African-American culture in particular. Freud's reading of Oedipus places ontogenesis in a culturally specific (Western, nuclear) drama: the boy's sexual demand for his mother and sexual rivalry with his father. This triangle is but one configuration of kinship structures and symbolic systems that engender subjective desire. Can we extrapolate from Freud's culturally specific narrative other family systems?

Anthropologists have long debated the universality of the Oedipus complex. Bronislaw Malinowski's *Sex and Repression in Savage Society* (1927) launched this debate by invoking the matrilineal (and patriarchal) Trobriand Islanders of Northeastern New Guinea. Malinowski found that Trobriand kinship represents the mother's brother as a boy's authority figure; correspondingly, the son "develops few ambivalent feelings toward the father" (Obeyesekere 71). Instead of rivalry with the father, the boy directs what we might call oedipal anxiety and aggression toward his maternal uncle, the kin member with most cultural authority over him. Malinowski concludes that since the boy's pattern of sexual and gendered socialization differs greatly from Freud's father-mother-child triad, we cannot simply "transfer" the Oedipus complex across cultures. Nonetheless, Gananath Obeyesekere has used cross-cultural variations in kinship structures to expand conceptions of the Oedipus complex. Without limiting the oedipal drama to Western, nuclear families, Obeyesekere argues that various configurations of kin members *do* determine the child's erotic and aggressive objects. These kinship structures comprise an Oedipus complex by inserting the child into its social order. In this respect, the Oedipus complex, while varying across cultures according to different models of kinship, is nonetheless constitutive of different formations of subjectivity (see Parsons 278).

Obeyesekere uses "the Oedipus complex" to denote how identity varies in kinship systems, but he expands Freud's framework by addressing power, not sexuality: "The centrality of the Oedipus complex lies in the structure of authority in the family, rather than in its sexual interrelations; consequently the Oedipus complex . . . varies with the type of family structure, especially in relation to the allocation of authority" (71). Obeyesekere reconceptualizes this complex as a drama about kinship, in which the child encounters affective ties and social authority. In this respect, Malinowski made clear the importance of power and authority for the subject's identifications—dimensions that Freud's emphasis on "the erotic nature of the son's ties with the mother and the sexual jealousy he has for the father" largely underplays (71).

Uncoupling links between authority and sexuality in family units not only gives the Oedipus complex more cultural specificity, but usefully severs this unit from biology. As Parsons writes, "Human societies do structure family patterns in different ways according to laws of kinship, or particular phrasings of the incest taboo, that by no means can be derived directly from the biological facts of mating and reproduction" (281). That the authority figure to whom the boy addresses his oedipal demand is not always physically present suggests that cultural symbolism can substitute psychically for "actual" experiences. For example, a Trobriand boy may internalize imagoes of his maternal uncle in ways that resemble Freud's oedipal structure, though the same boy may have little actual contact with this uncle. In this respect, we should not consider oedipal identification as a literal rendition of interpersonal relations: A child may identify with someone s/he has never met or who is no longer even alive.

Freud's recourse to the primal scene as an explanatory motif of masculine desire helps us gauge the intangible, unconscious processes that orient desire. At the same time, that Freud tried to universalize the Oedipus complex meant that he downplayed the significance of local, cultural factors such as the extended family. According to Obeyesekere, the Oedipus complex signals not the specific story of a boy's erotic demand for his mother and sexual rivalry with his father, but a child's general internalization and projection of desire, authority, aggressivity, and identification (24): "Sexuality, nurturance, domination and so forth are not simply engendered in the child's body; they are primarily products of his social relations in the family" (73).

Lacan's interpretation of the Oedipus complex focuses usefully on the constitutive basis of unconscious desire. Instead of describing the instinctual, universal *content* of man's unconscious desire, the Oedipus complex for Lacan indicates a *structure*, a "symbolic constellation underlying the unconscious of the subject," which causes the desire that must always be newly discovered in each case (Felman

103). For Lacan, Freud's Oedipus complex signifies a crucial metaphor of the West's familial structures.

If the Oedipus complex inaugurates a subject's desire relative to a specific social order, transposing it to Douglass's historically situated text does not reduce his desire to a question of incest and its prohibition. Since Douglass writes within and even aspires to the norms of the Euro-American social order from which psycho-analysis arose, his account usefully anticipates the Freudian/Lacanian paradigm of subjectivity. The *Narrative*'s similarities to European psychoanalytic models underscore that the social order not only regulates sexuality through mechanisms such as the incest taboo, but radically intervenes between the subject and its desire. Seen in this way, sexual desire for one's parents would indeed resist "formulaic universality" (Butler 76).

Family Values; or, The Economy of Kinship in Slavery

Douglass introduces the oedipal whipping scene in *Narrative* with a statement about his family origins. Although such a statement is typical of his autobiographical mod-els, Douglass's beginning atypically represents his father's name and his mother's body as absent: "My father was a white man. He was admitted to be such by all I ever heard speak of my parentage. The opinion was also whispered that my master was my father; but of the correctness of this opinion, I know nothing; the means of knowing was withheld from me. My mother and I were separated when I was but an infant" (48; see Niemtzow 117–18 and McDowell 198). For Cunningham, Douglass represents "his enslavement as the ontological dilemma of negation and absence" (112). We could consider this dilemma as a crucial element of slavery, or "natal alienation," from the legal decree that children of slave women do not inherit the name of their father, but rather "follow the condition of the mother":

> The whisper that my master was my father may or may not be true, and, true or false, it is of but little consequence to my purpose whilst the fact remains, in all its glaring odiousness, that slaveholders have ordained, and by law established, that the chil-dren of slave women shall in all cases follow the condition of their mothers; and this is done too obviously to administer to their own lusts, and make a gratification of their wicked desires profitable as well as pleasurable; for by this cunning arrange-ment, the slaveholder, in cases not a few, sustains to his slaves the double relation of master and father. (49)

Douglass argues that slavery is wrong because it leads white Americans to violate their laws of kinship: In cases of miscegenation, slavemaster fathers do not recog-nize their children. This law of kinship disenfranchises African-American slaves, since the cultural terms of citizenship and property depend on paternal recognition.[2] Douglass's personal circumstances therefore highlight one of the many material structures perpetuating slavery.

Douglass identifies kinship practices as a key sociolegal mechanism of slavery. Excluded from normative kinship patterns, the enslaved child "does become, under the press of a patronymic, patrifocal, patrilineal, and patriarchal order, the man/woman on the boundary, whose human status, by the very nature of the case, had yet to be defined" (Spillers 74). Because laws of inheritance apply principally to men, Douglass's masculine identity allows him to desire the authority of white men and to locate the cause of slavery in a loss of inheritance rights; the lack of his father's name signifies Douglass's overall disempowerment.

While this lack of paternal sanction has material effects on Douglass, it also greatly excludes him from symbolic meaning; his status as illegitimate deprives him of a lasting discursive position within "paternal Law." For Lacan, the child acquires language only by acceding to the symbolic order; the child must take up a masculine or feminine position in relation to that order. Whether male or female, however, the slave has no claim or clear relation to the phallus. Thus Douglass's lack of established paternity compounds his distance from the Father's name, frustrating his claim to masculine identification and his ability to speak from within his oppressive social order. His illegitimate status recurs discursively, for while slavery excludes blacks from political representation as citizens, it also excludes them from symbolic representation as subjects: "The master as a figure in discourse reserves to himself the masculine authority to generate meaning" (Cunningham 114). In this way, the Name-of-the-Father parses authority according to race and gender. Douglass must compensate for this lack to authorize his voice.

Douglass initially occupies no *socially* intelligible ground from which to speak: "To be a subject or 'I' at all, the subject must take up a sexualized position, identifying with the attributes socially designated as appropriate for men or women" (Grosz 148). In the Lacanian schema, an individual who does not accede to the paternal metaphor—that is, who is locked within the closed circuit of the mother-child dyad, and who remains outside social, linguistic, and economic exchange—is psychotic. Douglass clearly is not psychotic, but he nonetheless suggests that slavery confines the individual to a self-referential unit that obstructs the exchange necessary for symbolization and self-consciousness. In his famous comment on slave songs, he writes: "I did not, when a slave, understand the deep meaning of those rude and apparently incoherent songs. I was myself within the circle; so that I neither saw nor heard as those without might see and hear" (57). Here Douglass claims that the subjectivity he acquires as a slave differs radically from the subjectivity he achieves after literacy and liberation. Initially under slavery, his identity is nonreflective and presubjective. Following his master's explanation of why slaves are kept illiterate and from his own reading, however, Douglass begins to reflect on his unjust status; he acquires what Du Bois called a "double consciousness." Hearing Master Auld forbid Sophia Auld to teach him to read, Douglass "awakens" to consciousness; his master's words "sank deep into [his] heart,"

> stirr[ing] up sentiments within that lay slumbering, and called into existence an entirely new train of thought. It was a new and special revelation, explaining dark and mysterious things, with which my youthful understanding had struggled, but struggled in vain. I now understood what had been to me a most perplexing difficulty—to wit, the white man's power to enslave the black man. It was a grand achievement and I prized it highly. From that moment, I understood the pathway from slavery to freedom. (78)

This awareness of the operations of racial power, or double consciousness, is a defining condition of African-American subjectivity (Du Bois 2).

Under slavery, literacy assumes the role that language performs in the symbolic order: The ability to read paradoxically generates the sense of lack that positions the subject in relation to its social structure. While Lacan uses the paternal metaphor to explain the child's initial capacity for linguistic symbolization, Douglass uses it to explain the subject's access to discourse, particularly written language. As an African-American slave, he is not authorized to speak or write as such, much less to denounce slavery. By representing his exclusion from signification, however, Douglass begins properly to articulate his subjectivity; he appropriates symbolic dictates and thus partly subverts them. Indeed, by describing himself *as a slave*, Douglass resists the widespread assumption that slave identity is outside or beyond representation.

To authorize his slave subjectivity—an oxymoron in slave law—Douglass endeavors to appropriate normative masculinity. According to Jenny Franchot's superb analysis, Douglass authorizes his voice by fostering an ambivalent relation to the spectacle of his aunt's abuse: His "rhetorical exposure of the black woman's suffering body is crucial to his lifelong mission of disclosing the sins of the white fathers by turning slavery's hidden interiors into the publicized exterior of prose" (141). More important, however, "Douglass's description of [Hester's] whipping serves finally to make visible his heroic attainment of control, irony, and distance in the narrative voice" (148). Douglass vacillates between identifying as a slave to authenticate his narrative (and African-American identity) and shedding that identity to authorize his voice as a man. He authenticates his voice as Representative American Negro Man by temporarily aligning himself with his aunt. Yet his mimetic mastery of writing also allows him partly to suspend his enslavement:

Inscribing the Name-of-the-Father displaces his humiliation as a slave onto an African-American woman. Hester's "suffering provides him with his credentials as victim—critical to his self-authentication as fugitive slave-orator; her femininity enables him to transcend that identification" (Franchot 144).

Douglass equates his journey to freedom with a transition from slave to man, an achievement contingent upon his literacy. Literacy, in turn, generates a textual subject that largely requires an absence of feminine agency and speech: Hester does not speak; she only screams. Douglass's intended wife appears only after he has narrated his escape from slavery; he omits that her money financed his escape. Douglass also omits from his 1845 text incidents that illustrate his emotional vulnerability. In *My Bondage*, Douglass's "first introduction to the realities of slavery" is not the sight of Hester's tortured body, but his separation from his grandmother. After learning that he will no longer live with the woman who raised him, Douglass writes that he "fell upon the ground, and wept a boy's bitter tears, refusing to be comforted" (37). The image of a prostrate and "heartbroken" child, bereft of maternal love, replaces the 1845 account's image of a child silently witnessing his aunt's vulnerability. The 1855 text does narrate Hester's whipping some pages later, but the grandmother's loss is clearly formative: "The reader may be surprised that I narrate so minutely an incident apparently so trivial, and which must have occurred when I was no more than seven years old; but as I wish to give a faithful history of my experience in slavery, I cannot withhold a circumstance which, at the time, affected me so deeply. Besides, this was, in fact, my first introduction to the realities of slavery" (*Bondage* 37).

In *Narrative*, however, Douglass's self-appointed relation to patriarchal authority allows him to articulate the unrepresentable subjectivity of male slaves. In this respect, a gap emerges between his *recognition* of the place that paternal Law accords him and his *acceptance* of that place. Douglass indicates that beating the slavebreaker, Covey, widens this gap that literacy opened: "However long I might remain a slave in form, the day had passed forever when I could be a slave in fact" (113). This gap between an African-American's sociosymbolic position and his actual subjectivity offers some agency and resistance before the Law, though obviously he remains limited by laws. This psychic gap also suggests a foray into the inner workings of double consciousness, in which one can submit to the law while rehearsing for later defiance.

Chiasmatic Identifications

Douglass's introductory discussion of paternity *articulates* how the symbolic order can regulate a slave society, but the whipping scene *dramatizes* the process by which

Douglass learns his place in that order. This pairing, in the first chapter of Douglass's autobiography, of a description of the symbolic mechanism inscribing racial difference (the absence of the father's name) with an account of its enactment (the whipping scene) corresponds to the relation in psychoanalysis between the paternal metaphor as a mechanism of symbolic control and the oedipal drama that clarifies the subject's submission to that metaphor. While psychoanalytic theory explains—by way of the Oedipus complex—how the subject apprehends sexual difference, Douglass's whipping scene demonstrates how an individual also learns racial difference.

Slavery fragments kinship structures and precludes the type of nuclear family that Freud describes in the oedipal triangle, but Douglass's triad of master-aunt-self nonetheless composes a "family" unit in slave society. The white master is overdetermined as an oedipal father; he is the agent of a racist social order prohibiting Douglass not only from satisfying sexual desire, but from achieving basic autonomy, normative masculinity, self-determination, and access to language (literacy). The father/master also possesses sexual access to the mother. That Douglass speculates that his father is his master, irrespective of historical accuracy, forges a "family romance" that reproduces the patriarchal authority of American slave society.[3] Like the mother she replaces, Douglass's aunt is subject to the master/father's sexual demands. The whipping, Douglass implies, begins from the master's sexual jealousy; Hester would not stay away from a male slave with whom she was romantically linked. Consequently, the master

> took [Hester] into the kitchen, and stripped her from neck to waist, leaving her neck, shoulders, and back entirely naked. . . . After crossing her hands, he tied them with a strong rope, and led her to a stool under a large hook in the joist, put in for the purpose. . . . Her arms were stretched up at their full length, so that she stood upon the ends of her toes. He then said to her, "Now you d—d b—h, I'll learn you to disobey my orders!" and after rolling up his sleeves, he commenced to lay on the heavy cowskin, and soon, the warm, red blood (amid heart-rending shrieks from her, and horrid oaths from him) came dripping to the floor. (52)

These interrelations among master, aunt, and boy stage a scene that resembles Freud's account of the Oedipus complex. The whipping scene functions like a primal scene that triggers Douglass's "recognition" of racial difference from within the matrix of slavery's "family." The familial structure of Douglass's brutal scene ironically reinterprets proslavery rhetoric that likened the "peculiar institution" to the nuclear family. Douglass's nuclear "family" tells us something about the structures that legislate slavery, but it also signals Douglass's desire to represent himself within the frame of this legislation.

The whipping scene is primarily a visual event; that Douglass witnesses the whipping renders it formative:

> I remember the first time I *witnessed* this horrible exhibition. I was quite a child, but I well remember it. I shall never forget it whilst I remember any thing. It was the first of such outrages, of which I was doomed to be a *witness* and a participant. It struck me with an awful force. . . . It was a most terrible *spectacle*. . . . I was so terrified and horror-stricken at the *sight* that I hid myself in a closet, and dared not venture out till long after the bloody transaction was over. I expected it would be my turn next. It was all new to me. I had never *seen* anything like it before. (51, 52; my emphases)

The scene makes Douglass *recognize* his enslaved state; until this moment, he had been "out of the way of the bloody scenes that often occurred on the plantation," but he now "expected it would be [his] turn next" (52).

The function of sight bore other meanings in the nineteenth century, but I want to read this scene against two pivotal moments of seeing in Freud's account of ontogenesis to help clarify the role of fantasy and ambivalence in all sexual and racial identifications. According to Freud, the first crisis is when a boy sees female genitals; rarely does this "convince" him of women's castration. The second is the primal scene, in which a boy sees or imagines intercourse between his parents and again "discovers" women's castration. Douglass's whipping scene complicates this oedipal framework by placing racial difference crucially among the psychodynamics of sexual difference. To clarify this dynamic, we must revisit Freud's account of feminine and masculine castration.

According to Freud, castration anxiety usually assists the boy in "dissolving" his oedipal conflict and thus attaining masculine identification. The boy, however, does not at first believe that castration is a threat; he begins to fear it *only after he comes to accept female castration*: "To begin with the boy does not believe in the threat [of castration] or obey it in the least. . . . The observation which finally breaks down his unbelief is the sight of the female genitals. . . . Now his acceptance of the possibility of castration, his recognition that women were castrated, made an end of both possible ways [i.e., desire for each parent] of obtaining satisfaction from the Oedipus complex" ("Dissolution" 175, 176). We can infer from Freud that masculine identification hinges on a psychic belief in female castration. The girl's assumption of a feminine identity also hinges on her acceptance of women's castration, though this recognition initiates, rather than resolves, the feminine version of the Oedipus complex. For both genders, however, normative identification seems contingent on the belief that women are inferior to men; this belief appears to derive from the "fact" of their castration (that they don't have a penis).

This belief devolves on a visual event. In Freud's account, the sight of a woman's genitals precipitates castration anxiety in boys. Though this sight makes no immediate impression, the boy subsequently recalls this memory when his oedipal desire is impeded; he retroactively "realizes" that women are castrated:

> When a little boy first catches sight of a girl's genital region, he begins by showing irresolution and lack of interest; he sees nothing or disavows what he has seen. . . . It is not until later, when some threat of castration has obtained a hold upon him that the observation becomes important to him: if he then recollects or repeats it, it arouses a terrible storm of emotion in him and forces him to believe in the reality of the threat which he has hitherto laughed at. This . . . leads to two reactions, which may become fixed and . . . permanently determine the boy's relation to women: horror of the mutilated creature or triumphant contempt for her. ("Psychical" 21)

By contrast, the girl is supposed to "recognize" her lack immediately; we recall these now notorious lines: "She makes her judgement and her decision in a flash. She has seen [the penis] and knows that she is without it and wants to have it. . . . She begins to share the contempt felt by men for a sex which is the lesser in so important a respect" (21). In this scenario, assumptions about feminine inferiority are projected onto the female body, making gender difference a matter of sight and observation.

In the whipping scene, not only does the father figure represent the Law and the mother figure represent castration, but slavery and femininity seem to correspond as do freedom and masculinity. The aunt's powerlessness before the master mirrors the mother's castration relative to paternal Law. Seeing his aunt stripped to the waist, bound and beaten by his master, Douglass can disavow neither her lack nor her passivity. Although this scene's sexual content involves Hester's gender, it also implicates her race and status as a slave. As in Freud's account, Douglass discovers lack in the female body. However, Douglass clarifies better than Freud that the interpretation of sexual difference as lack derives from social context and its tyrannies.

Along what lines does Douglass identify? His perspective as "witness and participant" suggests that spectatorship is an active, even transformative, experience; the ambiguity of "participant" nonetheless begs a question about his precise role. What conclusions does Douglass draw from this sight of feminine humiliation? Does he identify along racial lines and perceive himself as similarly castrated— that is, as occupying a similar, "feminine" position—or does he distance himself from the slave's fate by identifying with his master's power? Douglass's gender implies identification with the master's authority; his race suggests identification with his aunt and her powerlessness. Like the boy who fears castration by his father, Douglass dreads that he will be whipped next; like the girl who internalizes a sense of inferiority, however, Douglass recognizes the slave's powerlessness as he passes through "the blood-stained gate" (51). Franchot puts this dilemma succinctly: "To achieve 'manhood' . . . is to forsake not only the mother but her race, whereas to achieve 'blackness' is to forsake the father and his virility" (142). How does Douglass resolve these cross-identifications?

Douglass's account of his spectatorship suggests that he identifies with *and* distances himself from his aunt's position. Like Freud's boy, Douglass is "horror-stricken" by the sight of her lack. This phrase implies sympathy and anxiety—a paralyzing fear of "seeing" femininity that recurs most clearly in the myth of Medusa. To distance himself from subjugation in slavery, and to avoid a sexual relation to the master/father by substituting for his aunt, Douglass appears to repress his identification with his aunt. All the same, slavery's racial structure runs counter to the "normative" oedipal dynamic, since it requires Douglass to identify with his "mother." Freud defines this psychic configuration as the "negative" Oedipus complex, or "feminine attitude," because the boy deems the father an object of desire, not a rival. Douglass's identification with the father is also blocked because, as a slave, he cannot claim the full benefits of masculine identity; this also endorses his "feminine attitude." Accordingly, the *Narrative*'s triangulated scene partly implies a homoerotic structure that requires enslaved African-American men first to identify with, then to desire, and always to fear, white men.

It is tempting to associate Douglass's "negative" or "feminine" Oedipus complex with the extenuating circumstances of slavery's mixture of race, sex, gender, and power. Yet Freud also interprets this "inversion" in a white European patient known as the Wolf Man. At one point in his tortuous way through the oedipal maze, the Wolf Man takes his father as an object of desire, thus identifying with his mother. Though Freud attributes this "feminine attitude" to an earlier "seduction" by his older sister—traumatic not because of a premature introduction to things sexual but because his sister's active behavior usurps the boy's gender role ("History" 210)—Freud explains that the Wolf Man's desire for his father is possible because he has not yet grasped the "fact" of women's castration. If the boy accepted women's castration, he would probably relinquish this "feminine" relation to avoid a similar fate. This argument clarifies that masculinity tends to equate male homosexuality with femininity. Although popular conceptions of the Oedipus complex assume that the boy's central task is to renounce the mother as an object of desire, fear of castration, in this case study, seems necessary to make the boy renounce his *father* as a comparable object.

Rerouting the Wolf Man's sexuality onto a masculine, heterosexual track seems to depend, as it does for Douglass, on appreciating the "fact" and price of women's castration. The Wolf Man grasps this price by witnessing (or fantasizing) his parents having sex: This primal scene "was able to show him what sexual satisfaction from his father was like; and the result was terror, horror of the fulfillment of the wish, the repression of the impulse" ("History" 221). Freud claims that the Wolf Man initially "misinterprets" this scene as an act of violence performed by his father against his mother, but he later "realizes" that his mother's passive, receptive position is normal and that castration is "a necessary condition of intercourse with the father" (231). This shift from "misinterpreting" coitus as violence to "realizing" that women's receptivity signifies castration does not eliminate associations of violence from the sexual scene, but it does ground them in natural law. This means not that heterosexual sex is tantamount to violence against women, but that in scenes in which coitus is psychically commensurate with gender inequality, women's disadvantage can appear as sexual victimization. Before the boy sustains his masculine identification, he sees the father's dominance as unjust and coercive. To assuage his terror of this domination, the Wolf Man renders the woman a natural receptacle for patriarchal force; after he discovers that she is castrated, the father's dominant posture appears psychically inevitable. In this way, the boy rescinds his identification with his mother to avoid *following her condition*.

This account of masculine identification tells us a great deal about Douglass's comparable dilemma. For instance, Douglass's account of his horror at the whipping resonates with Freud's description of the Wolf Man's initial horror at witnessing his parents having sex. Although fantasy clearly frames both scenes, violence in the first example is explicit; in the second, it is implicit (Cunningham 123). Douglass's *Narrative* stages the violence and coercion of the relationship between master and slave woman as an act of violence with a strong sexual undercurrent. Like the Wolf Man, Douglass wards off the terror of the master/father's authority by confining vulnerability to the (African-American) woman and by adopting a masculine identification. By revisiting the whipping scene as its author, Douglass controls the spectacle of the woman to confirm her status as a slave. While Freud's Wolf Man finally interprets the primal scene as proof of woman's castration, Douglass seems to attribute Aunt Hester's violation to her gender and race.

In this respect, the slave woman is an embodiment of slavery; indeed, her abused body is a standard motif of abolitionist literature. Although the *Narrative* states that men were also the victims of corporal abuse, with one exception Douglass describes horrific violence only against women. In addition to his account of Aunt Hester's humiliation, Douglass recounts that the "head, neck, and shoulders" of a young slave woman named Mary were "literally cut to pieces"; her head was "nearly covered with festering sores, caused by the lash of her cruel mistress" (80). Another "lame, young woman" was whipped "with a heavy cowskin upon her naked shoulders, causing the warm red blood to drip" (99). About the abuse he received, Douglass says only that he had been given "a number of severe whippings, all to no good purpose"—apparently, they did nothing to temper his defiance.

By depicting the bodies of abused slave women, Douglass conforms to a convention of abolitionist literature. Furthermore, Douglass clearly sympathizes with the tortured women and eschews self-indulgence by abbreviating descriptions of his own suffering. Yet he also defines agency as masculine by considering slave women passive victims. Describing his fight with Master Covey, to whom he had been sent in part for disciplining, Douglass contrasts his defiance with the other's passivity: He describes in detail his own whipped body to justify his violent response, which attests to physical power and self-control (Leverenz 109). Adding physical mastery to that of literacy, Douglass's pugilistic resistance "revive[s] within [him] a sense of [his] own manhood" and "inspire[s him] again with a determination to be free" (113). Christlike, Douglass undergoes "a glorious resurrection, from the tomb of slavery, to the heaven of freedom" (113); his sisters remain hung from their crucifixlike joists. Since " 'manhood' and 'freedom' function throughout Douglass's discourse as coincident terms," Franchot remarks, the black woman is left behind in bondage (153). Douglass's notable chiasmus—"You have seen how a man was made a slave; you shall now see how a slave was made a man"—seems to consign the woman to the position of slave in the slave/man binary.

Douglass's repeated accounts of slave women's—especially his Aunt Hester's—abuse in his three autobiographies have incurred charges that he is complicit with the master: For McDowell, he takes voyeuristic pleasure in recalling this abuse (203), while for Franchot, he "simulates the slaveholder's sexual abuse" by representing it (154). Douglass's compulsion to repeat this scene may indicate his partial identification with the master, but it may also attempt to control the loss of his aunt/mother as an object of desire and possible identification. As in Freud's account of the child who substitutes the presence and absence of an object for the mother's comparable appearances and disappearances, Douglass seems to diffuse his anger at slavery's abuse of women by attempting to create textual control. Thus while I have explored how Douglass's identity seems to require the passivity of black women, I do not mean that Douglass was insensitive to women's oppression, whether black or white: He strongly opposed the abuse of enslaved women and supported female suffrage. However, Douglass did break later with the suffragists when it seemed that black men would get the vote before black or white women. When forced to choose, he argued that black men needed such rights more than women did. He performed a similar triage in his *Narrative*, albeit unconsciously and indirectly.

If Douglass partly displaces his disempowerment as a slave by reducing slavery to his aunt's abused body and by engaging in compensatory linguistic representation of her abuse, he seems to cope with subjective lack by insisting on female castration and by deploying linguistic authority to maintain this truth. That Hester is castrated for Douglass may exemplify a psychoanalytic model in which all subjects are constituted by lack but male lack is usually repressed by mistaken assumptions that the father simply *is* the Law and that the penis *is* the phallus, etc. Douglass hints at this assumption and its symbolic compensation when he writes, "My feet have been so cracked with the frost, that the pen with which I am writing might be laid in the gashes" (72). In contrast to Hester's silent suffering, Douglass's abused body authorizes his speech (Franchot 154–55).

That Douglass's text seems to *need* women's castration and humiliation, in which women are reduced to a literally mutilated body, helps clarify a shift in psychoanalytic theory from Freud to Lacan. Douglass's *Narrative* uses the image of a castrated woman to foster fantasies of masculine control over meaning. The link between a woman's damaged body and a man's ability to make meaning demonstrates Lacan's claim that what Freud sometimes explained as anatomical fact (female castration) is really a symbolic condition for signification. Freud's oedipal drama of castration, in which the boy identifies with his father on the condition that he see his mother as castrated, is, for Lacan, an allegory for the lack that signals the subject's entry into language. In the oedipal scenario, the lack common to all subjects is projected onto the mother and the father initially appears uncastrated. In this way, the actual and symbolic father are conflated, as are the penis and phallus; masculinity bears a privileged relationship to the order of language. Under conditions of slavery, in which white men seem to approximate paternal Law, whiteness also has a privileged relationship to meaning. In such social formations, the symbolic order is linked to the phallus *and* to whiteness. That psychoanalysis privileges the phallus as signifier of desire highlights its presumption that the order of symbols is determined by gender and sexuality, and not by race.

That slave women's children were born into slavery, following the condition of the mother, helped ensure that African-Americans were barred from any meaningful relation to the symbolic order. As Silverman writes, "the kinship structure through which a particular symbolic order articulates the incest prohibition [is] capable of determining the ideological signifier through which lack is represented" (37). The scene of double consciousness dramatizes how ideologies of race and nation intersect with the symbolic order regulating sexual difference. As Douglass's text makes clear, racial identifications both constitute and frustrate gender identifications. The *Narrative* manipulates these contradictory identifications of gender and race according to the demands of public discourse on race; Douglass claims American citizenship by rewriting his relation to the Name-of-the-Father, thereby authorizing his voice as an abolitionist. Mapping these mutually constitutive identifications clarifies not only how race inflects the subject's relation to language and sexuality, but how Douglass, like Freud, circulated myths of a sufficient masculinity by projecting lack onto women. By exploring the intersection of racial and sexual differences in the process of subject formation, I propose further consideration of the relation between the social and the symbolic, as well as a rethinking of the terms and stability of symbolic Law.

ENDNOTES

I am grateful to Diana Fuss, Anthony A. Monsanto, Jr., Abdul Kareem Mustapha, Michael Newbury, and Timothy B. Spears for their helpful comments and suggestions.

1. Notable fictional and autobiographical texts containing such stock scenes include Frederick Douglass's *Narrative of the Life of Frederick Douglass* (1845), James Weldon Johnson's *Autobiography of an Ex-Colored Man* (1912), William Faulkner's *Absalom, Absalom!* (1936), Zora Neale Hurston's *Their Eyes Were Watching God* (1937), and Lillian Smith's *Strange Fruit* (1944).

2. In one of many observations on Douglass's uncertain beginning, Gates writes: "[F]or Douglass, the bonds of blood and kinship are the primary metaphors of human culture." Family ties are more than a metaphor in this text, however; "laws" of kinship structure human society on symbolic and sociolegal levels, both of which have material effects on individuals. Gates himself notes, in the case of slavery, that "patrilinear succession of the planter has been forcibly replaced by a matrilinear succession for the slave" ("Binary" 70).

3. "The profound ambiguity of this relationship between father and son and [between] master and slave persists, if only because the two terms 'father' and 'master' are here embodied in one, with no mediation between them" (Gates, "Binary" 70).

WORKS CITED

Andrews, William L. "The Performance of the *Narrative*." In Bloom. 165–82.

Bloom, Harold, ed. *Frederick Douglass's Narrative of the Life of Frederick Douglass*. New York: Chelsea House, 1988.

Butler, Judith. *Gender Trouble: Feminism and the Subversion of Identity*. New York: Routledge, 1990.

Cooke, Michael G. *Afro-American Literature in the Twentieth Century*. New Haven: Yale UP, 1984.

Cunningham, George P. " 'Called Into Existence': Desire, Gender, and Voice in Frederick Douglass's *Narrative* of 1845." *Differences* 1.3 (1989): 108–36.

Douglass, Frederick. *The Life and Times of Frederick Douglass*. 1910. New York: Gramercy, 1993.

——. *Narrative of the Life of Frederick Douglass, An American Slave, Written by Himself*. 1845. New York: Penguin, 1986.

——. *My Bondage and My Freedom*. 1855. Urbana: U of Illinois P, 1987.

Du Bois, W. E. B. *Souls of Black Folk*. 1903. Mineola, N.Y.: Dover, 1994.

Faulkner, William. *Absalom, Absalom!* 1936. New York: Vintage, 1990.

Felman, Shoshana. *Jacques Lacan and the Adventure of Insight: Psychoanalysis in Contemporary Culture*. Cambridge: Harvard UP, 1987.

Franchot, Jenny. "The Punishment of Esther: Frederick Douglass and the Construction of the Feminine." *New Literary and Historical Essays on Frederick Douglass*. Ed. Eric J. Sundquist. New York: Cambridge UP, 1990. 141–65.

Freud, Sigmund. "From the History of an Infantile Neurosis." 1918 (1914). Vol. 17 of *The Standard Edition of the Complete Psychological Works of Sigmund Freud*. 24 vols. Ed. and trans. James Strachey. London: Hogarth, 1953–74. 3–122.

——. "The Dissolution of the Oedipus Complex." 1924. Vol. 19 of *SE*. 173–79.

——. "Some Psychical Consequences of the Anatomical Distinction between the Sexes." 1925. Vol. 19 of *SE*. 248–58.

Gates, Jr., Henry Louis. "Binary Oppositions in Chapter One of the *Narrative*." In Bloom. 59–75.

Gates, Jr., Henry Louis, ed. *"Race," Writing, and Difference*. Chicago: U of Chicago P, 1986.

Grosz, Elizabeth. *Jacques Lacan: A Feminist Introduction*. New York: Routledge, 1990.

Hurston, Zora Neale. *Their Eyes Were Watching God*. 1937. Urbana: U of Illinois P, 1978.

Johnson, James Weldon. *Autobiography of an Ex-Colored Man*. 1912. New York: Hill and Wang, 1960.

Leverenz, David. *Manhood and the American Renaissance*. Ithaca: Cornell UP, 1989.

Malinowski, Bronislaw. *Sex and Repression in Savage Society*. 1927. Chicago: U of Chicago P, 1985.

McDowell, Deborah E. "In the First Place: Making Frederick Douglass and the Afro-American *Narrative* Tradition." *Critical Essays on Frederick Douglass*. Ed. William L. Andrews. Boston: G. K. Hall, 1991. 192–214.

Niemtzow, Annette. "The Problematic of Self in Autobiography: The Example of the Slave Narrative." In Bloom. 113–30.

Obeyesekere, Gananath. *The Work of Culture*. Chicago: U of Chicago P, 1990.

Olney, James. " 'I Was Born': Slave Narratives, Their Status as Autobiography and as Literature." *The Slave's Narrative*. Ed. Charles T. Davis and Henry Louis Gates, Jr. New York: Oxford UP, 1985. 148–75.

Parsons, Anne. "Is the Oedipus Complex Universal?" *The Psychoanalytic Study of Society* 3 (1964): 278–328.

Silverman, Kaja. *Male Subjectivity at the Margins*. New York: Routledge, 1992.

Smith, Lillian. *Strange Fruit*. New York: Reynall and Hitchcock, 1944.

Smith, Valerie. *Self-Discovery and Authority in Afro-American Narrative*. Cambridge: Harvard UP, 1987.

Spillers, Hortense. "Mama's Baby, Papa's Maybe: An American Grammar Book." *Diacritics* 17.2 (1987): 65–81.

Stone, Albert E. "Identity and Art in Frederick Douglass's *Narrative*." In Bloom. 62–78.

Wald, Priscilla. *Constituting Americans: Cultural Anxiety and Narrative Form*. Durham: Duke UP, 1995.

11

Nat Turner's Thing

Merrill Cole

Continuity's Omissions

In his important study *The Black Atlantic: Modernity and Double Consciousness*, Paul Gilroy attempts not only to account for the wide variety of cultural formations engendered by the African diaspora but to present the continuing tradition of black cultural articulation as a challenge and countertradition to modernity. Working within a cultural studies framework, Gilroy deemphasizes the localizing strategies of conventional ethnographic research to prioritize what James Clifford terms "the project of comparing and translating different traveling cultures" (107). Gilroy also follows W. E. B. Du Bois in insisting on "the intimate association of modernity and slavery" (53); history that excludes slavery fails to read modern society. To rectify Eurocentric historiography's neglect of transatlantic black culture, Gilroy aims to explore "the omissions and absences" (45):

> I am suggesting something more than the corrective inclusion of those black commentaries on the modern which have so far been overlooked by Western intellectual history. I intend not only to question the credibility of a tidy, holistic conception of modernity but also to argue for the inversion of the relationship of margin to center as it has appeared within the master discourses. (45)

Introducing "the slaves' perspective" as a singularly compelling counterdiscourse, Gilroy employs Frederick

Douglass and Margaret Garner as his "representative figures" (56). Their histories—Douglass' emancipation narratives and Margaret Garner's historical record,
the chief source materials for Toni Morrison's *Beloved*—epitomize black resistance to "the ethical darkness of slavery" (59). These accounts present "the idea of
a revolutionary or eschatological apocalypse," a redemptive "Jubilee" that, Gilroy
argues, imbues the written tradition of black modernity (56). Given this emphasis,
I find troubling Gilroy's almost complete disregard of Nat Turner.

Why does Turner, the leader of the most famous slave revolt in United States
history, appear only once in *The Black Atlantic*, in a sidelong reference? And why
does Gilroy's retelling of the past neglect to discuss *The Confessions of Nat Turner*,
arguably one of the most influential texts in the history of slavery? I contend that
the omission is symptomatic, indicating the upsurge of the unconscious that
Gilroy's continuist narrative must leave out in order to cohere. Moreover, I claim
that the elision hints at something intrinsic to *The Confessions of Nat Turner*, an
infectious "symptom" operating in both the text and the history of its reception.
To trace this "symptom," I use Lacanian psychoanalysis, which reads events that
traumatize linear and redemptive conceptions of history. Psychoanalysis insists on
what conscious reason cannot surmise—on what resists the most trenchant efforts
of interpretive recuperation. With attention to the disruptive event, to what it
terms "the symptom," psychoanalysis reconsiders trauma in a way that continuist
historiography, however diligent and all-embracing, necessarily cannot. Psychoanalysis attends to manifestations of the unconscious.

Intent on reading the history of slavery in terms of "the complicity of rationality with ethnocidal terror" (213), Gilroy halts before the terror that disturbs the
redemptive pieties, the "articulating principles" (191), structuring his approach. His
attachment to the project of "redemptive critique" (71) precludes his investigating
the murderous interpretive violence that *The Confessions of Nat Turner* details.
Whereas Douglass's narratives exemplify the possibilities of resolving the antagonism between reason and its outcasts, *The Confessions of Nat Turner* shows that the
constitutive complicity of reason and terror is less easy to undo. Gilroy's narrative
commitment to "a *changing* rather than unchanging same" (101) disallows the
recognition of *difference unamenable to continuity's appropriation* and refuses to take
into account the historical dismemberment announced by Turner's witness.

Instead, Gilroy finds Douglass's version of intellectual resistance to servitude
"exemplary" (58). Douglass "repeatedly calls for a greater Enlightenment capable
of bringing the illumination of reason" to slavery's dark circumstances (61).
Gilroy follows Douglass in focusing on the latter's struggle with Covey as the pivotal moment of his progress. In *Narrative of the Life of Frederick Douglass, An
American Slave, Written by Himself* (1845), this paradigmatic skirmish, in which

Douglass holds his own against a notorious " 'nigger breaker' " (Douglass 100), concludes with a message of hope:

> The battle with Mr. Covey was the turning-point in my career as a slave. It rekindled the few expiring embers of freedom, and revived within a sense of my own manhood. It recalled the departed self-confidence, and inspired me again with a determination to be free. The gratification afforded by the triumph was a full compensation for whatever else might follow, even death itself. He only can understand the deep satisfaction which I experienced, who has himself repelled the bloody arm of slavery. I felt as I never felt before. It was a glorious resurrection, from the tomb of slavery, to the heaven of freedom. (113)

This parable of spiritual progress underwrites the entire narrative: Douglass intends his "little book" to "do something toward throwing light on the American slave system" (159). Predating his escape from slavery, the turning point is the end of *subjective* servitude.

Although Gilroy criticizes Douglass's narratives for their masculinist and rationalist biases, he too emphasizes this skirmish, which he reads as the redemptive rewriting of "the dialectic of intersubjective dependency and recognition that Hegel's allegory presents as modernity's precondition" (68). In the Master-Slave dialectic, two uncivilized combatants meet before the advent of human society. One fighter submits to the other; one is recognized as master, and the other as slave. This pact, the rational accord founding society, is the sole condition by which the slave evades extinction. His subjective defiance matters not at all; only labor can bring him freedom.

According to Gilroy, however, Douglass challenges Hegel's canonical version of the myth in which "one solipsistic combatant . . . prefers his conqueror's version of reality to death and submits" (63). In slave narratives such as Douglass's, Gilroy asserts, the "positive preference for death rather than continued servitude can be read as a contribution of slave discourse on the nature of freedom itself" (68):

> The discourse of black spirituality which legitimises these moments of violence possesses a utopian truth content that projects beyond the limits of the present. The repeated choice of death rather than bondage articulates a principle of negativity that is opposed to the formal logic and rational calculation characteristic of modern western thinking and expressed in the Hegelian slave's preference for bondage rather than death. (68)

A violence that produces no death and results, at least directly, in little freedom, is easier to defend than the horror of Garner's infanticide, Gilroy's other example. Gilroy defers interpreting Garner's act, declaring that "[i]t is impossible to explore" the complex "issues of maternity" within the scope of his book (68). He declines to demonstrate precisely how the "negativity" of choosing death "*legitimises* these moments of violence" (my emphasis). How jubilee redeems violence, in its replacing reason with spirituality, goes unanswered. Gilroy also neglects to elaborate on how jubilee overcomes negativity with "utopian truth content."

To garnish intellectual support for Douglass's supposed revision of the Master-Slave dialectic, in which the defeated combatant now prefers death to slavery, Gilroy misquotes Jacques Lacan: " 'death, precisely because it had been drawn into the function of stake in the game [*sic*] . . . shows at the same time how much of the prior rule, as well as of the concluding settlement, has been elided. For in the last analysis it is necessary for the loser not to perish, in order to become a slave. In other words, the pact everywhere precedes violence before perpetuating it' " (Gilroy 63). Gilroy distorts Alan Sheridan's translation of Lacan to gerrymander the latter's meaning; he excises Lacan's complexity. This paragraph from "The Subversion of the Subject and the Dialectic of Desire in the Freudian Unconscious" actually reads as follows, without Gilroy's ellipsis:

> But precisely because it is drawn into the function of the stakes—a more honest wager than Pascal's, though it is also a question of poker, since there is a limit on how high one can raise the bid—death shows by the same token what is elided from a prior rule, and from the ultimate rule. For, in the end, the loser must not perish if he is to become a slave. In other words, the pact is everywhere anterior to the violence before perpetuating it, and what I call the symbolic dominates the imaginary, which is why one may ask oneself whether murder is the absolute Master. ("Subversion" 308)

Reversing Hegel's causal relation between violence and rational accord, Lacan does not argue that the loser morally *ought* to perish; instead, he emphasizes that the choice of a subjectivity free from symbolic violence, as Gilroy understands it, *simply does not exist*. If the slave does not die, she or he remains fettered to the pact. Only through death does the slave escape the pact, which is another name for the symbolic order.

Although Lacan maintains a distinction between two deaths, the physical death and the symbolic, "second" death ("Subversion" 325 n.11), Douglass's "inclination" (Gilroy 68) qualifies as neither: Douglass remains ensconced within the symbolic order he challenges. He not only consents to remain a slave for some time but maintains a lifelong intellectual negotiation, after physical emancipation, with the rational system oppressing him. Intent on reading Douglass against Hegel, Gilroy fails to acknowledge how Douglass sustains the Master-Slave dialectic: By accepting the "conqueror's version of reality" as modifiable, as *a changeable same* and thereby as preferable to death, Douglass confirms Hegel's Enlightenment myth. As I will show, *The Confessions of Nat Turner* better illustrates Lacan's objection to Hegel's triumphant rationality.

Turner briefly appears in *The Black Atlantic* in a passing quotation from Frederick Douglass's *Narrative*. Introducing Douglass's struggle, Gilroy writes, "this section of the narrative begins with Douglass being leased into Covey's care by Thomas Auld—his 'real' master. Having broken up the Sabbath school that Douglass had organized for his fellow slaves, Auld desired his slave to be 'well broken' lest he develop into 'another Nat Turner' " (61). Gilroy's sole reference presents Turner as an *unexplained* negative example, his account proceeding quickly to the paradigmatic encounter. Auld fears that Douglass's religious charisma will provoke something resembling Turner's insurrection. By not elucidating this analogy, Gilroy perhaps suggests that Turner is an inappropriate model and that his story might even interfere with Gilroy's project. While it is vital to elaborate on the scope of black cultural contributions to modernity, and to map the many continuities spanning the Atlantic Ocean, this essay contends that the history that is irrecoverable—that refuses to close up and suture, and that questions history itself—requires more subtle consideration.

Without attention to untranslatable otherness, cultural transmission continues in patriarchal fashion, with all the ugly connotations the word *patriarchy* suggests. Juxtaposing Garner with Douglass, Gilroy enlists "the work of feminist philosophers who have opposed the figuration of woman as a sign for the repressed or irrational other of rationality identified as male" (45), and he parallels this work to "an archeology of the icons of the blacks that appear as signs of rational disorder or as a means to celebrate the power of human nature uncorrupted by the decadence of the civilizing process. In either guise, blacks enjoy a subordinate position in the dualistic system that produces the dominance of bonded whiteness, masculinity, and rationality" (45–46). In his account of Hegel's dialectic, however, Gilroy employs Douglass "as a means to celebrate" a supposedly uncompromised resistance to slavery. Gilroy's instrumental use of Douglass's example belies the antirationalist agenda: Rather than challenging the interpretive system mandating domination, Gilroy reproduces it in a modified form. His search for redemptive continuity is patriarchal because it not only involves the transmission of tradition from father to son—from Douglass, as well as from such "representative figures" as Du Bois and Richard Wright, to Gilroy—but effaces the unrecoverable past. Determined to make coherent sense of slavery, Gilroy avoids historical trauma and subsumes otherness to the purposes of his critique.

Space for Desire

A history without spaces——without unrecuperable figures and events, without disruption or slippage, and without the unconscious and otherness—is a history bereft of possibility: If historical narrative inexorably plots the fulfillment of its own demands, resistance as such can only propel it. To make room for social change beyond the chain reactions of determinist causality, psychoanalysis acknowledges that historical law—like all discursive structures—disappoints logical consistency. Lacan names desire as the dynamic eluding epistemological capture. Desire's operation bars the text's access to self-reflexive knowledge, whether that "text" be a historical reading, a literary work, an individual, or a society. In his effort to produce a history capable of responding to his self-reflexive review, Gilroy erases, rather than acknowledges, the difficulty and partial irrationality of desire. For Gilroy and similar cultural historians, the exigencies of discursive sequencing and critical argumentation override examination of unsynthesizable detail, and figures who fail to meet the historian's explanatory standard ultimately fall by the wayside.

Failing to suture desire and fulfillment, discursive law cannot eradicate the resistance emerging from its constitutive self-contradiction. Instead, this law aggravates the antagonism it seeks to overrule because it irritates the wound it would heal, incessantly reexposing its symptom. In *Read My Desire: Lacan Against the Historicists*, Joan Copjec argues that historical readings rejecting the psychoanalytic concept of desire collapse society into its relations, failing to register the element that disrupts the self-reflexive closure of the system. Such readings lack lack; they try to collapse desire's divide by foreclosing the unconscious. Neglecting to admit the omissions, they plot causal relations as though the strategies of narrative continuity structured the very course of history. Their continuism cannot respond to "the *genealogy* of social spaces and the resistances to it" because they lack the psychoanalytic principle that "a regime's institution always in some way *negates* the regime it institutes" (10).

Stressing "the importance of ritual brutality in structuring modern, civilized life" (199), Gilroy fails to discern its traces in his writing. Though he argues for "the value of trying to revisit the sites of ineffable terror" (218), his "emphasis on the imaginative reappropriation of history" (222) forgets that the "ineffable," by definition, foils the most well-meaning of descriptions. Instead of providing the inexpressible a voice, his redemptivism doctors it for rational explanation. The Lacanian model he tangentially misappropriates, however, promises more to the study of "ritual brutality" than Gilroy admits. In *Reading Lacan*, Jane Gallop warns that "interpretation is always motivated by desire to have and desire to kill, which is to say, interpretation always takes place within a transferential situation" (27). Since interpretation is a manifestation of desire, a reading that disregards desire blinds itself to desire's constitutive play of mastery and servitude. On the one hand, transference names the process whereby the reader supports the illusion of a text's mastery; on the other hand, it presumes to comprehend the text from an interpretive position of mastery. Transference presupposes that knowledge inheres somewhere. Though no interpretation can circumvent transference, ignoring its operation "necessitates a violent reduction of the contradictory plurality" of the text under scrutiny (27).

Psychoanalysis offers a methodology that goes beyond redemptivism because it *reads the violence constituting interpretation*. Psychoanalysis counters presumptive models of continuity with the jouissance splintering progressive temporality. A structurally ambivalent French term designating suffering as much as pleasure,[1] "jouissance" names the state in which the egoic subject shatters with unsustainable enjoyment. In other words, the unconscious erupts. Although the word *enjoyment* may sound peculiar relative to slave revolt, I shall demonstrate how much it offers to historical study by providing a close, Lacanian reading of sections of *The Confessions of Nat Turner*.

Nat Turner and Lacan

Asked to explain the events leading to the August 1831 slave revolt in Southampton, Virginia, Nat Turner, the revolt's leader, recounts the signs portending that he "surely would be a prophet" (5). Among other indicators, Turner reads the characters of his "great promise" in "certain marks on my head and breast" (5). The recorder of his statement, Thomas C. Gray, cannot coerce a confession of guilt from the unrepentant prisoner. Instead, within textual brackets, he adds a debunking commentary on these physical marks: "[a parcel of excrescences, which, I believe, are not at all uncommon, particularly among Negroes, as I have seen several with the same. In this case, he had either cut them off, or they had nearly disappeared]" (5). Gray interrupts Turner's narrative to insert his own text: Condemning Turner's interpretation, he adds another, replete with racist ill will. Belittling Turner's scars marks *The Confessions of Nat Turner* in another way. The gesture of repetition—certainly not the only one in the text—suggests something more portentous about Turner's story than Gray can allow.

The insistent repetition characterizing Gray's reply to Turner responds to a dynamic inherent in Turner's testimony. Such insistence also colors the legal and journalistic reaction to Turner. Turner's execution reenacts his trajectory; in attempting to reinscribe justice in their own terms, the court and the newspapers unwittingly parody the insurrection, rendering questionable the call to justice itself. When one act of violence calls forth its own parody, the urgent calling forth itself—the voice of the superego—reveals its ferocity.

In *The Confessions of Nat Turner*, we see not only the insistence of excrescences but that of blood and revenge. The reiterative quality of the violence demonstrates its uncanny and symptomatic status, revealing a symbolic system grappling with the Lacanian real. The real cannot be integrated into symbolic reality; it is the site of the repressed desire that founds the symbolic order and threatens to undo it. As Renata Salecl explains in *The Spoils of Freedom*, "behind every ideology," behind every symbolic structuring of reality, "lies a kernel of enjoyment (jouissance) that resists being fully integrated into the ideological universe" (6). The real of slavery, of ethnocidal terror and subjugation, functions as Southern slave society's symptom—as the enabling condition threatening to undermine this society. By embodying this symptom, Turner is hardly incorrect to see his marks as a sort of prophetic heraldry. More than a metonym of his mission, these "certain marks" point to a complication that slave society cannot resolve, an excessive repetition irreconcilable to the order of social meaning. Salecl elaborates that the scene of unbearable jouissance, the locus of the encounter with the real, "is where fantasy comes into play: fantasy stages a scenario to conceal" the frightening kernel of enjoyment (6). Slavery ideology fantasizes that some should serve and others rule: Everyone is content when the servitude of the lesser serves the greater social good.[2] Turner disrupts this simple and rigid fantasy; I shall argue that he more closely approximates a personification of the death drive than does any stereotype of "the contented slave" (Oates).

In *The Sublime Object of Ideology*, Slavoj Žižek describes the symptom as "a certain signifier which is not enchained in a network but immediately filled, penetrated with enjoyment [jouissance]" (76). The symptom, the mark of the unconscious, refuses to represent what interpretive authority would define it as being; in the case of Turner's marks, the signifier fails to support the symbolization Gray imposes— black ignorance. Turner will not "renounce his symptom" (74); rejecting Gray's literalization, he repents of nothing. Gray hears in his nervous interpolation a reasonable explanation for Turner's marks. However, the place to which these signs point, the "late insurrection in Southampton," eludes him (3). Analogous to its executionary dispatches, Turner's revolt delivers a jolt to social reason's coherence. Just as Turner's crusade culminates in the murder of at least fifty-five whites, so his record enacts symbolic violence. *The Confessions of Nat Turner* reveals the social foundation *as* violence. Attempting to explain the strange raised marks that had once appeared on Turner's skin, Gray unwittingly recalls the insurrection's victims, claiming that Turner "had either cut them off, or they had nearly disappeared." Turner reads these marks textually, as signs; Gray, in his effort to disqualify Turner's sign-reading, ends up reproducing it.

By connecting Turner's actions with enjoyment, I am not implying that the slaves "enjoyed" their revolt, or that insurrection is a pastime. In *The Ethics of Psychoanalysis*, Lacan discusses the relation between transgression and jouissance, arguing that the latter registers an attainment of desire that shatters its possessor beyond the comfortable realm of social fantasy. How the subject, or society, deals with jouissance is an ethical question: "The moral dimension of Freud's theoretical elaboration is located nowhere else than in desire itself" (3). According to Lacan, "God is summoned" in a wide range of ethical accounts, as "the Other to whom [the] ordeal is addressed, in the last analysis its Judge" (4). The Father functions as judge not only in pious accounts such as Saint Augustine's and moral philosophy such as Kant's, but in the Marquis de Sade's putatively transgressive writings. These discourses invoke the Names of the Father: In one form or another, they call on patriarchal authority to justify their imperatives. The more a discourse relies on the moral voice of the Father, however, the more vicious its demands become.

If ever an "obscene and ferocious figure" of moral agency appears (*Ethics* 7), it is the voice calling Nat Turner. This superegoic agency functions as no civilized "moral conscience": "Whoever attempts to submit to the moral law sees the demands of his superego grow increasingly meticulous and increasingly cruel" (176). As Copjec explains, "Moral order is established, according to psychoanalysis, not in obedience to some reasonable or compassionate command to sacrifice our pleasure to the state but because we recoil before the violence and obscenity of the superego's incitement to *jouissance*, to a boundless and aggressive enjoyment" (92). For Copjec, Lacan teaches "the ethical necessity of hearing the otherness of this voice and of maintaining our distance from it" (98). Turner, on the contrary, closes the divide between the Father's voice and himself; he shows the immeasurable gain and the unspeakable terror that such collapse entails.

When Gray, exasperated by the fantastic turns of Turner's narrative, asks him, "Do you not find yourself mistaken now?" Turner replies, "Was not Christ crucified?" (8). This is Turner's full response to the question. Although Gray takes it as a proof of fanaticism, the logic of crucifixion serves as Turner's precise refutation of the case against him. In Gray's version of events, Turner takes his religion too far, beyond the law's proper limits. Nonetheless, the volume of Gray's maledictions against Turner—"atrocious circumstances" (3), "dreadful conspiracy" (3), "diabolical actors" (3) "ferocious band" (3), "barbarous villains" (11), and against Turner himself, whom he calls "warped and perverted" (13), and "fiend-like" (14, twice)—discloses the uneasiness of Gray's authority. When characterizing the insurrection as "this unparalleled and inhuman massacre" (14), Gray admits that he cannot integrate it into his symbolic reality.

To the Southern white community at least, Turner's insurrection takes on the dimensions of the Thing, which according to Lacan maintains itself "in the real" (*Ethics* 118). Not susceptible to symbolic integration, the Thing is a scrap of mundane existence embodying the horror of the real, which simultaneously structures and undermines the entire symbolic field. It is an emptiness, a hole, around which "intentions can always be wrapped" (132). The Thing is not the black man's penis, despite the pun my title introduces to modify the fantasy that it is: Although white American Southerners often castrated their black victims, imbuing the organ with myth, Turner is executed by the official "hand of retributive justice" (Turner 14), a hand not supposed to go below the belt. The castration that the law requires of Turner is symbolic, Turner's corpse serving as the text representing his symbolic castration. The circumstances of Turner's trial, however, suggest that his status has changed from that of a slave; his confessions are "fully and voluntarily made" (1). In a display of fetishistic logic—logic maintaining irreconcilable claims—the law demands that a piece of property display a certain degree of willful choice. The court knows that Turner is not a free man, but it insists on treating him as such for the purposes of justice.

Although the Chairman of the Jury names Turner's "the highest crimes in our criminal code" (15), Turner more accurately figures as the disruption of that code, the point where its articulation sputters. This attempt to render justice is a feeble echo of Turner's calling, a faulty mirroring of Turner's rhetoric. The verdict of guilty—"be hung by the neck until you are dead! dead! dead!—and may the Lord have mercy on your soul!" (15)—shows how interpretation takes place within a transferential relation. Transference creates the apparition of the Thing: Reiterating the terms of Turner's prophecy, the court relies on the slave's authority, investing him with the status of the terrifying real. As Copjec elaborates, "Confronted with the limits of our knowledge, we fictively add to the field of the Other, to the voice, an *X*, the mark of our non-knowledge. This simple addition is enough to eroticize the voice, to transform our relation to it to one of desire, of interpretation" (189). These erotics can be murderous, a situation more evident when lynching mobs gather. Projecting Turner as the Thing, his interpreters generate a violence incapable of grasping its object. The law destroys Turner physically but fails to effect his second death: It cannot efface the marks of insurrection because they constitute its limits; the hand of justice cannot grasp the real.

The law has seen its horrible double, a dimension Sigmund Freud interpreted when defining the uncanny as "that class of the frightening which leads back to what is known of old and long familiar" ("Uncanny" 220). Freud's term, *unheim-*

lich, possesses the same sort of semantic ambivalence as Lacan's jouissance: The uncanny is both intimate and irreducibly other. Freud shows that the uncanny involves "the phenomenon of the 'double' " (234), a repetition of the self serving as "the uncanny harbinger of death" (235). Reexperiencing the repressed reveals "the dominance in the unconscious mind of a 'compulsion to repeat' . . . powerful enough to overrule the pleasure principle" (238), a compulsion Freud links, in his 1920 study *Beyond the Pleasure Principle*, to the death drive.

In " 'I Shall Be with You on Your Wedding-Night': Lacan and the Uncanny," Mladen Dolar translates the uncanny into Lacanian terms. Its insistence is "the irruption of the real into 'homely,' commonly accepted reality. We can speak of the emergence of something that shatters well-known divisions and which cannot be situated within them" (6). The double, the manifestation of the Thing, is a figure of jouissance. An imaginary symmetry between Turner and his white interlopers leads each to characterize the other as possessing obscene enjoyment. Turner is compelled to murder the whites, to bring about "the great day of judgment" (7). They in turn have to render "retributive justice" (14) by executing Turner, and more blacks to boot. With violent superegoic voices on both sides, any moral judgment becomes problematic.

When Turner reads his mission in his scars, he (mis)recognizes himself as the subject of the Law. When he responds to the voice, however, he becomes the subject of the Law's mandate. Throughout Turner's confession, the Other, the Father, onto whom Turner has a transference, issues increasingly harsh commands. Turner lacks distance from this voice enjoining him to kill. According to Žižek, the superego is "an injunction which is experienced as traumatic, 'senseless'—that is, which cannot be integrated into the symbolic universe of the subject" (*Sublime* 37). Interpreting the injunction, Turner separates himself from the society to which he "belongs."

The difference between Turner's version of the law and the court's also suggests Lacan's distinction between the primordial, bad father of boundless enjoyment and the good, oedipal father that prohibits it. As Dolar explains, the drama of the double receives its paradigmatic enactment in Lacan's two fathers: After Oedipus, "The father takes responsibility for the loss [of jouissance], which makes him an ambiguous figure, subject to a lack and a split . . . producing the object that cannot fit into the paternal law. The Law offers words instead of things (instead of the Thing)" (15). The whites—Gray, the court, and the state of Virginia—operating in the name of this good father, concern themselves with a civil society and its slave system. Acting in the oedipal father's name, they attempt to eradicate unabidable jouissance, the excess they must destroy. However, the voice to which Turner responds is not what Žižek terms, in *The Metastases of Enjoyment*, "public

Law, the Law articulated in public discourse" (54). Rather, it is the superego, which "emerges" when the Law "fails" (54). Thus the Law, like the father, splits into asymmetrical parts—the written, which is public, and the voiced, which is super-egoic. Through brutal jouissance the superego effects "*the Law's suspension*" (55).

Whereas the whites imagine a harmonious society after destroying Turner, Turner offers no competing model of social good. During the insurrection, when he journeys to Jerusalem—which, appropriately, is both the heavenly city and its mundane representative near Southampton—Turner pursues apocalypse. For him, there is no compromise. He never articulates a final plan for his uprising; Virginia's little Jerusalem merely presents more whites to slay. The important goal is beyond this world; Turner imagines no new home for former slaves, no recon-ciliation after fighting, and no pact with the whites. Rather, the absolute register of his demand corresponds to the form of jouissance.

Lacan tells us that "*jouissance* implies precisely the acceptance of death" (*Ethics* 189). Thus while the court attempts to foreclose on this enjoyment by executing Turner, it simply fulfills his mission, reinvoking the trauma it would prohibit. Operating within the letter of the law—that is, with the name of the good but "insecure" father (*Ethics* 181)—the court defends against the resurgence of evil. As Lacan has argued, enjoyment in this form "is evil" (184). (This also explains the harshness of Gray's abuse.) The murder of the primordial father, the father-in-enjoyment, underwrites the efficacy of the law, which operates in his name. Turner's execution restages the mythic murder: He embodies unspeakable jouis-sance. The call to just retribution and to violence repeats, rather than eradicates, enjoyment. An "unfathomable aggressivity" (186) returns to menace the society in the form of those neighbors who are not quite neighbors, who could strike at any moment, and under the most unlikely circumstances—the slaves. After Turner, American society will live in fear of repeat performances of his struggle, of repe-titions unreadable within slavery's ideological fantasy.

The relentless character of Turner's sense of purpose—his refusal to express the slightest remorse or hesitation—deserves to be analyzed in psychoanalytic terms. To employ Lacan's famous phrase, Turner refuses to "give up on his desire," to express remorse or hesitation. For this, Gray labels him "a complete fanatic" for mass insurrection (13), framing in the language of insanity Turner's deviations from what society expects. By Gray's logic, the society is well, but the abnormal individual is ill. Gray pathologizes Turner as a victim "of early impres-sions" (13). To label Turner as delusional, however, requires that his vision be read as merely *subjective* fantasy.

A private fantasy, however macabre or absolute, has little power to influence history. Turner's relentless and unbending character nonetheless makes its mark.

Like the heroes Aristotle recommends for good tragedy in his *Poetics*, Turner reveals his character through action. Implacable negativity may also put Turner's revolt in the same dimension of tragedy as the fate of Sophocles's Antigone, which Lacan interprets in *The Ethics of Psychoanalysis*. Like Antigone, Turner willingly bears the lethal consequences of not compromising. The comparisons do not end here, however: Aristotle suggests that tragedy requires elevated speech, and Turner's language recalls the somber tonalities of the King James Bible. Additionally, as I shall show, Turner offers a visionary poetics that is his alone.

Regarding his purpose, Turner says, "even now, in this dungeon, helpless and forsaken as I am, I cannot divest myself of it" (5). Nothing shakes Turner's conviction that he "was intended for some great purpose" (5). Although the young Turner possesses "uncommon intelligence" (5), the leading sign of his chosenness is his spontaneous acquisition of literacy: "to the astonishment of my family, one day, when a book was shown to me to keep me from crying, I began spelling the names of different objects—this was a source of wonder to all in the neighborhood, particularly the blacks" (5–6). The authority of Turner's interpretive abilities derives from this miracle. He is able to read what others cannot; his relation to the word involves revelation. His peers believe in his "superior judgment . . . perfected by Divine inspiration" (6). Turner's calling leads him to follow the typical observances of biblical prophets: "Having soon discovered, that to be great I must appear so, I therefore studiously avoided mixing in society, and wrapped myself in mystery" (6). The essence of greatness consists of inculcating an enigma, an opacity signifying what mere appearance cannot show; as Žižek explains, " *'essence' itself is nothing but the self-rupture, the self-fissure of the appearance*" (*Sublime* 214; original emphasis). Removing himself from view, Turner self-consciously positions himself in the unseen, where mystery accrues.

"The Spirit that spoke to the prophets in former days" interpellates Turner (Turner 6). His utilitarian value disappears: "I would never be of any use to any one as a slave" (6). Rather than waiting for the Spirit to tell him what to do, he sets up the fantasy scenario that permits the Spirit to do its work: "I now began to prepare [the slaves] for my purpose by telling them something was about to happen that would terminate in fulfilling the great promise that had been made to me" (7). Turner achieves his purpose by first establishing the conditions that will make it possible: Repeating the words of the voice that prepares him, he readies fellow servants. The reinvocation of promise produces its fulfillment; recognizing himself in this call means realizing it. He ventriloquizes the superego.

The Spirit's claim is absolute. Fleeing slavery is not an option, because it would entail some form of compromise. Forbidding mundane, practical solutions, the

Spirit offers pitiless revelation: "I had a vision, and I saw white spirits and black spirits engaged in battle, and the sun was darkened, the thunder rolled in the heavens, and blood flowed in the streams; and I heard a voice saying, 'Such is your luck, such are you called on to see, and let it come, rough or smooth, you must surely bear it' " (7). The superegoic voice demands an apocalypse that does not conclude with a utopian vision. It calls for blood. It calls for tragic catharsis, in the malevolent terms of Lacan's "ritual purification" (*Ethics* 245).

Turner's climax of vision, which has no precise biblical precedent, occurs "while laboring in the field":

> I discovered drops of blood upon the corn, as though it were dew from heaven; and I communicated it to many, both white and black, in the neighborhood; and then I found in the leaves of the woodsy hieroglyphic characters, and numbers, with the forms of men in different attitudes, portrayed in blood, and representing the figures I had seen before in the heavens. And now the Holy Ghost had revealed itself to me, and made plain the miracles it had shown me—for as the blood of Christ has been shed on this earth, and had ascended to heaven for the salvation of sinners, and was now returning to earth again in the form of dew, and as the leaves on the trees bore the impression of the figures I had seen in the heavens, it was plain to me that the Savior was about to lay down the yoke he had born for the sins of men, and the great day of judgment was at hand. (7)

As Christ's blood was shed, so shall the blood of Southampton whites be shed too. This passage emphasizes blood's compulsive pull; in quick metaphoric substitution, one image supersedes another. As it changes to water, the blood incarnates the transformative power it signals.

Turner illustrates the perspective of the "Last Judgment" (*Ethics* 314), which opposes the utilitarian values of traditional ethics and its stance of moderation. This perspective, which Lacan reads in *Antigone*, is "the counterpart of tragedy" (*Ethics* 314): "it functions in the direction of a triumph of death" (313). In search of "true holiness" (Turner 7), Turner can be purified only on "the great day of judgment" (7). This doomsday perspective defies the "middle path" that, for Turner, is tantamount to chattel slavery. As Lacan emphasizes, the "morality of power" says to the subject, " 'As far as desires are concerned, come back later. Make them wait' " (*Ethics* 315). Turner refuses to wait. To dismiss his triumph as fantastic is to obscure both its logical progression and its real-world effects. No unmediated glimpse into the beyond, Turner's vision accords with the Book of Revelation's awful prophecies. Desire, pushed to this extreme, functions beyond the pleasure principle. Turner forms "his own relationship to death" (*Ethics* 295): "I heard a loud noise in the heavens, and the Spirit instantly appeared to me and said, the Serpent was loosened, and Christ had lain down the yoke he bore for the sins of men, and that I should take it up and fight against the serpent" (Turner 8). He then receives the call to action: "I should arise and prepare myself, and slay my enemies with their own weapons. And immediately on the sign appearing in the heavens, the seal was removed from my lips, and I communicated the great work laid out for me to do" (8). Turner's rhetoric compels. Instead of rejecting this call, the slaves embrace it. One who joins explains that "his life was worth no more than others, and his liberty as dear to him" (8). This echo of white American revolutionary bravado—"Give me liberty or give me death"—does not permit a happy choice: In the logic of the Last Judgment, liberty *is* death.

Turner's contingent advances from house to house, gaining members at each stop. He catalogs "the work of death assigned them" incident by incident (10). Although some details are gruesome, their numbing redundancy suggests little other than Old Testament genealogy. At one point, an entire family is killed, including "a little infant sleeping in a cradle, that was forgotten until we had left the house and gone some distance, when Henry and Will returned and killed it" (9). Later, the whites rally and send Turner's forces into disarray. In a series of battles, Turner's forces narrow down to Turner himself. He then evades capture for six weeks, hiding in "a hole under a pile of fence rails in a field" (12), near the scene of the first set of murders. The authorities expect Turner to flee, not return to the scene of the crime. Since Turner's continuing presence is in some sense inconceivable, no one sees him. The authorities can no more guess his whereabouts than they could predict the insurrection. They are blind to the symptom in their midst. When a hungry dog leads to Turner, the fugitive surrenders and is taken to the jail in Jerusalem.

At the end of his testimony, Gray asks Turner "if he knew of any extensive or concerted plan" (13). Although Turner's statement corroborates with "every circumstance" in the case (13), Gray finds it difficult to believe. The abolitionist and correspondent of Emily Dickinson, Thomas Wentworth Higginson, explains the Tidewater community's incredulity: "In all insurrections, the standing wonder seems to be that the slaves most trusted and best used should be most deeply involved. So in this case, as usual, men resorted to the most astonishing theories of the origin of the affair" (1898). Higginson himself highlights Turner's outrage, embellishing his account with a fictional journey through "Nat's" mind (1896). A story—whether of conspiracy, free-black influence, lack of biblical knowledge, whiskey, or nobility—appears necessary to fill the gaps. Even when the slave's subjectivity is taken into account (or appropriated, as in Higginson's text), Turner's narrative does not suffice. Gray searches for a conspiratory link between the Southampton insurrection and a concurrent one in North Carolina, questioning neither the justness of the institution inspiring both rebellions nor the shared social conditions compelling revolt across the South.

Gray ostentatiously recoils from Turner, whom he finds "still bearing the stains of blood of helpless innocence" (14). It is unclear whether the usage here is literal—whether Turner remains visibly stained. Gray draws his account toward conclusion with the story of "[t]he escape of a little girl" (14), a sentimental counternarrative to Turner's "little infant sleeping in a cradle": "Seeing the Negroes approached, she ran up on a dirt chimney . . . and remained there, unnoticed, during the massacre . . . she lay concealed until the next day; when, seeing a party go into the house, she came up, and, on being asked how she escaped, replied with the utmost simplicity, 'the Lord helped her' " (14). The little girl's story echoes Turner's. Where Gray would employ this anecdote to paint Turner in the worst possible way, he instead dips his brush in Turner's blood colors. This condemnation of Turner thus bathetically repeats his logic. Caught up in Turner's phrases, Gray's final two sentences tellingly lack logical consistency: "Few, indeed, were those who escaped the work of death. But, fortunately for society, the hand of retributive justice has overtaken them, and not one that was known to be concerned has escaped" (14). Does Gray claim that the whites who escaped from Turner did not evade his justice, or that the blacks not immediately killed by the whites' "work of death" were punished later? He likely means that only a few whites got away from Turner, but that no blacks responsible for the insurrection escaped. However, such an interpretation *does violence to the actual text*. The reader must dislocate language and force it into her or his meaning. Gray's ambiguous conflation of agents suggests not only the complete reversibility of these social roles but their self-contradictory constitution. Whose is the hand of justice? Who escapes? Who is fortunate? And what society is invoked?

The Voice That Would Condemn Him

In *Writing Diaspora: Tactics of Intervention in Contemporary Cultural Studies*, Rey Chow takes issue with psychoanalytic readings of blacks and modernity. Chow objects to the reading "of the native in the form of the symptom of the white man" (30). She faults Frantz Fanon because "his construction of the native is Oedipal" (31):

> Freud's question was "What does woman want?" Fanon, elaborating on the necessity of violence in the native's formation, asks, "What does the black man want?" The native (the black man) is thus imagined to be an angry son who wants to displace the white man, the father. While Freud would go on to represent the woman as

lack, Fanon's argument is that the native is someone from whom something has been stolen. The native, then, is also lack.

This Oedipal structure of thinking—a structure of thinking that theorizes subjectivity as compensation for a presumed lack—characterizes discourses on the non-West in a pervasive manner, including, occasionally, the discourse of those who are otherwise critical of its patriarchal overtones. (31)

Chow does not mention here that for psychoanalysis, *every* subject, Western or non-Western, is structured by lack. Whereas Fanon's reasoning may not provide an exit from oedipal conflict, dismissing the logic of oedipal violence in this offhand manner strikes me as dangerous. Although Chow claims to employ "Žižek's non-pejorative sense of 'symptom,' " which she glosses as "something that gives the subject its ontological consistency and its fundamental structure" (30), her reading fails to recognize that Žižek's Lacanian theory is incomprehensible without the dynamic of "fundamental, constitutive lack" (*Sublime* 53).

Chow is also mistaken in claiming that Fanon reads lack solely in the oppressed. For Fanon and psychoanalysis, lack constitutes both oppressor and oppressed: All subjects are split by unconscious desire, which speaks the language of the Other. As Lacan insists in *The Four Fundamental Concepts of Psycho-Analysis*, "*the unconscious is the discourse of the Other.* Now, the discourse of the Other that is to be realized, that of the unconscious, is not beyond the closure, it is *outside*" (131). Žižek elaborates, "The symbolic order is striving for a homeostatic balance, but there is in its kernel, at its very center, some strange, traumatic element which cannot be symbolized, integrated into the symbolic order—the Thing" (*Sublime* 132). This paradigm is not "subjectivizing" (Chow 312) but is rather a reading of desire that takes into account the transpersonal operation of the unconscious. The Other, the symbolic order, itself lacks; indeed, there is no position without lack. In her nondialectical reading of psychoanalytic lack, Chow too hastily reifies it. Unwilling to register how lack structures all subject positions and inheres in the social field, she neglects to consider the political and historical repercussions of these psychoanalytic arguments. In registering the unconscious's intractable alterity, psychoanalysis allows for no absolute or utterly consistent theoretical stance.

Creating a false dichotomy between "good" Žižek and "bad" Freud, Chow perpetuates the oedipal cycle she condemns. Although she endorses the concept of the Other that works "by combating the construction of the native as the straight-forward or direct other of the colonizer," she refuses to grant such theoretical complexity to Freud or Fanon. Working with Žižek's reading of Lacan's phrase "*les non-dupes errent*," she explains the fallacy of belief in a consistent Other. What Chow's analysis omits, however, is that Lacan's pun "*les non-dupes errent*" (Chow

52) is a homonym for "*les noms du père.*" Excoriating critics who take themselves, or the indigenous, as "the non-duped" (52), Chow fails to bring her contradictory discourse into account. *Writing Diaspora* makes conflicting demands, vitiating its own project to condemn other critical readings with the utmost severity. Assuming the role of a sort of superegoic voice for cultural studies, a voice whose demands are impossible to meet because they do not cohere, Chow herself enlists the Name-of-the-Father.

If I use Chow to point again to interpretation's inherent violence, I do not mean to situate my own reading as non-duped. My critique of Chow, as of Gilroy, derives from taking both their arguments seriously. With both critics, patriarchy answers back in one guise or another. The father has many names, and the very voice that would condemn him already speaks his language. The language of critical rivalry sustaining Chow's reading is precisely this superegoic voice, while Gilroy's stress on continuity entails patrilineal descent. This pernicious return of the repressed, in critics dedicated to a feminist and anti-imperialist agenda, is not something to dismiss lightly. According to Jacqueline Rose, "psychoanalysis gives us no absolute or consistent theory of violence" (70). Nonetheless, it does articulate—more than any other discourse—the always potentially murderous structure of desire.

There is a possible recuperative reading of *The Confessions of Nat Turner* that mobilizes Žižek's account of the symptom. Elaborating on "Hegel's theory of the role of repetition in history," Žižek observes that revolution "can only succeed as the repetition of a first failed attempt" (*Sublime* 60): "Historical necessity itself *is constituted through misrecognition*, through the initial failure of 'opinion' to recognize its true character—that is, the way truth itself arises from misrecognition . . . when [the event] erupts for the first time, it is experienced as a contingent trauma, as the intrusion of a certain non-symbolized Real; only through repetition is this event recognized in its symbolic necessity" (61). If we apply this logic, Turner's insurrection is the failed event guaranteeing slavery's end. While it is difficult to find an historical reading that takes Turner's use of language seriously, most accounts emphasize the symbolic charge of the insurrection itself. Such a reading is implicit in Stephen Oates's biography of Turner, *The Fires of Jubilee*, whose jacket blurb announces, "The bloody slave rebellion led by Nat Turner in Virginia in 1831, and the savage reprisals that followed, shattered beyond repair the myth of the contented slave and the benign master and intensified the forces of change that would plunge America into the bloodbath of the Civil War."

However, Henry Tragle, who compiled the source material for the rebellion as *The Southampton Slave Revolt of 1831*, doubts the full veracity of *The Confessions of Nat Turner*. Since "Every record that remains was generated by those against whom he fought," he states that the document "must be used with caution" (5). I agree with this warning, but it is crucial to note, as Tragle does, that Gray's incautious publication caused an uproar. Tragle observes that "There may have been localities where it was not permitted to be sold, because of its presumed incendiary character" (279). Whatever Gray's intention, *The Confessions of Nat Turner* escaped his control. If many Virginians wanted to suppress the story, they failed. It was picked up by, and launched the career of, abolitionist William Lloyd Garrison. Tragle documents "A Selection of Newspaper Accounts" that reveals the insistent, moralistic discourse enveloping the revolt.[3] The brutal persistence of this discourse, which recurred in words and deeds, predicted and called forth the carnage of the Civil War.

The question remains, What human price does redemption exact? Is there any exit from the circuit of blood? In his reading of revolution, Žižek admonishes that "as with Moses in Freud's analysis, this recognition-through-repetition always presupposes necessarily the crime, the act of murder" (*Sublime* 61). It "announces the advent of the Law, of the Name-of-the-Father" (61–62). Perhaps recuperation is inadvisable for *The Confessions of Nat Turner*, because Turner ethically rejects the social reconciliation that recovery underwrites. Copjec argues too, "It is only when the sovereign incalculability of the subject is acknowledged that perceptions of difference will no longer nourish demands for the surrender of difference to processes of 'homogenization,' 'purification,' or any of the other crimes against otherness with which the rise of racism has begun to acquaint us" (208). To grant Nat Turner "sovereign incalculability," to insist that his difference cannot be subsumed to the demands of interpretation, arguably is to try to grant his confessions the freedom for which he died. Racist violence arises when otherness becomes unbearable, when the need is felt to eradicate it in the name of some "father." Since psychoanalysis maintains the gap between desire and its fulfillment—and between the cause and its effects—Copjec's unsurmisable subject does not fall completely under the rule of the father. And while it is impossible entirely to evade the violence evoked by the Names-of-the-Father, as these names constitute symbolic reality, psychoanalysis teaches us the ethical value of paying constant attention to the operations of desire.

ENDNOTES

I would like to thank Tim Dean and Cynthia Steele for their encouragement and assistance with this project.

1. I am grateful to Tim Dean for this phrase.
2. Southern slavery ideology halts Hegel's progression at the point where the slave consents to labor. It would freeze the master and servant relation in happy stasis.

3. A full reading of the newspaper accounts exceeds the limits of this essay. I refer the interested reader to Tragle's documentation. Tragle also discusses the critical controversy surrounding William Styron's novel, *The Confessions of Nat Turner*. He remarks that numerous African-American writers criticize Styron for appropriating Turner's story, before illustrating the full extent of Styron's presumptuous ignorance. Styron, to my mind, is another unsatisfied reader of the text I want to bring into prominence. I therefore refer the interested reader to *The Southampton Slave of 1831: A Compilation of Source Material*.

WORKS CITED

Aristotle. *Poetics*. Trans. S. H. Butcher. *Critical Theory since Plato: Revised Edition*. Ed. Hazard Adams. New York: Harcourt Brace Jovanovich, 1992.

Chow, Rey. *Writing Diaspora: Tactics of Intervention in Contemporary Cultural Studies*. Bloomington: Indiana UP, 1993.

Clifford, James. "Traveling Cultures." *Cultural Studies*. Ed. Lawrence Grossberg, Cary Nelson, and Paula Treichler. New York: Routledge, 1992. 96–116.

Copjec, Joan. *Read My Desire: Lacan Against the Historicists*. Cambridge: MIT, 1994.

Dolar, Mladen. " 'I Shall Be with You on Your Wedding-Night': Lacan and the Uncanny." *October* 58 (1991): 5–23.

Douglass, Frederick. *Narrative of the Life of Frederick Douglass, an American Slave*. 1845. Ed. Houston A. Baker, Jr. New York: Penguin, 1986.

Fanon, Frantz. *The Wretched of the Earth*. Trans. Constance Farrington. New York: Grove, 1968.

Freud, Sigmund. *Beyond the Pleasure Principle*. 1920. Vol. 18 of *The Standard Edition of the Complete Psychological Works of Sigmund Freud*. 24 vols. Ed. and trans. James Strachey. London: Hogarth, 1953–74. 1–64.

———. "The 'Uncanny.' " 1919. Vol. 17 of *SE*. 217–56.

Gallop, Jane. *Reading Lacan*. Ithaca: Cornell UP, 1985.

Gilroy, Paul. *The Black Atlantic: Modernity and Double Consciousness*. Cambridge: Harvard UP, 1993.

Higginson, Thomas Wentworth. "Nat Turner's Insurrection." Vol. 1 of *The Heath Anthology of American Literature*. 2d ed. Paul Lauter. Lexington, Mass.: Heath, 1994. 1890–99.

Lacan, Jacques. "The Subversion of the Subject and the Dialectic of Desire in the Freudian Unconscious." *Écrits: A Selection*. Trans. Alan Sheridan. Ed. Jacques-Alain Miller. New York: Norton, 1977. 292–325.

———. *The Four Fundamental Concepts of Psycho-Analysis*. Trans. Alan Sheridan. Ed. Jacques-Alain Miller. New York: Norton, 1978.

———. *The Seminar of Jacques Lacan. Book VII: The Ethics of Psychoanalysis*. Ed. Jacques-Alain Miller. Trans. Dennis Porter. New York: Norton, 1992.

Morrison, Toni. *Beloved*. New York: Plume, 1988.

Oates, Stephen B. *The Fires of Jubilee: Nat Turner's Fierce Rebellion*. San Bernardino, Calif.: Borgo, 1975.

Rose, Jacqueline. "Margaret Thatcher and Ruth Ellis." *Why War? Psychoanalysis, Politics, and the Return of Melanie Klein*. Cambridge: Blackwell, 1993.

Salecl, Renata. *The Spoils of Freedom: Psychoanalysis and Feminism After the Fall of Socialism*. New York: Routledge, 1994.

Tragle, Henry Irving. *The Southampton Slave of 1831: A Compilation of Source Material*. Amherst: U of Massachusetts P, 1971.

Turner, Nat. *The Confessions of Nat Turner*. 1831. Transcribed Thomas C. Gray. Np: Ayer Company, 1994.

Žižek, Slavoj. *The Sublime Object of Ideology*. New York: Verso, 1989.

———. *The Metastases of Enjoyment: Six Essays on Woman and Causality*. New York: Verso, 1994.

12

"Savage Ecstasy":
Colonialism and the Death Drive

Christopher Lane

Parmi les plus mortelles douleurs, on est encore capable de joie.
                                    —Bossuet, qtd. in Gide, *Travels* 21

The only beast of burden is man.
  —Letter from M. Weber to M. Blum, qtd. in Gide, *Le Retour* 221

Jouissance comes easily to the slave, and it will leave the work in
bondage.   —Lacan, "Subversion" 308

"What desires can a person have who never sees anything
desirable?" This question surfaces in André Gide's discussion of African materialism. "The black races are
described as being indolent, lazy, without needs, and
without desires," Gide claims, "but I am inclined to
believe that the state of slavery and wretched poverty in
which they are sunk, only too often explains their apathy" (*Travels* 52n.). This is the Gide we recognize as
being appalled by French and Belgian colonialism; the
writer prepared to denounce European imperialism for
its cruel disregard of African suffering. This is also the
Gide some critics find amenable to postcolonial theory;
the writer committed to equalizing cultural relations
because he departs from the Congo and Chad quite
altered by his visit (see Walker, esp. 13 and 37).

   Much of *Travels in the Congo* (1927) is a conscientious
push to correct European myths of indigenous apathy.
Gide praises African dignity and self-sufficiency: The
sight of a well-organized village thrills him because it

promises a comfortable stay and enables him to revoke fantasies of African chaos. By limiting Africans' desires to a wish for "fair remuneration" and material well-being, Gide seems quite capable of answering Fanon's later question "What does the black man want?" (Fanon 8). Gide responds: "Every time that a well-stocked factory offers the native blankets, stuffs, household utensils, tools, etc., people are ingenuously surprised to see his desires aroused—if, that is to say, a fair remuneration of his work gives him the means of satisfying them" (52n.). The problem devolves on this "if," for Gide soon learns to his embarrassment that desire is not circumscribed by material parameters. *Travels* is thus beset by astonishing racial judgments—and by a corresponding *recoil* from Africa—which render Gide's pronouncements rather hollow. "The people here are very handsome, with clean, wholesome skins (at last!)," he remarks in a private aside to his reader, highlighting his aesthetic disdain for those who ignore French customs. These refrains compel us to ask, What does Gide want of Africa and of what does Africa consist for him?

Perhaps we can answer these questions only by asking where Europe, in turn, ends. For instance, in what sense can one visit a foreign land without having appraised it from afar? These questions obviously became more pronounced as cinema and television disseminated imagoes of African culture, but in 1925 the foreseen and the left-behind already beset Gide's pursuit of authenticity: "We never cease to feel that this is merely the prologue to our journey, which will not really begin till we come into more contact with the country" (18–19), he remarks in Dakar. To put this simply, Africa does not really begin for Gide with his arrival in Dakar. It is, he claims, "impossible to imagine anything less exotic or more ugly" (5). Gide may remark of the unfamiliar, "What joy to find oneself among Negroes!" (5), but Dakar and its citizens soon disappoint him, and the narrative *anticipates* Africa only by criticizing its uniformity, desolation, and failure.

Considering Gide's disappointment and his inability to observe Africa without foresight, let us repeat Gide's question with which we began, but from a different premise: "What desires can a person have who never sees anything desirable?" In one sense, postcolonial theory makes this question difficult to ask of a writer such as Gide, for his desire seems to blend so easily with the colonial structure that the two appear inseparable. We might address Gide's concerns more specifically with the simple retort, Who cares what Gide wants, given his inept grasp of African misery?

We must examine Gide's question, however, because it raises difficult issues of colonial intention that we cannot always explain by political mandates or economic policies. Although these factors are important to consider, they do not delimit the complex exchanges that surface repeatedly in colonial contexts (Pratt 160–62, 164). We might say that Gide's question highlights an economy, also grossly unfair, that exceeds issues of material wealth. This second "economy" involves a type of exchange, perhaps even a form of trade, whose goods and services are not always tangible, but whose effects are legible in Gide's *Travels* as fear, anxiety, fascination, repulsion, distress, pleasure, and embarrassment. None of these factors falls easily into a rubric for the politically correct. They probably cause us acute discomfort, but they recur with such persistence that we would only partly understand colonialism if like Gide we tried to pretend they do not affect us.

We can grasp the limits of Gide's colonial analysis only by considering what happens when he tries to account for French and Belgian racism by listing what might foster an African's satisfaction. The limits of materialist analysis surface when we realize that Gide's narrative gestures beyond obvious interest in colonial reform (see Lucey 155–56; Hargreaves 16). Indeed, the very idea of colonial *reform* returns us to what Gide and France want of Africa.

Such demands are enigmatic at the start of Gide's text. *Travels in the Congo* begins with a crisis of purpose that the journey's end only part resolves: "I think we are the only ones travelling 'for pleasure,' " he remarks on his opening page (3), before repeating the bemused curiosity of fellow travelers:

'What are you going out for?'
'I shall see when I get there.' (3)

Later, Gide tells us that "one doesn't travel to the Congo for pleasure [*On ne voyage pas au Congo pour son plaisir*]" (*Retour* 228), a statement we have ample reason to dispute, even contradict. If Gide has no obvious purpose or task, and pleasure is already doubtful or in scare quotes before he reaches Dakar, what is it he wants? Moreover, Gide's answer to his fellow travelers' question is not simply his own rationalization, though his purpose emerges precisely from insistent reminders that he has none.

It is tempting to present Gide's lack of purpose as the clearest indication of his desire—that is, as a grotesque manifestation of his ability to appear desireless—but even Gide resists a simple notion of conscious intention: "I have plunged into this journey like Curtius into the gulf. I feel already as if I had not so much willed it (though for many months past I have been stringing my will up to it) as had it imposed upon me by a sort of ineluctable fatality—like all the important events of my life" (4). Whether or not this remark strikes us as disingenuous, we cannot simply dismiss Gide's assessment of how Africa and Africans affect him. This lesson is frustrating but useful: We never escape racial fantasy in Gide's *Travels*, for we can access no "outside" from which to judge Gide's truth (see also Leiris). Interpretation prevails from within the scene of colonial desire. This does not mean that Gide's fantasies, or his capacity to symbolize them, are limitless; instead, a limit emerges within the narrative constraining what is internally credible and politically tolerable.

An example may clarify. Since his visit to the French and Belgian Congo resembles Conrad's journey to the second country, Gide invokes (and dedicates *Travels* to) *Heart of Darkness*, Conrad's 1899 novella: "This admirable book still remains profoundly true and I shall often have occasion to quote it. There is no exaggeration in his picture; it is cruelly exact; but what lightens its gloom is the success of the project which in his pages appears so vain" (11n.; see Putnam). As Gide realizes, however, history and fantasy do not progress in a simple course. Gide's statement about Conrad surfaces early in *Travels*, long before he ruminates on what, of the French and Belgian "project," has not succeeded—indeed, long before he ruminates on what colonial "success" might generally mean.

Gide later remarks: "Conrad in *Heart of Darkness* speaks admirably of 'the extraordinary effort of imagination that was necessary to make us take these people for enemies' " (174n.). By this point in *Travels*, however, Gide has already acknowledged the likelihood—perhaps inevitability—of colonial enmity. If *Travels* is not simply an exercise in pacifying aggression and racial hostility, Gide nonetheless reflects on his alternating pride and disgust at the Congolese, in ways that record what Gide cannot declare to them or other colonials. The reader overhears this disgust, listening with strange complicity to the fantasies that Gide represents by text, not speech, and even in writing Gide proceeds with difficulty, as if honesty would precipitate an epistemological crisis: "I find it difficult to finish my sentences, I am so afraid that if I really express my thought, I shall find no response to it" (52; see also Lacan's remarks in "Jeunesse" 750; Masson 67–70; Spurr 75).[1]

Gide repeats the question of his purpose—and thus of his desire—but *Travels* resolves neither. Part ashamed of his lack of purpose, and realizing that catching up on neglected classics is something he could do in France, Gide produces for himself a task that seems to excuse his colonial vacation: "I cannot get it into my head that I am charged with a mission and therefore an official personage. I have the greatest difficulty in puffing myself out to fill this role" (12; Darras 1–2).

Who has "charged" Gide with this mission? One answer lies in his conclusion that national loyalty ultimately prevails over his mixed intentions. If Gide cannot, and later will not, participate meaningfully in French colonialism, he nonetheless wants initially to function as a diplomat, commenting on French malpractice, smoothing out orders that get lost in translation, and partly excusing corrupt officials by fostering an image of France that renders that country's aims human and benign (for an overview, see Suret-Canale 307–54). At these moments, Gide loses all pretense at being impartial: "After such a long time spent in wandering through regions where everything was savage, formless, embryonic, inexistent [*sic*], it is the greatest joy to find oneself again in a village that is tidy, clean, and prosperous-looking; a decent chief, dressed in European clothes that are not ridiculous, in a freshly whitened helmet, speaking correct French—a flag run up in our honour—all of this moves me absurdly—almost to sobs" (135).

Since patriotism defeats Gide's criticisms of France's *inhuman* colonialism (my adjective is deliberate) and fosters his colonial identification, which would compel him eventually to despise the Congolese, Gide's narrative oscillates between idealizing and de-idealizing the indigenous. Correspondingly, *Travels* offers a complex account of racial identification and dis-identification that tells us a great deal about Gide's politically undesirable fantasies (Howard 837; Steel, "Gide" 56–59, 69). Here, for instance, is Gide's later, unequivocal declaration that his mission was ordained from without: "When I accepted this mission [!], I failed to grasp at first what it was I was undertaking, what part I could play, how I could be useful. I understand it now, and I am beginning to think that my coming will not have been in vain. During my stay in the colony I have come to realize how terribly the problems I have to solve are interwoven one with the other" (71–72).

One of these "interwoven" problems is Gide's demand to be driven to Bambio in a car, despite his knowledge that an overseer makes a group of women (some of them mothers) "work all night in order to repair the damage done by a recent storm and to enable us to pass" (67). Gide remarks of the women: "we had no heart to smile at them. These poor creatures, more like cattle than human beings, were in the streaming rain, a number of them with babies at the breast. . . . It happened more than once that the loose earth has given way and buried the women and children who were working at the bottom of the pit" (67). Not surprisingly, Gide critics find this passage excruciatingly embarrassing, yet they nonetheless defend him from absolute complicity with the French. Since Gide remarks on his having "no heart to smile at" these women, however, what *would* it have meant for him to wave at these human "cattle"? In this context, what jouissance would a smile or wave have signified?

This incident clarifies that Gide's wish to foster diplomacy antagonizes, not resolves, his "mission." The points at which his identification with the colonized fails produce other, extraordinary fantasies about indigenous enjoyment. In this way, we can begin to assess the "adventure" of psychic drives. As Lacan argued: "When you entrust someone with a mission, the *aim* is not what he brings back, but the itinerary he must take" (*Four* 179). Knowing that Gide hopes to return to France with anticolonial zeal, we can use Lacan's argument to clarify the vanishing points of Gide's identificatory struggle with the colonized. I shall quote Gide frequently to indicate both the fantasies ensuing from his struggle and the general limits of materialist and liberal-diplomatic accounts of European colonialism.

Let me begin by quoting Gide's address to an audience in Brussels after he had returned from the Congo:

> To the psychologist, these primitive races hold another interest [besides their lack of shame at being primitive (*ces races nues . . . qui n'ont point honte de l'être*)]. They teach civilized man to understand himself better. To know and see oneself better, one must first leave oneself [*il faut tout d'abord se quitter*]. By seeing one's country from abroad, one better understands one's own. It is at the heart of the African wild(er)ness [*C'est au sein de la sauvagerie africaine*] that I learn most about the European civilization to which we all belong, and for which we all work. One of the most peculiar characteristics of the indigenous of Central Africa, and, in general, of the tribes who live in a primitive state [*des tribus demeurées à l'état primitif*]—certainly, for our civilized European spirits [*nos esprits européens civilisés*], it is the hardest for us to admit—is their difficulty of separating themselves individually from their clans, tribes, and races. ("Conférence" 34–35; my trans.; see also Lévy-Bruhl's discussion of "*[L']Aversion de la mentalité primitive pour les opérations discursives de la pensée* 1–11)

This passage obviously defeats readings of Gide that praise his anticolonial transformation in *Travels*. Paradoxically, even cynically, Gide clarifies that his understanding of Europe conceptually *maintains* an image of Africa as primitive and savage. In this way, traveling to the heart—literally, the "bosom"—of Africa to experience savagery (*C'est au sein de la sauvagerie africaine* . . .) need not *unmake* a European if his politics aims toward self- and national reparation. This does not mean, of course, that the European's project necessarily succeeds or is altogether conscious. As we'll see, Gide learns more from colonial and psychic failure than he does from wandering and observing. However, the tension between what Gide pursues and what he discovers clarifies why he clings initially, and perhaps conclusively, to an identification with France.

Near the beginning of his journey, Gide represents Governor Lambline as exemplary of French behavior in the Congo: "I have had some very encouraging conversation with [the] Governor . . .; the admirable work he has accomplished shows what might be achieved by an intelligent and consecutive administration" (40). Many of *Travels*'s early passages deplore the practice of giving young Frenchmen authority in the colony before they have acquired appropriate experience. Gide bemoans how these colonials panic when their authority is questioned—how they "reign by terror" with "violent reprisals and cruelty of all sorts" (14). After seeing Governor Lambline's work, however, Gide leaves Bangui with a quieter conscience:

> The road is admirable; this word is always recurring under my pen, especially after a good night's sleep. I feel my heart and spirits as light as air, and my mind not over-stupid; everything I see enchants me. . . . The tree-trunks, no longer muffled in undergrowth, are visible in all their native nobility. . . . As we pass, all these people stand at attention and salute; then, if there is the slightest response, they burst out into shouts and laughter. When I waved my hand to the children as we were going through one of the many villages, they were in a frenzy of delight, jumping and dancing about wildly in a kind of delirious rapture [*c'est un délire, des trépignements frénetiques, une sorte d'enthousiasme joyeux*]. (41–42; *Voyage* 53)

Set against Governor Lambline's "intelligent and consecutive administration," however, are frequent descriptions of how the Congolese behave when the French are absent; these descriptions seem to indicate how the Congolese would act if the French had never colonized the country: "On the wharf a swarm of Negroes hurry about like black ants, pushing trucks before them. . . . Naked Negroes run about, shouting, laughing, quarreling, and showing their cannibal teeth" (7). Listening to a boatman's song, Gide remarks: "There was a wild beauty in this half-plaintive chant; a joyous play of the muscles; a farouche enthusiasm" (10). In French, *farouche* means savage, wild, and fierce as well as shy, timid, and coy; this adjective recurs several times in Gide's journals. Although Gide acknowledges French corruption, his remarks suggest that even corruption seems useful to impede a level of indigenous vigor and enthusiasm (and not just colonial discontent) that would override French governance. There is something about Congolese energy that leads Gide to oscillate between admiration and hostility, respect and disgust. *Travels* is never certain whether this enthusiasm will engulf, even cannibalize, the French in waves of unappeasable delight or fury.

For this reason, Gide characterizes the French as proponents of sublimation, calmly urging—and often ordering——the colonized to give up their jouissance for labor and trade. Clearly, the French are not without their own jouissance; as the Congolese realize, the French manifest this satisfaction beyond pleasure as colonial rapacity. If skimming off the profits of a country's or continent's natural resources is not sufficient evidence of jouissance on a mass scale, the idea of "reign[ing] by terror" surely clarifies that the policies to which colonialism aims (for instance, extracting products and wealth from a country by imposing foreign laws, language, and culture) can differ greatly from what colonials may desire as individuals and groups.

In this respect, what does it mean to *override* colonial law? If Gide presents the

French as proponents of sublimation, the Congolese symbolize for them pure drive. In his *Three Essays on the Theory of Sexuality* (1905), Freud also represents the ego as afraid that the drive will "override" its resistances as shame, morality, guilt, etc., and thus question its ability to regulate the psychic apparatus: "Disgust seems to be one of the forces which have led to a restriction of the sexual aim. . . . The sexual instinct in its strength enjoys overriding this disgust" (152). Should we define this enjoyment simply as the drives' pleasure in overcoming egoic resistance, or does bliss also obtain from finding oneself overwhelmed by "foreign," "alien," or simply unacceptable desires (Freud, *Inhibitions* 98)?

Here, we can draw a parallel with the lament Gide enunciates, some way into his journey: "My regularity has broken down" (26). Even earlier, he remarks: "I recognize a numbness—perhaps a diminution [in myself]. Eyes are less keen; ears duller; and they carry less far desires that are no doubt weaker. The important thing is that this equation between the urging of the soul and the obedience of the body should be maintained. Even when growing old, may I preserve within myself an undiminished harmony!" (17; see Barthes 87, 90–92). Both afraid and in awe of his new surroundings, Gide vacillates among the pleasures of novelty, the fear of discovery, and the ennui of repetition. Not surprisingly, while the indigenous sometimes appear benign and placid to him, they also apparently manifest a ferocious energy whose demand for satisfaction seems insatiable: "We were given an amazing tamtam [dance] in front of the rest-house of Moussareu," Gide remarks. "Admirable alternating songs tempered the enthusiasm and frenzy of the pandemonium and gave it rhythm and support [*tempèrent l'enthousiasme et la frénésie du pandémonium*]. I have never seen anything more disconcerting, more savage" (48; *Voyage* 61).

In *Paradise Lost*, Book II (1667), Milton has Moloch, Belial, Mammon, and Beëlzebub debate the future of evil in Pandemonium, a temple so named because it means "all evil demons" (*pan-dæmonium*) in Greek and Latin. Gide does not invoke Milton, but the comparison is nonetheless instructive: He claims to witness scenes that are "more disconcerting, more savage" than this "pandemonium." Indeed, Gide's fascination with the Congo stems partly from his inability to limit jouissance to Africans (Steel, "D'Angleterre" 59; Torgovnick 24, 28). As I suggested earlier, the French in their rapacity manifest a corresponding, if nonidentical ecstasy that colonialism realizes *and* resists.

Let us consider an incident that takes place over a number of days. On his way to Bambio, with Marc Allégret, his partner, and a series of porters who carry their luggage and both men in a *tipoye*, Gide observes flowers that remind him of Normandy: "I cannot describe my rapture and excitement" (69). The party reaches a village outside Bambio and finds a crowd of greeting villagers: "We shook hands with some chiefs who were lined up and standing at attention; and even, by mistake—such was our enthusiasm—with some common guards. We *played the part* of great white chiefs with much dignity, saluting with our hands and smiling like ministers on tour. One huge fellow, ridiculously dressed up in skins, was beating on a gigantic xylophone . . .; he was the conductor of the women's dance; these, singing and uttering savage yells, swept the ground before us . . .; it was a scene of delirium" (69; my emphasis).

The next day, Gide hears from Samba N'Goto, an interpreter, about a "ball" that occurred in Bambio some time earlier. The "ball" is named by M. Garron, a French settler whom Gide calls "a great hunter . . . bored to extinction [*il s'y ennuie à périr*]" (64; *Voyage* 86). The irony of this description surfaces when we consider that the "ball" was not a dance but a scene of torture that gave Garron and agents of the Compagnie Forestière an exquisite pleasure. According to Garron, between ten and twenty rubber-gatherers who worked for the Compagnie Forestière

> had not brought in any rubber the month before (but this month they brought in double, from 40 to 50 kilogrammes)—[so they] were condemned to go round and round the factory under a fierce sun, carrying very heavy wooden beams. If they fell down, they were forced up by guards flogging them with whips. The "ball" began at eight o'clock and lasted the whole day, with Messrs. Pacha and Maudurier, the company's agent, looking on. At about eleven o'clock a man from Bagouma, called Malongué, fell to get up no more. When M. Pacha was informed of this, he merely replied: "*Je m'en f—*" and ordered the "ball" to go on. All this took place in the presence of the assembled inhabitants of Bambio and of all the chiefs who had come from the neighbouring villages to attend the market. (70)

Although this scene is synecdochic of colonial trade and exploitation, it also attempts to symbolize a related but nonidentical drama about racial fantasy. Is it possible to represent this scene as an allegory of colonial enjoyment? The "ball" clarifies what is psychically at stake in extraction and expropriation, but Gide's palpable disgust of Pacha also emerges, I think, from the proximity between this "ball" and the white masquerade that he described immediately before in his journal: "We played the part of great white chiefs with much dignity, saluting with our hands and smiling like ministers on tour" (69; see Spurr 80). After copying Garron's account of the "ball" into his own diary, Gide declares: "My indignation against Pacha is naturally great, but the Compagnie Forestière *plays a part [rôle] in all this*, which seems to be very much graver, though more secret. For, after all, it—its representatives, I mean—knew everything that was going on. It (or its agents) profited by this state of things. Its agents approved Pacha, encouraged him, were his *partners* [*partie liée*]. It was at their request that Pacha arbitrarily threw into prison the natives who did not furnish enough stuff; etc." (71; *Voyage* 94; my emphases).

Since the Compagnie Forestière's representatives were Pacha's economic partners, Gide concludes, they were also his partners at this "ball," enjoying the spectacle of African suffering by likening the whole event to a dance. Our problem, however, is that Gide then declares his doubt, in the very next paragraph (as I cited above), about "what part I could play, how I could be useful" (71). We know that Gide recoils from this "ball" with horror—he writes to the Governor to say so. Yet his partial understanding of the intensity of colonial enjoyment—"I am terribly afraid, however, that this scene of the 'ball' was nothing exceptional" (71)—inadvertently connects with his "part" in observing and providing testimony; the "ball" therefore impinges on the rest of his journey:

> Impossible to sleep. The Bambio "ball" haunted my night. I cannot content myself with saying, as so many do, that the natives were still more wretched before the French occupation. We have shouldered responsibilities regarding them which we have no right to evade. The immense pity of what I have seen has taken possession of me; I know things to which I cannot reconcile myself. *What demon drove me to Africa* [*Quel démon m'a poussé en Afrique*]? What did I come out to find in this country? I was at peace. I know now. I must speak. But how can I get people to listen? . . . Have I been walking hitherto between high walls of falsehood? I must get behind them, out on to the other side, and learn what it is they are put to hide, even if the truth is horrible. The horrible truth that I suspect is what I must see. (72–73; *Voyage* 96; my emphasis)

The question is difficult to ask, but we must wonder what complex affinity joins Gide's account of the "ball" with his understanding of African misery. Gide's visual and fantasmatic complicity with colonial enjoyment prevails here and elsewhere, transforming the obligation to act—what Gide acknowledges as what "I suspect . . . I *must* see"—into a voyeuristic yearning quite similar to the "ball's" French onlookers: What "I suspect . . . I *want* to see." In this respect, *Travels* raises the difficult question When does colonialism inaugurate pleasure, *transporting* Gide to new heights of ecstasy from his knowledge of others' suffering?

This pun on "transport" recalls Gide's conscious stress on *not* smiling at the human "cattle" mending the road for him, but the whole affair also returns us to Gide's opening accounts of "Negroes hurry[ing] about like black ants, pushing trucks before them. . . . Naked Negroes [who] run about, shouting, laughing, quarreling, and showing their cannibal teeth" (7; see also Lucey's astute section on "transport" in *Gide's* 170, 174–80). Gide is quite obsessed by this analogy, likening the Congolese repeatedly to ants and termites (when they are not cattle or, later, baboons). Having described "swarms of natives bringing in their crop of rubber in great baskets" (44), for instance, Gide admires the deft industry of termites, who strangely have "abandoned" their "monumental" structures. Apparently, these works resemble

> mediæval castles or cathedrals with walls as hard as bricks and almost vertical. Or are these the work of a different *race* of termites? And have these termitaries always been rounded? And yet they all seem deserted. Why? It seems that another race of termites, whose buildings are on a small scale, now occupies the ground in place of the monumental ones. Some of these tumuli which I saw later had been cut straight through to make way for the road, and the mystery of their inside was displayed, with its passages, rooms, etc. I cursed the car for not letting me examine this matter more at leisure. (47; my emphasis)

Is this really, as Eric Marty claims, a "compassion[ate]" metaphor for African suffering (118)? The figurative links between insects and Africans seem to collapse when Gide represents the Congo's "settlement," or *colonia*, as a microcosm of human antagonism, not cooperation (see 47 and esp. 84); "culture" and "colonization" share a common etymological root. If the analogy between Africans and insects is deliberately political (and I'm not entirely sure it is), it also naturalizes, and perhaps "decatastrophizes," the substitution of one "race" of termites/ humans for another:

> Every thirty yards or so, there is a reed hut, half hidden by the foliage, and shaped like a pointed helmet. These garden-cities that lie stretched along the sides of the road are nothing but the merest mask of prosperity. The *race* that inhabits and overpopulates them is not a very fine one. Before it was subjected two years ago, its members lived scattered in the bush; the old people will not let themselves be *tamed*; they sit squatting on the ground like baboons and hardly glance up as the motor passes by; one never gets a salutation from them. The women, on the contrary, run up, waving and shaking their bundles; their sex (they are shaved) is sometimes hidden by a bunch of leaves. (47–48; my emphases)

Gide later has the leisure—or gall—to explore these human monuments. He describes indigenous huts whose interiority fascinates him; they display people at work who cannot see him watching. Here we might recall Gide's desire to "get . . . out on to the other side of . . . the high walls of falsehood . . . even if the truth is horrible" (73), but since he seems unaware that he is repeating his previous analogy, we must again quote him at length:

The rush mats are just high enough to allow a medium-sized man on horseback to see over them. As one rides by, one can look down upon the strangest privacies. This is the quintessence of the exotic. The beauty of the huts with their trellised roofs, edged by a sort of mosaic made with straw, is very great—*like the work of insects.* . . . The atmosphere is one of peace, forgetfulness, happiness; *the people here are all smiling; yes, even the suffering, even the sick.* (I remember an epileptic child in the first village of Bosoum; he had fallen into the fire and one whole side of his handsome face was frightfully burnt; the other side of his face smiled—an angelic smile.) (158; my emphases)

Again, is this analogy truly compassionate? First, the indigenous have no affect that is not also spectacle for Gide's hungry eyes (Gide, "Conférence" 31–32; Durosay, "Images et imaginaire" 12, 15). However, the boy's "angelic" response to trauma might easily reinscribe Gide's endless descriptions of Africa's "macabre" and "inhuman" elements. In this respect, how have critics managed to dissociate or conceptually remove Gide from this and other descriptions of colonial enjoyment?

Daniel Durosay, France's most prolific commentator on *Travels*, tries to juxtapose Gide's politicization with his initial pursuit of "erotism": "The departure for the 'Congo' had in effect progressively become, in the Gidean imaginary, a departure for a dreamed-up, Baudelairean land of natural liberty, of spontaneous erotism, of infinite sensuality" (Intro. to Allégret, *Carnets* 13; trans. Lucey). In this reading, the Congo rescinds Gide's selfish pursuit of pleasure by confronting him with the brute politics of exploitation: "The political and economic calamities of French Equatorial Africa having, in a manner of speaking, belied, demythologized the fantasm, and having determined Gide to embark upon a polemical campaign, the direction of the voyage tends (more and more as the writer's political commitment becomes more pronounced) to turn from egotism to altruism" (13; trans. Lucey).

Understandably, Michael Lucey finds such "simple narratives . . . insufficiently complicated" (153). He highlights passages in *Les Faux-Monnayeurs* (1925) and *Si le grain ne meurt* (1920; 1955) that contradict developmental accounts of Gide's politics, yet he also finds invaluable Marty's account of Gide's psychic ambivalence. For instance, Marty writes:

The journal [Gide] keeps throughout his trip [to the Congo and Chad] progressively ceases to be solely a collection of impressions or of sensations sublimated by a literary sensibility, in order to turn into an implacable account, a scrupulous and also revolted analysis of the economic exploitation and the poor treatment meted out to the blacks by the colonists. In fact, the quality of these two journals [*Voyage au Congo* and *Le Retour du Tchad*] is constituted precisely by the *alternation* of apparently insignificant notations on vegetation . . . fauna, climate, and human beings with remarks of an economic and social nature, but also with moments of compassion toward these mistreated peoples, or of disgust towards the French colonists. Gide discovers in himself a vulnerability, a wound caused by this spectacle, and which also becomes an obsession, an incandescent point that will subsequently mobilize his entire being. (117–18; Lucey's emphasis and trans.)

Marty's emphasis on oscillation and the "wound caused by this [African] spectacle" illuminates certain enigmatic moments in Gide's narrative. However, if it is textually and biographically incorrect to represent *Travels in the Congo* as Gide's political epiphany, it is also inadequate to claim that Gide's entomological analogies are simple "moments of compassion" or instances of disgust only at French colonialism. Consider, for instance, Gide's preposterous accounts of African dances:

> The women dance at the entrance to every village. This shameless jigging of elderly matrons is extremely painful to look at. The most aged are always the most frenzied. Some of them are like lunatics [*Certaines se démènent comme des forcenées*]. . . . The whole population crowds round one, pressing eagerly up to have the joy of shaking the hand one holds out—all shouting and laughing in a kind of lyrical demonstration of affection—almost cannibalism! [*C'est presque du cannibalism*] . . . . There were a good hundred . . . crowding round us with cannibal-like expressions of joy [*avec des manifestations de cannibales*], and so close as almost to suffocate us. (80, 99, 130; *Voyage* 106, 129, 162)

Marty and Lucey downplay or ignore these passages in order to redeem Gide through his anticolonial politics. This strategy requires both critics (and Durosay) not only to substitute narrative ambivalence for racial disgust, but to ignore the disturbing *compatibility* between Gide's humanism and his frequent recoil from African "savagery." To be sure, Lucey's reason for complicating Gide's politics stems from his unwillingness to endorse Gide's association of the unconscious and the abject with infantile states. Lucey writes:

> If I hesitate in what follows, as I have been hesitating throughout, to endorse developmental models (in favor of models that account for something like what Marty has called *alternation*), it is because a too quick recourse to developmental schemata often results in a moralizing abjection of the "undeveloped," "unconscious" early stage, whose political complexities then go unread in favor of a too celebratory identification with the virtues of a later moment. (154; original emphasis)

All this is undoubtedly true, yet Lucey's political dissociation of the unconscious from states of "savagery" ignores their fantasmatic cogency for *Gide*, ultimately protecting Gide's reader from the most gratuitous and politically incorrect elements of his work—one would never know these elements existed from reading Lucey's book. However disturbing the task or results, let us consider why Gide finds the "wound" of African savagery so compelling. For instance, he writes of another dance:

> It would be impossible to imagine anything more dismal and more stupid than this dance, unrelieved as it was by any breath of spirituality . . . repeated untiringly, they all go round and round . . . jigging their bodies as if they had no bones, bending forward, with their arms dangling and their heads shaking backwards and forwards like fowls. This is how they express their emotion—manifest their joy! By the light of the moon this obscure ceremony seemed the celebration of some infernal mystery; I stayed gazing at it for a long time, fascinated by it as by an abyss. (122–23)

What aspect of this "emotion" leads Gide to an abyss? Why indeed do such manifestations of "joy" almost unravel him, leading him to question not only his capacity for joy, but also why indigenous bliss—so crucial at other moments in *Travels* to relieving what Fanon calls "the racial distribution of guilt" (103)—seems here almost to *rob* Gide of pleasure? Recalling his fear of expressing his thought only to "find no response to it" (52), we can use Gide to revise simple psychologizations of black-white colonial relations; we must, however, examine these accounts before returning to Gide's text.

The type of reading Octave Mannoni, Frantz Fanon, and Joel Kovel offer of cross-racial envy, antipathy, and fear usually binds black and white men (invariably, it is men) in a Hegelian dynamic that misreads the fundamental asymmetry of all colonial relations (see Mannoni 18; Hegel 111–19; Masson 207–8; etc.). "The black man wants to be white," Fanon writes. "The white man slaves to reach a human level. . . . How do we extricate ourselves?" (9–10). How indeed?

In his section of *Black Skin, White Masks* (1952) entitled "The Negro and Hegel," Fanon also urges us all to "do battle for . . . a world of reciprocal recognitions" (218). "The only means of breaking this vicious circle that throws me back on myself," he writes, "is to restore to the other, through mediation and recognition, his human reality" (217). Fanon then italicizes a quotation from Hegel: "*they recognize themselves as mutually recognizing each other*" (qtd. 217). As many commentators of Fanon's writing have observed, however, there is another dimension to *Black Skin, White Masks* that resists this Hegelian sublation. Indeed, Fanon presents this other dimension at the start of his section on Hegel: "Man is human only to the extent to which he tries to impose his existence on another man in order to be recognized by him" (216). (Consider also Gide's famous argument: "*Moins le blanc est intelligent, plus le noir lui paraît bête*" [*Voyage* 21]; "The less intelligent the white man is, the more stupid he thinks the black" [14].) This additional dimension to Fanon's work—his emphasis on the unconscious—shatters Fanon's association of Hegelian sublation with interracial recognition (see 222). Fanon admits: "I am willing to work on the psychoanalytic level . . . the level of the 'failures,' in the sense in which one speaks of engine failures" (23).

Obviously, there are many dimensions of "failure" in the colonial scene. Perhaps the most fundamental for Fanon, however, is a failure of recognition between white and black: this contributes to the "Manicheism delirium" (183), or insoluble antagonism, in which colonialists and racists perceptually align whiteness with virtue and blackness with evil. Fanon claims repeatedly that whites and blacks are "sealed" by their perceptions (45, 218), which prevent them from "true recognition" in the Hegelian sense. But the failures he identifies at the level of fantasy and identification also create numerous "leaks." At one moment, Fanon writes, in response to "the white man's affective ankylosis," or paralysis: "I secreted a race" (122). In this respect, race approximates psychic trauma. Elsewhere, Fanon quotes Césaire on the character of Nazism: "It drips, it seeps, it wells from every crack in western Christian civilization until it engulfs that civilization in a bloody sea" (qtd. 90–91). In these passages, racism and prejudice seem almost anathema to subjectivity.

As a psychiatrist, Fanon was very receptive to the work of Sigmund and Anna Freud and of Jacques Lacan—more so, perhaps, than contemporary postcolonial theorists have acknowledged. Fanon approvingly cites Anna Freud's *The Ego and the Mechanisms of Defence* (1936) to interpret "why the black man cannot take pleasure in his insularity" (51; see also 59). He also quotes extensively from Sigmund Freud's account of trauma (see 143–44), while Lacan's theories of psychosis and the mirror stage, though somewhat literalized by Fanon, prove invaluable to him in explaining the persistence and astonishing intensity of certain racial imagoes (80, 161n.).

To be sure, Fanon finds Jung's work simplistic and inadequate to his needs. "Jung has confused instinct and habit" (188), he writes; "Jung consistently identifies the foreign with the obscure, with the tendency to evil" (190); "Personally, I think that Jung has deceived himself" (187; see also Torgovnick 29–42). We cannot fault Fanon here, yet Fanon crucially misreads Lacan, and says so—"On this point psychoanalysts [like Dr. Lacan] will be reluctant to share my view" (152)—by advancing a Hegelian/Sartrean model of alterity. Fanon states explicitly that after Lacan's theory of the mirror stage, "one can have no further doubt that the real Other for the white man is and will continue to be the black man" (161n.). This ignores that *méconnaissance*, or a failure of recognition, is central to Lacan's account of alterity ("Subversion" 310). Fanon writes: "We shall see that this discovery is basic: Every time the subject sees his image and *recognizes* it, it is always in some way 'the mental oneness which is inherent in him' that he acclaims" (161n.; my emphasis).

The point is not that Fanon chose not to follow Lacan *à la lettre*. As Fanon avowed in *Black Skin, White Masks*, "Earlier I referred to Jacques Lacan; it was not by accident. In his thesis, presented in 1932, he violently attacked the idea of the constitutional. Apparently, I am departing from his conclusions" (80). Certainly, Lacan *did* attack "the idea of the constitutional" with a "violen[ce]" that many recent critics accusing him of bogus universality appear not to realize (see McClintock 196; Butler 56–57). The point is that Fanon's partial fidelity to Lacan restores to the latter a Hegelian interest in sublation that Lacan also "violently" rejected. The very notion of a lack—or want—in being ("*manque-à-être*") (*Four* 29) renders Fanon's dream of a monument on which he "can already see a white man and a black man *hand in hand*" (222; original emphasis) unlikely to succeed *on a basis of a mutual recognition*. Denis Hollier therefore remarks of Lacan's mirror stage: "In this mirrored labyrinth, equivocation is law: the difference between ego and the other, between the victim and the aggressor, ceaselessly disappears" (9).

For this reason, Lacan's conception of "*L'Autre*," or Other, has no obvious relation to color.[2] This does not mean that Lacanian psychoanalysis is unable to address racism and prejudice, or that it is uninterested in either phenomenon. On the contrary, Lacan's refusal to portray racial difference as pure alterity fosters a more precise and historically subtle account of group identification and racial fantasy than we find in Hegelian accounts of whites and blacks, where both racial groups are locked in immutable conflict. For important reasons, then, Lacan does *not* simply or timelessly represent the black man as the Other; ironically, it is postcolonial theory, taking its notion of alterity from Hegel, Sartre, and Fanon, that produces this ahistorical and occidental account of racial difference.

The repercussions of Fanon's Hegelianism are nonetheless acute. While Fanon complains of being "sealed into thingness" (218) by white racism, he also aims toward "mastery of language" because it "affords remarkable power" (18). On one level, we can appreciate why linguistic mastery is threatening to white racism. However, Fanon also avows, at the beginning of *Black Skin, White Masks*, that "to speak is to exist absolutely for the other" (17). Ironically, Fanon is at his most "Lacanian" here, for he clarifies that we cannot limit the tyranny of prejudice to intentional racism; nor can we simply defeat it by "mastery of language": The signifier raises a further, generic dimension of alienation that implicates men and women of all races while exceeding their capacity for symbolic control. This is surely why Fanon claims "The Other will become the mainstay of [the white man's] preoccupations and his desires" (170), and why he states of the black man, "The goal of his behavior will be The Other (in the guise of the white man)" (154).

Considering this radical asymmetry, we can appreciate why Lacan character-ized desire as "a relation of being to lack. . . . It isn't the lack of this or that, but lack of being whereby the being exists" (*Seminar II*, 223). With this clarification, we can also understand Gide's preoccupation with African jouissance. Alongside the passage in *Travels* I cited earlier, in which Gide exclaims "This is how they express their emotion—manifest their joy! . . . I stayed gazing at [this infernal mys-tery] for a long time, fascinated by it as by an abyss" (123), we can place Lacan's question *Che vuoi?*, What does the Other want of me? ("Subversion" 312). Elsewhere, Lacan elaborates on this question: "What is my desire? What is my position in the imaginary structuration? This position is only conceivable in so far as one finds a guide beyond the imaginary, on the level of the symbolic plane, of the legal exchange which can only be embodied in the verbal exchange between human beings" (*Seminar I*, 141; see also Boothby 110–14).

This passage is replete with questions that recur throughout Gide's *Travels* and all colonial discourse. Yet the "guide" that Gide finds "beyond the imaginary" sur-passes all "legal exchange," as Lacan willingly concedes. It does so because Gide's desire is not *reducible* to symbolic exchange, even though he (and we) might wish to account for it in these terms. Jouissance is the cause of this self-surpassing, for it "guides" the subject to the "abyss" of its being. For this reason, the question "What does the Other want of me?" which recurs throughout Gide's *Travels* as a demand for purpose and orientation, seems for Gide to conflate the Other's jouis-sance with the menacing specter of African joy and revenge.

Slavoj Žižek put this well when he argued that "Fantasy appears . . . as an answer to '*Che vuoi?*,' to the unbearable enigma of the desire of the Other, of the lack in the Other, but it is at the same time fantasy itself which, so to speak, provides the co-ordinates of our desire—which constructs the frame enabling us to desire something. The usual definition of fantasy ('an imagined scenario representing the realization of desire') is therefore somewhat misleading, or at least ambiguous: in the fantasy-scene the desire is not fulfilled, 'satisfied,' but constituted (given its objects, and so on)—*through fantasy, we learn 'how to desire'*" (118; original empha-sis). Nonetheless, it must be asked: How can we tolerate a scenario in which the colonizer's fantasy clearly has such additional repercussions? Gide's naiveté is so distressing because it reminds us of fantasy's egregious narcissism. His identifica-tion balances precariously on these hostile fantasies, for the aggression and vio-lence accompanying identification hinge necessarily on the enigma of the Other's jouissance (for a related argument, see Anna Freud, "Identification with the Aggressor," *Ego* 118–22, 125–31).

Colonialism obviously compounds this antagonism, but it does not explain or delimit the *difficulty* of all structures of identification; this is a specific *and* generic argument. To put this another way, if we relied solely on material "guides" at this point, and not the ego-ideal, as Lacan advised (*Seminar I*, 141), we would find ourselves surprised by the surplus violence that constantly *escapes* colonial law (Copjec 215–16). We can illuminate this point by iterating Gide's dilemma about literal guides and transport in *Travels*. When he returned to France, Gide justified his having paid porters to carry him and Allégret in a *tipoye*,[3] though he complained at the time of discomfort and the difficulty he experienced in reading. At the time of his travels, too, Gide remarked: "A difficulty has arisen with our porters. They all want to leave. . . . [I]t is extremely difficult to get men to replace them; on the other hand, it seems *inhuman* of us to take these people much further away from their villages" (83; my emphasis). To push Marty's and Lucey's analyses further than they seem willing to go, let us note that Gide writes the following passage toward the end of his journey:

> A few smiles, a few kind words, have got the better of the porters' remissness. Yesterday evening they refused to go any farther. And now, in their enthusiasm, they declare they are willing to go as far as Douala. One old man, who was carrying the heavy cinema packing-case, was seized with a fit of excitement [*crise de lyrisme*]. He began rushing wildly about in every direction, laughing and shouting; off into the bush and then back again; spinning round on his own axis; darting up to a tree he caught sight of and striking it three times with a javelin he had in his hand. Had he gone mad? Not at all; it was merely lyrical excitement [*C'est du lyrisme, simplement*]. What we used to call "savage ecstasy" [*le transport sauvage*] when we were children. And at the time the *tipoye*-bearers—to get a *matabiche* [tip], no doubt—began thanking me, either separately or in chorus. They are no longer satisfied with calling me "Governor." They shout: "Thank you, Government, thank you!" (301–2; *Retour* 118)

According to Lucey, Gide's phrase "*crise de lyrisme*" "hints at a tentative, even fearful identification with this older porter, who somehow ironically fulfills Gide's desire both to be the spectacle and to see/film it" (179; see also Allégret, "Voyage" 37–38; Durosay, "Les Images" 63). This reading clearly obtains because the porter carries Allégret's camera, but it takes us only so far in understanding the condensed implications of "savage ecstasy." Let us ask, first, why Gide is so keen to downplay the possibility of this man's madness: "*C'est du lyrisme, simplement.*" And why does Gide's certainty at witnessing "merely lyrical excitement" implicate him in knowledge but lead him affectively toward dissociation?: The man's "excitement"— indeed, the porters' "enthusiasm"—never connects with Gide's perception of sublimity.

I think this asymmetry between Gide and the porters points up a dimension of colonial enjoyment that exceeds the tips, coercions, and material explanations we might otherwise invoke to comprehend this scene. If jouissance seems to manifest itself in the porter's "savage ecstasy," consider Gide's pride in being read synecdochically as colonial government—as the figure of France. Let me make clear that while the psychic motivations of every party might appear enigmatic in this and other scenes, they have powerful material effects. The point is less to *add* these volatile structures of fantasy and identification to colonial critique than to *rethink* how a careful understanding of such impersonal drives might alter our conception of colonialism—perhaps even imperial history.

Let us consider, for instance, why Gide concludes his *Travels* by reporting the following dialogue between a young French boy and girl as they all return to France on board the *Asie*. The girl remarks: "We French detest other nations—all of us French . . . don't we, George? . . . Yes, it's a peculiar thing about the French that they can't endure other nations." The boy responds obliquely, but with conviction: "I call a musician . . . a person who understands what he plays. I don't call a person a musician who bangs on the piano just like people kicking niggers" (375). Gide remarks: "And, as he added, with an air of authority, that they should 'be put an end to'—not the niggers, perhaps, and certainly not the people who kick them, but the bad musicians—the girl exclaimed indignantly: 'But then who will play for us to dance?' " (375).

Recalling the Compagnie Forestière's "ball" that so appalled and fascinated Gide, this exchange promotes a bleak conclusion, while allowing us to grasp the astonishing turbulence and psychic complexity of racial identification. Thus we can use Gide's text to open the terms of identification and racial fantasy and display their volatile determinants. In this respect, without leaving Gide behind us, we appreciate the genuine risk and radicalism of *Bound to Violence* (1968), Yambo Ouologuem's extraordinary novel, which ends more diplomatically with a game of interracial chess, but which also stubbornly repeats these inter- and *intra*racial antagonisms. As a fictional account of Sudanic Africa's colonial and even "precolonial" history, Ouologuem's novel, like Gide's *Travels*, sustains an astonishing inquiry into *le devoir de violence*: the characters' *debt* to violence as well as their urge to reproduce it in other forms. The narrator concludes: "One cannot help recalling that Saif, mourned three million times, is forever reborn to history beneath the hot ashes of more than thirty African republics" (181–82). These fragments characterize the novel's final section, "Dawn":

> The crux of the matter is that violence, vibrant in its unconditional submission to the will to power, becomes a prophetic illumination, a manner of questioning and answering, a dialogue, a tension, and oscillation . . . No solidarity is possible. Nor

purity. . . . . The law of justice and love is the only bond that is capable of uniting our irreducible diversities—from above. Down below, amid the strange fauna of the human passions, the lust for power and glory is at work. . . . The impossible part of forgiveness is that one must keep it up. (173, 175, 177, 181)

I do not wish to transmute Gide's problem into Ouologuem's text to foster a spurious universality. To follow Ouologuem in tracing African colonialism from the thirteenth century (the time of Arab mercantilism, with all of its racism and exploitation of Africans) to contemporary France does not mean that we must naturalize violence or exonerate Europe from its specific relation to imperialism. Like Ouologuem, however, and even the white South African journalist Rian Malan, I want to complicate the widespread assumption in postcolonial theory that denouncing Western violence gives us historical clarity or political power. It is Malan, for instance, who documents how South African whites and blacks "spiraled on down toward mutual annihilation. We always seemed to miss each other in the murk of our mutually baffling cultures and our mutually blinding fears" (276). Following this painful insight, and Fanon's and Ouologuem's comparable arguments, I contend that psychoanalysis does not impede our search for political answers, but it does implicate us all in "the racial distribution of guilt" (Fanon 103). Arguably, only an understanding of jouissance can "extricate" us from these violent reprisals and "baffling" exchanges.

ENDNOTES

1. Consider also Gide's opening words to "Journal du voyage au Maroc," which are very difficult to translate: "A new country allows one to experience a more sincere emotion. Whatever I experience here I want fully to interpret and understand. All of these emotions connect to some experience, and I would see fire in another's eye if I didn't know it was already burning [*je verrais le feu d'un autre œil si je ne savais pas qu'il brûlait*]" (66; my trans.).

2. I am grateful to Tim Dean for observing that in Lacan, "the Other has no color." This point surfaced in a discussion between Dean and Barbara Johnson at the 1989 MLA Convention in Washington, D.C.

3. See Volume II of Gide's *Journals*: "It seems to me . . . that the famous question of portage, which has been especially brought up, has not been examined calmly. Were I to astonish or even to inspire indignation in some people, I must confess, to be frank, that I cannot denounce the custom of portage. Its abuses are frightful. In itself I cannot consider it an evil. Besides, it seems to me inevitable. . . . The African native, moreover, submits to it without any protest, if the load that is imposed on him is not too heavy, and especially *if he is not taken too far from his village*" (33; original emphasis).

WORKS CITED

Allégret, Marc. *Carnets du Congo: Voyage avec Gide.* Intro. Daniel Durosay. Paris: Presses du C.N.R.S., 1987.

——. "Voyage au Congo." *Bulletin des amis d'André Gide* 16.80 (1988): 37–40.

Barthes, Roland. "Notes sur André Gide et son journal." *Bulletin des amis d'André Gide* 13.67 (1985): 85–105.

Boothby, Richard. *Death and Desire: Psychoanalytic Theory in Lacan's Return to Freud.* New York: Routledge, 1991.

Butler, Judith. *Gender Trouble: Feminism and the Subversion of Identity.* New York: Routledge, 1990.

Copjec, Joan. *Read My Desire: Lacan against the Historicists.* Cambridge: MIT, 1994.

Darras, Jacques. "Le Voyage en Afrique." *Ésprit* 128 (1987): 1–12.

Dedet, André and Christian Petr. "Le Voyageur en Afrique et son regard sur l'Autre." *Journal of European Studies* 22 (1992): 323–36.

Durosay, Daniel. "Les Images du *Voyage au Congo*: L'œil d'Allégret." *Bulletin des amis d'André Gide* 15.73 (1987): 57–79.

——. "Images et imaginaire dans le *Voyage au Congo*: Un film et deux 'auteurs.' " *Bulletin des amis d'André Gide* 16.80 (1988): 9–30.

Fanon, Frantz. *Black Skin, White Masks.* 1952. Trans. Charles Lam Markmann. New York: Grove, 1967.

Freud, Anna. *The Ego and the Mechanisms of Defence.* 1936. London: Hogarth, 1948.

Freud, Sigmund. *Three Essays on the Theory of Sexuality.* 1905. Vol. 7 of *The Standard Edition of the Complete Psychological Works of Sigmund Freud.* Ed. and trans. James Strachey. 24 vols. London: Hogarth, 1953–74. 135–72.

——. *Inhibitions, Symptoms, and Anxiety.* 1926 (1925). Vol. 20 of *SE.* 77–175.

Gide, André. "Journal du voyage au Maroc." 1923. *La Nouvelle revue française* 18.205 (1970): 66–71.

——. *Voyage au Congo.* Paris: Gallimard, 1927.

——. *Le Retour du Tchad.* Paris: Gallimard, 1928.

——. *Travels in the Congo.* 1927, 1928. Trans. Dorothy Bussy. Hopewell, N.J.: Ecco, 1994.

——. *The Journals of André Gide, Volume II: 1924–1949.* Ed. and trans. Justin O'Brien. Evanston, Ill.: Northwestern UP, 1987.

——. "Conférence de Bruxelles: Allocution prononcée le 22 mai 1928 pour la projection du film *Voyage au Congo*." *Bulletin des amis d'André Gide* 16.80 (1988): 31–36.

Hargreaves, Alec G. *The Colonial Experience in French Fiction: A Study of Pierre Loti, Ernest Psichari, and Pierre Mille.* London: Macmillan, 1981.

Hegel, G. W. F. *Phenomenology of Spirit.* 1807. Trans. A. V. Miller. New York: Oxford UP, 1977.

Hollier, Denis. "On Equivocation (between Literature and Politics)." Trans. Rosalind Krauss. *October* 55 (1990): 3–22.

Howard, Richard. "From Exoticism to Homosexuality." *A New History of French Literature.* Ed. Denis Hollier. Cambridge: Harvard UP, 1989. 836–42.

Kovel, Joel. *White Racism: A Psychohistory.* New York: Pantheon, 1971.

Lacan, Jacques. *The Seminar of Jacques Lacan, Book I, 1953–1954: Freud's Papers on Technique.* Ed. Jacques-Alain Miller. Trans. John Forrester. New York: Cambridge UP, 1988.

——. *The Seminar of Jacques Lacan, Book II, 1954–1955: The Ego in Freud's Theory and in the Technique of Psychoanalysis.* Ed. Jacques-Alain Miller. Trans. Sylvana Tomaselli, with notes by John Forrester. New York: Cambridge UP, 1988.

——. *The Four Fundamental Concepts of Psycho-Analysis.* 1973. Ed. Jacques-Alain Miller. Trans. Alan Sheridan. New York: Norton, 1978.

——. "The Subversion of the Subject and the Dialectic of Desire in the Freudian Unconscious." 1960. *Écrits: A Selection.* Trans. Alan Sheridan. New York: Norton, 1977. 292–325.

——. "Jeunesse de Gide ou la lettre et le désir." *Écrits.* Paris: Seuil, 1966. 739–64.

Leiris, Michel. *L'Afrique fantôme.* Paris: Gallimard, 1934.

Lévy-Bruhl, Lucien. *La Mentalité primitive.* 1922. 14th ed. Paris: Presses Universitaires de France, 1947.

Lucey, Michael. *Gide's Bent: Sexuality, Writing, Politics.* New York: Oxford UP, 1995.

Malan, Rian. *My Traitor's Heart: A South African Exile Returns to Face His Country, His Tribe, and His Conscience.* New York: Vintage International, 1991.

Mannoni, Octave. *Prospero and Caliban: The Psychology of Colonization.* 1950. Trans. Pamela Powesland. New York: Praeger, 1966.

Marty, Eric. *André Gide: Qui êtes-vous? Avec les entretiens André Gide–Jean Amrouche.* Lyon: La Manufacture, 1987.

Masson, Pierre. *André Gide: Voyage et écriture.* Lyon: Presses Universitaires de Lyon, 1983.

McClintock, Anne. *Imperial Leather: Race, Gender, and Sexuality in the Colonial Conquest.* New York: Routledge, 1995.

Milton, John. *Paradise Lost.* 1667. *Milton: Poetical Works.* Ed. Douglas Bush. Oxford: Oxford UP, 1966.

Ouologuem, Yambo. *Bound to Violence.* Trans. by Ralph Manheim of *Le devoir de violence.* 1968. Portsmouth, N.H.: Heinemann, 1971, 1986.

Pratt, Mary Louise. "Mapping Ideology: Gide, Camus, Algeria." *College Literature* 8.2 (1981): 158–74.

Putnam, Walter C. "Conrad, Gide, et le Congo." *Bulletin des amis d'André Gide* 16.80 (1988): 63–80.

Spurr, David. "Lire le Congo." *Bulletin des amis d'André Gide* 20.93 (1992): 73–81.

Steel, David. "Gide et Freud." *Revue d'histoire littéraire de la France* 77.1 (1977): 48–74.

——. "D'Angleterre en Afrique avec Marc Allégret." *Bulletin des amis d'André Gide* 20.93 (1992): 57–62.

Suret-Canale, Jean. *French Colonialism in Tropical Africa 1900–1945.* Trans. Till Gottheiner. New York: Pica, 1971.

Torgovnick, Marianna. *Primitive Passions: Men, Women, and the Quest for Ecstasy.* New York: Knopf, 1997.

Walker, David H., ed. *André Gide.* Harlow, Essex: Longman, 1997.

Žižek, Slavoj. *The Sublime Object of Ideology.* New York: Verso, 1989.

13

The Germs of Empires:
Heart of Darkness, Colonial Trauma,
and the Historiography of AIDS

Tim Dean

In an extraordinary review of David Denby's *Great Books*, Helen Vendler weighs in with her verdict on the contemporary culture wars. Assessing Denby's center-piece account of his Columbia University classroom discussion of *Heart of Darkness*, she remarks, "Perhaps it does students no harm to conduct bull-sessions about colonialism in class; but should Conrad be sacrificed to such an aim?" (37). Harvard poetry critic Vendler here distinguishes herself as perhaps the first critic in a century's worth of commentary on *Heart of Darkness* to suggest that Conrad's 1899 novella has nothing to do with colonialism. Even more remarkably, she dismisses any attempt to discuss *Heart of Darkness* in the context of colonialism as "anachronistic and patronizing" (37). While Vendler declines to enlighten readers of *The New Republic* as to what *Heart of Darkness* is really about, such absurd comments from so accomplished a critic permit us to take the temperature of current controversies over the literary canon, multicultural education, affirmative action, and political correctness. As Vendler accurately senses, Conrad's novella has become a test case in these debates.[1] The following account may be taken as an indirect intervention in such debates, since I shall discuss *Heart of Darkness* in relation to the popular racist idea that Africa is the *origin* of AIDS. Before proceeding, however, I would like to make clear that my argument about AIDS in Conrad's era isn't simply figurative or rhetorical, but is based on epidemiological and virological evidence of HIV in Africa at the turn of the century.

Conrad is a dream for psychoanalytic critics.   —Chinua Achebe 259

The kind of approach to *Heart of Darkness* that Vendler abhors is exemplified best not by Denby or the Columbia professors he represents in *Great Books*, but by a scene toward the end of *Apocalypse Now*, Francis Ford Coppola's 1979 film, in which Marlon Brando as Colonel Kurtz reads aloud from T. S. Eliot's 1925 poem "The Hollow Men." In a performance that no doubt wouldn't satisfy Vendler, Brando makes his way through the poem's opening section, but does not read its epigraph—how could he, when it is his own epitaph, "Mistah Kurtz—he dead"?

This uncanny moment is highly instructive. By selecting as his epigraph this line from Conrad, Eliot made it the second most famous sentence in *Heart of Darkness* (following "The horror! The horror!," which Ezra Pound a few years earlier had dissuaded him from using as the epigraph to *The Waste Land*). The line "Mistah Kurtz—he dead" achieved notoriety some half-century later, when Chinua Achebe entered it as evidence for the prosecution in his case against *Heart of Darkness*, in which he denounced Conrad as "a bloody racist" and recommended that the work be stripped of its canonical status. Achebe considers the line racist because it represents one of only two instances in the novella when Conrad deigned to confer the dignity of speech on the African natives; and in both instances he caricatures their speech as pidgin English, a racist stereotype. Although somewhat naive and unpersuasive in itself, Achebe's interpretation nevertheless initiated an intense critical debate about the status of race and racism in *Heart of Darkness*.[2] In recent years this controversy over Conrad's racism has moved from the ivory tower and taken center stage in the culture wars, in part because the terms of the debate, at least as Denby presents them, are more accessible to a wider audience—unlike, for instance, the earlier brouhaha over deconstruction (see Lehman).

Coppola's interpretation of Conrad, while partially consonant with Achebe's, is far more cogent, insofar as the scene of Brando reading "The Hollow Men" situates *Heart of Darkness* within what is perhaps the central modernist dynamic, thereby damning Eliot along with Kurtz. To enhance moviegoers' appreciation of the allusion, Coppola includes close-ups of other titles in Kurtz's miniature library: We see Jessie Weston's *From Ritual to Romance* and Sir James Frazer's *The Golden Bough*, two key sources for high modernism, particularly Eliot's version of it. Weston and Frazer haunt Anglo-American modernism because their late-nineteenth-century accounts of the symbolic journey and sacrifice necessary to rejuvenate a declining civilization offer mythic solutions to the crises of legitimation that characterize modernity. In *Apocalypse Now*, as in *The Waste Land* and *Heart of Darkness*, the journey upriver becomes an archetypal quest for the holy grail that will restore a diseased civilization to health and power. In this conception, the rise and fall of empires—whether Roman, British, European, or, most recently, American—can be superimposed on each another, just as the film's Academy Award-winning cinematography emphasizes the hallucinatory superimposition of images in Captain Willard's consciousness. Thus Coppola's representation of Kurtz quoting Eliot quoting Conrad against the background of *The Golden Bough* and *From Ritual to Romance* aligns Eliot with Kurtz to reveal the latter as a figure for the "ideal order" of Western civilization gone awry.[3] "All Europe contributed to the making of Kurtz" (*Heart* 50), says Marlow, in a formulation that strikingly anticipates Eliot's description of "the mind of Europe" as "an ideal order," a perfect canon (Eliot 38–39).

Once we recall that Eliot's "ideal order" refers not only to an arrangement of texts and a certain version of literary history, but also to a social order, an ideal set of cultural arrangements characterized by strict and stable hierarchies, then we can appreciate how this scene in *Apocalypse Now* uncannily prefigures our current critical conviction that the Western canon—especially its modernist exhibits—is deeply implicated in the history of colonialism. In this view, canon makers are also empire builders, and Kurtz's degeneration into insanity and mass slaughter may be read as the logical outcome of Western ideas about racial superiority, progress, and empire. Advanced most persuasively by Edward Said, in *Culture and Imperialism*, this view of the "Great Books" maintains not only that literary texts are inseparable from their sociohistorical contexts, but also, more pointedly, that literature performs the cultural work of rationalizing—while only occasionally challenging— imperial ambition. This postcolonialist elaboration of the fundamentally Marxian commitment to literature's ineluctable historicity tends to be accompanied, at whatever distance, by a correlative critique of historiography, based on waning faith in Western conceptions of universality and in the possibilities of historical objectivity. We might encapsulate these broad developments in the following formulation, to which most contemporary thinkers, Vendler excepted, would more or less subscribe: *Not only is fiction historical, but history is also fictive*, in the sense of its being a distillate of competing narratives rather than of objective recounting.[4]

While this general formulation may be attributable in part to the far-reaching epistemological implications of modernist experiments with narrative form, Conrad offers a quite specific perspective on the relation between fiction and history. Through my account of *Heart of Darkness*, I want to show how Conrad's perspective sheds new light on the racism debate, the history of colonialism, and even the historiography of AIDS—a context in which his novella has not previously been considered. In contrast to contemporary critics who elaborate the conditions of fiction's historical embeddedness, Conrad develops Henry James's essentially Aristotelian claims, in "The Art of Fiction," on behalf of fiction's testimonial superiority to history; in 1905 Conrad writes, "Fiction is history, human history, or it is nothing. But it is also more than that; it stands on firmer ground, being based on the reality of forms and the observation of social phenomena, whereas history is based on documents, and the reading of print and handwriting—on secondhand impression. Thus fiction is nearer truth" (qtd. in Kimbrough 231). Treating fiction as history, Conrad nevertheless inverts the contemporary critical tendency to view history as superior to fiction and literary texts as merely among the range of historical documents available for critical reconstruction of a given cultural epoch. It is not so much the historicity of fiction or the fictiveness of history that Conrad proclaims here; rather, his stronger claim seems to be that fiction becomes historical precisely when it is "based on the reality of forms"—that is, when fiction abandons the material world in favor of an ideal realm. To the degree that this intangible basis paradoxically represents "firmer ground," we are compelled to conclude that fiction is more historical than history.[5]

Although such claims on behalf of imaginative writing are themselves undoubtedly amenable to historicization, I am more interested in examining their rhetorical force and seeing how a psychoanalytic account of the connection between history and trauma furnishes new evidence for Conrad's thesis. For my purposes, the significance of trauma lies in its generating historically specific material effects whose cause, like Conrad's "reality of forms," is empirically unverifiable because it constitutively eludes direct observation. The psychoanalytic theory of trauma gives us a new way of understanding history and narrative that I would like to lay out briefly here. While physical trauma involves a violent rupturing of the body's surface or boundaries, psychical trauma involves rupturing the ego's boundaries. Since psychical trauma is defined in terms of ego-shattering, it follows that internal events, as well as external accidents, can induce trauma. The formation of the ego involves a gestalt, a perceptual moment that demarcates boundaries, separating off a portion of mental life that then always threatens to overwhelm the ego's borders. Thus the very structure of the ego renders it vulnerable to trauma, and although it is always possible to minimize one's exposure to external violence, it is far more difficult to evade one's own violent impulses or the desire to experience an ego-shattering intensity in sex.

Another way of putting this would be to say that while self-shattering is always potentially traumatic, it can also be pleasurable (see Bersani 29–50). As I hope to make clear, this inseparability of sexuality from trauma helps explain the belated temporality of trauma that is so crucial for an alternative understanding of history and narrative. Freud called this belated temporality *Nachträglichkeit* and used the term to describe how sexuality retroactively comes to be endowed with meaning after its premature emergence in childhood. The diphasic onset of sexuality—in which a period of latency separates the efflorescence of polymorphous childhood sexuality from its pubertal re-emergence—entails within fantasy a retroactive ascription of significance to impulses and events that exist primarily as repressed memories. As something that no child initially understands, sex is originally traumatic and becomes significant only *Nachträglich*, belatedly.

By extending this Freudian idea to describe the effects of the signifying chain as such (linguistic meaning is constituted retroactively), Lacan provides a less individualistic, more cultural framework for conceptualizing trauma. He aligns trauma with the order of the real—not reality, but that which resists symbolization. If psychical trauma is characterized by its overwhelming unmanageability, then in Lacanian terms trauma denotes whatever cannot be assimilated to the subject's symbolic universe. Once trauma is conceived in terms of a rupture in the symbolic order, we can grasp the notion that any trauma—even psychical trauma originating from one's own internal violence—is in part cultural and historical.

Indeed, psychoanalysis theorizes history through this concept of trauma. According to the logic elaborated most cogently by Joan Copjec, in *Read My Desire*, trauma gives rise to historically specific material effects whose cause remains elusive because resistant to symbolization. To put this in the more explicitly Marxian terms that Althusser develops from Spinoza, trauma names *the absent cause of history*, the force of the real in any symbolic network (Althusser 189). If historical causes escape direct observation, then this changes our understanding of the reading and writing of history. As Cathy Caruth explains in her recent meditation on the relations among trauma, history, and narrative, "Traumatic experience, beyond the psychological dimension of suffering it involves, suggests a certain paradox: that the most direct seeing of a violent event may occur as an absolute inability to know it; that immediacy, paradoxically, may take the form of belatedness" (91–92).[6]

Conrad's fiction indicates formally the impact and effects of colonial trauma—not through his direct representation of imperial atrocities but instead by his failure to represent. Approaching his novella by way of trauma, I hope to provide not only a more theoretical but also a more historical explanation of Conrad's notorious "obscurity"—that perennial critical problem which E. M. Forster noted in 1936 (136–41) and F. R. Leavis canonized as a critical judgment, in 1948 (177–80). If, as Lacan says, the real is not ineffable but is instead precisely structured, then the specificities of failing to represent the traumatic real must vary historically. And as Copjec argues in *Read My Desire*, it is incumbent upon cultural critics to read not only the diverse forms of representation produced at any given historical moment but also the diverse forms of representation's failures, those points at which the absent causes of history make themselves felt. Thus the following account of *Heart of Darkness* advances, along with interpretative and historical claims, two meta-critical theses: First, that the kind of imaginative writing we conventionally characterize as literature provides access to historical phenomena not readily accessible by other means; second, that psychoanalysis—far from being negligible because ahistorical, as current academic wisdom has it—may enhance this access to otherwise irretrievable historical states. When taken together, literature and psychoanalysis—rather than standing as the poor cousins of more sociological approaches in cultural studies—are in fact more historical than conventional historiographical methods.

However, it is necessary to acknowledge that psychoanalytic treatments of *Heart of Darkness* have, in practice, tended to be completely ahistorical. While Achebe maintained that "Conrad is a dream for psychoanalytic critics" (259), the history of criticism shows that psychoanalytic interpretations of *Heart of Darkness* have helped naturalize the novella's racist aspects (which Achebe was at such pains to make visible) by neglecting those dimensions of the story that betray Conrad's cultural biases and historical blind spots. If we characterize the debate governing Conrad criticism as involving a tension between "referential" and "symbolic" readings, then we must concede that psychoanalyses of *Heart of Darkness* fall squarely into the symbolic camp. Albert J. Guerard's early interpretation is representative:

> the personal narrative is unmistakably authentic, which means that it explores something truer, more fundamental, and distinctly less material: the night journey into the unconscious, and confrontation of an entity within the self. . . . It little matters what, in terms of psychological symbolism, we call this double [Kurtz] or say he represents: whether the Freudian id or the Jungian shadow or more vaguely the outlaw. And I am afraid it is impossible to say where Conrad's conscious understanding of his story began and ended. The important thing is that the introspective plunge and powerful dream seem true; and are therefore inevitably moving. (245)

In the symbolic or metaphorical mode of reading *Heart of Darkness*—as opposed to the referential or metonymic mode—Marlow's journey upriver is understood primarily in allegorical terms, as an introspective quest. And according to this mode of reading, the novella's title refers less to any geographical locale than to a universal human condition that Freud seems equally poised to diagnose (psychoanalysis's founding work, *The Interpretation of Dreams*, appeared the same year as *Heart of Darkness*). But, of course, Conrad's use of Africa as the backdrop for his exploration of European subjectivity is hardly innocent: As Achebe first noted, this setup is part of a long representational tradition in which Africa fulfills a subservient role as the "Other" at whose expense European identity is consolidated. Psychoanalytic interpretations of *Heart of Darkness* seem to perpetuate this setup by viewing its drama as an existential crisis (see Karl), rather than as an historical and political crisis engendered by colonial exploitation.

While we must admit that the type of psychoanalytic interpretations under discussion here are vulgarly thematic and uniformly reductive in their attempts to psychoanalyze either Conrad or his fictional characters, we might also appreciate the extent to which the tension between symbolic and referential readings is intrinsic to the novella itself. Conrad acknowledged this tension in 1902, when, in a letter to Elsie Hueffer, he responded to early reviews of *Heart of Darkness* thus: "What I distinctly admit is the fault of having made Kurtz too symbolic or rather symbolic at all" (*Letters* 2:460). Although Conrad is referring more to problems concerning Kurtz's characterization than to the dilution of referentiality in his novella, the question of Kurtz's symbolic status remains crucial. At no point in *Heart of Darkness* is this more the case than at Kurtz's death.

In accordance with the sacrificial quest motif he derives from high modernism, Coppola represents Kurtz's death as the climax of *Apocalypse Now*. In a scene that crosscuts with the ritual killing of a cow, Kurtz is assassinated by Captain Willard (Martin Sheen): The cow's head is hacked off at the same time as Brando's, thus making amply evident that Kurtz's death is a symbolic sacrifice akin to those promoted in Weston's and Frazer's mythic narratives. Yet Marlon Brando's massive physical presence in the film allows us to forget that, by contrast, Conrad's Kurtz wastes away until all that remains is his voice. When Marlow first sees him, Kurtz is so sick that he has to be carried by stretcher:

> I saw the man on the stretcher sit up, lank and with an uplifted arm, above the shoulders of the bearers. . . . He looked at least seven feet long. His covering had fallen off and his body emerged from it pitiful and appalling as from a winding-sheet. I could see the cage of his ribs all astir, the bones of his arm waving. It was as though an animated image of death carved out of old ivory had been shaking its hand with menaces at a motionless crowd of men made of dark and glittering bronze. (*Heart* 59)

In this virtually medieval tableau, Kurtz, reduced to the appearance of a skeleton, is pictured as always already dead. This representation of Kurtz's life and death as almost purely symbolic discourages us from finding anything but allegorical answers to the question, Of what does Kurtz die? But in the service of a different kind of psychoanalytic approach to *Heart of Darkness*, I would like to speculate that Kurtz dies of acquired immune deficiency syndrome.

While we can neither prove nor disprove the apparently preposterous hypothesis that Kurtz dies of AIDS, I propose it as a heuristic device to illuminate both the historiography of AIDS and the impact of colonialism, as well as the particular force of imperial ideology in *Heart of Darkness*. I shall advance the evidence for this retrospective diagnosis shortly, but I should make clear that by articulating the history of colonialism with that of AIDS, I hope also to suggest how specifically literary texts may help us conceptualize AIDS. In this respect, I largely concur with novelist Dale Peck's remark that "[t]he real solution to the AIDS crisis will be scientific, not imaginative. But until we have a cure, it is the imagination that must provide us with ways of dealing with the epidemic" (24). It is misleading to counterpose the scientific to the imaginative, because only imaginative science—along with experimentation and research support—will produce a cure. Nevertheless, Peck accurately assesses how necessary are imaginative conceptualizations of AIDS, including literary ones. Part of what makes AIDS so hard to conceptualize—even though some of us cannot stop thinking about it—is that we remain in the midst of the epidemic, without the benefit of adequate hindsight to grasp a trajectory leading to a cure.[7] It is for this reason that we can hardly afford not to consider any hypothesis, no matter how speculative, that may illuminate the epidemic's etiology.

After official recognition of a nosological entity, an extraordinary medical blindness to past instances of the disease is often uncovered.   —Mirko Grmek 116

Let us approach the hypothesis that Kurtz dies of AIDS by examining the details of Conrad's own six-month trip up the Congo River, in 1890, on which he based *Heart of Darkness*. When Conrad captained his steamship, *Roi des Belges*, upriver, the Congo Free State was in the grip of Belgian colonialism—a situation of quite unprecedented mismanagement and exploitation, including slavery, that lasted from 1876, when King Leopold II of Belgium finagled stewardship of what was misnamed an "Independent State," through 1908, when Leopold died and bequeathed the Congo to the Belgian people. Rather than ending Belgian exploitation, Leopold's death finally made official the Congo's colonial status. Strict Belgian rule continued in the Congo until 1960, when mutiny in the capital, Leopoldville (named the Central Station in *Heart of Darkness*), compelled colonial administrators to flee. Various rival native forces subsequently underwent a protracted and bloody struggle to fill the vacuum of power, until General Mobutu was installed as the nation's president in 1965. In 1971, as part of his project of nation-alization, Mobutu renamed the Congo "Zaire."[8]

According to recent epidemiological findings, Zaire is one of the twin epicen-ters of the AIDS pandemic, the other being New York City (Myers et al. 121–22). The first officially recognized case of AIDS in Africa involved a woman from Kinshasa (formerly Leopoldville) who died in 1977, five years before AIDS became known as such and six years before its etiologic agent, the human immuno-deficiency virus (HIV), was isolated. A retrospective diagnosis of AIDS also has been made for a Canadian who died in 1978, having received a blood transfusion two years earlier in Zaire (Grmek 134). By 1986, Kinshasa had been renamed again, this time as "the AIDS capital of Africa" (Prentice 3.14).[9] When new technology became available later in the 1980s, a Harvard team of scientists conducted tests on plasma collected from Zaire in 1959; twenty-one samples of this plasma tested pos-itive for antibodies to HIV-1, the virus believed to be responsible for the current AIDS pandemic (Nahmias, Weiss, and Yao; qtd. in Grmek 135).

Evaluating these findings, Mirko Grmek concludes that "HIV-1 or a close virus with similar antigenic properties was present in Zaire as early as 1959" (Grmek 135).[10] Although the date 1959 may seem astonishingly early to those accustomed to thinking of AIDS as a disease of the 1980s, it is actually a cautious estimate, since Robert Gallo's calculations backdate to the end of the nineteenth century the existence of HIV as a human parasite (Grmek 146).[11] However, I want to empha-size the date 1959 for several reasons: First, it represents the earliest verifiable date for locating HIV-1 in human tissue; second, the verification concerns plasma col-lected in Zaire; and third, 1959 represents the eve of Zaire's independence and hence of massive political upheaval and social reorganization in the former colony—an upheaval that, I shall argue, was instrumental in the emergence of AIDS. Finally, 1959 marks the date of a retrospectively diagnosed AIDS death in England—a widely publicized case involving a sailor whose tissue was frozen, after his inexplicable death in 1959, and tested positive for HIV in 1989, using the PCR (polymerase chain reaction) method (see Altman). The British case is also significant in this context because, like Conrad, the young man who died was a sea-man who traveled extensively; before his death physicians detected *Pneumocystis* pneumonia (PCP) and cytomegalovirus, coinfections that were highly unusual at that time but now are common in Westerners with AIDS (see G. Williams et al.). The British sailor initially fell sick with ulcers around his mouth and anus; although medical records indicate that he was unmarried, no concrete information about his sexuality survives (Altman).[12] For my purposes it is crucial that the date 1959 establishes the existence of HIV-infection in the Congo while that country was still under Belgian imperial rule. This does not make Zaire, or Africa, the *ori-*

gin of AIDS, but it does give us considerably more than a hypothetical rationale for connecting the history of European colonialism with the emergence of AIDS.[13]

Conrad's situation strengthens this connection. It may be helpful to recall that the atrocities of Belgian colonialism represented in *Heart of Darkness* coincide almost completely with contemporary historical reports by two other remarkable figures, both of whom were investigating conditions in the Congo during Conrad's time there. Given Patrick Brantlinger's argument that Conrad gleaned his information as much from European literature on Belgian colonial atrocities as from firsthand experience in Africa, this coincidence is hardly surprising (279–83). One of the contemporary investigators I shall discuss, George Washington Williams, was a distinguished African-American pastor, lawyer, politician, and historian who arrived in the Congo just three months before Conrad, though novelist and historian never met. Another contemporary investigator was Sir Roger Casement, an Irish diplomat employed by the British Foreign Office, whom Conrad met in June 1890. Conrad and Casement shared a room for two weeks in Matadi and maintained a friendship for many years thereafter. Casement was in the paradoxical position of a subaltern employed by the imperial overlord to investigate and expose colonial abuses elsewhere—that is, abuses perpetrated in Africa by an imperial power other than Britain. Casement later achieved notoriety when, during World War I, he went to Germany to recruit participants for the Easter Uprising in Ireland, in 1916. Arrested and tried for treason in England, Casement was thoroughly discredited by the Crown when he was "outed" as an inveterate homosexual who had initiated sexual adventures with hundreds of men across three continents. During his trial, the prosecution circulated copies of Casement's private diaries, which revealed how he had documented imperial abuses in the Congo while at the same time enjoying quite extensive sexual tourism there. The revelation of his sexuality prevented his being granted any reprieve and, after being convicted of treason, he was hanged (see Caserio).

Like many homosexual men of his period and class, Sir Roger had a particular penchant for sailors (see Singleton-Gates and Girodias 287); in 1890, when he met Casement, Conrad was still a sailor and not yet a novelist. Thus in light of Casement's diaries, Conrad's entry about Casement in his own *Congo Diary* takes on additional resonance. This *Diary's* opening entry, dated June 13, 1890, includes the following: "Made the acquaintance of Mr. Roger Casement, which I should consider as a great pleasure under any circumstances and now it becomes a positive piece of luck. Thinks, speaks well, most intelligent and very sympathetic" (Conrad, *Congo* 7). Whether "very sympathetic" means here what it *could* mean is ultimately unknowable; and although Casement was certainly what we would now call gay, Conrad was not. Yet in Africa at the turn of the century these categories of sexual identity did not exist; indeed, in contemporary Zaire they still hardly exist. One problem with Western constructions of "African AIDS" as a "hetero-sexual disease" is that, in countries such as Zaire, the everyday practice of male bisexuality compromises heterosexual masculinity *as an identity* far less than it does in the West.[14] As gay African-American novelist Samuel Delany quotes his Kenyan lover reporting, "There is no homosexuality in Africa: there you don't talk about it at all. You just do it!" (208).

Delany's anecdotal evidence, though somewhat simplistic, is useful for remind-ing us of the significant disparities between African and Western conceptions of sexuality. Despite these disparities, Conrad's turn-of-the-century narratives reveal a developed consciousness of the homosocial dynamics and homoerotic tensions that characterize all-male institutions, especially in colonial outposts and at sea. As Geoffrey Galt Harpham argues, in his remarkable recent study of Conrad, "con-sidered as a novelist of identification, Conrad qualifies as the greatest explorer of male-male attraction in the English language, far more interesting, subtle, and even candid than the elusive Wilde" (131–32). While the homoerotic interest in *Heart of Darkness* pales by comparison with Conrad's later sea stories, such as *Victory* (1915), it is far from absent in this earlier work. On more than one occasion Marlow expresses a marked jealousy of women associated with Kurtz, and when he finally meets Kurtz's "Intended" after his death, Marlow informs her, " 'Intimacy grows quickly out there . . . I knew [Kurtz] as well as it is possible for one man to know another' " (*Heart* 73). Is it mere coincidence that the entire narrative of *Heart of Darkness* is relayed from on board a ship named *Nellie?*[15]

Describing his fellows on board this motionless yawl, the anonymous narrator comments, "[b]etween us there was as I have already said somewhere, the bond of the sea" (*Heart* 8). Within the complex chain of narration and quotation that char-acterizes *Heart of Darkness*, the audience for Marlow's story is constituted as a fra-ternity. And while it is partly owing to the intense homosociality of "the bond of the sea" that nautical pursuits have always connoted homosexuality, this bond involves more than the lurking suggestion of "situational homosexuality" or the effects of single-sex social arrangements mandated by the Victorian gender ideol-ogy of "separate spheres" that permeates the novella.[16] More important for our consideration of *Heart of Darkness*, "the bond of the sea" supports imperial enter-prises, which depend on all-male institutions (see Lane 9, 25). We can therefore begin to appreciate how Casement's laying bare this dynamic in his diaries' recounting of numerous homosexual conquests in the colonies must have repre-sented an intolerable exposure of imperial ideology. Casement's diaries confirm in one genre what Conrad's fiction suggests in another—not only the reality of

Belgian economic exploitation in the Congo, but also less publicized forms of sexual interaction between colonial and subaltern subjects. The complex connections between these different forms of colonization and exploitation are crucial for the emergence of AIDS.

Africa, the continent out of which the Romans used to say some new thing was always coming . . .   —Conrad, qtd. in Kimbrough 145

Of the various figures publicizing imperial abuses at the turn of the century, African-American historian George Washington Williams was among the most vocal critics of Belgian rule. During his extensive visit to the Congo in 1890, Williams wrote a number of controversial reports, one of which was addressed to the President of the United States, Benjamin Harrison, explaining at length how the conditions of Belgian rule were "unjust, capricious and absolutely cruel" ("Report" 90). However, Williams' most publicized report was bravely addressed to King Leopold himself; it eloquently decried "the deceit, fraud, robberies, arson, murder, slave-raiding, and general policy of cruelty of your Majesty's Government to the natives" ("Open" 112).[17] Of the many abuses he detailed, Williams was concerned above all with the highly developed slave trade that Belgian agents in the Congo managed to maintain—in direct violation of the international agreement that had granted Leopold sovereignty over the Congo in the first place. Between the lines of Williams's reports we can read his sense of an African diaspora and his desire to spread the abolitionist message from the United States to Africa—even as we can read also his imperialist desire to "spread civilization" to "these poor children of nature," whom he contrasts with "educated blacks from the Southern United States" ("Report" 95), the latter of whom Williams recommends as the Congo's future governors. Williams thinks the Congo should be freed from despotic Belgian rule and subjected to enlightened African-American colonial rule. As with Conrad and Casement, Williams's critique of colonialism is riddled with paradoxes.

However, I think that the forms taken by Conrad's irony in *Heart of Darkness* suggest a greater self-consciousness than that of either Casement or Williams concerning the contradictions entailed in representing empire. Conrad's reference to *Heart of Darkness* as "part of the loot I carried off from Central Africa" (qtd. in Kimbrough 192) indicates his awareness of the paradox that representing empire, no matter how critically, is itself an imperial project. Rather than attempting to disavow this paradox, Conrad exposes it. He does so not simply by emphasizing the difference between imperialists and subalterns (or between humane imperialists and corrupt ones), but, more complexly, by emphasizing the division *within* colonial ideology itself—for example, as it is expressed in Kurtz's own report. In this respect we might say that Conrad permits Marlow to perform a protodeconstruction of Kurtz's text. Here is Marlow:

> All Europe contributed to the making of Kurtz, and by and by I learned that most appropriately the International Society for the Suppression of Savage Customs had entrusted him with the making of a report for its future guidance. And he had written it too. I've seen it. I've read it. It was eloquent, vibrating with eloquence, but too high-strung I think. Seventeen pages of close writing. He had found time for it. But this must have been before his—let us say—nerves went wrong and caused him to preside at certain midnight dances ending with unspeakable rites, which—as far as I reluctantly gathered from what I heard at various times—were offered up to him— do you understand—to Mr. Kurtz himself. But it was a beautiful piece of writing. The opening paragraph however, in the light of later information, strikes me now as ominous. He began with the argument that we whites, from the point of development we had arrived at, 'must necessarily appear to them [savages] in the nature of supernatural beings—we approach them with the might as of a deity,' and so on, and so on. "By the simple exercise of our will we can exert a power for good practically unbounded," etc. etc. From that point he soared and took me with him. The peroration was magnificent, though difficult to remember, you know. It gave me the notion of an exotic Immensity ruled by an august Benevolence. It made me tingle with enthusiasm. This was the unbounded power of eloquence—of words—of burning noble words. There were no practical hints to interrupt the magic current of phrases, unless a kind of note at the foot of the last page, scrawled evidently much later in an unsteady hand, may be regarded as the exposition of a method. It was very simple and at the end of that moving appeal to every altruistic sentiment it blazed at you luminous and terrifying like a flash of lightning in a serene sky: "Exterminate all the brutes!" (*Heart* 50–51)

The division within imperial ideology appears in Kurtz's report not simply as a disjunction between rhetoric and reality, but also as a disjunction between main text and footnote that points to the framing devices of Conrad's own narrative—that is, to the way in which Marlow's story, which occupies the vast bulk of the text, is itself being quoted by the anonymous narrator who begins the novella and who occasionally interpolates a comment into Marlow's tale. Practically the whole of *Heart of Darkness* is in quotation marks—the excerpts from Kurtz's report are being quoted in Marlow's report of his own journey upriver, which is itself an extended quotation within what we might call Conrad's report on his Congo experience. This citational structure establishes Conrad's ironic mode, and its complexity enables him to calibrate his irony to a remarkably fine degree.[18]

I would like to convey the potential of Conrad's ironic mode by focusing on the appeal, in the passage above, to the evolutionary rationale that legitimates imperial ideology ("we whites, from the point of development we had arrived at . . ."). The familiar notion that different cultures occupy different points along the timeline of Progress results from the mistaken transposition of a biological theory—evolutionism—into the realm of culture. What we might call this ideological catachresis enters domestic policy with the turn-of-the-century philosophy of social Darwinism, which had such an impact in the United States; in foreign policy it promotes a sense of responsibility on the part of more "developed" cultures to take civilization to what are perceived as the less developed. The "white man's burden" to spread civilization is understood as one of the duties accompanying the privileges of his advanced cultural development. Thus imperialism's cultural monism depends on a teleological conception of History and Progress consistent with linear narrative and a classical understanding of cause and effect.

This conception of cultural superiority, evolutionist history, and the colonial mission is implicitly criticized in *Heart of Darkness* by Conrad's protomodernist breakup of linear narrative form (in which one thing follows another according to a realist logic of causality and temporality). Furthermore, Conrad explicitly criticizes this conception by ironizing those figures, such as Marlow's aunt, who express "white-man's-burden" sentiments: "There had been a lot of such rot let loose in print and talk just about that time, and the excellent woman living right in the rush of all that humbug got carried off her feet. She talked about 'weaning those ignorant millions from their horrid ways,' till, upon my word, she made me quite uncomfortable. I ventured to hint that the Company was run for profit" (*Heart* 15–16). At this point early in the story, Conrad wields some fairly obvious irony by using quotation marks in a way that gestures toward the ironizing function of quotation throughout the novella. If passages such as this one encourage us to read all citation in *Heart of Darkness* in terms of "scare quotes," then Marlow's own narrative must be understood as vulnerable to the corrosive effects of irony, since quotation marks enclose his entire narrative.

This, I think, is how Conrad directs us to interpret Marlow's hyperbolic depictions when, like George Washington Williams, Marlow represents the Congo and the Congolese as culturally retarded. Achebe singled out the following passage as evidence of Conrad's racism:

> We were wanderers on a prehistoric earth, on an earth that wore the aspect of an unknown planet. We could have fancied ourselves the first of men taking possession of an accursed inheritance, to be subdued at the cost of profound anguish and of excessive toil. But suddenly as we struggled round a bend there would be a glimpse of rush walls, of peaked grass-roofs, a burst of yells, a whirl of black limbs, a mass of hands clapping, of feet stamping, of bodies swaying, of eyes rolling under the

droop of heavy and motionless foliage. The steamer toiled along slowly on the edge of a black and incomprehensible frenzy. The prehistoric man was cursing us, praying to us, welcoming us—who could tell? We were cut off from the comprehension of our surroundings; we glided past like phantoms, wondering and secretly appalled, as sane men would be before an enthusiastic outbreak in a madhouse. We could not understand because we were too far and could not remember because we were travelling in the night of first ages, of those ages that are gone, leaving hardly a sign— and no memories. (37)

This passage's final sentence figures in temporal terms Marlow's earlier characterization of Africa as "a blank space": For imperial eyes, Africa exists as space without geography, time without history. Yet Marlow concedes that there are very different kinds of blankness: " 'True, by this time it was not a blank space any more. It had got filled since my boyhood with rivers and lakes and names. It had ceased to be a blank space of delightful mystery—a white patch for a boy to dream gloriously over. It had become a place of darkness' " (11–12). Thanks to colonization, the darkness or obscurity that replaces "delightful mystery" leaves, like trauma, "no memories"—not because Africa lacks history, but because, on the contrary, the trauma of colonial impact forecloses the possibility of narrative history.

Reading *Heart of Darkness* in this way enables us to grasp that while Marlow's representation of the Congo's position in evolutionary time is, in the passage Achebe calls racist, perfectly compatible with the sentiments expressed in Kurtz's report, this compatibility already has been undermined in his own story—for example, by Marlow's ironizing his aunt's comment about "weaning those ignorant millions from their horrid ways." Such evolutionist sentiments are negated also by what Conrad expressed in a subsequent letter to Casement. When, in 1903, the diplomat wrote requesting the novelist's assistance in his Congo Reform Movement, Conrad replied, echoing George Washington Williams: "It is an extraordinary thing that the conscience of Europe which seventy years ago has put down the slave trade on humanitarian grounds tolerates the Congo State today. It is as if the moral clock had been put back many hours" (*Letters* 3:96). According to this letter, it is not so much that the Congo is culturally retarded and therefore needs European assistance as it is that Europe itself has regressed and therefore has no legitimate justification for imposing its cultural ideals on the Congo. Yet Conrad refused to join Casement's Congo Reform Movement, explaining that he was "only a wretched novelist inventing wretched stories" (*Letters* 3: 102). While some commentators have interpreted Conrad's refusal as betraying a failure of political commitment (Brantlinger 280), I read this letter as signaling Conrad's commitment to pursuing fiction's superior potential for the representation of historical trauma, since what he accomplished through the ironizing structures of *Heart of Darkness* surpasses the more direct and more highly rhetorical reports on the Congo published by Casement and Williams.

AIDS is certainly the most postcolonial of diseases.   —Samuel R. Delany 207

Here I would like to return to Williams, whose reports are significant not only because they confirm details of Congolese life represented in *Heart of Darkness*, but also because Williams notes the prevalence among the Congolese of what we now call Kaposi's sarcoma. Referring to "the most pestilential diseases, which often devastate whole communities of these hapless victims of their own filth" ("Report" 91), Williams remarks also on the "cutaneous diseases" suffered by many tribes (92)——an epidemiological phenomenon confirmed in 1984 by the Belgian pathologist Paul Gigase, who observed that in Zaire the indigenous population calls this skin disease *lumbabo*. According to Zaireans, "the incidence of this disease had not altered within human memory" (Grmek 114), even though what we now know as Kaposi's sarcoma was not isolated and described in the West until 1872, by the Viennese physician Moritz Kaposi.

It is necessary to acknowledge that Gigase's work on Kaposi's sarcoma in Zaire is one legacy of Belgium's imperial history. Epidemiological investigation of AIDS in Africa is complicated by the troubling continuities between imperial science and contemporary science; indeed, as with the evolutionary ideology that rationalizes imperialism, many contemporary AIDS discourses hinge on fantasies of origin. There exists an intensive, widespread conviction that AIDS always originates elsewhere and that certain populations, rather than specific practices, are primarily responsible for its transmission. These fantasies about how AIDS originates in the "Other"—whether gay men or black Africans—conform to the representational tradition delineated by Achebe in his critique of *Heart of Darkness*. Just as it is necessary to distinguish risk practices from the racist and homophobic notion of risk groups, so is it crucial to distinguish fantasies about the origin of AIDS from virological descriptions of the conditions of viral emergence. My contention is that recent distinctions within virology between *origin* and *emergence* radically disrupt the continuity between imperial science and much contemporary AIDS science in a way that clarifies the high incidence of Kaposi's sarcoma in Zaire.

Kaposi's sarcoma holds a unique position in the biomedical and epidemiological construction of AIDS.[19] A malignant dermatosis that characteristically takes the form of purplish skin lesions, Kaposi's sarcoma is crucially distinguished from cancer in that it does not metastasize; rather than a cancer, it is more accurately characterized as a multifocal neoplasm. Nevertheless, as the most visible and common presenting symptom of persons with AIDS in the West, it quickly was misnamed "gay cancer" in the early years of the epidemic. Previously confined to elderly Caucasian men of Mediterranean descent in its benign form in the West, Kaposi's sarcoma in persons under the age of sixty is now a sufficient criterion for a positive diagnosis of AIDS, *even in the absence of positive HIV antibodies*, according to current CDC definitions of AIDS. And although in the contemporary Western world correlation between Kaposi's sarcoma and AIDS is virtually one hundred percent, its correlation with seropositivity is significantly lower in Zaire, where KS was common before AIDS.

The inconsistencies involved in correlating Kaposi's sarcoma with AIDS represent just one example of the difficulties entailed in making retrospective diagnoses of AIDS. Furthermore, the difficulties in dating AIDS are not only empirical—for example, the fact that properly stored plasma is basically unavailable for antibody-testing from any period before the end of World War II. Rather, the difficulties involved in making retrospective diagnoses of AIDS are also epistemological and, I would claim, ideological. To clarify the nature of these difficulties, we need to distinguish between the virus believed to cause AIDS, the disease itself, and the pandemic it has recently generated. At a minimum, we are justified in maintaining that while the AIDS pandemic is new, HIV is not, though one or another of its more virulent strains may be. But this leaves unresolved the tougher question of how old the disease entity classified under the acronym AIDS might be. Epistemologically, AIDS could not have existed before the middle of this century, when disease as such was conceptualized in a way that would render AIDS invisible. Until recent developments in the life sciences, disease was classified according to the manifestation of clinical symptoms or pathological lesions. Since people with AIDS die with the symptoms and lesions that typify other diseases (what we now call "opportunistic diseases"), AIDS could not come into being as a nosological entity until medical epistemology altered: "Only then, between 1976 and 1980, did the intellectual and technological means needed to recognize and isolate the AIDS pathogen become available. This is the same period American health officials identify as the onset of the AIDS epidemic" (Grmek 56). For this reason, "AIDS does not present characteristic clinical manifestations that lend themselves to retrospective diagnoses" (Grmek 111). Remember that the acronym stands for Acquired Immune Deficiency *Syndrome*. A syndrome is not a disease in the conventional sense but a kind of pattern that requires an epidemiological—as well as an epistemological—gestalt in order to appear.

What, then, caused the AIDS epidemic to appear? According to Grmek, we have the triumph of bacteriology and the spectacular decline in infectious diseases throughout the twentieth century to thank for the emergence of AIDS: HIV "hides behind other diseases," he claims (160). In this respect, technological advances in Western medicine would have to be counted as part of the etiology of AIDS. But in the recent virological distinction between new and emerging viruses, we approach socioeconomic and cultural explanations of disease. Since the AIDS pandemic is a new phenomenon but HIV is not a new virus, HIV must be characterized as an *emergent* virus, one that has crossed species or geographical boundaries (or both) to create a new disease (see Henig; Myers et al.).

Epidemiological virologists now recognize that viral emergence results more from human behavior than from genetic mutation. New biomedical phenomena such as the AIDS pandemic are caused not by new viruses, but by viruses whose habitats have been disrupted by socioeconomic forces such as urbanization, militarization, changes in agricultural techniques, deforestation, escalating international commerce, changing medical practices, and globalization. The political, environmental, demographic, and economic changes that contribute to viral emergence are so wide-ranging that one recent account of emerging viruses proposes interdisciplinarity as a solution to the problem of etiology: "the study of viruses should be even more expansive, encompassing perspectives from totally different disciplines" (Henig 224). By now it should be clear that the profound socioeconomic disruptions wrought by imperial conquest *and by decolonization* typify the kind of large-scale changes that favor viral emergence. While international travel and tourism now represent significant paths for viral emergence, at the turn of the century colonists and sailors—such as Conrad himself—would have been the principal human vectors enabling viruses to emerge.[20]

The colonial and postcolonial history of Zaire is, in this respect, exemplary, since the terms of Belgian rule were designed to isolate the Congo; traffic in and out of the colony was kept to a strict minimum and the Congolese were forbidden access to education outside the territory. Congolese political organization was also forbidden until 1958 and then subject to stringent restrictions until 1959. This date indicates a very close correlation between viral emergence and the effects of colonial rule. The Belgians resisted any Congolese effort directed toward independence, so that, as one historian put it, "when the demand for independence came, the Congolese were without the trained leadership and political experience needed for successful self-rule" (Rice 134). For Zaire, the social and political disorganization resulting from decolonization had profoundly disruptive effects on kinship networks and sexual behavior—disruptions exacerbated by renewed sexual tourism. In this context, the virological distinction between new and emergent viruses justifies my characterization of colonialism as a *cause* of AIDS. And to the degree that virologists distinguish between origin and emergence, they thereby disrupt the politically disturbing continuities between imperial and contemporary science. In this respect, virology not only is a postcolonial science but implies a salutary counterimperial epistemology.

In order to refine this thesis, I would like to make one final point. As a blood-borne pathogen, the human immunodeficiency virus requires intimate contact for its transmission. The phrase "exchange of fluids," common in the discourse of AIDS education, is euphemistic in the sense that viral transmission actually involves some kind of physical trauma, a breaking or penetration of the body's surface (whether sexually or otherwise). Since "intimate contact" entails trauma, we might note that "contact" is the term used also to describe the traumatizing effects of one culture's encounter with another, especially when the relation between cultures is characterized by significant disequilibriums of power. Thus my final thesis is that colonial trauma entails sexual trauma, not that one is simply a metaphor for the other.

As Edward Said argues in *Culture and Imperialism*, it is only by appreciating the "intertwined and overlapping" histories of colonizer and colonized that we may "formulate an alternative both to a politics of blame and to the even more destructive politics of confrontation and hostility" (18). By means of this approach, we can grasp the history of AIDS and the role of colonialism in its emergence, since Conrad and Casement show how colonization involves a literal intertwining of imperial and subaltern subjects. Hence the emergence of AIDS, whose virus is commonly transmitted through sex, might best be understood as one legacy of the trauma of colonialism, the involuntary mixing of populations characterized by an imbalance of power. Furthermore, the disjunctive, anachronistic temporality of trauma, which Freud called *Nachträglichkeit*, ensures that trauma's legible effects are deferred and that trauma is thus constituted only retroactively. This temporal structure helps explain why HIV emerges at the moment of Belgian *de*coloniza-tion, around 1959–1960, as a belated consequence of colonial impact that consti-tutes colonialism *as* traumatic. The nonlinear temporality of trauma also throws into relief how Conrad's disjunctive narrative structure in *Heart of Darkness* is especially well formed to represent the effects of Belgian colonialism. Conrad enables us to see why imperialism should be counted a vital "cofactor" in the eti-ology of this new disease. And so while *Heart of Darkness* remains vulnerable to charges of racism, Conrad's novella permits us to grasp that Africa is not the ori-gin of AIDS—European colonialism is. Thus according to the psychoanalytic understanding of history that reconceives origins and causality in terms of the unsymbolizable, traumatic real, it is historically apposite—if not empirically veri-fiable—that Kurtz, the European colonialist par excellence, should be one of the first to die from what we now call AIDS.

ENDNOTES

For discussion of an earlier version of this paper, I thank the wonderful audience at California Institute of Technology, especially Kevin Gilmartin, Dori Hale, Claudia Klaver, Jeffrey Knapp, and Jennifer Tucker, as well as Cathy Jurca, who hosted my visit. Thanks also to Srinivas Aravamudan, Jason Friedman, Lauren Goodlad, Ranji Khanna, Chris Lane, and Michael Szalay for comments on a later draft. The composition of this paper was supported by a grant from the Royalty Research Fund, University of Washington, and I thank Colbey Emmerson for help with research.

1. Besides Denby and Vendler, see Graff 25–33, Said 19–31, and Searle 258–81, for significant, Conrad-centered interventions in these debates. Even apart from the culture wars, *Heart of Darkness* has been recognized as an exemplary occasion for considering competing critical interpretations: it was chosen, in 1989, to inaugurate the popular series "Case Studies in Contemporary Criticism" (see Murfin), in which a literary text is accompanied by five readings intended to represent different theoretical approaches—psychoanalytic, deconstructive, feminist, new historicist, and reader-response criticism. Significantly enough, in 1996 this inaugural volume was updated for a second edition, distinguished most notably by the replacement of the first edition's truly awful psychoanalytic interpretation (see Karl) with Patrick Brantlinger's important "cultural criticism" of *Heart of Darkness*.

2. Although in 1975 he called Conrad "a bloody racist," in 1988, when Achebe revised his essay for the Norton critical edition of *Heart of Darkness*, he softened the epithet to "thoroughgoing racist" (Achebe 257). Besides the essays on Conrad's racism that Kimbrough includes in the Norton edition (by Harris, Singh, and Sarvan), see also Hawkins, Watts, and Brantlinger for contributions to this debate.

3. In his very fine Marxian reading of the relationship between Conrad's novella and Coppola's film, Cesare Casarino explains: "Kurtz has to die not because his excessive methods, which are perceived as 'no method at all' by both Marlow and Willard, are extraordinary in the context in which he is working, but rather because they are the exaggeration of what are considered to be perfectly orthodox and normal methods. In other words, Kurtz brings to its extreme but logical conclusions the principles on which the institutions (the army, the trading company) function, thus implying that the inhumanity of which he is being accused is indispensable to the institutions' performance and existence" (101).

4. As one critic has summarized this way of thinking within literary studies, "what new historicists like Stephen Greenblatt have found most congenial in deconstruction is the way its effacement of the boundary between the literary and the nonliterary appears to encourage a reading not only of history itself as a kind of extended textuality but also of literature as an inescapably social practice, a practice no more privileged than any other" (Litvak 125).

5. In his excellent account of imperial rhetoric, David Spurr makes a similar claim, although without pursuing it: "*Heart of Darkness* has been read as incorporating the racism of men, like Conrad, who took part in the work of colonizing the Congo, while journalistic narratives like Henry Morton Stanley's *In Darkest Africa* (1891) can be read metonymi-

cally as part of a long history of representations of the Congo. The irony of this particular case is that *Heart of Darkness* tells us more about what the Belgian Congo was really like than any journalistic or historical account" (Spurr 10). By way of the psychoanalytic theory of trauma, I shall argue the slightly different point that it is precisely the way in which Conrad's novella *fails* to tell us "what the Belgian Congo was really like" that makes it more historically revealing than any journalistic account.

6. The classic psychoanalytic texts on traumatic states, in which Freud develops the *Nachträglich* (belated) temporality specific to trauma, are his 1895 *Project for a Scientific Psychology* and *Beyond the Pleasure Principle* (1920). While Lacan pursued the theory of trauma in terms of the unsymbolizable real, Laplanche (esp. chapter 2) elaborates the implications of belatedness particularly cogently for the psychoanalytic theory of sexuality. Useful expositions of the temporality of trauma also may be found in Chase (esp. chapters 7 and 8) and Caruth (esp. chapters 1 and 5). While Caruth is our leading literary theorist of trauma, see Felman and Laub (esp. 68–70) for the best account of the paradoxes entailed in witnessing and testifying to trauma.

7. As Suzanne Yang's brilliant account of the epistemology of Kaposi's sarcoma makes clear, this emphasis on cure is potentially counterproductive.

8. For details of Zaire's colonial and postcolonial history, I have relied largely on the condensed histories provided by Hennessy and Rice.

9. I am grateful to Chris Lane for furnishing me with copies of the Murtagh and Prentice newspaper reports. It is significant that New York City, the pandemic's other epicenter, is rarely referred to as "the AIDS capital of the world"—or even of America. As cultural studies critics Cindy Patton, Paula Treichler, and Simon Watney have argued, Western media constructions of AIDS in Africa tend to be unequivocally racist, often revealing "little or nothing of AIDS in Africa, but a very great deal about the changing organization of sexual and racial boundaries in the West" (Watney 118). Unfortunately, fantasies about the origin of AIDS in the "Other" are not restricted to the tabloid press (see Murtagh, Prentice, and Shoumatoff). From a Lacanian perspective, the rhetoric of blame that pervades discussions of the origin of AIDS—including Patton's, Treichler's, and Watney's critiques— betrays *imaginary* distortions that, in polarizing innocence and guilt, serve only to obscure the shared responsibilities and mutual interdependence of European nations and their former African colonies.

10. Grmek is an Eastern European physician, Director of Studies at the Sorbonne, and a highly respected historian of science. Of the more than a hundred books about AIDS that I have read, his *History of AIDS*, though not without its problems, still seems to me the best chronicle of AIDS's emergence, and I depend heavily on it in the present account.

11. Fairly reliable retrospective diagnoses of individual cases of AIDS can be traced back before 1959: "At least sixteen cases, published in American medical journals between early 1940 and June 5, 1981 (when the CDC announced their observation of *Pneumocystis* pneumonia in homosexuals), have been found to fit the present clinical definition of AIDS" (Grmek 121).

12. Grmek notes a coincident American case, in which a 48-year-old merchant marine

in New York City died rapidly of an atypical pulmonary condition, also in 1959: "Autopsy revealed *Pneumocystis* pneumonia. George Hennigar, the pathologist who did this post-mortem inspection and immediately recognized that the case was unprecedented, later said that, a posteriori, he considered a diagnosis of AIDS in this case was a 'strong possibility'" (Grmek 123).

13. For a critique of the epidemiology of AIDS in Africa, see Chirimuuta and Chirimuuta (esp. 142–44).

14. Writing for the London *Times*, Thomson Prentice insists: "In Africa, AIDS is essentially a heterosexually transmitted disease, as common among women as men. Homosexuality is rare, and dismissed as a contributory factor" (Prentice 1.14). The naive idea that since as many women as men in Africa are infected with HIV, homosexual practices are therefore practically nonexistent is surprisingly intransigent (see Akeroyd). Delany provides anecdotal counterevidence for homosexuality in Africa (207–8). More balanced pictures are given in McDermott et al., and A. Williams.

15. Although the history of the word "nellie" remains obscure, one lexicographer records it as meaning lesbian or male homosexual as far back as the mid-nineteenth century (Richter 150).

16. "Situational homosexuality" refers to sexual activity between ostensibly heterosexual men in the extended absence of "proper" sexual objects, especially in naval, military, and penal institutions. Such institutions were rationalized, in part, by the nineteenth-century ideology of "separate spheres," which held that men and women are so irremediably different as to operate in parallel universes. Marlow often articulates separate-sphere sentiments (see *Heart* 16).

17. Within a year of his visit to the Congo, George Washington Williams died, aged 41, from a mysterious wasting disease. His death certificate recorded as the cause of death *phthisis*, an outmoded medical term for a general wasting away of the body. The death certificate observed also that his right lung "had been wounded in the Egyptian war," which Williams's most recent biographer assures us is completely untrue (Franklin 225). This inaccuracy suggests that the available biomedical data were radically insufficient to explain why Williams died and that, in fact, the report should have read "Cause of Death: Unknown" in Williams' case. In the absence of any recognizable or isolable cause of death, Williams's physician effectively invented one. As a final parenthetical remark that may resonate with the diagnosis of *phthisis*, I note that in African countries such as Uganda, AIDS is known as "slim," on account of the wasting effects that accompany the disease and that, in a sense, make its presence visible.

18. As Robert Hampson indicates in his introduction to the new Penguin edition of the text, Conrad's judicious irony was necessitated in part by the magazine context in which he initially published *Heart of Darkness*, since he "had a fairly clear conception of the nature of his immediate readership: conservative and imperialist in politics, and predominantly male" (xxviii). I thank Kevin Gilmartin for drawing my attention to this point.

19. My thinking about the significance of Kaposi's sarcoma has benefited greatly from Yang.

20. G. Jean-Aubry notes that "Conrad's health was affected during all the rest of his life by his African expedition" (qtd. in Kimbrough 195).

WORKS CITED

Achebe, Chinua. "An Image of Africa: Racism in Conrad's *Heart of Darkness.*" 1977. In Kimbrough. 251–62.

Akeroyd, Anne. *Some Gendered and Occupational Aspects of HIV and AIDS in Eastern and Southern Africa: Changes, Continuities and Issues for Further Consideration at the End of the First Decade.* Edinburgh: Centre of African Studies, 1996.

Althusser, Louis et al. *Reading Capital.* Trans. Ben Brewster. London: NLB, 1970.

Altman, Lawrence K. "Puzzle of Sailor's Death Solved after 31 Years: The Answer is AIDS." *New York Times* (July 24, 1990): C3.

Apocalypse Now. Dir. Francis Ford Coppola. Paramount, 1979.

Bersani, Leo. *The Freudian Body: Psychoanalysis and Art.* New York: Columbia UP, 1986.

Brantlinger, Patrick. "*Heart of Darkness*: Anti-Imperialism, Racism, or Impressionism?" (1985). In Murfin, 2d ed. 277–98.

Caruth, Cathy. *Unclaimed Experience: Trauma, Narrative, History.* Baltimore: Johns Hopkins UP, 1996.

Caruth, Cathy, ed. *Trauma: Explorations in Memory.* Baltimore: Johns Hopkins UP, 1995.

Casarino, Cesare. "Historical Critique in *Heart of Darkness* and *Apocalypse Now.*" *Polygraph* 2–3 (1989): 94–113.

Caserio, Robert L. "Casement, Joyce, and Pound: Some New Meanings of Treason." *Quare Joyce.* Ed. Joseph Valente. Ann Arbor: U of Michigan P, 1998. 139–55.

Chase, Cynthia. *Decomposing Figures: Rhetorical Readings in the Romantic Tradition.* Baltimore: Johns Hopkins UP, 1986.

Chirimuuta, Richard C. and Rosalind J. Chirimuuta. *AIDS, Africa and Racism.* London: Free Association, 1989.

Conrad, Joseph. *Heart of Darkness.* 1902 (1899). In Kimbrough. 1–76.

——. *Collected Letters.* 4 vols. Ed. Frederick R. Karl and Laurence Davies. Cambridge: Cambridge UP, 1983–1990.

——. *Congo Diary and Other Uncollected Pieces.* Ed Zdzislaw Najder. New York: Doubleday, 1978.

Copjec, Joan. *Read My Desire: Lacan against the Historicists.* Cambridge: MIT, 1994.

Delany, Samuel R. "A Bend in the Road." *Yale Journal of Criticism* 7.1 (1994): 197–209.

Denby, David. *Great Books: My Adventures with Homer, Rousseau, Woolf, and Other Indestructible Writers of the Western World.* New York: Simon and Schuster, 1996.

Eliot, T. S. "Tradition and the Individual Talent." 1917. *Selected Prose of T. S. Eliot.* Ed. Frank Kermode. New York: Harcourt, 1975. 37–44.

Felman, Shoshana and Dori Laub. *Testimony: Crises of Witnessing in Literature, Psychoanalysis, and History.* New York: Routledge, 1992.

Forster, E. M. *Abinger Harvest.* New York: Harcourt Brace, 1936.

Franklin, John Hope. *George Washington Williams: A Biography*. Chicago: U of Chicago P, 1985.

Graff, Gerald. *Beyond the Culture Wars: How Teaching the Conflicts Can Revitalize American Education*. New York: Norton, 1992.

Grmek, Mirko D. *History of AIDS: Emergence and Origin of a Modern Pandemic*. Trans. Russell C. Maulitz and Jacalyn Duffin. Princeton: Princeton UP, 1990.

Guerard, Albert J. "The Journey Within." 1958. In Kimbrough. 243–50.

Hampson, Robert. "Introduction." *Heart of Darkness*. Ed. Robert Hampson. New York: Penguin, 1995. ix–xlix.

Harpham, Geoffrey Galt. *One of Us: The Mastery of Joseph Conrad*. Chicago: U of Chicago P, 1996.

Harris, Wilson. "The Frontier on which *Heart of Darkness* Stands." 1981. In Kimbrough. 262–68.

Hawkins, Hunt. "The Issue of Racism in *Heart of Darkness*." *Conradiana* 14.3 (1982): 163–71.

Haugh, Robert F. *Joseph Conrad: Discovery in Design*. Norman: U of Oklahoma P, 1957.

Henig, Robin Marantz. *A Dancing Matrix: Voyages Along the Viral Frontier*. New York: Knopf, 1993.

Hennessy, Maurice N. "The Congo Free State: A Brief History, 1876 to 1908." 1961. In Kimbrough. 79–81.

Karl, Frederick R. "Introduction to the *Danse Macabre*: Conrad's *Heart of Darkness*." In Murfin, 1st ed. 123–36.

Kimbrough, Robert, ed. *Heart of Darkness: Norton Critical Edition*. 3d ed. New York: Norton, 1988.

Lane, Christopher. *The Ruling Passion: British Colonial Allegory and the Paradox of Homosexual Desire*. Durham: Duke UP, 1995.

Laplanche, Jean. *Life and Death in Psychoanalysis*. 1970. Trans. Jeffrey Mehlman. Baltimore: Johns Hopkins UP, 1976.

Leavis, F. R. *The Great Tradition: George Eliot, Henry James, Joseph Conrad*. London: Chatto and Windus, 1948.

Lehman, David. *Signs of the Times: Deconstruction and the Fall of Paul de Man*. New York: Simon and Schuster, 1991.

Litvak, Joseph. "Back to the Future: A Review-Article on the New Historicism, Deconstruction, and Nineteenth-Century Fiction." *Texas Studies in Literature and Language* 30.1 (1988): 120–49.

McDermott, Jim et al. *Global HIV/AIDS: A Strategy for U.S. Leadership*. Washington, D.C.: Center for Strategic and International Studies, 1994.

Meyers, Jeffrey. "Conrad and Roger Casement." *Conradiana* 5 (1973): 64–69.

Murfin, Ross C., ed. *Heart of Darkness: A Case Study in Contemporary Criticism*. 2 eds. New York: St. Martin's, 1989, 1996.

Murtagh, Peter. "AIDS in Africa." *The Guardian* (Manchester) (Feb. 3, 1987): 25; (Feb. 4, 1987): 25; (Feb. 5, 1987): 19.

Myers, Gerald, Kersti MacInnes, and Lynda Myers. "Phylogenetic Moments in the AIDS Epidemic." *Emerging Viruses*. Ed. Stephen S. Morse. Oxford: Oxford UP, 1993. 120–37.

Nahmias, A. J., J. Weiss, and X. Yao et al. "Evidence for Human Infection with an HTLV-III/LAV-like Virus in Central Africa, 1959." *The Lancet* 1 (1986): 1279–80.

Patton, Cindy. "Inventing 'African AIDS.' " *Inventing AIDS*. New York: Routledge, 1990. 77–97.

Peck, Dale. "Ecce Homo: Leo Bersani's Grave Thoughts." *Voice Literary Supplement* 135 (1995): 15–17, 21 & 24.

Prentice, Thomson. "AIDS: Africa's New Agony." *The Times* (London) (Oct. 27, 1986): 14; (Oct. 28, 1986): 14; (Oct. 29, 1986): 14.

Rice, Lynne. "Zaire, from Colony to Nation: A Brief History, 1908 to 1987." In Kimbrough. 132–41.

Richter, Alan. *Dictionary of Sexual Slang*. London: Wiley, 1993.

Said, Edward. *Culture and Imperialism*. New York: Knopf, 1993.

Sarvan, C. P. "Racism and the *Heart of Darkness*." 1980. In Kimbrough. 280–85.

Searle, Leroy. *Democratic Literacy and the Politics of Reading*. Cambridge: Harvard UP, forthcoming.

Shoumatoff, Alex. *African Madness*. New York: Knopf, 1988.

Singh, Frances B. "The Colonialistic Bias of *Heart of Darkness*." 1978. In Kimbrough. 268–80.

Singleton-Gates, Peter and Maurice Girodias. *The Black Diaries*. New York: Grove, 1959.

Spurr, David. *The Rhetoric of Empire: Colonial Discourse in Journalism, Travel Writing, and Imperial Administration*. Durham: Duke UP, 1993.

Treichler, Paula A. "AIDS and HIV Infection in the Third World: A First World Chronicle." *Remaking History*. Ed. Barbara Kruger and Phil Mariani. Seattle: Bay, 1989. 31–86.

Vendler, Helen. "The Booby Trap." *The New Republic* (Oct. 7, 1996): 34–40.

Watney, Simon. "Missionary Positions: AIDS, 'Africa,' and Race." *Practices of Freedom: Selected Writings on HIV/AIDS*. Durham: Duke UP, 1994. 103–20.

Watts, Cedric. " 'A Bloody Racist': About Achebe's View of Conrad." *Yearbook of English Studies* 13 (1983): 196–209.

Williams, A. Olufemi. *AIDS: An African Perspective*. Boca Raton, Fla.: CRC P, 1992.

Williams, G., T. B. Stretton, and J. C. Leonard. "Cytomegalic Inclusion Disease and *Pneumocystis carinii* Infection in Adults." *The Lancet* 2 (1960): 951–55.

Williams, George Washington. "A Report upon the Congo-State and Country to the President of the Republic of the United States of America." 1890. In Kimbrough. 84–97.

——. "An Open Letter to His Serene Majesty Leopold II, King of the Belgians and Sovereign of the Independent State of Congo." 1890. In Kimbrough. 103–13.

Yang, Suzanne. "Speaking of the Surface: Psychoanalysis and the Texts of Kaposi's Sarcoma." *Homosexuality and Psychoanalysis*. Ed. Tim Dean. London: Macmillan, forthcoming.

PART III

Psychoanalysis and Race,
an Uncertain Conjunction

14
Wulf Sachs's *Black Hamlet*

Jacqueline Rose

The modern reader is unlikely to approach Wulf Sachs's *Black Hamlet* without suspicion. It is impossible today to read this account of the attempted analysis of a native diviner by a white psychoanalyst on his—that is, the analyst's—terms alone. Saul Dubow has described the historical, anthropological, and political world in which Wulf Sachs, the first practicing analyst in South Africa, made his extraordinary attempt (Intro. to *Black Hamlet* 1–37). In that world, seen through the prism of racist orthodoxy of the 1930s and 1940s, *Black Hamlet* appears to be an affront because of the offensive proximity it permits between black and white man. For the psychoanalytic establishment, Sachs's political boldness was admirable: "He was less frightened of change than others who in the presence of political confusion had chiefly observed their own qualms." But analytically speaking, *Black Hamlet* was no less out of bounds: "wholly unorthodox research . . . breaking every analytic rule" (Sadie Gillespie, Sachs's trainee and colleague, now a psychoanalyst in London, who picks out for special mention the fact that Sachs went to his patient's home) ("Wulf Sachs" 289; Gillespie 4).

The scent of scandal, however, changes with the times. The language of the pioneer has become more suspect; it is now commonplace to observe that what appears first as transgressive easily slides into a renewed form of control. To be a psychoanalyst in the 1920s was without question to occupy radical ground (neither "honorable or profitable" in Sachs's own words ["Mind" 5]). To be Jewish and a Socialist in South Africa was to invite insult and opprobrium on both counts (one of the grounds of reproach against the Jews in South Africa was that they championed, identified with, the blacks). To credit a black African with an internal world was to go against the creeds, not just of explicit racism but of medical science. But there are certain questions that, reading *Black Hamlet*, seem unavoidable today. In whose interests does Sachs's proceed? Or rather, given that in the colonial setting, to act in the other's interests was the problem rather than the solution (acting on behalf of blacks has been one of colonialism's strongest rationales), whose desire or fantasy are we dealing with here? What does Wulf Sachs *want* of John Chavafambira?—a question that has become customary in feminist rereadings of Freud. The 1957 *Evergreen* reprint of *Black Hamlet*—in a series list that included Simone de Beauvoir, Brecht, Genet, Beckett, D. H. Lawrence, Melville, and Henry James—began its blurb, "This is the true story of John Chavafambira," but Sachs himself goes to great lengths to explain how and why, at more than one level, he has made this story his own.

How, then, or from whose position, should *Black Hamlet* be read? In a sense the question is "academic," since even when it is Chavafambira's reported words we are reading, we cannot by-pass the voice of Sachs. But that does not stop us from trying out alternative positions or making other internal moves. What happens, for example, if the reader places herself on the side of the lame Maggie, John Chavafambira's wife, consistently and almost equally castigated by Chavafambira and Sachs alike? She stands in their way, warning and chastising (often called "nagging" in the text), convinced at the beginning and again by the end that no good can come of this relationship between the white doctor and the diviner: "No good will come of mixing black and white medicines. You're a *nganga* and must stick to it" (*Black Anger* 286). Against Sachs's emancipatory project of releasing John into agency in the modern political world, Maggie speaks in these moments from the place of the ancestors. She is, we might say, the voice of a collective conscience or even the voice of the dead (such self-placing in no sense exhausts her identity, which, like her husband's, shifts back and forth across the modern/traditional divide). It is as if her objections are there to remind us that the issue for psychoanalysis in Africa is not whether it can affect the individual (you can always affect an individual), but the relationship it establishes, or fails to establish, with the symbolic parameters of the group.

By calling his study *Black Hamlet*, Sachs inadvertently acknowledges that ancestry, lineage, dead fathers, and ghosts are the touchstones of psychic well-being, that the individual suffers—fails at one level to be constituted *as* individual—when her or his sense of inheritance and continuity is out of joint. Sachs chooses Shakespeare's *Hamlet* because of the remarkable narrative affinities between Hamlet's tale and Chavafambira's: the father dies, the uncle suspected of poisoning him marries the mother, the son feels deprived of the inheritance that should have been his ("he had a definite feeling of incompleteness, of being cheated of something infinitely precious"; 144). Sachs also chooses it because he reads in Chavafambira's reluctance to reclaim his destiny the same kind of halting, maimed agency that critics over the centuries have identified in Shakespeare's play.

And yet, in the course of the narrative Sachs tells, the light thrown from the one story to the other starts to cast itself back the other way. *Hamlet*—the play and the character—has often been taken as the first glimmer of Enlightenment man, a new figure of the human condition who, transcending that moment of emergence, stretches backward and forward through time. Universal because, in Sachs's own words, "with such piercing vision has Shakespeare searched the depths of his own, and at the same time, of all human nature . . . that centuries later men of every country, and of every race, have their own being moulded like wax in his hand" (*Psychoanalysis* 204). But other critics, such as Robert Weimann, have argued that *Hamlet* is at least partly a prenaturalist, prerepresentational text, one in which Hamlet's oddity as a character (prince, buffoon, madman in a seeming rotation of roles) serves as a reminder of the more collective, publicly shared forms of identity, which, at the time Shakespeare was writing, were historically on the wane (Weimann). Through John Chavafambira, we can reread *Hamlet* in this backward direction; that is, we can use this story to identify a form of personhood bereft once outside its collectively or ancestrally sanctioned domain: "the whole basis of the practise of medicine was shattered, unless identification, feeling of oneness with the father, with the ancestral spirits, were preserved" (163).

Over a period of four years in the 1960s, Marie-Cecile Ortigues, coauthor with Edmond Ortigues of *Œdipe africain*, practiced psychoanalysis in a hospital milieu in Dakar, Senegal. For this couple, a clinician and a philosopher, no treatment could proceed which failed to take these symbolic parameters as the base. As they see it, the Oedipus complex is, if anything, more rather than less present in Senegal than in the West. "Can one still talk of dissolving the Oedipus complex in a society where the main, public and permanent issue of life is explicitly defined in terms of the great oedipal themes: fecundity, ancestors, phallic omnipotence and the death of the father as progenitor of the law?" (90–91). But it is lived precisely publicly, collectively, mythically; it shares none of the characteristics of internalized guilt proper to Freud's oedipal child, "condemned" to live out the complex "in his personal fantasy world" (something of an advantage for the African, it is implied; 90).

If this limits the possibility of therapeutic intervention, it also focuses it. The purpose of the treatment, reported in detail in case after case, is to help the patient toward a benign reintegration of her or his symbolic legacy: "Thanks to the analytic dialogue, the possibility [for Talla, one of the central cases of the book] of distinguishing herself from her ancestors will come to be understood as a power which one inherits" (Ortigues 197). But what this also means is that the treatment moves in a dimension not strictly psychological. Talla's psychotherapy "reduces the psychological novel to a minimum and unfolds along the pure register of ancient tragedy spelling out the language of destiny" (191). Perhaps the appeal of *Hamlet* for the psychoanalytic critic lies here, too, in this shift from destiny to family romance. What is symbolic sacrilege, initiation, for Oedipus Rex, has started to move inward by the time of Shakespeare's play (in Freud's formula, *Hamlet* represents "the secular advance of repression in the emotional life of mankind" (*Interpretation* 264). Hamlet can be interpreted as someone whose motives are hidden from himself, someone who would act differently if he knew—if he could uncover the knowledge he somewhere already has—what was really going on in his mind.

The issue of knowledge is at the heart of the dialogue that unfolds between Chavafambira and Sachs. The stated contract between them is that they will impart to each other their medical secrets and skills. As *nganga* and psychoanalyst, they also have in common a certain relation to knowledge; against mainstream Western medicine (what psychoanalyst Jean Clavreul calls "*l'ordre medical*"), they share an emphasis on the symbolic dimension of psychic malaise. "How," Chavafambira asks when first confronted with a thermometer, "could a man be treated by a doctor who did not know his name nor the name of his father?" (162). The work of the *nganga* even has something of the character of a "talking cure" ("he achieved much merely by talking" [178] and "endless combinations and as many interpretations" [219]). But the idea of *self*-knowledge marks the limit to this common ground. In the course of their first meeting, Chavafambira insists "we can know everything through the bones, or through talking with our *midzimu*," but he adds, "it is true that I cannot throw the bones for myself" (73). We can read this moment as an acknowledgment—even a *nganga* cannot analyze himself (this is the starting premise of psychoanalysis, the exception arguably being Freud himself). Or we can read it as a graphic enactment of that point where psychoanalysis carves out its terrain by making self-knowledge—the idea of a self to be uncovered from the hidden depths—the object of desire, condition of its own possibility, and guarantor of the epistemic privilege of the West.

It is not strictly accurate, of course, to describe *Black Hamlet* as an analytic case (it would be immediately disqualified by the Ortigues, who make analytic treatment conditional on the *énoncé* of the patient, that is, his or her demand—and who insist that patient and informant are incompatible roles). Chavafambira is not Sachs's patient: "There were no therapeutic aims" (198). As Saul Dubow stresses, in the later version of the text Sachs goes to even greater lengths to insist on the absence of pathology, to rewrite Chavafambira's ailing in terms of socially induced and politically justified lament. And yet, if there is no disorder, there is without question—to modify slightly the title of one of Jacques Lacan's papers—a "progress of the cure" (Lacan). The Evergreen edition that called *Black Hamlet* "the true story of John Chavafambira" included commentaries on the same back page which offer the book above all in terms of its narrative *pull*, "as engrossing as fiction. . . . Any reader who gets as far as the second paragraph will not put it down." To read the text is to be driven by a sense of something unfolding, something that—again, as Dubow comments—twice reaches some sort of not quite plausible optimistic politicized end. One of the answers to the question of what Sachs wants from Chavafambira is, therefore, that as a native Chavafambira will come to understand racial injustice and fight it (*fight*, but not *break*, the law in one of Sachs's own later formulations) (*Black Anger* 276). It is one of the most extraordinary aspects of this narrative that psychoanalysis is offered here as a release or advance into freedom; this, we might say, gives a literal although unexpected meaning to the idea of the *progress* of the cure.

We should remember, however, that what Hamlet endlessly defers in Shakespeare's play is bloody revenge. If he appears in the psychoanalytic version as oedipal man—frozen by a confrontation, in the shape of his uncle, with his own patricidal and incestuous desires—it is his consequent failure to act, his inability to seize his political as much as his personal destiny, that is the point of the symptom and story. As Sachs reads *Hamlet*, the prince's murder of Polonius reveals him as an unconscious, or closet, revolutionary waiting to come out:

> In the unconscious, Polonius was identified with the tyrant aspect of Caesar, the Caesar who had to be killed by a revolutionary. Those who accept the basic mechanism of identification will understand the curious identification of Polonius with Caesar: "I did enact Julius Caesar. I was killed in the Capitol. Brutus killed me." . . . May I remind you of the generally negative attitude of Shakespeare to Caesar and his idealization of Brutus? (*Psychoanalysis* 205)

It must be unique in the history of psychoanalysis that the objective of a "treatment" is to induce in its subject the imagined capacity to kill (it is hardly the most familiar reproach).

Oddly then, *Black Hamlet* offers the spectacle of an analyst behaving more or less in the way feminist critics have demanded of Freud, notably in response to his first full-length analysis of a case of hysteria (the 1907 case of Dora). *If only* Freud had heard Dora's protest; *if only* he had read the social determinants, the hideously repressive, not to say abusive, machinery of her family and wider world; *if only* she had been allowed, as a woman, instead of the destiny of hysteria, to lead a political party like her brother Otto Bauer. *Black Hamlet* makes it clear that the analyst who does all this, who most fervently wishes for the patient's political emancipation, locks the patient into the imaginary world of his own demands—no less than did Freud, desiring Dora to desire her male suitor. If Chavafambira discovers political selfhood partly through Sachs, he does so at a cost. He becomes a political subject not just by leaving his kraal (from tribe to city, the migration that was the foundation of the new political urbanized black) but by mixing his medicines with those of the white doctor, against all dictates of ancestral law. His political self-discovery on behalf of his people is also an act of symbolic betrayal. Above all, it requires him, through the person of Sachs, to shed his distrust, a distrust Sachs himself acknowledges as legitimate, of the white man. It is one of the ironies but also an illuminating facet of *Black Hamlet* that Sachs, wooing Chavafambira in the spirit of nonracialism, finds himself up against a dilemma of linguistic communication not easily surmountable even with the best liberal intent. This suggests that if there is to be a rebirth of psychoanalysis in South Africa today, it will have to be in a form that, given the political legacy, can address the structural difficulties of language as much as the varieties of spoken tongue.[1] More obviously, the exchange between Sachs and Chavafambira takes place in the language of the colonizers—this marks its first and perhaps most crucial boundary— in which Sachs was wholly proficient and Chavafambira could only stumble his way (even if English was not Sachs's own first language—after Russian, and possibly German—Yiddish, it could have been his third).

"If the white man wants lies, why not tell him lies," Maggie comments in *Black Anger*, when she hears the true story of Sunshine, the young boy who had joined the family, fallen ill of pneumonia, and been tended by her and her husband until he died (315). He had contracted his illness on a prison farm, sent there when he refused to withdraw his complaint to the police that he had been sexually abused by his white employer: "He obeyed the white man's law. He told the truth" (314; truth in this context is the crime). Earlier in *Black Hamlet*, when Sachs asks Chavafambira if the native lies easily, he replies, "We don't like the white people. . . . We don't know what they will do with us. Therefore I don't care what I say to a white man if only I won't be punished. There is nothing bad in telling a lie if you don't cheat and don't do harm with it. Are you cross with me?" (197).

It is worth pausing here. Viewed psychoanalytically, these moments turn the interaction between Sachs and Chavafambira "*en abîme*" (an infinite set of cavities repeating and disappearing into each other). For Jacques Lacan, no statement captures more vividly the subject's relation to the unconscious than the statement "I am lying." This famous Bertrand Russell paradox—the utterance is immediately false if it is true—can only be disentangled, he argues, if you assume that there are two subjects at odds with each other, that of ego and that of unconscious, one of which is lying and one not. Chavafambira does not exactly say to Sachs, "I am lying"; in fact, "I don't care what I say to the white man" could be read as a version of psychoanalytic rule number one (say whatever comes into your head). But he comes very close to disqualifying the whole analytic dialogue, while capturing or mimicking something of the paradox that supports it. Psychoanalysis is, to use Paul Ricoeur's famous expression, a hermeneutics of suspicion. But what do you do when the patient, in an almost Brechtian moment of exposure, states: You have absolutely no reason to trust my words?

To the question of knowledge, we have therefore to add that of language and distrust. Or rather, we should notice how hostility across the racial barrier, which might seem to be the fundamental problem, is inseparable from the fully psychoanalytic question of what speech, in terms of its internal and external boundaries, is capable of. In what seems to be one of the crisis points of the text, Chavafambira loses his faith in Sachs: "His faith in me had broken down leaving a painful, open sore in his mind" (211). He sees Sachs's face in the faces of the detectives who come to interrogate the residents after the killing of baby twins in the yard. The identification seems logical. Compare Chavafambira's complaint about the detectives, "It seemed to John as if these white people put their meddlesome hands into his very thoughts," with the account by Sachs himself on the same pages of how he tried to get information from Chavafambira about the native beliefs involved in what had taken place: I had nevertheless continued to question him. . . . Day after day I questioned him . . . I was still not satisfied" (212–13).

Confronted, not surprisingly we might say, with unprecedented resistance and hostility from Chavafambira, "Doubts, uncertainties, conflicting thoughts and desires, were, like the nagging Maggie [*sic*], continuously with him," Sachs determines to end the crisis: "I must interfere and break down his resistance" (214–15). (Readers of "Dora" will recognize this tone, as well as notice the links among obduracy, the woman, and the open wound.) He explains to Chavafambira "the essence of the aggressive instinct, of the unavoidability and necessity of hating people who we believe to be hostile to us" (215). Hostility must out. Sachs gives Chavafambira license to hate him. Only on that basis will Sachs, he is sure, regain Chavafambira's unequivocal trust. The paradox here—again, one that goes to the heart of the analytic relation—is that by allowing himself to be the target of hostility, the analyst deflects and dissipates it. By making himself the object of aggression, he saves, so to speak, his own skin (this becomes the reproach of the later critics of Melanie Klein). No analyst is finally more *winning* than the one who invites the analysand's distrust: "I talked to him, day after day, until I won. . . . The material flew like a stream that has been artificially dammed. . . . He also introduced me fully and unreservedly into the secrets of his art" (215).

The difficulty, then, is not so much that the colonial situation makes analysis impossible; if anything, the problem works the other way around. *Black Hamlet* demonstrates the ruse of psychoanalysis. Analysis will not be thwarted (or, in the words of François Roustang, "psychoanalysis never lets go"). When Sachs's obituarist in the *International Journal of Psychoanalysis* suggests that his political fervor "blunted his perceptions as a scientist," he misses the point as I see it, on two counts ("Wulf Sachs" 298). Most simply, there is no analytic intervention without history and desire (*Black Hamlet* demonstrates this before anything else). Second, what appears as unorthodoxy or license is better read as insight or revelation, with implications that stretch well beyond this immediate case. In the "black-and-white" setting of the colonial story, analysis unavoidably confronts the ironies of its own predicament—not just the tragic but also the comic dimension of its own powers. Laughingly, in the company of his new political comrades, Chavafambira comments: "You know . . . for months and months I would talk to him lying on the sofa and he would just say 'Yes' . . . 'Very interesting' . . . 'Tell me more' . . . 'What do *you* think of it?' . . . It would make me so angry, so angry! I wanted to leave him so many times and never come back, so angry he made me with his silence" (*Black Anger* 304).

There is a famous joke by Heinrich Heine—Freud uses it to open *Jokes and Their Relation to the Unconscious*—about the poor lottery agent who boasts that the wealthy Baron Rothschild "had treated him quite as his equal, quite 'famillionairely' " (the unconscious knows that the dream of familiarity with a millionaire is a hoax) (*Jokes* 12–13). The night before Chavafambira meets Sachs, he dreams that King George came to Johannesburg. "Plenty whites and natives met him, the big man, the big King. All very friendly, natives and whites. . . . So sure was I that a white man would come to my help that I was not at all surprised when one day the white woman came to the yard and brought you" (*Black Hamlet* 194). A white man and white woman in the yard are, however, also the problem. As Sachs acknowledges, the presence of the anthropologist and the doctor compromises the inhabitants of Rooiyard and might even put them at risk.

The issue, then, is not one of awareness. Sachs recognizes the problem at several points in the text: "Why should he expect that the woman anthropologist and I should be any different? The truth is that he was quite right in that respect" (139). But he cannot break the circuit of his role. When Chavafambira is "on the verge of a nervous breakdown," remembering how "he had betrayed his own profession to me, association with whom seemed doomed to bring him to disaster," Sachs gives him "a soothing drug" and then takes him back to Johannesburg (Chavafambira had been attacked with a knife by an inmate of a mental asylum who accused him of cooperating with the white doctor, of *being* a white man [254]).

Even more striking is the shift that occurs when Sachs recognizes he has been treating Chavafambira as a "psychoanthropological specimen" and starts to see him as a "human being" for the first time—this is, as Dubow comments, a key turning point in the text (287). But at this precise moment, which has all the characteristics of a revelation, "A new man separated himself from the pages I was reading: the real John," Sachs then has another flash of insight, which arguably cancels out the first: "Then it struck me that his self-destructive actions might be the direct result of his sudden and abrupt severance from me" (287). No moment perhaps illustrates more vividly what literary theory would describe as the split between the *énoncé* (content or implied referent) and the *énonciation* (utterance or framing form) of the text: "John is a separate human being," and "You cannot do without me." No moment shows more strongly the predicament or demand of the humanist, whose recognition of the other as human has, above all, by that other, to be *seen*. Or, to use the language of surveillance and control, how can the surveilling subject, aware of past imperiousness, act on that awareness without literally *effacing* himself? Sachs remains *in loco parentis*. His dilemma captures the ambiguity of fostered, nurtured autonomy: "Go forward. Take my hand."

To the question put earlier, what does Sachs want of Chavafambira? one can suggest another reply. Or rather, to the first answer—that Chavafambira should fight racial injustice on behalf of his people—one can add another question: What does Sachs want in wanting that? Reading this dramatic sequence, it is hard not to conclude that it is a crisis in the analytic relationship between black and white, a fleeting recognition by Sachs of its impossibility, that Chavafambira's increased, and increasingly encouraged political consciousness will be called on to repair. Politics appears in this instance as a solution of sorts to a crisis of analytic faith; it would therefore be a mistake to read Sachs—along the lines of a demand frequently made of psychoanalysis—as discarding psychoanalytic blindness for political truth.

A specific psychoanalytic theory of primitive mental life runs beneath the surface of *Black Hamlet*. Sachs shares with Octave Mannoni, and with lesser known contemporary South African psychologists such as J. F. Ritchie, a belief in the dependency complex or psychic immaturity of the African, lifted from contemporary social theory ("he remained an infant throughout his life" [87]). Inside psychoanalytic literature, this belief can be traced back to Freud. In a famous passage in his 1914 paper "On Narcissism," Freud made an equation between the infantile unconscious and the mental life of primitives. They shared, he proposed, an over-estimation of the power of wishes and mental acts, "omnipotence of thoughts," a belief in the thaumaturgic force of words, and a technique for dealing with the external world, magic, "which appears to be a logical application of these grandiose premisses" (75). There is, as Gayatri Spivak has recently pointed out, something strange about this equation, not quite reducible to its obvious ethno-centrism. How can one proclaim the universal kinship of races, as Freud also does, and at the same time suggest that one race of people have been psychically left behind? Do primitives have children? A crazy question provoked simply by the fact that the child of the primitive is left so wholly out of the picture that you could be forgiven for thinking that they do not (Spivak 21). "Very little is known," Géza Róheim observes in his 1931 article, "Psycho-Analysis and Anthropology," "about the childhood of non-European races" (317).

In his 1924 debate with Bronislaw Malinowski about the universality of the Oedipus complex, Ernest Jones goes further ("Mother"). If the Oedipus complex does not appear to be visible in non-Western cultures, if the child manifests no hos-tility toward the father, it is because he has split that hostility and projected it onto the maternal uncle in order to save the also loved father from his unconscious rage. (This is the opposite of the Ortigues' concept of universality, since it makes social forms a derivative of individual psychology and downgrades the collective, sym-bolic dimension to the status of a purely secondary defense.) In an article on psy-choanalysis and anthropology written in the same year, Jones insisted that the equation between the primitive and the infant had been misconstrued, critics hav-ing missed the emphasis on the unconscious. The primitive is not being accused of acting like a child; what is at issue is "not so much a difference between adult and child as between two modes of thinking which are present in both. Stated in terms of values, this results in a greater respect for the mind of the child and a less respect for that of the adult" ("Mother" 128). No one is fully an adult, but some adults are less adult than the rest—although, as Jones himself puts it in the same article, the so-called primitive version is not unlike the British Constitution, which has "evolved a similar arrangement" by distributing hostile and idealizing sentiment between Prime Minister and King (165).

In all these discussions, there is one word that repeatedly recurs on all sides. The primitive "projects" the contents of his inner life onto the outside world. Only in this way, according to Jones, can the child rid himself of the impulses he most fears. Compare J. F. Ritchie's statement, "he tries to get rid of his hatred by an abnormal use of the instinctive mechanism of projection" (Ritchie 14) and that of Sachs, "he projected his trouble on others: enemies, witches, and bad luck" (*Black Hamlet* 223).

Psychoanalysis itself can, however, help us undo the ethnocentric components of its argument. We simply have to track its own internal usage of *projection* as a term. In his paper "The Unconscious," also written in 1914, Freud comes close to saying that the only way we have to convince ourselves of the reality of the other is to project our conviction of our own existence onto her or him (only by doing something similar are we likely to accept the idea of an unconscious in ourselves) ("Unconscious" 169). By the time we get to Melanie Klein, who was writing her most important work at the same time as Sachs, projection—properly *projective identification*—had become the driving mechanism of psychic life: we endlessly deposit unwanted parts of ourselves in others (one of the central ways we come to feel connected to them). In Melanie Klein's writings, the emphasis is much less on repression than in Freud's, and more on defense. It is at the point that repression is arguably being sidelined inside the psychoanalytic literature that it takes up its privileged residence in the unconscious of the West: "Repression among the really primitive races of mankind has neither the depth nor intensity of repression as we find it in Europe" (Róheim 309).

I would suggest that if one reads on through subsequent psychoanalytic thinking, the idea of the immaturity of the primitive can be turned on its head. Like woman, non-Western man becomes the excluded component of the theory that is trying to account for him. He is there to mark the limit of psychoanalytic insight (his exclusion is what allows psychoanalysis to keep its own boundaries in place). We could start counting all the things this primitive man is carrying, each of which it has become customary to read today as repudiated by—as too much for—Freud. From the oceanic feeling of oneness with the world, of which Freud famously expressed his incomprehension, compare Sachs on Chavafambira: "The whole basis of the practise of medicine was shattered unless identification, feeling of oneness with the father, with the ancestral spirits, was preserved" (163). To telepathy, which Freud first discounted but which crept back into psychoanalysis when he allowed for the possibility of unconscious transference of thoughts, compare Jones: "I for one cannot avoid the impression that they ['savages'] must at times possess a high capacity for divining the unconscious thoughts of their neighbours" ("Psycho-Analysis" 125; see also Freud, "Psycho-Analysis"; "Dreams"; for commentary, Derrida 3–41). To projection: for the Ortigues, identification (becoming the other) and projection (getting rid of part of oneself in the other) are the stuff of analysis, the only way for the analytic relation to proceed: "The fabric of the relationship between ourselves and our client is constituted through the complex and mobile play of reciprocal projections and identifications" (Ortigues 36).

Look again at the theory of the infantile projections of the primitive and, even in its own terms, it starts to turn back on itself. How can the Western observer recognize the presence of projection unless it is something still familiar to him, something he still *knows?* (It is a basic premise of psychoanalysis that nothing is ever completely left behind.) On what is the belief in the infantile nature of the primitive founded if not on a moment of projection? "In [*The Tempest*], the complex [of Caliban] must be a projection, for where else could it have come from?" (Mannoni, *Prospero* 20). In which case the theory immediately loses its founding distinction between primitive and civilized man. It is the observer's own fantasized childhood that he goes looking for when he takes off around the world: "The observer is repelled by the thoughts he encounters in his own mind, and it seems to him that they are the thoughts of the people he is observing. In any such act of projection the subject's purpose is to recover his own innocence" (20).

For Frederick S. Perls, a psychoanalyst who worked alongside Sachs for a time in South Africa before breaking away to become the founder of Gestalt therapy (according to his own account, he had been sent to South Africa to start a training program by Ernest Jones), projection is "typical of *modern* dissociated man" (my emphasis) and, together with flight, is the chief means of avoiding unwanted contact in the modern world (Perls et al., ch. 8, "Projections" 215). Sachs says of Chavafambira, "For him, no security—always flight . . . flight, always flight"; flight "was the line he chose whenever possible" (*Black Hamlet* 338, 236). But who, we might ask in the context of South Africa, is in fact fleeing whom? In her 1941 primer on South Africa, Sarah Gertrude Millin writes, "The history of a large part of the South Africans is a history of escaping from the next man" (8; a self-diagnosis, one might say, given the drift of her politics).[2] For Mannoni, projection and flight are the twin psychic poles of the colonial vocation: "Whatever one may think before analysis, it is himself man is looking for when he goes far away; near at hand, he is liable to come up against Others" (111).

One does not, of course, have to go that far to recognize that projection is an exemplary state of being and suffering in the West; that it can be discovered at the heart of the most valued emotional condition of so-called civilized man: "A certain resemblance, even while it evolves, exists between the women we love in succession. . . . These women are a product of our temperament, an image, an inverse projection, a 'negative' of our own sensibility" (Proust 894; my translation). And readers of modern literature will not miss the extent to which Sachs, in his repeated use of free indirect speech—thoughts in the words of the character, but using the form of the third person pronoun, which makes them belong ambiguously to character and narrator alike—projects himself into Chavafambira's mind: "Why was he oppressed like this? Why did he have to bear this burden of responsibility in this cheerless, inhospitable town?" "Why had he not told Mdlawini the truth?" "How greedy she was in her eating and drinking!" (124, 275, 299).

Behind every projection, an identification. There is, then, another way of reading *Black Hamlet*—one that would be in terms, not of controlling distance, but of a less stable proximity between Chavafambira and Sachs. As a Lithuanian Jew who arrived in South Africa in 1922, Sachs is both a colonial and a dispossessed subject (in no way does he simply embody the master narrative of the West). In the words of his obituarist, he had led a "wandering life" and had the "weary task of having to take his medical degree in three countries" ("Wulf Sachs" 288). Trained, according to various testimonies, by Theodore Reik, A. A. Brill, and possibly briefly by Freud, the passing of the legacy—as with Chavafambira, and as with so many analysts of his generation—was not smooth (see Dubow, Intro. to *Black Hamlet* n.3; Gillespie 3).

Likewise Chavafambira, who left Rhodesia for South Africa, trading his native kraal for the city, is a self-imposed exile from his native land, "cut off from the other natives," a "foreigner" wherever he goes (*Black Hamlet* 122, 125; *Black Anger* 299). Not just a Hamlet, Chavafambira is also in Sachs's eyes "an African Odysseus," "always restless, always discontented, always lonely" (*Black Hamlet* 289). Arguably, it is this latent identification that sparks the central moment of transformation in the text. When Sachs is accused by Tembu of being responsible for Chavafambira's arrest, he leaps internally—these words are unspoken—to his own defense: "Was I to place myself in the hands of these hostile men, and protest to them my innocence? Didn't I myself, a Jew, belong to a people ceaselessly driven from pillar to post?" (286). Who then, we might ask, in saving Chavafambira, is Sachs also trying to save? "We found ourselves as keen to save John as must have been the partisans of Dreyfus" (this remark is cut from the later version of the book; 292).

In his 1934 book, *Psychoanalysis: Its Meaning and Practical Application* (originally presented as lectures to the University of Witswatersrand) while discussing a male patient who had been a fervent supporter of women's suffrage, Sachs offers a moment that is hard not to read as his own self-analysis, the briefest recognition of the psychic-cum-historical pull of the native African for the Jew:

> As a Jew he felt the effects of anti-semitism very keenly, but, as an assimilated one, he could not join his fellow sufferers in an open fight and protest, by, for instance, joining a strong national movement. Instead he sympathized to a degree of identification with women . . . His interest in the equality of the sexes was really a manifestation of his demand for equality of races. So also we often find Jews who are fighters for someone else's national or racial rights. (*Psychoanalysis* 160–61)

Sachs was a Zionist, but one who only reluctantly conceded the need for a Jewish state (in a letter to Freud commenting on Freud's final work, *Moses and Mono-*

theism, Sachs argues that to become a nation would deprive the Jews of their defining character as a "mystery" to others and themselves).[3] He was also, like many of the Jewish community in South Africa, a radical—a Socialist, a champion of the oppressor, a supporter of native rights. According to Ellen Hellman, in her 1949 tribute to Sachs in the *Zionist Record*, he had, from his earliest days in Russia, been a rebel all his life (Hellman).

This Jewish self-placing is not unilateral; it does not come only from Sachs. Chavafambira says, "I read in the Bible that the Jews also refused to have Jesus, and believe in God. We are also the same" (*Black Hamlet* 174). At moments, the link follows the strangest of paths. Strangest of all is the episode where Sachs, sharing pig meat with Chavafambira on a return visit to his kraal, suddenly notices "the horrified stare of those present," which "reminded him" (Chavafambira) of the family's pig meat taboo; "John had unconcernedly consumed ham with me on many occasions" (311). What lore of his own fathers has Sachs himself forgotten?

It is important to place this side of the story in the specific context of South Africa, one that adds a further dimension to the history of race relations outlined by Saul Dubow. The period when *Black Hamlet* was written and published marked a period of rising anti-Semitism in South Africa, which started with the influx of Lithuanian immigrants in the 1920s. In 1930 Daniel François Malan, head of the National Party and subsequent apartheid leader, had passed his Quota Bill restricting immigration into South Africa from nonscheduled countries. No one had any doubt that it was aimed at the Lithuanian Jews; thereafter "a camel could have gone through the eye of a needle more easily than a poor Lithuanian immigrant would have entered South Africa for the first time" (Bradlow, qtd. in Shain 114). By the mid 1930s, anti-Jewish activities had, in the words of the Jewish Board of Deputies, "reached an unparalleled height" ("Report of the 11th Congress of South African Jewish Board of Deputies, May 1935," qtd. in Shain 144). In 1936 both Malan's Purified Nationalists and the United Party proposed Bills aimed at the activities and immigration of Jews. Milton Shain chooses 1937, the year of the publication of *Black Hamlet*, as the year in which "the Jewish Question" left the fringes and entrenched itself inside the white political mainstream.

For a long time, there had been low-level anti-Semitism in South Africa, especially among rural Afrikaners, who both identified the Jew with the ills of a modernity they had not learned to exploit (the city, finance, and modern trade), and also viewed them as the agents of a modernity they could not do without. But the Lithuanian immigrants—poor migrant workers entering South Africa at a time of rising unemployment and a new "poor whiteism" among Afrikaners—were seen as even more of a threat. The Jew served as the scapegoat of modernization; at once the pinnacle of capitalist achievement and also its dregs. "Even those who separated the acculturated and urbane Jew from the Eastern European newcomer exaggerated Jewish power and influence. Herein lay the convergence between the philosemitic and antisemitic view" (Shain 143). It is a story by no means restricted to South Africa, even if, as Shain argues, it predates South Africa's worst economic problems and Hitler's rise to power.

A Lithuanian Jew arriving in the 1920s, Sachs in fact sits uneasily across the two groups. Professional and European in preference and taste ("it pleased me to discover John's criterion of beauty to be no longer that of a primitive kraal-man, but of a Europeanized black man" 314), Sachs fulfills more than one stereotype of the acculturated Jew. As a doctor, he matches that of the new professional threatening to take over medicine and the law ("everywhere climbing to the top of the trees where the plums are to be found"); as a liberal who involves himself with the black community, he is closer to the "archetypical subversive," ignorant—in the words of one South African Party member in 1926—of the "relative position that should be occupied by the white man and the native" (Sir Abe Bailey, qtd. in Shain 134, 143; also J. S. Marwick, qtd. in Shain 124). But Sachs is nonetheless a Lithuanian, an Eastern European Jew of the second wave. To become a psychoanalyst in this context is perhaps above all to lay claim to the heart of Europe, to mold oneself unmistakably in its shape. The anxiety of that passage—from Lithuania to Western Europe, from East to West—gives a further dimension, I would suggest, to Sachs's wish to see Chavafambira enter the world of the newly educated, Europeanized black.

This dimension becomes even clearer if we move between the two versions of the text. The gap between the two books covers the period of the Second World War; South Africa entered the war on the side of the Allies after a famously narrow vote (the vote was 80 to 67 and split the governing party, providing the opening for the political triumph of the apartheid National Party in 1948). If the transition between *Black Hamlet* and *Black Anger* can be read, as Dubow suggests, in terms of Sachs's and Chavafambira's increasing political awareness (this is, note, Sachs's own reading of the shift), it also carries the burden of this other, unredeemed history. In *Black Anger*, during a discussion among Chavafambira's black comrades about the war, one of them, Dhlamini, speaks out in favor of the Germans: "The Germans would soon be in South Africa. . . . They were going to free the country from the Jews and the Indians and give their shops to the blacks." "You fools," answers Tshakada, "So—our local Nazis have suddenly discovered Black Aryans?" (302). Sachs then imports into the text the article by journalist and playwright H. I. E. Dhlomo, "African Attitudes to the Europeans," which he had published in his own journal, *The Democrat*, strengthening the Nazi reference to put this moment in perspective, to put Dhlamini in his place (Dhlomo). Dhlamini falls into the group of "neither/nor" Africans, "neither wholly African nor fully Europeanised," who have lost the spirit of tribal communism and "fall easy prey to . . . Nazi propaganda" (Dhlomo 21; *Black Anger* 303). (In the original the reference is not to Nazism but to appeasers, "the Municheers.")

Fritz Perls was also a migrant Jew, sent to South Africa by Ernest Jones, who, Perls writes, "did a magnificent job for the persecuted Jewish psychoanalysts" (these are the founding moments of psychoanalysis in Johannesburg which are therefore meaningless outside this history) (Perls, *In and Out* 41). In his autobiography, Perls predicts a future in which latent American fascism will come to the surface, sparing the Jew and taking as its new targets the Negro and the hippie. But "the Negro will not suffer it submissively, with cowardice as the European Jew did. He has tasted freedom, and flexes his muscles" (124). Although Perls was writing much later, this suggests another message, never explicitly articulated, to Sachs's postwar reworking of his text. Unlike the Jews—albeit with the help of this particular Jew—the blacks must save themselves.

There is a passage in *Psychoanalysis: Its Meaning and Practical Application* in which Sachs talks about violence in the mind. He compares the conflict between the different psychic agencies described by Freud—id, ego, and superego—to a state of revolution or civil war, ending either in dictatorship ("victory of the tyrannical Super-Ego") or disintegration of the nation or continuous revolt ("which, in the human psyche, will mean insanity"). It is, he says, the "primary aim" of psychoanalysis to stop "this continuous warfare" (*Psychoanalysis* 30). Place the two texts, the official psychoanalytic primer and the revolutionary case book, alongside each other, and the question one might be left with is, Which sounds the stronger note? (remember Hellman describing Sachs as a rebel all his life). For, if the first has the imprimatur of the master—a terse recommendation from Freud, which he allowed only after sending Sachs a set of objections which Sachs mainly ignored,[4] the second stands as the most effective caution to anyone who believes that war in the mind could be settled or that violence is something that psychoanalysis could hope definitively to repair. In relation to the passage from Sachs's psychoanalytic textbook, *Black Hamlet* returns, as it were, to the scene of the crime.

It is, as Dubow argues, too easy to dismiss Sachs's universalism as liberal illusion by simply lifting it out of the historical and political world of South Africa in the 1930s, when being a universalist and an antiracist liberal was to defy the predominant and deadly tropes of oppression. Hence the importance of Magnus Hirschfeld's *Racism*, with its claim to a founding and future unity of mankind, written in 1933–34 when Hirschfeld was in exile from Nazism. "There can be little doubt that mankind was a unity to begin with, and is destined to become a unity once more" (*Racism* 101; according to Freud's late diaries, in 1929–30 Sachs was also briefly in Berlin).[5] Universalism is always historical—always this or that universalism, never universal in itself. This is no less true of psychoanalysis, whose claims to universality were aimed first at the delusion of normality (we are all perverts at heart); at the racist boundaries of science (psychoanalysis makes no racial distinctions); and at a world that—in the case of France after Dreyfus, for example—was reluctant to let it through the doors. According to Elizabeth Roudinesco, Lacan, for all the scandal of his theories and person, could be accepted as the first great French psychoanalyst because, by placing Freud in the intellectual tradition of Descartes, he made psychoanalysis nationally recognizable and safe (Roudinesco).

Yet, to return to the start of this essay, the claim to universality has recently, for good reason, been put under strain. Reading Sachs today, we can see those moments when the assertion of universal kinship starts to look like a facet of colonialism, not *despite*, but *because of* itself. When Octave Mannoni wrote "The Decolonization of Myself," his own reply to *Psychologie de la colonisation* or *Prospero and Caliban* (almost contemporary with *Black Anger* but best known today for Frantz Fanon's crucial critique), he took issue with his own earlier universalism on these grounds (Mannoni, "Decolonization"; Fanon). It is not, he writes, the task of psychoanalysis to "join its cause" to those of "the old liberal [with a small 'l'] illusions" but to acknowledge the fact and the difficulty of differences—not pregiven, they acquire their meaning—in the world. "The real problem is not likeness, but difference. . . . The psychologist runs the risk of unintentionally playing the role of those valets in the commedia dell'arte , who act as go-betweens for their quarrelling masters and succeed in reconciling them until the moment when the masters, on speaking terms once more, rediscover the true motive for their quarrel" ("Decolonization" 294, 295; my trans.).

There is no point, he continues, telling the Jew or the black man that the label they suffer from does not signify or make any difference, since they know so well that it does. After all, it is pure Christian charity to love someone "regardless"; no one wants, except piously, to be loved because they are the same as everyone else. Loading the trauma of difference onto the black man, the white man can delude himself that there is or might be no trouble between men (a delusion the universalist shares). "The black man is in a position to see otherwise what is wrong in the way the whites (the least 'deluded,' the most 'human') have organized co-existence between men—including between the whites themselves—because it is he, the black man, who carries the weight, in that domain, of what isn't working" ("Decolonization" 298–99; my trans.).

For a long time, feminism has argued that one place to look for what goes on (and goes wrong) between men is their relation to women. I end therefore with Maggie, which is also where this essay began. This is a book about Hamlet (who could not act) and Oedipus (who was lame). But who is it who really drags her leg (her feet) in the text? "The power the lazy cripple exercised over her husband was amazing" (*Black Hamlet* 295). Who becomes the repository of Hamletism, the inability to act, while Chavafambira, under Sachs's tutelage, steps forth into his new world? "You lame bastard," Chavafambira is reported as shouting at her in the moment before he poisons her and thinks he has killed her—the moment Sachs reads as signifying that he is at last "ready for revolt" (298–300). What is the woman carrying for the rest of the players in this tale?

Chavafambira claims the legacy of his father through his uncle, but it was through the body of his mother, who would throw herself into convulsions, that the ancestors chose directly to speak (she was famous far beyond the borders of the kraal). Maggie's mother, Mawa, goes mad (Sachs diagnoses her as suffering from manic-depressive insanity) (246). The *ngoma* Emily, a vast monstrous body, talks directly to the spirits (Sachs diagnoses her as suffering from extreme hysteria [264]); seized by a policeman in the middle of one of her trances, she falls to the floor and dies. Although Sachs attempts a brief analysis of Maggie in the second version of his text, these women are beyond the analytic pale. In *Black Hamlet*, Wulf Sachs tries something historically exceptional, which, for that reason, is still a document for our time. It is not to underestimate that venture, or to give these women the status of "truth," to suggest in conclusion that they run rings around psychoanalysis, setting the limits to what it can do in Africa, making it impossible for psychoanalysis to have the last word. That there can be no last word—not psychically, not politically—is, however, also the fundamental principle of psychoanalysis.

ENDNOTES

1. One new development, the Psycho-Analytic Psychotherapy Study Group, is following a Kleinian path. See Hamburger.

2. For a fuller discussion of South Africa and its peoples, see Millin, *The South Africans*; for a critical analysis of her fictional writing, see Coetzee, "Blood."

3. Sachs to Freud, 1 August 1939, Freud Museum, London. I discuss this letter and Sachs's relation to the Jewish question more fully in chapter 2 of *States of Fantasy*.

4. Freud to Sachs, 14 March 1930; 7 March, 26 October 1932; 2 April, 9 December 1933 (Manuscript Division, Library of Congress).

5. The English edition of Hirschfeld's *Racism*, which appeared in 1938, was the first publication of the work (*The Diary of Sigmund Freud* 173).

WORKS CITED

Bradlow, Edna. "Immigration into the Union, 1910–1948: Policies and Attitudes." Ph.D. dissertation, U. of Cape Town, 1978.

Clavreul, Jean. *L'ordre medical*. Paris: Seuil, 1978.

Coetzee, J. M. "Blood, Taint, Flaw, Degeneration: The Novels of Sarah Gertrude Millin." *White Writing: On the Culture of Letters in South Africa*. New Haven: Yale UP, 1988. 136–62.

Derrida, Jacques. "Telepathy." 1981. Trans. Nicholas Royle. *Oxford Literary Review* 10 (1988): 3–41.

Dhlomo, H. I. E. "African Attitudes to the European." *Democrat* 1 (1945): 21 and 26.

Fanon, Frantz. *Black Skin, White Masks*. 1952. Trans. Charles Lam Markmann. New York: Grove, 1967.

Freud, Sigmund. *The Interpretation of Dreams*. 1900. Vol. 5 of *The Standard Edition of the Complete Psychological Works of Sigmund Freud*. Ed. and trans. James Strachey. 24 vols. London: Hogarth, 1953–74. 339–627.

——. *Jokes and Their Relation to the Unconscious*. 1905. Vol. 8 of *SE*. 1–238.

——. "On Narcissism: An Introduction." 1914. Vol. 14 of *SE*. 69–102.

——. "The Unconscious." 1915. Vol. 14 of *SE*. 159–215.

——. "Dreams and Occultism, Lecture XXX." 1933 (1932). Vol. 22 of *SE*. 31–56.

——. "Psycho-Analysis and Telepathy." 1922. Vol. 18 of *SE*. 195–220.

——. *The Diary of Sigmund Freud 1929–39: A Record of the Final Decade*. Ed. Michael Molnar. New York: Scribner's, 1992.

Gillespie, Sadie. "Historical Notes on the First South African Psycho-analytic Society." *Psycho-analytic Psychotherapy in South Africa* 1 (1992): 1–6.

Hamburger, Tony. "The Johannesburg Psycho-analytic Psychotherapy Study Group: A Short History." *Psycho-analytic Psychotherapy in South Africa* 1 (1992): 62–71.

Hellman, Ellen. "Dr. Wulf Sachs: A Tribute." *Zionist Record* 35 (1949).

Hirschfeld, Magnus. *Racism*. 1938. Ed. and trans. Eden and Cedar Paul. Port Washington, NY: Kennikat, 1973.

Jones, Ernest. "Mother-Right and the Sexual Ignorance of Savages." 1924. *Essays in Applied Psycho-Analysis*, Vol. 2: *Essays in Religion and Folklore*. London: Hogarth, 1951. 114–44.

——. "Psycho-Analysis and Anthropology." 1924. *Essays in Applied Psycho-Analysis*, Vol. 2. 165–73.

"J. R." "Wulf Sachs, 1893–1949." *International Journal of Psychoanalysis* 31.4 (1950): 288–89.

Lacan, Jacques. "The Direction of the Treatment and the Principles of Its Power." 1958. *Écrits: A Selection*. Trans. Alan Sheridan. New York: Norton, 1977. 226–80.

Mannoni, Octave. *Prospero and Caliban: The Psychology of Colonization*. 1966. Trans. Pamela Powesland. New Forward by Maurice Bloch. Ann Arbor: U of Michigan P, 1990.

———."The Decolonization of Myself." 1966. 327–35. *Clefs pour l'imaginaire*. Paris: Seuil, 1969. 290–300.

Millin, Sarah Gertrude Liebson. *The South Africans*. London: Constable, 1926.

———.*South Africa*. The British Commonwealth in Pictures Series. London: William Collins, 1941.

Perls, Frederick S. *In and Out of the Garbage Pail: Joy, Sorrow, Chaos, Wisdom: The Free-Floating Autobiography of the Man Who Developed Gestalt Therapy*. New York: Bantam, 1972.

Perls, Frederick S., Ralph F. Hefferline, and Paul Goodman. *Gestalt Therapy: Excitement and Growth in the Human Personality*. New York: Dell, 1951.

Ortigues, Marie-Cecile and Edmond Ortigues. *Œdipe africain*. Paris: Plon, 1966.

Proust, Marcel. *A l'ombre des jeunes filles en fleurs*. Paris: Pleiade, 1914.

Ritchie, J. F. *The African as Suckling and as Adult*. Livingstone, Northern Rhodesia: Rhodes-Livingstone Institute, 1943.

Róheim, Géza. "Psycho-Analysis and Anthropology." *Psycho-Analysis Today, Its Scope and Function*. Ed. Sándor Lorand. New York: Covici, Friede, 1933. 307–22.

Rose, Jacqueline. *States of Fantasy*. New York: Oxford UP, 1996.

Roudinesco, Elizabeth. *Jacques Lacan and Co.: A History of Psychoanalysis in France, 1925–1985*. Trans. Jeffrey Mehlman. Chicago: U of Chicago P, 1990.

Sachs, Wulf. *Psychoanalysis: Its Meaning and Practical Application*. London: Cassell, 1934.

———.*Black Hamlet*. 1937. With new introductions by Saul Dubow and Jacqueline Rose. Baltimore: Johns Hopkins UP, 1996.

———.*Black Anger*. New York: Grove, 1947.

———."The Mind of a Witch Doctor." *Book Find News* (Aug. 1947): 5.

Shain, Milton. *The Roots of Antisemitism in South Africa*. Charlottesville: U of Virginia P, 1994.

Spivak, Gayatri Chakravorty. "Echo." *New Literary History* 24.1 (1993): 17–63.

Weimann, Robert. *Shakespeare and the Popular Tradition in the Theater*. Trans. R. Schwarz. Baltimore: Johns Hopkins UP, 1978.

15

The Comedy of Domination: Psychoanalysis and the Conceit of Whiteness

Kalpana Seshadri-Crooks

> I have noticed . . . that my research demonstrating that race is merely a social and ideological construction helps little in getting taxis to pick me up late at night.
>
> —An African-American joke, qtd. in Roediger 1

Race and Psychoanalysis

It is no laughing matter to contend that colonialism has its humorous moments; even less amusing, perhaps, to propose that we view white racial identification as a joke. Without being facetious, I suggest that dominant racial identification—or whiteness—is implicated in Freud's theory of jokes, and that when threatened, such identification is susceptible to uncanny effects. I am not suggesting that we cannot read whiteness from other perspectives; rather, that the structure of jokes gives us access to the unconscious in a manner that usefully lays bare the mechanisms of racial identification and their ability to function in the colonial field.

Before I take up this argument, however, I must offer some disclaimers: This paper does not apply psychoanalytic concepts to issues of colonial domination and racism. (For studies that do, see Klineberg, Allport, and Kovel; also Lasker.) Instead, it is part of a larger project that assesses the uses and limits of psychoanalysis for discussions of racial subjectivity, specifically psychoanalysis's claim of global relevance. As a theory of subject formation resting on principles of sexual difference, psychoanalysis has universal aspirations that falter when brought to bear on issues of racial and colonial domination. This is so primarily because the discourse of race, to the extent that it is a modern European system of categorization, has significance only within Europe's cultural and political hegemony. When this discourse informs psychoanalytic theories of subjectivity, it radically limits and reorients notions of the subject as such (see Smith, Vardharajan, and Spivak).

Feminist psychoanalytic theorists now increasingly use psychoanalysis to address racialized subjectivity. Yet there has been much dissent among feminists and others engaged in antiracist work about the historical and cultural specificity of psychoanalysis. This dissent has challenged the individualist and familial bias of psychoanalysis, its often intractable claims of universality, its desire to privilege sex over other forms of difference, and the general hegemony of Western theories within which debates about psychoanalysis often seem symptomatic (see Gaines, Spillers, and Mama). Many Anglo-American feminists have noted the scandalous silence of feminist psychoanalysis about race (see Butler, Doane, Silverman, Abel, and Walton). With a few notable exceptions (for instance, Silverman and Walton), however, much of this exemplary work has focused on African Americans or other "people of color." In these discussions, whiteness often functions as an ontologically neutral category that advances a subject as raceless and unmarked as when "man" could appear as a genderless and universal term for humanity.

Emphasizing the constructed dimension of social categories and identities has led ideologically aware critics to attack the discourse of race in a haphazard and indiscriminate way, without clearly identifying the sources of power that preserve and reproduce racial distinctions.[1] As David Roediger, as well as Michael Omi and Howard Winant argued recently, insisting that race is a construct can translate rapidly into more-digestible claims that race is false consciousness; this insistence has worked well for conservative rhetoricians. Turning constructivism into voluntarism, these conservatives attack ameliorative strategies and social programs for racially disadvantaged groups.

Contrary to this voluntarism, I agree with Roediger that "the central political implication arising from the insight that race is socially constructed is the specific need to attack whiteness as a destructive ideology rather than to attack the concept of race abstractly. . . . [Since] *consciousness of whiteness also contains elements of a critique of that consciousness . . . we should encourage the growth of a politics based on hopeful signs of a popular giving up on whiteness*" (3; my emphasis). In an attempt to break the "hegemonic silence" (Walton 780) that has served either to trivialize or to reify racial identification, this paper places race and whiteness at the heart of Freudian theories of subjectivity.

We must take seriously that the modern discourse of race is a post-1400s

European invention, which differs markedly from other sociocultural hierarchies such as caste (*varna*) or occupational group (*jati*) in South Asia (Snowden, Bernal, Dumont, Gailey, and Nandy). As Roger Sanjek suggests in his Introduction to *Race*, race is a remarkable condensation of differences among social class, cultural practices, and language into physical appearance—specifically, skin color, facial features, and hair texture. He writes: "No other historical or ethnographic order . . . has been as globally inclusive in its assignment of social and cultural differences to 'natural causes' as has post-1400's racism" (2). Whiteness is a structuring principle of racial meaning; as a linguistic construct, it also subjects individuals to a phantasmatic identification that the body's surface seems to literalize. In this respect, we must consider whiteness per se and whiteness in principle as elaborate conceits.

The rich ambiguity of "conceit" is worth reviewing here. According to the *OED*, the word obtains from the idea of deception. Its meanings derive from an understanding of "personal opinion, judgment, or estimation." The more familiar use of "conceit" as "an overweening opinion of oneself; overestimation of one's own qualities, personal vanity or pride; conceitedness" dates from the seventeenth century. This word's figurative turn as a witticism, "a far-fetched turn of thought, figure, etc.; an affectation of thought" gained popularity in the seventeenth and eighteenth centuries. This alliance of belief, arrogance, and witticism makes thinking of whiteness as a conceit or linguistic knot quite appropriate.[2] To clarify our subjection to this conceit, we must note the reproduction of whiteness in the colonial scene, which offers the most "undisguised" view of race relations.

In the following section, I briefly locate the significance of race as a category of analysis by arguing for a more relational understanding of sexuality. I suggest that feminist accounts of sexual difference—despite their emphasis on the ideological or phantasmatic nature of identification—are necessarily incomplete to the extent that they downplay or ignore that racial identification is as crucial an element of subject formation. Using George Orwell's essay "Shooting an Elephant" (1935), I shall focus on a recurring moment when white identification gets reproduced in the colonial scene. My argument delineates the imbrication of whiteness and jokes, as well as the adjacency of jokes and the uncanny. On the one hand, the prevalence of "the white joke" sustains *and* threatens morbid arrangements of colonial power. The possibility of the joke's expression—usually signified by fears of native laughter—produces racial anxiety, and Orwell experiences this moment as uncanny. On the other hand, the containment of the joke can powerfully assist the reproduction of racial dominance. I intend not to collapse the differences between jokes and the uncanny, but to unearth why they sometimes coalesce in moments of intense racial anxiety. I hypothesize that this coalescence characterizes racial discourse; this combination may recur in other scenarios, but my primary concern is the reproduction of dominant whiteness.

Race and Sex

Feminist psychoanalysis has tended to prioritize discussion of sex over race. As Walton argued recently, the reasons for this can vary (779), but the result is an ongoing validation of the public/private split. In her excellent reading of "normative" sexual difference as a "dominant fiction," for instance, Kaja Silverman begins from an Althusserian premise that race and class identities are best understood as ideological interpellations. Later using Žižek's proposal that we consider "our" unconscious cathexis of the racially phobic figure, she states: "The emphasis which Žižek places on race is extremely welcome. The unconscious articulation of racial and class difference is facilitated, however, by the articulation of an even more inaugural difference, which we also need to conceptualize ideologically—sexual difference" (23).

That sex must be understood as phantasmatic belief is unquestionable; what is questionable is Silverman's assumption that sexual identity precedes racial identity because the former emerges in the family. This inadvertent chronologizing (I write "inadvertent" because Silverman charges Stephen Heath with the same infraction in his critique of Althusser [23]) hinges on the feminist axiom that sexual identity is both private and public, while race and class, insofar as they invoke a group or collectivity, belong only to the public domain. This designation of sex as primarily a familial narrative (and certainly more private than race or class) serves—contrary to Silverman's aspiration—to reinstate the public/private dichotomy, with all of its attendant problems. The foundational role Silverman assigns the family is clear in her discomfort with Laclau's positioning of "the people" at the center of ideological struggle:

> Laclau's formulation makes no provision either for the typical fantasy or the parental imago, and hence fails to account for that phenomenon without which it is impossible to manufacture a social consensus–belief. . . . It also locates at the center of the ideological domain a term which more properly belongs at its periphery. The category of "the people" exists in an intimate relation with a much more pivotal element of our "reality"—the family. It is from this element that it derives its affective force. (30)

I do not disagree with Silverman that the family is a site of psychic reality, but I do question the notion that we must separate the family from the people as a "much more" significant element of psychic reality. If we are to understand the reality of race, it must be granted coevality with sex; not to do so trivializes the effects of racial identification. This is especially crucial since, while everyday life regularly contests gender's "essential" meanings, nothing today seems more "real" than race: We see almost no challenges to race beyond the empty academic claim that it is a "construct." We can even attribute some of this refusal to consider race coeval with sex to the particularity of "whiteness" as an ideological structure.

Let me elaborate on this claim: Mary Ellen Goodman's pioneering work, *Race Awareness in Young Children* (1952), is an account of her ethnographic fieldwork dealing with four-year-olds and their acquisition and perception of racial identity. One hundred and three black and white children from New Dublin, New York, were tested by play activities and interviews for their nascent ideas about race and color. Goodman noted the children's varied levels of race awareness and their command of expressive vocabulary. While Goodman's observations about inter-racial attitudes among the children—on the eve of the *Brown* v. *Board of Education* decision—are now largely of historical interest and current research has super-seded them (see Holmes, Aboud), her findings about the acquisition of racial iden-tity have outlasted the effects of landmark legislation.[3]

Unfortunately, most scholarly attention has addressed the vexatious issue of black children's (secret and sometimes overt) predilection toward whiteness and their ambivalence toward their "blackness." Other researchers have found that regional and other variations alter these findings (see Clark 44–45, Aboud 37, and Holmes 54), but they have not commented at length on an interesting variable among black and white children. As Canadian researcher Francis Aboud puts it: "White children knew their label earlier than Black children. The Blacks knew their correct label only if they already perceived themselves to be similar to other Blacks, whereas some Whites had acquired their label before the perceived simi-larity and some after" (57). However, Robyn Holmes, whose young subjects gen-erally seem well adjusted to the "reality of their race," notes the following: "One major difference between European-American and African-American children emerged while they were creating and describing their self-portraits: All of the African-American children emphasized clearly the color of their skin when describing their pictures. By contrast, only two of the European-American chil-dren did. Most of the European-American children focused on other details and attributes in describing themselves" (49).

In some cases, as Goodman notes, black children willfully misused color vocab-ulary despite their otherwise precocious expressive ability. Goodman usefully reads such "resistance" as an index of aggression and wishfulness (55–59). We can therefore contrast black children's uneasy acceptance of their racial identity and their often conscious assimilation of racial discourse as yet another form of social regulation with Goodman's observation that white children do not come to "accept" their whiteness, but consider themselves always already white. In her chapter on white children, Goodman shows that their curiosity pertains not to themselves but to those they perceive as different:

> "Why is she that color? Is she sunburned? Can she change?" These questions and more have come from our children. They are conspicuously uniform in one respect: These white children do not ask about themselves—*why* their own color or the lack of it. They take it completely for granted, in the fashion of "primitive" tribesmen, that they are "the people." The others, those under the shadow of color, "they're different," as Paul P. explicitly puts it. Being different, they are, as Diane says, "strangers." (68)

Unlike African-Americans or other "people of color," who often represent their racialization as a conscious, historical discovery, access to whiteness is never available to anamnesis. This alerts us to the deep relation between whiteness and the unconscious and thus of the specificity of dominant subject formation. In Lacanian terms, the discourse of whiteness can be said to function as a condition of dominant subjectivity: It inserts the subject into the symbolic order. According to Lacan, this insertion entails a process of splitting, in which language invests the subject with an identity that is purely representational, thus alienating the subject from its "self" and engendering the unconscious. By acceding to the symbolic order—becoming gendered and raced as white, the subject-to-be is constituted as a speaking being (Lacan 284–85).

The particularity of white identity compels us to delineate the inextricable relation between sexual identity and racial identity. Thus we must do more than merely include the forces of public culture in pregiven theories of sexuality; we must discern how the seemingly extrafamilial signifier of race, which critics falsely consign to the public realm since it seems to invoke a collectivity, intersects with that of sex to produce the subject. This intersection asks us to reread theories of sexual identification in order to render visible the color of the law enforcing racial and sexual normativity at perhaps the same moment. Accordingly, my essay focuses on a moment when colonialism pointedly reproduces whiteness. Taking my cue from Fanon, I focus on a moment of intense racial anxiety as a gateway to analyze the structure of identification that is being threatened.[4]

My argument about the unconscious roots of whiteness and the successful reiteration of white identity hinges on a claim that identity is always partial and subject to failure. This failure occurs because, like sexual identity, the drama of race is not played out as a complete "event." As Judith Butler explains: "Identification is constantly figured as a desired event or accomplishment, but one which finally is never achieved; identification is the phantasmatic staging of the event. In this sense, identifications belong to the imaginary; they are phantasmatic efforts of alignment, loyalty, ambiguous and cross-corporeal cohabitation; they unsettle the 'I'; they are the sedimentation of the 'we' in the constitution of any 'I,' the structuring presence of alterity in the very formulation of the 'I' " (105).

This split between the I and the we, which is analogous to the subject's primary division in language (between the I that utters and the subject of the enunciation), internally ruptures whiteness between consciousness of being white and a desire to possess whiteness. Roediger seizes on this nodal point as a way to dismantle whiteness. Since the moment when whiteness is assumed has yet to be articulated, however, all we can reasonably do here is note the contingent reproduction of raced selves.

Is There a Joke in This Text?

In *Jokes and Their Relation to the Unconscious* (1905) and his 1927 essay "Humour," Freud draws analogies between jokes and dreams, especially concerning the process of *Entstellung*, or distortion. For Freud, this process, which usually involves condensation and displacement, characterizes joke- and dream-work. In "The 'Uncanny' " (1919), Freud also relates the uncanny to dreams, but nowhere does he note resemblances between jokes and the *unheimlich*. I suggest that these two concepts exist in almost complete isolation in Freud's theory primarily because the anxiety that yokes the two together violently, to borrow a term from Freud, is "*abseits*," or "out of the way": It is specific to the colonial scene. The differential of race—a factor of subject constitution and egoic identification that Freud professed no conscious interest in studying—produces this anxiety. Before making this apparently far-fetched claim, we must turn to language to discover the adjacency of jokes and the uncanny.

Much of Freud's argument about the uncanny rests on the etymological ambiguity of *heimlich* and *unheimlich*, "the meaning of which develops in the direction of ambivalence, until it finally coincides with its opposite" ("Uncanny" 226). Freud elucidates the point at which these words meld into each other—the fine line between familiarity and strangeness makes clear a deep relation between dreams and the uncanny. This ambiguous melding translates well into the English language; significantly, English offers another convergence between the canny and uncanny that proves useful for our purposes.

According to the *OED*, the English use the word "canny" to denote sly Scottish humor (see Weber). The same dictionary also gives us "mischievous and malicious" as synonyms for "uncanny." The canny and uncanny thus meld into each other over tendentious humor, or, in the words of the *OED*, "sly and malicious mischief."

Related meanings of "canny" as malicious mischief and sly humor are the source of a particular genre of "ethnic jokes" that Christie Davies identifies as referring mostly to Calvinists in Europe and Puritans (or Yankees) in the United States. According to Davies, we can attribute the European claim that Calvinists and other Protestant groups are "canny" to the fact that they "produced many of the merchants, entrepreneurs, and capitalists who laid the foundations of the modern industrial and commercial world. The hardheaded calculating spirit, the sense of work as a calling, the ascetic dedication to gaining, saving, investing . . . were conducive to their success in the marketplace, but for others there was a grim, joyless, over-competitive side, which they saw as the unacceptable face of Calvinism" (108–9). In this respect, the canny "other"—the Scotsman or Yankee —who is an extreme embodiment of capitalist virtue (opposed to disavowed sexuality, primitivism, or stupidity) is not other at all, but really an inflated or distorted version of the self. This fraught proximity joins the canny to the register of familiarity, disclosing a nexus of identifications that in a colonial situation has an uncanny potential.

The uncanny and jokes share many qualities, the most notable being the process of exposure. Exposure manifests itself in tendentious jokes that say something forbidden (*Jokes* 106) and in the uncanny as the persistence of secrets ("Uncanny" 225). Other structural connections include doubleness in the uncanny and the Janus face of jokes, recurrence of the same, repetition compulsion of the uncanny and repetition in mimicry; and the use of words or symbols like things. The uncanny and jokes also share in the rediscovery of something very familiar (*Jokes* 121; "Uncanny" 245); ignorance about the source of affect; automatism; and intellectual uncertainty about the object as animate or inanimate. When grouped around the idea of exposure, these elements converge as peculiar features of colonial and race relations. We shall see this convergence manifest itself in Orwell's anecdotal essays about British India.

Freud does not remark on the structural connections between jokes and the uncanny, but he does make a seemingly irrelevant joke in "The 'Uncanny'": "There is a joking saying [that] love is home-sickness" (245). This joke is meant to illustrate not the subject of the joke sentence—love—but its object: home-sickness, or more precisely, the home (*Heim*). Here home also stands for nation: "Whenever a man dreams of a place or a country and says to himself, while he is still dreaming, this place is familiar to me, . . . we may interpret the place as being his mother's genitals" (245). Freud's remarks do not answer the question What is love, but rather What is home(sickness)? The joke derives from the fact that the speaker does not enunciate "woman's genitals"; the listener must deduce this pun.

I seize on this moment in Freud's text primarily because it represents a peculiar juxtaposition of humor and the uncanny; It is difficult to differentiate one from the other. It is also not merely fortuitous that the joke's basis is the enigma of the Other: The punning substitution of a woman's genitalia or womb for home signifies her lack precisely because the home is a synecdoche for nation.

Significantly, Orwell's anecdotal essay "Shooting an Elephant" begins with an overwhelming sense of homesickness—a sentiment Freud has jokingly rendered as uncanny. But Orwell's homesickness apparently has little to do with nostalgia and everything to do with a hatred for his contradictory situation. Raymond Williams has sympathetically described Orwell's homesickness as "complicated": "He was stuck . . . between hatred of the empire he was serving and rage against the native people who opposed it and made his immediate job difficult" (3). Orwell's anecdote is especially interesting because explosive, uncontrollable laughter hovers menacingly at its margins. Orwell's principal concern is laughter—native laughter. When he is tripped on the football field, for instance, "the crowd yell[s] with hideous laughter" (148). The people also stand on street corners and jeer at him. Yet we *hear* no laughter in Orwell's text—sighs and gasps, perhaps, but no laughter. All the same, the irrepressible threat of laughter in this essay powerfully implies the circulation of an unspeakable joke in the text, whose narration and sharing might potentially dismember Orwell's white identification.

Jokes and the Comic

We must now recall some of Freud's salient points about jokes, especially their relation to comedy. This is necessary because laughter alone does not easily clarify whether a given statement or situation should be received as comic, a joke, or as a sign of humor. In *Jokes and Their Relation to the Unconscious*, Freud distinguishes among jokes (the verbal artifact), the comic (scenarios of excess physical exertion), and humor (the process of making light of a grave situation); above all, he insists on the need to distinguish jokes from the comic (9–13). Freud also divides jokes into two types of jokes: innocent (usually verbal jokes, puns) and tendentious (jokes usually engaging a thought or concept). He further subdivides tendentious jokes into obscene or sexual jokes that substitute for sexual contact (98)—these are also called "exposing jokes" (97)—and hostile or aggressive jokes "that open sources of pleasure that have become inaccessible" (103). (Freud also includes in the category of tendentious jokes those that target institutions in a cynical way [113] and skeptical jokes that question the certainty of our knowledge [115], but he does not devote much time to analyzing either of these specific kinds of jokes.) Freud's analysis of tendentious jokes is obviously the most pertinent for our critique of racial identification. Before we discern the uncanny joke of white identification, however, we must examine the persistence of comedy and its relation to racial jokes in colonial situations.

Among jokes, the comic, and humor, Freud argues that jokes alone bear a direct relation to the unconscious. Though humor and the comic sometimes overlap, they arise (he claims) from the preconscious (208).[5] He remarks further: "A joke is made, the comic is found—and first and foremost in people, only by a subsequent transference in things, situations, and so on, as well. As regards jokes, we know that the sources of the pleasure that is to be fostered lie in the subject himself and not in outside people" (181).

In his analysis of hostile jokes, however, Freud seems deliberately to ignore what today would be called the "ethnic" or "racist" joke. Freud deals only with those hostile jokes that evade internal and external obstacles to the expression of aggression: He focuses on jokes the powerless make to overcome the powerful (104) or rebuke them indirectly (the *Schadchen* jokes). While we can perhaps read Freud's circumscription as symptomatic of the vagaries of his Jewish identification,[6] his circumscription is nonetheless based on a notion of civil discourse that assumes social homogeneity: "[All] moral rules for the restrictions of active hatred give the clearest evidence to this day that they were originally framed for a small society of fellow clansmen. In so far as we are all able to feel that we are members of one people, we allow ourselves to disregard most of these restrictions in relation to a foreign people" (102).

Freud implies here that hostile jokes substitute for violence that is forbidden expression in civil society, just as obscene jokes substitute for spontaneous touching that moral law renders taboo. In both cases, repressed aggression—sexual and hostile (99)—is the joke's propelling force. In this respect, jokes thrive on moral and legal interdiction; they are in part produced and licensed by the law. Submission to this law, which produces the joke, also confirms the identities of the joker, victim, and listener. Thus in Freud's rather narrow conception of hostile jokes, racist humor—whether in a multicultural democracy or colony—becomes unthinkable (Neve 42). On the subject of anti-Semitic jokes, for instance, Freud was perfunctory: "The jokes made about Jews by foreigners are for the most part brutal comic stories in which a joke is made unnecessary by the fact that Jews are regarded by foreigners as comic figures" (111).

This peculiar disavowal of the racist joker (Freud implies that there is no such person, as there are no racist jokes per se) or, more properly, the comedian as joker (!), again elides the possibility of conceiving of racist jokes. The following exam-

ples from Blanche Knott's *Truly Tasteless Jokes* nonetheless attest to their existence: "What's the difference between a pothole and a black? You'd swerve to
avoid a pothole" (VIII.20); "What makes blacks so horny? Afro-disiacs" (VI.24);
"How come Pakistanis go around with their flies open? In case they have to count
to eleven" (VIII.38). That these are technically jokes and not comic stories is, I
think, indisputable. Yet Freud's basic exclusion of the racist joke, and his concern
to relegate it to the comic, demands that we reconceive the way such jokes function
in a multiracial, "liberal" democratic society: We must discover the relation
between such jokes and racist humor in the colony.

Racist jokes in a civil society often emerge from ethnic heterogeneity; surfacing
on the cusp between inside and outside, they also mark social boundaries by treating citizens as foreigners. We sometimes hear that such jokes are a healthy sign in
a civil society, in which interracial aggression is forbidden. For instance, Arthur
Asa Berger adopts this libertarian position when arguing about the United States:
"America is a nation of immigrants—each with different customs and traditions
and values—and is, par excellence, a breeding ground for ethnic jokes. Among
other things, these jokes help release aggressive and hostile feelings in people and,
in so doing, help facilitate the relatively peaceful coexistence of different ethnic
groups in America" (65).

A related view, which emphasizes the function of humor, concerns the hostile
joke as a "safety valve." Jerry Palmer discusses this in *Taking Humour Seriously*:
"In the 'safety valve' thesis the observation of a relationship between taboo and
humour leads to the conclusion that humour operates to release the pressure of
inhibition without affecting the application of the inhibition in non-comic circumstances" (61). In other words, the joke releases *and* contains antisocial impulses.
Accordingly, as Palmer observes, the joke surely has an ability to overturn social
norms and restrictions on hostility. The official proscription against aggression
perpetuates an economy of violence in which the displacement of hostility into
jokes creates further differentiation and hatred.

It is therefore important to acknowledge the joke's power, and to read it as
symptomatic of a rechanneling—not inhibition—of hostility. Not to do so would
idealize race relations, imagining that they are fully regulated by social inhibitions.
In material terms, this would deny the efficacy of language in reproducing racial
hostility, and the institutionalized oppression of "people of color," especially
"black" people. This idealization would also leave unaddressed the unconscious
structure of whiteness, which, following Etienne Balibar, we should understand as
"an active formation" (40) continuous with the racial structures of high colonialism and slavery.

I don't wish to enter into a debate here about the sociological meaning of jokes.

Both Christie Davies and Elliot Oring have usefully criticized attempts to read ethnic jokes as crude indicators of social relations and levels of hostility against specific groups (see esp. Davies 137); they contend that such arguments founder on inaccurate and inconsistent assumptions. While their claims are generally persuasive, Davies and Oring, wishing to preserve the spontaneity of the joking relationship, largely misconceive the debate itself by addressing the content of jokes and not the mechanism of joking, which reveals much more about ethnic identifications. Assertions that jokes are either responsible for or entirely innocent of racial oppression therefore move us unhelpfully from the joke's unconscious flirtation with the law to the joker's intentionality and his or her conscious deployment of jokes as insults. Indeed, to debate this issue in this way is to be deflected by the comic and to miss the joke. This deflection impoverishes our analysis of how variations in the dialectical pressure of aggression and inhibition—conditions of the joke—produce different joke situations indicating shifts in the history of racism and its common sense.

We can note these shifts whenever jokes recur in such ostensibly disparate situations as colonialism and modern, postcolonial society. Racist jokes in the former surface in an economy of inhibition and aggression. Yet we have reason to ask, What if the interdiction against the free expression of aggression were lifted, as in scenes of colonialism and slavery—that is, with "a foreign people" one governs? Freud does not consider this possibility. While democratic societies ostensibly prohibit acts of brutality, the compensatory idea of "free speech" allows jokes to reiterate racial identity and engender hostility. Recalling Freud, the relegation of racist humor to the comic also overlooks a salient aspect of race relations in a democratic society: the black man as aggressor rather than object of ridicule. ("What do you call a white man surrounded by three blacks? Victim. And what do you call a white man surrounded by three hundred blacks? Warden" [Knott Vlll.16].) This quite widespread representation of black men dramatizes the difference between racist humor in contemporary civil society and in the scene of European high colonialism, in which aggression is *not* forbidden and inequality and social fragmentation are structurally enforced and legislated. However, we shall see that with Orwell, who considered himself a "liberal" and an opponent of the empire, self-censorship of free aggression (which was something that he, like his character Flory in *Burmese Days*, could officially admit to his peers) leads to its displacement onto the elephant.

Let us recall that for Freud, nonconformity is the joke's optimal condition: "A particularly favourable occasion for tendentious jokes is presented when the intended rebellious criticism is directed against the subject himself, or . . . against someone in whom the subject has a share—a collective person, that is (the subject's own nation, for instance)" (*Jokes* 111). Whereas jokes are largely self-inflicted in Freud's conception, the comic is other-directed. This claim that the joke is predominantly dissident, and the comic reproductive of power relations, produces a unique reading of the colonial scene, as I will soon show. Freud's observation about the joke's reliance on inhibited hostility bears out in such a situation. We can see this in a quite exceptional instance of the misplaced joke—Mr. Fielding's taboo joke about "whiteness" in Forster's *A Passage to India* (1924). Since Fielding had been "caught by India late" (79) and "had no racial feeling" of which he was conscious (80), he is able to crack jokes:

> The remark that did him most harm at the club was a silly aside to the effect that the so-called white races are really pinko-gray. He only said this to be cheery, he did not realize that "white" has no more to do with colour than "God save the King" with god, and that it is the height of impropriety to consider what it does connote. The pinko-gray male whom he addressed was subtly scandalized; his sense of insecurity was awoken, and he communicated it to the rest of the herd. (80)

Most racial humor in the colony is—predictably enough—comic. The colonizer's need to infantilize the native to sustain the logic of the civilizing mission produces more comic stories than jokes. The existence of numerous novels, caricatures, and representations of natives in colonial literature well attests to these elements' comic importance. In a scenario of outright racial domination—whether colonialism or slavery—race relations are always "comic" and the other is figured derisively. Only when such domination is threatened—as in the antebellum South, the civil-rights movement in the United States, and independence movements (for instance, the prevalence of Gandhi jokes during the Indian freedom struggle)— are jokes possible while the other is in the process of being rendered criminal and not comical (see Michaels). Yet when interdictions against the free expression of hostility and aggression toward natives are lifted, as in many colonial situations, the only unspeakable topic is the foundation of "freedom" itself, which the conceit of whiteness grounds as a legislated inequality.[7] We recall that taboo is fallow ground for self-inflicted, hostile jokes.

The Reproduction of Whiteness

Concerning uncanny jokes, let me stress that I am not interpreting stereotypical moments when the other's laughter is experienced as demonic. In fact, this perception of "hideous" laughter, far from being specific to the colonial scene, is endemic to the gothic as well as such popular-cultural genres as horror films and crime fiction. This laughter, while undoubtedly caught up in notions of the uncanny, nonetheless gets dissociated from joke-work. I am focusing instead on the inherent performativity of the identity of the colonizer, who stages his authority with the paraphernalia of guns and ammunition. I rely here on Judith Butler's formulation: "The 'performative' dimension of construction is precisely the forced reiteration of norms. In this sense, then, it is not only that there are constraints to performativity; rather, constraint calls to be rethought as the very condition of performativity. . . . Performativity cannot be understood outside of a process of iterability, a regularized and constrained repetition of norms. And this repetition is not performed *by* a subject; this repetition is what enables a subject and constitutes the temporal condition for the subject" (94–95).

Consider now what Orwell says about the Burmese in "Shooting": "They were watching me as they would watch a conjurer about to perform a trick. They did not like me, but with the magical rifle in my hands I was momentarily worth watching" (152). The Burmese witness the reproduction of the colonizer's whiteness; any threat to that performativity will result in the literal failure of the subject's emergence. That such a failure might generate laughter suggests that there is a joke (the rediscovery of something very familiar?) suppressed in this iteration of identity, and that *"the white man" is both the subject and object of this joke*. Let us recall Freud's formula for the joke's transaction:

> Generally speaking, a tendentious joke calls for three people: in addition to the one who makes the joke, there must be a second who is taken as the object of the hostile or sexual aggressiveness, and a third in whom the joke's aim of producing pleasure is fulfilled . . . it is not the person who makes the joke who laughs at it and who therefore enjoys its pleasurable effect, but the inactive listener. (*Jokes* 100)

What does it mean to say that Orwell is the teller and victim of his own joke, a joke he dare not share? Possible moments of performative failure, which Orwell figures as exposure, are fraught with racial anxiety when the mask of authority begins to slip. This sense of failure refers to the constitutive split within whiteness, discussed earlier. Orwell articulates this split as the identitarian anxiety of "looking and feeling a fool" (151, 156), thereby expressing the self-division Freud suggests is endemic to the joking subject: "If one has occasion as a doctor to make the acquaintance of one of those people who, though not remarkable in other ways, are well known in their circle as jokers and originators of many viable jokes, one may be surprised to discover that the joker is a disunited personality, disposed to neurotic disorders" (*Jokes* 142).

While "disunity" or alienation of the "self" in language is constitutive of subjectivity per se (and for Freud the archetypal joker is a Jew who makes Jewish jokes), dominant white identity seems to rely on its inability to discharge the aggression of the joke's nonsense—its rhythm and rhyme—which is its true purpose and motivation (125–26). To revise Freud's economic metaphor slightly, the reproduction of whiteness would entail a tremendous expenditure of psychic energy, which the joke paradoxically can help conserve. ("We take note of the fact that *economy in expenditure on inhibition or suppression* appears to be the secret of the pleasurable effect of tendentious jokes, and pass on to the mechanism of pleasure in innocent jokes" [119].)

For Orwell in "Shooting," killing the elephant fundamentally contains this moment of discharge that threatens the subject with dismemberment and desubjectification. In an oft-quoted scene from "Shooting," for instance, Orwell speaks of the colonizer as

> a sort of hollow, posing dummy, the conventionalized figure of a sahib. For it is the condition of his rule that he shall spend his life in trying to impress the "natives." . . . He wears a mask and his face grows to fit it. I had got to shoot the elephant. I had committed myself to doing it when I sent for the rifle. A sahib has got to act like a sahib; he has got to appear resolute, to know his own mind and do definite things. To come all that way, rifle in hand, with two thousand people marching at my heels, and then to trail feebly away, having done nothing, no, that was impossible. The crowd would laugh at me. And my whole life, every white man's life in the East, was one long struggle not to be laughed at. (152–53)

The anecdote after all concerns a crisis averted; white identity is successfully reconsolidated.

Here we must contend with a prevalent reading of this essay, which claims that it exemplifies the Hegelian master-slave dialectic or, more narrowly, illustrates the master's paradoxical dependence on the slave. In *Domination and the Arts of Resistance* James C. Scott reads Orwell's inability to do the "logical thing" (10)— that is, his not shooting the elephant—as a sign of the master's compulsion to follow, which Scott calls the "public transcript":[8] "Orwell is no more free to be himself, to break convention, than a slave would be in the presence of a tyrannical master. If subordination requires a credible performance of humility and deference, so domination seems to require a credible performance of haughtiness and mastery. There are, however, . . . differences. If a slave transgresses the script he risks a beating, while Orwell risks only ridicule" (11).

Considering Scott's larger thesis that the hidden transcripts of the weak subvert the conformist imperatives of the powerful, this is a persuasive and necessary reading of Orwell's essay. However, my paper aims to prove that the risk Orwell faced in failing to perform was more than ridicule—that he was threatened with death and dismemberment. Given my concern with whiteness, to focus merely on the anxiety of ridicule would overlook the sustaining mechanisms of domination at work. To say that Orwell wants to contain native laughter is not incorrect; nor am I suggesting that we cannot read this anecdote as a record of native resistance to domination, which takes the familiar route of the lampoon (Freud has usefully described this process as unmasking [*Jokes* 201]). However, to focus on the broad workings of power alone ignores the contradictions of its specific manifestations. More important, such banal reasoning would lose sight of our larger problematic: how racial identification, and not merely its accompanying forms of power, emerges and recurs in such fraught scenarios. This problematic addresses specific questions: How is whiteness implicated in the joke's structure, and what are the psychic repercussions of the joke's public eruption? Additionally, what does being "white" mean, and how does racial classification function for "white" subjects? To answer these questions, we must consider Orwell's statements about racial difference.

Race, Class, and the Human

In his essay "Marrakech" (1939), Orwell is very candid about cultural and racial difference: "When you walk through a town like this . . . it is always difficult to believe that you are walking among human beings. All colonial empires are in reality founded upon that fact. The people have brown faces—besides, there are so many of them! Are they really the same flesh as yourself? Do they even have names? or are they merely a kind of undifferentiated brown stuff, about as individual as bees or coral insects? They rise out of the earth, they sweat and starve for a few years, and then they sink back into the nameless mounds of the graveyard and nobody notices that they are gone" (181).

Orwell's questions resemble a characteristic "intellectual" doubt about the uncanny—whether an object is really animate or inanimate. Yet though his doubt borders on the uncanny, it is not reducible to this phenomenon.[9] Our problem is to gauge how racial difference influences Orwell's notion of humanity. Lest we perceive his understanding of the "other" as class-specific, Orwell himself corrects us:

> All people who work with their hands are partly invisible, and the more important the work they do, the less visible they are. Still, a white skin is always fairly conspicuous. In northern Europe, when you see a labourer ploughing a field, you probably give him a second glance. In a hot country, anywhere south of Gibraltar or east of Suez, the chances are that you don't even see him. I have noticed this again and again. In a tropical landscape one's eye takes in everything except the human beings. It

takes in the dried up soil, the prickly pear, the palm tree and the distant mountain, but it always misses the peasant hoeing at his patch. He is the same colour as the earth, and a great deal less interesting to look at. . . . People with brown skins are next door to invisible. (183–84, 186)

Orwell is particularly useful in articulating the colonizer's relationship to race and class. He recognizes that race—not class or profession—primarily defines his sense of self. For instance, in *The Road to Wigan Pier* (1937), he claims: "In an 'outpost of Empire' like Burma the class question appeared at first sight to have been shelved. There was no obvious class friction here, because the all important thing was not whether you had been to one of the right schools but whether your skin was technically white. As a matter of fact most of the white men in Burma were not of the type who in England would be called 'gentlemen' . . . [but] they were 'white men,' in contradistinction to the other and inferior class, the 'natives' " (123–24).

Orwell is quite conscious here of being "white" and not just English (he often uses the term "European"). Yet he also admits that "brown" people's invisibility is "strange" and confusing. When he does recognize their humanity, it is always a surprise to him and *almost* uncanny. In "Marrakech" he finally sees a file of old women who regularly carry firewood past his house. Previously, he registered these women only as "Firewood . . . passing." Then one day, he claims that "for the first time" he notices them as "bodies":

Every afternoon a file of very old women passes down the road outside my house, each carrying a load of firewood. . . . It was only that one day I happened to be walking behind them, and the curious up-and-down motion of the load of wood drew my attention to the human being beneath it. Then for the first time I noticed the poor old earth-coloured bodies, bodies reduced to bones and leathery skin, bent double under the crushing weight. Yet I suppose I had not been five minutes on Moroccan soil before I noticed the overloading of donkeys and was infuriated by it. (185–86)

In his essay "A Hanging" (1931), Orwell also suddenly acknowledges the reality of an emaciated native prisoner. Walking on his way to the gallows, the man avoids a puddle, and Orwell is astonished by this man's humanity: "His eyes saw the yellow gravel and the grey walls, and his brain still remembered, foresaw, reasoned—reasoned even about puddles. He and we were a party of men walking together, seeing, hearing, feeling, understanding the same world" (46). Why is the other's humanity a shock here, an *almost* uncanny surprise? We must infer that in the extremity of colonial contexts, Orwell realizes that whiteness is coterminous with being human, and to be human one must basically be white.[10]

Judith Butler has argued relatedly that heterosexual identity, to the extent that it is assumed in compliance with the law, is based on the "regulation of phantasmatic identification" (97). This regulation, which enforces normativity by figuring "difference" as a monstrous outcome—castration or feminization for a man and phallicism for a woman—demands that we abject homosexuality. Butler writes: "The abjection of homosexuality can take place only through an identification with that abjection, an identification that must be disavowed, an identification that one fears to make only because one has already made it, an identification that institutes that abjection and sustains it" (112). In other words, the abjection of homosexuality enables, even produces, heterosexuality. "Heterosexual identification takes place *not* through the refusal to identify as homosexual but *through* an identification with an abject homosexuality" (112). Butler also claims that we can witness this logic of repudiation in the delineation of other hegemonic subject positions such as whiteness (112).

Butler's insight reconfigures whiteness—and the radical discontinuity with races on which it insists—as the abjection of racial others. However, we must modify this formulation before we can use it to illuminate racial identification. Butler's thesis that an abjection of same-sex desire founds heterosexuality relies on her interrogation of Freud's premise that desire and identification are mutually exclusive. Insofar as sexual desire is always deflected through prohibition and identifications are "multiple and contestatory," she writes earlier, "to identify is not [necessarily] to oppose desire" (99). Thus the recovery of the prohibited object is also the recovery of sameness: Identification functions as affiliation and connection. However, claiming racial sameness—especially in contexts of colonial domination—invokes universalist (as opposed to a practical) humanism, which Balibar demonstrates is entirely compatible with racism (63). We must argue instead that whiteness requires the abjection not of an identification with color per se (which would imply a shift from Butler's emphasis on relationships to objects), but with *whiteness* as a color (what Goodman has called the "brownness continuum" [224]) and with differences among humans. In this respect, white identification disavows crucial knowledge about difference, which brings it close to the structure of fetishism.

Reformulating racial abjection in this way is necessary to avoid another humanist trap: the incorporation of racial and cultural others. This divergence from Butler's model, which Butler anticipates (116), can be construed as the "ethical" moment in the critique of racial identification. I allude here to Emmanuel Levinas's critique of knowledge as the "relationship of the same to the other" (85) and his repeated emphasis on the subject's awareness of its responsibility to the Other. Levinas construes this "Other" as an unrecuperable alterity; he also advances an ethical relationship that does not presuppose interchangeability or community.

What's the Joke?

We can now return to the question of whiteness and the unspeakable joke. We discern the knowledge that whiteness abjects, by which it is haunted, in the threatened eruption of the uncanny joke. The unspeakable joke threatens to expose whiteness as a "ruse," to adopt Butler's term. The ruse is that whiteness is only a performance—not the essence—of authority; that as a color whiteness is but one element in a series of differences, and not the inaugural signifier of difference as such; and that whiteness is reducible to a metaphor that is produced in its citation of radical discontinuity—it does not constitute a stable presence. This joke is the colonizer's secret and it cannot be shared in "Shooting an Elephant" if colonial authority is to be reiterated. The following joke elucidates a similar premise:

> *The Elephant Joke*:
> There was once a Texan who had an unreasonable dislike of elephants. Realizing it bordered on a phobia, he consulted a psychiatrist, who told him it was a fairly common problem. "The cure is straightforward," said the shrink. "You have to go to Africa and shoot one." The idea appealed to the Texan, so he flew to Kenya and hired a guide to take him on an elephant hunting safari. The hunter's right-hand man turned out to be a native who in turn hired a bunch of his fellow tribesmen to spread out in a long line, beat drums and blow horns, and drive the elephants toward the blind where the hunters were waiting. As they waited, the noise grew louder and louder until out of the bush with much clanging and shouting burst the head beater. The Texan drew a bead and shot him right between the eyes.
> "What the hell'd you do that for?" bellowed the guide. "He's my best beater—I've worked with him for twenty years!"
> "If there's anything I hate worse than elephants," drawled the Texan, "it's big, noisy niggers." (*Tasteless* VI.86–87)

Let us now address a question I have postponed until now: What exactly is the joke in "Shooting an Elephant"? On a related note, given Orwell's anxiety about his authority, why not simply consider whiteness an ideology that produces native laughter from its inherent tendency to exaggerate differences? In other words, why isn't whiteness merely comic rather than a joke? To substantiate my thesis that whiteness is implicated in a joke structure, I will consider the particularities of the uncanny joke in "Shooting."

Let us recall Freud's claim that the threat of exposure is characteristic of jokes as they release unconscious inhibitions, whereas the comic is preconscious activity. There are two moments in "Shooting" when Orwell fears that uncontrollable laughter will erupt: First when he fears that he will not kill the elephant and thus perform as a true colonial. Second, when he fears that this failure will lead to his being trampled like the coolie: "A white man mustn't be frightened in front of 'natives,' " Orwell remarks, "and so, in general, he isn't frightened. The sole thought in my mind was that if anything went wrong those two thousand Burmans would see me pursued, caught, trampled on and reduced to a grinning corpse like the Indian up the hill. And if that happened it was quite probable that some of them would laugh" (153–54).

In both cases, Orwell fears that laughter will obtain from violence—that is, from killing or being killed. Thus he must manage this violence to suppress an uncanny joke about his whiteness. It is worth noting how the natives' laughter signifies this uncanny joke. Orwell's perception of the other in "Shooting" and in "Marrakech" is not wholly uncanny (that is, generative of fear and dread) until the loss of his difference emerges as a threat.

In "Shooting," for instance, the dead coolie whom the elephant has ground underfoot generates uncanny dread by his grotesqueness: Orwell first describes him as devilish and grinning. When Orwell realizes that he could end up like the coolie—that his skin might also be stripped clean, so he would not be identifiable anymore—he suffers an overwhelming sense of dread. What is anxiety-producing is the possibility of becoming like the other: The loss of difference here is the loss not only of whiteness and authority but of his humanity. This might induce laughter—the Burmese natives might perceive what Orwell perhaps already knows, that under his white man's mask he is just like them, their inhuman double, and *that* is uncanny. However, to idealize this exposure and deauthorization as a site of resistance in colonial discourse would be utopian. This moment signifies the extinction of meaning, because it promises not the pleasures of the imaginary (the refusal to obey the law), but literal death and dismemberment.

The elephant is the ambivalent figure of this meaninglessness, and thus of the joke nonsense that renders Orwell's anecdote an overdetermined elephant joke.[11] From this perspective, it is impossible to ignore the condensations and displacements that aggregate around the elephant. For instance, there are two moments in the anecdote when a marked slippage occurs between the threat that the crowd and elephant pose. When speaking of his need for an elephant rifle after encountering the coolie's gruesome corpse, Orwell admits: "It made me vaguely uneasy. I had no intention of shooting the elephant—I had merely sent for the rifle to defend myself if necessary—and it is always unnerving to have a crowd following you" (151). The condensation of the natives with the elephant in the last sentence registers in Orwell's use of the em-dash, for the peculiar aside following his main clause connects two entirely unrelated clauses.

When Orwell fears that being trampled like the coolie might induce laughter, his phrasing is again ambiguous: "The sole thought in my mind was that if any-thing went wrong those two thousand Burmans would see me pursued, caught, trampled on and reduced to a grinning corpse like the Indian up the hill" (153–54). In this sentence, the agent that pursues and tramples seems to be the Burmese, not the elephant: It is unlikely that an elephant would pursue—let alone "catch"—its prey with such single-minded determination. On the other hand, Orwell also seems unconsciously to identify with the elephant here. Given his perceived loss of agency in Burma—caught between theoretical hatred of the British empire and quotidian hatred of the Burmese who jeer at him—the elephant's rampage seems to displace his aggressive instincts:

> Early one morning the sub-inspector at a police station at the other end of town rang me up on the 'phone and said that an elephant was ravaging the bazaar. Would I please come and do something about it?. . . . The Burmese population had no weapons and were quite helpless against it. It had already destroyed somebody's bamboo hut, killed a cow and raided some fruit-stalls and devoured the stock; also it had met the municipal rubbish van and, when the driver jumped out and took to his heels, had turned the van over and inflicted violences upon it. (149–50)

Orwell's displaced aggression surfaces in his ability to find comic the elephant's dangerous rampage through the village. After the essay's racially strained begin-ning and the endearing description of the elephant as a "canny" creature, this lev-ity releases Orwell's racial tension. When he encounters the elephant, however, Orwell's empathy inhibits his duty to shoot it to protect the natives: "As soon as I saw the elephant I knew with perfect certainty that I ought not to shoot him [*sic*]" (151). In this face-to-face encounter, the elephant, to which Orwell previously referred with the neutral pronoun "it," is gendered as "him"; this again discloses Orwell's powerful displacement of instincts.

Orwell later represents the elephant as "a costly piece of machinery"; later still, it seems to possess such a "grandmotherly air" (153) that "it seemed to me that it would be murder to shoot him" (153). After the first shot, however, the elephant becomes "immensely old" (154)—as archaic as the joke itself that has been repressed. Here it would be tempting to unify the various condensations and dis-placements that center on the elephant by reading this object as a screen for the white joke (thus Abrahams and Dundes read the elephant generically as a metaphor for the black man). However, this analogy clarifies little about racial identification and is certain to limit interpretation of this rich but underexplored text.

To discern the meaning of the white joke, we must not be captivated by the comedy Orwell uses to disguise his aggression. Instead, we must discern that the comic functions in the colonial context not just as a façade for the joke (Freud suggests this generally of jokes and the comic [*Jokes* 181]), but as a veil that reveals *and* conceals the anxiety of colonial whiteness. As Freud argues about the relation between the comic and jokes: "If we fail to detect the joke, we are once again left only with the comic or funny story" (205). To put this more specifically, all comic stories about natives carry within them the anxious joke about whiteness. The particular deployment of this unspoken term, which the colonizer and colonized largely "agree" to avoid representing,[12] determines the immediate relationship between the white man and the native without affecting the structure of the joke. Let me conclude by illustrating this point.

The "risk" of native laughter has consequences even after colonialism's formal demise. Clifford Geertz makes this clear in his introduction to his essay "Deep Play: Notes on the Balinese Cockfight," with an anecdote about the moment he is accepted into a Balinese village. After a week or more, during which the villagers studiously ignore him, Geertz and his wife attend an illegal cockfight in the public square. The police break up the gathering and the villagers flee. In the ensuing chaos, which Geertz describes stereotypically, like a cartoon (414–15), he and his wife act on "the established anthropological principle, 'When in Rome,' " and also flee (413). "The next morning," writes Geertz,

> the village was a completely different world for us. Not only were we no longer invisible, we were suddenly the center of all attention, the object of great outpouring of warmth, interest, and most especially, amusement. Everyone in the village knew we had fled like everyone else. They asked us about it again and again, but quite insistently teasing us: "Why didn't you just stand there and tell the police who you were?" . . . "were you really afraid of those little guns?" As always, kinesthetically minded . . . they gleefully mimicked, also over and over again, our graceless style of running and what they claimed were our panic-stricken facial expressions. But above all, everyone was extremely pleased and even more surprised that we had not simply "pulled out our papers" . . . and asserted our Distinguished Visitor status . . . but had demonstrated our solidarity with what were now our co-villagers. (What we had actually demonstrated was our cowardice, but there is fellowship in that too.) (416)

Risking laughter, Geertz achieved exactly what he wanted—to penetrate "the inner nature" of Balinese society (417). Yet the entire possibility of comedy here (Balinese mimicry and Geertz's description of the police raid) derives from Geertz's and his wife's whiteness. Although Geertz downplays this factor, he does reveal it in an interesting moment. When he and wife flee the square, they seek refuge in a stranger's courtyard. In a resourceful moment, the stranger's wife serves them tea: "A few moments later, one of the policemen marched importantly into the yard, looking for the chief. . . . Seeing me and my wife, 'White Men,' there in the yard, the policeman performed a classic double take. When he found his voice again he asked, approximately, what in the devil did we think we were doing there?" (415).

This interesting conflation of gender with race, which Geertz attributes to the native, is part of the complex conceit that seems to render the native speechless. The barely acknowledged fact of Geertz's whiteness subtends the entire narrative—as the Balinese people's surprise at Geertz's "cowardice," the policeman's "classic double take," and the predictable representation of the natives as comic. Yet this scene does not convey white racial anxiety; on the contrary, Geertz aims to disavow his whiteness by refusing to perform the norm. There is a loss of agency here, but it does not derive, as Orwell and Scott insist, from being bound to racial performance—"the two thousand wills pressing [him] forward, irresistibly" ("Shooting" 152). Instead, the loss inheres in the dominant subject's limited and inconsequential decision *not* to perform, a decision to which the conceit of whiteness lends a solemn gravity.

I have argued that extremities of colonial domination sometimes expose the internal contradictions of whiteness. I have argued further that this exposure implicates whiteness in the structures of jokes and the uncanny, which reveals the unconscious basis of dominant racial identification. I am aware this argument may seem, at first flush, to render social change impossible, to the extent that I locate whiteness at the moment of the subject's accession to language. Yet I hope that disinterring the "white conceit," which defines even the most congenial moments of exchange, can renew our analysis and understanding of the hegemony of color as it prevails in the visual field.

ENDNOTES

I thank Homi Bhabha, Daniel Boyarin, Mark Bracher, Chris Lane, Paul Lewis, Robin Lydenberg, Frances Restuccia, Claudia Tate, and Jean Walton for rigorous critique of this article.

1. For example bell hooks's essay on whiteness, which, despite its attempt to incorporate black views of white identity, inadvertently reifies whiteness as an unquestionable category of racial difference.

2. The following quotation provided by the *OED* from Isak Walton's *The Complete Angler* clearly situates conceits in the realm of jokes: "Most of his conceits were either scrip-

ture jests, or lascivious jests: for which I count no man witty." This is not to suggest that we should reread the literary conceits of, say, the metaphysical poets as jokes, but to note that there is a family resemblance between the conceit and Freud's notion of the joke.

3. With regard to awareness, McDonald, who conducted a study similar to Goodman's at the Hanna Perkins school in Ohio (a therapeutic nursery and kindergarten), says: "Goodman quotes many individual examples from these four-year-olds. They differ hardly at all from our examples of Hanna Perkins children, twenty years later, from a large Northern city on the coast of the Great Lakes" (183).

4. I thank Homi Bhabha for teaching me to read Fanon in this manner. See his essays "Articulating" and "Interrogating."

5. In Freud's 1927 essay on humor, however, the distinctions begin to collapse.

6. See Sander Gilman's seminal article "Sigmund Freud and the Jewish Joke" on Freud's displacement of the Jewish joke onto the *mauscheln*. Elliot Oring also reads Freud's text as indicative of his ambivalence toward his Jewishness (see 94–111). See also Boyarin.

7. In *Pax Britannica*, James Morris quotes Sir Charles Dilke, who, sometime after the 1857 sepoy uprising against the British, reported "that a common notice in Indian hotels read: 'Gentlemen are requested not to strike the servants.' " Morris adds his own footnote to this: "Striking the servants, in an off-hand way, died hard in the Empire. In 1946, during my first week in Egypt, I boarded the Cairo train at Port Said with an English colonel of particular gentleness of manner and sweetness of disposition. As we walked along the corridor to find a seat we found our way blocked by an Egyptian, offering refreshments to people inside a compartment. Without pause, apparently without a second thought, the colonel kicked him, quite hard and effectively, out of our way. I was new to the imperial scenes, and I have never forgotten this astonishing change in my companion's character, not the absolute blank indifference with which the Egyptian accepted the kick, and moved" (137).

8. I thank Daniel Boyarin for this excellent reference. Scott's work is a significant contribution to theories of resistance and is a textbook of the various negotiations of colonial power.

9. Freud disputes Jentsch's view that the uncanny is produced mainly by "doubts whether an apparently animate being is really alive; or conversely whether a lifeless object might not in fact be animate" ("Uncanny" 3). While Freud acknowledges the importance of this doubt, he does not regard it as the central mechanism of the uncanny.

10. This is not to imply that Orwell was a "racist." A very good case has been made for him by Raymond Williams and Terry Eagleton to the contrary; nor am I interested in Orwell's individual pathology. In fact Orwell's self-consciousness about equating whiteness with humanness discloses his capacity to interrogate the transparency of racial discourse.

11. Abrahams and Dundes argue that elephant jokes, which exploded around 1963, were disguised antiblack jokes that whites told in the face of the civil-rights movement. However, Abrahams and Dundes's attempt to psychologize the joke as an oedipal narrative is problematic for reasons that I cannot take up here. For an excellent critique of Abrahams and Dundes's article see Oring 16–28.

12. In "Psychological," Wright contends: "It would take an effort of imagination on the part of whites to appreciate what I term 'the reality of whiteness' as it is reflected in the colored mind. . . . The many national states which make up that white world, when seen from the interior of colored life lying psychologically far below it, assumes [*sic*] a oneness of racial identity. This aspect of 'whiteness' of Europe is an old reality, stemming from some 500 years of European history. It has become a tradition, a psychological reality in the minds of Asians and Africans" (8).

WORKS CITED

Abel, Elizabeth. "Race, Class, and Psychoanalysis? Opening Questions." *Conflicts in Feminism*. Ed. Marianne Hirsch and Evelyn F. Keller. New York: Routledge, 1990. 184–204.

Aboud, Frances. *Children and Prejudice*. Oxford: Blackwell, 1988.

Abrahams, Roger and Alan Dundes. "On Elephantasy and Elephanticide: The Effect of Time and Place." *Cracking Jokes: Studies of Sick Humor Cycles and Stereotypes*. Berkeley: Ten Speed, 1987. 41–54.

Allport, Gordon W. *The Nature of Prejudice*. 25th Anniversary Edition. Reading, Mass.: Addison Wesley, 1979.

Balibar, Etienne and Immanuel Wallerstein. *Race, Nation, Class: Ambiguous Identities*. Trans. Chris Turner. New York: Verso, 1991.

Berger, Arthur Asa. *An Anatomy of Humor*. New Brunswick, N.J.: Transaction, 1993.

Bernal, Martin. *Black Athena: The Afro-Asiatic Roots of Classical Civilization*. New Brunswick: Rutgers UP, 1987.

Bhabha, Homi K. *The Location of Culture*. New York: Routledge, 1994.

——. "Interrogating Identity: Frantz Fanon and the Postcolonial Prerogative." In *Location*. 19–39.

——. "Articulating the Archaic: Cultural Difference and Colonial Nonsense." In *Location*. 123–38.

Boyarin, Daniel. "*Épater L'embourgeoisement*: Freud, Gender, and the (De)Colonized Psyche." *Diacritics* 24.1 (1994): 17–41.

Butler, Judith. *Bodies That Matter: On the Discursive Limits of "Sex."* New York: Routledge, 1993.

Clark, Kenneth B. *Prejudice and Your Child*. 1955. Boston: Beacon, 1963.

Davies, Christie. *Ethnic Humor Around the World: A Comparative Analysis*. Bloomington: Indiana UP, 1990.

Doane, Mary Ann. *Femmes Fatales: Feminism, Film Theory, Psychoanalysis*. New York: Routledge, 1991.

Dumont, Louis. *Homo Hierarchicus: An Essay on the Caste System*. Trans. Mark Sainsbury. Chicago: U of Chicago P, 1970.

Durant, John and Jonathan Miller, eds. *Laughing Matters: A Serious Look at Humour*. Essex: Longman, 1988.

Eagleton, Terry. "Orwell and the Lower Middle-Class Novel." *George Orwell: A Collection of Critical Essays*. In Williams. 10–33.

Fanon, Frantz. *Black Skin, White Masks*. 1952. Trans. Charles Lam Markmann. New York: Basic, 1967.

Freud, Sigmund. *Jokes and Their Relation to the Unconscious*. 1905. Vol. 8 of *The Standard Edition of the Complete Psychological Works of Sigmund Freud*. Ed. and trans. James Strachey. 24 Vols. London: Hogarth, 1953–74. 1–238.

———. "The 'Uncanny.' " 1919. Vol. 17 of *SE*. 217–56.

———. "Humour." 1927. Vol. 21 of *SE*. 160–66.

Gailey, Christine Ward. "Politics, Colonialism, and the Mutable Color of Pacific Islanders." *Race and Other Misadventures: Essays in Honor of Ashley Montagu in His Ninetieth Year*. Ed. Larry T. Reynolds and Leonard Lieberman. New York: General Hall, 1996. 36–49.

Gaines, Jane. "White Privilege and Looking Relations: Race and Gender in Feminist Film Theory." *Cultural Critique* 4 (1986): 59–79.

Geertz, Clifford. *The Interpretation of Cultures: Selected Essays*. New York: Basic Books, 1973.

Gilman, Sander. "Sigmund Freud and the Jewish Joke." *Difference and Pathology: Stereotypes of Sexuality, Race, and Madness*. Ithaca: Cornell UP, 1985. 175–90.

Goodman, Mary Ellen. *Race Awareness in Young Children*. New York: Collier, 1952.

Gregory, Steven and Roger Sanjek, eds. *Race*. New Brunswick: Rutgers UP, 1994.

Holmes, Robyn M. *How Young Children Perceive Race*. London: Sage, 1995.

hooks, bell. "Representing Whiteness in the Black Imagination." *Cultural Studies*. Ed. Lawrence Grossberg, Cary Nelson, and Paula Treichler. New York: Routledge, 1992. 338–46.

Klineberg, Otto. *Race and Psychology*. Paris: Unesco, 1951.

———. *Race Differences*. 1935. Westport, Conn.: Greenwood, 1974.

Knott, Blanche. *Truly Tasteless Jokes*. Vols VI and VIII. New York: St. Martin's, 1985.

Kovel, Joel. *White Racism: A Psychohistory*. 1970. New York: Columbia UP, 1984.

Lacan, Jacques. *Écrits: A Selection*. Trans. Alan Sheridan. New York: Norton, 1977.

Lasker, Bruno. *Race Attitudes in Children*. 1929. Westport, Conn.: Greenwood, 1968.

Levinas, Emmanuel. *The Levinas Reader*. Ed. Sean Hand. Cambridge: Blackwell, 1989.

Mehlman, Jeffrey. "How to Read Freud on Jokes: The Critic as Schadchen." *New Literary History* 6 (1975): 439–61.

Mama, Amina. *Beyond the Masks: Race, Gender, and Subjectivity*. New York: Routledge, 1995.

McDonald, Marjorie. *Not by the Color of Their Skin: The Impact of Racial Differences on the Child's Development*. New York: International UP, 1970.

Michaels, Walter Benn. "Race into Culture: A Critical Genealogy of Cultural Identity." *Critical Inquiry* 18.4 (1992): 655–85.

Morris, James. *Pax Britannica: The Climax of Empire*. Harmondsworth: Penguin, 1968.

Nandy, Ashis. *Intimate Enemy: Loss and Recovery of Self Under Colonialism*. Delhi: Oxford UP, 1983.

Neve, Michael. "Freud's Theory of Humour, Wit and Jokes." In Durant and Miller. 35–43.

Omi, Michael, and Howard Winant. "On the Theoretical Concept of Race." *Race, Identity, and Representation in Education.* Ed. Cameron McCarthy and Warren Crichlow. New York: Routledge, 1993. 3–10.

Oring, Elliott. *Jokes and Their Relations.* Lexington, KY: U of Kentucky P, 1992.

Orwell, George. "Shooting an Elephant." *A Collection of Essays.* 1945. New York: Harcourt Brace, 1953. 148–56.

———. "Marrakech." *A Collection of Essays.* 180–87.

———. "A Hanging." *An Age Like This: The Collected Essays, Journalism, and Letters of George Orwell.* Vol I. Ed. Sonia Orwell and Ian Angus. New York: Harcourt Brace, 1968. 44–48.

———. *Burmese Days.* 1934. New York: Harcourt Brace, 1962.

———. *The Road to Wigan Pier.* 1937. New York: Penguin, 1982.

Palmer, Jerry. *Taking Humour Seriously.* New York: Routledge, 1994.

Roediger, David. *Towards the Abolition of Whiteness.* New York: Verso, 1994.

Sanjek, Roger. "The Enduring Inequalities of Race." In Gregory and Sanjek. 1–17.

Scott, James C. *Domination and the Arts of Resistance: Hidden Transcripts.* New Haven: Yale UP, 1990.

Silverman, Kaja. *Male Subjectivity at the Margins.* New York: Routledge, 1992.

Smith, Paul. *Discerning the Subject.* Minneapolis: U of Minnesota P, 1988.

Snowden, Frank. *Before Colour Prejudice: The Ancient View of Blacks.* Cambridge: Harvard UP, 1983.

Spillers, Hortense J. "Mama's Baby, Papa's Maybe: An American Grammar Book." *Diacritics* 17.2 (1987): 65–81.

Spivak, Gayatri Chakravorty. "Can the Subaltern Speak?" *Marxism and the Interpretation of Culture.* Ed. Cary Nelson and Lawrence Grossberg. Urbana: U of Illinois P, 1988. 271–313.

Vardharajan, Asha. *Exotic Parodies: Subjectivity in Adorno, Said, and Spivak.* Minneapolis: U of Minnesota P, 1995.

Walton, Jean. "Re-Placing Race in (White) Psychoanalytic Discourse: Founding Narratives of Feminism." *Critical Inquiry* 21 (1995): 775–804.

Weber, Samuel. *The Legend of Freud.* Minneapolis: U of Minnesota P, 1982.

Williams, Raymond. *George Orwell.* Ed. Frank Kermode. New York: Viking Press, 1971.

Williams, Raymond, ed. *George Orwell: A Collection of Critical Essays.* Englewood Cliffs, N.J.: Prentice Hall, 1974.

Wright, Richard. "The Psychological Reactions of Oppressed People." *White Men, Listen!: Lectures in Europe, 1950–1956.* New York: HarperPerennial, 1995. 1–43.

16

Hitting "A Straight Lick with a Crooked Stick": *Seraph on the Suwanee,* Zora Neale Hurston's Whiteface Novel

Claudia Tate

Arvay was pretty if you liked delicate-made girls. . . . She had plenty of long light yellow hair with a low wave to it with Gulf-blue eyes. Arvay had a fine-made kind of nose and mouth and a faced shaped like an egg laid by a Leghorn pullet, with a faint spread of pink around her upper cheeks. . . . Arvay, young and white, and teasing to the fancy of many men. . . .

—Hurston, *Seraph* 4

I HAVE BEEN AMAZED by the Anglo-Saxon's lack of curiosity about the internal lives and emotions of the Negroes. . . .

—Hurston, "White" 169; original emphasis

Despite the tremendous popularity of the works of Zora Neale Hurston over the last two decades, *Seraph on the Suwanee* (1948) is still a marginal work. In her fourth and last published novel, Hurston returned to the topic that claimed her lifelong interest—probing "what makes a man or a woman do such-and-so, regardless of his color" (*Dust* 151). But unlike Hurston's *Their Eyes Were Watching God,* published eleven years earlier, *Seraph* has never enchanted its readers. In fact, the novel is generally understood by black literary scholars as a contrivance in Hurston's canon and in African-American literary scholarship.[1] This perspective undoubtedly results from Hurston's depiction of white protagonists instead of black ones. In the words of one prominent African-American literary scholar, Mary Helen Washington, *Seraph* is evidence of Hurston's "abandoning the source of her unique esthetic—the black cultural tradition"

(21). Washington goes on to say that Hurston "submerged her power and creativity" in this work (21).

I hope to refute these contentions by demonstrating that *Seraph* is very much a part of Hurston's persistent and compelling investigations of female desire and racialized culture.[2] With this novel, I argue, Hurston tried to please a white popular audience and herself by conspicuously constructing *and* subtly deconstructing the novel's white patriarchal narrative of romantic love with a couple of canny jokes about that culture's idealization of passive female desire and its conflation of race and class. To invoke Hurston's familiar maxim, she "hit a lick" at racism and sexism with the "crooked stick" of indirect but perceptive jest. For the purposes of this essay, I want to concentrate on *Seraph*'s investment in whiteness and only mention its critique of passive female desire, indeed female masochism, for the novel's white social milieu seems to be its most problematic feature.

One could generalize from my reading the importance of interpreting racial fantasies in literary texts that detail ethnic and racial tensions, desires, and identifications, noting that psychoanalysis provides useful critical strategies for understanding all of these concerns. In engaging psychoanalysis to read *Seraph*'s racial joke, we perceive not only Hurston's unstated punchline, but the irrational basis of social distinctions undergirding racial discrimination. Here and elsewhere, psychoanalysis exposes racism as an extenuated and pernicious form of tendentious jokes. Like the joke, racism is a compensatory system that defends a subject against a real or imagined lack. By granting us access to our deeply concealed individual and collective anxieties, psychoanalysis can help us understand how these anxieties affect our cultural histories. Before continuing my discussion, however, I must outline the plot of this under-read novel.

Seraph begins in 1905 in Sawley, a poor white town in Florida, and concludes around 1927 at sea, off the west coast of the state. The opening incident portrays the whole town's amusement in witnessing Jim Meserve court the peculiar Arvay Henson. On first seeing Arvay, Jim is sure that "[s]he just suited him . . . and was worth the trouble of breaking in" (8). However, Arvay believes that "this pretty, laughing fellow was far out of her reach," since she "was born to take other people's leavings" (24). To make matters worse, Arvay also suffers guilt from secretly "living in mental adultery with her sister's husband," Reverend Carl Middleton, on whom she has had a crush for five years (34). When he marries Larraine, however, whose robust manner and appearance everyone, including her parents, prefers to Arvay's slight form and timid manner, Arvay conceals her hurt feelings by "turning from the world" with "religious fervor" and then unconsciously repressing her sexual desire by developing hysterical convulsions (3).

In record time Jim proposes to Arvay, and she accepts even though she expects him to jilt her. Her insecurity then makes her behavior contradictory and causes Jim to think she has insufficient love for him. To remedy this dilemma, two weeks before their wedding day, Jim rapes Arvay and marries her immediately afterward without coercion. Arvay does not realize that this scenario is Jim's attempt to show his satisfaction with her and to bind her to him. She merely concludes that his extravagant charity causes him to marry her. The failure to recognize their mutual insecurities binds them in a sadomasochistic cycle of sexual aggression and submission, which the rape foreshadows. This defensive pattern of erotic attachment defines their marriage for more than twenty years.

Their first child, Earl, probably conceived during the rape, is retarded and slightly deformed. His abnormality suggests Hurston's censure of the rape. Weak and fearful of almost everything, he projects Arvay's insecurity. Even though she and Jim have two more children, Angeline and James Kenneth (called Angie and Kenny), who are not just normal but smart, very good-looking, and self-confident, Arvay devotes most of her energy to Earl, as her penance for "the way [she] used to be" (69). Since she cannot recognize her own virtues, she regards Earl as her child, while perceiving Angie and Kenny as Jim's children. When Earl is about eighteen, he sexually assaults a neighbor girl and is killed by a local man in an attempt to escape. Earl's death frees Arvay of her guilty burden but she continues to suffer acute insecurity.

During the marriage, Jim pushes his family up the social ladder. Although Arvay enjoys the financial security of Jim's ambition, she recognizes neither his motive nor his struggle to succeed. Entrenched in the passive-masochistic role of sexual submission, she cannot be confident of Jim's love. After Angie marries and Kenny goes to college, Arvay is relieved of most of her domestic duties. With time to reflect, she has more opportunity to justify her lack of esteem and to fantasize about Jim's abandoning her. According to her reasoning, she would then be free to return to her kind of folk in Sawley and live in confidence. Frustrated by Arvay's defensive behavior, Jim devotes more and more time to developing a shrimping business that takes him out of town. He also tries to invigorate the marriage by performing a stunt with a rattlesnake, but like his first effort to bind Arvay to him with rape, all he ends up doing is terrifying her. This final failure convinces him to leave her. Though he will support her indefinitely, he gives her one year to surrender passivity for "a knowing and a doing love" to save their marriage (262).

Before Arvay can plan a course of action, she receives a telegram from her sister stating that their mother is ill. Her mother's illness, which Arvay initially believes is not fatal, overshadows her "happy anticipation" of returning to Sawley. In her mind "[t]he corroding poverty of her childhood became a glowing virtue, and a state to be desired" (272). This idealization allows her to deny the pain of

Jim's abandonment. Instead she imagines that she will leave him by returning to Sawley. When Arvay arrives at her former home, her idealization confronts reality. Larraine is a "ton of coarse-looking flesh," Carl is a "drab creature," and their daughters are "mule-faced and ugly enough" (274, 275, and 276). If the Middletons' appearances and the dilapidated childhood home, with its odor of rat urine, are insufficient to make Arvay consider her life with Jim as a tremendous improvement, the invectives of Arvay's dying mother, Maria Henson, sharpen this comparison. She tells Arvay, "You and Jim sure is raised your chaps to be nice and kind. 'Tain't that a'way with Larraine nor none of her whelps." She and Carl, Maria insists, are just "like turkey buzzards" (280, 278).

Maria confesses to Arvay a lifetime of unfulfilled aspirations, as if to justify her subsequent request of her daughter. She asks to be "put away nice" on Sunday "with a heap of flowers on my coffin and a church full of folks marching around to say me 'farewell.' " Arvay assures her that she can put her "dying dependence" in her (280). By keeping her "sacred promise" to her mother, Arvay nourishes her self-confidence.

This climactic event makes Arvay realize she has "sense enough to appreciate what [Jim's] done, and [is] still trying to do for [her]" (309). She resolves to win him back. Arvay soon joins Jim on board his shrimp boat, the *Arvay Henson*. She displays her courage and tells him how proud she is of him. Through indirect discourse, the text reveals that Arvay at last perceives the insecurity behind Jim's aggressive mask. She realizes she was just as unaware of his "inner" self as she had been of her own ability.

Seraph's focus on white protagonists and female masochistic desire are startling departures from the stories of black female self-definition that are so prominent in Hurston's other writings. In fact, so great are these departures that the novel's pre-occupations appear as textual enigmas. By referring to psychoanalysis, a form of inquiry devoted specifically to interpreting concealed and puzzling meaning, I will attempt to unveil the novel's enigmatic whiteness to elucidate *Seraph*'s meaning and clarify its relationship to Hurston's other works. Psychoanalysis allows me to establish a dialectic between *Seraph*'s explicit surface content and its implicit deep significance, much as the human psyche constructs intelligible meaning by mediating between its conscious intentions and unconscious desire. By regarding the structure of *Seraph* "in some basic sense [like] the structure of the mind," I agree with Peter Brooks's claim that "there must be some correspondence between literary and psychic process"; that is, "aesthetic structure and form, including literary tropes, must somehow coincide with the psychic structures and operations they both evoke and appeal to" (24–25).[3] This viewpoint allows us to regard the discourses of *Seraph* as functioning like the conscious, preconscious, and unconscious domains of the psyche. By extending this argument, I will consider the novel's explicit and implicit discourses as analogous to those of Freudian joke-work, particularly those of the tendentious joke.

In *Jokes and Their Relation to the Unconscious*, Freud explains how the language of the joke initially incites bewilderment and subsequently produces illumination through the act of telling it. According to Freud, "jokes are formed in the first person" as "*a preconscious thought is given over for a moment to unconscious revision and the outcome of this is at once grasped by conscious perception*" (166; original emphasis). Like Freud's understanding of the tendentious joke, *Seraph* evokes pleasure by exploiting "something ridiculous in our enemy which we could not, on account of obstacles in the way, bring forward openly or consciously" (*Jokes* 103). Thus *Seraph* "*evade[s] restrictions and open[s] sources of pleasure that have become inaccessible*" (103; original emphasis).

When cast against Hurston's other writings, *Seraph*'s discourse on whiteness is bewildering. By regarding it as a part of the text's preconscious, like that of the joke, undergoing silenced or unconscious revision, we can clarify its meaning. The unconscious here would include the novel's stylistic and structural elements—for example, its repetitive words, tropes, circuity, exaggeration, ellipses, suspension, anticipation, retraction, negation, digression, irony, and causality. Although joke-work and other forms of unconscious discourses make use of the same structural devices of condensation, indirect representation, and displacement, "the techniques [of jokes] are explicit and overt and their opposition to accepted modes of conscious thought [is] clearly recognizable" (Oring 7). Unlike banter, the pleasure of the fully formed joke derives from its circumventing the censor to consciousness to express a prohibited thought. Unlike the joke, however, which strives for intelligibility, unconscious discourses seek obscurity and expression. For this reason they are more heavily veiled.

Freudian psychoanalytic tenets about compulsive repetition also help me identify *Seraph*'s recurring sentence—"I can read your writing"—as the inscription of the text's unstated demand that further directs my reading of its textual enigmas.[4] This sentence discloses Jim's ability to detect Arvay's desire despite her sexually repressed behavior; it also identifies the demand that Arvay fulfills at the novel's close when she accurately interprets Jim's concealed desire beneath his jesting, defensive behavior. Most important, though, this sentence demands that we examine *Seraph*'s textual content, which, like Jim's joking behavior, is not transparent.

By realizing that *Seraph* is a tendentious joke that has much in common with the carnivalesque text, we can synthesize the incongruity of the novel's plot, surface elements, and rhetorical features to clarify its social critique. In psychoanalytic literary terms, we can interpret the novel's meaning not only by reading its conscious or explicit plot and dialogue, but by deciphering its unconscious discourses of desire. Like Arvay, however, we readers will have to sweat because *Seraph* refuses to deliver its meaning in any simple way.

Seraph's white social milieu was probably the result not just of Hurston's effort to attract a Hollywood contract as a screenwriter, as several scholars have remarked, but also of a deliberate concession to publishers, who could not imagine a novel about a middle-class black family.[5] Shortly before Hurston began working on this novel, she tried to interest her publisher, Lippincott, in "a serious book [about a middle-class black woman] to be called *Mrs. Doctor*" (Hemenway 303).[6] No doubt Ann Petry and Dorothy West also encountered similar reluctance on the part of white publishers because they too were exploring the possibility of writing serious novels about the black middle class. West's *The Living Is Easy* and Petry's *The Narrows* appeared in 1948 and 1953, respectively. However, both works went out of print soon after their first printings.[7] These circumstances suggest that the black and white reading public not only expected black characters in novels by black authors; they also expected black authors to represent a homogeneous black folk. While black stereotypes were undoubtedly a part of Hurston's problem with Lippincott, her biographer, Robert Hemenway refers to her editor's disappointment with "the sloppiness of the writing" and the "strained quality in the prose." Hemenway then explains that Hurston blamed the rejection on Lippincott's decision "that the American public was not ready" for a book on "the upper strata of Negro life" (393). Hurston gave up on the book, and on Lippincott, to write *Seraph* for Scribner's. While Hurston's hope to make money off an enlarged audience for the book no doubt was another reason for writing about white culture, this social milieu, I contend, is not a contrivance, as many scholars have argued, but the result of Hurston's complex reflections and unconscious longings.

When Hurston identifies Jim as Black Irish, she partly clarifies the novel's racial coding. According to David R. Roediger, the label "Black Irish" refers to a mixed black/white heritage, resulting from the preponderance of Irish "intermixing with shipwrecked slaves" (4). The label also invokes mid-nineteenth-century racial stereotypes associated with the Irish. According to popular racial wisdom, "an Irishman was a 'nigger,' inside out" (qtd. in Roediger 133). Hurston's use of the term "Black Irish" suggests her familiarity with such stereotypes. *Seraph* draws on the derisive banter associated with the racialization of this ethnic stereotype to portray Jim and Arvay with white bodies and what her readers identify as black voices, because these characters speak recognizable Eatonville idioms (Eatonville was an all-black town). Thus Jim and Arvay seem to possess white exteriors and black interiors. In this respect, *Seraph* has two layers of meaning, which I attempt to read as a subversive and parodic joke by interpreting the literal and symbolic gap between these racial codes. The novel's unstated joke deconstructs absolute racial distinctions.

According to John Lowe, though, Jim and Arvay are decidedly white. Lowe insists that *Seraph* "is not simply a whitewashing of black characters," because "Crackers don't have a folk culture that memorializes actual events in history. Their stories and idioms bespeak a repository of folk wisdom, but one unconnected with history" (266). As evidence of this questionable insight, Lowe cites the following passage, which appears early in *Seraph*:

> Few were concerned with the past. They had heard that the stubbornly resisting Indians had been there where they now lived, but they were dead and gone. Osceola, Miccanope, Billy Bow-Legs were nothing more than names that had even lost their bitter flavor. The conquering Spaniards had done their murdering, robbing, and raping and had long ago withdrawn from the Floridas. Few knew and nobody cared that Hidalgos under De Soto had moved westward along this very route. (2)

Lowe argues that *Seraph*'s lack of concern with the area's social history is indicative of its white social context: "Obviously, African Americans would have more cultural strength in this connection, as so much of their oral tradition is tied to history." He concludes that Arvay's "family in Sawley seems adrift in time, much like the Lesters of Caldwell's *Tobacco Road*" (266).

I find Lowe's conclusion curious and inaccurate. Hurston's other novels do not seem intricately tied to history. Each focuses on character development; historical events are not foregrounded. In *Their Eyes*, Nanny's "highway through de wilderness" speech situates the novel at the turn of the century (when *Seraph* takes place as well). After this temporal reference, *Their Eyes* is also "adrift in time," indeed so much that if we could not surmise Janie's age relative to Nanny's, the courthouse scene could be set in either 1910 or 1930. We can approximate dates only by referring to the novel's internal generational history relative to the Emancipation. The same is true of *Jonah's Gourd Vine*: Slavery is the only historical marker. In fact, the novel withholds the date of Lucy's death, telling us instead that Isis is nine when her mother dies. In *Seraph*, as in the other two novels, the narrator identifies a post-Reconstruction setting by referring to Jim's background: "fortunes of the War had wiped Jim's grand-father clean" (7). The narrator also informs us that Jim is twenty-five when he arrives in Sawley and near fifty when he leaves Arvay. Moreover, the inscription of Arvay and Jim's children's birth dates in a family Bible provides clear historical markers. This ritual informs us, for example, that Earl is born in 1906, nine months after the story begins.

Rather than being cast adrift in time, then, *Seraph* is more attentive to dates than are the other novels. In addition, Lowe does not present any examples of a historically informed black folklore from Hurston's works to support his argument. He simply assumes that the "black oral tradition is tied to history" (266). Hurston's use of this tradition in her writings reveals black and white folklife as tied respectively to the historical facts of slavery and the Emancipation on the one hand, and the consequences of the Civil War on the other. On the basis of these three of Hurston's four novels, there seems to be no reason to conclude that white culture is any more or less ahistorical than black culture.

We do know, however, that Hurston was emphatic in her denunciation of racial stereotypes. She contended that rural, poor people—black and white—of the same southern region share the same dialect. In *Dust Tracks*, she further explained that all Southerners have "the map of Dixie on [their] tongue[s]." The "average Southern child, white or black, is raised on simile and invective. . . . Since that stratum of the Southern population is not given to book-reading, they take their comparisons right out of the barnyard and the woods" (98–99). Given her reluctance to racialize Southern dialect, Hurston must have intended *Seraph*'s white characters to sound like Eatonville blacks. This too was William Faulkner's intention in *The Sound and the Fury* (1929) when he has two unnamed white northern characters tell Quentin Compson that "He talks like they do in minstrel shows," by which they mean that Quentin "talks like a colored man" (137). Similarly, as urban blacks readily attest, when they speak the dialect associated with professional whites, they are accused of speaking "white." Thus when Jim and Arvay speak the phrases that the Eatonville blacks have already spoken in Hurston's earlier works, they must be speaking "black." Whether Sawley whites in fact sounded like Eatonville blacks seems a moot issue because the racial valence of the Eatonville dialect, designated as black in Hurston's prior publications, remains black regardless of the racial identity of the speaker.

Seraph invites us to see that conventional racial designations attributed to dialects and speakers are based on erroneous assumptions. Just as Hurston contended that poor blacks and whites living in the rural South spoke the same dialect, she also maintained that race was cultural rather than biological. In the unexpurgated version of "My People, My People," for instance, she insisted that "you can't tell who my people are by skin color" (*Dust* 216). If appearance is an unreliable indication of race, what can be said of speech patterns, especially those of characters in a novel? Race for Hurston would seem to be a questionable category. Indeed, her manipulation of allegedly fixed racial designations of the body and the voice probably gave her a great deal of pleasure. Nowhere would the pleasure be more intense than in *Seraph*, where she subverts multiple racial expectations. Since the characters in *Seraph* sound black, Hurston did not really abandon "the source of her unique esthetic–black cultural tradition" insofar as language is the medium of culture.

Despite Hurston's adoption of what we ultimately recognize as black vernacular for her white characters, she nonetheless relied on the assumptions associated with the privilege of whiteness to stage her critique of masochistic female desire. This setting facilitates her representation of the patriarchal demands of romantic love by avoiding the black people's problematic relationship to interracial masculine authority. In this way Hurston can connect Jim's love of Arvay and his financial success in Florida without taxing the credibility of her white and black readers. Hurston uses money similarly in "The Gilded Six Bits." But the few coins that Joe can bestow on Missie May make the act symbolic, whereas in *Seraph* Jim's economic gain is the physical proof that allows Arvay to set herself apart from her Cracker background, a developmental process that Lowe has explained with the assistance of Freudian theory on melancholia and joking.

While in this instance I agree with Lowe's analysis[8]—that is, if one were going to psychoanalyze a character like a person—I am arguing that Hurston's use of Freudian psychology in representing a character like Arvay is part of her deliberate and subversive commentary on female masochism, of which Arvay's whiteness is a necessary part.[9] Unlike many contemporary feminists who still persist in discussing woman apart from her racial identity, Hurston realized that she could not depict a woman without racializing her body, even as she problematized the very effort.

By realizing that *Seraph* has textual subjectivity that is analyzable, we can construct the meaning of the text's whiteness and appreciate Arvay's flawed personality. She is, after all, a character whose newfound wisdom, at the novel's close, informs the reader how to decipher *Seraph*'s meaning. Just as she learns to read Jim's jesting words, we must detect and read the novel's joking humor. For *Seraph* is a long satirical joke about notions of cultural and biological purity that probably serve Arvay's and possibly Hurston's aggressive ego defenses with pleasurable affect (Oring 97).

Psychoanalysis enables us to appreciate the double valences inscribed in this novel's metahumorous carnivalesque discourses. In addition to producing humor, these conciliatory and subversive discourses engender parody. In this way *Seraph* unsettles the unquestioned social relationships between blacks and whites, women and men. The novel highlights Jim and Arvay's unacknowledged dependency on black idiom, labor, companionship, and folk wisdom as well as their reliance on sadomasochism and sexual bondage. By also acknowledging Jim's successful business endeavors in language that seems like flattery, indeed cajolery, Arvay learns to manage Jim to her advantage. Compared to the spirited, aggressive, and censoring humor of Arvay's earlier invectives, however, her new language of sweet regard seems rather shallow.[10]

While the external whiteness of the novel's central protagonists controls the discourse of social mobility, Jim and Arvay's exploitation of black folk wisdom controls the novel's plot. For example, after listening to Joe Kelsey, his black friend, Jim finds what he believes to be a way of making Arvay love him—that is, by raping her just before marrying her, as discussed above. When Arvay returns from her mother's funeral, determined to win back her husband, for instance, she seeks the assistance of Joe's son, Jeff, and his wife, Janie, by taking "up an attitude that she would have died before adopting before she went away" (313). They respond to the changed Arvay by commenting:

> "I declare, Miss Arvay, but you sure is folks."
> "Sure is," Jeff added sincerely. "Just like Mister Jim, ain't she, Janie? And everybody knows that Mister Jim is quality first-class. Knows how to carry hisself, and then how to treat everybody. Miss Arvay's done come to be just like him."
>   The reflection upon her past condition escaped Arvay in the shine and the gleaming of the present. (314)

While the text preserves the class entitlements for racial demarcation, it signifies the mutual respect between the Meserves and the Kelseys, a perspective further emphasized on Jim's shrimp boats. When Arvay boards one of the boats, for instance, she notices "white and Negro captains were friendly together and compared notes. Some boats had mixed crews" (323). These factors, combined with the protagonists' speaking black but appearing white, suggest a masquerade. We see a connection here between the protagonists' psychic and social identities that becomes problematic when we try to place them in the novel's racially defined and polarized codes of the real South.

Racism not only segregated black people from white in the real South of Hurston's epoch; it also prescribed servility for all black subjects. For them to appear equal to white subjects in Western culture, they would have to assume white masks, as psychiatrist Frantz Fanon has argued in *Black Skin, White Masks* (1952). Undoubtedly, Hurston could appreciate Fanon's contention because she seems to have masked Arvay and Jim in a related way.

Arvay's observations about her own changed racial perspective and the racial equality on the microcosm of the boats contribute to *Seraph*'s racial fantasy. Hurston constructs this fantasy by violating the presumption of a black social context, thus periodically inverting the white social context so that in many ways it resembles the masquerade of Bakhtin's carnival. According to Bakhtin, the masquerade works out "*a new mode of interrelationship between individuals*, counterpoised to the all-powerful socio-hierarchical relationship of noncarnival life" (23). Like the participants of this carnival, the appearances, gestures, and speech of Arvay and Jim "are freed from the authority of all hierarchical positions" (Bakhtin 23).

Seraph's refusal to center a black social milieu—and its corresponding delight in repeatedly calling the white characters "Crackers" while self-consciously placing black folk idioms in their mouths—carnivalizes the presumption that discernible racial differences are the natural basis of segregation and discrimination. Such racist presumptions oppressed Hurston all her life. Flaunting her circumvention of the racist social censor in *Seraph* must have given her a great deal of pleasure.

Hurston seems to have been almost the only one to have appreciated *Seraph*'s racial transgressions. Her black readers have been much too troubled by her switch to white characters to share this pleasure. And her white readers, who already enjoyed her apparent endorsement of dominant cultural myths about patriarchal virtue and female romantic submission in *Seraph*, probably would have liked it even better had she published the work under another name, thereby making the novel's connection to black culture less tangible.

Whether Hurston calculated correctly the demands of Hollywood we shall never know. She was falsely arrested for sexual misconduct shortly after the novel's publication. When the Baltimore *Afro-American*, in a sensational account of the indictment, used an excerpt from *Seraph* (Jim's statement "I'm just as hungry as a dog for a knowing and a doing love") to confirm Hurston's "perverse" sexual aggression, and subsequently defended its position by presuming Hurston's guilt, *Seraph* became entangled in the controversy. By the time the charge was dismissed, the damage was irreparable: Hurston and her readers neglected the novel.[11] Ironically, the novel that started out as Hurston's joke on her resistant readers ended up playing a cruel joke on her.

Seraph's whiteface masquerade can be seen as a meditation on—indeed a deconstruction of—modern racial binary classifications. What initially appears as a regressive racial fantasy is actually a revolutionary text that condemns racial categories and restrictions. Like the "carnivalized" body that Bakhtin described, the white bodies of *Seraph*'s protagonists, with their black-speaking voices, are not closed, complete, defined, or totalized social entities. Since Arvay and Jim repeatedly transgress the boundaries of their presumed racial categories, they are neither entirely white nor black.

This radical commentary is lost on those who do not recall that all of Hurston's works refuse to consider race as a serious category. In "How It Feels to Be Colored Me," for example, Hurston insisted that "[a]t certain times I have no race, I am *me*" and "in the main, I feel like a brown bag of miscellany propped against a wall" (155). She further trivialized race by regarding it as a contest and by describing her colored body as painted: "[m]y face is painted red and yellow and my body is painted blue" (153, 154). *Seraph*'s whiteface masquerade also engages in such racial bantering. Even as this masquerade performs the presumption of racial difference, it also symbolizes a revised social self and a reformed society in which race is not a fixed, quintessential characteristic.[12] The indeterminacy of race—the refusal of this novel to validate absolute racial distinctions between black and white dialect, culture, and people—is the basis of *Seraph*'s subversion—its implicit joke on both black and white readers.

To be a joke, *Seraph* must have a punchline that defeats the censor, construed here as racist ideology. For "[a] joke without a punchline is no joke" (Oring 82). We can detect the punchline by looking for "what is seemingly incongruous" becoming "appropriate" (83). This novel appears to endorse two contradictory racial conventions: the segregation of black and presumably pure white bodies, on the one hand, and visibly white bodies talking black on the other hand. White readers have tended to read Jim's and Arvay's bodies as racially white and to disregard their black voices, even though both are the effects of language (Jim and Arvay are not real people but characters in a novel). Black readers have read these incongruities as contrivances to justify marginalizing the novel. Both groups of readers know how to interpret these apparent contradictions, however. For these characteristics identify racial hybridity that has been projected onto, and therefore inscribed in, textuality. According to real, time-honored racial conventions, white-black racial hybrids *must be* black! The punchline is then: These white folks are black! Much like *Puddn'head Wilson* (1894), by Samuel Clemens, in which the presumptions about the absolute meaning of racial difference turn out to be a cultural fiction, *Seraph* unsettles the validity of time-honored racial ideologies. This is *Seraph*'s seditious joke on racialism, matched by its subtle but nonetheless radical critique of romantic love, which I discuss elsewhere.[13] In both instances, Hurston appears to uphold the racial and sexual conventions of her day. Yet she presents them in such a way that they insinuate their own internal contradictions and thereby collapse.

ENDNOTES

1. If African-American scholars mention *Seraph* at all, and many have not, they categorically regard it as the least of Hurston's works. For example, three black scholars writing in the wake of the Black Power and Black Aesthetic movements tie the novel's defects to its racial posture. Davis claims that the novel "lacks the racy Negro folk speech and seems more highly contrived. No matter how much Miss Hurston knew about Florida poor whites, she instinctively and naturally knew more about Florida Negroes, and the difference shows in this novel" (118). More recently, feminist literary scholars Wall and

Washington endorse Davis's viewpoint. Wall contends that *Seraph* "represents an artistic decline" and that "Hurston was at her best when she drew her material directly from black folklore; it was the source of her creative power" (391). Washington speculates that Hurston wrote "this strange book to prove that she was capable of writing about white people." Washington goes on to judge the book as an "awkward and contrived novel, as vacuous as a soap opera" (21).

2. *Seraph* not only draws on Hurston's personal observations about what she calls the slavery of love in *Dust Tracks*, but presents her critique of the orthodox Freudian viewpoint of masochism "as an expression of feminine nature," a perspective with which Hurston was undoubtedly familiar ("Economic Problem" 257). As John Lowe explains, "Freud was a favorite topic during the Harlem Renaissance and in New York intellectual society in general during the twenties and thirties" (271). "Hurston's mentor Boas," Lowe adds, "no doubt introduced her to Freud as early as the twenties, but other friends like Van Vechten were aficionados as well" (273).

3. Brooks contends "that the structure of literature *is* in some basic sense the structure of the mind—not a specific mind, but what the translators of the *Standard Edition* of Freud's Works call 'the mental apparatus' . . ., a term which designates the economic and dynamic organization of the psyche, a process of structuration" ("The Idea" 24–25).

4. For elaboration on the compulsion to repeat, see *Beyond* and "Remembering."

5. Wallace Thurman wrote several Hollywood screenplays featuring white characters to address class issues. As Klotman explains, Thurman, Langston Hughes, and Hurston learned "that the 'Negro' may have been in vogue in Hollywood in the thirties, but it was still the cardboard Negro, the Imitation-Judge Priest-Green Pastures GWTW Negro" (qtd. in Klotman 91).

6. According to her biographer, Hemenway, no extant copy of the manuscript exists.

7. *The Living Is Easy* (1948) and *The Narrows* (1953) were reissued in 1975 and 1971, respectively, with the resurgence of black nationalism and the women's movement. Both novels are currently in print.

8. Arvay displays an assortment of symptoms. *New York Times* reviewer Slaughter identifies her as a hysterical neurotic. Since her feelings of dejection arise from narcissistic deficiencies, I would instead identify her core problem as a narcissistic personality disorder. A manifestation of this problem would include melancholy and other neuroses. See Kohut 229–38.

9. Freudian theory ascribes passivity to the female even in matters of aggression. For elaboration, see Freud, "The Economic." In chapter 5 of *Psychoanalysis and Black Novels*, I argue that the character of Arvay contributes to *Seraph*'s subversion of then-accepted views on the naturalness of female masochism.

10. duCille also comments on Arvay's altered speech pattern, claiming she has abandoned the speech pattern of a "Cracker" and assumed the discourse of "a coquette" or "a southern belle." Moreover, she uses her newfound language to flatter Jim's ego (140).

11. For an account of the trial, see Hemenway 319–25.

12. Here I adapt Castle's argument: "Even as the masquerade assumed its place in

English society, it reified a sometimes devolutionary, sometimes revolutionary anti-society founded on collective gratification. Its profuse, exquisite, difficult imagery symbolized a revision, not just of the psyche, but of culture itself " (74).

13. See chapter 5 of my *Psychoanalysis and Black Novels*.

WORKS CITED

Bakhtin, Mikhail. *Problems of Dostoevsky's Poetics*. Ed. and trans. Caryl Emerson. Minneapolis: U of Minnesota P, 1984.

Baltimore Afro-American. 23 Oct. 1948: 1–2.

Brooks, Peter. "The Idea of a Psychoanalytic Literary Criticism." *Psychoanalysis and Storytelling*. Cambridge: Blackwell, 1994. 20–46.

Castle, Terry. *Masquerade and Civilization: The Carnivalesque in Eighteenth-Century English Culture and Fiction*. Stanford: Stanford UP, 1986.

Davis, Arthur. *From the Dark Tower: Afro-American Writers 1900 to 1960*. Washington, D.C.: Howard UP, 1974.

duCille, Ann. *The Coupling Convention: Sex, Text, and Tradition in Black Women's Fiction*. New York: Oxford UP, 1993.

Fanon, Frantz. *Black Skin, White Masks*. 1952. Trans. Charles Lam Markmann. New York: Grove, 1967.

Faulkner, William. *The Sound and the Fury*. New York: Vintage Books, 1987.

Freud, Sigmund. *Jokes and Their Relation to the Unconscious*. 1905. Vol. 8 of *The Standard Edition of the Complete Psychological Works of Sigmund Freud*. 24 vols. Ed. and trans. James Strachey. London: Hogarth, 1953–74. 1–238.

——. "Remembering, Repeating and Working-Through." 1914. Vol. 12 of *SE*. 147–56.

——. *Beyond the Pleasure Principle*. 1920. Vol. 18 of *SE*. 7–64.

——. "The Economic Problem of Masochism." 1924. Vol. 19 of *SE*. 157–70.

——. "Female Sexuality." 1931. Vol. 21 of *SE*. 223–46.

Hemenway, Robert E. *Zora Neale Hurston: A Literary Biography*. Urbana: U of Illinois P, 1977.

Hirsh, Marianne. *The Mother/Daughter Plot: Narrative, Psychoanalysis, Feminism*. Bloomington: Indiana UP, 1989.

Hurston, Zora Neale. "How It Feels to Be Colored Me." 1928. *I Love Myself When I Am Laughing . . . : A Zora Neale Hurston Reader*. Ed. Alice Walker. Old Westbury, N.Y.: Feminist, 1979. 152–55.

——. *Jonah's Gourd Vine*. 1934. New York: Harper and Row, 1991.

——. *Their Eyes Were Watching God*. 1937. New York: Harper and Row, 1990.

——. *Dust Tracks on a Road*. 1942. New York: Harper and Row, 1991.

——. *Seraph on the Suwanee*. 1948. New York: Harper and Row, 1991.

——. "What White Publishers Won't Print." *I Love Myself When I Am Laughing . . . : A Zora Neale Hurston Reader*. 169–73.

Klotman, Phyllis. "The Black Writer in Hollywood, Circa 1930: The Case of Wallace

Thurman." *Black American Cinema*. Ed. Manthia Diawara. New York: Routledge, 1993. 80–92.

Kohut, Heinz. *The Analysis of the Self: A Systematic Approach to the Psychoanalytic Treatment of Narcissistic Personality Disorders*. New York: International UP, 1971.

Lacan, Jacques. "The Agency of the Letter in the Unconscious or Reason since Freud." 1957. *Écrits: A Selection*. Trans. Alan Sheridan. New York: Norton, 1977. 146–78.

Lowe, John. *Jump at the Sun: Zora Neale Hurston's Cosmic Comedy*. Urbana: U of Illinois P, 1994.

Oring, Elliott. *The Jokes of Sigmund Freud: A Study in Humor and Jewish Identity*. Philadelphia: U of Pennsylvania P, 1984.

Roediger, David R. *The Wages of Whiteness: Race and the Making of the American Working Class*. London: Verso, 1992.

Slaughter, Frank G. "Freud in Turpentine." *The New York Times Book Review* Vol. 48 (1948): 24.

Tate, Claudia. *Psychoanalysis and Black Novels: Desire and the Protocols of Race*. New York: Oxford UP, 1997.

Wall, Cheryl A. "Zora Neale Hurston: Changing Her Own Words." *American Novelists Revisited: Essays in Feminist Criticism*. Ed. Fritz Fleischmann. Boston: G.K. Hall, 1982. 370–93.

Washington, Mary Helen. "A Woman Half in Shadow." *I Love Myself When I Am Laughing. . . : A Zora Neale Hurston Reader*. 7–25.

17

"Nightmare of the Uncoordinated White-folk": Race, Psychoanalysis, and H. D.'s *Borderline*

Jean Walton

Because psychoanalysis seems to have become *the* discourse of sexual difference, it seems tautological to say there is a "psychoanalysis of sex." Far less obvious is the claim that there might be a psychoanalysis of race. Neither Freud, his colleagues, nor most of his successors considered it axiomatic that the racial fantasies often surfacing in analysis might in turn clarify the racialization of every subject. Yet in psychoanalytic theory and its modernist uses, racial images proliferate that are intimately bound up with these fields' accounts of sexual difference. How might a psychoanalysis of race complicate the apparent preeminence of a psychoanalysis of sex? To put this another way, can we elaborate a psychoanalysis of race without first exploring what we might call the "race of psychoanalysis"?

Insofar as psychoanalysis and modernism were mutually constitutive, in their attempts both to secure and disrupt conventional gender identity, I want to make the following claim: We can understand how psychoanalysis is both "raced" and "racializing" by considering how some of Freud's claims about the "civilized" and the "primitive" were appropriated by a group of white modernists.

Among Europe's experimental films from the 1920s and '30s, perhaps none offers a more fascinating conjunction of psychoanalysis and representations of race than *Borderline*, the expressionist, interracial melodrama produced by the POOL group and directed by Kenneth

Macpherson. The film starred Paul and Eslanda Robeson, imagist poet H. D. (Hilda Doolittle) and her lesbian companion, Bryher (Winifred Ellerman).

The POOL group derived from an artistic and domestic ménage à trois among H. D., Bryher, and writer-photographer Macpherson, who married Bryher to conceal his romantic involvement with H. D. in the late '20s. This group published several books on cinema and the first English-language journal devoted to film as an art form, *Close-up* (1927–33); it also produced four experimental films, of which *Borderline* seems to have been the most ambitious. Much of the POOL group's interest in film consisted in exploring its potential as a psychoanalytic apparatus for rendering unconscious processes.

Among the contributors to *Close-up* was analyst Hanns Sachs, who wrote regularly on psychoanalysis and film; the group was particularly excited by *Secrets of a Soul*, German director G. W. Pabst's expressionistic attempt to translate the rudiments of Freud's "talking cure" into visual narrative (see Konigsberg). All of the films the POOL group made explicitly concern psychoanalytic concepts (see Friedberg). Less consistently, the group preoccupied itself with the politics of racial representation in film, devoting at least one issue of *Close-up* to reviews and articles about problematic depictions of blacks in popular American and British cinema.[1] As Susan Stanford Friedman observes, Macpherson and Robert Herring (the latter another contributor to *Close-up*) were also "part of the white crowd for whom 'the Negro was in vogue.' They regularly visited Harlem on their trips to the States with Bryher and brought back to Europe all the latest in black writing and music" ("Modernism" 98).

Herring introduced Paul and Eslanda Robeson to H. D.'s circle in the late '20s, and eventually the POOL group persuaded the Robesons to take time from their hectic touring schedule to act in *Borderline* while it was shot in Switzerland. It was Paul Robeson's second film role since he had appeared in Oscar Michaux's *Body and Soul* in 1924. Though *Borderline* was not particularly well received when it was first released (owing as much to its psychoanalytic preoccupations as to its putative antiracism), the film has since drawn the attention of a number of scholars with divergent critical concerns. A brief synopsis of its diffuse yet significant plot, its explicit engagement with psychoanalysis, its avant-garde aesthetic, and its interracial content will make clear this interest.

Borderline is an expressionistic depiction of the sexual and racial tensions that develop in a small European village when two heterosexual couples—one white, one black—play out the interpersonal problems arising from the white man's sexual involvement with the black woman. In the short "libretto," passed out at the initial screenings of the film, we are told that in a small "borderline" town, anywhere in Europe, Pete, a negro, is working in a cheap hotel café. His wife, Adah, who had left him some time previously, has arrived also in the same town, although neither is aware of the presence of the other.

Adah is staying in rooms with Thorne and Astrid. Thorne is a young man whose life with Astrid has become a torment to them both. Both [are] highly strung, [and] their nerves are tense with continuous hostility evoked by Thorne's vague and destructive cravings. He has been involved in an affair with Adah, and the film opens with the quarrel which ends their relationship.[2]

As Pete (Paul Robeson) reconciles with Adah (Eslanda Robeson) in a series of out-door scenes, Astrid (played by H. D., using the pseudonym "Helga Doorn") and Thorne (Gavin Arthur) quarrel until Astrid is accidentally stabbed to death. The drama between the two couples is intercut with scenes from the hotel's restaurant, over which a lesbian couple seems to preside (a butch-looking, cigar-smoking Bryher plays the café's manageress, while Charlotte Arthur is the femme barmaid). In this interior setting, we see townspeople discussing the interracial affair while the barmaid encourages general drinking and merrymaking, the manageress soberly keeps the books, and a gay-coded piano player (Robert Herring), with a photo of Pete propped next to him, accompanies the action with what is doubtless jazz music. Before her death, Astrid jealously castigates Thorne in the café, stirring up the racist sentiments of the villagers by calling him a "Nigger Lover" and seeming to make a pact with a witchlike old lady, who later says that if she had her way, "not one negro would be allowed in this country." These scenes are intercut with exterior shots of the village and surrounding countryside, where the black couple reconciles in natural, rustic settings.

Astrid's death leads to further racial hatred by the townspeople until Adah voluntarily leaves and Pete is ordered to depart by a letter from the Mayor. Before leaving, Pete appears with Thorne in a scene of mutual forgiveness; they shake hands, and, as the libretto puts it, "they both realise that what has happened has been beyond them, and brought about by external circumstances—that enmity has been among others, and they themselves mere instruments for its consummation" (150). We next see Pete waiting alone at the train station. Final shots inside the café indicate that "order" is restored now that the black characters have been exiled from the white village. Overall, the film indicts the villagers' racist triumph; it also implies, however, that Thorne (unlike the other characters) has undergone a transformation as a result of these events and has worked through his inner conflicts. In this sense, the film privileges his subjectivity over that of the other characters.

Critical attention to *Borderline* has been diverse, characterizing the film as feminist, modernist, a psychoanalytic experiment, a lesbian or queer text, a white representation of blackness, and as a significant moment in Paul Robeson's film career (see, respectively, Friedberg; Friedman; Morris; Weiss; Cripps; Dyer). Yet in almost every case, emphasis on one aspect of the film's significance inevitably eclipses its other elements by downplaying their interdependency. For example, Anne Friedberg's discussions of the film, arguably the most detailed and exhaustive of sources on the POOL group's activities, focus on *Borderline*'s production, contexts, and troubled reception, but do not extensively interpret its racial diegesis. On the other hand, Richard Dyer's treatment of Paul Robeson's crossover star status in *Heavenly Bodies* provides perhaps the most astute, though brief, analysis of the film's racial politics, noting how "little an active role the Paul Robeson character has in the narrative" and how the "highly complex use of montage only reinforces this inactivity" (132). While his treatment of the film focuses on its white construction of black masculinity, Dyer also notes in passing the presence of gay- or lesbian-coded characters in the film ("the dyke style of the innkeeper and her woman friend, for instance, and the piano player with the photo of Pete/Robeson on his piano" [132]) and suggests that there are homoerotic elements in the film's resolution. Yet Dyer's exhaustive coverage of Robeson's career makes it impossible for him to explore in depth *Borderline*'s amalgamation of sexual and racial difference as both were imagined by its white modernist creators.

How do white fantasies of racial difference inform and underwrite *Borderline*'s psychoanalytically inflected modernist challenges to a conventionally gendered and sexed status quo? By interpreting *Borderline* and its accompanying texts, I shall modify the standard feminist question that many H. D. scholars ask: What difference do women writers and filmmakers make in the related projects of modernism, psychoanalysis, and cinematic representation? This essay extends that question by asking, In what way do these women's fantasies of racial difference inflect their gendered differences in these projects?

We should note immediately that *Borderline*'s composition and structure already complicate these questions. For instance, although H. D. and Bryher portrayed Macpherson as *Borderline*'s artistic genius, the film was a collaborative effort insofar as the two women defined the characters they portrayed and took over the daunting job of editing the film when Macpherson became sick after the shooting. They also wrote interpretive and explanatory texts to accompany the film (thus influencing its reception) and doubtless contributed to the film's artistic conception and sexual/racial politics, even though they downplayed these politics by highlighting the film's formal properties. We know that in their personal lives, H. D. and Bryher challenged sexual, gender, and domestic conventions, and that H. D. habitually transposed her personal experiences into her literary projects, writing what critics and biographers call "romans à clef" that feature her lovers, friends, and closest associates. Yet as I suggested above, little has been written about *Borderline* as a type of "film à clef": The film explores the preoccupations, desires, and interrelationships of white modernists that are "projected" onto their black acquaintances. The film also partly makes clear the forms of racial and sexual difference that surface in a cinematic venture designed to *counter* the blatantly racist productions of the American film industry.

This group's preoccupation with racial politics was concomitant with its intense interest in psychoanalysis for its affirmation of the role of the unconscious in creativity and its availability as a discourse of sexual difference. *Borderline* aids our interpretation of a racial account of psychoanalysis, modernity, and neurosis. In her introduction to H. D.'s *Borderline* pamphlet, for instance, Friedman notes that "H. D. wrote openly about her identification with Robeson as a fellow expatriate American in her privately printed sketch 'Two Americans' and covertly about her erotic attraction to him in the poem 'Red Roses for Bronze' " ("H. D." 89). We might wonder how such identification and desire—primary psychoanalytic constituents—relate to how H. D. incorporated Robeson into the film's expressionist text and used him, via formal techniques, as a "foil" to offset the psychic complexity of her own character.[3]

"Into the Labyrinth of the (White) Human Mind"

As scholars of the POOL group have observed, H. D., Bryher, and Macpherson greatly admired Pabst's psychoanalytic experiment *Secrets of a Soul*; they also worked closely with analyst Hanns Sachs, who contributed articles on film and psychology to *Close-up*. Bryher had been in analysis with Sachs since 1928 and H. D. would be analyzed by him in 1931, before starting analysis with Freud in 1933. Both women closely read the psychoanalytic journals to which Bryher had subscribed since the early 1920s (Friedman, *Penelope's* 287).

In an article entitled "Film Psychology," published in *Close-up* in 1928, Sachs analyzed scenes from Eisenstein to demonstrate how a film's diegesis "consists of closely interwoven psychological coherencies," which become visible only if a film "can externalise and make perceptible—if possible in movement—invisible inward events" (11). Sachs suggested that such "limited mimetics" as facial expressions might better be replaced by focusing the camera on evocative objects or the "small unnoticed ineptitudes of behaviour described by Freud as symptomatic actions" (11). Only in this way could film become "a kind of time microscope . . . [that] shows us clearly and unmistakably things that are to be found in life but that ordinarily escape our notice" (12). Accordingly, film functions as an analyst—as "a new way of driving mankind to conscious recognition" of those things that would otherwise remain unconscious (15). Like the POOL group's other film projects, *Borderline* was conceived in part to continue what Sachs argued was the intrinsically psychoanalytic nature of Eisenstein's films. *Borderline* (and certainly H. D.'s assessment of it in her pamphlet) was also greatly informed by Freud's observations on sexuality, repression, and neurosis. The film accentuates Freud's ideas with a racialized white/black binary that places the black subject beyond the "civilized."

In an article written after the first public screenings of *Borderline*, Macpherson explained that the POOL group had contributed a technical innovation to the project of "driving mankind to conscious recognition" of the unconscious:

> I decided to make *Borderline* with a "subjective use of inference." By this I meant that instead of the method of externalised observation, dealing with objects [as in Sachs's discussion of Eisenstein], I was going to take my film into the minds of the people in it. . . . To take the action, the observation, the deduction, the reference, into the labyrinth of the human mind, with its queer impulses and tricks, its unreliability, its stresses and obsessions, its half-formed deductions, its glibness, its occasional amnesia, its fantasy, suppressions and desires. (294)

Like much contemporaneous psychoanalytic discourse, Macpherson posited a universal "human mind" whose essential labyrinthine nature is shared by male and female, black and white. The film, we are told, gives the effect of entering "into the minds of the people in it"; thus we would expect to know much about the consciousness of each protagonist. In practice, however, the film distinguishes greatly among the minds it "probes"; it deploys montage techniques to enter repeatedly (if somewhat mechanically) into certain minds (Astrid's and Thorne's) but not others. In this way, the film aims to give Astrid and Thorne the type of complexity that Macpherson described in his article. We enter Pete's mind less frequently, and often then only because its "placidity" (the way in which it is "conversant with nature") contrasts with the turbulence of both white protagonists. Adah remains very much a cipher, functioning as an external stimulant who triggers the psychic responses of others (Thorne's conflicted desire, Astrid's jealousy, Pete's overflowing joy); she is never rendered as a subject herself.

This asymmetry between "white" and "black" emerges from the POOL group's racial understanding of Freudian psychoanalysis. H. D. and Bryher doubtless were familiar with the thesis linking neurosis to repressed sexuality in Freud's 1908 paper " 'Civilized' Sexual Morality and Modern Nervous Illness." After summarizing Erb, Binswanger, and Krafft-Ebing on the deleterious effects of modernization on the "nervous system," Freud argues in this essay that such claims "prove insufficient to explain the details in the picture of nervous disturbances": "They leave out of account precisely the most important of the aetiological factors involved." "If we disregard the vaguer ways of being 'nervous' and consider the specific forms of nervous illness," Freud adds, "we shall find that the injurious influence of civilization reduces itself in the main to the harmful suppression of the sexual life of civilized peoples (or classes) through the 'civilized' sexual morality prevalent in them" (185).

Freud begins this article by invoking Ehrenfels, who "dwells on the difference between 'natural' and 'civilized' sexual morality. By natural sexual morality we are to understand, according to him, a sexual morality under whose dominance a human stock is able to remain in lasting possession of health and efficiency, while civilized sexual morality is a sexual morality obedience to which, on the other hand, spurs men on to intense and productive cultural activity" (181). Unlike the authors Freud later cites, Ehrenfels apparently correctly attributes "damaging effects" to "civilized sexual morality," though he misses a "particular one whose significance [Freud] will . . . discuss in detail in the present paper . . .[:] the increase traceable to it of modern nervous illness—of the nervous illness, that is, which is rapidly spreading in our present-day society" (182). Freud then questions the distinction between "natural" and "civilized" desire, in which the former appears "unrepressed" such that "a human stock is able to remain in lasting possession of health and efficiency" through "selection by virility" (181, 182), while the latter is a compulsory monogamous heterosexuality that can lead to both "productive cultural activity" and neurosis (181). Considering how race and sexuality intersect in *Borderline*, H. D. and the POOL group frequently and unthinkingly reproduce this distinction between the "natural" and "civilized," with its apparently explanatory account of cultural attainment and neurosis, as a white/black binary: The film's black characters connote a "natural" sexual morality that largely evades the repressive influence of "civilized" (read "white") moral codes.

"Dark Daemon" and "Uncoordinated White-folk"

In her pamphlet on *Borderline*, H. D. makes racial distinctions among the characters to which the film seems largely impervious; she does so while trying to downplay the film's racial politics:

> Macpherson . . . is, in no way whatever, concerned personally with the black-white political problem. . . he says, "here is a man, he is black," he says, "here is a woman also of partial African abstraction." He says, not "here is a black man, here is a mulatto woman," but "here is a *man*, here is a *woman*." He says, "look, sympathize with them and love them" not because they are black but because they are man, because they are woman. (112)

The text is contradictory here: If racial distinctions are not important components of the characters' constructions, why specify that Adah is "of partial African abstraction"? H. D.'s insistence on Adah's "mixed" race seems to correlate closely to Adah's position between two racially coded extremes: At one pole we see what H. D. calls "the half world mondaine, Astrid with Thorne, her lover" (110). Here whiteness connotes "overcivilized." At the other pole, we watch Pete, the "very earth giant," the "earth-god," the "great river," the "ground under all their feet" (111–12); his blackness apparently precedes civilization. Further, Pete's designation as "earth" and "god" removes him from the category that dwells between: the human. His precivilized nature renders him prehuman.

Another passage in H. D.'s pamphlet suggests that these extremes confirm a susceptibility to moral corruption among whites and a premoral, primordial, godlike innocence among blacks, with Adah occupying an ambiguous and unstable relation to both extremes:

> Pete and Adah escape from their little room and stand on a hill slope. Like a dream, the great negro head looms disproportionate, and water and cloud and rock and sky are all subsidiary to its being. Like a personal dream, gone further into the race dream, we see (with Pete) hill and cloud as, on that first day, created. Dream merges with myth and Pete, regarding a fair heaven far from the uncreated turmoil of that small-town café, says quite logically, "let there be light." *Light has been, it is obvious, created by that dark daemon, conversant with all nature since before the time of white man's beginning.*
>
> His small sweetheart in her little shop-bought, pull-on soft hat is complement to this radiant figure. *She has sinned, she is not altogether god-like,* but she is created on the hill slope with him, *apart from the nightmare of the uncoordinated white-folk.* (122; my emphases)

The "shop-bought" hat (a product of white civilization) seems to encode Adah's "white" blood: In the film's logic, this "white" blood renders her capable of sinning, which is to say, of making decisions in a moral realm. Conversely, Pete's "godlike" blackness exempts him from this "moral realm"; apparently, his mind is prehuman and does not correspond to Macpherson's "human labyrinth." Adah is thus an unrepresentable link between white and black, civilization and nature, moral and premoral; her mixed blood seemingly overdetermines her sexual liaison with a white man. If in this film her whiteness makes her capable of sin, her sin is paradoxically to desire whiteness. The film cannot fully represent this paradox. While Adah therefore signifies a structural and thematic link between black and white, her interiority is not adequately explored. She becomes the untheorized ground, or excluded middle, on which the black/white opposition of *Borderline* is predicated.

Given this unintelligible middle ground, the film cannot represent Adah's psyche via its experimental montage techniques. What the film *does* represent are the interior states of mind at either end of this white/black, moral/premoral spectrum: those of Astrid and Pete. These characters structurally resonate with each other insofar as the technique of "clatter montage" constructs them more insistently than it does the other characters (see Friedberg, "Approaching"). Indeed, H. D. draws attention to how this technique (used to reveal or externalize each character's mind) makes visible the essential differences that mark their psyches. In the first section of her pamphlet, she remarks: "The giant negro is in the high clouds, white cumulus cloud banks in a higher heaven. Conversely, his white fellow-men are the shadows of white, are dark, neurotic; storm brews; there is that runic fate that 'they that live by the sword shall perish by the sword.' Or as here applied, 'they that live by neurotic-erotic suppression shall perish by the same'" (112).

Linking racial types metaphorically with clouds, H. D. portrays Pete as "white cumulus" and the *white* characters as "dark, neurotic" by virtue of their behaving like storm clouds). Later, referring to the rapid montage sequences, she explains how the film's white/black binary recurs, juxtaposing Pete with a waterfall (akin to the white clouds) and Astrid with the "knife" or neurotic sword by which she perishes:

> The minute and meticulous effect for instance that Mr. Macpherson achieves with Pete, the negro and the waterfall, or the woman Astrid with the knife, are so naturalistic, I should say so "natural" that they seem to the uninitiate, sheer "tricks" or accidents. The effect of the negro, Pete, against the waterfall is achieved by a meticulous and painstaking effort on the part of the director, who alone with the giants of German and Russian production is his own cutter and will not trust his "montage" to a mere technician, however sympathetic. . . . The same sort of jagged lightning effect is given with Astrid with her dagger. The white woman is here, there, everywhere, the dagger is above, beneath, is all but in her heart or in the heart of her meretricious lover. (118–19)

As H. D. implies, the "clatter montage" technique—"achieved by the meticulous cutting of three- and four- and five-inch lengths of film and pasting these tiny strips together" to suggest a flickering double exposure (119)—links the two "opposite" characters on whom it is used most frequently: Astrid and Pete. That these two characters never appear in the same frame or, indeed, in the same scene, heightens their status as contraries: Their positions on the continuum of "civilized" and "natural" apparently are so far apart that it is impossible to imagine them occupying the same cinematic space. As Astrid's "opposite," however, Pete is indissolubly tied to her as the blackness that the film abjects to confirm her "purity."

FIGURE 17.1
Pete (Paul Robeson) photographed against the "natural" backdrop of cumulous clouds. *Beinecke Library, Yale University.*

The two scenes H. D. describes represent peaks of erotic intensity: in Pete's case, a "natural" eroticism conveyed by his joyful merging with the elements (waterfall, sky, rocks, and trees; see figure 1); in Astrid's case, a "repressed" eroticism that results in the frenzied, neurotic manipulation of the knife leading to her death scene (see figure 2). Pete reunites with Adah in a series of shots that track them wandering through the village's quaint cobblestoned lanes and into the countryside. We see several picturesque shots of this countryside—trees, buildings nestled in the mountainside, a horse and cart. We then see Pete reaching down to pull Adah up to the "hill side" H. D. celebrated in her pamphlet. Presently, the film gives us several panning shots of a waterfall, rushing river, and trees; the frequency of the cuts increases until the montage reaches "clatter" speed. At this point, the waterfall is juxtaposed with Pete's profile set against a bank of clouds, which exteriorizes his "overflowing joy" at being with his "sweetheart" again. The rapid montage sequence ends with several longer shots of his beaming face against the sky; toward the end of one of these shots, the camera pans down from his face to Adah's, which rests on his breast (see figure 3).

Later, after several shots establishing the white couple's fretful ennui in their rooms (Astrid endlessly adjusting a Victorian shawl; Thorne lying on his bed in the

FIGURE 17.2
Astrid (H. D.) clenches her hands in "neurotic-erotic suppression." *Beinecke Library, Yale University.*

next room; Astrid sitting motionlessly next to a record she has put on the Victrola, feeling neglected no doubt while Thorne strokes and nuzzles the cat), Thorne prepares to leave, carrying a suitcase. Astrid clutches her shawl tighter and stares at him from across the room, her eyes glistening with frustrated tears. Here we get a shot, from her perspective, of the suitcase: The camera zooms in on this object; then, in a brief clatter montage sequence, the film intercuts shots of the suitcase with barely discernible frames of Adah's face. This indicates either that the suitcase belongs to Adah or that Thorne is going to her. Interestingly, although this montage sequence also involves a character's face, this technique does not give us the character's psyche, but that of the montage's presumed "viewer": Astrid. Adah's face functions as the index for the "labyrinth" of a white woman's mind, but never as the threshold of Adah's own psyche.

At this point, Astrid enters into what we might call a "masquerade" of femininity, following Joan Rivière's essay of the previous year, "Womanliness as a Masquerade" (1929). According to Rivière, women who engage in public displays of competence in a professional arena reserved for men may follow that display with flirtatious behavior toward men they perceive as hostile to their proficiency. By seducing "father figures" in their male audience, these women, according to Rivière,

FIGURE 17.3
Pete (Paul Robeson) reconciles with Adah (Eslanda Robeson), in her "shop-bought hat." *Beinecke Library, Yale University.*

hope to ward off retaliation for "stealing" the penis that is rightfully a man's. In this context, "womanliness" is a compensatory—not essential—behavior; the masquerade offers self-protection in a patriarchal social sphere. Yet the analysand that most preoccupies Rivière has fantasies of being attacked by a "negro" whom she would seduce and then hand over to the "authorities": "This phantasy . . . had been very common in her childhood and youth, which had been spent in the Southern States of America; if a negro came to attack her, she planned to defend herself by making him kiss her and make love to her (ultimately so that she could then deliver him over to justice)" (37). The true "father figures" in this imagined scenario set in the "Southern States of America" would not be the attacking "negro," but the white male authorities representing "justice." To propitiate the (white) fathers, the white woman fantasizes that she can substitute the black male body for her own. This suggests that the "masquerade" involves a degree of identification and desire across imagined racially defined differences—indeed, a trafficking in the eroticized black male body (see Rivière, and Walton, "Re-Placing").

In a bid to prevent Thorne from reuniting with Adah (whose face, juxtaposed on the suitcase, indicates that Thorne prefers another "womanliness" to Astrid's), Astrid flies across the room in her "feminine" shawl, clutches Thorne, and hangs

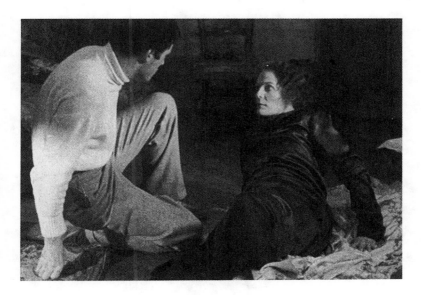

FIGURE 17.4

Thorne (Gavin Arthur) and Astrid (H. D.) in their room, after Astrid's "masquer-ade" of death. *Beinecke Library, Yale University.*

from his neck. She then collapses to the floor and lies there in stricken contortion, her eyes staring lifelessly. Dropping the suitcase, Thorne kneels at her side, obviously frightened that she has somehow died as a result of her nervous crisis (see figure 4). When she mockingly snaps back to life, he deliberately walks around the table, sharpening a pencil with a knife at crotch level, as if to assert once and for all that he does indeed have the phallus. A little later, Astrid picks up the same knife and jabs it into the air very close to Thorne. Here the "clatter montage" technique recurs to imply an intrinsic link between Astrid and the knife. That Astrid threatens Thorne with the knife signifies that she has relinquished her (unsuccessful) masquerade of death and is now desperately plying the phallus. The rapid montage sequence juxta-poses the knife with Astrid, some daffodils on the table, and glimpses of Thorne's face and hand as the knife cuts him. The sequence continues until Thorne wrestles the knife from Astrid's hand; the two of them collapse once more onto the floor.

As H. D. suggested, this scene is meant to convey a cause-and-effect relation between "living" and "dying" by the sword. From this, we understand that these "uncoordinated white-folk" live and die by "neurotic-erotic suppression": The erotic *is* the phallus for which "civilized" white protagonists compete against a background of "natural," black supporting characters.

FIGURE 17.5
Kenneth Macpherson (behind camera) shoots a scene
with Paul Robeson (right), assisted by *Borderline* cast
and crew. *Beinecke Library, Yale University.*

Black Screens, White Filmmaker

The film's phallic symbolism does not properly acknowledge that *Borderline*'s
white male filmmaker flourishes by the sword; H. D. presents Macpherson in her
pamphlet as the film's consummate editor. H. D.'s pamphlet also reiterates over

and again that Macpherson has mastered film directing. According to H. D., his expertise derives from being a master with the "sword"—as the splicer and editor of film. However, since Macpherson became sick after shooting the film, H. D. and Bryher, the film's lesbian collaborators, did much of its remaining editing. They were also largely responsible for what they felt was its most innovative aspect—its clatter montage. H. D. nonetheless claimed that Macpherson "is his own cutter and will not trust his 'montage' to a mere technician, however sympathetic" (119).

Considering the film's imaginary in tandem with H. D.'s commentary, we find that those who "die by the sword" are palpably a gendered *and* raced category: If it is the white man's prerogative to be the sword's master, the white woman takes the fall for this "mastery." In this respect, it is not entirely true that "he who lives by the sword must die by it," for in this film women and blacks die or disappear by the sword: Astrid is literally killed by the knife over which she and her male counterpart struggle; Pete and Adah are subsequently exiled from the community. Only Thorne regains some tranquillity from these violent abjections. At no point does the film allow us to imagine that Pete and Adah (or, indeed, Paul and Eslanda Robeson) "liv[e] by the sword." The result of the POOL group's racial application of the primitive/civilized binary explored in Freud's essay: While the black characters seem "immune" to neurosis, they are barred from creative achievement, for this is reserved for the "civilized" genius that H. D.'s pamphlet extols (see figure 5).

Beyond this structural exclusion, by the '20s and '30s filmmaking's apparatus was thoroughly raced, as a passing reference to lighting techniques in independent filmmaking, published in *Close-up*, attests. In a 1930 article in *Close-up* entitled "This Year's Sowing," Oswell Blakeston quotes Basil Emmott on how to handle lighting situations. When it comes to the question of close-ups, Emmott says, "to get any god-damned effect that has some vitality you must shoot through the cracks of two niggers. This ensures the lens being in shadow and allows you to turn lamps where you will" (483). The footnote to an asterisk in the text after the word "niggers" shows no more understanding of this term's racist meaning than does the passage itself. The note simply informs us that "a 'nigger' is a black screen, used to shield the camera from rays of light" (483n.). Accompanying this article, in typical *Close-up* fashion, are stills of the faces of Paul and Eslanda Robeson, and H. D.; the Robeson shots are labeled: "Two characteristic studies of Paul Robeson, famous negro singer and actor, in *Borderline*, a POOL Film, directed by Kenneth Macpherson." Considered with the photos, the racist term for the black screens is both a personal insult to the Robesons and a structural problem for the POOL group's racial dynamics. Moreover, although film stills in

Close-up are often juxtaposed with unrelated articles, these stills function as examples of close-up lighting, illustrating Emmott's remark that "lighting should alter for each face."

This remark implies that "Negro" faces require different lighting conditions than do "white" faces. I suggest however that lighting does not simply *respond* to differently raced faces, but greatly assists in the *construction* of this difference's meaning. If "lighting should alter for each face" so that our racial understanding of each face alters, the apparatus itself offers a racial account of its elements' division of labor. A beam of light is thus directed "through the cracks of two niggers" onto the face in question. Syntactically, this sentence reads as if the "cracks" *belong* to the "niggers," rather than referring to the space between them. In this way, the screens are not merely personified; they are also racialized, perhaps even sexualized (they have "cracks"). *Close-up*, which Macpherson edited, seemed unaware that contemporaneous film discourse harbored the racism that he wanted his film to combat. Moreover, H. D.'s suggestion that Pete is a "daemon" creator of "light" can be understood as an ideological inversion of cinema's racial apparatus: "Dream merges with myth and Pete, regarding a fair heaven far from the uncreated turmoil of that small-town café, says quite logically, 'let there be light.' Light has been, it is obvious, created by that dark daemon, conversant with all nature since before the time of white man's beginning" (122).

In this depiction, Pete's blackness removes him from the world of light only to present him as the creator of light: In a system determined by light, the center is imagined as the blackness that makes light possible. In this ideological figure, an unilluminated "dark daemon" precedes the "white man's beginning" in light; alternately, the "daemon" is ludicrously praised as a creator. Meanwhile, Macpherson—who places his lights between the black screens that his colleagues (and perhaps he himself) call "niggers"—"creates" the light illuminating Pete's "mythic" appearance on the hillside.

In the character of Pete, racial blackness combines, via clatter montage, with the waterfall to suggest a gushing that the film does not suppress—a naturalness that somehow escapes neurosis. He and Adah do not, like Astrid and Thorne, "liv[e] by the sword" or by "neurotic-erotic suppression," for their sex lives apparently are uncomplicated, untainted by civilization and its discontents. By corollary, unlike the white male filmmaker and his white collaborators, Pete and Adah do not consciously determine the images they present.

H. D. extended this white fantasy of the black mind's premoral, natural, "sexual" quality from Pete to Robeson himself, as her fictional account of him in "Two Americans" attests:

His least movement was so gracious, he didn't have to think things out. Nevertheless with an astonishing analytical power, he did think. That was the odd thing about Saul Howard, he did think. He had a mind, a steadfast sort of burning, a thing that glowed like a whole red sunset or like a coal mine, it was steady, a steady sort of warmth and heat, yet all the time intellectual; *he thought not as a man thinks.* Paula Howard, his wife, thought more as white folks, consistently, being more than half white . . . (H. D., qtd. in Guest 199; my emphasis)

In this thinly veiled fictional portrait, the narrator gives Robeson (as Saul Howard) an ability to "think," but only if his mind resembles a "thing" that glows like a "sunset"—a natural, nonhuman element. Interestingly, H. D. does not write, "he thought not as a white man thinks," but simply, "he thought not as a man thinks." This implies that the standard for human thinking is a tradition of white thinking, from which Robeson's blackness necessarily excludes him. H. D.'s next sentence reinforces this suggestion: She tells us that Paula Howard, standing in for Eslanda Robeson, "thought more as white folks, consistently, being more than half white." Like Adah in *Borderline*, Paula in "Two Americans" occupies a middle position between black and white, the human and nonhuman, the civilized and precivilized.[4]

Borderline and H. D.'s accompanying pamphlet consistently conflate actors with the characters they play; we see this when Barbara Guest, H. D.'s biographer, describes the film as

a mêlée of emotional difficulties, threats of departure, false loves, exaggerated despair. The comic relief is supplied by Bryher, who is quite at home with a fat black cigar in her mouth, going about the business of adding up the cash, while the others seek to destroy themselves. Through it all stalk the sincere and loving couple, Robeson and his Essie. The Robesons finally get out of the film by walking off into the mountain while H. D. writhes upon the floor in a death agony in imitation of the final act of *Jeanne Ney*. (197)

Guest describes the film almost entirely in terms of whether various actors/characters are "at home" or "outsiders" in its realm:

Robeson does not fit in. He is too much himself. He is not a "borderline" person, even if it is rationalized that being black makes him so. He is very much a part of the world. His personal beauty and the strength of his character tend to dominate the film, mostly because Robeson seems unaware of the psychological overtones of the film. He must have been a great admirer of Eisenstein, and may have been suggested by that director for the role, but he has no concept of the scenario of the film, nebulous as it was. (196–97)

Since Guest never explains how she knows that Robeson has "no concept of the scenario of the film," we must conclude that she derives this impression from his performance. She takes her cue from H. D.'s pamphlet in assuming that the Robesons are not "borderline," like the white characters, insofar as Thorne's "perverse" sexual drives (which his excessive drinking and interracial desire signify) and Astrid's sexual jealousy both denote their borderline status. This denotation represents the Robesons as "standouts or outsiders among a group of borderliners" precisely because they are not marked by "perverse" or "unwholesome" sexuality: They represent a healthy, heterosexual couple untainted by the neuroses that inform (white) civilization.

Guest's remarks suggest that the cinematic effect of "natural" sexuality derives from the Robesons "naturally" exuding this phenomenon while the film was shot. She also implies that Robeson does not "act," since he is "too much himself"; allegedly, his "personal beauty and the strength of his character" dominate the film, not his conscious method of playing a part. How indeed could he act when he is "unaware of the psychological overtones of the film" and "has no concept of the scenario of the film"? Guest refers to "Robeson and his Essie" as a "sincere and loving couple" stalking through a film full of self-destructive white people. This suggests not that Pete and Adah are "sincere and loving" characters in *Borderline*, but that what Guest presumes is the Robesons' "sincere and loving" marriage contrasts radically with the white couple's tormented relationship.

Considering biographical accounts of the Robesons' life at the time, we cannot maintain this fantasy of them as an "unaware" but "sincere and loving" presence in the film (see Duberman). A diary entry by Eslanda Robeson clarifies that the Robesons knew enough about *Borderline*'s scenario to find its racial dichotomy between white and black psyches ridiculous and offensive: "Kenneth and H. D. used to make us so shriek with laughter with their naive ideas of Negroes that Paul and I often completely ruined our make-up with tears of laughter, and had to make up all over again. We never once felt we were colored with them" (qtd. in Duberman 131).

From the Robesons' perspective, that "Negroes" are naive is a preposterous white fantasy; the white filmmakers "make up" these black actors' faces so that their blackness contrasts sufficiently with their counterparts' whiteness. Robeson's "natural" presence in the film obviously is due to the filmmaker's calculated techniques. When the Robesons realized what Macpherson and H. D. wanted them to portray, however, their laughter ruined this construction's make up so that it had to be reapplied. Clearly, Macpherson and H. D. received their laughter good-naturedly, for Eslanda adds that "we never once felt we were colored with them"— that is, that Paul and Eslanda's puncturing of white naiveté never induced hostility or resistance. However, the Robesons' implicit critique of the POOL group's racial fantasies ultimately went unheeded in *Borderline*, since this group's "naive ideas of Negroes" remained part of the film's fabric and white reception.

I have argued that the POOL group adapted Freud's gendered (and implicitly raced) accounts of sexual repression, neurosis, and cultural achievement, inserting them into a cinematic machine that reproduced an already established racial binary. This binary resonates with a problematic Freudian account of female sexuality and subjectivity that many feminists have critiqued. Excluded from (or, in Adah's case, misguidedly covetous of) the "moral" realm of whiteness, Pete and Adah (and for their white observers, the Robesons too) occupy a terrain that Freud, in his account of the superego, largely reserved for women and girls. Freud claimed that "the level of what is ethically normal [in women] is different from what it is in men. Their super-ego is never so inexorable, so impersonal, so independent of its emotional origins as we require it to be in men" ("Some" 257). In Freudian terms, that Pete and Adah occupy a precivilized and premoral realm correlates with their "underdeveloped" superegos, for they are not fully initiated into the symbolic order, which is determined as much by whiteness as by the phallus. Pete and Adah's absence of neurosis, and their resultant inability to achieve culturally, endorses this reading.

I haven't sufficient space to explore how the film's distinctions between hetero- and homoeroticism complicate these racial and cultural metaphors. As *Borderline*'s precivilized characters, Pete and Adah (and, by extension, the Robesons themselves) seem to display a natural heterosexuality that requires no repression; conversely, Astrid and Thorne appear neurotic precisely because, as products of modernization, their (problematic) heterosexuality is achieved only by repressing underlying homoerotic impulses. The butch/femme lesbian couple and gay-coded pianist who preside over the café's public space reinforce this reading of white heterosexuality. Like Pete and Adah, these characters seem decidedly less neurotic than the white heterosexual couple; their emotional health is predicated on their *un*repressed—or perhaps successfully sublimated—homoerotic desire. As I argue elsewhere, the queer matrix that these characters represent ensures a homoerotic subtext that complicates *Borderline*'s "straight" account of interracial desire (see Walton, "White"). One might say that the queer-delineated space of the café "hosts" the "straight" plot, and that the white couple is "queered" by its trajectory through that space. The black couple remains unproblematically heterosexual throughout the film, however, though Robeson's body seems to function as the "natural" black flesh precipitating the white characters' "perverse" desires. While the black characters are "available" to the white characters and filmmakers as catalysts for sexual, psychological, and aesthetic transformation, the reverse is not true.

By linking neurosis, racism, and a form of perverse heterosexuality, H. D. and her collaborators arguably intended *Borderline* to illustrate the limits of white civilization-as-modernity. Insofar as the film primitivizes black characters, living "by the sword," or by "neurotic-erotic suppression" is the sad fate of whites only. It is also their privilege, however: According to the Freudian model that the POOL group adapted, when the "erotic" is *sublimated* and not "suppressed," the white subject can become an exceptional artist, writer, or filmmaker. Cultural achievement is thus the alternative—perhaps even the solution—to white neurosis. Moreover, in the POOL group's imaginary, only white subjects have homoerotic impulses that *need* repression or sublimation; since blacks are statically heterosexual in this film, they have no need to sublimate or suppress their impulses. In this respect, *Borderline* gives us the impression that modernism—or, perhaps more specifically, the "gendering" and "queering" of modernism—was an exclusively white prerogative.

ENDNOTES

I thank Jim Morrison for launching this project by inviting me to present on *Borderline* at the Society for Cinema Studies conference in Spring 1995. I also thank Abigail Child and Melissa Ragona, whose enthusiastic conversations with me about the film helped at the early revisionary stages. Thanks to Lee Ann Brown, Mary Cappello, Lise Carlson, and members of the URI Experimental Film Discussion group, for their shared interest in experimental cinema, and to my undergraduate and graduate students at the University of Rhode Island for helping me see the film with new eyes every time I taught it. The URI Council for Research kindly granted me summer support so that I could continue my work on race and psychoanalysis. This article is dedicated to the memory of Marjorie Keller.

1. Introducing *Close-up* 5.2 in "As Is," Macpherson calls for "The negro documentaire of the negro. . . . The negro as an observer of himself. As his own historian. As his own agitator" (90). Arguing that "international film" is most authentic when the director is indigenous to the country or "race" he is trying to depict (only a Pabst can accurately depict Austria, for example), Macpherson asks us to consider the "negro film" and "decide whether you think international cinema is here going to mean a thing when a white man directs, no matter how charmingly, blacks so that they must always seem to be direfully dependent on white man's wisdom" (87). At the same time, Macpherson (soon to be a "white man" director) claims to be able to discern superior race traits in the "loose racial hands" of black actor Stepin Fetchit: "These so utterly not incantationish gestures are unselfconsciousness, perfectly inherited greatness of race and of race mind. . . . We can

scrap every trained toe waggle of a ballerina for the very least of these movements. Making this greatness articulate for the cinema is the fascinating pioneer work of somebody" (88). As we shall see, the *Borderline* project was Macpherson's attempt to avoid, as a "white man" director, the pitfalls he anticipated in this editorial; Robeson was to become the vehicle for expressing what he took to be the inherent "unselfconsciousness" of the black race, in contrast to the overconsciousness of the white.

2. At the first screenings of *Borderline*, the POOL group handed out a one-page plot synopsis, calling it the film's "libretto," which suggests that the group wanted the film to appear in part as a visual (but silent) operatic performance, built around a bare narrative outline (Friedberg reproduces the libretto in full; see "Writing" 150). One should not confuse this libretto with the longer interpretive pamphlet that H. D. published after the film's release, entitled simply "Borderline."

3. In "Modernism" Friedman takes up the question of H. D.'s erotic attraction to Paul Robeson, but focuses exclusively on her short story, "Two Americans," her poem, "Red Roses for Bronze," and the interpretive pamphlet she wrote on *Borderline*. While drawing on H. D.'s pamphlet, my discussion concerns more directly her role in the eroticized racial representation in the film proper.

4. See Friedman, "Modernism," for a more sympathetic reading of "Two Americans."

WORKS CITED

Blakeston, Oswell. "This Year's Sowing." *Close-up* 6.6 (1930): 482–85.

Cripps, Thomas. *Slow Fade to Black*. New York: Oxford UP, 1977.

Duberman, Martin Bauml. *Paul Robeson*. New York: Knopf, 1988.

Dyer, Richard. *Heavenly Bodies: Film Stars and Society*. New York: St. Martin's Press, 1986.

Freud, Sigmund. " 'Civilized' Sexual Morality and Modern Nervous Illness." 1908. Vol. 9 of *The Standard Edition of the Complete Psychological Works of Sigmund Freud*. Ed. and trans. James Strachey. London: Hogarth, 1953–74. 181–204.

———. "Some Psychical Consequences of the Anatomical Distinction Between the Sexes." 1925. Vol. 19 of *SE*. 248–58.

Friedberg, Anne. "Writing about Cinema: *Close-up*, 1927–1933." Ph.D. dissertation, New York University. October 1983.

———. "Approaching Borderline." In King. 369–90.

Friedman, Susan Stanford. "Modernism of the 'Scattered Remnant': Race and Politics in the Development of H. D.'s Modernist Vision." In King. 91–116.

———. *Penelope's Web: Gender, Modernity, H. D.'s Fiction*. New York: Cambridge UP, 1990.

———. "H. D. (1886–1961)." In Scott. 85–92.

Guest, Barbara. *Herself Defined: The Poet H. D. and Her World*. New York: Doubleday, 1984.

H. D. "*Borderline*." (Interpretive pamphlet about *Borderline*.) London: Mercury, 1930. In Scott. 110–25.

King, Michael, ed. *H. D., Woman and Poet*. Orono, Me: National Poetry Foundation, 1986.

Konigsberg, Ira. "Cinema, Psychoanalysis, and Hermeneutics: G. W. Pabst's *Secrets of a Soul*." *Michigan Quarterly Review* 34.4 (1995): 519–47.

Macpherson, Kenneth. "As Is." *Close-up* 12.5 (1930): 293–98.

Morris, Adalaide. "The Concept of Projection: H. D.'s Visionary Powers." *Signets: Reading H. D.* Ed. Susan Stanford Friedman and Rachel Blau DuPlessis. Madison: U of Wisconsin P, 1990. 273–96.

POOL. *Close-up* (Special Issue on Blacks in Cinema) 5.2 (1929).

Rivière, Joan. "Womanliness as a Masquerade." 1929. Ed. Victor Burgin, James Donald, and Cora Kaplan. *Formations of Fantasy*. London: Methuen, 1986. 35–44.

Sachs, Hanns. "Film Psychology." *Close-up* 3.5 (Nov. 1928): 8–15.

Scott, Bonnie Kime, ed. *The Gender of Modernism*. Bloomington: Indiana UP, 1990.

Walton, Jean. "Re-Placing Race in (White) Psychoanalytic Discourse: Founding Narratives of Feminism." *Critical Inquiry* 21 (1995): 775–804.

——. "White Neurotics, Black Primitives, and the Queer Matrix of *Borderline*." *Out Takes: Essays in Queer Theory and Film*. Ed. Ellis Hanson. Durham: Duke UP, forthcoming.

Weiss, Andrea. *Vampires and Violets: Lesbians in Film*. New York: Penguin, 1992.

18

Bonding Over Phobia

David Marriott

I think I have sufficiently emphasized that the unconscious is the unknown subject of the ego, that it is misrecognized [*méconnu*] by the ego, which is *der Kern unseres Wesens* [the core of our being] . . . The core of our being does not coincide with the ego.

—Lacan, *Seminar II* 43

But I too am guilty. . . . There is no help for it: I am a white man. For unconsciously I distrust what is black in me, that is, the whole of my being.   —Fanon 191

I know I am black. Even so, I occasionally fantasize and dream about being colorless, or at least invisible. Often I allow myself the comfort of placing this confused identification in my experience of everyday life, as if racial visibility and violence existed solely in the public domain, or only inside the heads of some hate-filled white people rather than in the minds and fantasies of black people. This is not, however, simply a case of displaced desire or social persecution. An unoccupied seat next to me on a full train sharply reminds me not only of white racial fears and anxieties about somatic contagion, but of how my life has been shaped by an introjected and anxiety-producing fear of being attacked—both within and without—by phobic intrusions. This evacuated space represents a place where whites care to—or dare—not go, a space that a type of X ray might reveal as black alienation and psychic dispossession. On these occasions, an unoccupied seat can help one recognize an apparently immutable cycle of white projected fear and black social invisibility. One also recognizes in oneself a violent desire to fend off this intrusion, either by glaring at one's frightened aggressors or by putting an end to this sickening charade by looking at oneself *as if one were in their place.*

I don't think I am overstating my case. Nor am I trying to articulate a black existential fear of nothingness. Instead, I am trying to outline the interstices of cultural fantasy and racial anxiety, abjection and desire; in the above example, these interstices pair or bond racially segregated social surveillance with black obsessional neurosis. Taking as its primary theme racial misrecognition, my essay asks how we can understand black identity when, through an act of mimetic desire, this identity already gets constructed as white. If the act of identification produces a fractured doubling of self, how can we distinguish what is interposed from what is properly desired?

To engage these questions, imagine the following scenario: A black analysand is in session with his white psychoanalyst—an encounter with multiple connotations, of course, and one rife with racial anxiety—discussing his traumatic experience of seeing himself, and being seen, as black in a series of racist encounters. As the analysand is talking, giving no thought to the pain or disruption which his talk of racial fear may be giving to his analyst, he suddenly realizes—inexplicably, uncritically—that the experiences he's describing don't concern him at all, but someone else lying in his place. Lying there enthralled by this double, who appears to be white, he is completely surprised by the analyst's announcement that it is the end of the session. He leaves the room in a daze, promising to himself not to return. A week later, he does.

The experience of being taken over by a racial *imago*—of being intruded upon, displaced, and fixated by an imaginary double—recurs in many accounts of black identity and identification. The disorientation and trauma this displacement produces suggest that an unconscious that seems to be "white" has displaced a conscious black identity. A number of difficulties arise from this too hasty account of racial intrusion, however, though the most crucial is also the most banal: the commonplace but no less intractable phenomenon of having a phantom unconscious that appears to hate you, because it undermines your psychic well-being. In light of this imaginary bonding between racial self and intrusive imago, it is difficult to say where the phobia in this scenario actually resides—whether in transference, incorporation, introjective or projective identification. Yet the sense of having an internal screen—of presenting an internal frontier where ego and imago can meet—is irreducible here.

I shall introduce two further examples of this encounter, the first a four-year-old girl fixated by her image in a mirror, the second a famous Martinican psychiatrist reflecting, in more or less analytical discourse, on an encounter with a French

boy. In both examples, the sense of being hated from within also seems inseparable from the condition of being hated from without:

> A four-year-old Negro girl in the Arsenal Nursery School in Pittsburgh used to
> stand in front of the mirror and scrub her skin with soap. When gently diverted from
> this she began to scrub the mirror. Finally, when induced to paint instead, she first
> angrily filled sheets of paper with the colors brown and black. But then she brought
> to the teacher what she called "a really *good* picture." The teacher first could see only
> a white sheet, until she looked closer and saw that the little girl had covered every
> inch of the white sheet with white paint. (Erikson, "Memorandum" 648)

> "Look at the nigger! . . . Mama, a Negro! . . . Hell, he's getting mad. . . ."
>   My body was given back to me sprawled out, distorted, recolored, clad in mourn-
> ing in that white winter day. The Negro is an animal, the Negro is bad, the Negro is
> mean, the Negro is ugly; look a nigger, it's cold, the nigger is shivering, the nigger
> is shivering because he is cold, the little boy is trembling because he is afraid of the
> nigger, the nigger is shivering with cold, that cold that goes through your bones, the
> handsome little boy is trembling because he thinks that the nigger is quivering with
> rage, the little boy throws himself into his mother's arms: Mama, the nigger's going
> to eat me up. (Fanon 113–14)

In these two scenes a suppressed but noticeable anger and confusion arises in
response to the intruding other—a response partly deriving from the realization
that the other, as racial imago, has already occupied and split the subject's ego.
Reading these two passages makes us aware how intrusion may be experienced as
an irreparable psychic separation of the ego, which internally splits the subject
between what Melanie Klein has termed "good" and "bad" internal objects, such
that the sense of displacement is all the more acute. Both accounts suggest that the
pain or anger that intrusion provokes derives not from something missing, but
from the addition of something undesirable and dirty that fragments the body by
destroying all positive semblances of self. The aggressivity this intrusion
unleashes introduces a new dynamic into the structure of the personality as
described above, for the symptom involves the self's desire to hurt the imago of the
body in a passionate bid to escape it.

Fanon's example in *Black Skin, White Masks* (1952) recollects an actual event as
it occurred—there is no doubt that the black psychiatrist traipsing round the streets
of Paris is Fanon himself. It is he who experiences the child's look of racial fear as
a painful inner splitting and anguished self-obliteration. On the other hand, this
sense of intruding violence shattering the ego seems to be damaging someone else,
as if, for a moment, Fanon were merely an actor in a mise-en-scène and not the ter-

rifying nigger he sees reflected in the boy's eyes. He sees but does not recognize this imago as himself—as if a counterpart were performing in his place in this "racial drama" (150). Fanon's public humiliation and loss of prestige derive not from the discomfort of provoking fear in a child, but from how that child's words and look strip him of whatever imaginary coherence or identity he may have had, leaving him in a crumpled, traumatized and amputated heap of fragmented parts; he "haemorrhages" a deplorable quantity of black blood. Other spectators of this scene, including the child's mother, seem to confirm, rather than dispel, Fanon's shame—shame because despite Fanon's (and others') high opinion of himself, he is reduced to the imago of a cannibal and there is something genuinely frightening about cannibals—something primordial and unreconstructed but frightening nonetheless—and something projected onto him.

Fanon realizes that he performs the role of intrusive racial imago for the white child, yet he cannot easily unburden himself from this scene without indulging in a pitiful denial of his blackness. Fanon's inability to escape this look of fear that imprisons, overwhelms, and designates him—combined as this inability is, say, with an awareness that the boy's persecutory assault is prompted by genuine fear rather than a desire to abuse—produces a state of confusion as to what exactly he has lost. After all, the strange paradox of seeing someone presumably looking directly at you but enthralled by an image of someone else seems to typify the sense of unreality dominating this exchange, of everything being out of place. It is as if all the scene's spectators act out predetermined roles in a racial phantasmagoria while discovering, for the first time, their interchangeability as counterparts with no beginning and no end. Consequently, Fanon gives the child a "tight smile" as he passes, steeling himself against the brutal intrusion of the other's perspective. Fanon's loss of the wherewithal to express hurt in this situation is arguably the cruelest deprivation of all.

Symbolically, Fanon knows that any black man could have triggered the child's fantasy of being devoured that attaches itself to a fear of blackness, for this fear signifies the "racial epidermal schema" (112) of Western culture—the unconscious fear of being literally consumed by the black other. Neither the boy nor Fanon seems able to avoid this schema, moreover, for culture determines and maintains the imago associated with blackness; cultural fantasy allows Fanon and the boy to form a bond through racial antagonism. Mournfully seeing himself trapped and reflected in the eyes of the little French boy, Fanon describes himself as "arriving too late," as being displaced by and intruded upon by racial hatred and phobia that fix him as an imago. The picture of the black psyche that emerges from Fanon's description of this and related incidents is one that is always late, never on time, violently presented and fractured by these moments of specular intrusion. The child's combined fear and anxiety—at the level of identification—acts as a stain on Fanon that may never go away. The scene's overwhelming alienation—the literal fear and trembling it engenders, the foul language that despoils—is traumatic for Fanon. He retains in memory the boy's fear of being eaten, of literally being turned into shit by an organic communion with the black body. Generally, this absorption of the black body into a fecal object is one of the most depressing and melancholic fantasies ensuing from the psychodynamics of intrusion.

The question of unconscious belatedness, discussed earlier, is also relevant in my first example—the girl's obsessive concern with her mirror image. From Erik Erikson's description above, we learn that the girl has tried many times to remove physically what we can call a stain from both her body and its mirror image, as though her specular alienation were indeed not only ritual but a compulsion. And how did her teachers' respond? By a series of diversions and inducements, we are told, as if the expression of the girl's phobia through paint were somehow less troubling—for her teachers—than her obvious physical alienation before the mirror. Such inducements may have been therapeutically designed to offset the girl's more isolated sense of alienation in front of the mirror. Yet the girl also seems enraged by something continuing to cover her image despite all her efforts to remove it.

Curiously, in the description above it is not clear whether the girl's partial search for something hidden, in part at least, "beneath" her body and mirror image—something her scrubbing away might reveal—is a consequence of what these mirror images effectively screen out or what they fail so desperately to reveal. It is also unclear whether her reluctance to turn away from the mirror image of her body (she has to be distracted and then induced) is a refusal to give up on something this image seems to hide, or, more complexly, something this image fails to reveal and symbolize. The trace of this failure seems to remain with that white sheet covered over with white paint, the outcome of a loss involving pain and destitution. So it is not at all clear whether the girl offers us the fantasy of a screen or secret, or even a combination of both. Whenever she scrubs the image it seems to remain the same, and she eventually gets angrier and transfers her need for solace onto the teacher, implying "isn't this a really good picture of myself, isn't it a truer representation of myself than those dirty black images and what they reveal?" (648).

According to Erikson, in whose 1964 essay "A Memorandum on Identity and Negro Youth" the above scenario appears, this girl is punishing and denying her black body precisely because she unconsciously believes herself to be white. The girl's fantasy is not simply an imaginary or delusionary identification with whiteness: It represents the intrusion, into her unconscious, of phobias that racist cultures project onto the bodies of black people. The clash between seeing oneself—and being seen—as black manifests itself in the form of an "aggravated identity-confusion," whose symptom is a disabling hypochondria that the girl's attempt to scrub herself white fully illustrates.

In its recapitulation of themes previously announced in Erikson's *Childhood and Society* (1950), the "Memorandum" suggests a link between black unconscious fantasies and racial imagoes. However, while the girl's racial identity seems to conflict with how she is represented culturally—whether at the level of a racial self and imago or of unconscious and cultural fantasy—Erikson suspends this conflict by advancing an historical articulation of black identity and hypochondria. He reads the girl's confused racial identity, which produces a "hypochondriac invalidism" and "total self-eradication" of the ego, as an example of how "infantile drive control (cleanliness) and social self-esteem (color) are associated in childhood" ("Memorandum" 648). Initially, the link between black infantile drive control and social esteem is not clear. Yet Erikson considers this association traumatic for the black child, for blacks allegedly have been asked historically to assume the burden of white racist representation:

> Negro babies often receive sensual satisfactions which provide them with enough oral and sensory surplus for a lifetime, as clearly betrayed in the way they move, laugh, talk, sing. Their forced symbiosis with the feudal South capitalized on this oral-sensory treasure and helped to build a slave's identity: mild, submissive, dependent, somewhat querulous, but always ready to serve, with occasional empathy and childlike wisdom. But underneath a dangerous split occurred. The Negro's unavoidable identification with the dominant race, and the need of the master race to protect its own identity against the very sensual and oral temptations emanating from the race held to be inferior (whence came their mammies), established in both groups an association: light–clean–clever–white, and dark–dirty–dumb–nigger. The result, especially in those Negroes who left the poor haven of their Southern homes, was often a violently sudden and cruel cleanliness training, as attested to in the autobiographies of Negro writers. It is as if by cleansing, a whiter identity could be achieved. . . . Three identities are formed: (1) mammy's oral-sensual "honeychild"—tender, expressive, rhythmical; (2) the evil identity of the dirty, anal-sadistic, phallic-rapist "nigger"; and (3) the clean, anal-compulsive, restrained, friendly, but always sad "white man's Negro." (645–46)

This "forced symbiosis" between U.S. plantation slavery and black orality leads to a "dangerous split" in black (and white) identities, resulting in a series of bizarre liturgies around which black—especially migrant—identities have formed. Black identity experiences the trauma and despair of racist rejection because of its "unavoidable identification" with white culture—an identification against which whites must defend themselves owing to the dangerous temptations of black oral-sensuality. Underlying this psychohistory of racial hatred is a conflict the legacy of which blacks will never be able to throw off—they cannot love themselves as black but are made to hate themselves as white. The dangerous split in black identity between black abjection and white superegoic ideal thus registers as a failure of the black ego to accept the reality of its abjection. This failure of adaptation, in which the ego does not synthesize the historical splitting of black identities, condemns blacks to neurotic regression in hypochondria. The ensuing division between identity and identification manifests itself as one between bodily ego and unconscious fantasy.

However, Erikson's reading of American racial history goes much further than a straightforward psychoanalytic account of racial intrusion: It manages to equate the campaigns for Civil Rights, racial equality, and desegregation (remember the "Memorandum" was published in 1964) with black hypochondriac neuroses, thus explaining the latter as the inevitable outcome of black civic attempts to acquire forms of white social authority. Are we meant to assume, against Erikson, that the aberrant forms of the girl's ego—expressed in traumatic aggression—are complicit with a narcissistic injury and loss whose appearance stems from the combined history of racial enslavement and black demands for racial equality? Are we also meant to assume that a fantasy of dirt underlies the girl's neurosis—as signaled by the wider culture's association of blackness with uncleanliness, a racial fantasy in which the experience of having a black body is tantamount (at the level of both unconscious and cultural fantasy) to being smeared with shit?

If so, then the choice for blacks, according to Erikson's reading, is as follows: For black instinctual demands to be recognized and valued, rather than condemned, they must be compromised by the black ego's successful adaptation to the realities of American society. The question is whether blacks, undergoing this "long and painful inner reidentification" (648), could unburden themselves of the image of the black body in fantasy—as shit, for example—when this adaptation takes place. Could such adaptation to social demands, given the bleak, frenzied, and ghostly presence of racial imagoes that afflict these demands, really absolve blacks of intrusion given what these demands reveal—the sick bonds of phobia whose trauma remains with the black subject? But what could the full liberation of black libidinal adaptation have meant in the 1960s (the decade of black civil rights), when a mass outbreak of white racial (and sexual) fears in extreme forms of racial violence tried to deny such liberation, at least as equated with the fulfillment of social wants and aspirations?

There are immense complications here, so it is hardly surprising that Erikson's reading sounds like a reductive—if not a naive—psychohistory of racial conflict. An interesting point of comparison nonetheless emerges in the work of Kenneth and Mamie Clark. Working in Chicago during the 1940s, these black social psychologists conducted on black children a series of tests using primarily dolls. Their research was later to prove instrumental in the 1954 case of *Brown v. Board of Education*, a case brought by the NAACP in its campaign legally to desegregate schools.

The Clarks' doll tests aimed to measure how racism and segregation damaged the self-esteem of black children aged three to seven. These tests involved showing the children four identical dolls—two brown and two white. The children were asked eight questions: the first four—"Give me the doll that you like to play with," "Give me the doll that is a nice doll," "Give me the doll that looks bad," and "Give me the doll that is a nice color"—were designed to test preferences. Requests five ("Give me the doll that looks like a white child"), six ("Give me the doll that looks like a colored child"), and seven ("Give me the doll that looks like a Negro child") were meant to test the children's knowledge of racial differences. The final request, "Give me the doll that looks like you," was meant to show racial self-identification. The Clarks' tests revealed that by the age of three or four, the children could correctly select the dolls that "looked like a white and like a colored child." However, when requested to "Give me the nice doll," half of the children chose the white doll; and half chose the brown doll in response to the request "Give me the doll that looks bad." A cause of particular concern was that a third of the children effectively "misidentified" themselves as white when demonstrating a marked preference for the white doll—a preference decidedly more noticeable in children aged three and four years than at a later age (remember that the girl at the Arsenal Nursery School is also aged four).

To the Clarks, this preference signified a confusion, even a loss of racial identity; for the narcissistic choice of the white doll necessarily involved "a concomitant negative attitude toward the brown doll" (608). Obviously, we simply do not know who or what these children imagined themselves to be; when asked why they preferred the white doll, however, some of the children replied " 'cause he's white" or "pretty." Conversely, the brown doll was rejected with the words " 'cause him black" or "ugly," or, more revealing, because he "got black on him." If the former suggests a form of psychic tautology (and I'm not sure what could solicit such identification if not racial fear and white superegoic authority), the latter suggests a look marked by both positive and negative desire.

Observing the trauma provoked by these eight requests, some of which left the children inconsolable and convulsed in tears, Kenneth Clark wrote, "Some of these children, particularly in the North, were reduced to crying when presented with the dolls and asked to identify with them. They looked at me as if I were the devil for putting them in this predicament. Let me tell you, it was a traumatic experience for me as well" (qtd. in Kluger 318). Again, the symbols of racial intrusion on display here ensure that the children cannot defend themselves in their identifications from the affects of reactional neuroses. These tests, prefaced as they were by the children's exposure to their phobic representation in the wider culture, unleashed feelings of rejection, psychic splitting, negativity, and trauma. Given these children's profound ambivalence, it is not surprising that a mixture of disavowal and fixation, of concealment and revelation, should seep into the spectacle they present of black alterity. Having had their demands for love denied at the level of their own visual image, these children (rather like the girl at the Arsenal Nursery School) seem to carry a burden of representation that they perceive but do not understand. Such examples of cultural alienation and psychic dereliction complicate Erikson's earlier reading of black childhood self-eradication in terms of a tension between libidinal adaptation and social life—unable to develop black self-love these children are forced to hate themselves as white.

It is no coincidence that the girl in Erikson's "Memorandum," whom he presents as an example of ego disintegration, came from a desegregated school located in the North where racial tensions in the 1950s and 1960s were particularly acute. Despite its intention to explain why the girl's confused racial identity hinges on an "unavoidable identification" with racist cultural fantasy, Erikson's reading utilizes the same stereotypical racial fantasies. The intrinsic fault of black drives, he implies, is that they are oral-sensual or sadistic anal-compulsive *before* that traumatic (although unavoidable and necessary) identification with culture. The appeal of this opposition prevails throughout Erikson's account of black identity's alleged difficulties with ego synthesis. Proceeding from this account's implicit assumptions, he issues a warning: A crisis in this identity will emerge if black mothers, in their search for "Anglo-Saxon ideals," "create violent discontinuities" in their children—or, if black children, in their pursuit of ego autonomy, learn to "disavow their sensual and overprotective mothers" (648). Paradoxically, this warning entails concern for the black ego's possible alienation from the libidinal, unconscious structures that apparently help produce culture racism in the first place. Erikson can thus view the phobic effects of black misidentification as secondary to internal psychic factors, or else reappropriate these effects as illustrating an intrinsic fault in black libidinal development. An explanation of what it means to be seen as black, or to see oneself as black, apparently requires nothing more than this developmental schema of the dangers of black orality. And the phobic aberrations of this schema derive from elements in black child care and the passing on—to the child—of a pathological racial unconscious.

Erikson seems to forget that black people experience racial fantasies as intrusive because such fantasies are felt to be inescapably and all-pervasively *there*; the black unconscious is always late. There is nothing spectacular or mystifying about this sense of belatedness; in racial dramas the pain of displacement effectively eradicates a sense of self preceding the traumas of intrusion. But this pain, in turn, can manifest itself as a melancholic reaction to being taken over by someone else's anxiety or phobia, an intrusion that violently evacuates the subject. The trauma resulting from this abduction hurts all the more. I'm thinking in particular of Fanon because the form it takes (via a type of nominal indicator or racial deictics—"look, a Negro!") is so impersonal, leaving an empty space where before there was arguably a self, or at least a proper name. This derelict and evacuated psychic space, governed by a subject reduced to a nervous and miserable silence (Fanon remarks "I could no longer laugh"; 112), attests to a loss for which the black subject has no witnesses: "I was denied the slightest recognition" (Fanon 115).

It may not be too fanciful to suggest that the black ego, far from being too immature or weak to integrate, is an absence haunted by its and others' negativity. In this respect, the memory of a loss is its only possible communication. Yet if there are no witnesses to offer atonement—or to deny or prevent the internal and external injury of intruding phobias—could such mourning ever console those black mourners? In these circumstances, having a "white" unconscious may be the only way to connect with—or even contain—the overwhelming and irreparable sense of loss. The intruding fantasy offers the medium to connect with the lost internal object, the ego, but there is also no "outside" to this "real fantasy" and the effects of intrusion are irreparable.[1] Here we can return to Fanon's own account of racial intrusion and how it affects both white and black psyches.

As I discussed earlier, the intruding double is experienced in fantasy as the subject's internal displacement—a turning of the subject inside out through the breaching of an internal enclosure or screen. The irreducible uncertainty between what is outside and what is inside constitutes the frontier where ego and imago meet. In an extensive footnote to *Black Skin, White Masks*, in which he questions the separation of unconscious and cultural fantasy to clarify racial identification, Fanon tries to analyze this aporia in light of clinical observations on black Antilleans' self-representation in dreams and color neuroses: "In the Antilles perception always occurs on the level of the imaginary. It is in white terms that one perceives one's fellows" (163). This confusion of self and other, which Fanon considers a "normal" consequence of alienation caused in racial intrusion, relegates skin color to the status of an empirical accident, a neurotic maneuver designed to keep the outside out and the inside in. That is why these Antilleans, as fantasists, are particularly germane to Fanon's diagnoses of racial neuroses. Beginning with a notion of the specular counterpart—"*l'imago du semblable*," derived not from Freud but from Lacan's theory of the mirror stage and the imaginary—Fanon speculates whether the aggressivity directed at the racial imago of the other derives from the subject's own internal aggressivity:

> It would certainly be interesting, using the Lacanian notion of the *mirror stage*, to ask to what extent the *imago* of his kind or counterpart [*semblable*] built up in the white youngster at the usual age would be subjected to undergo an imaginary aggression with the apparition [*apparition*] of the Black Man [*du Noir*]. When the process described by Lacan is understood, there can be no more doubt that the true Other of the White Man [*Autrui du Blanc*] is and remains the Black man [*le Noir*]. And vice versa. (131; trans. mod.)

It is worth noting—although I do no more than note—that Fanon's understanding of *le stade du miroir* derives from Lacan's 1938 article in *Encyclopedie française*, "Les complexes familiaux," where Lacan discusses "*l'imago du semblable*" regarding narcissistic, specular identification and the "intrusion complex," and the oedipal identification proper to the parental (i.e., paternal imago (*Complexes* 88–112). Lacan's account of the ego's *imaginary* genesis, in which it fantasizes unity from observing the body's reflected image, interested Fanon because it binds the ego to primitive libidinal drives. Since for Lacan, "Everything pertaining to the ego is inscribed in imaginary tensions, like all the other libidinal tensions. Libido and ego are on the same side" (*Seminar II* 326), Fanon explores this equivalence via the symbolics of racial intrusion or "breaching." The ego's constitution and the subject's ensuing process of identification can explain racial aggressivity, for the ego is initiated into representation by the specular image of the other—the rival "other" it loves and hates, and with which it ambivalently identifies. Claiming that "the true Other of the White Man is and remains the Black man," Fanon suggests that the imago of the black other is an instinctual component of the white psyche, linked inextricably to the psychic processes in which aggressive drives associated with phobic anxiety and fear become psychically effective through a racial object or delegate.

Fanon's "sociodiagnostic" of the racial neuroses and their "anomalies of affect [*les anomalies affectives*]" locates these neuroses at a point where aggressive cultural and psychic fantasies seem to converge (12). If we follow through the logic of this convergence, recalling the traumatic aggressivity of the girl before the mirror, aggressivity itself represents a kind of constitutive fantasy. Fanon's analyses of interracial trauma pronounce this fantasy as the irruption of the "unidentifiable, the unassimilable" in the rival other, an irruption receiving significant attention in *Black Skin, White Masks*. The metaphors of breaching, staining, and contamination that Fanon invokes to conceptualize the ego's imaginary and racial capture suggest that the ego experiences racial difference as a violent rupture of bodily ego.

Additionally, these metaphors relate to a fantasmatic intrusion of the black (or white) imago. As part of the ego's origins, this imaginary intrusion receives its stimulus from the sight of the black other, a sometimes unbearable vision signifying a dangerous violation of white bodily integrity.

This sense of violation is crucial to understanding white racial violence, in which the ego represents the imago through phobia. Fanon refers to this imaginary identification as follows: "A few years ago, I remarked to some friends during a discussion that in a general sense the white man behaves towards the Negro as an elder brother reacts to the birth of a younger. I have since learned that Richard Sterba arrived at the same conclusion in America" (157). Sterba's article, "Some Psychological Factors in Negro Race Hatred and Anti-Negro Riots," first published in 1947, analyzes the unconscious motives of white analysands who participated in, or who were affected by, Detroit's race riots of June 1943. In his discussion of these analysands' dreams, Sterba suggested that racial phobias derive from repressed sibling rivalry. Playing the role of an imaginary younger sibling in these unconscious fantasies, Negroes are represented as "unwelcome intruders" (412).

To be sure, the turning outward of aggressivity in real racial violence did allow these analysands to satisfy their destructive drives through a substitute object—the Negroes who happened to be on the streets during the actual riots.[2] Sterba discerned in the analysands' dreams attempts to offset their oedipal anxieties: Apparently, they could satisfy their repressed hatred of the white father only by the real and symbolic murder of black men. This allowed positive feelings for the father to remain intact, while ambivalent emotional ties to the father were allowed to appear—as a cultural and unconscious fantasy of racial intrusion—through substitute objects. The question nonetheless remains, What did the black men suffering real injury because of these ties make of this desire, which tried to sacrifice them to protect the prestige of the white father? Put slightly differently, Did the role these black imagoes performed allow the desire for real racial murder on the outside to intrude on these dreams of paternal hatred, and in a way that is not simply described as an example of fantasy becoming real?

We can demonstrate this issue by focusing on what I earlier called the proximity between a failed mourning and the role of aggressivity in racial intrusion. If black men must die so that the aggressive structure of white repression and sublimation of libidinal drives can remain in place, why aren't these deaths mourned as a loss in the dreams of Sterba's white analysands? If they cannot mourn the resonance of such a loss, is it because the loss as such for them did not occur? Far from being a form of disavowal, could not these dreams—in becoming real—reveal the fixations where culture and unconscious fantasy become inseparable? Rather than concealing a secret, unavowable loss, this example of an unconscious failure to mourn surely points up a more general truth concerning the place of the black imago in the white unconscious—a place marked by murderous aggression and a phobic transferral of feelings of loss onto the black other.

This place is also marked by the eruption of unconscious hatred into the real and, conversely, by the breaking in of a murderous real into the white (and black) unconscious. Such bonding in real fantasy allows the subject to negotiate aggression and loss while ensuring that the imago of blacks carries the imaginary "work" of this dreaming. This may explain why, finally, the shadow of white racial phobia continues to fall across the black unconscious via the sick horror of a double intrusion: fixation and aggressivity. It may also explain why the etiology of racial prejudice must be located elsewhere—not solely in the public domain. To fathom the mechanisms and structures of racially violent fixations and obsessional neuroses, it is not enough to point out the oppressive experience of the social and its myriad forms of institutional violence against black people. One must also explain the effects of unconscious fantasy and identification on racial identity. Insofar as cultural and unconscious fantasies are experienced as real, exclusively psychoanalytic or culturalist readings must be abandoned for us to appreciate the authority and persistence of these racial imagoes in white and black identifications.

So imagine the following scenario:[3] A white analysand is free-associating on the word "black" before his black analyst. He is embarrassed because he can think only of negative words and mental associations; for some unknown reason, the word doesn't seem to conjure up any positive quality. Despite his attempts at repressing it, the word "nigger" urges itself to the forefront of his mind, refusing to go away. He utters it, conscious of his own spiteful fury, and with as much venom as he can muster—he has never, to his knowledge, used this word before. The analyst shows no response. Now even more embarrassingly conscious of his own stupid, blind, and violently impotent rage, the analysand thinks of another phrase: "black nigger." The association seems right; it seems to fit. What is more, it seems to mean something, but it is not a phrase the analysand wants to utter here. He utters the word "death" instead—a classic association, so banal and obvious, but reassuring nonetheless. The analyst nods with obvious enthusiasm and urges him to continue.

ENDNOTES

I thank Vicky Lebeau and Jacqueline Rose for their helpful comments and criticism.

1. For an account of Fanon's concept of "real fantasy" see Lebeau's as yet unpublished paper "Psychopolitics: Frantz Fanon's *Black Skin, White Masks*." I am indebted to her reading of the dreamwork in relation to these "*phantasmes réels.*"

2. In these riots, racial hatred was "directed at male Negroes only" (Sterba 412).

3. Compare Fanon: "Over three or four years I questioned some 500 members of the white race—French, German, English, Italian. I took advantage of a certain air of trust, of relaxation; in each instance I waited until my subject no longer hesitated to talk to me quite openly—that is, until he was sure that he would not offend me. Or else, in the midst of associational tests, I inserted the word *Negro* among some twenty others. . . . From this result one must acknowledge the effect of my being a Negro: Unconsciously there was a certain reticence" (166–67).

WORKS CITED

Clark, Kenneth and Mamie Clark. "Racial Identification and Preference in Negro Children." *Readings in Social Psychology.* Ed. Eleanor E. Macroby, Theodore M. Newcomb, and Eugene L. Hartley. London: Methuen, 1966. 602–11.

Erikson, Erik H. *Childhood and Society.* 1950. 2d ed. New York: Norton, 1963.

———. "A Memorandum on Identity and Negro Youth." 1964. *A Way of Looking at Things: Selected Papers from 1930–1980.* Ed. Stephen Schlein. New York: Norton, 1989. 644–59.

Fanon, Frantz. *Black Skin, White Masks.* Trans. Charles Lam Markmann. New York: Grove, 1967. *Peau noire, masques blancs.* Paris: Editions Seuil, 1952.

Kluger, Richard. *Simple Justice: The History of Brown v. Board of Education and Black America's Struggle for Equality.* London: Deutsch, 1977.

Lacan, Jacques. *Les complexes familiaux dans la formation de l'individu: Essai d'analyse d'une fonction en psychologie.* 1938. Paris: Navarin, 1984.

———. *The Seminar of Jacques Lacan, Book I: Freud's Papers on Technique 1953–1954.* Ed. Jacques-Alain Miller. Trans. John Forrester. New York: Cambridge UP, 1988.

———. *The Seminar of Jacques Lacan, Book II: The Ego in Freud's Theory and in the Technique of Psychoanalysis 1954–1955.* Ed. Jacques-Alain Miller. Trans. Sylvana Tomaselli. New York: Cambridge UP, 1988.

Sterba, Richard. "Some Psychological Factors in Negro Race Hatred and in Anti-Negro Riots." *Psychoanalysis and the Social Sciences* 1 (1947): 411–27.

Contributors

Gwen Bergner is Assistant Professor of English at West Virginia University. Her essay on Fanon recently appeared in *PMLA*. With Nicole Plett, she has also contributed to *Moving Words, Re-writing Dance* (Routledge, 1996). She is currently completing a manuscript on psychoanalysis and racial subjectivity in American literature.

Daniel Boyarin is Taubman Professor of Talmudic Culture in Near Eastern Studies and Women's Studies at the University of California, Berkeley. His books include *Carnal Israel: Reading Sex in Talmudic Culture* (California, 1993), *A Radical Jew: Paul and the Politics of Identity* (California, 1994), and *Unheroic Conduct: The Rise of Heterosexuality and the Invention of the Jewish Man* (California, 1997).

Merrill Cole is a Ph.D. candidate in English and the Program in Criticism and Theory at the University of Washington. He has published essays in *Discourse* and *Literature Interpretation Theory*.

Tim Dean is Assistant Professor of English at the University of Illinois, Urbana-Champaign, and, during 1997–98, a Fellow at the Stanford Humanities Center, where he is working on a book to be titled "Modernism and the Ethics of Impersonality." His *Beyond the Couch: Sexuality, Psychoanalysis, and Cultural Politics* is forthcoming from SUNY Press.

Jacques Derrida is Directeur d'Études at the École des Hautes Études en Sciences Sociales, in Paris. He is the author of many books, including *Psyché: inventions de l'autre* (Galilée, 1987),

The Other Heading: Reflections on Today's Europe (Indiana, 1992), *Passions* (Galilée, 1993), *Specters of Marx: The State of the Debt, the Work of Mourning, and the New International* (Routledge, 1994), *The Gift of Death* (Chicago, 1995), *Archive Fever: A Freudian Impression* (Chicago, 1996), *Résistances de la psychanalyse* (Galilée, 1996), and *Politics of Friendship* (Verso, 1997).

Christopher Lane is Associate Professor of English at Emory University. He is the author of *The Ruling Passion: British Colonial Allegory and the Paradox of Homosexual Desire* (Duke, 1995) and of recent essays in *Diacritics, American Literature, Modern Fiction Studies*, and *The New Statesman & Society*. In Fall 1998, U of Chicago P will publish his next book, *The Burdens of Intimacy: Psychoanalysis and Victorian Masculinity*.

Alphonso Lingis is Professor of Philosophy at Pennsylvania State University. He is the author of many books, including *Excesses: Eros and Culture* (SUNY, 1983), *Libido: The French Existential Theories* (Indiana, 1985), *Deathbound Subjectivity* (Indiana, 1989), *The Community of Those Who Have Nothing in Common* (Indiana, 1994), *Foreign Bodies* (Routledge, 1994), and *Sensation: Intelligibility in Sensation* (Humanities, 1996).

Julia Reinhard Lupton, Associate Professor of English and Comparative Literature at the University of California, Irvine, is coauthor with Kenneth Reinhard of *After Oedipus: Shakespeare in Psychoanalysis* (Cornell, 1993) and author of *Afterlives of the Saints: Hagiography, Typology, and Renaissance Literature* (Stanford, 1996). Her essay in this collection is part of a work in progress, "Before Culture: Race and Religion in Renaissance Drama."

David Marriott teaches critical theory and black cultural studies at Queen Mary and Westfield College, University of London. He has published in *Textual Practice* and contributed to *Understanding Masculinities* (Open, 1995). He is currently writing *Black Male Fantasies*, forthcoming with U of Edinburgh P.

James Penney is a graduate student in the Literature Program at Duke University. He is currently researching a dissertation project entitled "Philosophies of Perversion," which engages psychoanalytic theory as well as French literature and philosophy.

Amit S. Rai teaches literature at Eugene Lang College, New School for Social Research. His work has appeared in *Screen, Diaspora, Oxford Literary Review,* and *South Asia Research*. He is currently completing a manuscript on the colonial contexts of Victorian desire, narrative, and governmentality, entitled *The Imperial Bedroom*.

Jacqueline Rose is Professor of English at Queen Mary and Westfield College, University of London. Her books include *The Case of Peter Pan; or, The Impossibility of Children's Fiction* (Macmillan, 1984), *Sexuality in the Field of Vision* (Verso, 1986), *The Haunting of*

Sylvia Plath (Harvard, 1992), *Why War?—Psychoanalysis, Politics, and the Return to Melanie Klein* (Blackwell, 1993), and *States of Fantasy* (Oxford, 1996).

Kalpana Seshadri-Crooks is Assistant Professor of English at Boston College. She is presently working on a book entitled *Imperial Incarnations: Race and Psychoanalysis in the Colonial Context* and is coediting (with Fawzia Afzal-Kahn) a collection of essays on Postcolonial Studies. She has published articles on colonial theory in *Cultural Critique, Ariel,* and *South Asian Review.*

Charles Shepherdson, currently a Fellow at the Pembroke Center, Brown University, has contributed to many different collections and journals, and is the author of *Vital Signs: Nature and Culture in Psychoanalysis* (Routledge, 1998).

Claudia Tate is Professor of African-American and American Literature at Princeton University. She is the author of *Domestic Allegories of Political Desire: The Black Heroine's Text at the Turn of the Century* (Oxford, 1992) and *Psychoanalysis and Black Novels: Desire and the Protocols of Race* (Oxford, 1997). She has also edited *Black Women Writers at Work* (Continuum, 1983), *The Works of Katherine Tillman* (Oxford, 1991), and *The Selected Works of Georgia Douglas Johnson* (G. K. Hall, 1996).

Jean Walton is Associate Professor of English at the University of Rhode Island. She has published essays in *Contemporary Literature, New Orleans Review, College Literature,* and *Critical Inquiry,* and has contributed to *The Lesbian Postmodern* (Columbia, 1994). She is writing a book on psychoanalysis, feminism, and white fantasies of racial difference.

Suzanne Yang is a candidate for the M.D. degree at the University of California, San Francisco. Her areas of clinical work have included the psychiatric treatment of combat veterans with post-traumatic stress disorder and of homeless persons with severe mental disorders such as schizophrenia. She is editor (with Juliet Flower MacCannell) of *ANaMORPHOSIS: Journal of the San Francisco Society for Lacanian Studies,* and has contributed essays to *JPCS: Journal for the Psychoanalysis of Culture and Society* and *Homosexuality and Psychoanalysis* (Macmillan, forthcoming).

Slavoj Žižek is Senior Researcher at Slovenia's Institute for Social Sciences, University of Ljubljana, and is Slovenia's Ambassador of Science. His many books include *The Sublime Object of Ideology* (Verso, 1989), *For They Know Not What They Do: Enjoyment as a Political Factor* (Verso, 1991), *Tarrying with the Negative: Kant, Hegel, and the Critique of Ideology* (Duke, 1993), *The Metastases of Enjoyment: Six Essays on Woman and Causality* (Verso, 1994), and *The Indivisible Remainder* (Verso, 1996). He has also edited, with Renata Salecl, *Gaze and Voice as Love Objects* (Duke, 1996).

Index